The Theosophical Enlightenment

SUNY Series in Western Esoteric Traditions
Edited by David Appelbaum

The Theosophical Enlightenment

by
Joscelyn Godwin

STATE UNIVERSITY OF NEW YORK PRESS

ILLUSTRATION CREDITS: 1.1: National Gallery of Wales, Cardiff (private collection). By permission of the owner. 1.2: By permission of Towneley Hall Art Gallery and Museums, Burnley Borough Council. 2.3, 3.3, 3.4, 7.2: By permission of the National Portrait Gallery. 7.1: By permission of the Galleria degli Uffizi, Firenze (Collezione degli Autoritratti). 8.2: By permission of the Board of Trustees of the Chevening Estate. 11.1: By permission of the Grand Lodge Library and Museum, Freemasons' Hall, London. 11.2: From F. King, *Modern Ritual Magic* (Bridport: Prism, 1989). By permission of Prism Press. 13.2: From the Hertfordshire Record Office. By permission of Lord Cobbold. 15.1: Miscellaneous Papers (Rammohun Roy), Rare Books & Manuscripts Division, The New York Public Library, Astor, Lenox and Tilden Foundations. By permission. 16.3: From *H.B. of L. Textes et documents secrets de la Hermetic Brotherhood of Luxor* (Milan: Arché, 1989). By permission of Laszlo Toth. 17.1: Private collection. By permission of R. A. Gilbert. 17.2: Photograph by Paul Brunton. By permission of Kenneth Thurston Hurst.

Published by
State University of New York Press, Albany

Printed in the United States of America

For information, address State University of New York Press,
State University Plaza, Albany, N.Y., 12246

Production by Cathleen Collins
Marketing by Nancy Farrell

Library of Congress Cataloging in Publication Data

Godwin, Joscelyn.
The theosophical enlightenment / by Joscelyn Godwin.
p. cm. — (SUNY Series in Western esoteric traditions)
Includes bibliographical references and index.
ISBN 0-7914-2151-1. — ISBN 0-7914-2152-X (pbk.)
1. Theosophy—Great Britain—History. 2. Occultism—Great Britain—History. I. Title. II. Series
BP545.G63 1994
299'.93'094109034—dc20 94-1572
CIP

10 9 8 7 6 5 4 3 2 1

To Leslie Price and James A. Santucci

Contents

Illustrations

Preface

This is an intellectual history of occult and esoteric currents in the English-speaking world, from the early Romantic period to the early-twentieth century. The Theosophical Society, founded in 1875 by Helena Petrovna Blavatsky, holds a crucial position as the place where all these currents temporarily united, before diverging again. The book's ambiguous title points to my thesis that Blavatsky's Theosophy owed as much to the skeptical Enlightenment of the eighteenth century as it did to the concept of spiritual enlightenment with which it is more readily associated.

I have limited my field to the English-speaking world, referring to foreign developments only when they impinge directly on it. There are several reasons for this. First, a complete history of nineteenth-century esotericism would make an impractically large book. Second, I have treated elsewhere many aspects of French esotericism during the same period. The third and most important reason is that the two crucial events of the period happened in America (the birth of Modern Spiritualism in 1848 and the founding of the Theosophical Society), while their fullest intellectual consequences were worked out in Britain.

This book combines new information drawn from obscure periodicals, books, and manuscripts with a general overview whose intention is to entertain as well as to instruct. At times it condenses the more specialized work of other scholars, such as the doctoral dissertation of Marsha Keith Schuchard; at others, it offers material never explored before, such as the Stanhope-Lytton correspondence on crystal-gazing, or the survey of Paschal Beverly Randolph's life. The subject of esotericism is so new to humanistic scholarship that no conventions yet exist for its treatment. I respect my sources sufficiently to allow that their world, so different from that of most academic studies, has a right to be exhibited on its own terms. At the same time, I do not conceal the fact that I consider many of them deluded and deluding.

The book is in three parts. Chapters 1–4 are concerned with the revisionist approach to myth in the seventy years around 1800. Set in motion by French Enlightenment ideas, this became a vehicle for those who sought a universal view of history, mythology, and world religions without being bounded by biblical fundamentalism or Christian supremacy.

Chapters 5–9 are a history of the occult sciences in England from the 1780's to about 1850.

From Chapter 10 onwards, the characters and topics become interrelated in a web of increasing complexity. Chapters 10–13 focus on the themes of spiritualism, secret societies, esoteric Christianity, and Rosicrucianism. With the entry of Madame Blavatsky, a rift begins to open between the Western occultists and the proponents of Eastern doctrines, especially Buddhism. The last chapter examines some of the extensions of both schools into the twentieth century.

A NOTE ON TERMINOLOGY

The primary sources of this book are late eighteenth- and nineteenth-century writings in which certain terms are used in multiple senses and ambiguous ways. Without imposing rigid meanings on them, I use these terms within the following guidelines:

Theosophy and *Theosophists*, with a capital T, refer to Blavatsky's society and its members.

theosophy and *theosophers* refer to the tradition of religious illumination exemplified by Jacob Boehme and his followers, including John Pordage, Jane Leade, William Law, Louis-Claude de Saint-Martin, Franz von Baader, and Anne Judith Penny. A few Theosophists, such as C. C. Massey, were also theosophers.

esoteric and its derivatives *esotericist, esotericism,* always presuppose the existence of a corresponding *exoteric* body of knowledge or doctrine, such as a scriptural text or a religious ritual. The esotericist's object is to penetrate the surface meaning in order to reach a secret and superior knowledge. Esoteric Judaism is called Kabbalah; esoteric Islam, Sufism. The theosophers were esoteric Christians. After 1880, Theosophy centered around what was called "esoteric Buddhism."

The *occult sciences* in the West include astrology, alchemy, ritual magic, practical Kabbalah, certain breathing and sexual practices, and various forms of divination. Some developments of Mesmerism and spiritualism may also be included.

Occultism as a concept dates only from the mid-nineteenth century, as the term for the pursuit of occult science in deliberate opposition to the prevailing beliefs of scientific materialism. Thus, although Sir Isaac Newton was an alchemist, and Johannes Kepler was an astrologer, they were not occultists. Blavatsky used the term loosely, sometimes meaning "esotericist" as defined above. But not all Theosophists were occultists: many of them are better described as philosophers and students of comparative religion.

ACKNOWLEDGMENTS

The research for this book was mainly conducted during a sabbatical year in England. I am grateful, as ever, to Colgate University, especially to the Research Council for a grant, and to my colleagues in the Music Department. The staff of the following libraries were invariably helpful to me: Bibliotheca Philosophica Hermetica (Amsterdam), Bibliothèque Municipale de Lyon, Bibliothèque Nationale (Paris), Boston Public Library, the British Library, Cambridge University Library, Colgate University Library, the College of Psychic Studies (London), Cornell University Library, Dr. Williams's Library (London), Grand Lodge Library at Freemasons' Hall (London), the Harry Price Library at Senate House (University of London), the Swedenborg Society (London), Hertfordshire County Record Office, Letchworth Public Library, New York Public Library, the Warburg Institute Library (London), the Wellcome Institute Library (London), and York Public Library.

I would also like to thank Christopher Bamford for hospitality, conversations, and loan of books, William Breeze for material on Allan Bennett, Richard M. Brown for his views on these "nineteenth-century byways," Christian Chanel for material on Max Theon and the H.B. of L., M. H. Coleman for the material by Emma Hardinge Britten, John Robert Colombo for information about Hydesville, John Patrick Deveney for conversations and material on Randolph, Sybilla Jane Flower for an invaluable conversation on Bulwer-Lytton, Janet Godwin for reading the manuscript, Bishop T Allen Greenfield, D.D. for material on Davidson, Paul Johnson for conversations, loan of books, and the example of his own research, Stephen Lloyd for introducing me to Cosway and his circle, Dr. Christopher McIntosh for hospitality, conversation, and the loan of his dissertation, Adam McLean for leading me to Dr. Williams's Library, Roger Nyle Parisious for sharing his Golden Dawn researches, Leslie Price, Founder of *Theosophical History,* for first interesting me in Theosophical history and for his unfailing helpfulness, Prof. James A. Santucci, Editor of *Theosophical History,* for encouraging and defending my research, Prof. Marsha Keith Schuchard for materials on Blake and others, Nicolas Tereshchenko for sharing unpublished discoveries, and André Vanden-Broeck for his friendship and example.

Parts of this book have previously appeared in *The Hermetic Journal, Theosophical History,* and *The Occult Observer.*

ONE

The Worship of the Generative Powers

In the late spring of 1777, when much of the world was at peace, a young English gentleman was enjoying a scholarly and aesthetic tour of Sicily. The island lay somewhat off the beaten track of the usual "Grand Tour," and Richard Payne Knight (1751–1824) was hoping to make his reputation by bringing back pictures and descriptions of its classical remains. Two other gentlemen accompanied him. The senior member of the party was Philipp Hackert, a German painter; the other was his pupil, a wealthy English amateur named Charles Gore. The two artists made sketches on the spot that were elaborated, on their return, into finished watercolors of the Lipari Isles, the volcanoes Stromboli and Etna, the ruins of Segesta, Selinus, Agrigento, and Syracuse. Knight kept the journal, which he embellished with classical learning. It passed from Gore into the hands of his friend Johann Wolfgang von Goethe, who followed a similar route ten years later.[1]

Knight was the son of a Herefordshire clergyman who had retired in middle age, surprising everyone by marrying his servant (a carpenter's daughter) and raising a family in his own large manor house. Richard was sufficiently sickly as a child to be kept at home and spared the experience of boarding school. After his father's death in 1764 he was sent to a tutor, and became a keen Greek scholar. His foreign tours took the place of a university education. The death of an uncle had meanwhile made him heir to his grandfather, a self-made man whose fortune had come from ironworks. Knight thus entered manhood in a state of intellectual and financial freedom and with a combination of sensitivity and sensuality that invite comparison with his contemporary William Beckford.[2] Although his fortune was far more modest, he was, like Beckford, a builder, a collector, a traveler, an author—and a pagan.

Figure 1.1. *Richard Payne Knight (1751–1824), by Nathaniel Hone.*

Knight had been to Italy at least once before, in 1767[3] or 1772, presumably on a conventional tour of the mainland sites. His journey in 1777 was more serious in intention, undertaken for research as well as for pleasure and the broadening of the mind. Intensely responsive to the Sicilian atmosphere and to the interplay of natural scenery with classical remains, he was appalled by the contrast presented by the modern denizens. Heirs to a thriving civilization that had once filled the island with theaters and splendid temples, the Sicilians now lived in dismal poverty and abject superstition. Knight could see only one reason for their decline: the baleful influence of Christianity. His was not merely the self-righteous reaction of an Anglican to the abuses of Rome, in an era when English vicars would argue from the pulpit that the Pope was the Antichrist: it was a thoroughgoing rejection of what he called the "sour mythology of the Christians."[4]

The broad and tolerant Anglican church did not often provoke the furious anticlericalism of a Voltaire, but in Knight's case the spectacle of Sicilian Catholicism led to a contempt for priestcraft as a whole. No doubt this attitude had psychological roots as well, connected with the clergyman father who had died when Richard was thirteen. In this passage from Richard's diary, the Reverend Knight and his way of life are indicted, by implication, along with the Sicilian clergy:

> The Ecclesiasticks are immensely numerous & possess above one third of the Island, which being totally exempt from Taxes, the rest is of course heavily burdened. However the bigotry of the Sicilians is such, that an attempt to tax them, would be unpopular, as the reduction of their number has been found to be. Their influence is so great, that all inquiry or improvement of every kind is checked. Men, who gain vast emoluments of the blind belief of a few incomprehensible Mysteries, are naturally very jealous of every thing, that can tend to dissipate the cloud of darkness which protects them. Weak as human reason is, it would be sufficient in its lowest state to penetrate the thin veil of Priestcraft, if People only dared think; but the greatest Part of Mankind believe because they have never had the Courage to ask their own understandings, whether they believe or not.[5]

We will return to Knight and to the blossoming of these sentiments in creative scholarship, after making a digression that will explain the milieu that nourished his work. It was probably on an earlier tour of Italy that he first met Sir William Hamilton (1730–1803), whose embassy in Naples was an obligatory stage for English travelers even before the arrival in 1786 of the glamorous Emma (the second Lady Hamilton, who became Nelson's mistress). Sir William, who had acquired a fortune along with his first wife, was avid for vases and other classical antiquities and had assembled a magnificent collection, which he sold to the fledgling British Museum. The cataloguing and publication of these vases were entrusted by Hamilton to a certain "Baron" d'Hancarville, the pen-name of Pierre François Hugues (1719 or 1729–1805), a learned rascal of the Casanova type. The four folio volumes that appeared in 1766–67 were a tribute to the Italian engravers and printers, but d'Hancarville's own contribution was a mixed blessing. A feast for the eye, the work became progressively more confusing to the mind as d'Hancarville changed his mind about his editorial policy, wrote long-winded discourses on the progress of the arts, and forgot half-way through to add an English translation to his French text. His conclusion, which must have gratified his patron, was that many of the scenes on Hamilton's vases referred to the Eleusinian Mysteries, whose great secret was the unity of God. This, d'Hancarville thought, was the key to the universal religion of antiquity, which had been brought to classical Greece from the Phoenicians and Etruscans by way of Orphism.[6]

Orphism and the Mysteries were magnets for those who investigated ancient religion, whether in a spirit of reverence or of disdain. A similar effort to d'Hancarville's appeared in 1772: *L'Antiquité dévoilée par ses usages* attributed to the skeptical mythographer Nicholas Boulanger (1722–1759) but rewritten by the Baron d'Holbach, most extreme of the atheistic *philosophes* of the French Enlightenment. This explained the Mysteries as having taught, through impressive displays, the survival of the soul after death—a belief not generally held in the ancient world until proclaimed by Christianity.[7] But the Orphics taught an even more esoteric doctrine: that of the past and future destructions of the world, and of the eventual death of the gods themselves. In this respect, says Boulanger, Orphism resembled the system of the Brahmins, with their successive creations and destructions of the globe.[8] Boulanger's own theory of origins traced all religious observances to memories of the last such cataclysm, the almost-universal Deluge.

To attribute to pagan religions two of the central doctrines of Christianity, namely monotheism and the immortality of the soul, was a strategic move in the Enlightenment's campaign to strip Christianity of its pretensions to uniqueness. This was welcomed both by atheists such as Holbach and by deists or pantheists such as Knight.

The Hamilton vase collection, as published, gives only an inkling of another aspect of pagan art and myth that had fascinated connoisseurs since the Renaissance, namely the sexual element, which is so carefully avoided in most Christian iconography. The recent excavations of Herculaneum had turned up a surprising number of erotic objects, especially ithyphallic statuettes and gems with scenes of sexual intercourse, to add to the examples already secreted in the museums of Rome and Florence. While the collectors of these artefacts, such as Sir William Hamilton, Charles Townley,[9] and Payne Knight, derived a certain humorous pleasure from forbidden fruits, these eighteenth-century gentlemen were not merely prurient, but scholarly and anthropological in their interests. They were the sort of people who, as boys, had discovered the obscene lyrics in the Greek Anthology—but only because they could read Greek.

Far from being a mere career diplomat, Sir William Hamilton was a natural researcher. He had already taken advantage of living near Mount Vesuvius to become an expert in vulcanology; now he was curious about local vestiges of paganism. One of these came to his attention in 1781, when he learnt how the feast of Saints Cosmas and Damian was being celebrated in the remote town of Isernia, in the Abruzzo. Apparently wax exvoti representing the male organs were taken to church, chiefly by women, who then dedicated them with kisses—presumably with prayers for successful pregnancy. At the same time, those who suffered from diseases of those parts had them anointed directly by the priest. Entranced by the news of this survival of the worship of Priapus, the Roman god of fertility, Hamilton made the pilgrimage to Isernia in the hope of witnessing the ceremony. But it had been suppressed in the meantime by an overzealous bishop, and the disappointed tourist had to be content with acquiring some of the wax objects, euphemistically known as "big toes."

Hamilton wrote of his discovery to his learned friend Sir Joseph Banks, the longtime President of the Royal Society, and in 1784 he came to London bearing his trophies, still said to lurk somewhere in the British Museum. Banks was also Secretary of the Society of Dilettanti, which voted to print Hamilton's letter for private circulation among its members, together with another letter on the same subject from "a person residing at Isernia." The Dilettanti had been founded in 1732 by Sir Francis Dashwood and a group of young bucks who had been to Italy (the qualification for membership) and enjoyed drinking together and talking about their experiences there.[10] Their meetings had a neopagan and libertine atmosphere, which, although not so extreme as that of the other club for which Dashwood was famous, allowed the indulgence of interests that outsiders might have found shocking.

D'Hancarville had meanwhile established himself in Paris, his work for Hamilton (from which he derived all the monetary profit) giving him entry to the rarefied circles of aristocratic connoisseurs. He found a collaborator of his own stamp in the Abbé Gaspar Michel Leblond (1738–1809), sublibrarian of the Mazarin Library. Together they produced three erotic works that enjoyed several reissues in French and English.[11] These were luxurious picture-books for private cabinets, illustrating antique gems with sexual themes; some copies are hand-colored. It is said that the plates in the third volume were engraved by the Duc d'Orléans, a notorious rake and later a revolutionary under the name of "Philippe Egalité,"[12] whom we will meet among the London occultists in Chapter Five.

In the book on the secret cult of Roman women, d'Hancarville protests that this is far removed from crude pornography. "The Ancients," he wrote, "did not look upon the pleasures of love with our eyes . . ."; they "could attach no kind of turpitude to actions which they regarded as the goal of nature and the height of felicity."[13] In the spirit of his century, d'Hancarville's libertinism, combined with antimonastic prejudice, was given vent in the following observation: "One might have considerable difficulty in deciding who better deserves the worship of mortals: a gallant woman who, following her temperament, has passed the best days of her life receiving and giving pleasure; or one who has ceaselessly destroyed through discipline and loathing a body formed by nature for another purpose, and deliberately filled her life with disgust, suffering, and sourness."[14] Was his tongue in his cheek when he went on: "The cult of the true God has dissipated that of a crowd of Divinities, whose example naturally led men to corruption; but it has not entirely restored them to the practice of civic and moral virtue"? Surely it was, for he concludes: "How can one reconcile the idea of a religion founded on kindness and clemency, yet which still rigorously condemns such natural pleasures, and ones to which we seem driven by an irresistible urge."[15]

D'Hancarville's next field of activity was London, where he became the resident scholar and curator for Charles Townley (1737–1805), member of the Dilettanti and owner of the finest collection of antique sculpture in the country. Under the pretext of illustrating and commenting on items from Townley's cabinet, the Frenchman now developed his theories on ancient symbolism into a fully fledged system, published anonymously in 1785 as *Recherches sur l'origine, l'esprit, et les progrès des arts de la Grèce.* In typical Enlightenment fashion, he believed that he was at last placing the study of antiquity on a scientific basis, by the "entirely new method" of founding it on "principles."[16] The first of these principles was that the world had originally had "one cult, one theology, one religion, and very likely one language."[17] The main symbols of this primordial religion were the Bull and the Serpent, both representing the Creator God. Over time, their statues gradually took on human lineaments, until people found themselves worshipping purely human figures and believed these to be the gods: hence the birth of idolatry and polytheism.[18] The primordial religion supposedly left its stamp on the arts of China, Tartary, and India, from all of which Townley's collection could furnish illustrations. Thanks to his connections with the East India Company, Townley had even acquired an erotic sculpture torn from a cave temple at Elephanta. It is comical to see d'Hancarville confidently reading his own cosmogonic theories into Tibetan paintings of wrathful deities,[19] or an Indian map of the Ganges.[20] He only has to see a triangle on a Chinese bronze plaque to be sure that it refers to the cult of Apollo and Diana.[21]

One traveler to the Far East had reported seeing a Japanese icon of a bull attacking an enormous egg with its horns.[22] D'Hancarville thought that this corresponded to the Orphic myth of the World Egg: the bull was the first being, Protogonus, bringing the material world out of chaos.[23]

Figure 1.2. *Charles Townley with his secretary Pierre-François Hugues d'Hancarville and his friends Charles Greville and Thomas Astle, by Johann Zoffany, painted 1781–83.*

Later the bull was personalized as Bacchus, a "mythological phantom" subsequently identified as the Scythian leader who carried this cult across Asia; it survives in India as the cult of the cow and of "Brouma."[24] (How it got to Japan, he does not explain.) D'Hancarville saw the Mysteries as having revealed the secret theology to their initiates, despite its degradation into idolatry among the common people. This primordial system comprised three beings: a God who is the principle of all, exemplified by fire or a pine cone; a Son, as the supreme force or generator whose action brought the material world out of the darkness of Chaos; and Love, through which all creatures received life.[25]

This brief summary gives little indication of the disorganization of d'Hancarville's thought, which emerges as a muddle of scattered learning, marshalled by sporadic attempts to impose on it an Orphism colored by Christian theology. He must have picked up ideas in Paris from two other mythographers whom the Abbé Leblond helped in their researches: Antoine Court de Gébelin (author of *Le Monde Primitif,* 1775–1784) and Charles Dupuis (author of *L'Origine de tous les cultes,* 1795), to whom we will return in Chapter Two. Yet d'Hancarville's efforts were an integral part of the movement with which this chapter is concerned, which expressed itself in the instinctive homage paid to the beauty and mystery of ancient artefacts by projecting onto them a person's own deepest convictions about God and the universe. It was just that in d'Hancarville's case, these were not particularly deep.

Richard Payne Knight shared with the Frenchman a freethinker's attitude to religion, an interest in forbidden subjects, and a desire to unveil the secrets of antiquity. The Dilettanti, as we have heard, had agreed to publish Hamilton's account of the Isernian customs, but nothing had yet come of it. In 1785, Knight again visited Sir William Hamilton in Naples, and the next year he published a book-length essay, "A Discourse on the Worship of Priapus and its Connexion with the Mystic Theology of the Ancients," within the same covers as the accounts of the modern Priapic rites of Isernia. Although pride of place was given to Sir William Hamilton's letter, the addition of Knight's essay and its engraved plates made the whole into a substantial quarto, which was printed for the Society of Dilettanti in 1786, in an edition of about 250 copies. It was distributed only to members, and, if they wished, to one friend of each.

I suspect that Hamilton found in Knight a much more congenial mind than d'Hancarville's, and that he encouraged the publication of the younger man's work. The *Discourse* acknowledges the Frenchman's work with brief courtesy, but owes nothing to it except possibly the determination not to make such a mess of the subject. Knight had the advantages of being a sympathetic reader of the Neoplatonists and understanding their efforts at theological synthesis. As a Greek scholar who had already written

An Analytical Essay on the Greek Alphabet (published 1791), he had no need for the translations of his contemporary Thomas Taylor, who was bringing Iamblichus, Plotinus, Porphyry, and Proclus to the attention of English readers, much as Ficino's translations had brought them to Latin readers three centuries earlier. Knight was impatient with the "most exquisite ingenuity most wantonly wasted" of Taylor's beloved Proclus,[26] but he respected the "ancient Theologists" in general. He claimed to follow in his analysis the "true Orphic system," which he thought was probably the "true catholic faith."[27] It so happens that Taylor's first major work was also a translation and interpretation of the Orphic Hymns, and was published in the following year, 1787.

Besides Orphism, Knight also admired the pure theism of the eclectic Jews such as Philo, and the theology of the *Bhagavad Gita,* which he knew in Charles Wilkins's translation of 1783 (see Chapter Fifteen). Otherwise his study of Indian religious ideas was based on the reports of recent travelers (he cites Sonnerat's and Niebuhr's *Voyages*), and on a few Indian artefacts that he had seen, chief of which was Townley's fragment from Elephanta showing a man and a woman enjoying oral intercourse. Knight had it engraved for his *Discourse,* his commentary showing his fundamental seriousness: ". . . the action, which I have supposed to be a symbol of refreshment and invigoration, is mutually applied by both to their respective organs of generation, the emblems of the active and passive powers of procreation, which mutually cherish and invigorate each other."[28]

This interpretation gives a preview of the metaphysical system that forms the basis of Knight's *Discourse.* It is founded on Plutarch's *Isis and Osiris,* the primary source in antiquity for the kind of ecumenical theology that men of the Enlightenment found so attractive. At the summit is "the God of Nature, the First, the Supreme, the Intellectual,"[29] who as generator of the universe is symbolized by the phallus. This supreme god is creator, destroyer, and renovator; but "it must be observed, that, when the ancients speak of creation and destruction, they mean only formation and dissolution."[30] Knight recognized in the *Bhagavad Gita* "the same one principle of life universally emanated and expanded, and ever partially returning to be again absorbed in the infinite abyss of intellectual being."[31]

This emanating process, Knight explains, takes place through a division of the active and passive functions of the Deity, the Creator being both male and female.[32] The two functions manifest as the divine essence, and universal matter; we know them respectively as the life-force and the substance of the earth, the first invigorating the second to bring forth living beings. All images of copulation, therefore, signified in the purer, pre-Christian era the power of the infinite being; while the act itself, far from being shameful in any of its varieties, was a copy of the universal process, and hence as sacred and joyful as Nature itself.

Nothing shocked Knight. Of the temple prostitutes and sacred orgies reported by Herodotus, he writes:

> These acts of devotion were indeed attended with such rites as must naturally shock the prejudices of a chaste and temperate mind, not liable to be warmed by that ecstatic enthusiasm which is peculiar to devout persons when their attention is absorbed in the contemplation of the beneficent powers of the Creator, and all their faculties directed to imitate him in the exertion of his great characteristic attribute. To heighten this enthusiasm, the male and female saints of antiquity used to lie promiscuously together in the temples, and honour God by a liberal display and general communication of his bounties.[33]

Even Herodotus's account of the ritual copulation of a woman with a goat at Mendes in Egypt, and Townley's Roman statuette of a satyr with a she-goat, moved Knight only to a semblance of religious respect. Of the former he suggests: "It was one of the sacraments of that ancient church, and was, without doubt, beheld with that pious awe and reverence with which devout persons always contemplate the mysteries of their faith, whatever they happen to be . . ."[34] And should anyone object, he would only have had to point to the "Christian" ceremonies of Isernia.

At a time when the discovery of Indian erotic art was commonly regarded, even by those without missionary interests, as proof of the depravity of Hindus in comparison to Europeans, Knight was one of the very first to assert the unanimity of Hindu doctrine with the "ancient theology" of Egypt, Persia, and the West. Moreover, his sexual interpretations of everyday objects should be recognized as the first adumbration of Sigmund Freud's theories. The spires and pinnacles with which our churches are still decorated derive, says Knight, from the ancient solar obelisks still found in the North of England (referring to menhirs), which represent the sun's rays as well as the phallus; happily their mystic meaning is forgotten, he adds, or the Reformers of the seventeenth century would have destroyed them.[35] Knight discriminates between the two types of ancient monument, obelisk and pyramid.[36] The obelisk is the symbol of Light, Creation, and the god Osiris. The pyramid, on the contrary, symbolizes Fire, Destruction, and Osiris's murderer Typhon. From the union of the two forces springs "the goddess *Harmony,* who was the physical order of the universe personified."[37]

It required a sophistication rare in Knight's or any era to distinguish these twin forces of creation and destruction from the subjective pair of "good" and "evil." Knight had no truck with Plutarch's idea of an original evil principle, calling this "an error into which men have been led by forming false notions of good and evil, and considering them as self-existing inherent properties, instead of accidental modifications, variable with every circumstance with which causes and events are connected."[38] Nor could he take seriously the Neoplatonic concept of a deity "beyond Being," calling it an entertaining specimen of metaphysical theology, "a study very generally, and very deservedly, neglected at present."[39]

Knight could not, and surely had no wish to, separate his philosophy from the compassion aroused by seeing the Catholic Church in action. He defends the theory of emanation as having at least excluded "two of the greatest curses that ever afflicted the human race, dogmatical theology, and its consequent religious persecution."[40] In the same breath he praises the Roman Empire for its tolerance, saying that the early Christians were persecuted not for their religion but for civil crimes, treason, or their own intolerance.[41] Thus he joins the more famous infidels of his century, such as Voltaire and Edward Gibbon, in turning the tables on the Christians, who had changed a teaching of love into one of the most oppressive institutions the world had ever known.

Personal experience in Catholic France had lent emotional force to Knight's convictions. While Voltaire had his Calas (the Protestant judicially murdered, whose reputation and family the philosopher did so much to save), Knight had his Desrues. He was in Paris in the winter of 1777 when Bury Desrues was executed with the refinements of cruelty typical of the Ancien Régime, apparently on a false charge, which his widow was then forced into corroborating. Knight writes movingly in his political poem, *The Progress of Civil Society* (1796), of his horror at these events.

Knight's *Discourse* enjoyed a notoriety out of all proportion to its distribution, and its reputation followed him throughout his career—not that this troubled him. The outrage felt by less open minds on encountering it may be judged from that of Thomas James Mathias, author of a popular verse treatise *The Pursuits of Literature* (1794). It seems very unlikely that Mathias read, much less understood, Knight's neopagan essay; the mere sight of the plates was enough to move him to this diatribe:

> A friend of mine would insist upon my perusing a long disquisition in quarto, *On the Worship of Priapus* (printed in 1786) with numerous and most disgusting plates. It has not been published, but distributed liberally. As I hope the treatise may be forgotten I shall not name the author, but observe, that all the ordure and filth, all the antique pictures, and all the representations of the generative organs, in their most odious and degrading protrusion, have been raked together, and copulated (for no other idea seems to be in the mind of the author) and

> copulated, I say, with a new species of blasphemy. Such are, what we would call, the records of the stews and bordellos of Grecian and Roman antiquity, exhibited for the recreation of antiquaries, and the obscene revellings of Greek Scholars in their private studies. Surely this is to dwell mentally in lust and darkness in the loathsome and polluted chamber at Capreae."[42]

This is the first example—and we will be seeing many more—of the fury that our philosophers could arouse.

Knight's reputation in the wider world of culture rests on two things quite distinct from his Priapic theories. The first is his original approach to country house design and landscaping, which he put into practice in the building of Downton Castle, Herefordshire, from about 1773 to 1785. Contrary to current practice, Knight built an asymmetrical, castellated house, set in natural rather than artificial grounds. He elaborated on his principles in *The Landscape, a Didactic Poem* (1794). The second thing, which absorbed most of Knight's income after Downton was built, was the collection of classical statuettes, medals, coins, and gems, and old master drawings and paintings. His wish was that his classical objects should pass, after his death, to the British Museum, where they can now be seen. But few visitors notice them because of the superior attraction of the Elgin Marbles and other large exhibits. Knight made a fool of himself by being the only connoisseur of his day to despise the Elgin Marbles and advise against their acquisition; he was accused of fearing that they would eclipse his own little treasures, and mocked for preferring to spend three hundred pounds on a "Black Beetle" (presumably a scarab).[43] This is not the place to fill in all the details of his life; but it is appropriate to shed some further light on his character, which he revealed in a series of intimate letters to his fellow antiquary Lord Aberdeen, covering the period from 1805 almost to his death.

In 1796 Knight had already remarked that marriage was usually unhappy because of its indissolubility.[44] By 1809 he was reconciled to remaining single and childless, and gave Downton over to his brother Thomas Andrew. Thereafter he divided his time between his London house in Soho Square, where he kept his collection, and Stonebrook Cottage, a surprisingly modest house on the Downton estate. His philosophical devotion to Nature, as expressed in the *Discourse on the Worship of Priapus,* was more than a pose, for Knight was in love with the country: not, like many of his class, as a venue for shooting and hunting parties, but as the place where man serves as the gentle custodian of Nature and contemplates her in solitariness. To the end of his life, Knight would walk several miles a day, probably during what he calls the "most beautiful hours" of six to eight A.M. and five to seven P.M.[45] He was a tireless planter of trees, and felt sad when he visited Scotland in 1812 and saw the mass fellings at Hamilton.[46] He complained that his fellow gentry "really do not know what a delightful planet this is or what a delicious portion of it has fallen to the lot of us grumbling Englishmen."[47]

Knight described his life at Stonebrook Cottage as spent "in as perfect happiness as my Nature is capable of—wandering through my romantic woods planning and executing improvements every morning, and enjoying my old books in undisturbed tranquility every evening."[48] Aberdeen must have teased him about his bucolic solitude, for Knight replied with an eloquent and amusing letter that brings his character most vividly to life. His single state evidently did not prevent him from conducting priapic researches on a practical level:

> Do not imagine that I am in any danger of becoming a lovesick swain in my cottage—I am either too old or too young; and, were it not so, am so bristled over with Greek that Cupid might as well point his arrows at a porcupine. Indeed I believe that love, such as poets and novel writers have imagined and described never frequented any cottages but those ideal ones of their building. At least my experience, which has been very long and extensive, never found any in them, but of a sort which was to be bought ready made. Of this I get enough to keep my thoughts at Home, (and a little now sufficing) in a very secret and comfortable way—not of course without some suspicions, but without any glaring scandal. The Rustics are not nice, so that a small endowment gets a Husband when a cloak is wanting. I have however of late been fortunate in Borrens; and since the Army has been put into Barracks, and our soldiers been quartered at Ludlow the greater Evil has never visited us. Before, the arrival of a Regiment always spread contagion around, and poor Cupid was again put under the tuition of Mercury [referring to the treatment for venereal disease], who in the interpolated Tale of the Odyssey expresses the most eager desire to share with Mars in the Favours of his Mother, as he has since done most abundantly.[49]

Inured though he was to criticism of his Discourse, Knight must have regretted that the theories advanced in it were not more readily accessible. In later life he took the opportunity to give them a more mature and comprehensive form in a second treatise on symbolism: *On the Symbolical Language of Ancient Art and Mythology* (1818).[50] The matters broached in the *Discourse* now take their place as merely part of an ancient and universal language of signs. As to its origins, Knight explains that ancient religion was divided between the "natural" form (we would call it exoteric), common to all peoples and consisting in the worship of the sun, moon, stars, earth, and elements; and the esoteric or "secret mystic system" found in the more civilized countries and reserved to hereditary priesthoods.[51] The latter taught more exalted and philosophical views of deity and the human soul and revealed them to initiates in the Mysteries.

Possessing in the system of emanations the esoteric key, Knight found himself able to interpret virtually any ancient myth or visual symbol. One can easily imagine the pleasure it gave him to "read" the coins, intaglios, statuettes, and artefacts to which he had dedicated his fortune and to see everywhere reflected the sublime principles of cosmogony. Reading in the *Odyssey* the famous myth of Venus and Mars caught in Vulcan's net, he perceived "a mystic allegory, signifying the active and passive powers of destruction and generation fixed in their mutual operation by the invisible exertions of the universal agent, fire."[52] Handling his collection of scarabs, he recalled that "The Aegyptians are said to have represented the pervading Spirit or ruling providence of the Deity by the black beetle . . ."[53]

Knight's esotericism was a speculative system of cosmogony, devoid of any consequences for personal growth beyond the dispelling of superstitious ignorance. It would have been laughable for him to assume the mantle of initiate (except among the Dilettanti, for whom he designed togas). Consequently, while his finely honed taste permitted him to shock the bourgeois mentality with his display of phallic objects, it did not give him any sympathy with occult or mystic pretentions. He was vigorously contemptuous of astrology[54] and indifferent to the angelic hierarchy of the Kabbalists and magicians.[55] Apuleius's famous epiphany of the "sun at midnight" during his initiation into the mysteries of Osiris, was, to Knight's urbane reading, nothing but the revelation of the sun's dual power, destructive as well as generative.[56] Any attribution of immense antiquity or mysterious, lost knowledge aroused his skeptical side: he rejected Jean-Sylvain Bailly's belief that a highly scientific civilization had existed in antediluvian times.[57] The "ancient" Egyptian system, as retailed by Greek and Roman writers of the Christian era, seemed to Knight a recent invention imposed on them by the Egyptian priesthood, owing more to Plato than to indigenous tradition;[58] the *Zend Avesta* recovered by Anquetil Duperron, merely the concoction of modern Zoroastrians.[59] In matters of scholarship, Knight was a modern man.

The authors of works on the origins and principles of ancient religion inevitably project their own views onto their subject-matter, whether through a negative attitude that throws into relief their own, superior creed (or unbelief), or through a warm enthusiasm. Moreover, the choice of images and language for the expression of this metaphysics always reveals the writer's own personality and tastes. Knight was a freethinking Deist with an aversion to dogmatism of any kind. Thus his first principle is the agnostic one: that it is impossible for the human mind to conceive of Infinity. He found an echo of his sentiments in his beloved classical world, and in parts of the modern Orient. Of the Chinese, he wrote that "as their creed, like that of the Greeks and Romans, remains undefined, it admits of no dogmatical theology, and, of course, of no persecution for opinion."[60] And in the *Bhagavad Gita* he admired the sentiment of the incarnate deity Krishna: "Even they who worship other gods worship me, although they know it not."[61] He himself seems to have considered the most salient of the Supreme Being's attributes to be the universal principle of desire, leading to harmony.[62] This was the philosophy of Knight as we know him from his letters, at peace with his environment and with himself.

Knight's humanism made him distrust established religion and its ministers, seeing there a universal tendency to bigotry and deceit. His severest censure was reserved for the "sanguinary fanaticism, and [. . .] horrible enormities of massacre, pillage, and persecution, which had been consecrated by the religion of Mohammed; and which everywhere attended the progress of his followers, spreading slavery, misery, darkness, and desolation, over the finest regions of the earth . . ."[63] The regions in question were India, where Knight was hard put to find any satisfactory religious solution for the people. Brahminism with its caste system, while preferable to Islam, he found socially deplorable, for "in no instance in the history or man, has the craft of imposture, or the insolence of usurpation, placed one class of human beings so far above another, as the sacred Brahmins, whose souls are approaching to a reunion with their source, are above the wretched outcasts . . ."[64] Yet he could hardly favor the efforts of the Christian missionaries, either morally or politically, knowing that the light of the Gospel, with its message of equality before God, would eventually break not only the caste system but the colonial system as well.[65] Leaving the reader with this prospect, he concludes the *Symbolical Language* on an elegiac note, urging the preservation of Greek and Roman antiquities as the unique and probably unrepeatable zenith of human achievement.[66] In bequeathing his collection to the nation, Knight was paying the proper tribute to the highest thing he knew.

While Richard Payne Knight was working on his interpretation of the worship of Priapus, another scholar halfway across the globe was wrestling with similar problems. Sir William Jones (1746–1794), supreme court judge at Calcutta, wrote in 1784 the work that marks his transition from philologist to mythographer: the essay "On the gods of Greece, Italy, and India." Jones's thesis was the common one, for his time, of cross-cultural identity: the gods of these different nations resembled each other because there had been contacts in one direction or another. Often applied to Greece and Egypt, this theory was now to be tested on the fresh ground of India. Drawing on Plutarch, as Knight was doing, Jones surmised that the Egyptian Isis and Osiris were equivalent to the Hindu god Ishwara and his consort Idi, and both pairs to "the Powers of Nature considered as Male and Female."[67] This is exactly the thesis of Knight's *Discourse.* As for the more lurid elements of both religions, Jones found no moral depravity in the sexual symbols of Hinduism, any more than in the Egyptian phallic rites reported by Herodotus: they were crude and literalistic, maybe, but based on a respectable, if pagan metaphysic of the dual energies of Nature.

Jones's essay was published in the inaugural volume of *Asiatic Researches* (1788), and no doubt passed beneath the eyes of some of Knight's readers. A couple of years later, one Reuben Burrow gave timid voice in the journal to another idea that corresponded to Knight's, and which would pervade the mythographic literature of the nineteenth century: the interpretation of ancient monuments as phallic symbols. Burrow suggested that the pyramids of Egypt, the "pyramids" lately discovered in Ireland, and probably the Tower of Babel were all "images of Mahadeo."[68] Mahadeo or Mahadeva ("great god") was a name given to the Hindu god Shiva, whose primary symbol, found in all his temples, was the lingam or phallus. Burrow adds that Cleopatra's Needle and the Devil's Bolts at Boroughbridge probably have some religious origin. Thus the new evidence from India was being brought into the same circle of ideas as Knight had outlined.

Knight had already laid considerable emphasis on the double nature of ancient sexual worship, and on votaries of the female as well as the more prominent male organ. Confirming Knight's suspicion that all he found in the West could be corroborated from the Orient, *Asiatic Researches* next offered a Hindu myth that exceeded all his hopes. It was Lieutenant Francis Wilford who published a summary of it in 1792, in his article "On Egypt and other countries . . . from the ancient books of the Hindus." Wilford was a bold, speculative scholar: so much so, that Sir William Jones felt obliged to add an afterword to his article, saying that he was not entirely convinced by it. But no issue was taken with the myth itself, attributed to the *Servarasa,* of the dual creation of the human race by Shiva and his wife Mahadeva (or Parvati). It told that in the course of mythic time, the two groups became polarized as the *Lingajas,* or devotees of Shiva and his lingam, and the *Yonijas,* devotees of Parvati and her yoni. Their rivalry erupted in war, from which the Yonijas emerged victorious. Wilford's Brahmin pundits told him that they were now called the Yavanas (who exist in modern times as an obscure tribe in Orissa), and that the point of difference between the two groups was that the Yavanas insist on the primacy of the female, not the male parent in producing perfect offspring. Wilford comments that both parties of the conflict were known in Greece, where the yoni was worshipped at Eleusis, and also to the Hebrews, whose periodic lapses into Canaanite phallicism are testified to by their scriptures. He adds that a third, median sect was introduced to Greece by the "Pelarsgi," whose symbol represented the union of both sexual organs, under the concealing symbolism of the boat Argo, or else of the navel or *omphalos*.[69]

Wilford's account of this prehistoric sexual schism was reprinted verbatim in Edward Moor's influential *Hindu Pantheon* (1810).[70] In France, it was taken over by Fabre d'Olivet in his *Histoire philosophique du genre humain* (1822), without giving any indication of the source, presenting it rather as revealed prehistory and thus introducing it into the French esoteric tradition. By that time, it made little difference that Wilford was shown to have been sorely misled by his pundit informants, to an extent that discredited nearly all of his work.

Like many skeptical scholars, Francis Wilford devoted his energies to excavating precisely the kind of material that is seized upon by the makers of occult systems and presented by them as dogma. He argued in his book-length "Essay on the Sacred Isles of the West" that the legendary "White Island" of the Hindus was none other than Britain. It did not take much to move it a little further West, and make it into lost Atlantis. Again, in his "Remarks on the names of the Cabirian Deities, and on some words used in the mysteries of Eleusis," Wilford pointed out that the mysterious words that closed the mysteries, "Konx, Om, Pax," were the same as the Sanskrit "Cancsha, Om, Pacsha," pronounced at every transaction,[71] thus suggesting a primordial, world-wide system of mystery initiations.

For all his arcane interests and bizarre theories, Wilford had little respect for the tradition he studied. In 1798 he published an article "On the Chronology of the Hindus," whose explicit object was to overthrow "their monstrous system, which I have rejected as absolutely repugnant to the course of nature, and to human reason. Indeed their systems of geography, chronology and history are all equally monstrous and absurd."[72] Wilford was still unable to accept a greater age for the world than the six thousand years fixed by the divines: one of the current bones of contention that stuck in the craw of even the best scholars of the 1790s.

The early volumes of the *Asiatic Researches* were hard to obtain (being printed in Calcutta), but the writings of Sir William Jones, which were the most important of their contents, were published separately and read in every academy of the Western world. Whereas Oriental philosophies and religions had hitherto been known only from isolated documents and travelers' tales, Jones and his colleagues ensured that they would henceforth be described in a proper scholarly manner. No longer dismissible as heathen superstitions, Oriental wisdom now cried out for integration into the world view of anyone concerned with mythography, religious origins, and esoteric studies. But this incurred a painful collision with the thinking habits of Christian culture, not least that of prudery in sexual matters.

Such was the case with another influential Indianist, the Rev. Thomas Maurice. In his seven-volume *Indian Antiquities* (1793–1804), Maurice writes of the Hindu lingam worship: "Our pity and abhorrence are at once excited by the emblem under which they represented, in this recess [of a Shiva temple], the Supreme Creator."[73] Obliged, as a clergyman, to base all human history on the Bible, Maurice attributed this degenerate superstition to Noah's bad son Ham, whose legacies of phallic, serpent, and sun worship, and human sacrifice had migrated to India from Egypt with his descendants, the Cushites.[74] But Maurice, like Wilford, was a preserver and transmitter of this degeneracy, and, not least, of the memorable story of how Shiva's lingam cult began.[75] The myth tells that the god Shiva was wandering around the world, naked as usual, when he came upon a group of ascetics performing their devotions. Amused by them, Shiva uttered indecent and insulting remarks, whereupon they cursed him, and his phallus dropped off. Poor Shiva roamed the earth in his mutilated state, while his distracted wife Parvati followed, singing songs. When eventually the missing part turned up, it had grown to monstrous size and was endowed with life and motion. The sacred lingam was now cut into thirty-one pieces, each a perfect replica of the original, which were distributed around earth, heaven, and hell. Shiva himself was reborn entire.

This myth rivals Zeus's castration of Kronos and the masturbation of the Egyptian sun god Ra as the story least likely to induce respect for the gods of the heathen. It did not take a very advanced mythographer to detect a similarity to the Egyptian myth of Isis, wandering the earth in search of the lost phallus of Osiris, nor to the many myths of mutilated and resurrected savior-gods, such as Dionysus, Attis, and Adonis. Correspondences between the Oriental religions and Christianity also forced themselves on these early researchers: Wilford wrote on the parallels between the lives of Jesus and Krishna, and on the identity of the crucified and resurrected Hindu hero Salivahana.[76] This could have but one meaning to him, as the Jesus-Krishna parallels had to Sir William Jones: that the Indians had acquired them from early Christian missionaries, just as they had borrowed myths and symbols from Greece and from Egypt. There was really no alternative, so long as all humanity was believed to stem from Noah's Ark, in the third millennium BCE. But once the age of the earth was pushed beyond the biblical boundary, these parallels became perilous indeed, for they could be, and were, used to support the contrary thesis: that Christianity was only a borrowing from Hinduism.

After Payne Knight, there was one man who proclaimed the phallic theory loud and clear: the short-lived Irish scholar Henry O'Brien (1808–1835), author of *The Round Towers of Ireland.* Coming from a completely obscure background, O'Brien did not even learn English until he was twelve. Then someone took his education in hand and enabled him to attend Trinity College, Dublin. Here he discovered, of all things, the *Asiatic Researches,* and determined on the vocation of a scholar.

Scattered throughout Ireland are some hundreds of round towers of unknown age and purpose, tall and slim, with conical roofs and with their only entrance sometimes many feet above the ground. When in December 1830 the Royal Irish Academy offered a gold medal and fifty pounds for the best essay on the origin and uses of these curious monuments, O'Brien felt that the summons had come that would draw him out of poverty and oblivion. Having grown up near a ruined tower at Bally-Carbery, which the peasants called "The Temple of Delight," he had sought out several others, read everything written on the subject, and already made up his mind as to its origin and use.[77] Confident that no one could possibly know more about round towers than he, the young antiquarian embarked on a five-hundred page prize essay.

The Round Towers of Ireland was finished by 1 June 1832, the deadline for the Academy's competition. It is a sprawling and incoherent work, into which O'Brien poured every ounce of his learning and opinions, whether they had to do with the subject or not. He had conceived the notion that the round towers dated from the colonization of Ireland from the East, and that they belonged to the oldest religion on earth, at the same time phallic, fiery, and "Budhist," stellar and solar.

O'Brien introduces into his book several themes from *Asiatic Researches:* the disquieting presence of the lingam in Indian temples, the story of Shiva losing his phallus, the sexual schism and the victory of the Yavanas, and the crucifixion of Sulivahana. He shows the relationship between fire, sun, and phallic worship, much as Payne Knight had done. Then he plays his ace: *Budh* in Irish means both phallus and sun; therefore "Budhists" are phallicists! To confirm this, O'Brien quotes a tenth-century Irish annal, which calls the round towers *Fiadh-Nemeadh. Fiadh* is etymologically the same as *Budh;* and *Nemeadh* means "consecrated." Therefore these buildings are "consecrated lingams."[78]

O'Brien could get away with this because the Western ignorance of Buddhism was still so abysmal (a theme to be developed in Chapters Thirteen and Fifteen). He sums up, not unjustly, the prevailing view of his time: ". . . if you look into any encyclopedia or depository of science for a

Figure 1.3. *Henry O'Brien (1808–1835), from* The Round Towers of Ireland, *1898.*

definition of the word 'Budhism,' you will be told that 'it is the doctrine of solar worship as taught by Budha.'"[79] However, the young scholar did not agree with this. Certainly the sun and moon were the first objects of worship for fallen humanity; but the Eleusinian and other Mysteries taught their initiates the great principles of generation and procreation, using the appropriate symbols.[80] Budhism was not solar but phallic worship.

How did O'Brien suppose that this cult had come to Ireland? From Persia, he says, for "Erin" is the same as "Iran." This was not quite as insane as it may sound, since in O'Brien's time there was much speculation on Irish origins from Phoenicia, Scythia, Central Asia, and even Chaldaea. For example, General Vallancey had stated that the mysterious personages of Irish legend, the *Tuatha-de-danaan,* were identical to the Persian sorcerers called *Pish-dadan.*[81]

O'Brien was constitutionally unable to agree with any other scholar. Chiding Vallancey for his ignorance, the young expert says that if Tuath signifies the phallus, Pish or Puzza means the vulva, the two of them being "the actual regulators of the solar universe."[82] Then he introduces Wilford's story of the schism between the lingajas and yonijas, and uses it to support his theories of migrations from India to Iran, Egypt, and Ireland, where the lingajas triumphantly erected the round towers as emblems of their cult.

O'Brien devoted many obscure pages to Christianity and its symbols, to which he had an ambiguous attitude. He revered the Jesus of the Gospels, yet could not believe that earlier religions were un-Christian. The many instances of crosses and crucifixions from pre-Christian Europe, India, and Mexico, made him suspect that Jesus had not been the only crucified savior. Moreover, he found that the cross was repeatedly associated with "Budh." In veiled terms, O'Brien conveys the message that the crucified saviors were those who through mortification and self-denial overcame sexual temptation and attained inner purification.[83]

In confirmation of this, O'Brien found, somewhere in the *Asiatic Researches,* an inscription from Gautama's Indian birthplace, Budda-Gaya, that seemed to refer to an earlier avatar than Christ. Every Irish cowherd, says O'Brien, knows what *Budh-gaye* means:

> *Budh-gaye,* then of the Irish, or *Budha-gaya* of the Hindoos, means *Phallus telluris, i.e.* the *generativeness of the earth,* or *the earth's prolific principle.* This I have before demonstrated to have been the object of adoration to the ancients; and have furthermore shown, that one of the individuals, in whom this idea was personified, had suffered crucifixion as a mediator for sin.[84]

The crucified Christ was therefore both a phallic symbol and an exemplar of sexual abstinence. The vulva, likewise, was an ambiguous symbol, for "in the *sacred, i.e., Irish* language, the word *Sabh,* has three significations—firstly, *voluptuousness,* or the *yoni;* secondly, a *snake,* or sinuosity; and, thirdly, *death* or life!"[85] O'Brien explains that one is saved from the death of sin or concupiscence by the Redeemer, who took birth through the very place that caused one's sorrow.[86]

At the end of 1832, O'Brien learnt that his essay had not won him the gold medal, but a second prize of twenty pounds. Far from thinking himself lucky that the Royal Irish Academicians had even recognized his eccentric theory, he became a thorough nuisance, complaining loudly that the winner, Dr. Petrie, was a political choice. Early in 1834 the disappointed scholar published his essay himself as *The Round Towers of Ireland (or the Mysteries of Freemasonry, of Sabaism, and of Budhism, for the first time unveiled),* prefacing it with all his whining letters to the Academy. For a second edition, dated from London in September 1834, he removed the subtitle and prefatory letters, and added a dedication to the Marquis of Lansdowne, who had now become his patron; O'Brien was probably tutoring his children.

O'Brien was a brilliant young man whose psychological problems might have been mollified by age and approbation. But a sudden fatal illness took him in the summer of 1835, aged twenty-six. Richard Carlile, the freethinker, called his death "a lamentable instance of genius smothered and murdered by ignorant and wicked mystery."[87] *The Round Towers of Ireland* may be flawed, but it was the only English-language treatise on the sexual theory of mythology to appear between Payne Knight's *Discourse* of 1786 and the revival of these ideas in the 1860s. It was probably the first Irish work to incorporate, however inappropriately, the new knowledge of the *Asiatic Researches.* A work entirely *sui generis,* it deserves a place among the "curiosities of literature" that can still surprise and delight the dilettante.

The 1860s saw a renewal of interest in the phallic theory of religions, not among anthropologists or academic historians but in the coteries of Freemasons, self-styled "Rosicrucians," and collectors of erotica. Robert Martin, M.D., presented the whole complex in 1860 to the readers of the *Freemason's Magazine and Masonic Monitor:* the male and female principles, phallic worship in the Bible, revolting rites in Hindustan, and the etymologies of "Bro. O'Brien."[88] Knight's *Priapus* was reissued in 1865 in an edition of 125 copies, enlarged by the antiquarians Thomas Wright, Sir James Emerson Tennent, and George Witt, who brought the subject up through the Middle Ages and added many illustrations.[89] The publisher was John Camden Hotten, a specialist in erotic literature who issued Hargrave

Jennings's *The Rosicrucians, their Rites and Mysteries* a few years later (see Chapter Thirteen).

Another book that kept the phallic theory alive was Sellon's *Annotations on the Sacred Writings of the Hindus* (1865). Captain Edward Sellon (1817/18–1866) was a naval officer who took advantage of his posting in India to gain a wide experience of native women. A thorough atheist, his violent life ended in suicide, leaving behind a poem to his mistress with the epigram "*Vivat Lingam. Non Resurgam.*"[90] Appropriately enough, it was Sellon who took in hand the arrangement of Knight's phallic objects in the British Museum.[91]

His reconstruction of the history of religions begins with the monotheistic worship of *Brühm Atma,* "Breathing Soul." In time, he says, this was given the material emblem of a phallic stone, as symbol of the productive power. Next came the adoration of the elements, especially fire; then polytheism entered with the worship of the three emanations Brahma, Vishnu, and Shiva. The almost universal tendency to deify heroes, creatures, the heavenly bodies, and every attribute of the Supreme Being, from Love to Murder, led to the historical religions, including those demanding human sacrifice. Besides drawing on the *Asiatic Researches,* Sellon relates the practices of the Hindus to the current craze for Mesmerism or animal magnetism (see Chapter Nine), for example in his closing sentence: "During Puja, the Yogini is supposed to be in a *magnetic sleep,* wherein like the Sibyls among the Ancients and modern clairvoyants, she answers questions in a delirious manner, and is supposed to be for the time inspired by the deity."[92]

Sellon makes a special point of the phallic nature of the Hebrew religion, of the name of JHWH as a graphic emblem of the sexual organs and the Ark of the Covenant as what he calls a "Linyoni," concluding that there was no people more obsessed with every sexual perversion than the Jews.[93] Similar views would reappear with H. P. Blavatsky (see Chapter Fourteen), who wrote in one of the essays destined to complete her *Secret Doctrine* that "in its hidden meaning, from *Genesis* to the last word of *Deuteronomy,* the *Pentateuch* is the symbolical narrative of the sexes, and is an apotheosis of Phallicism, under astronomical and physiological personations."[94]

The two-volume *Ancient Faiths Embodied in Ancient Names* (1868) of Thomas Inman, M.D., also belongs to the philophallic school of interpretation, though most of it is merely an etymological dictionary.[95] Inman's clinical experience gave him fresh insights into why the ancients chose certain symbols to represent the male or female organs, and made him unsqueamish in describing them. One of his leading ideas is an explanation of why so many religions have a male Trinity, while the Great Goddess or Celestial Virgin stands alone: it is because the male sexual organs are conspicuously triple (penis and two testicles), while the female is single. To protect unlearned Christians from so blasphemous an analogy, Inman leaves the key paragraphs of this theory in Latin.[96]

Inman's erudition and his numerous illustrations were raided by Hargrave Jennings and John Davenport. We will treat Jennings at length in Chapter Thirteen. Davenport (1789–1877) was a poor scrivener who led a precarious existence teaching Oriental languages and writing hack literature. His *Aphrodisiacs and Anti-aphrodisiacs* (issued in 1873) was sold by Hotten in London and by Bouton in New York (the publisher of Blavatsky's *Isis Unveiled*); it was intended to be a sequel to Knight's *Discourse,* and in its first part gathers what had now become a common stock of phallic fable.[97] Davenport's writings were ransacked in turn by the Bath publisher, Robert H. Fryar, for an "Esoteric Physiology Series" which he issued in the late 1880s. The series comprised four works: (1) the twelve erotic engravings of Giulio Romano, called *Situations gracieuses;* (2) *Sexagyma,* a digest of the works of John Davenport; (3) D'Hancarville's *Veneres uti observantur in gemmis antiquis,* (4) Colonel Fanin's *Peintures, Bronzes, et Statues erotiques du cabinet Secret* of the Royal Museum of Naples; (5) Knight's *The Worship of Priapus* with *An Essay on the Worship of the Generative Powers during the Middle Ages of Western Europe* (by Thomas Wright). Fryar says that they were "withdrawn from circulation in 1889, in deference to the National Vigilance Association."[98]

Fryar played an indispensable role in the background of the Hermetic Brotherhood of Luxor, whose importance to the history of occultism at the end of the nineteenth century will emerge fully in Chapter Sixteen. The sexual doctrines of Paschal Beverly Randolph (see Chapter Thirteen) were an essential part of the Hermetic Brotherhood of Luxor's teachings. Fryar was the British agent for manuscript copies of Randolph's sexual writings, and he also published the first advertisement for the "H.B. of L." in 1884. His reissue of Knight and D'Hancarville was not just a venture in learned pornography, but part of a serious stirring of interest in a long-suppressed topic. For the H.B. of L., the proper use of sex was the royal road to occult power and spiritual development, both in this world and the next.

As this book proceeds, it will become clear that the nineteenth century's search for new modes of spiritual enlightenment was intimately linked with the moral and philosophical "Enlightenment" that began in early eighteenth-century France. This chapter has provided one illustration. A handful of erudite libertines, taking advantage of a climate which allowed them to advertise their nonbelief in Christianity, fastened on sex as the universal explanation of mythology and religious origins. A hundred years later, their work provided the theoretical basis for an order of practical occultism.

The next chapter will trace a different, though parallel effort, also moving from France to England: the solar theory of religious origins. Beside the phallic and the solar theories, we might have considered other British mythographers such as Andrew Ramsay,[99] for whom they were aspects of the One God; Thomas Blackwell,[100] for whom they were powers of Nature; Jacob Bryant,[101] for whom all the pagan gods were really Jewish patriarchs; George Stanley Faber,[102] for whom they were deified mortals; John Leland[103] and John Landseer,[104] for whom they were the heavenly bodies, etc. The reason they do not appear here is because, with the possible exception of Blackwell, these were Christians who took the Bible as the bedrock of their system. My interest here is in those who did not, and consequently had to thread their own way through the cluttered alleyways of ancient faiths.

TWO

The Cult of the Sun

This chapter begins a year later than the European tour of 1777 that opened Payne Knight's eyes to the evils of Catholicism and the society it condoned. It was on 18 May 1778 that Charles François Dupuis (1742–1809), an obscure professor of rhetoric at the Collège de Lisieux, Paris, was struck by the idea whose elaboration would occupy all his working life: that the twelve signs of the zodiac, that perennial enigma, were nothing but an allegory of the yearly cycle of agriculture.[1]

Not the most exciting idea, one would have thought—but for Dupuis to have recorded the date on which it came to him, it must have been an epiphany. Perhaps it resembled the illuminations that came to his contemporaries Charles Fourier, Hoëné Wronski, and Fabre d'Olivet, and inspired them to build their systems of universal order. Dupuis was to do the same, after his fashion. Though devoid of any esoteric, mystical, or even religious impulse, he pursued his *idée fixe* with the devotion of an illuminate who holds the key to the world's mysteries, as indeed he believed himself to do.

Just as Knight found the key to his sexual metaphysics where it had lain for centuries in the pages of Plutarch, so it was the fifth-century encyclopedist Macrobius who set the precedent for interpreting all religions as originally zodiacal and solar. In his *Saturnalia,* Macrobius relates the signs of the zodiac to the twelve labors of Hercules, the sun god who works all year, dies at the winter solstice, and is reborn from his ashes in the spring.

Was this, Dupuis wondered, the answer to a question that had so vexed scholars: Where do the signs of the zodiac come from? A mythographer of the generation preceding Dupuis, the Abbé Noël-Antoine Pluche, in the first volume of his *Histoire du Ciel* (1739–1741) had tried to

Figure 2.1. *Charles-François Dupuis (1742–1809), from* Abrégé de l'origine des cultes, *1836.*

relate the zodiacal animals to the farming activities of each month. In 1773, Antoine Court de Gébelin had combined these with the Labors of Hercules, to arrive at the following synthesis:[2]

The Nemean Lion - Leo - July - heat needed for growing crops
The Lernaean Hydra - Virgo (with Spica, the ear of wheat) - August - reaping the many-headed stalks of wheat
The Erymanthian Boar and the Repulse of the Centaurs - Libra - September - equality of day and night at autumn equinox; slaughter of pigs
The Ceryneian Hind - Scorpio - October - hunting season
The Stymphalian Birds - Sagittarius - November - shooting migrating flocks
The Stables of Augeias - Capricorn - December - month of rest and cleaning
The Cretan Bull and the Foundation of the Olympic Games - Aquarius - January - Carnival games
The Mares of Diomedes - Pisces - February - cruelty of coldest month
Hippolyte's Girdle - Aries - March - victory over short nights
The Cattle of Geryon - Taurus - April - fecundity
The Capture of Cerberus - Gemini - May - month of Eleusinian Mysteries, with descent to the Underworld
The Apples of the Hesperides - Cancer - June - fruit harvest

But for all its ingenuity, Court de Gébelin's system was unconvincing. It leaves several of the signs unexplained, and the labors are neither in the traditional sequence, nor true to life in any climate.

In order to correct this, Dupuis had to make two bold assumptions. First, he supposed that the beginnings of astronomy, hence the origin of the zodiac, had occurred not in the temperate zone but in tropical Egypt, where unique farming conditions obtain on account of the Nile's annual flood. Dupuis's second assumption concerned the way in which the zodiac signs align with the months of the year. He began by asking what signs might originally have marked the solstices and equinoxes, the four corners of the year. Libra, he guessed, must have been an equinox, because it obviously symbolizes the equality of day and night. But which equinox was it? In conventional astrology, the sun enters Libra on the 21st of September, the autumnal equinox. This puts the vernal or spring equinox in Aries, the sign of the Ram or frisky lamb, aptly followed by Taurus which rules the month of plowing with oxen. So far, so good. But things were quite different in Egypt. Plowing takes place there in November, after the Nile has enriched the soil and subsided. Could the zodiac once have been aligned in exactly the contrary position, with Libra, not Aries, at the spring equinox?

When Dupuis tested this hypothesis, he found that the majority of the signs agreed with Egyptian agriculture:

Libra: March, spring equinox
Scorpio: April, apparently the time of unhealthy airs and winds
Sagittarius: May, possibly the war season, though even Dupuis admits that this is a weak explanation
Capricorn: June, summer solstice, with the sun at its highest point, like a mountain goat. Alternatively, if Capricorn is taken to be a sea creature (like a sea goat or the Indian Makaram), it rules the first of three "watery" months, covering the 100 days of the Nile flood
Aquarius: July, a watery sign for the Nile flood
Pisces: August, similar to Aquarius
Aries: September, autumn equinox, pasture emerges (for flocks) after the retreat of the flood
Taurus: October, ground ready for plowing with oxen
Gemini: November, ?
Cancer: December, winter solstice, when the sun goes back on its tracks, "crabwise"
Leo: January, the lion symbolizing the energies of the returning sun and growing vegetation
Virgo: February, harvest (Virgo centers on Spica, the ear of wheat)

The only trouble with this arrangement—and it was a considerable trouble—was that the solstices and equinoxes had not occurred in those signs since about 13,000 BCE. Nowadays the objection would be that Egyptian civilization did not exist at so early a date. In the eighteenth century, it was that the world did not exist. As mentioned at the end of Chapter One, the biblical barrier of circa 4000 BCE for the age of the world was not easily broached, least of all by a poor scholar who depended on the approval of the "second estate"—the clergy—for the furtherance of his career. Dupuis was no landed gentleman like Knight; his *Mémoire* would never have seen the light, as it did, as part of De Lalande's great treatise on astronomy if he had not been willing to excuse himself from the suspicion of heresy in the following summary:

> It thus seems that the first part of this Memoir has proved that Astronomy comes from a unique source; that it was born on the banks of the Nile, even at the Tropic; that it subse-

> quently spread among the different peoples of the world at various epochs; and that the state of the skies at the time of the distribution of the zodiacal signs as we still know them was as follows: the summer solstice corresponded to Capricorn, while the spring equinox, the most universally observed among all peoples, was then marked by the hieroglyphic sign of the Scales.
>
> The epoch of this invention would far exceed the limit fixed by our chronologists for the creation of the world; and this would be a strong objection against the hypothesis, if one were obliged to assume that the Precession of the Equinoxes has been identical over all of time. But might not the disturbance that occurred at the universal Deluge have changed the appearance of the fixed stars? This is something that we can never know; and so we are compelled to draw our conclusions following the chronology accepted today. Thus we make nothing depend on the antiquity of our epoch, so as not to contradict sacred traditions, nor the opinion of the interpreters whom it is always our duty to respect.[3]

Dupuis steers clear of attributing any religious validity to the speculations of early peoples. He says that ancient man "lost the knowledge he had received from God," and worshipped what he saw in the heavens.[4] This was man's first error, leading to a cult of the stars of which astrology was the regrettable consequence. As Dupuis sums it up, "The worship paid to the Soul of Nature, united to the cult of the Sun, the Moon, the stars, and other agents of Divinity, has formed the religion of practically all the peoples of the world."[5]

This, again, was not entirely original. The anti-Christian Boulanger had suggested that the patriarch Enoch (Gen. 5:22–24), who lived 365 years and did not die, was simply the Sun. With the help of fantastic etymologies, Boulanger went on to identify this figure with Noah, Hermes, and even with Saint Peter, remarking that the pagan gods were not the last to get into the Christian Paradise![6]

To Dupuis' credit, he resisted the temptation to base his theories on etymology, that hoary mainstay of mythographers which is so easy to twist to any desired purpose. His work is based solely on coincidences of imagery. He found the zodiacal cycle reflected in the episodes of Bacchus's life, as told by Nonnus, as well as in those of Cadmus, Phaeton, and of course Hercules. He promised his readers that they would find fuller details in a larger, forthcoming book.

Dupuis worked on these "details" for another dozen years, during which his career flourished. He obtained the chair of Latin Eloquence at the Collège de France, was elected to the Académie des inscriptions et belles-lettres, and entrusted with important administrative duties. Even Frederick the Great, the great patron of Enlightenment thought, heard about the work in progress and offered Dupuis a professorial chair in Berlin, but died (in 1786) before the offer could be taken up. During the French Revolution Dupuis entered politics, representing the Département of Seine-et-Oise at the Convention. This interrupted him, he writes, just as he was about to revise his work; then came the terrifying post-revolutionary upheavals. He found himself constantly spied upon, all his letters being opened. In a moment of despair, he resolved to burn his manuscripts, but they were saved by his wife. Eventually he deposited them with a craftsman who had made the globes to illustrate Dupuis's theories, so that the work might survive even if the author did not. The most compromising part, the essay on Christianity, apparently existed only in a manuscript copy belonging to a friend of thirty-six years, Le Tellier, who suffered the very fate that Dupuis feared.

Dupuis's own reluctance to expose himself to the possible consequences of publishing a controversial work—for who could tell whether the anticlerical atmosphere of the Revolution might not give place to a different fanaticism?—was overcome by Abbé Leblond, the same Mazarin librarian as had helped Court de Gébelin and d'Hancarville. In 1794 Leblond persuaded the Club of the Cordeliers (a vigilante group devoted to the Rights of Man) to rush Dupuis's work through the press. *L'Origine de tous les cultes, ou Religion universelle* (Paris, An III [1795]) shows no sign of its troubled origins, being a handsomely illustrated production issued in three quarto or eight octavo volumes.[7]

In his earlier *Mémoire,* Dupuis had said that man's first error—meaning the first divergence from a primordially revealed religion—was embodied in the famous inscription on the temple of Isis at Saïs: "I am that which was, is, and will be. No mortal has yet lifted my veil." He promised that his larger work would develop the theme of how the ancient fables were a veil thrown over the operations of Nature.[8] Thus he stands first in the line of self-proclaimed unveilers of Isis, which would include Godfrey Higgins (*Anacalypsis* [Greek for "unveiling"], 1833–36), J. C. Colquhoun (*Isis Revelata,* 1836), W. Winwood Reade (*The Veil of Isis,* 1861), and H. P. Blavatsky (*Isis Unveiled,* 1877).

What did this passionate scholar find beneath the veil? Nature, and nothing but Nature. Dupuis refused to occupy himself with questions such as "Does God exist?" or "Is the soul immortal?" The answer to the first seemed evident to him (he says evasively), but he protested that he was nothing but the chronicler of others' ideas. In an (unconscious?) parody of the Protestant attitude to the Bible, he wrote: "Every man has, like myself, the right to pay attention to nothing but himself and Nature, and to determine what relations he thinks he should have with her, without any intermediary."[9]

By intermediaries, Dupuis alludes to the so-called revealed religions and their authorities, to which he had paid lip-service in his *Mémoire.* Now he states outright that these religions are all "the daughters of curiosity, ignorance, self-interest, and imposture."[10] They and their gods are nothing but human inventions. If anything is to be considered as a god, it is the natural universe itself; and so it was to the pagans. Contrary to received belief, says Dupuis, early man did not first have the idea of a divinity, then materialize it in the heavens and in natural objects (as he had said in his *Mémoire,* following orthodox prehistory): man's first ideas came, as they do to all of us, from the senses.[11]

In his mixture of anticlerical polemic with classical erudition, and in his ultimate pantheism, Dupuis was the intellectual brother of Richard Payne Knight. Like the Englishman, he held in highest reverence not the personal Creator God but the Anima Mundi, the enlivening force in Nature. Among the ancients he respected Pythagoras, for whom God was extended in every part of the world like the human soul in the body. Dupuis says that Pythagoras perceived the correspondence between the macrocosm and the microcosm, but never posited a Creator outside the universe.[12] In this, the Samian philosopher agreed with the universal faith of all ancient peoples, who knew no gods but the heavenly bodies,[13] and at first worshipped them in all their grandeur on mountain-tops, with no need for temples or images.[14]

Like Payne Knight again, Dupuis recognized without embarrassment that the ancients also worshipped the generative organs, both male and female, seeing these as symbolizing the active and passive parts of Nature.[15] But whereas the libertine Knight could accept the bestial ritual of Mendes as a sacrament, symbolizing the union of the human with the divine, Dupuis remarks contemptuously that only religion could sink so low as to make girls copulate with a goat.[16]

It was the Egyptians, Dupuis thinks, who probably contributed more than any other people to the whole religious baggage of priests, temples, and organized ceremonial.[17] Deceived by priestcraft, people gave themselves up to illusion, just as even wise men today will resort for cures to quacks. Then the legislators, thinking people so foolish that they could only be governed by illusions, applied religion to politics and morality. The result was the tyrannical pact between priest and kings, which a Frenchman of the eighteenth century knew all about. Once established, religion used every resource to impose itself: magic, ceremony, dance, music, and threats all played a part. But "as for us, who live in an age when the French cannot and will not be deceived any more, we must draw our laws from the springs of justice and everlasting reason. It is time to see at last whether the people, as they resume their rights of sovereignty, will suffer themselves any longer to be fooled like children, or like slaves."[18]

Dupuis refused to countenance the utilitarian argument for religion as being good for the common people's morals. If religion is false, he says, it is false for everyone without exception, and useless to all alike. To speak otherwise is to say that the truth is only good for a few, while error is better for the majority. "Let us render human reason its due: Nature has planted the basis of morality in its bosom."[19] He dismissed the Mysteries of the ancient world in the same breath as modern priestcraft, saying that in Egypt, their first home, their purpose was merely to strengthen piety and to give consolation in the face of death.[20] Dupuis recognized that they were concerned with immortality and the posthumous journey of the soul, its purifications and metempsychosis,[21] but these adventures of the soul were nothing more to him than the projection of the annual battle of the sun with the principle of darkness; souls, being of the same substance as the Father of Light, were assumed to suffer analogously.[22]

Here we reach the central theme of Dupuis's book, and the "origin of all religions" of its title: they are all to be traced to the passage of the sun through the twelve signs of the zodiac. Picking up the threads of interpretation from his earlier *Mémoire*, he stretches them to the limit, and beyond, as he uses this theme as a universal key to mythology.

In the third volume, Dupuis drops his long-awaited bombshell: the application of the selfsame key to Christianity. He distances himself, he says as he prepares us for it, as much from the believers who accept everything as from the skeptics who believe nothing; he prefers to sift the true from the false. "Filled with respect and love for the truth, we are going to seek her in the very depth of our sanctuaries, and we will remove the mysterious veil that covers her. Perhaps, once again, we will discover Nature."[23] In the process, he promises, he will free Christ from his two natures: "The people make him both god and man; the philosophers of today, merely a man. We will make him neither a god, much less a man; for the sun is as far from the human as it is from the divine nature." [24] Jesus Christ, in a word, is the sun, and his life is nothing but an allegory of the sun's course through the zodiac, from birth, through crucifixion on the cross of the solstices and equinoxes, to resurrection. Thus the Christian religion is just another distorted representative of the great, original religion of Nature—but with what dire consequences for its hapless sectaries! "The love of religion produces intolerance; charity towards one's neighbor makes the religious man spy on others' faults; under the pretext of groaning over the weaknesses of others, he publicizes and exaggerates them; and the crimes which are imputed to them are frequently nothing but acts of reason."[25]

An early biographer of Dupuis wrote that he was "born poor and died without a fortune, leaving as the sole bequest to his widow the reputation of an upright man and a paradoxical scholar."[26] One of the most endearing things about him is the dedication of his great work to his wife. He wrote it, he tells her, when there were still "great ones" around, but refused to spoil his first pages with a grovelling dedication to any of them. Instead, his book appears under the auspices of Hymen (the Goddess of Marriage) and Erato (the Muse of History). He reminds his wife that she saw the work's germ and its development; agreed to go abroad to publish it; saved it from the flames when he was incensed by the literary people who were persecuting "enlighteners." She had lived with him through sixteen years of research, and twenty-two of continual happiness. Finally he thanks her for her love of himself and of books; and for her admiration of Voltaire, to whom she devoted whatever time she had left.

The same biographer remarks that Dupuis's work was "a partisan book, which some defended fiercely, others refuted to their advantage, and which soon, abandoned by both parties, fell flat for want of praise and criticism to sustain it: the usual lot of all works which are either too superficial or too weighty to keep themselves alive in the opinion of men of good sense."[27] Dupuis's abridgement in one volume, *Abrégé de l'Origine des Cultes* (An VII/1798) had more success, comprising extracts from the work and the all-important theory of Christianity. The latter was several times translated into English.[28]

Dupuis was fortunate in seizing the one moment when such a work could be published in France. For all the anger it generated, it did not prevent him from continuing in his academic and political posts. Sadly, he did not live to enjoy the small property near Dijon to which he retired with his family in 1809.

Most of those who encountered Dupuis' ideas had done so even before his *Origine de tous les cultes* appeared, through *Les Ruines des empires* (1791) by his friend Constantin François de Volney (1757–1820). Unlike the ponderous volumes of Dupuis, Volney's book was lively, concise, and as fresh as the latest news from revolutionary France. Like his other works on Near Eastern travel and ancient history, it was quickly translated and published in England and America,[29] where it has been kept in print to this day by small presses devoted to the secularist cause.

The *Ruins* became one of the foundational works of freethought in the English-speaking world, causing its author's name to be coupled with that of Voltaire as religion's greatest foe. Under the literary guise of a world conference of religions (such as was to convene in Chicago a century later), Volney gives each one the chance to condemn itself out of its own mouth. As in Dupuis's work, Christianity takes its place as just one among many: it is described as "Christianity, or the Allegorical Worship

Figure 2.2. *Constantin François de Volney (1757–1820), from L. A. Thiers,* The History of the French Revolution, *1881.*

of the Sun, under the cabalistical names of Chrish-en, or Christ, and Yesus or Jesus."[30] In a few pages (Dupuis had taken a few hundred), Volney outlines the Christian mythology as a dramatization of the constellations Virgo, Boötes, Perseus, Serpens, Aries, etc. He then concludes with a free discussion in which his delegates demonstrate, through mutual abuse, that all religions have the same aim, namely the duping of the people by a professional priesthood.

Volney, like Knight and Dupuis, was a worshipper at the temples of Reason and Nature. As a counterbalance to the polemic of *Ruins*, he set out his constructive policy in a little book, *The Law of Nature, or Catechism of a French Citizen* (1793), also much read in England and America. He admits that there is a revealed religion: it is revealed by God in the nature of things. This religion (1) is just, the punishment being proportionate to the transgression; (2) is pacific and tolerant, because all men are brethren, and equal in rights; it advises peace and toleration, even for their errors; (3) is of itself sufficient to make men happier and better; (4) reveals the existence of a god undefiled by the passions of human nature. Worship of this divinity consists entirely in action, i.e., in obeying the rules that maintain the order and harmony of the universe.[31]

Volney rejects Rousseau's savage utopia, in which men are neither happy nor free, lacking the philosophy that gives insight into the laws of nature. He approves the moral rectitude taught by the Gospel, and concludes his book:

> Preserve thyself.
> Instruct thyself.
> Moderate thyself.
> Live for thy fellow creatures in order that they may live for thee.

The opposition to Dupuis and Volney, or for that matter to Voltaire himself, took little account of their natural religion and compassionate morality. So infuriating was their attack on the Judeo-Christian tradition that it was easier to counterattack by calling them inaccurate names like "atheist," and by blaming the French Revolution on them.

One example of this is John Prior Estlin, in his *Nature and Causes of Atheism* (1797), who applied this term to anyone who did not know "the one true God": thus the pagans who worshipped Diana at Ephesus were atheists,[32] and so were Dupuis and Volney who set out to prove that Nature is God.[33] Estlin makes two points that do have some historical and psychological worth, respectively. The first is that Dupuis, in tracing the worship of nature and natural (including astronomical) objects, is really writing about idolatry, not religion.[34] Even if Dupuis were to prove that the origin of all worship was the religion of nature, says Estlin, this would not disprove the Author of nature;[35] one cannot be a rational being without admitting an intelligent author of the universe. The second point is that Dupuis cannot distinguish Christianity from the Roman Catholic Church. Estlin writes with the Anglican complacency that the Frenchman can scarcely be blamed: "Accustomed from the earliest period of life to consider *Superstition* as *Religion,* and *Popery* as *Christianity,* it is not to be wondered at, that the association in his mind should have become indissoluble, and that disgusted with whatever had appeared to him under the form of religion, he should have rejected it altogether."[36] Estlin then argues that, just as Dupuis "proves" Jesus Christ to have been merely the sun passing through the zodiac, one could argue that Julius Caesar's invasion of Britain never took place: it was nothing but an allegory of the sun passing through Aquarius and Pisces to enter the vernal equinox. This was the first of many parodies of the solar theory.

A weightier critic of the French mythographers, the chemist and Unitarian Joseph Priestley (1733–1804), met Volney in London and evidently liked him. Priestley was no orthodox spokesman. He was an Arian, rejecting the divinity of Christ and the doctrine of the Atonement. At various times he was a dissenting minister, a materialist, a supporter of the French Revolution (which caused his house to be destroyed by a mob), a vegetarian, and a confident expecter of the Second Coming of Christ by 1814 at the latest. His chemical theories of a semimaterial, fiery stuff called "phlogiston" led to the discovery of oxygen. In 1797, while taking refuge in Philadelphia from the violent reactions of the English to his politics, Priestley published a letter chiding Volney for writing his *Ruins.* He called the work a firebrand, causing infidelity especially among young persons, and denigrating a religion which is of such value, especially in helping us to face death.[37] While Volney does seem to acknowledge the principle of intelligent design in nature, how can he not see the resemblances of the Book of Nature to revealed religion? "My studies," writes Priestley with justifiable pride, "have been pretty equally divided between that book, and another, which I doubt not is from the same author, bearing marks of wisdom, and having the same great object, the moral instruction of mankind."[38]

Two years later, Priestley weighed into Dupuis, as part of a *Comparison of the Institutes of Moses with those of the Hindoos and other ancient nations . . .* (1799). Priestley calls Dupuis's *Origine de tous les cultes* "Certainly the most extraordinary production of the present, or of any preceding age, and the *in plus ultra* of infidelity."[39] He resents Dupuis's slights to revealed religion, the omission of a god external to nature, and the dating of astronomy's origins to 15,000 BCE, contrary to the chronology of Moses.

Priestley's belief in universal restitution (the eventual salvation of every creature) and in moral progress after death made him a gentle opponent of unbelief, unlike the fire-and-brimstone preachers or even the arrogant Anglicans of the universities. In his *Comparison* he writes that God delights in the education of men, and that he could not possibly allow men of such perverted power as Alexander the Great, Julius Caesar, Voltaire, Rousseau, or Hume to be lost forever: whatever their state of mind at death, their capacity for improvement was not destroyed.[40] In this he anticipates the doctrine that the spiritualists would popularize half a century later: that no soul is lost, but that all, good and bad alike, participate in a grand scheme of education, of which life on this earth is merely one "grade."

The primary exponent of the solar theory of religions in England was Sir William Drummond K.C., F.R.S., F.R.S.E. (1770?–1828). He was a member of the international circle of connoisseurs and interpreters of ancient mythology mentioned in Chapter One, whose representatives in England were members of the Society of Dilettanti. Already at Christ Church, Oxford, in 1787, Drummond had made his mark in an aristocratic "speaking society."[41] He married in 1794 the wealthy daughter of Charles Boone, M.P.,[42] and entered Parliament in his turn as a Tory. A longtime friend of Sir William Hamilton, Drummond succeeded him as resident at Naples in 1801. He also replaced Lord Elgin for a few years at Constantinople; but his diplomatic career, though it took him through eventful times, was a short one. He retired in 1809, spending most of the rest of his life abroad.

Sir William Drummond was England's answer to Volney and Dupuis. He, too, was an anticlerical deist, a convert to the solar and zodiacal origin of religion, a philologist and researcher of origins. But Regency England was not Revolutionary France. Like Volney, Dupuis, and Knight, Drummond was at least a temporary politician, but a conservative one who believed that the British constitution was the surest guarantee of the liberties of mankind against such assaults as had taken place, under the sign of Liberty, in France.[43] By the end of the eighteenth century, the longstanding British contempt for the French seemed doubly justified. On the one hand there was the horrible example of oppression by the monarch, the aristocracy, and the Roman Catholic Church—terrors that Britain had escaped thanks to Magna Carta, the Civil War, and the "Glorious Revolution" of 1688. On the other hand, there was the mess that the French had made as soon as they rid themselves of these oppressors. Yet while one might sneer at one's neighbors across the Channel, there was the irresistible lure of French intelligence and "reason," especially in its liberating criticism of a Christianity that fewer and fewer thinking people were able to take at face value.

Drummond was of one mind with the French *philosophes*, but only once, in his notorious book *Oedipus Judaicus*, did he flaunt his contempt for religion. Usually he was more discreet. In the following quotation that

Figure 2.3. *Sir William Drummond (1770?–1828), by Arminius de Meyer.*

ends the Preface to his anodyne *Academical Questions* one can sense his true thoughts, but only if one understands the codewords of 1805, when "prejudice" could refer to Christian orthodoxy, "reason" and "philosophy" to the ideals of the Enlightenment:

> Prejudice may be trusted to guard the outworks for a short space of time, while Reason slumbers in the citadel; but if the latter sink into a lethargy, the former will quickly erect a standard for herself. Philosophy, wisdom, and liberty, support each other; he, who will not reason, is a bigot; he, who cannot, is a fool; and he, who dares not, is a slave.[44]

I said that Drummond was discreet. Perhaps the word should have been hypocritical: the reader may judge from the following incident. In the *British Critic* of 1806, Drummond wrote (anonymously) about a controversy at the University of Edinburgh: should the law still demand that a professor, before installation, declare his obedience to the Church? The chosen candidate had refused to do so. Far from supporting this stand on behalf of religious freedom, Drummond says that "though we have certainly no partiality to the peculiar dogmas of the Westminster confession, we are decidedly of the opinion, that in every christian country, the established instructors of youth ought to profess the established faith."[45] However, when writing to his confidant Lord Aberdeen, who was then a precocious scholar of twenty-one, Drummond confessed:

> I was obliged to cant most abominably for the British critic; but have done as well as I could. I was afraid after all that they would have seen through my fervent zeal for our holy religion. But fortunately the article was admitted without any remarks.[46]

It is the "fortunately" that disturbs. Drummond did not have to get his articles accepted: he was no penny-a-liner.

In 1811, Drummond caused to be printed, but not published, his best-known work: *The Oedipus Judaicus*, which, like Knight's *Discourse on the Worship of Priapus*, was intended only for private circulation but leaked out to cause alarm and disgust among the self-appointed guardians of public morality. As one reviewer said, "It could only be brought out occasionally, when the servants were busy, and the children a-bed—lest a single glance into one of its pages should either excite plebeian horror, or produce too early a contempt for old fashioned opinions."[47]

Oedipus Judaicus is a set of essays, of varying degrees of finish, dealing with some episodes in the Hebrew scriptures that are hard to take literally. Drummond's interpretation, in every case, is that these passages conceal an esoteric meaning concerning the sun, the zodiac, and the other heavenly bodies. Taking advantage of, and sometimes issue with, the erudition of Athanasius Kircher,[48] Jean-Sylvain Bailly, Charles Dupuis, and Sir William Jones, Drummond treats six passages. (1) The blessing of Jacob on his twelve sons in Genesis 49 is interpreted as symbolic of the zodiac. (2) Abram's battles with the kings in Genesis 14 is interpreted as the conquest by monotheism of the gods of "Tsabaism" (Sabaeanism), who are the heavenly bodies. (3) The Tabernacle in the Wilderness, and Solomon's Temple, are both shown to be elaborate symbols of the physical cosmos. (4) The invasion of Canaan by Joshua loses its literal and intolerably cruel meaning by being read as the passage of the sun through the zodiacal signs. This is assimilated to the self-identification of the Twelve Tribes with the signs, and explained as part of Moses' plan to defuse the false religion of the Sabaeans by explaining the true machinery of the heavens. (5) and (6) are sketches of how astral symbolism can also be read into the Book of Judges and the ceremony of the Paschal Lamb.

Few readers would have been offended by these scholarly commentaries, stuffed with Hebrew and other languages, had not Drummond chosen to open it with a Preface in a far different style. This Preface enjoyed a separate career in pamphlet form, taking its place in the canon of freethought with the works of Volney, Thomas Paine, Mary Wollstonecraft, and Robert Owen. Here is a representative paragraph from it:

> To a small circle I think myself at liberty to observe, that the manner in which the Christian readers of the Old Testament generally choose to understand it, appears to me to be a little singular. While the Deity is represented with human passions, and those none of the best;—while he is described as a quarrelsome, jealous, and vindictive being;—while he is depicted as a material and local God, who dwelt on a box made of Shittim wood in the temple of Jerusalem;—they abide by the literal interpretation. They see no allegory in the first chapters of Genesis; nor doubt, that far the greater portion of the human race is doomed to suffer eternal torments, because our first parents ate an apple, after having been tempted by a talking serpent. They find it quite simple, that the triune Jehovah should dine on veal cutlets at Abraham's table; nor are they at all surprised, that the God of the universe should pay a visit to Ezekiel, in order to settle with the Prophet, whether he should bake his bread with human dung, or with cow's dung. They believe the facts to have happened literally as they are stated; and neither suspect, nor allow, that the language of the sacred writers upon such occasions may be entirely figurative. Very different is their mode of interpreting these same Scriptures, when they think there is any allusion made to the kingdom of Christ. Then they abandon the literal sense without scruple, and sometimes, it may be thought, without consideration. The Rabbins learn with astonishment, that the Song of Solomon, for example, is a

> mere allegory, which represents the love of Jesus for his church; and that the lady, whose navel was like a round goblet, not wanting liquor,—whose belly was like a heap of wheat, set about with lilies,—whose nose was as the tower of Lebanon, which looketh towards Damascus,—and who promised to her well-beloved, that he should lie all night betwixt her breasts,—was not Solomon's mistress but the Church, the spiritual spouse of Christ.

What most offended was Drummond's flippant manner. Even Lord Byron wrote to his friend Hodgson in 1811: "How much unhappiness may not the author of the erudite infidel work of this accomplished writer have to answer for . . . ?"[49] A whole series of attacks and counterattacks followed publication, from which the Rev. George D'Oyly emerged as Drummond's most articulate opponent. While nothing is duller to read than most religious controversy, some of the points scored by these contestants are worth recording, especially as they touch on the issues of the next chapter, which concerns blasphemy.

D'Oyly first reproached Drummond for "profane and indecorous banter" and "light and indecent ribaldry" unbecoming to a member of His Majesty's Privy Council.[50] Although *Oedipus* had been published privately, D'Oyly thought it unjust that in this way "a man of fortune may remain secure from any animadversions, while he is poisoning the public mind with the most noxious trash, is undermining the best interests of society, and tearing up the most sacred feelings, religious, moral, and political."[51] Besides, D'Oyly went on, the *Oedipus Judaicus* is little more than a plagiarism from a "French infidel writer, Dupuis" (which was a fair jibe), himself a plagiarist from Volney (which was not).[52]

Just as Dupuis had been reproached for mistaking the superstitions of Rome for the essence of the Christian religion, so D'Oyly insists that Christians do not nowadays believe any of the nonsense that Drummond imputes to them. They do not, for instance, consider the Supreme Being to be a local, material deity with human passions.[53] One cannot read literally such epithets as "jealous," "angry," or "repentant"—no Christians do.[54] A later critic who wrote as "Q.R." emphasized this primary objection, and complained that Drummond had said not a word on the noble and sublime descriptions of God that also abound in the Old Testament.[55]

Drummond defended himself in two lengthy rejoinders: at least, they are presumed to be by him, though they pretend, under the name "Vindex," to be by an ally. In the first of these, he protested the dragging out into public view of a private work, and this "upon principles, which, if generally adopted, would soon destroy all confidence between man and man;—would fill every breast with suspicion and distrust;—and would establish the authority of an inquisition, little less terrible than that which sends its victims to the stake."[56] *Oedipus Judaicus,* said Vindex, had been given by the author to between thirty and fifty friends, mostly at their pressing wish.[57] (A later critic said that copies had also been surreptitiously placed in important libraries, hence introduced deliberately into the public domain.[58]) *Oedipus Judaicus,* says Vindex, was not an attack on the Scriptures, but on particular interpretations of them;[59] Drummond's sneers were not at the clergy, but at bigots.[60] Certainly the author had borrowed ideas from Dupuis, especially from his astronomical tables and calendars. But Vindex pointed out that there is no Greek, Hebrew, Syriac or Arabic in Dupuis's work, whereas *Oedipus* fairly bristles with them.[61] As for Drummond's own religious position, "He has expressed his belief in the existence, and his reverence for the attributes, of God, in the strongest terms. There is not a passage in the book, in which he has spoken disrespectfully of Christ, or of the Christian religion."[62]

More than that, Drummond showed himself a devoted reader of the Book of Nature. D'Oyly may have scolded him for insolence in considering Jehovah to concern his mighty self with a flea's foot, but:

> Every thing that lives and moves in nature bears testimony to the existence of a first intelligent cause. Every creature furnishes a proof of the necessary existence of a Creator, because every creature shows in itself, that there is a final cause of its being. The structure of the smallest insect displays such mechanism as can alone be attributed to skill and design. In contemplating, therefore, the formation of the smallest insect, I feel myself compelled to acknowledge that I behold a work of the Deity, and a proof of his power.[63]

As for D'Oyly's ingenuous remark that no Christian takes seriously Jehovah's so-called "wrath," or his "hardening of Pharaoh's heart," Vindex warns him that he attributes a sophistication to Sunday-school children that even a bishop does not show.[64] He concludes by saying that when D'Oyly has made some proper study in Oriental languages, then he will deign to discuss Drummond's knowledge of them with him.

This was a tactical error on Vindex/Drummond's part. D'Oyly happened to be the Christian Advocate to Cambridge University and a Fellow of Corpus Christi College. It did not take him long to consult his colleagues and ascertain that Drummond's knowledge of Oriental languages and astronomy was quite poor. Most seriously, he showed that according to the latest scholarship (not the theories of Bailly on which Dupuis had relied), the Zodiac of twelve signs dated from no earlier than Alexandrian times, about the third or second centuries BCE: hence it could not possibly have been known to the writer of the Pentateuch.[65]

Drummond tied himself up in knots as he tried to answer this new attack with *Additional Letters to the Rev. G. D'Oyly,* ascribed to "Vindex, Biblicus, and Candidus" (1813 or 1814). This enabled "Q.R.," evidently a friend of D'Oyly, to enumerate Drummond's scholarly misdemeanors:

1. He is nothing but a servile copyist from Dupuis.
2. He began in a prejudicial manner, by setting aside any possible historical meaning of the Paschal institution.
3. He garbled the Rabbis' account of the astronomical Ram, saying exactly the opposite of what they say.
4. His idea that the Paschal institution comes from an Egyptian one hinges on the identification of a festival in which a ram was worshipped with one in which a ram is sacrificed to another object of worship.
5. He copied an erroneous passage on Epiphanius from Dupuis.[66]

These charges were difficult to deny and embarrassing to admit to. Drummond held his peace, but his work continued to make waves. A few years later another Cambridge divine, the Rev. George Townsend, published a scholarly lampoon: *The Oedipus Romanus; or, an attempt to prove, from the principles of reasoning adopted by the Rt. Hon. Sir William Drummond, in his Oedipus Judaicus, that the Twelve Caesars are the twelve signs of the Zodiac. Addressed to the higher and literary classes of society.* Townsend begins ironically: "I pretend that the Roman historians, Tacitus, Suetonius, etc., had their esoteric, and exoteric doctrines: they are enigmatical writers, and concealed certain truths from the vulgar under the disguise of a most candid, and impartial statement of facts."[67] He assumes that there was a primordial language, discoverable by etymology: "like a suit of chain armor, it bends at pleasure over every part of an hypothesis; and defends a new system, by guarding against the intrusion of all the darts and arrows of facts and history. . . ."[68]

The *Oedipus Romanus* is a very good parody of Drummond's methods, or of any other single-minded systematizer. Using the linguistic roots of that pious mythographer, Jacob Bryant, Townsend shows how the name of Caesar is composed of *Cai* = mansion, and the honorific *Sar. Julius* is obviously *Helios* = sun. Therefore Julius Caesar is nothing more or less than the Sun's House.[69] With evident relish he proceeds to turn the rest of the Roman Emperors into allegories of the signs of the zodiac. Then, with more solemnity, he explains why he has undertaken the task of writing against Drummond and his kind:

> These poisoners of the springs of moral happiness, these enemies of the virtues and peace of man, seem not to have

> anything themselves at stake, and pervert every talent in their endeavour to plunge others into a fearful abyss of doubt and uncertainty. . . . The peculiar doctrines of Christianity, the Trinity, the incarnation, and the atonement, cease to exist—Morality becomes a matter of convenience, principle a dream; the laws of God chimerical, the laws of man expedient—All in this life is coldness, selfishness, and vanity; and, at its close, oblivion and eternal sleep.[70]

I think that Drummond found the reactions to his *Oedipus Judaicus* a chastening experience. At all events, he was anxious in his later works to avoid treading on ecclesiastical toes. In his *Memoir on the Antiquity of the Zodiacs of Esneh and Dendera* (1821) he argues against the accepted date for the Creation of 4004 BCE, but only because he prefers the authority of the Septuagint to the Hebrew text, into which he thought errors had crept. The Septuagint gave him 5390 BCE for the Creation, 3128 for the Deluge,[71] and this at a time when the far greater age of the earth was being freely discussed.

Drummond argued in his *Memoir* that at a remote time there seems to have been knowledge of the sun as the center of the planets, the rotation of the earth, the eliptical orbits of comets, and probably the telescope and microscope: a once mighty system of natural philosophy whose fragments were gathered by the Greeks Thales, Pythagoras, and Democritus.[72] Who were these early sages? Drummond hardly seems to be the same person as wrote the mockeries in *Oedipus Judaicus* when, with the words "If we believe, let us not believe by halves," he says that it was the Antediluvians who made this great progress in knowledge: easily enough, since they lived up to 900 years.[73]

One might think this sarcastic, but the context does not allow for that. Still less does the fact that the same chronology underlies Drummond's last work, *Origines* (1824–29). He sketches the subsequent history of religion as follows. Already before the Deluge, men lapsed into Sabaeanism, and this false religion reasserted itself among the descendants of Noah. The Sabaean apostates had a doctrine of emanation that led in turn to the polytheism and avatars of Brahmanism, even to metempsychosis. Heaven became the great God, earth the great Mother. Thence came phallic rites and impure mysteries that "modern decency hesitates to mention, and refuses to describe."[74] Far from praising this theory of emanation, as Payne Knight had done, Drummond blames it for all the confusions of the spiritual with the material that mark heathen religion, culminating in the worship of animals by the Egyptians.[75]

The last volume of *Origines* is signed the 27th March, 1829, two days before Drummond's death. Near its end, he writes with greater warmth towards the ancient apostates:

> That there exists only one God, and that God is a perfect and beneficent Being, both reason and religion sufficiently teach; but of the Divine nature, of the substance of the Deity, or of the manner of his existence, the human mind is inadequate to form any just conception. We can affix no clear ideas to omnipotence, omniscience, infinity, eternity.
>
> Under these circumstances we ought not too severely to blame the Tsabaists, if they represented immaterial natures by material types.[76]

Memoirs of Sir William Drummond's years of retirement in Italy record his conversation as not only erudite but brilliant and playful. The Countess of Blessington (whom we will be meeting again) described him as a high-minded gentleman with a *politesse de la vieille cour.* He read and wrote all day and much of the night, the sofas and floor being covered with books, while Lady Drummond occupied herself with her toilette, lapdogs, and social calls, and lavished her vast wealth on the poor of Naples.[77] Lord Holland, who met the Drummonds in 1825, wrote in his journal: "Sir William Drummond is agreable and very good-natured. His house is magnificently mounted and his dinners excellent. He hates the Bible, but has more spite against the Old than the New Testament. His wife is the image of old Queen Charlotte, and nearly an idiot."[78] In the course of several dinners, Lord Holland observed that Drummond, who by now was thin and emaciated, resembling the old Voltaire ("a likeness that flatters him a good deal"), "says everyone is mistaken and wrong, but he never supplies the facts he tries to destroy by any theories of his own, and his science seems only to be founded on the mistakes and ignorance of others."[79]

To the Countess of Blessington, when she made her last visit to him in Rome, "He spoke to me of his approaching end with calmness; said he should have liked to have had time to finish the work in which he is engaged; and observed that it was a blessing, for which he was penetrated with gratitude to the Most High, that his mind still survived the wreck of his body, and enabled him to bear, if not to forget, the physical sufferings entailed by disease."[80]

The *Oedipus Judaicus* did for the solar theory of religion what the *Discourse on the Worship of Priapus* had done for the sexual theory. Both works were published privately and anonymously, by freethinking gentlemen scholars. Both caused a scandal. But it was not necessary to have obtained or read either of these rare books, in order to learn what they had to say. In Knight's case, this would have been through gossip (who in the House of Commons did not known that the Honorable Member for Ludlow had written a book on phallic worship?). In the case of Dupuis and Drummond, it was through popularizers such as Robert Taylor and Richard Carlile, whose efforts to enlighten the middle and lower classes led to their prosecution and imprisonment for the crime of blasphemy.

THREE

The Blasphemers

During the turbulence following Sir William Drummond's *Oedipus Judaicus,* one of his critics pointed out that a man less well-protected had recently been pilloried for publishing no worse a book.[1] This was a reference to the first of a wave of prosecutions for blasphemy, some of which, like Drummond's book, arose directly out of Dupuis's attack on Christianity.

Blasphemy was, and still is, an ill-defined concept. That much has become clear from the two *causes célèbres* of recent times, the London *Gay News* trial in 1977, and the Salman Rushdie affair. It usually means the denial or mockery of things or persons held by some to be sacred; thus the degree at which it becomes offensive depends on the latter's susceptibilities, while the making of it a crime depends on their power. Blasphemy may be interpreted to include the profession of atheism—the ultimate insult to a personal God!—and as such was punishable by death under the Mosaic Law, the Code of Justinian, the laws of England until 1677, and the laws of Scotland until 1825. But this does not mean that the death penalty was regularly applied in any of these cases: the last executions for heresy in England were in 1612.

By the period with which this book is concerned, the idea of blasphemy as a crime in itself had taken second place to that of political subversion through "blasphemous" attacks on the established religion. Judges in the 1760s laid down the principle that there was no prosecution in England for religious opinion, bringing an end to the cases brought against deists who denied Christ and the church. From 1769 until 1812, there were only seven blasphemy prosecutions in England, some of them ending in acquittal.

The paranoia following the French Revolution changed the situation drastically. One immediate result was the suppression of "revolutionary"

THE

AGE OF REASON,

Part-the Third;

BEING

AN EXAMINATION

OF THE

PASSAGES IN THE NEW TESTAMENT QUOTED FROM THE OLD, AND CALLED PROPHECIES,

CONCERNING

JESUS CHRIST.

TO WHICH IS PREFIXED,

AN ESSAY ON DREAMS.

ALSO,

An Appendix,

CONTAINING

THE CONTRADICTORY DOCTRINES

BETWEEN

MATTHEW AND MARK;

AND

MY PRIVATE THOUGHTS ON A FUTURE STATE.

By THOMAS PAINE.

London:

PRINTED AND PUBLISHED BY R. CARLILE, 55, FLEET STREET.

1819.

Figure 3.1. *Title page of Thomas Paine's* Age of Reason, Part Three, *1819, published by Richard Carlile.*

literature, including the books of Thomas Paine (1737–1809), author of *Common Sense, The Rights of Man,* and *The Age of Reason.* In 1797, the newly formed "Proclamation Society," led by the abolitionist William Wilberforce, secured the conviction and a year's imprisonment for Thomas Williams, for having sold one copy of *The Age of Reason.* Paine was now living in France, where, like Dupuis, he had been an elected delegate to the Convention and narrowly escaped the guillotine. He wrote an open letter to the judge, Mr. Erskine, questioning the nature of Williams's crime. He pointed out that:

> Socrates, who lived more than four hundred years before the Christian era, was convicted of blasphemy, for preaching against the belief of a plurality of gods, and for preaching the belief of one god, and was condemned to suffer death by poison. Jesus Christ was convicted of blasphemy under the Jewish law, and was crucified. Calling Mahomet an impostor would be blasphemy in Turkey; and denying the infallibility of the Pope and the Church would be blasphemy at Rome. What then is to be understood by this word blasphemy? We see that in the case of Socrates truth was condemned as blasphemy. Are we sure that truth is not blasphemy in the present day? Woe, however, be to those who make it so, whoever they may be.[2]

The Age of Reason was written to pass the time while Paine was imprisoned in Paris and likely to be executed. It breathes the spirit of Paine's Quaker forebears, whose rejection of Christian dogma and theology did not impair their reverence for God; its "blasphemy" consists in treating the Bible as literature, Jesus as a historical figure, and fundamentalists as fools. It is no more offensive than Gibbon's *Decline and Fall of the Roman Empire.* The real reason for the ban on its publication was Paine's role in both the American and French Revolutions.

Several years later, in 1812, Paine's further essays were collected for publication as the third and fourth parts of *The Age of Reason.* Daniel Isaac Eaton, a bookseller, published Part Three, "An Examination of the passages in the New Testament, quoted from the Old, and called Prophecies of the coming of Jesus Christ." Paine's intention was to show how specious were the efforts of the Evangelists to find prophecies of later events in the Hebrew Scriptures. After a trial marked by the aggressive and overbearing conduct of the prosecutor, Lord Ellenborough, Eaton was sentenced to eighteen months' imprisonment and a monthly appearance in the pillory.

The authorities of the time justified the suppression of freedom of speech by a sentimental concern for the state of mind of the masses. Evidently they had cause for concern, for when Daniel Eaton was brought out to the pillory at Charing Cross, the profane mob did not pelt him with stones and rotten eggs, but cheered and applauded him. But this only increased the determination of pious people in high places to stamp out this wave of "atheism." From 1812 until 1828, there were sixty-two prosecutions for blasphemy in England. A famous sign of these times was the expulsion of Percy Bysshe Shelley from Oxford for his pamphlet *The Necessity of Atheism* (1811). It does seem unfair that Shelley, Drummond, and other upper-class freethinkers did not suffer much for their ideas, while Shelley's Irish servant was jailed for six months in 1812 for distributing his master's *Declaration of Rights,* and in 1821 the unauthorized publisher of Shelley's *Queen Mab* (an *Age of Reason* in verse) was sentenced to four months' imprisonment.

The victory of Waterloo and the elimination of all threat from France was a hollow one for the people of England. Two harsh winters following 1815 brought near-famine, but Lord Liverpool's government (1812–1827) was unresponsive. Parliament was manned by landowners whose Corn Laws deliberately kept the price of bread high and prevented the importation of cheaper foreign wheat. Trade unions had been illegal since 1799, and the working classes—now flocking from the farms to the factories—were cruelly suppressed when they tried to draw attention to their plight. At Derby, three laborers were hanged and beheaded in 1817 for their part in an insurrectionary march that had probably been started by a government *agent provocateur.*[3] On 16 August 1819 came the Massacre of Peterloo, Manchester, when cavalry charged at a huge crowd of peaceful protestors, killing and wounding men, women, and children by the hundred. Meanwhile the Prince Regent unconcernedly pursued his career of spendthrift philandery, outdoing any modern royal scandal with the prosecution of Queen Caroline in 1820–21.

In the interests of the network of connections that overspills the chapters of this book, I interpose here the sentiments of Richard Payne Knight on the occasion of Peterloo. He wrote to Lord Aberdeen from his country cottage on the Welsh border:

> Happily we have no Reformers here:—at least none whose Projects of Reform extend further than to Mills and Markets; and when Corn is plenty they remain quietly at work in their coalpits. In the year of scarcity I was however obliged in conjunction with a brother Magistrate to order a Charge of Cavalry against them, which they sustained most sturdily with their Pike axes and iron cranes; but after many hard blows and cuts were overpowered, their Leaders taken and transported, without any loss of life; but both Magistrates and Volunteers have kept themselves sober, and therefore proceeded with all due

> forms of law; for which they got no thanks, as these drunken Boobies of Manchester have for their silly and lawless precipitation. [. . . The colliers also sent] their female auxiliary, whom they emply'd more skilfully by sending them to seduce their Antagonists the night before: but our Heroes with equal Gallantry cuckolded them in the evening and sabred them in the morning; and 'tis said the Skirmish of Venus left more lasting scars upon some of them than that of Mars did on others.[4]

Among the oppressions of the Liverpool government were the hindrance of public education, and a prohibitive tax on newspapers and pamphlets, on the principle that the restless classes had better be kept ignorant if not illiterate. An underground press immediately mushroomed, and the humbler type of printer and bookseller came under suspicion. It was in this context that the Attorney General saw fit in late 1818 to institute blasphemy proceedings against William Hone (1780–1842). Hone was certainly no atheist, and no enemy to Christianity, but he was a political gadfly. Pamphlets and broadsheets poured from his press—he had to keep them pouring to support his family of seven children—attacking the government, the sinecured clergy, the Prince Regent (his special bugbear), and the Corn Laws that were pushing poorer folk than himself over the brink of starvation.

Hone's mistake, if it was a mistake, was to express his outrage at this state of affairs in the form of three parodies: *Wilkes's Political Catechism,* a parody of the Anglican Catechism, including the Ten Commandments and the Lord's Prayer; *The Litany;* and *The Sinecurist's Creed,* a parody of the Athanasian Creed. While political dissent was still grudgingly protected, Hone's parodies, published in 1817, opened a loophole for the prosecuting authorities, who screamed blasphemy.

Hone stood trial for three days, on three separate charges. Unable to afford a lawyer, he made a stirring self-defense, standing in his shabby suit and speaking for upwards of six hours each day. His defense was based on the fact that ecclesiastical parodies of this type had a long historical justification, and that no one took them as denigratory to the sacred texts. Why, Martin Luther himself had written a parody of the First Psalm; and there were countless recent instances, including many current political cartoons using biblical imagery, that had gone unpunished. Lord Ellenborough, the Lord Chief Justice, who presided over the second and third trials on 19 and 20 December 1817, stretched his privileges to the limit in instructing the juries to find Hone guilty. The Attorney General, summing up at the final trial, said that "he felt it his duty to the public to institute this prosecution, with a view to prevent the issue of such publications in future as were calculated to undermine the religion of the country, and

THE

THIRD TRIAL

OF

WILLIAM HONE,

ON AN

Ex-Officio Information.

AT GUILDHALL, LONDON, DECEMBER 20, 1817,

BEFORE

LORD ELLENBOROUGH AND A SPECIAL JURY,

FOR PUBLISHING

A PARODY

ON THE

ATHANASIAN CREED,

ENTITLED

"THE SINECURIST'S CREED."

Ninth Edition.

LONDON:

PRINTED BY & FOR WILLIAM HONE, 67, OLD BAILEY;

AND SOLD BY ALL BOOKSELLERS.

1818.

PRICE ONE SHILLING.

Figure 3.2. *Title page of* The Third Trial of William Hone, *1818.*

so to destroy the basis of morality, comfort, happiness, and prosperity."[5] Lord Ellenborough's last words to the jury held up before them the bogeyman of French republicanism: "if such publications as that before them were not prohibited and punished, the country was too liable to be deluged by irreligion and impiety, which had so lately produced such melancholy results in another nation."[6] But for all their threats, Hone emerged with the jury's verdict of "Not guilty," to be received by a jubilant throng in the streets. Within days he was selling verbatim transcripts of his three trials at a shilling each.

Hone's acquittals were a landmark in the battle for the freedom of the press. But relieved as he was, Hone was genuinely upset by his parodies being called blasphemous, as he had had no intention of mocking religion, only of using forms of words familiar to all as a vehicle for his political criticisms. In preparing his defense, he had help from a wide circle of scholarly friends and customers of his bookshop, including the collector Charles Townley, Payne Knight's friend. In the process, Hone learnt about a body of virtually unknown religious literature, to which he gave publicity in his books *The Apocryphal New Testament* (1820) and *Ancient Mysteries Described* (1823), which is mostly on the miracle plays of the Middle Ages.

After his trials Hone withdrew his parodies, best-sellers though they had become, "rather suffering privations than reviling the religion of his country or injuring Christianity, the poor man's charter."[7] He even came to regret having published the uncanonical Apocrypha, when in the 1830s he became a keen member of the Weigh-House Chapel, a dissenting church.[8]

If Hone repented his offenses to religion, there were those who relished them. Richard Carlile (1790–1843), another pamphleteer, printer, and political radical, had also been imprisoned in 1817 for selling parodies on the Book of Common Prayer. After Hone's acquittals, Carlile reissued the parodies that Hone had withdrawn, and published the still banned *Age of Reason*, now extended to four parts, and other works by American deists such as Elihu Palmer's *Principles of Nature*. The "Society for the Suppression of Vice and Immorality" (a new incarnation of the Proclamation Society) brought an action against him in 1819. This gave Londoners the entertainment of another spectacular trial, at which Carlile read from Paine's book and picked out some embarrassing quotations from the Bible itself, thus ensuring that the most offensive passages would have to be published in the court report. Sentenced to three years' imprisonment and a fine of 1500 pounds, he refused to pay the fine and was consequently jailed for six years. His wife, sister, and nine of his shopmen were also imprisoned for continuing to sell Carlile's publications. While

Figure 3.3. *Richard Carlile (1790–1843). Artist unknown.*

in Dorchester Gaol, the Carliles managed to continue their work, issuing numerous pamphlets, articles, open letters, and a periodical called *The Republican.*

In a letter of 1 April 1821, Carlile writes:

> I am attached to truth, and prejudiced towards falsehood as far as either is comprehensible to my mind. I am not more

> prejudiced against Christianity than Judaism, or Paganism, or Mahometanism. I view the whole in the same light, and have a deep rooted conviction that whatever is called religion, is mischievous to mankind.[9]

Carlile did not yet trouble himself with any God that might or might not exist: the evidence of nature was sufficient for him to conclude that "we should consider ourselves but as atoms of organized matter," coming and going like the clouds.[10] Nor did he think that Bacon, Newton, or Locke, in their later life, had had any other ideas of the Christian religion than his own; they had just had to dissemble their beliefs.[11]

Released from prison in 1825, the irrepressible Carlile instantly reprinted the offending books. But the Society for the Suppression of Vice had given up the unequal struggle with the followers of Thomas Paine. Henceforth, the crime of blasphemy had to contain abusive or outrageous language, not just the denial of Christianity. Carlile's subsequent imprisonments in 1831–33 and 1834 were for a political libel and for his refusal to pay church rates. In all, he spent over nine years in jail.

Carlile's interests extended to two further domains which became the peculiar care of freethinkers in the nineteenth century: the rights of women, and the plight of the insane. I do not know whether Carlile's *Every Woman's Book,* published in *The Republican* on 6 May 1825, was the first manual of birth-control methods in the English language, but it was certainly a pioneering work. Reissued as a separate booklet, it argues first that "It is a barbarous custom that forbids the female to make advances in love . . . Why should not the female state her passion to the male, as well as the male to the female?"[12] The sad results of our conventions, thinks Carlile, are embittered old maids and bachelors who "belong to a sort of sub animal class."[13] Even for the married, there are problems: "What a dreadful thing it is that love cannot be enjoyed, without the danger of a conception; when that conception is not desired, when it is a positive injury to the parties and to society."[14] But there is a simple means to avoid the horrors of abortion and infanticide, which Carlile describes three times in order to avoid any misunderstanding: the use of a vaginal sponge tethered to a ribbon. Apparently this had been alluded to by John Stuart Mill, the Utilitarian philosopher, and introduced into England by Robert Owen, the utopian magnate of whom we will hear more shortly. Owen had even gone to Paris to find out exactly how French women prevent unwanted conceptions.[15]

Carlile's concern for the insane led to his investigation of the Bethlem Asylum (now, appropriately enough, converted into London's War Museum). He accused its staff severally and by name in a long pamphlet of 1831, *A New View of Insanity,* which details the horrible cruelty of some, and the utter lack of understanding of all of them. Carlile calls insanity "that almost-universal disorder of the human race," and writes that if he knew a sane man living, he would dedicate the book to him; but as it is, he dedicates it to the insane. Obviously he was playing with two different meanings of the term: first, the universal refusal of human societies to regulate their affairs in a peaceful and unoppressive manner; second, the situation of individuals driven from the ranks of their fellows for their inability to conform to behavioral norms. The causes of insanity are two, according to Carlile: "ill-managed physical love," and religion. As for their cure: "Kindness is the healing and subduing principle. I hate hell, and those who preach it."[16] Godfrey Higgins, who will dominate the next chapter, also worked for this cause.

While in jail, Carlile obtained the materials for an exposé of Freemasonry, giving in *The Republican*, vol. 12 (1825) the texts and passwords of the three "blue" or "Craft" degrees (Entered Apprentice, Fellow Craft, Master Mason) and the Royal Arch. Not a man to do things by halves, he dedicated to King George III this "complete exposure of the mummeries of the association of Freemasons, of which you are the self-styled Grand Patron." This was expanded, without the ruder editorial remarks, into a *Manual of Freemasonry* that became a stock-in-trade of masonic publishers. Carlile's motives were mixed. First, he had come to conclude that since there was no great masonic secret, the famous secrecy of the Craft was a social blot that had better be removed. Second, Freemasonry was under royal patronage, which had protected it from the Act of Parliament of 1799 that banned all other secret societies; to attack it was part of Carlile's campaign against royalty and its privileges. Third, he was always in need of money and publicity.[17] He began by borrowing his opinions from Thomas Paine, whose posthumous "Essay on the Origin of Free-Masonry" Carlile had published in 1819, and who had written there:

> The Christian religion and Masonry have one and the same common origin, both are derived from the worship of the sun; the difference between their origins is, that the Christian religion is a parody on the worship of the sun, in which they put a man whom they call Christ, in the place of the sun, and pay him the same adoration which was originally paid to the sun . . .[18]

These were the views of a dutiful pupil of Volney and Dupuis, and for a time they sufficed Carlile, too. But after his release from six years' imprisonment, in 1825, Carlile became rather religious and mystical. One of his first actions was to pay the half-crown fee to become a licensed preacher. He detected in the ancient mysteries something of real value that required a "revelation." By the late 1830s, he believed that this unveiling was the glory of his time; that it was "*modern infidelity*, which is really becoming *the light of the world,* which *is the light, life, and knowledge needed,* and which is morally, scientifically, and properly speaking, the true *Eleusis or Advent,* or HE THAT SHOULD COME."[19]

Science had now become Carlile's god, and he had become its prophet, even the incarnation of the new Logos of Reason.[20] Lacking any scientific education, he had a layman's awe for the wonders of technology, all seemingly brought about by the application of human intelligence. His prose lost its former hard edge; his thoughts grew woolly, as he wrote that "The advent of the Jewish Messiah, the advent of Christ, and the advent of a reasonable state of society, in which mystery and superstition shall yield to plain practical science, in the constitution of the human mind, are to be one and the same reality, the moral of the mystery of Judaism, Christianity, and Masonry."[21]

A fresher mind, at this point, was that of Robert Owen (1771–1858), the cotton magnate, reformer, and socialist. His astounding success in running his mills at New Lanark (Scotland) on utopian lines had attracted the attention of many important people in the teens of the century, including the royal Dukes of Kent (father of Queen Victoria) and Sussex. Owen was on the brink of success in attracting serious attention to his philanthropic schemes when he stepped out of line by declaiming too loudly against religion. He was dropped by his patrons in Parliament, and moved his theatre of activity to the United States, where many Owenite communities were founded.

Owen bridges the Regency period, when the intransigent opposition to religion went hand in hand with philanthropy, feminism, and left-wing politics, and the period after 1850, when the new religion of Spiritualism changed everything. In his vigorous old age, Owen declared himself a convinced Spiritualist, claimed to have been a medium since his birth, and continued his conversations with the spirits of his old friends the Duke of Kent, Thomas Jefferson, and Benjamin Franklin. Thus he constellates several of the themes of this book.

Robert Owen was too canny to court prosecution for blasphemy, but in a landmark speech of 20 October 1830, to a London audience of over a thousand people, he made his position clear. There are four classes of human being, Owen said. The first are the Believers: strong in morals, weak in intellectual faculties. The second are the Unbelievers, the worldly wise who support religion as being good for other people. The third class comprises the Open Unbelievers—deists, atheists, and skeptics—who yet do not perceive the laws of nature as relevant to man, either as an individual or in the social state. Finally, in Class Four, are the "Disbelievers in all past and present religions, but believers in the eternal unchanging laws of the universe, as developed from facts derived from all past experience; and who, by a careful study of these facts, deduce from them a religion of

Figure 3.4. *The Rev. Robert Taylor (1784–1844). Engraving by T. Smith.*

nature." These people possess the highest degree of intellectual and moral faculties.[22] But what do they find, when they set out to understand, and then to benefit the world? They discover, says Owen, "that the religion of the world is the sole cause now of all the disunion, hatred, uncharitableness, and crime, which pervade the population of the earth; and that, as long as this ignorant and worldly religion shall be taught to mankind, it will be utterly impracticable to train men to love one another, or to have common charity for each other." [23]

It was in this climate, when large audiences would flock to hear such denunciations of the Establishment in the names of Reason and Science, that the most important figure of this chapter flourished. This was the Reverend Robert Taylor (1784–1844), whose deliberate flirting with the blasphemy laws earned him the sobriquet of "The Devil's Chaplain." Taylor's background was not quite so humble as those of Hone and Carlile: his father was a prosperous ironmonger. Robert was trained for medicine and admitted to the College of Surgeons in 1807. He immediately changed his vocation and studied for the church, graduating from St. John's College, Cambridge in 1813 and being ordained a priest. No sooner was he installed as curate of Midhurst, Kent, than he began to have doubts, caused by reading deistical books, and for some years vacillated between the ministry and school teaching. When he wrote about his dilemmas to Dr. Buckner, the Bishop of Chichester, the latter replied that gentlemen, naturally, do not believe in the marvels and mysteries of revealed religion, but that these are necessary to keep the public quiet.[24] He advised the troubled curate not to rock the ecclesiastical boat. This was not enough for Taylor, who in 1824 left the Church of England and set up his own deist ministry.

Taylor's sermons, of which specimens were later published in *The Devil's Pulpit*, were a delightful entertainment to his congregation, but the authorities were not amused. As soon as his reputation had begun to grow, he was indicted for "conspiracy to overthrow the Christian religion."

Taylor stood his first trial for blasphemy on 24 October 1827, and was adjudged guilty on 7 February 1828. He was fortunate to live in England rather than in France, where the government of Charles X had recently (1826) passed laws instituting the death penalty for this offence. He appeared at his trial in his priestly robes, accompanied by a band of elegant young women. In his own defense he said:

> I am not an Atheist; I am not a Christian, neither am I a hypocrite. I am in my heart and soul a Deist. In the cause of Deism I have suffered what, in any other cause, would be accounted a real martyrdom. For Deism I have incurred the loss of natural

> relations and friends, of property, of liberty itself, and have held my life, and my life's comfort, of inferior consideration to the great duty of inculcating just and worthy notions of the Supreme Being on an insulted and priest-ridden people . . .[25]

Confined in Oakham Gaol, Taylor gained in leisure what he lost in comfort, and succeeded in completing two books. *The Syntagma,* which means "a systematic treatise," was published in 1828. It is a scholarly investigation of Christian origins, and a proof from the want of acceptable evidence that Jesus Christ never existed, but is merely a personification of virtue. Thus the whole apparatus of belief and of the churches erected on it falls to the ground.

The second book was *The Diegesis* (which means a "statement of the case"), finished in February 1829 and published in 1833. The purpose here was to prove that this religion, whose supposed founder never existed, was besides entirely unoriginal. Taylor's main targets are the ecclesiastical historians Lardner and Mosheim, who had made their scholarship subservient to superstition and dogma.

In the *Diegesis* Taylor contrasts the fictitious Gospel and the theologies of St. Paul and the early Fathers with the universal and tolerant paganism that had hitherto prevailed under the *pax Romana.* One of his themes is the infection of the new faith with the exclusivism and intolerance of the Jews: a tiresome tribe, according to Taylor, whose history began only after the Babylonian captivity in the sixth century BCE. The key to his argument is that "Everything of Christianity is of Egyptian origin."[26] Taylor had by now read Godfrey Higgins's *The Celtic Druids,* which we will treat in the next chapter, and was full of admiration for that work; he also knew the *Asiatic Researches.* Consequently his *Diegesis* contains much on the Essene origins of Jesus, and on the identity of Christ with Krishna.

Upon his release in 1829, Taylor joined forces with Richard Carlile, and the two set out on an "Infidel Mission" through the north of England. Returning to London, Taylor took over the Rotunda, a large circular building in Blackfriars Road. The domed ceiling was decorated with the signs of the Zodiac, appropriately enough since Taylor had now at last discovered Dupuis and become the greatest popularizer of the zodiacal theory of Christianity. This could have been done in a sober and pedagogical spirit, but then no crowds of fashionable people would have flocked to the Rotunda for their Sunday morning edification. Here is an extract from Taylor's sermon on Easter Sunday, 1831. After announcing that he was going to commit "the unpardonable sin against the Holy Ghost, the sin of being rational,"[27] he explained that the "Blood of Christ" is nothing but the autumn vintage, shed at the equinox, when the sun begins to lose its power:

So that he [the sun] is represented as *Christ taken down from the Cross,*" a dead man, with all the blood drawn out of him, that precious blood which he shed for us men, and for our Salvation, when he "came down from Heaven."

And where is his blood? Why, where should it be, but in that "*Cup of Salvation,*" standing upon that sacramental table, just as it was drawn out of the Bacchanalian barrel, on which the Ivy-crowned Bacchus sits like a drunken boy at the good vintner's shop. And as I feel a little bit bloodthirsty just at this moment; and as the Catholic clergy very sensibly held, that there was no occasion to give up the cup to the laity, I shall, with your permission, keep the cup to myself, hoping that your faith will be satisfied, by seeing me drink it as your representative. (*Drinks.*)

"And now," in the sublime poetry of Watts' Hymns, as sung in a hundred chapels and churches, in this infinitely *be-chapeled* and be-churched metropolis:

"and now I drink my Saviour's blood, (*Drinks.*)
I thank thee, Lord, 'tis generous wine;
Mingled with love, the fountain flowed
From that dear bleeding heart of thine.—(*Hymn* 18.)

This soul-reviving wine,
Dear Saviour 'tis thy blood: (*Drinks.*)
We thank that precious flesh of thine,
For this immortal food,"—(*Book* 3, *Hymn* 17.)

Or, as I have read those lines of Dr. Watts plagiarized, and but little altered, in the composition of quite as good a poet as Dr. Watts—the Rev. Dr. *Towzer*, a famous hand at doggerel:

"'Tis the same blood, in wine or swipes [beer],
'Tis God's own blood, we vow;
And when we feel it in our tripes,
We feel we don't know how."[28] (*Drinks.*)

This parody of the Eucharist was altogether "over the top." Taylor was indicted on 4 July 1831 for this and five other blasphemous statements in his sermons, convicted, and sent to Horsmonger Gaol. Following Carlile's example, Taylor consistently refused to give sureties for his good behavior or to pay fines. Nevertheless, he was released in 1833, and a tremendous reception greeted his return to the pulpit, where he spiced his performance with recitations from Shelley and Shakespeare. But he did not occupy it much longer. After marrying a wealthy admirer, he retired to the island of Jersey, leaving Richard Carlile to convert the Rotunda into his own home. Taylor later practiced as a surgeon in France, and died in Tours; but there is no substance to the unkind rumor that he converted to Christianity on his deathbed.[29]

The blasphemy trials of the first decades of the century cast far more opprobrium on the prosecutors than on the defenders, who showed a moral backbone and a thirst for martyrdom of which any Christian might be proud. The Unitarian W. J. Fox, preaching a sermon on 24 October 1819 about Richard Carlile's trial, was disgusted with the rejoicings of Christians at his conviction, as if it were a Waterloo victory over infidelity.[30] This prosecution, Fox said, virtually rescinded the protection granted to Unitarians in 1813, making Unitarianism again an offense. He knew of no evidence that Christianity was part of the law of England. Parts of English Common Law, such as trial by jury and the hanging of felons, went back to our Gothic ancestors, for whom *preaching* Christianity might have been an offence! Besides, if Christianity were the law of the land, then the law of England should enforce *all* the tenets of the faith—including the rendering of good for evil.

Fox confirmed the Bishop of Chichester's admission to Taylor, saying that many of the lower classes were honest unbelievers, while many upper-class people were concealed unbelievers, thinking Christianity a useful superstition to keep the lower classes in order.[31] It seemed to him that Christianity was being protected not because it was true, but because it was established. But that was a very dangerous precedent to set. Islam, for that matter, was an established religion in some parts of the world; had Christianity any business to interfere there?[32] "Christians," he concluded, "make your religion more defensible; not in itself, that cannot be, but as exhibited in your opinions and practices."[33]

There was one last wave of prosecutions for blasphemy in 1841, brought by the Bishop of Exeter, Henry Philpotts, against an atheist weekly, Charles Southwell's *The Oracle of Reason.* Southwell and his successor G. J. Holyoake were both imprisoned for abuse of the Old Testament; Holyoake got six months for suggesting that God, like a retired officer, should be placed on half-pay. His daughter died of starvation while he was in prison. But as the nineteenth century went on and the French Revolution faded from memory, the opinions and practices even of atheism did not seem so frightful, since some atheists were seen to behave as exemplary citizens, with a more than average concern for their fellows. By 1846, freethinkers had won the right to publish their views, and prosecutions ceased. The secularist movement was becoming an accepted part of the political Left, and Mrs. Grundy found a new outlet for her energies in persecuting the advocates of birth control. Apart from a few soap-box orators jailed for profanity in 1918–21, Britain's blasphemy law was laid to rest until the *Gay News* trial of 1977.[34]

One of the many commentaries on that trial was written by Sangharakshita (D. P. E. Lingwood), a well-known English Buddhist. Although in this book I generally avoid modern commentaries, preferring to let my sources tell their own story, this one makes an important link with the subject of my final chapter. Among other results of the trial, Sangharakshita reported the revival in 1978 of the "United Order of Blasphemers," originally founded in 1844. He was concerned at the revival of archaic laws that allowed *Gay News* to be convicted on the simple grounds that one "sympathizer with Christianity" had been shocked and disgusted by the poem in question.

This vague and subjective definition of the crime left Buddhists, especially, in an equivocal position. As Sangharakshita says,

> It is well known that the notion of a personal God, the creator and ruler of the universe, has no place in the Buddha's teaching, and that throughout its history Buddhism has in fact rejected the notion as detrimental to the moral and spiritual development of mankind. But such a rejection is undoubtedly painful to the feelings of a great many Christians and sympathizers with Christianity: it shocks and disgusts them. Under the present interpretation of the law any Buddhist bearing public witness to the truth of this fundamental tenet of Buddhism, whether in speech or in writing, therefore runs the risk of committing the crime of blasphemy and being punished accordingly.[35]

Of course, he adds, it seems very unlikely that a Buddhist would be prosecuted for propagating his religion in twentieth-century Britain. But as recent efforts to remove the likelihood altogether by repealing the blasphemy laws have failed, it follows that there are those who would not be averse to applying them. "This is hardly surprising. Christians have never been remarkable for their tolerance, and after the events of 1977 and 1978 no Buddhist,—no non–Christian, in fact,—can feel really safe so long as the blasphemy laws remain unrepealed."[36]

Sangharakshita analyzes the state of mind of a Christian, especially a Catholic, who is required to believe in a non–existent God and in much other nonsensical theology. Using the insights of Jungian psychology, he finds that these cause an inner tension that would break out in blasphemy, were it not unconsciously repressed and, in consequence, projected onto other people.[37] He compares the present situation with the projections of blasphemous fantasies onto the Templars in the early fourteenth century, then later onto the so-called witches. (At the time of writing, there is a similar outbreak going on in the United States concerning "Satanic ritual child abuse.") "Therapeutic blasphemy" may be needed to dissolve such conflicts, says Sangharakshita, defining it thus:

> In order to abandon Christianity completely,—in order to liberate himself from its oppressive and stultifying influence,—it may be necessary for the ex-Christian not only to repudiate Christianity intellectually in the privacy of his own mental consciousness but also to give public expression in words, writing, or signs to his *emotional* rejection of Christianity and the God of Christianity, i.e. it may be necessary for him to commit blasphemy.[38]

But this is what the law now longer allows. It permits decent controversy and the assertion of atheism, but not the abuse and ridicule of religion that "therapeutic blasphemy" requires. Worse, the law now threatens to be extended to cover non-Christian religions such as Judaism and Islam. Under these circumstances, Sangharakshita concludes, no Buddhist can feel entirely safe.[39]

The concepts stated with such clarity by this English Buddhist help us understand the minds and actions of Knight, Dupuis, Volney, Drummond, Owen, Carlile, and Robert Taylor. Their work was a form of therapeutic blasphemy, in which by publicly breaking various sexual and religious taboos they freed themselves from their Christian indoctrination. And just as Sangharakshita regarded this as merely a prelude to the realization of a true philosophy, namely that of Buddhism, so we will find that an anti-Christian housecleaning preceded the spiritual quests of many of the spiritualists, occultists, and Theosophists who occupy the following chapters.

FOUR

The Shoemaker and the Squire

In moving from the complacent infidelity of Payne Knight and Sir William Drummond to the missionary zeal of Richard Carlile and Robert Taylor, we have traced in miniature the sociology of unbelief in the early nineteenth century. Ideas tossed around in the Society of Dilettanti and published in expensive books took no time at all to filter down to the popular level, where a ready audience was found for their assault on Christian orthodoxy. France had of course set the precedent for this kind of development, with Voltaire and the Encyclopedists as the instigators, and the Paris *canaille*, enthroning a prostitute on the altar of Notre Dame, as the unfortunate conclusion.

The situation was different in England, for two reasons. First, the Church of England was not seen, any more than the Crown, as particularly oppressive or villainous, so that Voltaire's cry of "*Écrasez l'infâme!*" would have fallen on deaf ears. Second, there was already by 1800 an artisan class eager for self-improvement and education, who responded to the stirrings of religious doubt with curiosity, not brutality. They were the people who refused to further humiliate Daniel Eaton as he stood in the pillory, and cheered the blasphemies of Carlile and Taylor as they went on their infidel crusade. These small tradespeople and clerks were literate, intelligent, and well able to see through hypocrisy, especially that of their social superiors.

This chapter presents an ill-assorted pair of mythographers. Mackey is the perfect illustration of the artisan-savant, while his contemporary Higgins continues in the aristocratic mold of Knight and Drummond. Both of their *oeuvres* grew out of the *Asiatic Researches* and the late eighteenth-century creators of universal theories, facilitated by a climate that permitted dissent from biblical fundamentalism. Looking to the future, Mackey's system of cosmic cycles survived to be included in the teaching documents of the Hermetic Brotherhood of Luxor (1880s), while Higgins's great book, *Anacalypsis,* has more than a casual resemblance to Blavatsky's *Isis Unveiled* (1877).

Samson (or Sampson) Arnold Mackey (1765–1843), a resident of Norwich, had been apprenticed to a shoemaker at eleven, then had spent many years as a soldier, presumably in the lowest ranks. In 1811 he returned to his trade and settled in his native city as a "journeyman shoemaker," renting a small attic for his business and home. The rest of his life was one of hard work, poverty, frustration, and finally the almshouse. Looking back on it, he wrote:

> What a forlorn creature a man of genius is that happens to be a poor man possessing a communicative turn of mind, and a Fortitude capable of surmounting those difficulties that had impeded the career of every other European of his Age, that had attempted to penetrate the Mist that obscured the history of Antiquity.[1]

What made Mackey different from the millions of laborers and petty tradesmen, and similar to the much more privileged person who shares this chapter with him, was that his life had an intellectual purpose. He had a theory, a piece of knowledge that answered many of the enigmas of the universe, and which he felt it his philanthropic duty to share. Much later, with I know not what justification, it would be said that he was the pupil of an initiate of the Hermetic Brotherhood of Luxor. The reader will discover more about this matter in Chapter Sixteen. But Mackey could perfectly well have hatched his great idea on his own.

Almost as soon as he came to Norwich, in 1812, he began trying to offer his knowledge to the world, but want of money prevented him from publishing anything until ten years later.[2] It was not until 1822 that his first book, *The Mythological Astronomy of the Ancients Demonstrated,* appeared, with the first exposition of his theory. Mackey's books have survived as curiosities, with their volvelles tied with cobbler's thread, no doubt by the author's own gnarled fingers. But what are they all about? The readers of his first and fundamental book might have had some difficulty in grasping this great idea, because the author, following the fashionable example of Payne Knight, Erasmus Darwin, and other contemporary scholars, chose to write it in the form of a poem with prose commentaries. Since he could not, or would not state his theory plainly and clearly, I shall do so here.

Mackey's theory concerns the inclination of the earth's axis and its changes over long spans of time. Astronomers have known at least since

Figure 4.1. *Diagram from S. A. Mackey,* The Mythological Astronomy, *1823.*

classical times that the earth's axis rotates once in about 25,920 years, pointing successively at different stars, of which the current one is Polaris, the North Star. One result of this cycle is the "precession of the equinoxes," according to which the spring-point of the sun moves around the twelve signs of the zodiac, spending about 2,160 years in each sign.[3]

Ever since calculations of the axial inclination have been recorded, that is to say since Hipparchus in the second century BCE, it has changed very little. In Mackey's time it was reckoned to have diminished less than a degree since the creation of the earth about 6,000 years ago, which to most astronomers made it inconsequential. Mackey thought otherwise. He had drawn the logical conclusion from this diminution: that the earth's axis describes not a circle but an alternately expanding and contracting spiral, each turn comprising one cycle of the precession of the equinoxes, and at the same time altering the angle of inclination by four degrees. The earth's polar axis currently points 23½ degrees away from the celestial pole, but for Mackey this was only a temporary station. In earlier times, he believed, the inclination was much greater, to the point at which it lay in the same plane as the earth's orbit around the sun.

The axial inclination as we know it is the cause of the seasons of the year. When one hemisphere is tilted more towards the sun, that hemisphere has summer, and when away, it has winter, etc. The greater the angle of inclination, the more pronounced the contrast of the seasons would be. At the maximum angle, each hemisphere would be pointed directly at the sun day and night during the summer, and pointed away for weeks on end during the winter. These extremes of light and dark, of heat and cold, would be virtually insupportable for life as we know it. In Mackey's words, it was an "age of horror" for the planet. Conversely, if the axial angle were to continue to diminish in the future, eventually it would be perpendicular to the ecliptic (or coincident with the celestial pole, which is the same thing), and there would be no seasons on earth, but a perpetual spring and a "golden age." Then the cycle would begin again.

Mackey gives no indication of his sources. An autodidact, he was an avid reader of journals and popular digests and could easily have come across the idea of the steady diminution of the angle of inclination. His originality lay in drawing conclusions without any fear of exceeding the canonical age of the earth. While we have seen Sir William Drummond extending this from about 6,000 to nearly 8,000 years, few men of the time dared to think, as Mackey could, in terms of millions. Calculating on the basis of each precessional cycle of 25,920 years changing the angle of axial inclination by four degrees, Mackey dates the Age of Horror at 425,000 years in the past, the Golden Age about a million years ago, and its recurrence 150,000 years from now.

Mackey is a good example of the indirect effect of the *Asiatic Researches*, for he crossed this psychological barrier after reading of the immense time-cycles of the Hindus, and after finding a book by a clergyman who proposed an earth age of 140,000 years. This precedent gave him the courage to publish his own views.

It was one thing to extend the age of the earth to a million years and more, but Mackey went further still by attributing an analogous age to the human race. It was essential to his system of mythography that the Age of

Horror should have been witnessed and survived by a few human beings, its dreadful memory passing into the mythology of every land. Mackey probably did not know how closely his approach resembled that of Nicholas Boulanger (mentioned in Chapters One and Two), for whom the Deluge was the catastrophe whose memory had entered the collective unconscious and emerged as the dominant theme of myth and religion alike. Both mythographers anticipated modern discoveries of the persistence of collective memories, while Mackey's estimate of the age of homo sapiens at about a million years approaches current ones.

When Mackey lectured on his theory at the Philosophical Society of Norwich, the main objection was to these excessive lengths of time, and to the thought that the Hindus might have known more about them than Europeans. Mackey retorts that "The Hindus knew the country which we call America, and knew the earth to be round long before the Christians of Italy put Gallileo into prison for life, for saying it was so."[4] He describes one of his critics as gesturing "like a pig in a hurricane," and summarizes the objection of another in a doggerel rhyme:

In this soft purling cadence of tone
    Did his streamlet of eloquence flow;
'Till he said that a toad in a stone
    As much as a Brahman might know.
For perchance through a hole in the rock
    The toad might Aldebaran see;
And might, where he ask'd what's o'clock,
    Give an answer as ready as he.[5]

Like many an autodidact, Mackey hurt his case by riding his hobbyhorse to the limit. Every myth or legend he came across seemed to illustrate the experiences of mankind under the changing conditions of the shifting axis. All solar myths referred to the apparent behavior of the sun; serpent myths, to the spiral path of the pole. The different volves of the spiral were always mythologized as intelligent beings,[6] which explained away all the stories of the gods and their progeny. All numbers in theogony and myth referred to celestial mathematics, which Mackey believed to have been fully understood by the priest-astronomers of antiquity. As he sums it up: "I have shown that the mysteries of the ancients were but poetical expressions recording the operations of the Elements and the appearance and disappearance of the celestial bodies as they were regulated by the different angles of the Pole."[7]

Mackey's religious convictions were akin to those of the other people treated so far in this book. This is a deliberately vague statement, since convictions shift in the course of life, and are not easy to ascertain in cases as poorly documented as some of our personages. We can however define them negatively. They did not believe in a personal God who intervenes in human affairs, nor in the Scriptures as a divine revelation, nor in Jesus Christ as the only Son of God. Yet they were not atheists, while both Nature and Reason were sacred to them.

Mackey's god was internal, not external to nature: it was the energy that powers the world-machine and imbues it with inexorable laws of action and reaction. As for the clergymen who attributed the cataclysms in the natural order to the ferocity of an angry Jehovah, in his view they were the real blasphemers.[8] He complained of how the scientific authorities of his time mixed up the religion of nature with a revealed religion "wholly of human invention."[9] A particular bugbear was Sir Richard Phillips, author of an anti-Newtonian *New System of Physics.* Phillips apparently refused to allow matter to possess gravitation for fear of imbuing it with power, lest matter be made equal to God. Mackey retorts:

> May we not ask, why is this strain of seeming piety introduced? why blend Science with Metaphysics? why call matter inert? If God be All-in-all, as Christians as well as Philosophers admit, then, every portion of matter must be some part of God, and may not that inherent property of matter which we call attraction, be some portion of The Divine Spirit, which enliven that matter?[10]

Mackey's distaste for the clergy, like Payne Knight's, was part and parcel of his humanitarianism. He says that: ". . . of all the Frauds that have been practised, on a national scale, those that are said to have proceeded from the mouth of God have produced the greatest calamities: it is these pious frauds that have, in reality, set a man at variance against his Father, and overturned all the harmony of society."[11] The title of the book from which this is quoted comes from a saying of Voltaire: "He is man's best friend who undeceives him." With the French philosopher, Mackey blames the situation not only on the Christians but on their Jewish forebears. Reading the Hebrew Scriptures in the light of an ancient learning that Mackey believed to stretch hundreds of thousands of years into the past, he was forced to the conclusion that "The Jews, who were an illiterate, malignant, and petty people, appear to be foremost on record among pious murderers."[12]

As for Jesus, Mackey admired him as a man teaching the most sublime morality, like Confucius. Both were deists, he says, only Jesus unfortunately came to a people far different from the Chinese, who had sense enough to know that "a man, however wise, however prudent and scientific, is not a God."[13] This was hardly fair play, for it was not the Jews who deified Jesus! But Mackey was not a fair player: a monomaniac on the brink of destitution cannot afford that luxury. He explains that the Jews were divided into two sects: the Sadducees, who were traditionalists with no doctrine of the immortality of the soul, and the Pharisees, whose name derives from Pherezia, that is, Persia.[14] These "dupes of Persia" acquired thence the doctrine of immortality, and also the Hindu myth of Christna, who is nothing but a personification of the sun at a certain point of the (Mackeyan) axial cycle. The consequence was the mistaken identity of the man Jesus with (1) the Hindu Christna, (2) the sun, and (3) God. "He that first attached to the moral character of Jesus, the astronomical attributes of Christna, the Hindoo symbol of the departing Sun, and his re-appearance in the constellation of Virgo, deserves the most severe reprobation."[15] By the time of Mackey's last work, in 1839, the blasphemy persecutions had blown over and he could allow himself a therapeutic laugh at the expense of this confusion, writing of "*Jao*, the great *fabricator* of the universe, whom the Greeks have converted into *old Joe the Carpenter*, who was married, as they say, to the virgin, before he knew that she was in the family way."[16]

Living in East Anglia and without the means to travel, Mackey had little contact with the savants of his day. Norwich, however, was one of England's major cities, and gentlemen there noticed the learned shoemaker and opened their libraries to him after the appearance of *The Mythological Astronomy* in 1822. In subsequent works he was able to take advantage of the *Asiatic Researches*, as Knight had done, to refine his interpretations of Hindu myth. Mackey knew and admired Voltaire and Volney sufficiently to quote them on his title pages. Dupuis's work reached him late and at second hand; he accepted the Frenchman's interpretation of the zodiac as reflecting the Egyptian agricultural year, "which proves that the story of the virgin and her child, was known to the Egyptians more than a Million years back."[17]

The Freemasons also noticed Mackey. A prominent masonic figure, Hippolyto Joseph Da Costa, knew him personally. Da Costa was born in Brazil, initiated into Freemasonry in Philadelphia, and persecuted for his adherence in Lisbon, from which he escaped thanks to the British presence in Portugal. Coming to London, he published an account of his adventures in 1811, then, inspired by the example of Dupuis, wrote a *Sketch for the History of the Dionysian Artificers*.[18] This small book told that the masonic lodges and temples were symbols of the great temple of the universe; that the trials of the aspirant in the dark, etc., represented the Sun's "sufferings" in winter; and that the solar cycle was itself a symbol of the descent and ascent of the soul. Following Jean-Sylvain Bailly, Da Costa explained some of the ancient myths by tracing their origin to certain latitudes, including polar ones where the sun is actually invisible for several days in winter. But all of his symbolism, like Dupuis', assumed the current relationship of the earth to the sun, and was therefore based on the annual cycle alone.

Mackey claimed that ". . . on the appearance of my book, on the *Mythological Astronomy of the Ancients,* his book on the *Dionysian Artificers* was called in. . . ." Manly Palmer Hall, the modern editor of Da Costa, writes that the latter "evidently planned the preparation of a considerable volume, but the larger work, if actually written, never saw print." [19] This, and the extreme rarity of Da Costa's *Sketch,* supports Mackey's proud assertion. Mackey goes on to say that his theory was henceforth recognized by many Freemasons as the one containing the true knowledge of their mysteries. Consequently, his membership was eagerly sought; but he refused, citing as obstacles his poverty, the terrors of the Third Degree, and the oath of secrecy that he would be obliged to take. He is careful to add that his refusal of the Freemasons' invitation in 1824 had nothing to do with his reading of Richard Carlile's polemics.[20]

Since Mackey would not consent to initiation, the Freemasons then offered to found a special "Order of Urania" based on his discoveries and symbolism (his second book having been called *The Key to Urania*), to ensure that his science would be protected by a respectable body of men. This was conclusive for Mackey: he would not have his knowledge "buried beneath the Tyler's sword." (The Tyler is the masonic officer who guards the privacy of the Lodge.) Like Socrates, who refused to be initiated into the Eleusinian Mysteries because his tongue would thereby be tied, Mackey did not want his own revelations to be controlled by others. He concludes this account of his experiences with Freemasonry:

> And thus I remain
> DEPUTY GRAND MASTER
> OF MY OWN LODGE,
> THE LODGE OF URANIA,
>
> Into which all may be admitted male and female that possess Genius and Learning; and from whence has irradiated that refulgent Light, which explains every ancient mystery; and which can never again be extinguished, though *Cambyses* returns.[21]

As for the veiled system of morality of which Masons are so proud, Mackey says that "we find a system equally beautifully given us by the Grand Master, Jesus, without a veil." [22]

Some London readers of Mackey's early works suggested that the author should move to the capital, take a shop in Holborn, and publish his own works, selling astronomical instruments and books, and Oriental literature. Richard Barrow, an "eminent surgeon of Hounslow" who wrote to Mackey on 9 June 1824 with these suggestions, promised that "your system must in time destroy the present ridiculous and circumscribed chronology," and added that Mackey should always put "Journeyman Shoemaker" on his publications: "Nature has given you a Patent of Nobility, and you need no other."[23] If Mackey had followed this advice, he would have come into contact with other minds that were sifting through ancient astronomy and mythology without the constraints of biblical fundamentalism. Perhaps he would have become less cabined in his own system and his own self-righteousness and not felt the need to issue ukases from his cobbler's shop against all those foolish enough not to know about his system. He did make at least one trip to London, for we find him there in Soho on 20 December 1830, giving a lecture that showed why there was so much more water in the southern hemisphere than in the northern.[24] He is said to have had interviews with the Duke of Sussex and the Duke of Somerset.[25] But he was to end his days in a Norwich almshouse.

In 1836, Mackey wrote a spirited attack on the geologist J. J. Gurney, describing himself as "old and almost blind and frequently without the common necessities of life."[26] Nevertheless, in his last work, three years later, he was still sticking to his guns as the only true interpreter of the Book of Revelation. "And this truly sublime astronomical allegory had never been opened by any body but the poor old Shoemaker of Norwich, who is now cribbed into No.4, Doughty's Hospital, Calvert Street, which he deems a kind of paradise."[27]

A few years after Mackey's death, *Note & Queries* carried a number of reminiscences of the courageous old shoemaker. One contributor, called "M," wrote that "in the year 1827 when prosecutions of blasphemy were leading thousands to see what could be said against Christianity [. . .] some friends of mine recommended the works of a shoemaker at Norwich named Mackey, who said he had completely shown up *the thing*."[28] (The reference, as "M" makes clear, is to the prosecution of Robert Taylor.) A female contributor, "F.C.B.," knew Mackey between 1826 and 1830, when he was trying to supplement his income by giving "orrery demonstrations" in his lodgings, presumably illustrating his theories of the axial change and its consequences. She saw him again in Doughty's Hospital around 1840, "surrounded by astronomical apparatus, books, the tools of his former trade, and all kinds of strange litters." The old man would not talk freely to a woman, but F.C.B. did her best to find out how he had come by his ideas. He mentioned the mythographer Jacob Bryant, the Indianist Thomas Maurice, and the *Asiatic Researches*, especially the essays of Francis Wilford. But all his study had been solitary: "He had evidently read and studied deeply, but alone; his own intellect had never been brushed by the intellects and superior information of truly scientific men, and it appeared to me that a vast deal of dirt had accumulated in his mind."[29] Finally, another inhabitant of the almshouse, J. Dawson, wrote to say that after Mackey's death, all his manuscripts had come to him, including an account of his life; he also knew of a half-length portrait. And that is the first and last ever heard of those relics.[30]

Faithless to the end, Mackey concluded his life's work with a passage on the resurrection of the body and the life everlasting. These, he said,

> relate to eternal laws of Nature. The body dies, rots, and becomes vegetable; the vegetable becomes animal, and so on, world without end; which must be life everlasting.
>
> If all the scientific allegories in the Bible, were explained in this manner, it would greatly add to the mental happiness of mankind all over the earth.[31]

There is something moving in the picture of Mackey turning from his day's labor at the cobbler's last to read avidly in a borrowed copy of the *Asiatic Researches.* Sir William Jones and his Christian colleagues would have been appalled to learn that one of the fruits of their labors would be to reinforce a working man's contempt for religion. But Dupuis and Volney, those infidel Frenchmen, would have been delighted at the thought of a *sans-culotte* thirsty not for blood but for the knowledge that makes him free.

Great as were the worldly barriers that separated Mackey from Godfrey Higgins (1772–1833), the squire of Skellow Grange, these two men would have found much to agree upon if they had ever met. A common dislike of "churchianity" and a contempt for the priesthood of all nations would have provided genial common ground for them, as would a shared fascination with cyclical chronology and a touching faith in etymology as an instrument of proof. But while they surely had acquaintances in common, probably among the masonic brethren who were so interested in Mackey, the shoemaker apparently never saw the three quarto volumes that constitute Higgins's monument: *The Celtic Druids* (1829), and the two volumes of *Anacalypsis* (1833, 1836). Higgins, for his part, mentions Mackey's theory of the Christian fish symbol with approval, and qualifies its author as "a very profound-thinking shoemaker"[32] and a credit to his caste. For Mackey's vortices and gyres, it seems, he had less respect.

Higgins was the son of a country gentleman with property in Skellow, near Doncaster, Yorkshire. He attended Trinity Hall, Cambridge, and the Temple in London, but was kept short of money by his father and never completed either course of study. He inherited Skellow Grange upon his father's death about 1799, married in the early 1800s, and joined the Yorkshire militia to prepare for Napoleon's threatened invasion of England. He rose to the rank of Major, but a severe illness caused his retirement

Figure 4.2. *Godfrey Higgins (1772–1833), from Hailstone,* Portraits of Yorkshire Worthies, *1869.*

about 1808, after which he devoted himself to local philanthropy and to study. Several addresses to electors and to the two Houses of Parliament bear witness to a vigorous campaigner for the humane treatment of the insane, and to a conscientious squire concerned for the well-being of the countryside and all its inhabitants, however humble.

For all his regional activities, Higgins was a considerable traveler, making two journeys to Rome and one to Naples. He was in Rome for Christmas and the opening of Jubilee Year in 1824–25. Among the other places he visited were Paris, Geneva (in spring 1824), Milan, Venice, Bologna, Siena, Cumae, Pompeii, and Loreto and Ancona on the Adriatic Coast. Other journeys took him to Dublin, where he pursued his researches into Catholicism, and to the Scottish Highlands, including the isles of Staffa and Iona. He had a London residence in Keppel Street, conveniently near the British Museum, and often visited Bath. This much one can glean from statements and allusions in *Anacalypsis.*

Higgins was never able to make the journey to Egypt and the East, which he was sure would place the capstone on his philosophy of history. At the time of writing *The Celtic Druids,* he had engaged an Armenian monk to be his guide and was impatient to depart. He describes his circumstances in that book, with the intimacy and openness that make him a pleasure to read:

> The only daughter of the author, the kindest and most affectionate of children, is happily married. His only son, the comfort and pride of his parent's declining years, is at man's estate. The author is a widower, only 53 years of age, and is in good health. *The game is yet upon the cards.* Who knows but he may live to see the mountains of Ararat, or the city of Samarcand! [33]

But the Armenian guide had died by the time the Preface to the work was written in January 1829, and the voyage was postponed—forever, as it turned out.

The first volume of *Anacalypsis* was sent to press from October 1830, and printed bit by bit, being completed in April 1833. Work on the second volume proceeded, but Higgins only lived to correct the first four sheets before dying on 9 August 1833. His son Godfrey Jr. undertook to issue the whole work, employing an unnamed editor who lived in Homerton (near Cambridge) and finished his work on 4 June 1836. In the course of the work Higgins mentions some twenty persons as his friends, most of them further qualified as, for instance, Thomas Taylor, "my learned and excellent friend." [34] For all his contempt for the cloth, a number of them were clergymen. The others included a Mr. Salome of Bath, who was Higgins's tutor in Hebrew. One story told him by Salome became a *locus classicus* for Higgins's theory of Hebrew as the oldest language of mankind. Salome had witnessed an affray at the East India Company's docks involving some Malayan sailors, and had been astonished to recognize their language as his own.[35] The same Jewish friend also brought Higgins into contact with the inhabitants of the London ghetto, eliciting these remarks:

> The Jews, as a race, are very handsome; they take after their ancestor Cristna. Nothing is more easy than to distinguish a thorough-bred Jew or Jewess. And it is very greatly to the honour of the Jewish matrons that the family likeness or national peculiarity should have continued so long. It gives me great pleasure to see this hitherto oppressed and insulted race regaining their station in society. I hope that all distinction in civil rights will very speedily disappear.[36]

Another friend, the Rev. Dr. Joseph Hunter, preserved some of Higgins's letters together with a brief memoir. Hunter had met him in Bath (attending Higgins's wife, who fell ill and died there), and thereafter saw him frequently at Skellow Grange, Bath, Oxford, and London. In the 1820s, Higgins paid Hunter for some genealogical researches; by 1830 he was sending the doctor regular bulletins on the progress of *Anacalypsis,* with asides such as the following reaction to the coup-d'état in France:

> What glorious news from France. I only hope they will make Orleans king. This I wish as a man that is a being of the genus *Mannus.* As an Englishman I should wish for Bordeaux then the government will be weak & the country a prey to faction & all kinds of mischiefous intreagues [sic] & in no respect dangerous to us. Orleans I think will never be so foolish as to accept the regency. Then who are they to have?[37]

Orleans, son of Philippe Egalité, did mount the throne as the "citizen-king" Louis-Philippe (1830–1848); we will hear more of him in Chapter Five.

Higgins's political and religious views were shared by one man whom he does not presume to call a friend, but with whom he had important relations: the Duke of Sussex (1773–1843), sixth son of George III. I have already mentioned him in connection with Robert Owen and Samson Mackey. An intellectual and consequently a misfit in his family, Sussex had spent his youth wandering round the Continent, meeting Sir William Hamilton in Naples and attending Göttingen University, where he began a lifelong interest in Hebrew and biblical studies. Estranged from his father through an unapproved marriage in Rome, the Duke supported the abolition of the slave trade, the emancipation of Catholics, Jews, and dissenters, the abolition of the Corn Laws, parliamentary reform—in short, the entire liberal agenda of his time. In the world of learning he was President of the Society of Arts and of the Royal Society; and he became Grand Master of the United Grand Lodge of England at its inception in 1813.

Richard Carlile, in his exposure of Freemasonry, records an intriguing incident concerning Higgins, the Duke of Sussex, and himself:

> The late Godfrey Higgins once observed to me, without explanation, that there were but two Masons in England—himself and the Duke of Sussex. I put in a claim to be a third. He asked me to explain, on the condition that he was not to commit himself by any observation. I did so, as here set forth. He smiled and withdrew.[38]

In an earlier edition of the work (1831), Carlile dates the incident to "last year" and admits the Rev. Robert Taylor as a fourth.

The Duke of Sussex's Grand Mastership marked the union of the two streams of English Freemasonry, the "Ancients" and "Moderns," who had been bickering for much of the previous century. One of his main objects was the de-Christianizing of the rituals and ceremonies, so as to make the Craft answerable to its universalist claims. Like Higgins, he felt a particular friendship for the Jews. The Jewish Lodge at Frankfurt, formed under Napoleon's protection in 1807, turned to him when it found itself oppressed by an aggressive Christian Masonry, and the Duke granted it a new, unrestricted charter in 1817.[39] Since he had moved in the same circles of scholarly freethinkers as Payne Knight, Hamilton, and Drummond, it seems very likely that Sussex, while nominally a Christian, had developed similar views about the origins of religion, and that he saw Freemasonry as preserving a relic of the time before priestcraft, schism, and dogma.

Such was certainly Higgins's opinion. He himself became a Freemason only after writing *The Celtic Druids,* though he had already decided that Freemasonry was a survival of the ancient esoteric schools. He considered that, while it would not refuse to admit a simple deist, Freemasonry was particularly suited to reunite Jews, Christians, and Muslims in recognition of the essential unity of their religions. Higgins deliberately curtailed his masonic ambitions, refusing to join either the Rosicrucians or the Knights Templar, "that I might not have my tongue tied or my pen restrained by the engagements I must have made on entering the chapter or encampment. But I have reason to believe that they are now become in a very particular manner what is called exclusively Christian orders . . ."[40]

Higgins used Freemasonry, as he used his travels, to further his researches into the mysteries of antiquity. One of these was the similarity of the words "Chaldees," the astronomer-priests of the Near East, and

"Culdees," an order of Druids who had survived in England long into the Christian era. Using his newly acquired rights of entry,

> After I had been led to suspect, from various causes, that the Culdees [. . .] were Masons, I searched the Masonic records in London, and I found a document which upon the face of it seemed to shew that that Lodge, which was the Grand Lodge of all England, had been held under the Cathedral in the crypt, at York. In consequence of this I went to York, and applied to the only survivor of the Lodge, who shewed me, from the documents which he possessed, that the Druidical Lodge, or Chapter of Royal-Arch Masons, or Templar Encampment, all of which it calls itself, was held for the last time in the crypt, on Sunday, May 27, 1778.[41]

Higgins obtained these documents, some of them written in runes, and deposited them with the Duke of Sussex. Presumably they were surrendered willingly by their custodian, Mr. Blanchard, because they proved the antiquity that the York Lodge had always claimed over London. Higgins evidently respected the Duke as a repository of the true secrets of masonry, and the British Constitution as its guarantee:

> Why do the priest-led monarchs of the continent persecute Masonry? Is it because they are not entrusted with its secrets; or, because their priests cannot make it subservient to their base purposes? All these are questions I may ask, gentle reader; but *all* I may not answer. If you be not satisfied, ask his Royal Highness the Duke of Sussex: he can answer you IF HE CHOOSES. But this I may say, it is not every apprentice or fellow-craft who knows all the secrets of Masonry.
>
> Masonry is not inimical to priests, or kings, or religions; but though it is not an *active* enemy, it is no friend to bad priests, or bad kings, or bad morals. Masonry is patronized by the Royal family, and by many priests in Britain. The reason of this is no Masonic secret. It is because the princes of Britain are not, and desire not, to be the tyrants of their country, and because among the priests of Britain are to be found many who are neither fanatical nor base; but, on the contrary, men possessed of every virtue, and whose misfortune it may be, but not whose fault, to belong to their pernicious order.[42]

. . . which is damning the clergy with very faint praise!

So what were these secrets? As few readers will want to find out by reading the 1500 pages of *Anacalypsis*, I will make a cogent story out of what is scattered throughout the two volumes. Naturally this will be a selective summary, dwelling on themes that recur in our other writers.

"In the beginning," all the planets revolved around the sun in the same time and the same plane. The pole of the earth coincided with the pole of the heavens, and the Arctic regions were warm. The direct act of God, infusing life into matter, occurred somewhere in Northern Asia, long before the biblical chronology allows for the Creation. The first race of mankind was black, and its first religion, either revealed or developed over a long time, that of Emanation. In this system, "the One," which is neuter and unknowable, first emanates "Wisdom," which is the divine plan of the universe; also, from another aspect, polarizes into a Creator and a Destroyer; or, again, into a Trinity of Creator, Preserver, and Regenerator. Thereupon ensues a chainlike series of emanations, including lesser gods and human souls, each containing a particle of divinity. Higgins is not systematic in his treatment of any of this, but he shows how these and a few other principles inform every known religion.

The earliest race was of one faith, one color, and one language, and spread over the entire globe. The most relics of it are to be found in Buddhism, which Higgins believed to be incalculably ancient. The Negroid features of Gautama's statues seemed to him proof of this, as also the blue-faced Krishna, the black-faced Osiris, and the black images of the Virgin and Child in many Catholic churches. This showed him that it is nonsense to regard the black race as inherently inferior. In those distant times the length of the year was 360 days; the month, 30; the precessional cycle, 36,000 years; and the only metal known was gold. Thus there was no money, no weapons, and it was indeed a Golden Age when none killed, even for food. The simple and beautiful offering of Melchisedek—bread and wine—was the only sacrament.

The basic doctrines of this period, which have all survived in one form or another to the present, were the immortality of the soul, metempsychosis, the final reabsorption of all things in the One, and the periodic renewal of worlds. An interest in the latter led the ancient sages to study astronomy and cosmic cycles, enabling them to make preparations for the all-but-universal Deluge that upset the orderly solar system and brought about the ruin of the primordial world.

There have been at least three partial deluges, caused by the earth's meeting with a comet. As a result of the last one, which washed over the Pyramids, the length of the year, month, and precessional period all changed. Two cycles were rediscovered by the Chaldeans: that of the astrological ages of 2,160 years each, and the "Neros Cycle" of conjunctions of the sun and moon at the spring equinox. The Neros period was at first thought to be 666 years, then 650, then 608, until finally the correct length was established at 600 years. All of these numbers are commemorated by significant names and phrases in the languages where the letters have numerical equivalents. Such was the work of the "esoteric" priesthoods, while exoteric doctrines were given to the common people.

The changes from one cycle to another were marked by wars, schisms, and messianic expectations. Among the most important of these was the schism between the worshipers of the male and those of the female principle. The Jews, from Abraham onwards, were strict followers of the "lingam" sect, while their opponents in Palestine were of the "yoni" persuasion. Other conflicts arose in every land between the indigenous population, usually blacks, and the invaders who descended from "Noah," i.e., from a group of lighter-colored deluge-survivors who spread from the east of the Caspian Sea. One such conflict was between the ancient, black, vegetarian Buddhists and the aggressive, white, Himalayan Brahmins, leaving bad feeling in India to this day.

The most venerable symbol of the One has always been the visible sun, and all religions are therefore, on one level, forms of solar worship. Christianity is no exception, the crucifixion of its solar Christ symbolizing the sun crossing the celestial equator at the vernal equinox, or between two astrological ages. Numerous other crucified saviors corroborate this myth and its meanings. The religion of Jesus of Nazareth, on the other hand, is the most admirable moral teaching, coming from an Essene who was by that token a "Buddhist," i.e., a representative of the primordial, esoteric religion. Higgins does not hesitate to declare himself a Christian, in the sense of taking as exemplar this Nazarene who was probably never crucified but lived to the age of fifty. But he abhors the work of Saint Paul and of all his priestly followers.

At the time of Jesus' birth, the eighth Neros cycle since counting had begun was coming to an end, and messianic expectations were running high both among the esotericists who understood astronomy, and among the people who were led on to expect great events. Caesar and Augustus were both considered as possible ninth avatars, and their stories were tailored to fit, just as Jesus' was, after the event. Thus the idea that the twelve Caesars are a solar myth may be truer than the Rev. Townsend thought, when he proposed it in jest.

Around the year 600, another such cyclical point occurred, contributing greatly to the success of Mohammed, who was seen as the tenth and last avatar of a larger 6,000-year cycle. Once again, in 1200, the end not only of an age but probably of the world was due. The Crusaders had long been preparing Palestine for the expected return of Christ; Joachim of Fiore was predicting the Age of the Holy Spirit; the Pope was taking steps to recognize Islam, if it should become necessary; but by 1260 nothing cataclysmic had happened, and it remained for a few sectaries to claim that Saint Francis, or Genghis Khan, had been the avatar.

All of the above constitutes what Higgins styles "the Mythos": an evolving and migrating body of esoteric knowledge, concealed in numbers and names, taught in the Mysteries, and still known in the secret conclaves of the Vatican.

The myth of an avatar every 600 years had virtually died with the disappointments of the thirteenth century, but not quite. The next date would have been 1800, or 1824 if the more venerable 608-year cycle were followed. Higgins noted that a spate of millenial teachers had arisen in his own time, predicting the end of the world and claiming important status for themselves: he mentions especially Irving, Brothers, Walmesley, and Joanna Southcote. And then there were Napoleon, and the present Emperors of Austria and Russia, whose ambitions may have been fueled in part by an awareness of the Mythos. Moreover, not only were the first years of the nineteenth century the start of a new Neros cycle; they also saw the end of the Piscean and the start of the Aquarian Age. Higgins does not date the latter, but leaves the reader to make the simple calculation of adding 2,160 to the start of the Piscean Age, 350 BCE. That would give 1810—surely the earliest date ever proposed for the Age of Aquarius.

Higgins himself was anything but a sensationalist, and had no patience at all with occultism, ancient or modern. The purpose of life, for him, was the cultivation of virtue, in order to be more speedily reabsorbed into the One. This realization was the greatest wisdom of the ancients; indeed, their "secret doctrine" was nothing else, however often it had been lost, or covered in irrelevant accretions by self-seeking esotericists. Higgins believed in progress because of the blows dealt to a jealous and exploitative priesthood, first by the invention of writing and second by that of printing, which had saved Europe from the fate of theocratic Tibet. In his own lifetime, he had seen the end of the pretensions of kings to a "divine right" founded on the Mythos. Given such views, it is not difficult to guess which of the authors mentioned in previous chapters he liked and disliked. He was a keen supporter of Jean-Sylvain Bailly; he quotes with approval Dupuis, Drummond, and Knight, and defends Wilford, whose reputation had been ruined because a Brahmin foisted forged scriptures on him. Sir William Jones and the Reverends Maurice and Faber, on the other hand, earn censure for "pious frauds" in concealing the proto-Christian elements in Hinduism.

At one point of his second volume Higgins writes:

> I must fairly admit, that I cannot read what I have written without an indescribable melancholy. In what a state of

> delusion have four-fifths of mankind been kept, and still are kept, by the dishonesty of the remainder; and, in the teeth of my humble and feeble efforts, I fear always will be kept! But, at all events, I have done my duty; I have endeavoured, with no little labour, to draw aside the veil. I know what I deserve; I fear, I know what I shall receive, from my self-sufficient and ignorant countrymen. But yet, a new aera is rising. There still is hope in the bottom of the box.[43]

This talk of a new era may not have been taken in any high-flown sense by Higgins himself, but his mythos of historical cycles may well have excited some readers with a more credulous frame of mind. In Chapter Seventeen we will review this possibility and some of its consequences.

One trembles at the disservice done to an author by reducing his book by a factor of several hundred. But if I were to give *Anacalypsis* the summary it deserves, together with dozens of indispensable quotations, Higgins's book would leave no room for my own. I will now cast an eye over his lesser works.

The Celtic Druids anticipates *Anacalypsis* in many of its ideas: the one primordial race of Bailly; the ancient black empire which once ruled Egypt and all of Asia;[44] its language and its alphabet as parents of all known ones; the identity of Druids with Chaldaeans, Brahmins, Magi, Pythagoreans, Essenes—but not yet with Buddhists! Higgins also accepts the prevalence of solar and phallic worship in all religions, both illustrated by the prehistoric monuments of the British Isles. A standing stone is phallic; a stone circle, solar. A large portion of the book is given to illustrations of these, and to accounts of them by others. Read before *Anacalypsis, The Celtic Druids* is a mind-opening work. It was the subject of Higgins's one serious contemporary review, by an anonymous contributor to *The Southern Review* of Charleston, South Carolina.[45] But *Anacalypsis*, which so eclipses its predecessor, appears to have been completely ignored by the learned journals of the day.

Higgins's nonpolitical writings are completed by two smaller books, which since they are not available in modern reprints I summarize here. They are not so much interesting in themselves, as in the kind of opposition they aroused, which shows that in England's great seats of learning the Enlightenment was still barely a glimmer.

Horae Sabbaticae, completed on the 25th of January 1826 and published the same year, is a plea to lift the Puritan gloom from the British Sunday. As a magistrate, Higgins must have found himself in the uncomfortable position of having to enforce laws he disagreed with, particularly those that forbade any sort of Sunday entertainment, recreation, and trade—laws far stricter than those of the Catholic countries of Europe, or even of Calvinistic Geneva.[46] Most of Higgins's argument is from Scripture, citing especially Jesus' own breaking of the sabbath and his implicit abolition of it in his Summary of the Law (Luke 18:18–22). Higgins recommends that here, as in everything, Christians should follow the example of their master. Against the argument that the sabbath owes its origin to the seventh day of Creation, he says that there is no evidence for its observance by the Patriarchs.[47] Besides, Sunday was the day on which God started his work, not finished it.[48]

Thus far, *Horae Sabbaticae* might have taken its place among dull theological treatises. But it carried a sting in its tail:

> What does all this prove? It proves that, generally, reason has nothing to do with religion. And that men are of that religion, which their priest and their nurse happen accidentally to profess. This observation will offend many persons; but it is, notwithstanding, perfectly true.[49]

Offense was duly taken. A Doncaster neighbor of Higgins's, Henry Standish, was upset by the devaluation in the *Horae Sabbaticae* of public worship in favor of private devotion. Standish was very wary of leaving people to do their praying by themselves. He confessed a liking for stage plays, but was horrified by the prospect of their taking place on Sunday. As far as the disparity between Moses' teaching and Jesus' went, Standish wrote that "the fact is, that the New Testament and the Old Testament must be combined together so as to deduce a consistent whole. . . ."[50] He did not, however, attempt this Sisyphean task.

The Rev. T. S. Hughes, Christian Advocate for Cambridge University, also felt obliged to speak up for orthodoxy, as his predecessor Estlin had done against Sir William Drummond. Hughes excused Jesus' sabbath-breaking (though he could not bring himself to call it that) as intended to show "a proper distinction between the great moral duties and the overstrained observance of ritual institutions."[51] But most of Hughes's letter to Higgins is on biblical scholarship, as he expounds on septenaries in Judaism and paganism, on the times of day of the Apostles' and Saint Paul's meetings, etc. Hughes was keen for Sunday not to be gloomy, but at cricket and football he absolutely drew the line.[52]

Higgins must have read these with amused interest, and when he could spare the time from *Anacalypsis*, he issued an enlarged edition of *Horae Sabbaticae* (1833). One of the things he had now learned was that the whole subject of sabbath origins had been fully discussed at the Reformation and settled by the churches of both sides according to the "unsophisticated doctrine of the Gospels and Epistles."[53] He also learned that he had "the excellent society of Quakers" on his side, as well as many scholarly divines. Higgins recalled that when he was visiting Geneva, he had been shown the place where John Calvin, aged 70, used to play football with the boys after Sunday services.[54] All of this made the legal enforcement of Sunday observance in Britain even more untenable.

With the patronizing attitude of their class, some of Higgins's friends had admitted to him that the sabbath was only a human institution, but added that it would be bad for public morals to let this be known. Higgins replied to this with the righteous anger of a defender of truth, in almost the same terms as we have heard from Dupuis and Mackey:

> So then, at last, the people are to be humbugged into obedience to the law of the land, and to the performance of their duty. This is in good keeping with this age of cant and humbug. A pious fraud is to be practised to keep the people in order!
>
> No; let the people know the true nature of their rights and their duties; let them know how far they are bound by the law of God.[55]

The other minor work was designed to stir up the minds of the Asiatic Society's members: *An Apology for the life and character of the celebrated prophet of Arabia, called Mohamed, or The Illustrious* (1829). It was a practical step towards the reconciliation already noticed in connection with Higgins's Freemasonry, in order, he says,

> to abate the mischievous spirit of intolerance which has hitherto existed between the followers of Jesus and those of Mohamed, by shewing that the religions of both, however unfortunately changed by time, are the same in their original foundation and principle. If the author should succeed in the slightest degree in exciting or increasing a brotherly feeling towards the professors of the Mohamedan faith, so many millions of whom are our fellow-subjects, he will be amply rewarded.[56]

Higgins begins with the disconcerting reminder that the accusations against Mohammed by the Christians are no more evidential than those made against Jesus by the Jews.[57] Among the positive aspects of the Prophet's character, even Christian scholars (though the facts are gall and wormwood to them) admit his mildness and good manners; applaud his ban on games of chance and wine; his faithfulness to a wife fifteen years his senior; the charity he enjoins to the poor (not just tithes to be paid to priests) and his kindness to animals; his doctrine of works, not faith; and his intelligible and simple theology. Higgins is most moved by Mohammed's persecution by the priests and rulers of his day, which he likens to that of Socrates, Pythagoras, Moses, Luther, and Jesus.[58] This stirs him to a diatribe more eloquent than any in *Anacalypsis* against those who compelled Mohamed to take up the sword in self-defense—and all their kind:

> What a stupendous effect has arisen from the folly of these few miserable priests of a contemptible religion [Meccan paganism]! What miseries have been brought on the world by this pernicious order of men! In all ages and in all nations, the priests have been the enemies of the happiness of mankind. To them may almost all the great revolutions of the world be traced. . . . It is not to the philosophers and the Carbonari, that the late revolutions of France and Spain are to be attributed, but to the murderers of the family of the Calases, and to the heads of the Inquisition. Nor are Ferdinand and Miguel the persons to whose charge the miseries of Spain and Portugal ought to be laid. They are but the creatures of the priests; they are only what the priests, who have the sole merit or demerit of every action of their lives, have made them. An established priesthood has all the dangers of a corresponding society. All hierarchies have been raised to the height which they acquire at first by good conduct in the priesthood. They rise by the prudent behaviour of good men in humble life to wealth and power; these once obtained, bad men get possession of the power, and the order then becomes the curse of the world.[59]

One of the best commendations of Mohammed's religion is its absence of such a hierarchy: "How happy it would have been for Europe if the religion of Jesus, in a similar manner, had forbidden the use of priests or priesthoods!"[60] Higgins reminds his readers that it is priests who have imprisoned Carlile and Taylor;[61] that the Pope and the Archbishop of Canterbury have never spoken out against the African slave trade;[62] and that there is nothing half as infamous in Islam as the Inquisition, or the murder of millions in Mexico and Peru.[63]

Higgins devotes a long section to Mohammed's own reverence for Jesus, and to the Prophet's belief that he was sent in fulfilment of Jesus' promise of a Paraclete or Comforter—interpreted by Christians as the Holy Spirit. Even if Mohammed was mistaken about his own prophetic status, Higgins thinks him no worse, and certainly no less sincere, than Joanna Southcote, Swedenborg, or Wesley.[64] Mohammed may have genuinely believed that he was "moved by the Spirit," as the Quakers call it. Possibly he was convinced of his paracletic function by the coincidence of his name with prophecies in the Gospel of Barnabas and in Haggai. But whatever his beliefs and/or delusions, says Higgins, Mohammed was no impostor.[65]

In conclusion, Higgins tells of the advice he himself gave to a young Egyptian sent to England by the Pasha for his education, who had been warned that he would be damned if he did not become a Christian.

> Remain in the religion of your ancestors. . . . No person, whose mind has not been corrupted by education, can doubt the truth of the Hindoo doctrine, that God is equally present with the pious Jew in the synagogue, the Christian in the church, the Mohamedan in the mosque, and the Brahmin in the temple.[66]

Higgins's open-mindedness in defending the religion that had long been the anathema of Christians is admirable. But it was not entirely unjust when a local clergyman, the Rev. P. Inchbald, objected that the underplot of the work was to weaken the claims of revelation and to attack Christianity.[67] Commending Higgins's good work in reforming asylums, Inchbald advises that country gentlemen should attend to agriculture, not theology.[68] He then shows the quality of his own theology by ranting against the Mohammedan creed that "All is from God," saying that "consequently, evil, not less than good, is ascribed to God as its author,—a doctrine which, in whatever system it obtains, shakes to the foundations both religion and morals."[69] Again we sense the fear that if the truth were told, the castle might come tumbling down. Inchbald surely was not ignorant of the passages in the Bible that ascribe evil as well as good to God—to say nothing of the dreadful crimes dictated by Jehovah to his people. Higgins, like other philosophers, had put his finger on a sore point: that while Jesus had chosen his audience and apostles from the "lower orders," the Church now considered the truth too dangerous for popular consumption.

Another Yorkshire clergyman, the Rev. George Wyatt, took Higgins to task for his prejudices against priests, telling him to "reprimand the delinquent priests but not the institution."[70] Quite fairly, he adds an Appendix on all the Imams, Sheiks, Cazims, Katibs, etc., who constitute a virtual priesthood within Islam. More hurtful was the letter of R. Mackenzie Beverley, a neighbor who teased Higgins for his leanings towards Islam, reminding him of all the "sausages, black-puddings, excellent ham, and delicious port wine of Skellow Grange."[71] Beverley, who wrote part of his pamphlet in Higgins's own breakfast-room,[72] thought that "The only excuse for [Mohammed] is that he was doing evil that good might come,"[73] and dropped Higgins from his acquaintance. In *Anacalypsis* Higgins let his "former friend" know what he thought of his conduct.[74]

So the arguments went on, each one fired by a prejudice that came down, in the end, to whether or not the arguer was at home in the

Christian Church. Such matters are never to be settled by logical or scholarly persuasion: they are, rather, a touchstone for the wisdom of the heart. Higgins could open his heart to Mohamed and his religion, and his reward was tolerance. His critics could not, and their reward was the confirmation of their own narrowness. Perhaps it made them better churchmen. As to who emerged the better Christian, that depends on how the term is taken. The way in which Higgins took it is evident from the words with which he concluded the *Anacalypsis*:

> In the time of Tiberius appeared a man of the name of John. He was a Nazarite, of the monastic order of the Pythagorean Essenes, and lived the life of a hermit. He was put to death by Herod, for rebuking him for his vices. About the same time lived a person, who was his cousin, whose original name has probably been changed, like that of Abraham, Jacob, Joshua, Pythagoras, &c., but who has since been known by the name of JESUS CHRIST. This person was also a Nazarite, of the same sect or monastic order—the Pythagorean Essenes. He, like his cousin John, was a philosopher, a teacher of morality and of reformation of manners to his Jewish countrymen. He was put to death by the priests of the Pharisees, the prevailing or orthodox sect, at that time, in Judea, against whose vices he loudly declaimed, and whose hypocrisy he exposed. He was a person of a most virtuous life and amiable manners—the Socrates or Pythagoras of his day. We know that he taught a very strict and pure morality, the unity of God, the immortality of the soul, and that this life is only a state of probation for a state of future existence, in which every person will be rewarded or punished according to his merits or demerits. These are the facts which we know respecting Jesus and his doctrines,—and as I believe that the facts are real, and that the doctrines are true, I consider that I am his follower, his disciple, and *a Christian*.[75]

At this point the reader may agree that the gulf between shoemaker and squire has widened again. There is a seigneurial grandeur to Godfrey Higgins, a serene command of immense learning which, even though often stuffed into the bottomless pit of etymology, carries him through vastnesses of time and space yet never obscures the "one thing needful." Mackey's self-proclaimed uniqueness, by contrast, is a caricature, the more pathetic in view of his crippling disadvantages. Both men threw out a challenge to their age: to reimagine the past, free from the blinkers of habit and obedience and thus to meet the future with a clearer eye. Both were ignored in their own time and forgotten in ours, perhaps because the process was already further advanced than they thought. The negative part of the process, that is: for the consensus of the secular nineteenth century would leave a cold void in many a soul.

At this point of my story, the destructive work has been completed, like a city block levelled for a new building. We have been listening to a group of people emancipated from infantile beliefs, whose intellects were free to take a bird's-eye view of all of human aspiration. Such people make excellent magistrates and diplomats, brave martyrs for freedom, diligent scholars, but there is not an artist or a poet among them, much less a mystic. In the next chapters we will turn to those in whom freethinking was only the base for new modes of spiritual aspiration: people who felt a thirst that could only be satisfied by the direct encounter with other planes of being. For convenience, I refer to them as the occultists.

FIVE

Magicians and Revolutionaries

The land of John Dee, Robert Fludd, and Elias Ashmole has never lacked practitioners of the occult sciences, even if at times they have lain very low. At the end of the seventeenth century, for instance, there was that curious character Thomas Britton (1644–1714), who held musical evenings in the loft above his London coal-store. Famous for having invented the institution of the public concert, Britton welcomed many eminent musicians (including Handel) and their aristocratic patrons up the narrow stairs to his music-room. Like a Renaissance prince who would keep a salon for artists and connoisseurs, while reserving for a handful of intimate friends the finest of his music and his most precious objects, so Britton had a deeper layer of private life behind his concert-giving: that of a magician and a practical alchemist. Two sales of Britton's library, held in 1694 and 1714, uncovered a large collection of grimoires, alchemical manuscripts, and the virtually complete works of Maier, Heydon, and Vaughan. Ron Heisler, the most diligent student of the Rosicrucian tradition in England, has drawn attention to one lot in the 1694 sale:

> a large Magical Circle, with the divine names of Gods, Angels, Spirits, etc., being 7 foot square, and fairly drawn on Vellum pasted to Cloth and rolled up, together with two Magical Tables or Leaves about a yard square each, the one containing abundance of Chaldy and Magical Characters or Letters with the several Names of God about Triangles [. . .] the other Table contains the Spirit Pamerfiels [. . .] hansomely stained into Cedar Wood. Also two Cherubims Heads on Pedestals. There belongs also to this famous magical collection, a round solid Christal Glass, 3 inches and more diameter, and fixed on

> a solid Brass Stand. Four more globular and solid green Glasses with holes at the top, all fixed in Tin Candlesticks. A very strange Lamp in Tin in several divisions, and with 7 lights above 2 foot in length. Another Lamp in Tin with 3 lights, in the fashion of a Semicircle. A magical Staff about 7 foot wreathed about with white and black. Five pair of holy Slippers, all stained with several Red Crosses. A magical Table with a Pyramidical Triangle, drawn on a Sheet of Parchment. The form of an Instrument to command by magical Invocations, Constringations, etc., any Spirit [. . .] and to bring in an instant of time, any hidden Treasures of what kind soever [. . .] A brief Introduction explaining the Uses of the magical tables. The practice of the East Table. The regal invocation, together with the practice of the West, North, and South Tables . . .[1]

This was not a casual assemblage, but a fully equipped cabinet for working angelic magic in the Dee-Kelly tradition, including a portable magic circle, tables of the four directions suitably inscribed, and crystals in which the spirits would appear. In Thomas Britton's collection we have a passing glimpse of people who still took the tradition very seriously, although Ashmole and the Vaughans were dead, and the Royal Society no longer a front for an "Invisible College" of Hermeticists and alchemists. There is no doubt that individuals and tiny groups have been working in this way without interruption from Britton's period to the present, and that those who announce, or even leak, the fact to the public are the exception rather than the rule.

The indigenous stream of British magic, with its Christian Kabbalistic principles, received a strong infusion in the 1740s in the person of Samuel Jacob Chayyim Falk (c. 1710–1782).[2] Falk was born in Galicia (Poland) into a messianic community inspired by Sabbatai Zevi. He became a noted *Ba'al Shem* ("Master of the Divine Name," a term for a practical Kabbalistic magician[3]) and narrowly escaped being burnt for heresy in Westphalia. Escaping from Germany, he came first to Holland in the 1730s, then in 1742 arrived in London where he stayed until his death. Falk ran a secret school in his own house in the East End, maintaining an alchemical laboratory on old London Bridge (which was then lined with houses), and traveling sometimes to France. A diary of one his servants survives for the period up to 1750, which shows that he was involved with Theodore, pretender to the throne of Corsica, in the attempt to restore the latter's fortunes through magical and alchemical means. Falk is described as drawing magic circles, lighting candles by sevens, drawing Kabbalistic diagrams, wielding a sword, and sounding the shofar (the ram's horn trumpet of Jewish ritual). He seems to have vacillated between poverty and riches, at times literally pawning his shirt, yet ending his life in a fine house on Wellclose Square, furnished with a private synagogue and bequeathing a beautiful silver Torah case to the Great Synagogue of London.

It is not certain how far Falk was of the Sabbatian persuasion. The Sabbatians had their own rules, which allowed them to transgress those of orthodox Judaism, and in general to appear other than they were.[4] Falk's way of life was certainly unorthodox. He mixed freely with Christians, to the extent of seeming to have some agenda of his own, probably within Freemasonry. The upright Jewish community of London looked askance at this mysterious immigrant until he was taken up by Aaron Goldsmid, founder of a distinguished family of financiers and philanthropists.[5] It is no coincidence that two of Goldsmid's sons became intimates of the Duke of Sussex, whose attempts to dechristianize English Freemasonry and whose friendship to the Jews were mentioned in the last chapter.

Very suggestive circumstances have led Marsha Keith Schuchard, in her peerless study of occultism and literature,[6] to conclude that Samuel Falk was probably the master in Kabbalism to two far better-known figures: none less than Swedenborg and Cagliostro. After he became known as a seer, Swedenborg (1688–1772) took pains to present all his doctrines as having come to him directly from the spirit worlds. But Prof. Schuchard's research has uncovered a very different Swedenborg from this idealized self-image. Already as a child, he discovered a technique of breathing that he combined with prayer. Possibly it was this that led to an early meeting with unnamed "other minds" who opened his inner vision. His short book *Of the Infinite* (1734) tells of his collaboration with these minds, and hints at some religiosexual experience akin to those described by Boehme and in the Kabbalah (which he later denied having read).[7] In 1736, when he was living in Amsterdam in close relations with the Jewish community, this technique led to powerful visions of light, which he called "the Sign."

In Amsterdam, Swedenborg also took up automatic writing, and became increasingly preoccupied with the metaphysics of sex: something more freely discussed by Kabbalists than by Swedish Protestants. Loving intercourse between man and wife was, for these Jews, an essential part of the Friday night ritual, seen as reflecting the ecstatic creative act of God through his Shekinah and as hastening the reunion of the male and female principles. Prof. Schuchard suggests that the combination of breath control, Hebrew studies, the Kabbalistic exegesis of the Bible, and a preoccupation with sex all point to an involvement of Swedenborg in Kabbalistic visionary methods, specifically those of Abulafia.[8]

The Magus of Stockholm had a long connection with England. When he left Sweden after his graduation, in 1710, he had spent two years

Figure 5.1. *Emanuel Swedenborg (1688–1772), by Edwin Roffe, from* Compendium of Swedenborg's Theological Writings, *1896.*

in London and Oxford, probably joining a Jacobite masonic lodge. After travels that took him to the Jewish communities of Hamburg, Prague, and Rome, he came to London again in 1744, entering the semi-secret society of the Moravians. This movement was led by Count Zinzendorf, who pursued a mysticopolitical ideal of hastening the millenium by uniting Christians and Jews via Kabbalism.[9] Here Swedenborg pursued further his automatic writing, breath control, and ecstatic trance, taking part also in the sexual activities that were borrowed from the Sabbatians.

During Swedenborg's London visit, he stayed for ten weeks in a tavern on Wellclose Square, going out every morning on some unspecified business. It was there, in April 1745, that his better publicized mission began, with the angelic order to "Eat less food!" Thereafter his contact with the spirit worlds was direct and quite matter-of-fact. Without any modification of his sober and methodical character, Swedenborg became the taxonomist of other worlds, seeing with the greatest of ease through what to others was an impenetrable veil and writing it down in the eighteen volumes of *Arcana coelestia.* His teachings did away with the literal interpretation of the Bible and the doctrine of the Atonement. He accepted pre-Christian revelations, praised Mohammed, and detested the Catholic Church. Building on the Hermetic world view of a graduated universe, its levels linked by correspondences, and on the Kabbalistic vision of all this as the macrocosmic body of God, Swedenborg asserted the dignity of man and the spiritual destiny of the individual as an adventure that stretches far beyond death.

A significant part of this adventure, as Swedenborg was to teach in *Conjugial Love* (1768), is the persistence of sexual activity. In the Latin version of the work, "he revealed with unusual explicitness the breathing and meditation techniques of Yogic-Cabalism that could produce a prologed erection and state of orgasmic trance."[10] He explains that in the spirit worlds the soul will be able to hallucinate for itself a spiritual body in which to enjoy more exquisite sensations than it ever tasted on earth.

On the one hand, the Swedenborgian revelation does away with many of the things that made Christianity unacceptable to men of the Enlightenment, while on the other, it anticipates the spiritualism of the next century. Swedenborg did not use pentacles, candles, scrying-glasses or talismans, because he did not have to. If two of the primary objects of ceremonial magic are to converse with angels and to know the hidden causes of things, then from 1745 onwards, Swedenborg was every inch a magician.

As for Cagliostro, Prof. Schuchard produces evidence to implicate him also in Samuel Falk's plans, to the extent of suggesting that it was Falk who sent him out on the mission of Egyptian Freemasonry, which

***Figure* 5.2.** *Alessandro Cagliostro (1743–1795), after Francesco Bartholozzi.*

would be both his glory and his downfall.[11] Alessandro Cagliostro (1743–1795), reputedly the last man to have died in the dungeons of the Inquisition, came to London first in 1772 after an adventurous career as a healer and alchemist all around the Mediterranean. He may have met Swedenborg there, who was cogent to the day of his death; he certainly became an admirer of the Swede, and on his next visit to London, in 1776, kept company with the Swedenborgians and with Falk's circle. Cagliostro's next mission, in 1779–1780, was to Germany, the Baltic, Russia, and Poland, where his first Egyptian lodge was founded in Warsaw.[12] Then he propagated the Egyptian Rite of Freemasonry on a grand scale in Strasbourg, Bordeaux, Lyon, and Paris (1785). His enemies, such as Catherine the Great of Russia, made it quite clear that they knew of his connection with Falk.[13]

Throughout his travels under various pseudonyms, Cagliostro made flamboyant claims for himself concerning the Elixir of Life, the Philosopher's Stone, the regeneration of the body, clairvoyance, and healing. A greater contrast to the character of Swedenborg cannot be imagined. But Cagliostro was successful enough as a healer to earn the gratitude of hundreds of poor, and several very rich persons. His motive seems to have been the foundation of a higher Freemasonry above all sects and schisms, which would restore the patriarchal religion under which Adam, Seth, Noah, Abraham, etc., were in direct communion with God, and eventually lead mankind back to the state enjoyed before the Fall. To this end, his Egyptian Rite freely admitted Jews, and, in contravention of all masonic custom, women.

Cagliostro's rite actually was not Egyptian at all, except in its decor: its rituals and lectures were populated not by Isis, Osiris, and Thoth, but by the Jewish Patriarchs, Solomon, the seven archangels of the Apocalypse, and the Greek gods understood alchemically.[14] Its great allure over common Freemasonry was that its initiations were truly magical, in the sense of obtaining communication with angels. Cagliostro himself did not pretend to this art, but required a sensitive subject, usually a young girl or boy. Here is a contemporary account:

> Cagliostro founded an Egyptian Masonic Lodge in the house [in Basel] of Herr Sarasin, whose younger daughter was then a child of nine. Each time she was consecrated for the Work and served as child [*Wayse*, lit. "orphan"] or medium to receive the manifestations. Generally, these manifestations of the Powers would take on a form similar to what a painter can do, in a bright and beautiful style. The Master on the throne or someone else would ask the child questions, which the child would forward, and then receive answers that went far beyond a

> child's horizon. I could see clearly from the surroundings that all this went on without any physical or optical apparatus; there was no mirror, no incense visible.[15]

In the initiation of the Master's grade, the seven archangels were summoned by name, and the child received from them comments about the candidate's suitability. In the established lodges, especially in Paris, the working naturally took on a much grander air, with theatrical costumes and a tabernacle in which the child was enclosed.

In 1786, after having been wrongfully implicated in the Diamond Necklace affair, Cagliostro was jailed for a time in the Bastille. On his release, he came to London and published a *Letter to the French People* in which he prophesied the fall of the Bastille and of the monarchy, and a revolution which would reestablish the ancient patriarchal faith in 1800[16]—the very date of the Neros Cycle that fascinated Godfrey Higgins.

On his arrival in London in November, 1786, Cagliostro was welcomed by the eccentric Jewish convert Lord George Gordon (1751–1793), who lent him his coach and accompanied him everywhere. Famous for his anti-Catholicism which had indirectly sparked off the "Gordon Riots" of 1780, Gordon had been to Paris, perhaps with Cagliostro, in 1782, and felt a deep hatred of Bourbon despotism. He was delighted at the humiliations caused by the Necklace affair.[17] Like Cagliostro, he ended his days with a long prison sentence, in Gordon's case for libelling the British Government and the Queen of France in defense of his friend—not in the dungeon of the Castello San Angelo, however, but in Newgate Prison, where he was brought kosher food and entertained his friends daily. These friends included the Duke of York, whose band came too and played revolutionary songs; the Duke of Clarence (later William IV); the ubiquitous Duke of Sussex, known as the "Philo-Semite"; also political radicals such as Daniel Isaac Eaton, whom we have encountered among the "blasphemers."[18]

Cagliostro's other chief friend in London was the Royal Academician, Philip James de Loutherbourg (1740–1812). The son of a German court painter, de Loutherbourg had been championed by Diderot and elected to the Paris Academy of painting at the age of twenty-two.[19] Coming to England in 1771, he made a great impression with his work for David Garrick's theater in Drury Lane, where his innovations made him the father of modern scene-painting and the inventor of many stock devices for light and sound effects. De Loutherbourg had known Swedenborg personally and painted him, and remained a lifelong Swedenborgian (though we shall see that this was a loose term); he had followed the career of Anton Mesmer from 1778 onwards; he met Cagliostro in 1783 at the Strasbourg lodge of the "Amis Réunis." Back in England, he settled in Hammersmith in 1785 and applied himself to the practice of Mesmerism and the search for the Philosopher's Stone. Cagliostro stayed in his house during his visit to London. The mute witness to de Loutherbourg's quest is the catalogue of his comprehensive occult library, which was especially strong in Renaissance Hermeticism, Behmenist theosophy, and French alchemy.[20]

De Loutherbourg was nothing if not eclectic in his religion. He attended Baptist chapels, revivalist meetings, Swedenborgian services, and joined Cagliostro's Egyptian Rite. He was a founding member of Duché's "Theosophical Society" of 1783 (see below), and a friend of the millenialist healer Richard Brothers. In 1789, persuaded that the divine power could work through him as well as them, de Loutherbourg started giving free magnetic (or mesmeric) healing at his house. Mainly because of the loud publicity given by one of his cured subjects, Mary Pratt, he was besieged by patients, as many as three thousand crowding before his doors. Inevitably, some of his cures failed, and after six months' excitement the crowds became ugly. The de Loutherbourgs prudently left England for a while. They escorted Madame Cagliostro to Switzerland (her husband having left already), then, when the Cagliostros imprudently stepped onto Papal soil, returned to England, where Loutherbourg painted until his death.

After Swedenborg and Cagliostro, the most eminent person named as a pupil of Samuel Falk was the Duke of Orléans, later Philippe Egalité (1747–1793). We have briefly mentioned him in connection with D'Hancarville's erotic publications. He was a frequent visitor to London, and a crony of the Prince of Wales (later George IV). The whole Orléans family, ever since Philippe's great-grandfather the Regent, was notoriously involved in the black arts. Philippe is recorded as having told how, at Raincy, a Jew once led him into a thicket where a phantom appeared to him. "He had a conversation of more than an hour with this real or phantasmic figure, whose hand sealed an iron ring around his neck. He showed us this ring, but did not confide further in us what had been predicted to him, contenting himself by saying: 'The matter is of the highest importance; but it is a mystery.'" Viatte, the historian of French occultism who gives this account, adds that the Jew in question was none other than Falk, and that the talisman was supposed to obtain the crown for its possessor.[21] Another version of the story[22] has Falk give Orléans in London a ring of lapis lazuli for the same purpose. Just before his execution, Philippe sent the ring via a Jewish friend to his son, who duly became King Louis-Philippe in 1830—to the delight, as we have seen, of Godfrey Higgins and of every other liberal in Europe.

Swedenborg had died in London in 1772, and, as always happens in such cases, the disciples made up their own versions of the master's teachings. Two main currents ran through the English Swedenborgian movement. The first was religious, the second occult. On the religious side, it is important to recognize that Swedenborg was first and foremost a Christian, albeit of his own peculiar bent. The general trend of Enlightenment thinkers was towards the humanization of Jesus, respecting him either as a moral exemplar, as most of the deists did, or else as a divinely inspired prophet, as the Unitarians (and Muslims) did. But the Jesus of Swedenborg is not even the Son of God: he *was* the one God, walking in Palestine as he had walked in the Garden of Eden. Swedenborg writes in *Arcana coelestia:* "it pleased Jehovah to present Himself actually as He is, and as He appears in heaven,—namely, as a Divine Man. For every part of heaven conspires to the human form. . . ."[23] It is impossible to exaggerate Swedenborg's anthropomorphism, only to excuse it as having arisen as a result of visions of a Kabbalistic type. The books of the *Zohar* entitled "The Greater Holy Assembly" and "The Lesser Holy Assembly" analyze an anthropomorphic god-figure, Macroprosopus, right down to the hairs of his beard. If one follows diligently a course of Kabbalistic meditation, one might well have visions of the same sort, and draw the inevitable conclusions.

Swedenborg's religious followers, however, did nothing of the sort. Their leader in London was the Rev. Robert Hindmarsh (1759–1835), a Wesleyan by upbringing, who read *Heaven and Hell*, found that it "explained everything," and inserted a newspaper advertisement in December 1783 inviting admirers of Swedenborg to meet in a coffee house. In 1787 they were joined by the energetic Manoah Sibly, and in January 1788 the Swedenborgians opened their own chapel in Eastcheap, where Wesleyans would often come as visiting preachers. Hindmarsh published a journal in 1790–1791, *The New Magazine of Knowledge concerning Heaven and Hell, and the Universal World of Nature.* It included information on "horrid murders," astronomy, science, and monsters, but Hindmarsh cautioned against practice of the occult sciences. For one thing, he said, the divinatory arts are unreliable, otherwise we should find their practitioners becoming very rich! Astrology and magic doubtless have their foundation in truth, but as used today they are perversions of the divine order. There is nothing to be gained in paying attention to whatever influences the stars and planets may have. If we believe that God governs all things, then they are governed by love and wisdom. If we think that Nature governs them, they are governed by the dead material forces of heat and light. But can the dead govern the living? Consulting the planets is therefore taking Nature in place of God.[24]

Hindmarsh also wrote against Jacob Boehme, contesting those who put him on the same level as Swedenborg. He found Boehme uncouth and obscure, whereas Swedenborg was clear and orderly. Admitting that he did not own any of Boehme's works, Hindmarsh surmises that the

German cobbler wrote under the "natural light," rather than under divine inspiration, and was like a moon to Swedenborg's sun.[25] Here again we have a rejection of nature and of what it can teach us, in contrast to the deists for whom it was the only revelation of the divine intelligence. The Rev. Hindmarsh was equally averse to palmistry and to the doctrine of transmigration. He recalls a visit around 1789 by a Scots physician, Dr. Sinclair, who wanted to talk about the New Church. As Hindmarsh mentioned that he doubted astrology and palmistry, the doctor offered to read his palm, and told him that he would drop dead in twelve months. The minister smiled complacently. A year later, Dr. Sinclair dropped dead of apoplexy in a Birmingham bookshop. Thus "When we paint in imagination the fate of another, we may be only contemplating our own."[26]

Hindmarsh understood transmigration to mean the rebirth of humans in animal bodies, and says that, like astrology, it is the perversion of the true doctrine, lost more than a thousand years before Pythagoras taught it. It has to do with the science of correspondences and the general laws of the spiritual world, where Swedenborg had seen depraved souls *appearing* as dogs and other animals.[27]

Hindmarsh was at pains to separate his Swedenborgian church from the occultists, and to make it a dissenting church of an unthreatening type, with prayers, hymns, and a paid hierarchy. He had a vested interest in this, as a professional clergyman who had lost his footing in the Wesleyan ministry.

Very different motives lay behind the Swedenborgian study-group that the Rev. Jacob Duché ran in his Lambeth home from 1778–1792, and whose existence is well-known to Blake scholars. Duché was an American of Huguenot extraction, and had been Chaplain of the Continental Congress of 1774. Already immersed in the writings of Jacob Boehme and William Law, he came to London in 1777 after a quarrel with the Founding Fathers (he did not want the two countries to split apart), and immediately made his way into the Swedenborgian community. By 1783 he was leading a study-group called the "London Theosophical Society," a significant title because "theosophy" at this period meant the doctrine of Jacob Boehme and his followers. The members included de Loutherbourg, the Marquis de Thomé (who propagated the Swedenborgian Rite of Freemasonry), the Swedish alchemist-Freemason Augustus Nordensköld, Swedenborg's French translator Benedict Chastanier, the artists John Flaxman, William Sharp, and very probably William Blake. They were visited in 1787 by Cagliostro and Louis-Claude de Saint-Martin.[28] Prof. Schuchard has drawn out the many threads that associate these people with Thomas Paine and other exporters of American revolutionary ideas to France.

The American and French Revolutions, however differently they turned out, rested on certain common principles of radical philanthropy that found their most congenial home in Freemasonry. Their iconography and mottoes supply undeniable evidence of this, visible to this day on the currency of both countries. After the American success, and before the French fiasco, the *éminence grise* of the movement in England was General Charles R. Rainsford (1728–1809), whom Prof. Schuchard calls "the Ashmole of the eighteenth century."[29] He was a cousin and close friend of Sir Joseph Banks, the President of the Royal Society to whom Sir William Hamilton's letter on the "worship of Priapus" was addressed. As a member of the Royal Society and the Society of Antiquaries, Rainsford was *persona grata* in London's intellectual and cultural circles. His military career often took him abroad, and always seemed to favor his involvement in Freemasonry. As early as 1745, when serving in Flanders, Rainsford became close to the Duke of Cumberland (nephew of George III and Grand Master from 1782 to 1790). From 1745 to 1751 he was with the Coldstream Guards in London and had the leisure to pursue his occult and Freemasonic contacts. In particular, he acquired the reputation of being an authority on the *Ba'al Shem.* In 1758 he was Private Secretary to the Governor of Gibraltar, and in 1761 co-commander in Germany with the Duke of Brunswick. Along with Hesse-Cassel and Hesse-Darmstadt, Brunswick was one of the most strongly masonic of the German ruling houses. In 1762 Rainsford served a year in Portugal, returning in 1763 to become a Member of Parliament under the patronage of the Duke of Northumberland, another Freemason. In 1772 we find him in Rome, receiving alchemical processes from an Italian adept, Gasparo Landi. For years Rainsford collaborated on alchemy with another Fellow of the Royal Society, Peter Woulfe, who became a Swedenborgian, an Illuminé of Pernety's Avignon order, and a follower of the apocalyptic prophet Richard Brothers. Back in uniform, Rainsford was commanding the troops in the Hague as they embarked for the American War in 1777.

Rainsford retired from public life in 1782, but only to pursue with more energy his complicated schemes for world unity and enlightenment. In that year he and Benedict Chastanier published a call to alchemists, Kabbalists, and Freemasons to join a new "Universal Society," intended to "conciliate all Doctrines, and even all interests, making constant use of all its talents and directing all its energies to the general wellbeing of the whole Earth, and the particular advantage of the country in which it is established."[30] Artists were particularly urged to take part in this enterprise; one who responded immediately was Richard Cosway, who will play an important role in Chapter Seven. The Universal Society collaborated closely with foreign illuminates, having close ties in France (through Chastanier) and in Sweden (through Nordensköld), and soliciting for members in the United States. The Theosophical Society of Duché was the exoteric wing, as it were, of this Universal Society,[31] hence the confusion of exactly who belonged to which group.

Rainsford's complicated schemes next took him to Algiers, where he found some curious manuscripts relating to the Society of the Rosy Cross (though it went under a different name there), and was initiated into it. In 1784, the lodge "Les Amis Réunis," otherwise called the Philalethes ("lovers of truth") summoned a general Convent of Freemasons in Paris. Cagliostro was of course invited, but demanded that all the other groups pay obeisance to his Egyptian Rite, and that the Philalethes burn all their records, which they had generously offered to make available during the conference. That was the kind of difficulty Cagliostro made for his would-be friends. The Duke of Brunswick led the German delegation, and General Rainsford the English one, which included several of the London Swedenborgians. For the rest of the 1780s, Rainsford was busy with an elaborate network of correspondence in England, France, and Sweden, in pursuit of his goals.

All of the General's spare time must have been taken up by the study and copying of texts on the occult sciences. At Rainsford's death his copies passed to his friend the Duke of Northumberland, with the result that they remained in Alnwick Castle, safe but unknown for almost two hundred years. Ron Heisler and Adam McLean have begun researching these manuscripts, and have found a collection of hundreds of texts in five languages treating, in order of prevalence, alchemy, Kabbalah, magic, religion (especially the Druses), science, the Tarot, Rosicrucianism medicine, and astrology, taken from manuscripts and rare published works.[32]

Despite his profession—or perhaps because of the issues of life and death with which it faced him—General Rainsford was of a gentle and philanthropic nature, keen only to do his duty to God and his neighbor.[33] His mission had no egotism in it: it was of the essence of Freemasonry, if one allows that essence to include the cooperation of spiritual forces in the human enterprise. His initiation into Algerian "Rosicrucianism" and his involvement with Falk point to the movement for union of the three Abrahamic religions—Judaism, Christianity, and Islam: an ambition shared by many occultist Freemasons on the continent of Europe. Perhaps this was a development of the Renaissance idea of a *prisca theologia* common to all faiths, but without their gloss of Christian supremacy that patronized the pagans and wished for the conversion of Jews and Muslims. Godfrey Higgins, who hoped to visit Syria and Egypt before he died, would later remark that Freemasonry seemed ideally suited to bring about this reconciliation; he made his own contribution to it by defending Mohammed.

The initiatic journey to Islamic soil has been a repeated theme of European esotericism, ever since the Templars settled in Jerusalem and the mythical Christian Rosenkreuz learnt his trade in "Damcar" (Damascus). We find it in the lives of Paracelsus and Cagliostro, then, as travel became easier, in a whole host that includes P. B. Randolph, H. P. Blavatsky, Max Theon, G. I. Gurdjieff, Aleister Crowley, René Guénon, R. A. Schwaller de Lubicz, and Henry Corbin. There was very likely some element of this in Napoleon's Egyptian campaign of 1797, when he announced to an astounded audience that he, too, was a Muslim; then returned to Paris to convene the Jewish Sanhedrin and to reinstate the Christian clergy.

Returning now to the London Swedenborgians, we will look more closely at two brothers who exemplify the alternative paths of religion and occultism, but without the excesses and hostility generated by Hindmarsh. Manoah Sibly (1757–1840) was born of Calvinistic Baptists. His mother died when he was eleven, and his father refused to send him to school or college. Mothered by his elder sisters, he educated himself, and by the time he was nineteen knew Latin, Greek, Hebrew, Syriac, and shorthand, and was writing biblical criticism. He had invented his own system of shorthand, based on his study of Hebrew: like that language, it had no vowels. At first this prodigy of learning worked with his wife as a bookseller, specializing in the occult. They had eleven children, seven of whom died. After also keeping a school for a while, Manoah secured a job as a professional shorthand writer. He took down trials at the Old Bailey, and worked on the law circuit for the City of London. He would transcribe his notes in his bookshop, while conversing with customers who knew that this was the best place to find books on astrology, magic, and alchemy. In 1797, Manoah secured a job with the Bank of England, where he worked as an exemplary employee for forty-three more years, being Principal of the Chancery Office for the last twenty-five.

This much for Manoah Sibly's outward life. His inner life seems to have gone the same way, from restless activity to a long calm. At twenty-three he joined a congregation of Baptists similar to his parents' sect, but he could never accept the doctrine of Atonement. After four or five years, he split off and formed a private group of about fifteen people, who worshiped on their own for nine months. Then, near despair of ever attaining spiritual knowledge, he was introduced by a virtual stranger to Robert Hindmarsh's New Church. This was in 1787. Like a flash of lightning, at the very first meeting Manoah realized that he had found the truth. He preached his own first sermon on Good Friday, 1788, in the newly-acquired chapel. At first reluctant to enter the ministry, his calling was confirmed by a dream and he was ordained in 1790.[34]

Manoah soon found Hindmarsh's church too clerical and restrictive. In about 1793 he seceded, and in 1803 opened a new church near the

Bank, in Ludgate Hill. He preached there twice every Sunday for the rest of his long life.

Ebenezer Sibly, M.D., (1751–1799) is a more shadowy figure than his brother, but left a more lasting memorial in the form of several quarto volumes on astrology, herbalism, medicine, and the occult sciences. His medical degree was from the Aberdeen Medical College; he also belonged to Mesmer's Harmonic Philosophical Society in Paris. Both his large works are dedicated to the Freemasons, whom he joined in 1784. Allen G. Debus, in his important analysis of Ebenezer's work, shows how it tried, not unsuccessfully, to marry traditional Hermeticism with what seemed in the 1780s to be the vanguard of science. In Prof. Debus's words:

> it would be quite incorrect to dismiss Sibly simply as an occultist. It is true that he was deeply convinced of the need to search for truth in the works of older alchemists, natural magicians, and astrologers. He wrote with conviction of the vital spirit and the *anima mundi*—and of sympathetic forces that bound together the great and small worlds. Yet, Sibly also felt comfortable with the most recent scientific journals and he sought to accommodate this research to his own world view. Heberden, Newton, Priestley, and Lavoisier were no less important to him than Aristotle, Hermes Trismegistus, Khunrath, and Paracelsus. Even more important, the recent work of Mesmer seemed to offer the most powerful proof of his own cosmic interpretation of man and nature.[35]

Viewed from the other shore of the occult divide, Sibly's great work, *The Complete Illustration of the Celestial Art of Astrology* (4 vols., 1784–1792) was of dubious value. Ellic Howe writes that "Sibly extensively plagiarised the works of seventeenth-century authors because he had nothing new to say about astrology. Again, if the book sold reasonably well and was reprinted within two decades of his death, it was because it was the only easily available major treatise on the subject."[36] This was also the opinion of the one occult journal of the time, *The Conjurer's Magazine* (later *The Astrologer's Magazine and Philosophical Miscellany*).[37] Like the discovery of Thomas Britton's clandestine activity, this magazine opens up a narrow but surprising vista on a small group of people practicing the occult sciences with great application and seriousness. These experts, identified only by initials and pseudonyms, could tell at a glance that Sibly did not even plagiarize from the best sources and that he pirated from borrowed, unpublished translations.[38]

The fourth part of his magnum opus is titled: "Distinction between astrology and the wicked practice of exorcism. With a general display of

Figure 5.3. *Ebenezer Sibly (1751–1799), from* A New and Complete Illustration to the Celestial Science of Astrology, *1784.*

witchcraft, magic, and divination." It explains Sibly's theory of spirits which, following Swedenborg, he believes to be living in their own world that is neither heaven nor hell, but a prelude to one or the other. His essential point is that it is only the wicked spirits that can be summoned through magic and exorcism and answer questions: no one can compel the blessed spirits to appear. They watch us, but are not subject to spells and conjurations.[39] Sibly gives the names of the seven good angels who watch over human affairs, and of the seven corresponding evil (or infernal) spirits. He explains that the latter have made few appearances on earth since the coming of Christianity. They had more access to mankind when the world was under the wrath and jealousy of the Father. When God's wrath was removed by Christ, Satan's power in the world decayed, so that pacts with the Devil are exceedingly rare today. However, the non-Christian nations of Asia, Africa, and America are still deluded and bewitched by him, and we must hope for the Gospel to be preached there.[40]

It is clear enough from this that Ebenezer Sibly was anything but emancipated in the sense of the deists, pantheists, and orientalists of our first four chapters. He had moved straight from the Calvinism of his youth to Swedenborgian Christianity, and united this with the native traditions of magic and astrology. In the same treatise he gives an outline of evocations and exorcisms, with engravings of magical instruments, but omits the essential details that might allow an "evil-minded" person to try it.[41] He tells the cautionary tale of Thomas Perks, a young man who did so at the end of the seventeenth century and was rewarded by terrible apparitions and lifelong sickness.[42] All of this commerce with spirits is "infernal" magic, whereas for Sibly the only licit type is the "natural" magic that is inherent in the occult properties of Nature.[43] Hence the bulk of his work is devoted to astrology and herbalism.

Sibly's other major work, *A Key to Physic and the Occult Sciences* (1792), is a more systematic attempt to unfurl the Hermetic world view from its first principles in a rational belief in God. Reason and Nature appear to have been sufficient resources for this, though Sibly does not hesitate to quote a scriptural passage if it seems apposite. Swedenborg is nowhere mentioned, but Sibly's dualistic system is evidently derived from his. In the first place beneath God is the all-pervading *Anima Mundi* or "Universal Spirit of Nature," which is the vehicle for influences to travel through the levels of the cosmos.[44] This is the foundation for all action at a distance, ranging from the dispensation of God's own Providence to the influxes of astrology and animal magnetism. It acts on "one catholic or universal matter, called corpuscles or atoms, filling all space, which is an extended, impenetrable, and divisible, substance, common to all bodies, and capable of all forms. . . ."[45] This is the *materia prima* of the alchemists, taking on all forms, including living bodies, and manifesting the sympathies and antipathies infused into them by their corresponding archetypes, including the planets. To illustrate the workings of the system, Sibly proffers a curious mixture of "marvels"—he had seen people vomit up monsters[46]—with contemporary experimental science (accepting Lavoisier's oxygen as the vital air).[47]

In a long section on the animal and vegetable kingdoms, Sibly shows a humanitarian dislike of dissection, even of the humblest creatures, and a respect for the sensitivities of plants. His book includes attractive plates of sea anemones and *animalculae* seen through the microscope. From this he moves up the chain of being to man, dwelling especially on the mysteries of human reproduction. This puzzled Sibly greatly until he concluded that the seminal fluid does not enter the uterus directly during intercourse, but is absorbed through the walls of the vagina. (He evidently equated the sperms seen under the microscope with the tiny creatures found in stagnant water and did not consider them essential to the matter.) Pregnancy comes about when the seminal fluid is carried by the bloodstream to the ovum. As an agreeable side effect, this absorption improves the feminine temperament:

> the sallow and inanimate female, by coition, often becomes plump and robust, and beautiful and active, while the widow, or married worman, deprived of commerce with her husband, gradually returns to the imperfections and peculiarities of single life; and that the ancient virgin, all her life deprived of this animating effluvia, is generally consumed with infirmity, ill-temper, or disease.[48]

Sibly's view of sex is almost as mechanistic as his astrology, but he was a doctor, after all, and most of his *Key* is devoted to diseases and their cures, with a prominent plug for his own Solar and Lunar Tinctures, for men and women respectively. It was all part of his scientific yet Hermetic approach, in which the formative forces of the unseen world permeate the visible one, and in which the skillful practitioner can harness them through the new technique of animal magnetism, or through the venerable craft of the herbalist.

Sibly's *Key* was issued with an *Appendix to Culpeper's British Herbal*, containing descriptions and engravings of exotic plants and a table of instructions for gathering herbs at the appropriate planetary hour. This was one of the most firmly entrenched principles of natural magic, and one of the clearest applications of the doctrine of correspondences. For private use, Sibly made his own table of correspondences, called the "Rotalo" or the "Wheel of Wisdom." An example survives,[49] copied from Sibly's manuscript in 1824 by Frederick Hockley (of whom we will be hearing much more). The wheel consists of concentric circles divided in eight sectors: one for each of the planets and the various things ruled by them, and one containing the names of these categories. It seems doubtful that the gentle Sibly ever put into practice the sympathetic magic described alongside the diagram. For example, the influences of Venus are captured by murdering a pigeon, taking out its heart, and cutting off some of one's own flesh. But the Rotalo and its copyist supply a bridge between the Renaissance diagrams of correspondences, used in conjunction with the Art of Memory, and the fullest development of this principle by members of the Hermetic Order of the Golden Dawn (see Chapter Eleven).

As a pendant to this chapter, I will show how the circles of magicians and revolutionaries in the 1780s impinged on one man of a rather different color: William Beckford (1760–1844), the author of *Vathek* (1786), a solitary masterpiece of picaresque orientalism. Beckford became the richest young man in England when his father died in 1770. His fortune came from slave-worked plantations in the West Indies, which he never visited and which caused him only passing regrets. Educated by tutors, he came under the influence of Alexander Cozens (c. 1717–1786), painter and sometime tutor at Eton, who was born at Saint Petersburg and had trained in Rome. Cozens had opened a fashionable drawing academy at Bath, not far from Beckford's family seat at Fonthill. His characteristic painting technique was to put blots on the paper, then develop these random patterns into landscapes: an artificial stimulus to the imagination known to artists from Leonardo da Vinci to Max Ernst.[50] Cozens taught the teenage Beckford drawing, but more importantly escorted the susceptible youth on a voyage, at once scholarly and thrilling, to the world of the *Arabian Nights* and of Oriental mythology.

In 1777 Beckford made his first European tour, to Switzerland. His enormous wealth assured him of a welcome by important people everywhere, including the aged Voltaire. Back in England with little to do, he fell in love with a boy of ten, William Courtenay (later the Earl of Devon). Then Louisa Beckford, the wife of his fox-hunting cousin Peter, fell desperately in love with him. Both affections were returned to a degree, but neither was easily consummated: William Beckford and Louisa were seldom alone together, while the boy was at school, or else guarded by his parents and no fewer than eleven sisters.

On Beckford's second European tour of 1780–1781, which he chronicled in one of the masterpieces of travel literature (*Italy, with Sketches of Spain and Portugal*), he was the guest of his mother's cousin, Sir William Hamilton. Although Sir William took a fatherly interest in the young man, it was the first Lady Hamilton who gave Beckford her time and her affection. Their relationship had the confidentiality that sometimes occurs between a very young man and a middle-aged woman, who will listen and advise sympathetically while he tells her things his mother must never know: in Beckford's case, a homosexual affair he had had in Venice, and which Lady Hamilton urged him never to repeat, for "eternal infamy [. . .] attends the giving way to the soft alluring of a criminal passion."

What scared Beckford far more was the prospect of his coming-of-age, which should by virtue of his fortune lead to Parliament, public life, and surely a peerage. After the noisy, official birthday celebrations were over and he was left alone at Fonthill, he determined to have his own private celebration and to give the party to end all parties at Christmas, 1781. In daily letters, Beckford and his cousin Louisa flaunted their paganism and their wickedness to one another, using the imagery of human sacrifice and black magic as they planned the event. To secure the presence of William Courtenay, their "little victim," was their joint object, which was achieved with the connivance of the tutor Cozens.

For this Christmas party, Beckford engaged three of the finest singers in Europe, including his favorite, the castrato Pachierotti, with whom he had spent much time in Italy. Their part was to provide unseen music, to waft through the vast rooms of Fonthill (the Palladian mansion, not the Gothick one that Beckford himself built). He also hired de Loutherbourg to supervise the lighting and to turn the whole house into a theatrical setting. De Loutherbourg probably took the opportunity to try out the techniques of his "Eidophysikon," a sound and light display which was shown in London in 1782 and praised by Reynolds and Gainsborough. Beckford, Louisa, Courtenay, and a handful of young companions spent three days and nights immured in this artificial paradise, into which no old, ugly, or servile face was permitted to intrude. The rooms were suffused by incense smoke, the richest foods and wines were provided, and the whole lit by de Loutherbourg's skill with a delicate roseate glow.[51] Fifty years later, Beckford was still dwelling in memory on the scene, which crystallized all the human and aesthetic passions of his youth and which provided the inspiration for his novel of the Caliph Vathek.

Magical dabblings were part and parcel of Beckford's orientalism, which was aesthetic and erotic, rather than spiritual. His contemporaries were aware of them, but more concerned with his sexual misconduct. Beckford's biographer Guy Chapman surmises that after the scandals that exploded around Beckford and Courtenay in late 1784, he "could only rebut the charge of sodomy by an admission of the charge of anti-Christian practices and Oriental magic."[52]

Before those events, which were to drive Beckford out of England for ten years, he was a lion of both the London and the Paris salons. His letters mention the Swedenborgian violinist François-Hippolyte Barthélémon and the painter "Dicky" Cosway. He was in Paris early in 1784 at the crest of the occult wave, before the condemnation of Mesmerism by the Academy, the entanglement of Cagliostro in the Diamond Necklace affair, the failure of the Philalethes' Convention, and the suppression of the Illuminati of Bavaria.

On his previous visit to Paris, in 1781, Beckford had met Charles-Nicholas Ledoux (1736–1806), an architect of the fantastic and utopian school. Now, in 1784, Ledoux offered to show the young man his greatest work:[53] ". . . the most sumptuous apartment I ever erected—it belongs to a revered friend of mine, whose thoughts, words, and actions are not of the common world—his habits, his appearance, his garb are peculiar—very peculiar—so much so indeed, that he never wishes to manifest himself—unless to persons born under peculiar influences." The revered friend having given his approval, one day in late January or February Beckford was taken in a closed carriage to a hidden château about an hour's drive from Paris, whose entrance was concealed amongst immense woodpiles.

Now began "a mysterious occurrence which reduces to insignificance all Loutherbourg's specious wonders . . . something unaccountable, I was going to say superhuman—something that 'froze my young blood' and made me gasp and writhe as if under the actual and immediate pressure of some horrid occult influence." Passing through several chambers, Beckford at last reached the magnificent salon and was introduced by its architect to "a formal looking old man of small stature, but imposing presence," dressed in an antique silken suit, who invited Beckford to study the works of art in the room. The most striking of the many treasures was a colossal bronze cistern standing on a green porphyry base, filled to the brim with clear water. Beckford writes:

> As I stood contemplating the last gleams of a ruddy sunset reflected on its placid surface—the old man, risen at length from his stately chair, approached—and no sooner had he drawn near, than the water becoming agitated rose up in waves. Upon the gleaming surface of the undulating fluid,—flitted by a successsion of ghastly shadows, somewhat resembling, I thought, the human form in the last agonies of dissolution—but as these horrid appearances passed along with inconceivable swiftness, I distinguished little, quite sufficient, however, to impart a thrill of terror to my whole frame it never experienced before.

Beckford's reaction ("This is most frightfully extraordinary," he said) did not commend him to the initiates, and he was dismissed. As Ledoux, stony-faced, was leading him out, he heard an unseen choir chanting and saw a taper-lit chapel. He could distinguish the words of the chant as "a passage of the magnificat which declares the mighty fallen and the meek exalted." Ledoux informed him that "this truly sacred edifice is set apart for a high, tho' not entirely a religious purpose," but refused to answer any more questions: Beckford had failed the neophyte's test.

The surprise that the visions in the pool caused Beckford are proof, I think, that he had not done anything very exciting in the way of crystal gazing or magical evocation at that notorious Christmas party. Nor does he ever appear to have tried such things again. As for the general credibility of the account, it must be added that this letter of 1784 survives only as it was rewritten long afterwards. The elderly Beckford would read his best letters out to particular friends: they had become literature, in which the distinction of truth from artifice was irrevocably lost. He added this note to it:

> I have strong reason to suspect that this austere, grim-visaged old man was the identical personage who, not long before the out-break of the French Revolution conducted the wretched D. of Orleans into the dismal dreary plain of Villeneuve St. Georges—where—at midnight—surrounded by horrible phantoms—a talismanic ring was given him, in which having placed a Macbeth-like confidence, he was led on step by step to the fatal scaffold.[54]

Remembering that Samuel Falk died in 1782, we can instantly dismiss the idea that he was the old man in question. But it is likely that the story has a core of truth, and that the architect and Freemason Ledoux, perhaps alerted by de Loutherbourg, saw Beckford's talents, wealth, and taste for mystery as a fine prize for the movement that involved most of the characters in this chapter. It is not impossible that magical rites were performed in which those sentiments of the Magnificat were proclaimed, with the intention of bringing about the abasement of the mighty and the filling of the hungry. Beckford, however, signally lacked the philanthropic virtues, and probably the "philalethean" ones, too. Neither magician nor revolutionary, he was useless to anyone but himself.

SIX

Neophytes and Initiates

The deceptive dawn of the 1780s, when William Beckford still found it bliss to be alive, and to be young, very heaven,[1] was cruelly cut off by the guillotine. The course taken by French politics in the years following the demolition of the Bastille on 14 July 1789 was not at all what the Freemasons of the Enlightenment had in mind. After the "Terror" and the execution in 1793 of King Louis XVI, Queen Marie-Antoinette, and Philippe Egalité, came the declaration of war on England and the threat of invasion. Pitt's government responded by suspending the Habeas Corpus act, enabling the judiciary to carry out summary arrests of anyone suspected of treachery. In 1794 came the celebrated trials of Horne Tooke and other members of the harmless "London Corresponding Society" on a charge of high treason, and their acquittal. Treason in those years of paranoia could mean the mere advocacy of parliamentary reform or universal suffrage. The situation was not helped by the fact that King George III was insane, and the heir to the throne a scheming womanizer.

Into this atmosphere of suspicion came, in 1797, the publications of the Abbé Barruel (*Mémoires pour servir à l'histoire du Jacobinisme*) and his Scottish counterpart John Robison (*Proofs of a Conspiracy against all the Religions and Governments of Europe, carried on in the secret meetings of Free Masons, Illuminati, and Reading Societies*), proclaiming that the French Revolution had been a masonic plot against Church and State, with the Illuminati of Bavaria as the villains-in-chief. Every secret society came under suspicion, especially those with "illuminated" leanings. It was a time for magicians to keep their heads down. Consequently the later 1790s are a desert, compared with the open activity of the 1780s. While much activity must have gone on unrecorded, we have only a couple of symptoms of the continuing organization of secret schools for the pursuit of occultism.

In the last chapter I mentioned the *Conjurers'* (later the *Astrologers'*) *Magazine*, which began in 1791 as the forum for a small coterie of astrologers and devotees of the occult sciences: *conjurers* of spirits, of course, not *conjurors* or stage magicians. It published stories ("The Necromancer"), readers' letters, conjuring tricks and kitchen-table experiments,[2] elementary instructions in astrology, horoscopes of current disasters (especially events in France), thoughts on witches, rainbows, twins, animal magnetism, lives of ancient philosophers, and political remarks. Its editorial policy was anti-Catholic, anti-Sibly, anti-Swedenborg; its astrology rather mechanistic, as in an article on "First Principles of Occult Philosophy asserted and proved upon Atomical principles." The editors were trying to cleanse the occult sciences of superstition and assimilate them to the vanguard of natural philosophy.

An exception to this reductionist attitude was the contribution of William Gilbert, a Londoner who specialized in the manufacture of talismans.[3] Like Ebenezer Sibly, Gilbert underlined the importance of the correct astrological timing in preparing magical aids. He charged high fees for his services and announced his ambition in May 1792 to start a college at his house. But there was no follow-up to this invitation, and early in 1794 the *Astrologers' Magazine* ceased, its organizers probably scared by the political witch-hunt that was afoot.

The next announcement of this kind came in 1801 from Francis Barrett, as a note in his book *The Magus, or Celestial Intelligencer.*[4] He promises that those who become his students—no more than twelve allowed—"will be initiated into the choicest operations of Natural Philosophy, Natural Magic, the Cabala, Chemistry, the Talismanic Art, Hermetic Philosophy, Astrology, Physiognomy, &c. &c. Likewise they will acquire the knowledge of the *Rites, Mysteries, Ceremonies,* and *Principles* of the ancient Philosophers, Magi, Cabalists, Adepts, &c."[5] He gives his address in Marylebone and his visiting hours, and offers to answer letters on these subjects.

We know of one pupil of Barrett's: a Dr. John Parkins of Grantham, Lincolnshire, who became a teacher in his turn. Barrett prepared a manuscript for Parkins in May 1802: "Directions for the invocation of spirits, and an essay on spiritual vision," which was accompanied by a crystal that Barrett had consecrated.[6] In this manuscript he wrote:

> I have observed your constancy and attention—if you will be my Disciple or Scholar, signify the same by letter & I will try thee whether thou art fit—if so I will initiate thee into the highest Mysteries of the Rosycrucian Discipline—but it will be necessary for thee to come to London where I am to take the *Oath.*[7]

In the essay, Barrett explains that "the Ancient Magi amongst their philosophical researches into Nature & Magic discovered a possibility of

Figure 6.1. *Francis Barrett, from* The Magus, *1801.*

communicating with Celestial, Astral, & inferiour spirits . . ." Thus they got knowledge of future events, of nature and its elemental inhabitants. But in order to attract the spirits into communion, a material medium was necessary. Some magi used thick fumigations to form an artificial or temporary body. The spirit's appearance caused a shock to the system of the beholder, bringing on sickness and trembling like the approach of death; then the magus was "rapt up as it were into a delirious Ecstasy of soul." Barrett says that this mainly applies to the use of the magic circle, but that there is another, less stressful form of invocation, also helped by suffumigations. He advises that all aids are useless unless the magus concentrates and follows the rules of abstinence; and that spirits come more readily to an unfrequented house. He closes with the words: "Wish not for riches but to learn some secret whereby you may assist your fellow Creatures."

This private communication of Barrett's carries an air of authority, as if he has had experience of what he is writing about. So does *The Magus,* at least to the naïve reader. But that book is nothing but a plagiarism in disguise. Three quarters of *The Magus* consists of selected chapters, only, from Henry Cornelius Agrippa's *Three Books on Natural Magic,* taken from the English translation of 1651, and of the spurious *Fourth Book* of Agrippa, published in English in 1655, which included Peter of Abano's *Heptameron* (on the conjuration of spirits). The section on Magnetism comes from the English edition of J. B. van Helmont's works (1662, 1664); that on Natural Magic, from Agrippa and from Giambattista Porta (*Magia naturalis,* English edition, 1658). Barrett names these authors in passing, but deliberately gives the impression that they are the least of his many sources, and that he has translated all this material himself.

The source for the seventeenth-century books used by Barrett to compile *The Magus* was the library of Ebenezer Sibly, which at Sibly's death on 30 October 1799 had passed first to his nephew, then to the bookseller and publisher Lackington, one of the biggest dealers in London. Many of the books were bought by another, smaller bookseller, John Denley (1764–1842), who had a small shop in Covent Garden and specialized in the occult. It is easy to reconstruct what happened. Barrett borrowed the books from Denley, transcribed them, and then offered his version to Lackington for publication. *The Magus* was duly published by Lackington, Allen, & Co., at "The Temple of the Muses," Finsbury Square, while Denley was not even given a complimentary copy.[8]

The holograph manuscript of the greater part of *The Magus* is in the Wellcome Institute Library in London. It carries a note by W. Gorn Old (the astrologer "Sepharial") that should be recorded in Barrett's favor, to the effect that, while *The Magus* as published teems with mistakes in Hebrew, these errors are absent from the manuscript. Another interesting thing about it is that on the title page Barrett has inserted the letters "FRC" after his name, evidently as an afterthought. He may have decided that it would be a good idea to present himself as a "Frater Rosae Crucis," since he called his hotch-potch of occult lore "the highest Mysteries of the Rosycrucian Discipline." However undeservedly, the book was a success, not in bringing Barrett fame and fortune, but in carrying a numinous reputation for a century and more. Unlike Sibly's works, it did not go into several editions, but became a bibliophilic rarity. It was a finely printed quarto, full of diagrams and strange alphabets, and adorned with the one and only original contribution of its compiler: the delicious colored engravings of devils, portraying Apollyon, Belial, Theutus, Asmodeus, the Incubus, Ophis, Antichrist, Astaroth, Abaddon, and Mammon.

There is nothing in Barrett's book to say where these grotesque portraits came from, except that he was their designer and R. Griffith their engraver. But they do have a kind of context. One of the attractions of the *Conjuror's* and *Astrologers' Magazine* was a supplement of engravings from Lavater's *Physiognomy*, the founding document of another occult science which was attracting much attention at the time. Physiognomy is based on the doctrine of correspondences, for it assumes that mental, emotional, and spiritual qualities are reflected in the lineaments and proportions of the head and face. Lavater's specimen heads—several hundred of them—were engraved by Henry Fuseli, assisted by his artist friends William Sharp and William Blake. Prof. Schuchard points out the connections among the heads of various human and semihuman types in Lavater, the diabolic heads in Barrett, the astrological heads in John Varley's *Zodiacal Physiognomy* (see next chapter), and the "visionary heads" drawn by William Blake from his own supernatural vision.[9] Barrett's devils are visionary heads of the same type, their ugliness reflecting their evil nature. Considering the weight given in *The Magus* to the practice of crystal-gazing or scrying, that may have been the source of them.

For all that Barrett misrepresented his material, *The Magus* did offer the public a fairly complete occult manual, which taught the principles of arithmology and correspondences, planetary and Kabbalistic magic, and scrying technique. A series of potted biographies of "great magicians" completed the work. There was stuff aplenty there for aspiring magi, as well as for the gothic novelists who were part of the same reaction against classicism and pure reason.

Barrett's claim to be a Rosicrucian now demands scrutiny, for there was no "Fraternity of the Rosy Cross" as such in the England of 1800. One possibility is that Barrett received the title from Dr. Sigismund Bacstrom, a more serious character altogether. Bacstrom had traveled the world as a ship's surgeon; he, too, was an F.R.C., and had a charter to prove it, dated 12 September 1794 from the island of Mauritius. A. E. Waite has analyzed this charter and the branch of the society it seems to represent. Two notable things about it are: (1) that it it asserts belief in the "Grand Atonement by Jesus Christ on the Rosy Cross stained and marked with his blood for the redemption of Spiritual Nature"; and (2) that the Society admits women. Therefore it can have had nothing to do with the Freemasonic movements treated in the previous chapter, since they welcomed non-Christians while excluding women. Bacstrom (as he was later to relate to Alexander Tilloch) was initiated by Comte Louis de Chazal, a French alchemist and *grand seigneur* resident on Mauritius, then ninety-seven years old. The initiation took place privately, by word of mouth, after a period of study. Three years later we find Bacstrom conferring an identical form of initiation on Tilloch, a Scotsman and editor of the *Philosophical Magazine*.[10] The charters in each case state that the neophyte has been found worthy by just one member, and enjoin him, before his death, to initiate one or at most two successors.

According to Ron. Charles Hogart, who has catalogued the Bacstrom manuscript collection of the late Manly Palmer Hall, Dr. Bacstrom was born in 1740 or before; lived in Amsterdam from 1763–1770; came to London around 1775, then again between 1790 and 1808. In 1798 he was living in Marylebone and doing alchemical work with a considerable circle of adepts and aspirants. The simplest (and kindest) interpretation of Francis Barrett's "F.R.C." is that he was initiated in due form by his Marylebone neighbor. But Barrett's interest in magical evocation was very far removed from the doctor's experiments, which mainly concerned the universal panacea and the elixir of life.[11] No death date is recorded for either man.

We may have, with Barrett and Bacstrom, the anachronistic situation of roaming "Fellows of the Rosy Cross" who have each met only their own initiators and hence cannot be said to belong to a society in any normal sense. Waite concludes that the order in question must go back to before the formalized, ceremonial Rosicrucianism of the later eighteenth century.[12]

The Rosicrucian Order into which Godfrey Higgins refused initiation was something quite different. Waite effectively squashes the idea that there was an independent, formalized Rosicrucian order functioning in England in the 1830s, and suggests that what Higgins was alluding to was simply the "Knights Rose-Croix" degree of high-grade Freemasonry.[13] Higgins's aversion to Christian supremacy would have made the ritual of this Eighteenth Degree of the Ancient and Accepted Rite intolerable to him. But he knew of other contemporary Rosicrucians, about whom he had the following to say:

> The Rosicrucians of Germany are quite ignorant of their origin; but, by tradition, they suppose themselves descendants of the ancient Egyptians, Chaldaeans, Magi, and Gymnosophists; and this is probably true. They had the name of *illuminati*, from

> their claiming to possess certain secret knowledge, and, from their secrecy, they were also called *invisible brothers.* They use as a mark of distinction or monogram the three letters F.R.C., which probably means *Fratres Rosi Crucis.* Luther took for his coat of arms, a cross rising from a rose. They are said to hold that an universal spirit pervades all nature, which they call Argheus [presumably Paracelsus's *archaeus*]. Here is evidently the Indian Argha. Under an old Carthusian convent at Baden, is a very curious series of secret prisons; they are said, in the town, to have belonged to the Inquisition; but I have not been able to discover that it was ever established there. On this account, and for some other reasons, I am induced to suspect that they belonged to these *invisible brethren.*[14]

This passage seems to me deliberately naïve, as if Higgins is hinting at something beyond the words. What are the "other reasons"; and did Higgins go himself to Baden and see these cellars? Possibly his reference is to the brand of Rosicrucianism that had existed on the Continent of Europe not many years before. This was the Golden and Rosy Cross (Gold- und Rosenkreuz), a German order first described by Sigmund Richter in 1710. In the course of the eighteenth century, it developed into an aristocratic fraternity with elaborate rituals and a special interest in practical and spiritual alchemy. As Christopher McIntosh writes in his history of the order, "it upheld faith against scepticism, revelation against reason, Christian doctrine against deism or paganism, monarchy and established hierarchy against democracy, tradition and stability against change and progress."[15] It did not admit Jews. Its ideals, in short, were as different as could be from those of the mythographers of our first four chapters.

The Gold and Rosy Cross appears to have had no English members and was virtually extinct by 1793. But there was an offshoot of it that connects more directly with the movements described in the previous chapter. In 1780 or 1781 an ex-member of the order, Hans Heinrich von Ecker und Eckhoffen (1750–1791), left to found his own order, the "Ritter des Lichts" (Knights of Light) or "Fratres Lucis" (Brothers of Light). The impulse for this splinter-group was Ecker's initiation by a Franciscan monk who had spent many years in Jerusalem and learnt Kabbalistic secrets of alchemy and magic from a Jewish sect there. While the work of the Fratres Lucis was predominantly alchemical, and its rituals still close to those of the Golden and Rosy Cross, its terminology and symbolism were Kabbalistic. Thus it formed another channel for the influence of Jewish esotericism on the occult Freemasonry of Europe.

Although the Fratres Lucis were not allowed to take part in the great Convention of Freemasonry at Wilhelmsbad in 1782, Ecker's order attracted important figures, especially after he reorganized it under the name of the "Asiatic Brethren." This refounding took place in Vienna, with the assistance of a Jewish businessman, Ephraim Joseph Hirschfeld, and a converted Jew, Baron Thomas von Schönfeld. Their contribution was, respectively, to translate the original Hebrew documents on which the order was founded and to give it a strong infusion of Sabbatianism: for Schönfeld had been a follower of Sabbatai Zevi's cult. Other influences were the early works of the Christian theosophist Louis-Claude de Saint-Martin, and the alchemical theosophy of Georg von Welling. All the members, who included personages as important as Prince Carl von Hessen-Cassel, took Jewish names, while the antinomian principles of Sabbatianism appeared in the ritual eating of pork with milk. Jacob Katz, the authority on Hirschfeld, points out that this ecumenism made rather greater demands on the Jewish than on the Christian members.[16] Yet the abandonment of Jewish ritual and Mosaic prescriptions were as much in the spirit of the rational Enlightenment as the demotion of Jesus Christ in Deism. Only by giving up their exclusivities could members of either faith meet as equal human beings, thence to set out together on the esoteric adventure of alchemy and magic.

Ecker died in 1791, leaving the Asiatic Brethren in an uneasy position vis-à-vis official Freemasonry. Schönfeld had gone to France in 1790 and joined the Jacobins. He was guillotined in Paris on 5 April 1794, the same day as Danton.[17] Hirschfeld returned to Germany and settled near Frankfurt, where he was still hoping to reconstruct the order until his death in 1820.[18]

In the Asiatic Brethren we have a Kabbalistic-theosophic order with the intention of Jewish-Christian reconciliation which, though it seems to have had no actual counterpart in England, was fully in the English spirit. In the German-speaking lands it stood firmly on one wing of the debate over whether Jews could be Freemasons, i.e., whether Freemasonry was or was not Christian in its essence. The German mainstream was on the Christian side, refusing to accept as regular any lodges with Jewish members. It required the authority of Napoleon, after his conquest of Germany and Austria, to change the situation.

The Napoleonic invasion forced the Germans to give civil rights to the Jews. One consequence was the founding, in 1807, of a Jewish lodge in Frankfurt am Main under the aegis of the French Grand Orient. The Frankfurt lodge was called "Zur aufgehenden Morgenröthe" ("The Rising Dawn") or simply the *Judenloge* (Jewish lodge), and included Jews and Christians, some of whom had been in the Asiatic Brethren. Its clientele was predominantly young, rich, and politically progressive; its goals social, not spiritual,[19] as far as most of the members were concerned. The pressing need of European Jewry was to be accepted as equals in society; sharing in the three craft degrees of Freemasonry should have been one of the most open roads to such acceptance. A few Jewish members, however, did pursue the higher grades (Rose-Croix, etc.), notwithstanding their Christian language,[20] while Hirschfeld still dreamed of resurrecting the Asiatic Brethren's rites within the newly founded lodge.[21]

After the defeat of Napoleon, every kind of difficulty was put in the Jewish lodge's way by the German authorities: oaths on the Gospel were required, the Christian Scottish Rite was instituted, and eventually Carl von Hessen-Cassel ordered the lodge disbanded. To the chagrin of the local Freemasons, the Jewish lodge appealed to the Duke of Sussex, who gave it a charter in 1817 from the United Grand Lodge of London (as mentioned in Chapter Four). This was satisfactory up to a point, though it left the Aufgehende Morgenröthe isolated and shunned by German Freemasonry, defeating its ecumenical object.

There has been speculation that Edward Bulwer-Lytton was initiated into this Frankfurt Jewish lodge. William Wynn Westcott, cofounder in 1888 of the Hermetic Order of the Golden Dawn, claimed in a lecture on the Rosicrucians that:

> The late Lord Lytton, the author of "Zanoni" and "The [sic] Strange Story," who was in 1871 Grand Patron of our Society, took very great interest in this form of Philosophy, although he never reached the highest degree of knowledge; for public reasons he once made a disavowal of his *membership* of the Rosicrucians, but he had been admitted as a Frater of the German Rosicrucian College at Frankfort on the Main; that College was closed after 1850.[22]

Bulwer-Lytton (1803–1873)[23] will henceforth be a central figure in this study. In Chapter Eleven we will dispose of the rumor of his membership in Westcott's society, the Societas Rosicruciana in Anglia or S.R.I.A. But that is not what is at stake here. Gérard Galtier, the historian of Egyptian Freemasonry, suggests as a hypothesis that Lytton, who was never made a Freemason, was initiated into a branch of the Asiatic Brethren that was still operating in the Frankfurt region, probably during his visits to Germany between 1841 and 1843.[24] Lytton confided in a letter of 1872 to Hargrave Jennings that he himself, unlike current pretenders to Rosicrucianism, possessed the "cipher sign of the 'Initiate,'" and stated that the "Rosicrucian Brotherhood" still existed, only not under any name recognizable by outsiders.[25] This seems to support Mr. Galtier's suggestion that some Asiatic Brethren survived underground after their movement's apparent demise. Just as Ecker's original foundation of 1780 had been intended as an improvement upon the Gold and Rosy Cross, made in the ecumenical spirit of the first Rosicrucians, so its survivors in the 1840s might still have believed themselves to be the true holders of the

Figure 6.2. *Edward Bulwer-Lytton (1803–1873), by Alfred d'Orsay, from* Falkland and Zicci, *1875.*

Rosicrucian lineage: secretive and invisible, as the early seventeenth-century founders had been.

At this point we must learn more about Lytton's attitude to the occult before he went to Germany. Every researcher into Lytton's esotericism has to start with his novel, *Zanoni,* and so shall we.[26] The book was finished in January 1842, but its theme goes back to 1825, when Lytton made the initial sketches for it. Themes from it appeared in a short story, *The Tale of Kosem Kosamim the Magician* (1832), and about half of the text in *The Monthly Chronicle* during 1838, under the title *Zicci.*

The Opening scene of *Zanoni* is set in the occult bookshop of "D——" in Covent Garden (evidently a reference to Denley's shop), and purports to be transcribed from a ciphered manuscript acquired from an old gentleman encountered there. Later we realize that the old gentleman was the young artist Clarence Glyndon, one of the protagonists of the story. How far this fictitious author's opinions are Lytton's own is a moot point; but with that reservation I shall assemble a group of themes and allusions that have a certain integrity about them, and whose exposition Lytton felt had led, in retrospect, to his favorite among his novels.[27]

Readers must look elsewhere to discover the plot of *Zanoni*; I am concerned with the opinions and theories for which the plot is a support. First, the book gives a clear sense of discrimination between good occultism and bad. It rejects Mesmer and Cagliostro as profiteers, associating them (quite unjustly) with the errors of the *philosophes* and deists; it praises Louis-Claude de Saint-Martin alone among the eighteenth-century illuminates. The story is set in the years 1791–93, culminating with the bloody rule of Robespierre and his execution on 10 Thermidor (28 July 1793). The revolutionaries are painted in the worst of colors, their iniquity, true to the doctrines of physiognomy, reflected in their physical ugliness. Lytton's initiates hate their impiety, atheism, and dogma of *égalité.* Why is the latter so abhorred? Because the whole of the universe is a hierarchy, from the archangel to the worm; and because it is human inequality alone that holds out the hope of progress. "The wiser the few in one generation," says Zanoni, "the wiser will be the multitude in the next!"[28]

Besides Glyndon, the narrator, artist, and neophyte, the characters of *Zanoni* include two Chaldean initiates, apparently the only two left on earth of a high and ancient order. This is not the Rosicrucians, but an older and more illustrious order of which the Rosicrucians are a branch. It pays especial respect to the teachings of the Platonists, the Pythagoreans, and Apollonius of Tyana. Evidently it is not Christian, as the Rosicrucians are. The two initiates are Mejnour, the senior one, and Zanoni, who has been on earth only five thousand years. While sharing in the same occult knowledge and possessing the secret of indefinite life, these two differ markedly in character. Mejnour inhabits the body of an old man, with every earthly passion extinguished, in order to accomplish the transmutation of man into superman. His ambition is:

> to form a mighty and numerous race with a force and power sufficient to permit them to acknowledge to mankind their majestic conquests and dominion; to become the true lords of this planet, invaders perchance of others,—masters of the inimical and malignant tribes by which at this moment we are surrounded; a race that may proceed, in their deathless destinies, from stage to stage of celestial glory, and rank at last among the nearest ministrants and agents gathered round the Throne of Thrones. What matter a thousand victims for one convert to our band?[29]

Mejnour works at his plans with "cabala and numbers," sitting in Olympian calm behind the scenes and cycles of human history, indifferent to others' weal or woe as he is indifferent to his own. Lytton would caricature the results of such an enterprise in his late novel, *The Coming Race.*

Zanoni is an equally mysterious character, but one who becomes less superhuman as the plot unfolds. There is much of the Comte de Saint-Germain about him: Zanoni is also a cosmopolite, a "noble traveler" who has seen the world (his servants come from India) and its history; a man who has achieved the elixir of life, who gives away priceless gems and stuns the public with his mystery and his wealth, coming and going as he pleases. In a humorous parody of Godfrey Higgins's methods, Lytton explains the etymology of Zanoni's name as referring to the sun-god.[30] Zanoni's choice is to enter the maelstrom of human passion, losing his occult powers in the process but gaining what his master Mejnour has rejected: love and death. The message of the work is that the love of human beings for each other, and their acceptance of death, are things of incalculable value, not to be surpassed even by the highest initiate. It is left for the reader to notice that this message is also that of Christianity.

The novel is an encyclopedia of ideas about the occult sciences. In pointing out the extreme ugliness of the French Revolutionary leaders, Lytton supports the thesis of physiognomy. Herbalism is mentioned reverently, along with the general value of research into the mysteries of nature. The doctrines of universal sympathy, of secret affinities in nature, and of hierarchical planes of being permeated by an omnipresent Mind are essential to *Zanoni,* as to any Hermetically influenced work. The multiple planes include those that can only be explored out of the physical body. Therefore ascesis is necessary to the aspirant, refusing the demands of the flesh in order to live in the soul and work with the imagination. The artist can do this as well as the mystic; a Platonic subtheme of *Zanoni* is the sacred nature of art, if only inspired by the "Ideal."

At one point the narrative is interrupted by an "erasure in the manuscript" which immediately puts one on the alert. What is Lytton pointing our attention to with this transparent device? The words surrounding the gap are:

> Glyndon was surprised to find Mejnour attached to the abstruse mysteries which the Pythagoreans ascribed to the occult science of NUMBERS. In this last new lights glimmered dimly on his eyes; and he began to perceive that even the power to predict, or rather to calculate, results, might by—
>
> * * *
>
> But he observed that the last brief process by which, in each of these experiments, the wonder was achieved, Mejnour reserved for himself, and refused to communicate the secret.[31]

Lytton's biographers record one and only one instance in which he practiced one of the occult sciences himself: it was geomancy,[32] a form of divination by throwing pebbles (or making random marks on paper) and making deductions from the pattern they make. The subject of the consultation was Lytton's friend Benjamin Disraeli, for whom he predicted a career of public and political success that was unimaginable at the time (1860). Possibly this is what Mejnour was doing.

The world view of *Zanoni* is of a universe populated by beings at every level: not just the physical series from galaxy to microbe that was currently exciting Victorian scientists, but an unseen hierarchy which could, by the proper means, be rendered perceptible. The lowest of them are the spirits of the four elements: the Gnomes, Undines, Sylphs, and Salamanders of Paracelsus and of the *Comte de Gabalis.* No friends to humankind, these were believed by earlier magicians to be fiends, and their pacts with them to be drawn with the Devil. But no man can sell his soul, says Zanoni, for "in every human creature the Divine One breathes; and He alone can judge His own hereafter, and allot its new career and home."[33]

This immortal part of man is called by the Neoplatonic term *augoeides,* which manifests when "the sphere of the soul is luminous, when nothing external has contact with the soul itself; but when lit by its own light, it sees the truth of all things and the truth centred in itself."[34] Thus man is tripartite, consisting of body, soul, and the *augoeides* or indwelling Divine Spirit.

The magus can command the elemental spirits, but more importantly he can establish contact with higher beings. Zanoni twice summons a celestial apparition called "Adon-Ai," from whom he has learned all his wisdom. In Cornelius Agrippa's *Natural Magic,* Book II, Chapter x, we read (as surely Lytton did) that the lowest of the ten divine emanations is called *Adonai Melech*; that it works through the blessed souls immediately below the ninefold angelic hierarchy to give knowledge, understanding, wisdom, and prophecy. Adon-Ai disputes with Zanoni at the point at which the initiate has decided to renounce his ascesis and embrace human love; when Zanoni is obdurate, the Son of Light smiles. On the second apparition of Adon-Ai, the spirit gives his blessing to Zanoni's decision, for by now he has also embraced human death, which Adon-Ai calls "the sublimest heritage of thy race,—the eternity that commences from the grave."[35] It would presumably be in this eternity that Adon-Ai himself lived, so that by dying, Zanoni was entering the state of his spiritual master and becoming a "blessed spirit" in his turn.

The philosophy of *Zanoni* includes no idea of reincarnation. In their first interview, Adon-Ai points out to Zanoni the disadvantage of falling in love with a woman who will soon die, leaving him, the proud possessor of the elixir of life, to live for ages after her: "Through what grades and heavens of spiritualized being will her soul have passed when thou, the solitary loiterer, comest from the vapours of the earth to the gates of light?"[36] Ironically enough, the butcherers of the Revolution are quite correct when they say *"Il n'y a que les morts qui ne reviennent pas!"*[37]

Finally there is the famous "Dweller of the Threshold," whom both Glyndon the neophyte and Zanoni the adept have to face and overcome. This is a hideous personification of one's past thoughts and evil tendencies, which even if not perceived lures the aspirant towards disaster. In modern parlance, it is the subconscious. The only way to conquer it, as Zanoni teaches to Glyndon and demonstrates himself, is by overcoming one's fear and persisting in one's resolve to cling to virtue, come what may. Then two paths are open: one, the path to seraphic detachment such as Mejnour has achieved; the other, the path by which one becomes as a little child again, which is Zanoni's choice.

Zanoni was much read and discussed, especially in France and Germany (where many of Lytton's works were translated). Lytton's friend Dickens, in *A Tale of Two Cities* (1859), borrowed *Zanoni*'s climactic theme of a man who gives his life at the guillotine to save his friends. In French literature, the hero of the *Comte de Monte Cristo* of Alexandre Dumas *père* (1844) has suspiciously Zanonian characteristics. But perhaps the theme of the noble traveler was simply in the air. George Sand, more esoteric than Dumas, made use of it in *Consuelo* (1842–44) and its sequel *La comtesse de Rudolstadt* (1843–45). The game of tracing influences I leave to the literary critics. But as far as esotericism in Victorian Britain is concerned, there is no more important literary work than *Zanoni*, and, as the following chapters will show, no more important figure than Bulwer-Lytton.

Does *Zanoni* show any evidence to support the theory of Lytton's initiation into an occult lodge? None, to my mind—though this does not eliminate the possibility that he was initiated in Germany after the book was published. There is nothing in *Zanoni* that a voracious reader of occult literature could not have learned at second hand. The concept of the Dweller of the Threshold is the only one that is entirely original, and even that could have been invented by the novelist's fertile imagination, or else—as I think more probable—discovered through personal experience.

Lytton's philosophic initiation began when the library of his scholarly grandfather, Warburton Lytton, passed through his house in 1811 and the precocious eight-year-old got "ankle-deep in the great slough of Metaphysics."[38] While at preparatory school, he was befriended by the Rev. Chauncey Hare Townshend, a wealthy cleric occupied with mesmerism and magnetic experiments;[39] they would meet again at Trinity Hall, Cambridge. At fifteen, Lytton could write such lines as:

> What! is it solitude to hold
> Rich commune with the soul's high po'wr?[40]

In 1825–26, visiting Paris for the first time, Lytton found himself on the brink of a nervous breakdown. He abandoned the social whirl of the Faubourg Saint-Germain and retreated for some months to Versailles, where he saw nobody and spent ten hours a day riding in the country. It was probably during this period that the event took place which he later described to his friend Forster:[41]

> I know by experience that those wizard old books are full of holes and pitfalls. I myself once fell into one and remained there forty-five days and three hours without food, crying for help as loud as I could, but nobody came. You may believe that or not, just as you please, but it's true!

Can one doubt that he knew the Dweller of the Threshold all too well? But this does not make Lytton a Rosicrucian. If there is any truth at all in the early seventeenth-century publications that started the whole business, it is that Rosicrucians are (1) Christian, and (2) invisible. Lytton certainly espoused the Christian virtues—that is one of the themes of *Zanoni*—but he expressed the wish to be buried in unconsecrated ground: an extremely unconventional desire for a member of the British establishment.[42] He was only made a Christian after his death, when his son Robert was unable to resist the glamor of interring his father in Westminster Abbey. Also, he was anything but anonymous and quite willing to talk (to the right sort of person) about his attitude to the occult sciences. He was open-minded in comparison to the average skeptic, but detached and wary in comparison to the enthusiasts. We will see illustrations of this in later chapters. At this point it is sufficient to say that Lytton was a highly self-aware and intelligent man, whose world view refused to be constrained by "beliefs" of any kind.

This chapter began with the question of why Francis Barrett put the letters "F.R.C." on the title page of his *Magus.* I will end it with another question, so as not to give the impression that the Rosicrucians are easily to be disposed of. What can one say, for example, when one comes across a manuscript concerning crystal-gazing bearing the ownership signature "Randolph Oxley, G. M. of the Rosy Cross 1841"?[43] This manuscript is the work of Frederick Hockley, apparently made for a man who was not just F.R.C. but a self-styled "Grand Master" of the order. Perhaps a better informed or more ingenious scholar than I will solve this one, keeping in mind that the Fraternity of the Rosy Cross appears to have had at least as many "Grand Masters" as rank-and-file members!

SEVEN

Artists and Astrologers

We heard in Chapter Five that General Rainsford's Universal Society addressed a special call to artists to join in his enterprise of occult ecumenism. An extraordinary number of English artists, if they did not answer that precise call, were involved in occult matters during the fifty years around 1800.[1]

Everyone knows about William Blake, and if little place is given him here it is solely because his esotericism has been so exhaustively studied by Kathleen Raine and Marsha Keith Schuchard. Students of art history will also know of Fuseli, Flaxman, and Samuel Palmer. This chapter shows the relation of these and other artists to the world of the previous chapters, and moves forward to the occult revival of the 1820s.

The Swiss-born Henry Fuseli (1741–1825) was friends with Lavater in Zurich before he came to England in 1763. We have noted that Fuseli was the principal illustrator of Lavater's physiognomy and a contributor to the early *Conjurer's Magazine*. His success in England, where he stayed on, encouraged by Sir Joshua Reynolds, to become a Royal Academician, was built on his illustrations to Shakespeare and Milton, though his reputation nowadays is mainly as a protosurrealist, a painter of erotic fantasy and dreamland. Large-scale paintings such as the different versions of "The Nightmare" portray not just the creatures of dream and the unconscious, but the waking evocations of the magician—like Barrett's diabolical heads. Prof. Schuchard says that Fuseli's paintings are the clearest pictures of "magnetic ecstasy" as it was achieved by the somnabulists of Mesmer and Puységur (see next chapter); other commentators have seen in them an anticipation of Freud's theory of dream and the subconscious mind.

When we read Blake's epigram to Fuseli:

> The only Man that e'er I knew
> Who did not make me almost spew
> Was Fuseli: he was both Turk & Jew—
> And so, dear Christian Friends, how do you do?[2]

we can detect a link on the part of both artists to the philosemitic movement within and without Freemasonry, and a companion in Blake's Christianity of the Imagination that was mystical, sexual, and ecumenical.

John Flaxman (1755–1826), another Royal Academician, was the classicist to Fuseli's romanticist. His best-loved work must be his decorations to the jasper and basalt ware of the Wedgwood Pottery, which are still sold today. Some of their Grecian themes were copied from d'Hancarville's catalogue of Sir William Hamilton's collection (see Chapter One); Flaxman knew both men.[3] His numerous tomb sculptures and book illustrations (of Homer, Dante, etc.) show him to be another careful student of the physiognomic science. But if his work seems nowadays to breathe a rather cold neoclassicism, Flaxman's private life involved him with mysteries. For example, he belonged to the Rev. Duché's study-group of the 1780s. He invited Thomas Taylor to give twelve lectures on Platonic philosophy in his house, probably around 1788. In 1796 he created an illustrated poem, *The Knight of the Blazing Cross,* as a gift for his wife; inspired by fantasies of medieval chivalric orders, it tells of a knight who attains the spiritual realm, then returns to earth for the good of mankind. He made a personal examination of Swedenborg's exhumed skull in 1817. Near the end of his life, in 1822, he collaborated with Blake on illustrating the *Book of Enoch*: a work known in occult circles ever since James Bruce had brought it from Ethiopia in 1773.

We have already encountered Philip James de Loutherbourg, the magnetic healer and friend of Cagliostro, the creator of special effects for Garrick's theater and of supernatural atmospherics for William Beckford. De Loutherbourg seldom had the opportunity to bring his occult interests out in his art: he was too busy producing battle scenes and "sublime" landscapes. However, his many contributions to Macklin's great illustrated Bible (published in seven volumes from 1800 to 1816) included some Kabbalistic emblems, with Hebrew letters, so arcane that the editor included an eight-page explanation of them.[4]

De Loutherbourg's involvement with the theater is more relevant to these themes than might at first appear, since it was in the theater that alternative realities could become most palpable to the ordinary person. This was a great Shakespearean epoch, when the supernatural, the grotesque, and the Hermetic qualities of the Bard were no longer bowdlerized to suit Augustan taste. Fuseli's illustrations are sufficient evidence of that. There was a thirst for the beyond, for the absolutely other, which drew the Romantics to Shakespeare as it drew them to Gothic architecture, to Ossian, to India and Egypt. Where could those honest folk who knew nothing of drugs, somnambulism, or magic satisfy that thirst? In the theater, just as they do today in the cinema. And the more realistic—or surrealistic—it could be, the better. De Loutherbourg's "Eidophysikon" was designed to give everyone a taste, at a shilling a time, of the alternative reality that Beckford's friends had enjoyed. A contemporary painting of it shows a setup resembling a puppet theater, with benches for the audience and a harpsichord for incidental music. The image is evidently that of "Satan arraying his Troops on the Banks of the Fiery Lake, with the raising of the Place of Pandemonium; from Milton," which was accompanied with terrifying effects of thunder and lightning.[5]

A fourth artist, ignored by the history books today, is the portrait-painter and miniaturist Richard Cosway (c. 1740–1821). Coming from obscure origins, he won prizes at the Society of Arts from 1755–1760 and contributed regularly to the Royal Academy from 1770–1787.[6] His wealth came from his fashionable portrait business, and from dealing in pictures and antiques. A short man, excessively vain and given to extravagant dress, Cosway's greatest attraction was his wife, the former Maria Hadfield. Her parents kept a hotel in Florence that was a favorite resort of the English on the Grand Tour; she also exhibited paintings at the Royal Academy, spoke five or six languages, and played the keyboard to perfection. When she married Cosway, she was given away by his friend Charles Townley, the collector and employer of d'Hancarville (see Chapter One). Entirely chaste, Maria's admirers included Thomas Jefferson, who spent idyllic days with her in and around Paris in 1789, and the Prince of Wales, who attended the Cosways' smart parties in Pall Mall during the later 1780s. There he might have encountered his friend Philippe Egalité, who stayed at the Cosways during his visits to London. Richard Cosway was a strong supporter of the French Revolution and, as we have seen, an early adherent of General Rainsford's Universal Society.[7] He is named as one of those who attended Thomas Taylor's lectures at Flaxman's.

The Cosways' house had a noteworthy past as the "Temple of Health" of Dr. James Graham (1745–1794),[8] a successful magnetic healer who had employed Emma Lyon (later to become the second Lady Hamilton) to pose in mud-baths and to impersonate the goddess Hygeia; he also offered the services of a "celestial bed" to stimulate potency and fertility. Cosway fell happily in with the Graham style, entertaining on a grand scale and regaling his guests with lectures on occult subjects. He practised magnetic clairvoyance, diagnosing his friends' ailments; he communicated telepathically with his wife while she was traveling in Europe

Figure 7.1. *Richard Cosway (c. 1740–1821), self-portrait.*

with Flaxman and Bartolozzi. At a Royal Academicians' dinner, he announced that he had had a visit from William Pitt, who had died four years previously. The late Prime Minister, Cosway said, was "prodigiously hurt that during his residence on earth he had not encouraged my talents."[9] If all this shows a man self-obsessed, it is only fair to add that

Cosway was one of the first and firmest supporters of a poorer but far greater artist, William Blake.

Like de Loutherbourg, Cosway was a keen collector of books and manuscripts on the occult sciences, of which the sale catalogue has been preserved. They included the rare *Theosophical Transactions* (1697) of the Philadelphian Society, a group of Behmenists; manuscripts of Dr. John Pordage, one of that group; Kabbalistic drawings of Dionysius Andreas Freher; a manuscript on angel magic attributed to Peter Paul Rubens, and other magical texts. Cosway himself reputedly kept a hired room for his own raising of spirits, with a magic circle inscribed on the floor, but he never showed it to the idle or the curious.[10] The Fourth Earl Stanhope, who knew Cosway in his youth, told an anecdote of how Lord Lyttleton had once sent for the artist to draw, from his description, an apparition that he had seen.[11]

One of Cosway's engraved self-portraits shows him robed, in dramatic stance, with a Kabbalistic book in his hand bearing a Hebrew inscription meaning "His name is Esau."[12] Far from obvious in its meaning, this may refer to "the Way to Esau," the spiritual path taught by Jacob Frank (1726–1791), the last leader in the Sabbatean movement.[13] Frank was another proponent of the union of Jews, Christians, and Muslims and perhaps the most notorious teacher of a secret, licentious path. After accepting baptism in the interests of his program, Frank ended his days (from 1786 or 1787 onwards) holding court in Offenbach, near Frankfurt: home of the Asiatic Brethren, whose founding member, Schönfeld, was one of Frank's disciples. Gershom Scholem writes that in Frank's usage, "Esau or Edom symbolizes the unbridled flow of life which liberates man because its force and power are not subject to any law."[14] Moreover, in Kabbalah Esau and his land of Edom are symbolic of the Gentile world, as opposed to the land of his twin brother Jacob, father of the Twelve Tribes of Israel. For Cosway to identify himself, in Hebrew, as Esau might be a statement of solidarity and brotherhood with the Jews whose secrets he was making his own.

In 1824, the elderly William Blake became the center of attention and affection of a group of young artists nearly as eccentric as himself, calling themselves the "Ancients" on account of their idolization of the past. The most distinguished members of the group were Samuel Palmer, Edward Calvert, and George Richmond, whose exquisite images of an idealized countryside mark a precious moment in the history of English art; others included Francis Oliver Finch, a Swedenborgian, and Frederick Tatham, an Irvingite who took Blake's widow in.[15] On their visits to Palmer's house at Shoreham, Kent, the group were known by the locals as the "Extollagers," because it had got around that they were doing astrology. Under Blake's spell they talked of animal magnetism, ghosts, and clairvoyance,[16] and doubtless much else.

Samuel Palmer, whose artistic reputation stands the highest of the group, met Blake in 1824 through his future father-in-law, the painter John Linnell. From that year dates his remarkable sketchbook, now in the British Museum, which contains scenes of a hallucinatory quality that he was never to recapture. I suspect that the unprecedented style of these sketches came from Palmer's discovery of a new technique for stimulating the imagination: scrying or gazing into a glass ball or crystal. The evidence lies in the annotation of a small but finely executed pen sketch:

> I saw in my spec. glass the most wonderful miniature which note I well nor heedless let it slip. In it these 3 textures struck upon the eye instantly. 1st the firm enamel of a beautiful young face, with 2nd going down from the forehead smooth & unbroken over the shoulders, Hair, wondrous sleek, and silkily melting (in long hairs more thin than man can do) into 3rd, a background of the crisp mosaic of various leaved young trees thinnishly inlaid on the smooth sky—so that there was an extreme soft between two kinds of hards. . . .[17]

The resulting sketch has the intense and minute detail characteristic of some scryers' perceptions. This raises the interesting possibility that some of Palmer's finished works, especially the six incomparable sepia drawings of 1825 in the Ashmolean Museum, may have had a similar origin in artificially conjured visions; and that his abandonment of the process accounts for the change of style on which art historians have always commented. In Palmer we may have the rare case of an artist who crossed the boundary between the self-contained use of the imaginative faculty—which, heaven knows, is sufficiently fertile of wonders—and its projection onto an external object, here a glass or crystal.

The last artist to be considered in this chapter is John Varley (1778–1842), a great ox of a man whose energy and eternal optimism charmed Blake and excited the social butterflies. Varley was a watercolorist whose landscapes are some of the finest in the genre. His living came mainly from being London's most fashionable teacher of painting. Sometimes he made 3,000 pounds a year; at other times he was arrested for debt. He lost a fortune on a failed invention to do with carriage wheels. Obsessed with astrology, he would start every morning by calculating his transits, and always did his friends' horoscopes. Quite a number of his predictions came true. His biographer, Adrian Bury, says that "He knew no definite God or creed. He bowed to no sect, he took no private road, but looked up through Nature to Nature's God."[18]

Varley connects with our story at three distinct points. First, he was brought up in the shadow of the Third Earl of Stanhope (1753–1816). John's father Richard Varley (died 1791) was tutor to the Earl's young

Figure 7.2. *John Varley (1788–1842), by William Blake.*

son. His uncle Samuel Varley, a watchmaker and jeweller, was a collaborator with the Earl in experimental science, and received a handsome legacy on the Earl's death, including his mechanical equipment. Stanhope became a Fellow of the Royal Society in 1772, and was an inventor of genuine talent. In collaboration with Samuel Varley, he formed a "Chemical and Philosophical Society" that met at Hatton House, to which Josiah Wedgwood and other famous men belonged. It was the forerunner of the Royal Institution of Great Britain, founded in 1800 as "a Public Institution for diffusing the knowledge and facilitating the general introduction of useful mechanical inventions and improvements; and for teaching, by courses of philosophical lectures and experiments, the application of science to the common purposes of life."[19] When one notices that Sir Joseph Banks was very active in founding this body, that Richard Payne Knight was a life subscriber, and that the annual subscriptions were collected by William Drummond, the world which we are exploring in this book begins to seem a rather small place. The freethinking mythographers were also involved in the intellectual powerhouse of the Industrial Revolution.

The Third Earl of Stanhope was a revolutionary in another sense. He was chairman of the "Revolution Society," formed in 1790 out of sympathy with the French. A Freemason, he was friendly with Philippe Egalité on the latter's visits to London, and was accused by Robison of complicity in the Freemasonic plots against Church and State. He was known as "Citizen Stanhope," and only saved by his rank from serious harm.

Stanhope's daughter, Lady Hester Stanhope (1776–1839), developed an early interest in astrology and the occult, which was to come to full flower in her later life, when she lived as the uncrowned queen of the Druses in Syria. John Varley, who was two years younger than she, and grew up as a fatherless child in the shadow of the Stanhopes' family seat at Chevening, Kent, may have shared in her interests quite early on. Another possibility, suggested by Prof. Schuchard, is that he learnt his astrology from Ebenezer Sibly.[20] In either case, Varley was connected from his youth with the radical and occultist Freemasons of the late eighteenth century.

Second, John Varley was a friend of William Blake, although the two men did not meet until John Linnell introduced them in 1818. Blake, with his prophetic gift, did not have much time for Varley's more laborious astrology, but it was in Varley's house that he drew the famous visionary heads in 1819, staring into space and recording what he saw there. Possibly the astrology of the Shoreham Ancients came through Varley, who was always happy to teach others.

From this period, and specifically from the encounter with Blake, came Varley's unfinished treatise on "zodiacal physiognomy."[21] The work was intended to comprise four volumes and to contain *inter alia* "the establishment of Christianity and the abolition of the worship of heathen gods, shown to have accompanied the processional [sic] motion of particular fixed stars."[22] Evidently Varley had discovered the train of thought of the mythographers whom we have traced in Chapter Two. His zodiacal physiognomy is based on the correspondence of people's birth signs to their physical features, which he illustrates with five plates of human and demonic heads. I quote a lengthy extract concerning the planet Uranus (discovered in 1785 and then called "Herschel"), which shows the confluence of Varley's occult interest with his awareness of the latest discoveries of science; he was, after all, the nephew of an inventor, and an inventor himself.

> Aquarius is a mystical, astronomical, astrological, occult, and scientific sign, of which the Herschel planet is its lord and ruler; and symbolically (like those occult sciences) beyond the general natural view of mankind: and its satellites bear some analogy to the singularity attached or imputed to the votaries of those pursuits or studies, from the extraordinary circumstance of their moving in a retrograde direction, and nearly perpendicular to the plane of his orbit. As the antient students and professors in the earlier periods of the judicial science were compelled to resort to the severest and closest study, in caverns, closet, or confined dwellings, which last are astrologically known to be signified by the earthy sign Virgo, the significator also of that part of the body which contains the bowels, this explains the allegory of Uranus' children being confined by him in the bowels of the earth; and their rebellion is symbolical of the repugnance and opposition of the active, commercial, saturnine portion of society, to the pursuit of the occult sciences, which imposed such restraints on their youthful or their active habits. But as the dominion of the world was acquired by Saturn's trading people, who by virtue of his real and true dominion in the feminine accumulating sign Capricorn, became the wealthy and powerful directors in the commonwealth; they—still believing erroneously, while ignorant of the Herschel planet's existence, that the sign Aquarius was Saturn's masculine and superior house, more as conferring intellectual preeminence than worldly gain—stifled in their birth the predilection for those pursuits which belonged to Aquarius, as being ultimately injurious to worldly power and estimation. Here then is the meaning of Saturn's devouring his male children as soon as born.[23]

Far-fetched as Varley's interpretation may be, it is in the respectable lineage of Dupuis and Drummond, tracing ancient astrological beliefs to some rational basis.

Elsewhere in the book Varley tells of his sessions with Blake, and of the latter's conversation with the ghost of a flea. For all his sympathy with the prophetic poet, Varley was no mystic; his brand of astrology was as rational as the politics of Citizen Stanhope. But he set up no barriers to the possible. In later life he reappeared in the fashionable world to become the sage of the Countess of Blessington's salon, which will be described in Chapter Nine. I turn now to the astrological revival, in which Varley played a large part.

In Chapter Five I mentioned the silence of the occult sciences during the antirevolutionary fervor after 1793. Barrett's *Magus* of 1801 stands in splendid isolation: nothing else of the kind was printed until the end of the Napoleonic Wars came in sight. Astrology was the first science to reappear, with a monthly journal, *Mentor Stellarum,*[24] which ran for less than a year in 1813–14. There was nothing very occult about it: it belonged to the rational, deterministic wing of astrology that demanded mathematical skill rather than a mystical frame of mind. *Mentor Stellarum* ("Teacher of Stars") provided the basic interpretive equipment for budding astrologers to begin their own horoscope reading; it carried articles on the calendar, herbalism, Uranus, the diminution of the obliquity of the ecliptic, and poetry both by Thomas Taylor, and addressed to him. (Taylor the Platonist was an astrologer, and a friend of Blake.) One of the contributors was Henry Andrews of Royston, who identifies himself as the longtime editor of Moore's, Partridge's, and other almanacs. These had never ceased publication, being a profitable monopoly of the Stationers' Company and indispensable at a time when sailors were still obliged to steer by the stars. But in the new journal, Andrews writes at a more learned level, showing himself to be a student of the golden age of English astrology: the mid-seventeenth century. He recommends Lilly and Coley as the best authorities in the language.[25]

The circle of astrologers who produced *Mentor Stellarum* were associated with the *Conjurer's* or *Astrologer's Magazine* of twenty years before, for they now reveal several of the identities of contributors to that journal. One of them was John Harris, a gentleman who possessed a profound knowledge of astrology, learnt as a boy from his father. It was he (said the *Mentor*) who discarded the wrong notions that the seventeenth-century astrologer Partridge had imbibed from Placidus; Harris also introduced the use of new aspects (semi-square, quintile, sesquiquadrate, biquintile) from Kepler.[26] This shows us one way in which serious astrology had been passed down in the eighteenth century.

The other astrological sally of 1813–14 was the work not of a group but of a single man, John Corfield (born in London, 1767). His first effort to launch an astrological journal had as its main attraction the nativity of Napoleon. Corfield showed a proper hostility to the infidel French in the title: *The Antijacobin Review, and true Churchman's Magazine.* Here, in July 1813, Corfield writes that he has studied astrology for thirty years,[27] so from the age of sixteen. He bewails the poor state into which the art has fallen in modern times, as compared to its heyday in Alexandria and China. The main shortcoming of modern astrology, he says, is inaccuracy in recording the time of birth, where an error of only four minutes can lead to an error of a full year in later deductions. He illustrates his principles with a corrected nativity of Napoleon, on the strength of which he predicts peace in 1814.[28]

Corfield went on to produce *The Urania, or, the Philosophical and Scientific Magazine* in 1814, in which, for lack of collaborators, he wrote the readers' letters as well as the editor's answers to them.[29] The single other contributor was Thomas Taylor, whose works are lavishly advertised and quoted from. He writes a letter outlining the hierarchy of the Neoplatonists, and his nativity is given. This was during the period when Taylor was at work on his Proclus translation, and published nothing for three years. Spurned by the academic classicists, he perhaps grasped at the straw of Corfield's journal as a vehicle for his Platonic teachings.

Corfield was a solitary eccentric, who must have had some private means since he says that he lost 500 pounds by these two astrological publications.[30] Possibly he was a vegetarian, like Taylor (and Shelley), for he writes in his commonplace book:

> What makes the English so phlegmatic & melancholy but the extreme use of animal food—What renders the Welsh so hot & choleric but cheese & leeks—the French derive their levity from soups, frogs & mushrooms—the Italian diet gives jelousy & revenge—the warm & solid diet of Spain, may endow profound gravity; but at the same time they suck in with their food, the intolerant vice of pride.[31]

Further evidence of the rationalist trend in astrology comes in the *Complete Dictionary of Astrology* of James Wilson, "Philomath," and the same author's edition of Ptolemy's *Tetrabiblos.*[32] Wilson's philosophy is as follows:

> Man was never intended to possess the gift of Prescience in perfection, nor would it add to his happiness. Nevertheless, there is a certain affinity in nature, whereby every part and particle belonging to it is connected with and dependent on the rest, and which, however imperceptible it may be to shallow or prejudiced understandings, is as obvious to the man of observation as his own existence.[33]

Wilson was a physicalist, but his definition of matter included a very fine "fluid" that emanates from the planets through space, wholly imperceptible except by its effects. He was anti-Newtonian, because his own theory made action at a distance unnecessary. This fluid, in his view, accounted for astrological influence and for other forms of divination, manifesting as "sympathy." He explains:

> this occult sympathy was and is the source of every species of divination, which, notwithstanding the silly common place gibes of imitative writings, and the frauds of its knavish professors, is really founded in nature and truth. The mind, when anxiously and steadily fixed on knowing the result of an undertaking has, from the tripod to the teacup, always been gratified, if a proper intelligent system was adhered to.[34]

Wilson's standpoint made him paranoid on two fronts. On the one hand, he despised Ebenezer Sibly, because of his superstition and inaccuracy. On the other hand, he considered the lawyers and statesmen of the "Society for the Diffusion of Useful Knowledge" (founded in 1825 by Lord Brougham) to be blockheads, because they rejected astrology while being ignorant of it.

A certain type of astrologer has always yearned to be accepted as a scientist. James Wilson's theory of a universal fluid as the vehicle of causation was shared with many scientists of his day. Another type of astrologer, no less scientific, has a more religious approach to his art. We have an example from this period in Thomas Oxley, who speaks of "that sublime Science, Modern Astrology, which above all books and all other learning, gives us the most enlarged and the most elevated views of the power, wisdom, and goodness of the Omnipotent and All-wise Creator."[35]

Oxley was a practical man who would have got on well with the diffusers of useful knowledge. To put beside Lord Stanhope's micrometer, Varley's carriage-wheels, and Graham's balloon, he invented a "self-reefing and unreefing paddle wheel" and an "expanding screw propellor."[36] Oxley was also the inventor of a plansiphere (spherical model of the heavens) that saved the trouble of calculating from ephemerides. He believed that he had discovered the true theory of astrology, consisting in the mathematical doctrine of probabilities. It was this that the ancients had discovered empirically and the moderns refined through better observation. Oxley was indifferent on the question of planetary influence: whether or not that is the cause, he says, astrology does work. He admits that there may, in fact, be no connection of cause and effect; but that since so many coincidences have been observed, they must not be from chance, but from some higher laws set up at the Creation.[37] This resembles Leibniz's doctrine of pre-existent harmony, while also anticipating C. G. Jung's doctrine of synchronicity, the acausal connection of events which was Jung's explanation of how astrology worked.

A third type of astrologer is most interested in getting knowledge of hidden things: the future, other worlds, spirits, etc. Astrology then takes its place among the occult sciences of alchemy, geomancy, arithmology, scrying, necromancy, and ceremonial magic. To this type belonged the man who more than any other was responsible for the occult revival of the early nineteenth century: Robert Cross Smith (1795–1832), known as "Raphael."

Smith's first effort was a pamphlet on geomancy, *The Philosophical Merlin*, published in 1822 and sold by the bookseller Denley.[38] It pretended to be the translation of a manuscript belonging to Napoleon, similar to the *Book of Fate* published in the same year,[39] and showed how to predict one's future geomantically with the minimum of knowledge and complication.

In 1824, again anonymously, Smith started a popular astrological magazine called *The Straggling Astrologer*, published at fourpence every Friday afternoon. The title conveyed the idea of an independent and curious wanderer. The magazine aimed to attract people to astrology by including poems, weekly predictions, and comments on topical and political events. Sometimes it went a little too far, as with an article on how a man could discover astrologically whether his fiancée was a virgin; this necessitated an apology and a promise never again to offend the fair sex. Offense was also given by publishing the King's horoscope, though this was no longer a capital offense. The *Straggling Astrologer* took a stand against Caroline, the queen of George IV accused of adultery; and against the current rage of infidelity. With great hoopla, it engaged the services of "H.R.H. Princess Olive of Cumberland" to write a regular column. Better known as Mrs. Serres, this pretender to royal blood had learnt natural and occult philosophy from her grandfather James Wilmot, of Trinity College, Oxford.[40] Mademoiselle Normand, of Paris, a well-known prophetess, was also named as a collaborator. In short, *The Straggling Astrologer* exploited the combination of high moral tone, sexual titillation, and snobbery that has never failed the popular press.

The editors of *The Straggling Astrologer* were well aware of the mythographical questions of the day, and made a special effort to praise John Landseer's *Sabaean Researches* for explaining the solar nature of pagan deities. They took the opportunity to make a veiled slur on the priesthood, by the time-honored strategy of accusing the priests of antiquity of faults prevalent in modern times. Here is a passage about the priests of Bel or Baal:

> But wonderful as it may seem in our time, the priests of those days were very fond of what is commonly called "good living"; and for the sake of securing it snugly to themselves, they

> succeeded in making the king and people believe, that Bel and the Dragon were the only deities of the world.[41]

In the eleventh number of *The Straggling Astrologer*, on 14 August 1824, there is an announcement to the effect that the "Mercurii" have promised their cooperation, these being a society of scientific gentlemen, for some time privately established for the promotion of occult science; they are men of wealth and genius who have applied themselves intensely for years, toiling through ancient manuscripts in search of wisdom. In the last number (30 October) the Mercurii offer to buy books on occult philosophy, especially geomancy and magic; they are few and select, their meeting place a secret.

It is a fair guess that Richard Cosway had been one of these Mercurii before his death in 1821. *The Straggling Astrologer* printed an article on talismans, transcribed by Cosway from a manuscript in the British Museum, and extracts from a magical manuscript of Rubens formerly in Cosway's possession. Perhaps Thomas Taylor was another member of the group. We have already noticed his presence in the abortive astrological magazines of 1814, and *The Straggling Astrologer* gives two of his translations of Orphic Hymns. As the magazine closes, the publisher, William Charlton Wright, announces *The Prophetic Almanack; or, annual abstract of celestial lore* for 1825, from the manuscripts of Sir Wilson Brachm, "KTR, Humanist" (whom I am unable to identify), as well as the observations of J.V., who must be John Varley.

On the demise of this weekly magazine, Smith started a monthly: *Urania; or, the Astrologer's Chronicle, and Mystical Magazine,* "edited by Mercurius Anglicus, Jun., The Astrologer of the Nineteenth Century, assisted by the Metropolitan Society of Occult Philosophers" as well as by the "Members of the Mercurii" and the "Philosophic Lyceum." Like Francis Barrett in the *Magus,* Smith gave his address and offered to answer questions. Among the many astrological articles, some of them quite technical and many associated with English history and current events, we find the "Nativity of Mr. Blake, the Mystical Artist." Blake, says the accompanying article, has a curious intercourse with the deceased and has a poem recited by the spirit of Milton; "and the mystical drawings of this gentleman are no less curious and worthy of notice, by all those whose minds soar above the cloggings of this terrestrial element, to which we are most of us too fastly chained to comprehend the nature and operations of the world of spirits."[42] Smith adds that he has met Blake several times (doubtless introduced by Varley), and was delighted by his conversation, his extraordinary faculties, and his absence of superstition.

In *Urania,* Smith makes the first of his predictions for the coming year, apparently using not only astrology but geomancy. Thereafter he would publish these separately as an annual almanac, *Raphael's Prophetic Messenger,* always prefacing the text with a folding, hand-colored plate that shows with fine surrealistic effect the emblematic persons and objects that embody his prophecy. In every subsequent issue, he analyzes the previous year's illustration and shows its accuracy. The almanac continued after Smith's death and continues even today, though it has become much less interesting to read. Ellic Howe, in his study of Smith, has traced the identity of the astrologers who assumed Smith's cloak and his sobriquet of Raphael.[43]

Smith was a millenialist. Already in *The Straggling Astrologer* he had predicted that towards 1849 the Jews would assemble and rebuild Jerusalem; that a golden era would commence at the close of the nineteenth century, but not before earthquakes, famine, and war had destroyed one third of humanity. He saw the commencement of the apocalyptic period in the conjunction of 1821, ushering in "the world's greatest sabbath which will be seen a rule of theocracy."[44] The title page of the *Prophetic Messenger* for 1828 says that its purpose is to prepare mankind for the coming of Christ's kingdom on earth. Smith shared the sentiments that Samuel Palmer's biographer attributes to the painter and most of his friends during the same years: "he saw the future in a sinister Apocalyptic light, with the land shrouded in horror and great darkness, men's hearts failing them for fear, nation rising against nation, and the reign of Antichrist about to begin."[45]

Such times are good for astrologers. Smith's apocalyptic timetable left him plenty of time for his own enterprises, which were many, various, and presumably lucrative, in an era when almanacs sold by the hundreds of thousands.

After the failure of the *Straggling Astrologer* and of *Urania,* Smith gathered up their sheets and sold them as books. The *Straggling Astrologer* was now entitled *The Astrologer of the Nineteenth Century,* "sixth edition." Later in 1825 appeared a much enlarged and lavishly illustrated "seventh edition." This work rivals Barrett's *Magus* as the occult compendium of its time, incidentally putting Barrett in his place as merely "an intelligent writer on magic."[46] The subtitle tells all, or nearly all: "The Master Key of Futurity, and Guide to Ancient Mysteries, being a complete system of occult philosophy. Embellished with five Beautifully Coloured Plates, and 90 Illustrative Engravings of Horoscopes, Hieroglypics, and Talismans. By the Members of the Mercurii: Raphael, the Metropolitan Astrologer; the Editor of the Prophetic Almanack; and other Sidereal Artists of First-Rate Experience."

The Mercurii, severally or collectively, had acquired Richard Cosway's occult library on his death in 1821, and made it available to Smith. One of these persons went by the name of Philadelphus, and was a friend of Cosway's.[47] He provided Smith's magazines with extracts from the English Behmenists of the seventeenth century, especially from Pordage's manuscripts and from the *Theosophical Transactions* of the Philadelphian Society. Philadelphus shows his hand in remarking that Pordage's system of heavens is very much like Swedenborg's.[48] Another possible member of the Mercurii is the aeronaut and alchemist George W. Graham, who helped Smith set up his business.[49] Finally there was John Varley, who furnished nativities and other manuscript material.

While *The Astrologer of the Nineteenth Century* does have sections on astrology, it is more concerned with the other occult sciences, especially the glamorous ones of raising spirits: elemental, angelic, and those of the dead. Many instances are described, some illustrated by the engraver Cruickshank. Smith says that evocation was not considered sinful, so long as one did not enter into a compact with the entities.[50] Spirits could be invoked in magic circles, such as Cosway had in his private room, or they could be called into magic mirrors. Smith illustrates a large mirror mounted on a pedestal with the words "Tetragrammaton" and "Elohim" on its base, reputedly identical to the "Urim and Thummim" of Moses.

Smith published several other books, all of which mix practical instruction in astrology or some divinatory science with anecdotes and wonders. He was playing to a public whose appetite for armchair occultism had been whetted by gothic novels, and which was beginning to look for real experiences, if only of fortune-telling. The gothic conceit serves as framework for Smith's *Royal Book of Dreams* (1830), purportedly taken from a fifteenth-century manuscript that he bought from a laborer who had dug it up near Bristol. The book was rudely bound in wood and adorned with enormous clasps with death's heads, scythes, and "sundry Monkish emblems of mortality."[51] It treated of "the arte magicke," "charmes," "the arte negromancye," etc. Most of it was defaced, but Smith did not grieve at this, "for I have ever held such superstitions as unlawful, and as far remote from the pure science of the stars as light is from darkness."[52] However, he did find a legible treatise on how to read one's dreams and interpret them by a combination of ciphers and geomancy, which Smith explains in this book.

A similar conceit accounts for the "Oracle of Pythagoras" in Smith's next book, *The Lady-Witch of Raphael* (1831): he says that it came from a manuscript unearthed at Pompeii, of which he acquired a copy from the collection of Belzoni, the Egyptologist and showman. The Oracle consists of nine hundred answers; one finds the right one by manipulating a magic square, the age of the moon, and one's own name. *The Lady-Witch* is another "omnium gatherum," containing poems, literary fantasies, anecdotes, divination, nativities, and advertisements for toothpaste. It was dedicated to Queen Adelaide, but whether with or without permission, one cannot tell.

Smith was obsessed with divination, but it seems that he withheld his greatest treasure from publication. This exists as a manuscript book,[53] secured by a lock, entitled: "*The Art of Secret Astrology*, containing the horary reign of the celestial intelligencers, [sic] Elections of Fortunate & Unfortunate Times; for commencing, pursuing & finding any Undertaking; & also the important secret whereby may be most certainly known the Thoughts, meaning, & intent of any person whatever, at any stated time either of making Proposals, visits, letters, &c. &c. &c And whether they come as friends or enemies. This last great Discovery, has never yet in any age of the World, nor at any time whatever been communicated, except by select *oral* testimony." It is a table of planetary rulerships of the hours of the day, taking into account that such hours are irregular, being the twelfth part of the time between sunrise and sunset. Hence in the winter the nocturnal hours are much longer than the diurnal ones. Smith gives a table of timings, and indicates which hours can be relied on as always good, or always bad.

Smith's writings have little to offer on that most profound of the occult sciences, alchemy, beyond saying that there are nearly a hundred alchemists in London. But one of his books, *The Familiar Astrologer* (completed 1828, published 1831), contains a remarkable pair of essays on "The Philosopher's Stone" by John Palmer (1807-1837; no apparent relation to Samuel).[54] This young adept claimed to have studied at the Institut de France under the chemist Nicolas Vauquelin, with Baron Thénard, Guy Lussac, Dumas, and at the Sorbonne.[55] At first he went by the pseudonym of "Zadkiel the Alchemist" (not to be confused with "Zadkiel the Seer, i.e., R. J. Morrison), but on Smith's death in 1832 he became the second "Raphael," and continued the *Prophetic Almanac*.[56]

Palmer introduces his first essay by saying that the famous chemists Sir Humphrey Davy and Dr. Woolaston pursued alchemy for a considerable time, thereby throwing light on their main chemical discoveries; they were constantly buying books from a Mr. Wagstaff, who had the choicest collection of alchemy and occult manuscripts in England. Mr. Wagstaff told Palmer that he had been credibly informed of a series of experiments conducted at the Royal Mint to ascertain the growth of gold and its chemical foundation. This is further evidence of the broad-minded interest in rejected knowledge on the part of scientists around 1800, but it may go back much further than that, to the time when the Master of the Mint was the great alchemist Sir Isaac Newton.

Palmer now writes on the strength of his own knowledge of alchemy. The metals in mines, he says, do grow and increase. Their root is neither metallic nor mineral, but partakes of both, and arises from the putrefaction and decomposition of both mineral and vegetable bodies. It is soft and maniable, variable in color, and so common that there is not a child ignorant of it. It is common in fields and marshy places, where one does not have to mine it, but may frequently find it at the depth of a man's leg. This is the "Vase."[57]

Palmer goes on to say that before the operations commence, the Philosopher's Loadstone must be discovered, in order to attract the astral spirit and give it substantial form. He will only say that it takes the form of a cross, the sign of redemption from which the Philosophers prepared their medicine that restores man to his primitive state. The proper time to collect it is from the 20th or 21st of March to the 20th of June, gathering it after sunset when the moon is at or near full, and there is no strong wind. The student should turn to the north, and "if the student has been fortunate enough to divine the attractor of this fluid, let him seek it in *a mine of thirty years standing*, and he will then be able to obtain the spirit in the form of a viscous fluid." This fluid, carried to the highest pitch of concentration and fermentation, like condensed fire, is the Stone of the Magi.

In his second essay, Palmer instructs the alchemist to divide the mineral matter into pea-sized pieces, and water it with "our liquid" forty to fifty times. Thereupon it becomes clammy, smelly, and black: this is the Crow's Head. Then with gentle heat it turns to the white Philosophical Mercury. One should imbibe this seven times, then a white substance will form a cottony mass on top. The pulp below is prepared, and becomes red and sulphurous. Together they constitute the Philosophic Marriage of the red man with the white woman. Next come forty to fifty imbibitions in astral water, which makes the matter become blacker than black (the reign of Saturn), then a powder of a brilliant whiteness. The reigns of moon, Venus, Mars, and the sun succeed, leaving a red powder. Now all that remains is the process of mulitiplication. Palmer concludes by saying that if time allowed, he would show the relation of alchemy to religious mysteries and ceremonies, and how mythology has taught this art in enigmas.

The clarity of Palmer's account is rare in the alchemical literature; for its period, it is unique. I suspect that he obtained his knowledge in Paris, perhaps in the same circles that produced the *Hermès Dévoilé* of Cyliani (1832).

Once the concerns of the Mercurii and of other underground seekers had been brought into the open—at least into the limited openness of Raphael's readership—, there was a gratifying response from the public, measurable by the number of publications now appearing. Something must have been felt even in the wider literary world. 1830 was the year in which the aged Sir Walter Scott published his *Letters on Witchcraft and Demonology*, to which Sir William Brewster, the physicist, replied with his

Letters on Natural Magic. William Godwin contributed a similar work of informed skepticism in his *Lives of the Necromancers* (1834). These early 1830s were years that tried the English nation sorely, leading many pious folk to conclude that because their country was going through a constitutional crisis, the end of the world must surely be at hand. Little did they know that they were sailing into the placid waters of the Victorian era.

Two streams of this resurgence of occultism are of particular importance. One is "animal magnetism," almost synonymous with Mesmerism. In the next chapter, a brief account of the British magnetisers will show how science and the occult regretfully parted company at mid-century. The other stream centers on crystal-gazing or scrying, and will be taken up in Chapter Nine.

EIGHT

Animal Magnetism

The history of animal magnetism in Britain goes back at least to the seventeenth century, when the idea of sympathy as a healing principle was expounded by Robert Fludd, Sir Kenelm Digby, and other disciples of Paracelsus. The example most commonly remembered is their "weapon-salve" or "powder of sympathy," a gruesome mess for smearing not on wounds but on the objects that caused them. The idea of sympathy existing between objects or bodies was a natural and defensible one within their Hermetic world view. Sympathy or resemblance between the Above and the Below held together the entire cosmic hierarchy and was the archetype of the invisible bonds that permeated the phenomenal world.

In the later eighteenth century, with its confidence in experimental science, it seemed as if these bonds of occult sympathy might at last become manifest. Newton had gone as far as to quantify certain of them, with his theory of gravitation. He had also posited the ether as an insensible medium for influences, a premise that would survive until the time of Einstein.

To Newton's gravitation, the Austrian doctor Franz Anton Mesmer (1734–1815) added the concept of "Animal Gravity," a force that works on and in our bodies through substances more subtle than matter.[1] Mesmer's doctoral dissertation had taken as its subject the influences of the planets, treating them from a purely physical point of view but allowing that they may well influence the human body, just as the moon does the tides. As his medical practice developed, he became convinced that he was able to harness this force and employ it for healing. Sometimes he used magnets and other appliances, at other times simply his own hands, placed on the patient or waved in magnetic passes. In either case, he believed that the operative agent was an imponderable "fluid."

In 1778, Mesmer moved his practice to Paris and created sufficient interest for an official committee of the Royal Academy of Sciences to be formed for the investigation of his theories. The committee included Jean-Sylvain Bailly, Antoine Lavoisier, Dr. Guillotin, and Benjamin Franklin. Their report, published in 1784, was disastrous to Mesmer's reputation, for it implied that he was a quack. This was the inevitable conclusion from a point of view that considered only the physical theory (which could not be experimentally proven) and ignored the psychological dimension of his therapy. No depositions were accepted from the many patients of all classes who claimed to have been healed by Mesmer.

Today we can appreciate better the roles of Mesmer's personality, the atmosphere of his healing salon, the expectations of the patients, and the part played by imagination and suggestion in his cures. Their efficacy is taken for granted in a more psychologically aware era. But if we have this awareness, it is thanks to those who followed in Mesmer's footsteps and developed, in the teeth of the medical establishment, the techniques of hypnosis and the theory of the unconscious mind. No one had heard of those in 1784.

The Academy's condemnation did nothing to prevent the spread of Mesmer's theories and practices in England, beginning in 1785. They were first imported by a character who styled himself "Monsieur le Dr. John Bell, Member of the Philosophical Harmonic Society at Paris, Fellow Correspondent of Court de Geblin's [sic] Museum [. . .] and the only Person authorized by Patent from the First Noblemen in France to teach and practise that Science in England, Ireland, &c."[2] Bell had probably paid the hefty fee to learn Mesmerism from the master himself and sworn not to reveal its secrets. In both London and Dublin, he used an oaken tub, eight feet in diameter, standing on four glass insulators: evidently a copy of Mesmer's *baquet*, used to amplify the magnetic fluid and to feed it out to a circle of patients. Bell believed that any animate or inanimate body could be magnetized or "electrified," to increase its action, but counseled practitioners against trying to cure any of the more serious diseases.

As we know from earlier chapters, London in the 1780s was a happy hunting-ground for adventurers in the occult sciences, and no doubt Dr. Bell did as well as any of them. A second emissary from the Harmonic Society, Dr. de Mainauduc, made a proposal in 1785 for the foundation of a London "Hygeian Society" for ladies to be incorporated with the one in Paris.[3] This was perhaps what emerged as James Graham's "Temple of Health" in Schomberg House, Pall Mall, with its Magnetic Throne and Celestial Bed (see Chapter Five).[4] De Mainauduc himself arrived in England in 1787.[5] He was a male midwife, and had been a pupil of Charles Deslon (or d'Eslon), one of the foremost French medical men to espouse Mesmer's doctrines. De Mainauduc's first advertisement was for twenty ladies to pay him fifteen guineas each for a complete "exhibition" and treatment. Such was his success that he was able to raise the price to between twenty-five and 150 guineas,[6] thus emulating his teacher Deslon, who, it was said, had cleared 100,000 pounds.[7]

Those who learned the Mesmeric art from de Mainauduc also had to pay. George Winter joined his distinguished students (who included the painters Cosway and de Loutherbourg) by paying twenty-five guineas, plus five guineas for the use of the room, and signing a bond in the sum of 10,000 pounds with an affidavit not to reveal the secrets during de Mainauduc's lifetime.[8] Winter was far from being a convinced disciple. While he accepted that the principles of sympathy and antipathy were part of God's system of nature, and that Mesmer had revived an ancient system of healing, the method taught by de Mainauduc was not a universal panacea. Winter kept a register of more than a hundred cures that he was unable to effect through animal magnetism, but which responded to conventional medicines.

We have already noted the success that de Loutherbourg had with magnetic healing in 1789, using no further apparatus than his own hands and will. Richard Cosway, never one to do a thing by halves, claimed to have attained a state of "somnambulistic lucidity," which enabled him to see a hole in a friend's liver; the story reached George III, who was much amused by it.[9] Mention of "lucidity" takes us beyond the original Mesmerism to the developments of the Puységur brothers. In 1784 the Marquis de Puységur and his brother, Count Maxime, having learnt the master's techniques with mixed success, retired to their country estate at Busancy. In an atmosphere very different from Mesmer's physically and psychically overheated salon, they worked outdoors. Their subjects were not wealthy neurotics (not that all of Mesmer's were), but their own peasants; not people in search of new sensations, but ones who were genuinely ill. Moreover, they had no need or desire to make money.

Mesmer's healing process typically caused the patient to pass through a violent phase called a "crisis," for which a specially padded room was set aside. Nowadays one can also understand the therapeutic value of overcoming inhibition. But the Puységurs' subjects, perhaps not so inhibited to begin with, entered instead into a calm, sleeplike condition. What made this truly extraordinary was that in this "somnambulistic" state they were able to speak with an authority unknown to them when waking, and to diagnose their own ailments. Moreover, somnambulism often brought extrasensory perceptions, hence its description as "lucid." Experiments along these lines led to far different results from anything that Mesmer had envisaged (he disliked what the Puységurs were doing), soon crossing the borderline from medicine into the supernatural. From being patients, the somnambulistic subjects had become mediums.

John Bell had a garbled idea of the Puységurs' methods: he wrote in 1792 that there was a kind of crisis called "luminous," named for the sect of *Illuminés.*[10] This was precisely the sort of association that blackened the whole practice in the public mind, as the 1790s ran their course and anything French and "enlightened" became anathema. For different reasons, Mesmerism was also eclipsed in France. The historian and psychical researcher Frank Podmore explains that it was tarred with the brush of the aristocracy and by the fact that many early adherents had also been disciples of Cagliostro.[11] Consequently, Mesmerism did not revive in either country until after the fall of Napoleon.

In Germany, in the meantime, mainly thanks to the apostolic enthusiasm of Lavater, Puységur's version of Mesmerism had excited the *Naturphilosophen* such as Franz von Baader, Johann Friedrich von Meyer, and J. J. von Görres. Baader, the most profound and influential of the group, concluded that in somnambulism or "magnetic ecstasy" one is in quite a different, magical relationship with the world. The ecstatic subject enters a different sphere of being, a higher and more universal condition of life, which follows different rules from those of the ordinary one; it relates to the bodily senses as an organic being compares with an inorganic one. In such a state, clairvoyance is not to be wondered at. Baader criticizes the skeptics and materialists who confuse the two states through basing them both on the same, physical foundations.[12]

There was a tension in Germany between those like Baader, who regarded somnambulism as a way of exploration of the soul-world, and those who fought to keep science clean of mysticism. For the Romantics, it was a gateway to another and a higher world; for the scientists, it was a question of fluids requiring further research. D. G. Kieser, of the University of Jena, reviewing Baader's work, urged his colleagues to preserve their intellectual freedom in the face of natural laws that have not yet been grasped, and not to give way to the pious sentimentality infecting all departments of life.[13] This was understandable in 1817, when the recent "Holy Alliance" of the Russian, Prussian, and Austrian Empires seemed to threaten a revived theocracy and the suppression of freethought. Reviewing the situation in Europe three years later, in 1820, Prof. Eschenmeyer of Tübingen University found it very disappointing. In France, he says, there is no scientific research at all: all animal magnetism there is done by laymen. England and Italy are a tabula rasa, while in America there is nothing.[14] In Prussia, however, a mesmeric hospital had already been operating in Berlin since 1815.[15]

The torch of Mesmerism in France was relit by J. F. P. Deleuze, Librarian and Professor of Natural History at the Jardin des Plantes and a pupil of the Puységurs from prerevolutionary days. His *Histoire critique du magnétisme animal* (1813) emphasized the role played by the human will and introduced the ideas of what would today be called hypnotic and posthypnotic suggestion.[16] Deleuze brought Mesmerism back into the public forum, and eventually it was taken up again by the medical world. Experiments were tried at the Hôtel-Dieu hospital in 1819–20, some of which succeeded in curing otherwise hopeless cases of "hysteria." In the following year a Dr. Recamier performed the first surgical operation on a mesmerically entranced subject. Somnambulists came to be employed in medical practices for diagnosing, while in trance, the ailments of others. Eventually the Royal Academy of Sciences agreed to a second official commission, whose report, published in 1831, at least did not outlaw animal magnetism, but encouraged further investigation. This lukewarm report was suppressed, being circulated only to the Academy members, but in 1833 an English translation, with 150 pages of commentary, was published by J. C. Colquhoun (died 1854), an advocate at the Scottish Bar.[17]

The revival of animal magnetism in England was due to another layman, Richard Chenevix, F.R.S. (died 1830), a chemist and mineralogist "of large fortune."[18] Chenevix had encountered animal magnetism in Germany in 1803–04, but had become finally convinced of its reality by the experiments of Abbé Faria in Paris, which he witnessed in 1816.[19] The Portuguese Faria was a flamboyant character who had traveled in India; he did not believe in magnetic fluids, but in the will power of one person working on another. Spurning even the use of passes, he would simply order his patients to go to sleep.[20] Chenevix achieved numerous cures, at first of epileptic children in Ireland, then of patients in the Wakefield Asylum in Yorkshire.[21] This hospital, incidentally, had been founded in 1818 through the efforts of Godfrey Higgins; I wonder whether it was he who facilitated Chenevix's experiments there, of all places. In 1829 Chenevix published "On Mesmerism, improperly denominated Animal Magnetism" in several numbers of the *London Medical and Physical Journal* and was allowed to demonstrate his methods in some of London's hospitals.[22] He was able to mesmerize patients even from another room, and to make them carry out commands that he expressed only in his own thoughts. But his death in 1830 prevented further investigation of these marvels.

Colquhoun included in his translation of the French Commission's report an analysis of six states of animal magnetism by C. A. F. Kluge.[23] These were: (1) the waking state; (2) half sleep, or impending crisis; (3) magnetic sleep; (4) perfect crisis or simple somnambulism: the patient reawakened in a very peculiar connection with the external world; (5) self-intuition or clairvoyance: the patient can inspect him- or herself internally, and prescribe remedies; (6) lucid vision, leading to universal lucidity. Colquhoun found the higher states to be a powerful argument for the independence of the soul, and hence for its immortality.[24] He was a believer in the universal, subtle fluid as a link between soul and body, and found in it, as Ficino and the Renaissance Platonists had found in their *spiritus*, a reconciliation of religion and natural philosophy. Three years later, in 1836, he published *Isis Revelata: An Inquiry into the origin, progress, and present state of animal magnetism.* By a pleasing synchronicity, this work with its title meaning "Isis Unveiled" appeared in the same year as Higgins's *Anacalypsis,* which alludes to the same Egyptian goddess of Nature. Among the immense quantity of information on ancient and modern phenomena, Colquhoun remarks that clairvoyance (the fifth and sixth states) is not yet known or appreciated in Britain, whereas on the Continent of Europe it is almost universally admitted.[25]

Two other mesmerizers who worked outside the medical profession in these years were friends of Bulwer-Lytton. In Chapter Six, I mentioned Chauncey Hare Townshend, a clergyman who lived mainly on the Continent. Lytton wrote of him: "He was a young man when I was a boy at school at St. Lawrence. He then lived with his father at Ramsgate. He had won a prize poem at Cambridge and later had a volume of poems. His beauty of countenance was remarkable at that time. Those who knew Byron said it was Byron with bloom and health. He grew plain in later life—an accomplished man—but effeminate and mildly selfish."[26] When Lytton went up to Trinity Hall, Cambridge, he found Townshend there on a visit, but was hurt when the older man showed no interest in him. Later their friendship was renewed, and they exchanged occasional letters on Mesmerism until the 1860s.

Townshend conducted experiments in Mesmerism at Cambridge in 1837, putting his patients into trance by staring fixedly at them with his hands on theirs, or on their knees, then moving his hands up and down in an ellipse; his book *Facts in Mesmerism* has charming illustrations of couples doing this. Like Colquhoun, he compares the backward and prejudiced attitudes of England to those of the Continent, especially Germany (he was writing from Innsbruck). The reasons were plain to him: Mesmerism had been discovered by the wrong kind of person, lacking candor and philosophical strictness. If only a Newton or an Arago had discovered it![27] The other misfortune, Townshend thought, was the erroneous assimilation of early Mesmerism to science, with the assumption that it had a specific and physical cause or power. Privately he added to Lytton: "Of one thing I assure you—the subject possesses vast literary capabilities."[28] Lytton would make good use of this advice twenty years later, in *A Strange Story.*

The next mesmeric visitor from the Continent was another aristocratic amateur, Baron Jules Dupotet de Sennevoy (1798-1881). As a medical student, Dupotet had been one of the mesmerizers in the Hôtel-Dieu experiments of 1820. He had served on the 1831 commission and succeeded in 1837 in getting permission to practice in England. He gave exhibitions in Wigmore Street, where many physicians practiced, and at University College Hospital. Earl Stanhope (the Fourth Earl, on whom more below) was instrumental in getting Dupotet a hearing, and it was to him that the Frenchman dedicated his *Introduction to the Study of Animal Magnetism* (1838), calling the Earl's voice the sole one raised in his defense.[29] It was probably these exhibitions that prompted Townshend to try his hand in Cambridge the same year.

Dupotet divides animal magnetism into three separate schools, of which he belonged to the third: (1) the original school of Mesmer in Paris, very Epicurean (in the materialistic sense), assuming a universal fluid; (2) the Lyon school of the Chevalier de Barbarin, together with the Swedish and German branches: Platonic in its philosophy, believing that phenomena are caused by the effort of the soul, hence called "spiritualists"; (3) Puységur's school at Strasbourg: experimentalists who combine the treatment of the first school with the psychical teachings of the second. The schools differ in theory, he says, but all have the same results.[30] Having done his work in England, Dupotet returned to France, where he published a *Journal du magnétisme* from 1845 to 1860.

With Dupotet's departure, the torch of Mesmerism was left in the hands of Stanhope's friend John Elliotson (1791–1868). Besides a large private practice, Elliotson could style himself in 1832 "M.D. Cantab., F.R.S., F.R.C.P.; Physician to the Royal Hospital of St. Thomas and to the Royal Society of Musicians; President of the Phrenological Society, and Hon. Member of the Phrenological Society of Paris; Professor of the Principles and Practice of Medicine in the University, &c., &c."[31] He had watched Chenevix's work in 1829 and was convinced that more than mere imagination was involved in it, but did not pursue it further until Dupotet arrived in England.[32] Then he gave it his whole life.

Elliotson's first exhibitions, at University College Hospital, used as their subjects a pair of young Irish sisters, Jane and Elizabeth Okey (or O'Key), who were hospitalized for epileptic fits, spontaneous delirium, and catalepsy. A large part of his research had to do with how to magnetize them, in a misguided attempt to pin down the workings of the elusive fluid. For example, Elliotson would magnetize a coin by touch or passes, then the coin would be put with a group of untreated ones. As soon as the girl picked out the magnetized coin, she would go into a trance. The girls clearly exploited the situation. While magnetized, they whistled, gabbled in unknown languages, teased eminent visitors, and told unsuitable stories,[33] none of which redounded to the credit of the new therapy. One detail is interesting in view of the later spiritualists' craze for exotic spirit-guides: Elizabeth Okey, when asked questions she could not answer, would refer them to her "Negro" and report his answers.[34]

For a while *The Lancet*, Britain's foremost medical journal, deigned to allow a lively discussion of Elliotson's work. But more rigid experiments began to cast doubt on the reality of the magnetic energy and this,

Figure 8.1. *Animal Magnetism: The Operator putting his Patient into a Crisis. From E. Sibly,* A Key to Physic and the Occult Sciences, *1814.*

together with the girls' frivolity and cheating, caused the hospital to request Elliotson to stop his mesmeric work there. In 1838 he resigned from his academic and hospital positions. He worked henceforth as an evangelist for animal magnetism, as a private practitioner, and as the editor of a journal, *The Zoist* (1843–1856), which is a fascinating chronicle of its times.

If, as Townshend said, Mesmerism was unfortunate in its founder, it was doubly so in having Elliotson as its chief proponent in the British medical world. He was a short, pugnacious man of great physical and moral energy, quick to anger and adept in mocking his opponents, whereas what was needed was a smooth diplomat. He was also antireligious at a time when most medical men paid at least lip-service to the established church, and keen to keep "mysticism" out of Mesmerism and its twin science, phrenology.

A word must be said here about phrenology, or as Elliotson called it, "cerebral physiology": the analysis of character through studying the shape of the skull. Branching out from Lavater's physiognomy, phrenology had been invented around 1800 by two German doctors, F. J. Gall and J. K. Spurzheim, and had come to England shortly afterwards. Elliotson himself was the founder of the Phrenological Society in 1824, and it is probably he who, in the opening article of his magazine, addresses the phrenologists thus:

> We say to Cerebral Physiologists, grapple with nature, cease speculating on the unseen, the unknown, the unfelt, the chimerical. Limit yourselves to the consideration of practical questions and apply the knowledge you accumulate. Separate the conjectural and the plausible from that which is established truth, embrace the latter and defend your position regardless of the consequences. Be Philosophers. Cease drawling forth *misereres* over the fading remnants of spiritual theories; the offspring of infant brains; the vestiges of an intellectual chaos, a period of ignorance and superstition; and rejoice at the approaching indications of man's emancipation from the incubus of error.[35]

However, Elliotson was not a simple secularist, but was only keen to keep science and religion from interfering with one another. This is why he rejoiced that his own University of London, unlike those of Oxford and Cambridge, did not require church membership.[36] He writes in 1845:

> I have all my life sought for facts only, and never felt inclined to frame hypotheses [. . .] I have advocated the truth of phrenology only as far as I have ascertained the facts by careful observation: and have not defended, nay, have greatly doubted, much that passes current among phrenologists. He *knows* that on mesmerism I have never speculated:—never gone beyond the plain facts which I carefully observed. The same love of fact has made me advocate materialism. I see that the living brain thinks and feels; and I have never indulged in the hypothesis

> that, not it, but a something altogether imaginary, called soul or spirit, thinks and feels and does all that our experience plainly tells is done by the brain, while we are being completely deceived by our *fancied* experience. The Spiritualist is a man of lively imagination and predilection for hypotheses. [. . .] I carefully shew that a materialist may believe in God and a future state, and that the evidence for the latter must be revelation not philosophy: and quote great divines of this last opinion.[37]

In the same year, one R. R. Noel wrote to the *Zoist* from Rosawitz in Bohemia, to say that up to now the predominant view in Germany had been that the brain is the instrument of an immaterial mind, but that materialism and necessity were beginning to be seen as the only true and consistent views for scientists.[38]

Like many secularists, Elliotson was a passionate humanitarian. He wrote vigorously against capital punishment and cruelty to animals. Public executions, he says, brutalize both executioner and audience. For murderers, he recommends perpetual imprisonment, but adds that those in solitary confinement should at least have an animal or bird for company, and books.[39] It was natural for such a person to be especially interested in Mesmerism as a painkiller and to be outraged at the refusal of the medical establishment to consider so humanitarian a resource.

A great impetus to this use of Mesmerism came in 1845 through the publication of James Esdaile's work in India. Esdaile was a young surgeon in charge of a charity hospital at Hooghly. Finding that he was able to put patients into mesmeric sleep, he began to use this for his operations. In six years, he performed 261 major operations, removing tumors of a size scarcely to be believed, and being rewarded by the survival of nearly all his patients.[40] Much of the *Zoist* is devoted to describing and discussing Esdaile's work, which was encouraged by the Governor-General of India, Lord Dalhousie, and by patrician Hindus such as the Tagores.[41] Despite the official rejection in England of mesmerically induced anaesthesia, Elliotson could remark in 1847 on a new wave of openness, saying that an increasing number of surgeons and dentists were using Mesmerism to prevent the pain of operations.[42]

Just as Mesmerism was riding this wave, a new kind of anaesthetic arrived in England from America: ether, which had the great advantage of being physical, quantifiable, instant and universal in its efficacy (its side effects were another matter). The medical profession could now ignore the claims of this too-mysterious Mesmerism with a good conscience. The Mesmerists seem to have reacted by turning their attention to the more occult aspects of their science. One of these was the clairvoyance that had been spontaneously demonstrated by Puységur's patients and by many after them. In 1844 a young French clairvoyant, Alexis Didier, came to England and gave exhibition sittings over seven or eight years, making a substantial amount of money for himself and his mesmerizer, Marcillet.[43] Townshend was one of those who wrote to the *Zoist* to describe Alexis's wonders while in trance: he could read books blindfold, predict political events, detect thieves, etc.[44] Even the famous stage-magician Robert Houdin confessed himself baffled by what he witnessed in private sittings with Alexis, and Houdin knew more than anyone alive about how to produce apparent phenomena.[45] Alan Gauld, the historian of hypnotism, uses the Didier case to evaluate the whole question of "supernatural" powers, saying that if they can be discounted in Alexis's case, there is no point in considering them in any other case. After a careful analysis of the alternatives, Gauld reluctantly concludes that magnetic somnambulists "did sometimes acquire and transmit information which they could not have come by in any of the ordinarily recognized ways."[46]

It was in Germany that these psychical phenomena blossomed into mysticism. Heinrich Jung-Stilling (1740–1817) describes how, when subjects are able to be taken by repeated magnetizing or stroking beyond the passive, magnetic sleep, they enter a more elevated and very agreeable state: "The exaltation of the inner man rises in many persons to such a height, that they come into connexion with the invisible world, and they very frequently reveal hidden mysteries, and also remarkable things, which are taking place at a distance, or will shortly happen."[47] Jung-Stilling regarded this state as resembling, and in fact proving, the state of the soul after death, when it loses all connection with the sense-world and finds itself among beings of its own affinity: hopefully its friends, the Saints, and the Redeemer himself.[48]

Jung-Stilling was Professor of Political Economy at Heidelberg and Marburg Universities, and a friend of Lavater, Herder, and Goethe. His *Theory of Pneumatology,* which was published in English translation in 1834, was the work of a convinced Christian, written both as a rational analysis of psychical phenomena and as a warning against dabbling in them. "Animal Magnetism," wrote Jung-Stilling, "is a very dangerous thing. When an intelligent physician employs it for the cure of certain diseases, there is no objection to it; but as soon as it is applied to discover mysteries, to which we are not directed in this life, the individual commits the sin of sorcery—an insult to the majesty of heaven."[49]

Beside the figure of Swedenborg, who was apparently able to visit the spiritual world without being magnetized, the Germans of the Romantic era had some striking examples of this type of soul-traveling. One was Anne-Catherine Emmerich, whose vaticinations were collected by the poet Clemens Brentano. Another was Friederike Hauffe (1801–1829), known as the "Seeress of Prevorst," who was studied by the doctor-poet Justinus

Kerner. He first magnetized her in 1826, in the attempt to cure her from convulsions and other ailments, which beset her throughout her short and sickly life, then stayed to listen to the awe-inspiring revelations that she gave when in trance.

The Seeress of Prevorst lived in familiarity with the phantasms of the dead. Many came to her for help in matters concerning their surviving relatives. Moreover, she was the focus of poltergeist activities: knocks, raps, and flying furniture. Lastly, she gave in trance a remarkable series of cosmological teachings, illustrated by charts of circles and wheels, with a text in an unknown script. This was supposedly the primordial language of mankind, which the Seeress (and other German somnambulists) would speak; Kerner perceived in it a kinship to Hebrew. As the psychical researcher Frank Podmore points out, important features of later Spiritualism and Theosophy are already present here: converse with the dead, raps, the revelation of a cyclical cosmology, and the *Ur*-language.[50]

The story of the Seeress of Prevorst was published in English, in abbreviated form, by Catherine Crowe in 1845. But the cosmopolitan Mesmerists did not need to wait so long, being fully aware of developments on the Continent. This brings us back to Lord Stanhope,[51] the patron of Dupotet, and to his peculiar foreign entanglements.

Philip Henry, the Fourth Earl (1781–1855) was the son of Charles "Citizen" Stanhope (the Third Earl), which was not an easy destiny. Just in case England should enjoy a revolution of the French type, Charles made his children learn useful trades or professions. The *Medical Times* reported that Philip had been apprenticed to a surgeon-apothecary in Canterbury; his obituary in the *Zoist* said that he had been a brickmaker and signed himself thus in the census.[52] In any case, he was interested in medicine from his early years, as he himself told the members of Elliotson's London Mesmeric Infirmary.[53] In his youth he also knew Richard Cosway, whose pretentions as a healer were mentioned above.[54] Utterly incapable of getting along with his eccentric father, who kept him virtually imprisoned at the family seat of Chevening, Kent, he was helped by his half-sister Hester to escape in 1801. In 1806 there was a lawsuit between Philip (as Lord Mahon) and his father, as a result of which he was disinherited of all the Third Earl's disposable property.

Even after he succeeded to the family property and title when his father died, unreconciled, in 1816, Philip Henry Stanhope was beset by financial difficulties. A recent biography by Johannes Mayer has shown how he solved these by acting as a secret agent for the government of William Pitt. Mayer traces Stanhope's travels around Europe, particularly in the German states, and his involvement with the contested thrones of France and of Baden. Like his father, Philip joined many causes and tilted at many windmills, but entirely contrary ones. Whereas the Third Earl had

Figure 8.2. *Philip Henry, Fourth Earl of Stanhope, (1781–1855).*

been a friend of the Orléans family and a supporter of Louis-Philippe, the Fourth Earl gave his allegiance to the Bourbons and the reactionary Charles X. He said of himself: "I am, as you well know, one of those old-fashioned Tories, who wish that Rights may be respected, all Property may be secured, and that ancient Institutions may be preserved."[55]

Stanhope was anti-High Church, anti-Poor Law, anti-Catholic emancipation, anti-opium trade, and, to the disgust of his Kent neighbors, cared nothing for country sports. His enthusiasms included flying in balloons, teetotalism, and universal suffrage. He was Vice President of the Society of Arts and, like the Second, Third, and Fifth Earls, a Fellow of the Royal Society—giving him ample opportunity to meet most of the principals of our study. His interest in science and medicine led him to become President of the Medico-Botanical Society, to which he gave annual addresses from 1829 onwards. In the first one, he voiced the good Paracelsian idea that the Creator has stocked the earth with plants, and that it is up to us to find out their therapeutic uses.

As we have seen, Stanhope had watched Dupotet's trials at London University and felt that he must defend them against medical prejudice. He himself was a magnetic practitioner: he cured epileptics and gave a course of treatments to his servants and the village people at Chevening.[56] Aubrey Newman, the biographer of the Stanhopes, says that the Earl got into trouble through an over-generous nature. This is exactly what Philip would have wanted to hear about himself, but it cannot have been the only cause of his strange involvement with Kaspar Hauser.

Kaspar or Caspar Hauser (1812–1833) appeared in Nuremberg in 1826, apparently lost and unacquainted with every facet of normal life. Under the care and tutelage of several worthy citizens and professors, he eventually told of how he had spent his youth shut up alone in a cell and fed only bread and water; that he was finally taught a few words and how to sign his name, then set loose in the streets. This rare specimen of a "natural man" untouched by civilization was a godsend to theorists in the Rousseau tradition, and Kaspar attracted much attention. He had abnormally keen senses, and a passionate aversion to eating meat and to cruelty of any kind, gratifying believers in the moral superiority of the "noble savage." It was in October 1829 that Stanhope, traveling in Germany, heard about Kaspar and of an assassination attempt (some said a self-wounding) that had occurred a few days before. Stanhope first met him on 28 May 1831 and for a time was often in his neighborhood. In September the Earl returned to Nuremberg and for two months saw Kaspar daily. He took on an obligation to the city of Nuremberg to be responsible for Kaspar's safety and wanted to take him away as his ward. But instead, Kaspar was moved to Ansbach to become an apprentice, where after a time Stanhope ceased to visit him. Only after Kaspar's assassination (some said suicide) on 17 December 1833 did Stanhope return and speak to people who had known him. By now the Earl was convinced that Kaspar had not told the whole truth about himself and that he was in part an impostor. Kaspar's death a few days after receiving a stomach wound seemed to him to have been the result of suicide, caused by the fact that his story was beginning to break down. Stanhope's final opinion was that Kaspar had been a journeyman tailor or glover from the Austrian side of the River Salzbach.[57]

The account from which this is summarized was written by Stanhope soon after Kaspar's death in response to a book by Anselm von Feuerbach (1775–1833), formerly Stanhope's friend. As President of the Court of Appeals in Ansbach, Feuerbach took responsibility for Kaspar's welfare. He came to believe in the rumor that the boy was the heir to the House of Baden, abducted in the cradle, and replaced by a sickly baby who died shortly afterwards. Everything he observed in Kaspar served to confirm this belief, whereas to the Earl much of what Feuerbach reported about the boy was simply wrong.

Stanhope's efforts to adopt Kaspar Hauser only increased his reputation among his fellow Mesmerists for "philanthropy and Christian kindness."[58] We will meet him again in the next chapter, as an old man still prying into mysteries. But after the Earl's death in 1855, Kaspar's guardian and tutor G. F. Daumer published his own "revelations," in which he virtually accused Stanhope of conspiracy to murder. Daumer's theory was that the boy was probably from an aristocratic English family that had connections in Hungary, or vice versa; that he was in Hungary as a young child when it was decided to abduct him and let him die of privation, no doubt for the sake of a great inheritance that would go to someone else. But the plan went wrong. He did not die, and his captors, unwilling actually to murder him, brought him to Germany and turned him loose in Nuremberg, expecting him to disappear into the lower classes or the army. As publicity and researches about Kaspar grew, the conspirators became worried, and when he gave signs of remembering his youth (recognizing Hungarian words, for instance), they decided to act. Daumer notes that Stanhope was in the city when the first attack was made on Kaspar, and that he may well have been in Ansbach at the time of the murder. The most Daumer will allow the Earl is that he was perhaps not acting in his own interest, but in that of a relation or friend who was the original criminal.[59]

Daumer's thesis was taken up by Jacob Wassermann, author of a popular historical novel: *Caspar Hauser, the Enigma of a Century* (first published in German, 1908). Wassermann devotes many pages to misrepresenting Stanhope (whom he confuses with the Earl of Chesterfield) as a monster of depravity, who having squandered his family fortune was reduced to murdering inconvenient heirs. His account was accepted by

Anthroposophists because Rudolf Steiner, the founder of Anthroposophy, accorded to Kaspar Hauser a major role in the spiritual history of Europe.[60] I will digress on this here, because of the bearing it has on the theories of occult conspiracy to be introduced in Chapters Ten and Eleven.

Johannes Mayer, an Anthroposophical scholar whose recent book examines every facet of Stanhope's and Hauser's relationship, proves beyond reasonable doubt that Hauser was really born in 1812 as the son of Stéphanie von Baden, née Beauharnais, and her husband the Grand Duke of Baden.[61] He suggests that the motive for the abduction and faked death was that this boy was the son of Napoleon's adopted daughter, hence the French Emperor's possible heir. The Bourbons (eventually restored as Louis XVIII and Charles X) would have had most to gain from the removal of the child. By the time Kaspar appeared in Nuremberg, his father's line had been succeeded by that of his uncles, whose legitimacy was in turn under challenge from the neighboring kingdom of Bavaria. A true male heir to the Grand Duchy of Baden would have inconvenienced both of these factions.[62] Stanhope's circumstantial involvement with all of these people, and his constant traveling around Germany, put him at the center of the intrigues around the mysterious youth.

The political center of Rudolf Steiner's theory concerning Kaspar Hauser is that it was he, and not William I of Prussia, who was to have been the collaborator with Bismarck in the unification of Germany. "Was to have been" presumes a plan behind European history; Kaspar's imprisonment and untimely death presumes its frustration by earthly powers. These are two very large presumptions. But prince or not, Kaspar was no ordinary *Bursche.* There are many contemporary witnesses to his beautiful personality, unspoilt by his cruel treatment. G. F. von Tucher, his first guardian, wrote: "Everything I have found in him, including his natural piety and freedom from self-consciousness, gives most fully the picture of the first human beings in Paradise before the Fall." His teacher Daumer called him "the heavenly appearance of an angelically-beautiful, angelically-pure soul."[63] The descriptions of Kaspar's purity of soul and his unjaded appreciation of the beauty of the world put one in mind of the youthful German Romantics such as Novalis, the painter Philipp Otto Runge, and Franz Schubert.

But what became of that impulse? One could almost say that it died with Kaspar Hauser in 1833. Steiner seems to have thought that if a German Romantic, rather than a Prussian soldier, had acted as midwife to a united Germany, that precious germ of Romantic spirituality might have lived and flourished. The Anthroposophist Paul Allen remarks: "in the spiritual individuality of Caspar Hauser we are confronted with a higher Being who doubtless had a task of greatest importance to accomplish upon earth," and one whose murder had incalculable consequences. Allen adds: "It becomes ever clearer that had Caspar Hauser, born under the sign of the Archangel Michael, 'the fiery Prince of Thought,' been able to unfold those spiritual impulses necessary for the progressive development of mankind, the dagger plunged by Hitler into the heart of Middle Europe, with all its catastrophic consequences for humanity, might have been averted."[64]

Steiner does not actually accuse Earl Stanhope of complicity in Kaspar Hauser's murder, as Daumer and Wassermann did, but he hints at a rivalry behind the scenes between the esotericists of Central Europe and the Anglo-Saxons. He says that the latter had been grimly determined since about 1600 to dominate their spiritual epoch (the "Fifth Post-Atlantean," in Steiner's system) and to act as nurses for the succeeding epoch, which was destined to be that of the Slavic peoples. Steiner said in a lecture of 1916: "Just as the Romans were the wet nurse in spiritual connection to Western and Central Europe, so the Anglo-Saxons were to be the wet nurse for the Eastern European peoples and lead them over to their later spiritual life."[65] Evidently Steiner felt that this Anglo-Saxon hegemony had been a disaster, because it had led first to spiritualism, with its false teachings about the soul's destiny, then to a Theosophical Society that spurned Christianity in favor of the East. But since Steiner himself was a Central European occultist, a Christian supremacist, and a disillusioned member of the Theosophical Society, he is hardly a disinterested witness.

Conspiracy theory is anathema to the historian, but indispensable to the history of occultism. It is of the very essence of the occult world view that earthly events are not the result of material cause and effect alone, but that they are influenced by other levels of being. The occultist automatically seeks for a "higher" cause, both in the great happenings that change the course of world history, and in small happenings such as the Kaspar Hauser episode that lack a normal explanation. By raising Hauser to a figure of cosmic significance, Rudolf Steiner unites the two types.

Animal magnetism, in turn, is of the essence of occult conspiracy theory, which hinges on the possibility of deliberate action at a distance and the implanting of ideas in people's minds. There is no need here for the clumsy apparatus of mundane conspiracy theory, such as the Abbé Barruel and John Robison attributed to the network of Illuminati and Freemasons. The occult adept is imagined to work directly on the minds of leaders, who only appear to be directing the destiny of nations. If the destinies in question are not as tidy, or as benevolent, as this scenario would suggest, the reason is plain: evil adepts also possess these powers. The wars on earth then reflect a "war in heaven."

NINE

Visions in the Crystal

One of the themes of Chapters Seven and Eight was the way in which the occultists of the post-Napoleonic period picked up the threads that had fallen in disarray in the 1790s. This chapter traces another of these threads: that of divination through the crystal, or scrying. It is one of the most widespread forms of occultism, practiced since antiquity in almost every known culture.[1] The English tradition has the famous examples of Roger Bacon, whose magic mirror and brass head were the wonders of a superstitious age, and John Dee, with his "shew-stones" of various types, at least one of which is now in the British Museum. After Meric Casaubon's exposé of Dee's angelic conversations, there were surely those who, rather than mocking the Doctor, sought to emulate him. The works of the astrologer William Lilly and of John Aubrey, the collector of gossip and strange lore, describe or illustrate scrying crystals adorned with the names of archangels, as used in the later seventeenth century.

Like ceremonial magic, with which it was closely linked, scrying persisted even in the era of rationalism. The sale of Thomas Britton's magical collection (see Chapter Five) included a "solid round Christal glass," as well as apparatus for the reputedly more perilous method of evoking spirits by means of a magic circle. One of the "Dr. Rudd" manuscripts in the British Museum, transcribed by Peter Smart between 1699 and 1714, illustrates a mirror whose back is inscribed with Hebrew names, and whose purpose was the invocation of the Nine Hierarchies of Angels to visible appearance.[2] Raphael, the leader of the nineteenth-century astrological revival, preserves an "Extraordinary narrative of a celebrated astrologer of the last century."[3] The unnamed author tells that he once lodged in the house of a watchmaker's widow in Little Britain (a small district of the City of London), where an astrologer had formerly lived. The tenant had a dream vision of his predecessor and felt a dreadful shaking of the room. He then discovered a cabinet which he had seen in his dream, with a secret drawer containing the astrologer's manuscripts bound in vellum. They showed that he had once studied geomancy, the crystal, conversing with spirits, the use of sigils, and foretelling by a magic mirror. In 1750, however, he had given up everything but astrology. The secret drawer also contained sigils, mystical jewels, and thin plates of gold and silver inscribed with angelic names in Greek and Hebrew. There was in particular a case of solid gold one inch square, with seven Chaldaic names bordering a large clear crystal, accompanied by instructions on vellum, "A Call to the Crystal." It is very likely that this narrative gave Bulwer-Lytton one of the themes of his splendid ghost-story, *The Haunted and the Haunters.* Crystal-gazing was at the center of the occult revival of the early nineteenth century. It was the perfect occult science for a certain type of investigator. Unlike alchemy, it did not require daily work in an expensive laboratory. Unlike astrology, it needed no mathematics. It was less challenging to the nerves than evocation in a magic circle, and its equipment was more easily concealed. But it was far more exciting than geomancy or the other 'mancies, and, at least as it had developed in England, it seemed to offer no affront to Christian faith.

Although this chapter deals only with the scrying of named individuals, mostly active in London and in touch with each other, there must have been more crystal-gazing going on in the provinces than ever came to light. As a single example that may be the tip of an iceberg, there is a report from 1866 of the practice among the working classes in Lancashire: glass balls the size a hen's egg were sold in Manchester, and much used by women to see what their husbands were up to.[4] The "Mr. P." who reported this to the *Spiritual Magazine* was headmaster of a national school in Lancashire. He had discovered that the local sexton and his son were seers, but that they had not told him because they thought a schoolmaster would never believe in it. They even had a book telling the planetary spirits which presided over the days of the week.

In the metropolis, scrying became popular in the early nineteenth century among the Mercurii and the friends of Francis Barrett, whose *Magus* had included instructions.[5] We know that Barrett consecrated crystals for the use of his pupils (see Chapter Six), and that it was Barrett's circle—taking this in the broadest sense—that initiated the most persistent crystallomancer of the century, Frederick Hockley (1808–1885).[6]

The circumstances of Hockley's birth and parentage are unknown, but like many devotees of the occult sciences, he began his studies and practices at a young age: by his own admission, he was given a crystal and began scrying at fifteen or sixteen, in 1824. Hockley evidently did not go to university; he earned his living as a partner in a firm of chartered accountants in the City.[7] Before becoming established in that profession, he worked for Denley the bookseller, copying manuscripts and doubtless doing other jobs.[8] In Chapters Five and Six, we noted in passing that he was the copyist of Sibly's *Rotalo* (dated 1824) and of Randolph Oxley's manuscript on crystal-gazing. All his life, Hockley made beautiful copies of magical works, sometimes illuminated, which can be seen in various libraries.[9] He wrote down all his own conversations through the crystal, preserving them in thirty volumes (of which six are known to survive), which he would show to very select friends. He was an avid collector of books and manuscripts, acquiring from Denley the manuscripts of Ebenezer Sibly and of Barrett's *Magus*, and also those of Bacstrom mentioned in Chapter Six (now in the libary of the late Manly P. Hall in Los Angeles).[10]

Hockley was not clairvoyant. Like John Dee, Cagliostro, and Max Theon, he had to collaborate with a "speculatrix" or scryer, to whom he dictated questions to be put to the spirits that the scryer could see in the crystal. He approached his work in the most pious and Christian frame of mind, always prefacing and closing it with long prayers as a safeguard against contact with evil spirits.

Hockley believed that use of the crystal had originated with the Jews, who were given it by divine command under the appellation of the Urim and Thummim (Exodus 28:30).[11] He disagreed strongly with the equation, pursued by some skeptical writers in the *Zoist*, of what is said by spirits in the crystal with what is said by mediums in mesmeric trance. The latter, says Hockley, is mere suggestive dreaming, in which the magnetizer's thoughts are picked up by the medium. Surely John Dee was not so besotted (says Hockley) as not to have noticed, over twenty years' scrying, if the responses had been merely the embodiment of his own thoughts. On the contrary, the phenomenon has a much closer connection with the spiritual world than the rationalists of the present day like to think. Hockley had no doubt that some of the spirits were real, departed human beings. He became quite familiar with one of them, a Spanish monk who had been tried for sorcery and burnt in 1693. Another communicator purported to be a living man, Captain Anderson, who was in the Crimean War and had a crystal with him through which he told Hockley of his misadventures.

Hockley found it reassuring that the spirits tended to keep the same prejudices and religious beliefs in the spirit-world as they had had on earth: if they all said they'd become Roman Catholics, or Anglicans for that matter, there would be something to worry about! Hockley envisaged the soul as embarking on a long period of further education in the spirit world, "and when it becomes illumined by the divine mind, and capable of solving *our* doubts, being placed beyond the reach of mortals however magnetic."[12] Such a one was the "Crowned Angel of the Seventh Sphere," a very communicative spirit whom Hockley contacted in 1854 through

Emma Louise Leigh, the daughter of his landlord in Croydon who worked for Hockley from the age of thirteen until she died at twenty.[13] The "C.A." dictated a complete metaphysical and cosmological system—much of it now lost—and converted Hockley from Unitarianism to a more traditional belief in the Trinity and the Virgin Birth of Christ. Apparently even the "illumined" spirits preserve their doctrinal prejudices.

This is how Hockley conceived of the mechanics of scrying:

> The writing which is seen in the Mirror is done by the Spirit forming the letters in his mind as each word passes through his mind, so they take the form of a reality and appear—the Seer who sees and the Spirit through whose mind these ideas pass, are for the time one, but they are united by so slight a cord that the least thought jars it, when it is jarred the writing appears small, and when quite severed the writing disappears until the bond is again completed—they see with the Spirit's eyes, and they read what is impressed upon the Spirit's mind.[14]

This exactly resembles the process by which the "Mahatma Letters" (see Chapter Fifteen) are said to have been conveyed from Koot Hoomi and Morya to the early Theosophists. In the Mahatmas' case, the process entailed a further stage of "precipitation" onto paper by the "seer," who was not a medium but an initiate in training.[15]

Hockley's long experience brought him into contact with most of the people of his age who were interested in the art of scrying. On the scientific side, he collaborated with the Fourth Earl Stanhope,[16] who paid an optician to make Hockley two artificial crystals made from powdered rock crystal and brass.[17] Hockley in return gave Stanhope a black mirror, which made objects and writing appear larger, but was "in some degree injurious to the eyes."[18] He himself had most success using the traditional "crystal ball," a pure spherical rock-crystal.

Hockley was discreet, keeping his crystal manuscripts under lock and key but not unwilling to talk about his unusual pursuit to serious researchers. He made representations to the *Zoist* in the 1850s and gave an interview to the London Dialectical Society during their investigation into Spiritualism in 1869. He showed them a crystal in a silver ring, mentioned that he had about 1,000 books on occult science, and told them his favorite story:

> Some time ago I was introduced to Lieutenant Burton by Earl Stanhope, and he wished me to get him a Crystal, with a spirit attached. I also gave him a black mirror as well, and he used that in the same manner as you would a crystal. You invoke the person whom you wish to appear, and the seer looks in and

> describes all, and puts questions and receives answers. Lt. Burton was greatly pleased and went away. One day my seeress called him into the mirror. She plainly recognized him, although dressed as an Arab and sunburnt, and described what he was doing [. . . Later, Burton] assured me it was correct in every particular and attached his name to the account I had written down at the time, to certify that it was true.[19]

Richard Francis Burton (1821–1890) had contacted John Varley after being sent down from Oxford in 1841 and was fascinated by the astrologer's theories.[20] In 1842 he went to India for six years and became invoved in yoga, drugs, and magical eroticism (he later translated the *Arabian Nights*). Burton wanted a crystal because his plan, which he actually carried out in 1853, was to penetrate the forbidden city of Mecca, disguised as an Indian magician from Alexandria.[21]

The "attaching" of a spirit to a crystal, mentioned in the above quotation, was the same ritual referred to by Barrett as "consecrating." Crystals were dedicated to different types of spirits, usually classified after the seven planetary angels, according to the type of information desired. For finding hidden treasure, Jupiter might be of assistance; for seeing one's beloved, Venus, etc. Hockley also made use of free or unconsecrated crystals.

Hockley kept severely aloof from any form of black magic, but he knew all about it. He disclosed certain spells to one of his friends, a Church of England clergyman, who not only tried it out but published the fact in his anonymous book of memoirs, *The Great Secret* (1896), adding that even now, the terror he felt was still palpable.[22]

From 1853 to 1855 Hockley had a long correspondence with Robert Owen. The social reformer, whom we met fulminating against religion in Chapter Three, was now a convinced spiritualist, and had been publicizing his communications from various great men of the past. These came not through a crystal but through the more modern channel of a trance-medium, Mrs. Hayden. Foremost among Owen's advisers was his old friend the Duke of Kent (1767–1820), the father of Queen Victoria. Although Owen had already been scolded by Prince Albert, in 1848, for pestering the Queen with letters, he could not resist writing to her again about these conversations.

The Crowned Angel meanwhile told Hockley that Owen was utterly mistaken: that he was communicating not with the real Duke of Kent, but with an evil, earthbound spirit. The C.A. offered a form of exorcism with which to call its bluff and dismiss it. Hockley informed Owen of this; Owen thanked him for his advice, but persisted in believing his "Duke of Kent" to be genuine. Far from wanting to keep the matter secret, he published his correspondence with Hockley in his *The New Existence of Man Upon the Earth* (1855),[23] but tactfully inserted blanks where the C.A. had named the evil spirit. This was none other than the Queen's jealous uncle Ernest Augustus (1771–1851), Duke of Cumberland and later King of Hanover, who had insulted Prince Albert and was even suspected for a time of having tried to poison the Queen.

In Hockley's crystal manuscripts, as copied (against his directions) by Francis and Herbert Irwin, there is a report that sheds further light on this episode, and on crystal-gazing in general. I have numbered the paragraphs for easy reference.

> [1] Victoria Regina
> [2] I very much wish to know whether I am to become a writing medium, as I wish to communicate with my father the Duke of Kent—Owen tells me he has heard him rap.
> [3] I have been informed by the C. A. that it is not your Fathers spirit but the evil Spirit of your uncle the late King of Hanover that visits him—
> [4] Oh indeed then I should be very sorry to have anything to do with such things. My husband Prince Albert is also very anxious about the crystal—he has one in his possession but he does not thoroughly understand it—he would be very glad for you to give him any information about it—are you not acquainted with Mr I——g one of my pages
> [5] "Yes and if Mr Gerding will give you my address I will give H.R.H. full instructions upon the subject or Earl Stanhope will give you my address upon your application to him."
> [6] I do not know Earl Stanhope he does not attend court
> [7] Oh then I will enquire about you when I return to Windsor Castle-and if I can find you out I will certainly send for you—
> [8] I thank you
> [9] Victoria Reigns
> [10] Victoria Reigns[24]

Recent scholarship has poured cold water on the attempts made since the 1860s to enroll Queen Victoria to the spiritualist cause.[25] But this document, if taken at face value, seems to show her and Prince Albert in the thick of it. What is one to make of this? Having analyzed it at length elsewhere,[26] I propose the following scenario.

Hockley is holding a session with his seeress, Emma Leigh. Suddenly she announces the appearance in the glass of Queen Victoria [1]. The figure of the Queen speaks [2] into the medium's clairaudient ear, which the medium repeats verbatim to Hockley. He replies [3], and the Queen asks for advice about Albert's crystal [4]. Now Hockley exercises discretion. The Crowned Angel has already put him on his guard against lying spirits, and besides, the protocol for personal contact with the monarch is to go through a courtier: one does not give the Queen one's address in a Croydon boarding house. Hockley does, however, know Earl Stanhope [5]—but the Queen does not [6]. In [7] the Queen's simulacrum announces that she is returning to Windsor; then the medium hears (or reads) the twice-repeated motto at the close [8–10].

If this is what happened, the whole episode may have been a projection from Hockley's unconscious mind, perceived clairvoyantly by the medium. Hockley knew already of Owen's letter to the Queen; he might have known a page at court, who could have told him of Prince Albert's owning a crystal. The Crowned Angel had given Hockley a priceless piece of gossip from the spiritual world, namely that the Queen's wicked uncle was masquerading as her noble father, and fooling a famous man like Robert Owen. Hockley must have been longing to tell her himself, but that was unthinkable. His bottled-up desire projected itself in the form of the flattering request to help the Sovereign and the Prince Consort in their occult researches, after which he must have sat back to await the summons to Windsor. Although it never came, he believed that he had had a real interview with Queen Victoria, and showed the record to the Irwins as one of his prize communications.

Even when deflated in this way—and I would not insist that this is the only explanation—the "Victoria Regina" episode remains full of historical and psychological interest.

Hockley was justly described by a friend as "the most all-round occultist" of his time.[27] His long magical career provides the link between the era of the Mercurii and that of the Golden Dawn sixty years later. Naturally, he was not the only one who took up scrying under the influence of Denley's bookshop and its familiars. Another was Lieutenant Richard James Morrison, R.N., (1795–1874), who became the foremost authority on astrology after the death of Robert Cross Smith in 1832.[28] Morrison had retired from the Navy on half-pay and married a baronet's daughter. As Ellic Howe says, "a highly-educated man with a wide range of rational and irrational interests, he became well known in London society and was welcomed in a good many fashionable houses. . . ."[29] Writing under the name of Zadkiel (the Hebrew name for the angel of Jupiter), Morrison started publishing an annual almanac in 1830 (for the year 1831), at first called *The Herald of Astrology*, later *Zadkiel's Almanac*, which followed Smith's example in varying the technical part (astrological tables and pedagogy) with an attractive icing of marvels and occultism.

Astrological tables are always calculated geocentrically, because they take the point of view of the earth's inhabitants, not those of the sun.

Figure 9.1. *"Zadkiel" (Richard J. Morrison, 1795–1874).*

When it comes to astronomy, however, the astrologers who use these tables are heliocentrists, like most people since the time of Newton. But there have been exceptions, and Morrison was one of them: he was certain that the earth does not move. To combat the system of Newton (condemned by Morrison as a man "bitten by Epicurian Atheism"[30]), Morrison published a book in 1868 called *The New Principia; or, True System of Astronomy*. Like Tycho Brahe in 1600, Morrison believed that the sun and moon go around the stationary earth, while the other planets are centered on the sun. He accepted Kepler's eliptical orbits, but rejected the astronomers' estimate of the planetary distances: the sun, he says with sanguine confidence, is 365,006 miles from the earth; the moon only 36,828 1/2.[31]

Morrison was a Christian supremacist of a strong but not a particularly bigoted type. He spurned the "puritanical, formal rites" like the Sabbath, as opposed to the "pure religion of the heart." He hated the "atheism" of Robert Owen, the blasphemers, and the "revolting Malthusian philosophy" (a euphemism for birth control). But the idea of a community based on love of one's neighbor appealed to him; he found such principles in the work of Charles Fourier.[32]

Given his psychological makeup, it is not surprising that Morrison was led far up the garden path when he started to play with Mesmerism and scrying. In his almanac for 1841 he gives a long report of discoveries made through "E.A.," a young woman of seventeen who answered questions while in mesmeric trance. She gave forth a whole cosmology, resembling Swedenborg's in that she could see the spirits of the dead, each dwelling in its appropriate planet. But whether because of the source, whatever it was, or because of the questions Morrison asked it, the revelations were far inferior to those of Hockley's Crowned Angel. Morrison was obsessed with knowing what had happened to various celebrities after their death. E.A. told him where such as Voltaire, Henry VIII, and the Buddha were now to be found, what they now looked like, and what their state of mind was. She also informed him that the tides are not caused by the moon, but by water expanding under the flow of electricity; that the Round Towers of Ireland were built for astronomical observation; and that the Millenium would come in about thirty years' time.[33]

Ten years later, in his almanac for 1851 (now selling 57,000 copies), Morrison favored his readers with a long series of visions provided by a spirit called "Orion" through Lady Blessington's crystal. From this source the inquisitive Lieutenant learned much gratifying gossip. Naughty George IV was making good progress in the spirit world: since 22 May 1842, he had graduated from purgatorial Venus to heavenly Jupiter, but had yet to join "good old George III" in the highest heaven of the Sun. Alexander the Great was due to be released from his punishment "next Sunday." Judas appeared, looking very wretched, and asked to be let go from the crystal. Sir Isaac Newton promised that astrology would be taught in some of the colleges of England before twenty years had passed. King Solomon, when asked whether he had understood astrology, replied "Yes, but not so well as you do." Socrates appeared, wearing coarse, striped peg-top trousers, and recommended as the best means to obtain wisdom "Astrology, Phrenology, and Prayer." He said that he now accepted Jesus Christ as the Messiah, and wished the scryer a happy thirteenth birthday. As far as the future was concerned, Orion said that Louis Napoleon would never be King of France: he would be assassinated, and the Comte de Paris would eventually reign. A dreadful three-year war was due to break out in 1855, 1856, or 1857, with America, France, Russia, Sweden, and Denmark on one side, England, Turkey, Germany, Hungary, and Norway on the other. England's side was (of course) going to win.[34]

At the time of these consultations with Orion, there was great public interest in the fate of Sir John Franklin, the explorer who had departed on a search for the Northwest Passage and of whom nothing had been heard. Sir John himself appeared in the crystal on 4 February 1850 with the reassuring news that he was well, but short of provisions. Orion reported again on 1 March that the Franklin Expedition was doing well, and was now NW of Melville Island.[35] Unfortunately the discovery of the Franklin Expedition's diary and remains in 1859 showed that Sir John had died in 1847: he should already have been on a planet.

Given that the spirits in crystals of even the highest pedigree were liable to give out such rubbish, it may seem astonishing that anyone bothered with them. The same may be said of the revelations of young persons in a state of "somnambulistic lucidity": they often reflected the most unexamined prejudices of the gentlemen who were controlling them.

There were three intersecting circles of scryers during the 1830s to 1850s. The first, of which we have had a sampling in Hockley and Morrison, were Christian scryers in the Dee tradition who sought knowledge of the spiritual world. A second one consisted of socialites, centering on Lady Blessington's salon. It must have had offshoots in many upper-class houses where crystal gazing became an after-dinner entertainment, until the craze for Spiritualism and table turning took its place in the 1850s. The third circle was scientific and will be treated last.

Marguerite Gardiner, the Countess of Blessington (1789-1849), in some ways resembled Emma Hamilton and Maria Cosway: she too had come from an undistinguished background but managed, through a combination of beauty, charm, and intelligence, to become the central attraction of one of the great salons of her day. We met her briefly in Chapter Two, reporting her impressions of the aged Sir William Drummond. That was during her years of residence on the Continent. Before that, she had married the First Earl Blessington in 1818, and held court in the early 1820s in St. James's Square. John Varley was one of her familiar visitors there.[36] After the Earl's death, Lady Blessington took to novel and magazine writing to support herself in her accustomed style—much as Bulwer-Lytton was doing, and, on the other side of the Channel, the Baroness Dudevant (George Sand).

In 1836, Lady Blessington moved into Gore House, a grand Kensington residence that had belonged to William Wilberforce, on the site now occupied by the Albert Hall. It was here that Bulwer-Lytton, his friend

Figure 9.2. *Marguerite, Countess of Blessington (1789–1849), after Sir Thomas Lawrence.*

Benjamin Disraeli, the Fourth Earl Stanhope, John Varley, and many other luminaries gathered to dabble in the occult sciences. In the walled gardens was a pavilion where the exquisite Count Alfred D'Orsay lived and did his portraits, which (says Michael Sadleir)[37] made him just enough money to keep himself in gloves. One work of his that has survived is a fine drawing of his fellow dandy Bulwer-Lytton, done in 1837. Just as Lytton was responsible for the rule of black evening-dress for men (which caught on after his novel *Pelham,* 1828), so Lady Blessington started the fashion of having a centerpiece of fruit and flowers on the dining-table, instead of some silver or gilt monstrosity.

Lady Blessington was a voracious collector of every kind of object and, one might say, person. After her financial ruin and flight to France, the sale of her effects by the bailiffs lasted twelve days.[38] Long afterwards, Bulwer-Lytton called her "his dearest friend."[39] Over a hundred of her letters to him survive, spanning the period from 1824 to 1849. They are intimate and consoling, and show a true friendship during the period when Lytton suffered miserably from financial uncertainty, electoral defeat, and persecution by his estranged wife.

Soon after Lady Blessington started entertaining at Gore House,

> A craze for occultism seized on the company. Headed by Bulwer and Disraeli, they plunged into discussion and experiment. They listened entranced to Varley's stories of his extravagant friend William Blake; they debated the pros and cons of witchcraft and spiritualism; they even tried their hands at crystal-gazing with the help of a famous crystal given to their hostess by Nazim Pasha.[40]

Nazim Pasha was presumably a high official of the Ottoman Empire. In 1835 he wrote to Lady Blessington in French, sending her a book on medicine and music composed by the Sultan.[41] The famous crystal was a four-inch sphere of pure rock-crystal, consecrated to Michael, the archangel of the Sun.[42] Among other notable visitors to Gore House was Louis Napoleon, Bonaparte's nephew, during his London exile in 1838–1840 and 1846–1848; he also visited Lytton at his retreat, Craven Cottage in Fulham. When Napoleon returned to France after the Revolution of 1848, his court became a similar focus for society occultists, but he gave nothing to "poor Alfred Dorsay,"[43] who had nurtured such high expectations of him. Another foreign intimate of the Blessington-D'Orsay household was Prince Dwarkanath Tagore, grandfather of the poet Rabindranath, who came there in 1842.[44] He and his family were interested in Mesmerism, and all signed the petition to Lord Dalhousie to support the work of Esdaile at his Mesmeric Hospital in Calcutta.[45]

The scrying of the Gore House set was not of the pious and prayerful type practised by Hockley or Morrison. While the presence of Varley and others from the days of the Mercurii counted for something and provided the know-how, the socialites' interest was probably aroused by the lively discussion in literary magazines of the *Account of the Manners and Customs of the Modern Egyptians* (1836) by Edward Lane (1801–1876).

Lane's book contained a thrilling description of scrying through a boy-seer, staged by an Arab magician in Cairo. After receiving Lane and preparing talismans and incense, the magician called a boy off the street, drew the magic square of Saturn on the palm of the boy's hand, and poured a little ink into it. With the magician holding his hand (which, Lane remarks, reminds us of animal magnetism[46]), the boy told of what he saw. The vision began with an apparently traditional sequence of events, including a sweeper, an army, a bull-slaughter, and a feast. Then Lane and his friends asked to see Lord Nelson, Shakespeare, and some of their friends, all of whom were described more or less satisfactorily. Nelson was missing his left arm, but that, said the magician, was because apparitions in the ink are reversed as in a mirror.[47]

Several other Europeans visited the same magician shortly afterwards, including Lords Prudhoe (afterwards Duke of Northumberland), Lindsay, and Nugent, and were mostly rewarded with similar phenomena. Years later, Lane became skeptical, for he discovered that all the successful visitors to the Cairo magician had used the same interpreter: Osman Effendi, an ex-Scottish soldier converted to Islam. Lane suspected Osman of having made it all up—the visions of Shakespeare, etc.—to please his fellow Britishers.[48] This still did not explain how Lane himself, an Arabic scholar, could have been deceived.

Probably the most adequate definition of scrying is that of Theodore Besterman: "Scrying is a method of bringing into the consciousness of the scryer by means of a speculum [mirror] through one or more of his senses the content of his subconsciousness, of rendering him more susceptible to the reception of telepathically transmitted concepts, and of bringing into operation a latent and unknown faculty of perception."[49] Besterman, later a devoted Voltairean, did not come lightly to the last part of his conclusion. He found himself forced to it by the numerous cases in which something has been seen in the crystal that could have been neither in the scryer's mind, nor in that of the questioner's. The Hockley-Burton experiment is one of the most persuasive examples of this type, but the Morrison-Franklin incident shows how unreliable it is.

We come now to the third category of crystal-gazers, those motivated by scientific curiosity. The first prominent man of science to take scrying seriously was Stanhope's friend William Gregory (1803–1858), M.D.,

F.R.S.E., and Professor of Chemistry in the University of Edinburgh. With Gregory's entry onto the scene, the era of gentlemanly enthusiasm began to give way to that of dispassionate psychical research.

Gregory's first interest was in animal magnetism, of which he learned in 1827 through a Dr. Coindet of Geneva, who lent him books on the subject. Being under the impression that it was a skill limited to a few individuals, Gregory did nothing about it until 1842 or 1843, when he tried to magnetize and found that he could do it himself. He could not deny the reality of the clairvoyance that sometimes occurred in magnetic sleep, but he needed a scientific basis with which to account for it. This he found in the theories of Baron von Reichenbach, proponent of the "Od" force. Gregory translated Reichenbach's weighty book from the German, and believed that this odic or odylic force, universally diffused, was the vehicle for clairvoyance and other phenomena. As a chemist, he was interested in the idea that certain substances could concentrate this energy or substance. Rock crystal was one such: Gregory guessed that it was the combination of its odylic influence with the effect of gazing that threw the subjects into a conscious magnetic state, and caused them to see visions in it. When he wrote his *Letters to a Candid Inquirer, or Animal Magnetism* to the Eighth Duke of Argyll in late 1849, Gregory knew of four such crystals that had the property of making children or young persons see visions: one of them was Lady Blessington's, which he says was now owned by Morrison; a second belonged to Lord Stanhope; and another was his own.

Given his chemical approach to the question, Gregory did not approve of artificial crystals, nor of the "magnetized" glasses made in England and sold at a high price to the ignorant. Generally, he says, these are no good except for females who see lovers in them. But he admits that the mere process of gazing renders one more or less lucid and may induce higher states such as exstasis.[50] A more effective substance was that of the smooth, black mirrors used in the Middle Ages, which Baron Dupotet had apparently rediscovered. These, says Gregory, were probably highly charged with odyle, and besides, the dark room, the odors of balsam and narcotics would naturally have led to visions. John Dee had one such mirror, made from jet; it had been owned by a former Duke of Argyll.[51] Dupotet found that the most exciting visions arose in a mirror of charcoal. Others used water, as we have seen in the example of William Beckford (see Chapter Five); Hockley and Lord Stanhope both favored, for certain of their scryers, a spherical glass bottle of water such as Cagliostro had used. Then there was the Arab custom of using ink. Gregory's conclusion was that the whole phenomenon needed very much to be studied scientifically, just as light and electricity were being studied.

The only person known to have associated with all three of the crystal-gazing circles named above is Lord Stanhope. The Kaspar Hauser affair was now long behind him, but his interest in anomalies continued. He told William Gregory that he had experimented with three crystals, assisted by fifteen children of different ages and sex and by seven women, who had seen visions impossible to be attributed to memory, and who had no disposition to deceive.[52] Stanhope was friends with Hockley; he visited Gore House. On 17 January 1853 he wrote to Gregory with a summary of his experiments and conclusions, which is so comprehensive and intelligent that I give it in full here.

> I have deferred to write to you until I was able to communicate the conclusions which I have deduced from a careful and patient investigation, that has now been continued, with very little intermission, for many months, of the phenomena exhibited by Crystals. They are as follows.
>
> 1. A great number of persons, both Adults and Children, have seen in them Visions, some of which were of an extraordinary nature, and such as could not have been suggested by memory.
>
> 2. Those Visions differ in some instances very much from ordinary Dreams, by the length of their duration, by the vivid light and brilliant colours which are occasionally exhibited, and by the nature of the objects that are shewn.
>
> 3. Some persons, few in number, see in Crystals Figures of the human form, each of which when called by its Name exhibits always the same appearance. They are called Spirits.
>
> Those Figures appear, at least in my Crystal, without using any particular Form, termed a "Call" or "Charge."
>
> 5. Writing in printed characters, are also seen by the same persons in Crystals as Answers to the Questions that are asked.
>
> 6. Those Answers are not the results of "Thought Reading" for they often differ from the opinions of those who ask the Questions.
>
> 7. In a few cases correct information has been obtained on events taking place at a distance, but this may have been the effect of spontaneous Clairvoyance, for Mesmerism has been carefully avoided.
>
> 8. The Visions and Writings that are exhibited cannot be explained by Mesmerism which has never been used, or by the influence of Crystals, for the same phenomena are shewn by a globular Bottle, made of thin and fine Glass, without any

defects and blemishes, filled with distilled Water. The Bottle which I use is 3 3/4 inches in diameter.

9. The appearance of those Visions and Writings is not to be explained by natural causes, and is therefore to be considered, in the strict sense of the term, as Supernatural.

10. No means have been yet discovered by me of ascertaining the truth or falsehood of the Answers when given.

11. No reliance can be placed on those Answers, as they have often been found to be erroneous, and even inconsistent with each other, and in some instances full of equivocation and evasion.

12. The Answers are not invented by my Seer who is a very artless, trustworthy, young woman, and who is often much struck by their incongruity, although she is quite unaccustomed to critical enquiries.

13. The Visions and Writings seen in Crystals are however important as they prove to persons who might not otherwise by convinced the existence of a Spiritual World, though the Answers which are received may be undeserving of credit.

14. Those Visions and Writings have an objective, and not merely a subjective reality, for they are not seen except the eye is properly directed, and except the intensity of the light is accurately regulated.

15. It is very interesting to ascertain, if possible, the reasons,

a. that some persons have the faculty of seeing Visions and Writings, while most others do not.
b. that erroneous and contradictory Answers are returned, when those of a contrary nature would, in all respects, be far more suitable to the purpose.

and also to learn

c. the proper means of testing them when they appear.
d. from what beings the Answers proceed.[53]

Stanhope sent Lytton a copy of this letter, at the same time lending him his artificial crystal and its stand, and urging him to keep them as long as he wanted. He gave Lytton the address of William Hockley, and recommended talking with him, "as he has been occupied for many years on subjects which excite your attention; but he can be seen only on Sundays, for he is engaged every week day in the City."[54]

Stanhope also offered to lend his seer, Susan Cook, suggesting that she could stay in the London house of Stanhope's son, Lord Mahon, while working with Lytton. Apparently Hockley's "Crowned Angel" was among the twenty or so spirits that spoke to Susan and displayed writings to her in the crystal. The peculiarity of the Crowned Angel's writing was that each letter was composed of blue and white dots with a red border.[55] Stanhope also urged Lytton to come and visit him at Chevening, promising to meet him whether he came by road or rail.

Lytton and Stanhope were both engaged in serious researches into crystal vision during the early 1850s, but that was only one wing of their activity. Another concerned the "modern spiritualism" of table-turning and raps, recently brought from America by Mrs. Hayden and witnessed by them both. This will be treated in Chapter Ten. The great question arising from both types of phenomenon, and also from the lucid visions of animal magnetism, was whether the communicating entities were truly what most of them claimed to be: the spirits of dead men and women.

Another very busy and well-connected occultist, Kenneth R. H. Mackenzie (1833–1886), was also researching into crystallomancy in the early 1850s. His conclusions are a little different from Stanhope's, but equally skeptical as to the communications from the dead. He gave them early in 1878, in a paper on "Visions in Mirrors and Crystals" to the British National Association of Spiritualists,[56] a group of serious and educated spiritualists whose activities more resembled psychical research than séances. Mackenzie told them that he had taken up crystal-gazing mainly because he was unable to attain clairvoyance in the normal waking condition, and thought trance clairvoyance undesirable. The crystallomancer, he went on, discovers a new and peculiar world with its own laws and order. These were the same in John Dee's time, in the time of William III,[57] and today in the reign of Victoria. The spirits do not pretend to be the highest authority. They are bound by "harmonic laws" and respectful of the Creator, and apparently live active and educative lives.

Mackenzie started his work with the crystal in 1851, after meeting a gentleman in a bookbinder's shop who took him to his home and showed him this new world of beauty. The seeress was a lady of about nineteen, of "average education," who looked into a silvered mirror; a few words spoken emphatically and sincerely were the only charm employed. The sessions lasted for two hours, during which different spirits would come and go. Mackenzie prepared questions, and collected over five thousand answers from her. But, like his instructor, he himself was unable to see anything.

Mackenzie's instructor was almost certainly Frederick Hockley. The younger man writes of "his friend's" vision of Captain Burton, afterwards confirmed; of his instructor's "several essays" dictated through crystals and mirrors, of remarkable philosophical interest but not infallible. Once, Mackenzie said, he went with a scryer to look in John Dee's crystal in the British Museum, and she saw the city of Prague! His years of unbiased research led him to a definite idea of the spirit world and its inhabitants who, he insisted, were not the same as the "subhumans" or elementaries of the occultists.[58]

Earth, Mackenzie explains, is surrounded by several luminous spheres that are interpermeable, with several conditions of spirit life. The lowest level is "unpurified" and bound to matter. Next come the elementary powers of nature, which are only half human. Then comes a luminous earth in which, like a mirror, a universal record of everything is preserved; it is there that our spirit-doubles go when they act on us in dreams, and thence that predictions come. Outside this sphere are the higher spirits, whom we can contact only when in a superior condition of being and able to pass what Lytton calls the Dweller of the Threshold, free from superstitious dread. These purified spirits are in general ignorant of us and our needs, but some of them work for us by warning, never preventing. They set no importance on creeds, knowing that in our future life errors will be corrected, and that "the universe, being infinite in expansion, allows space, or rather states in which all opinions may be held."[59] The spirits have no tolerance for sin, but they say that there is no eternal punishment. Mackenzie fears that his audience may think him too credulous, but tells them that he is simply reporting what he has heard, being unwilling to deny something just because it is inexplicable in the present state of knowledge.

A long book might be written about nineteenth-century crystallomancy. This chapter has concentrated on its role in the lives and thought of people active in the fields treated in other chapters. Crystal working clearly played a great part in their researches, providing them with a gateway to another world (in whatever sense), whether directly or through the use of a medium. It connected with animal magnetism and with the revelations of somnambulists, the main difference being in the apparatus or procedure used to induce clairvoyance. Sometimes the scryer was magnetized as a preliminary; in France, hashish was often used. When used with rituals and with the intention of communing with angels, scrying formed a branch of ceremonial magic in the Judeo-Christian tradition. It stimulated the scientific imagination, at a time when some "natural philosophers" were not quite ready to exclude incomprehensible phenomena from consideration. Lastly, to some experimenters it seemed to offer a channel of communication with the dead, hence a promise of their own survival.

TEN

Hydesville and After

Just as exoteric history has its great battles and revolutions, so the history of esotericism has certain events that change the face of the subject forever. Two of these fall within the purview of this study: the beginning of Spiritualism in 1848, and the founding of the Theosophical Society in 1875.

"Modern Spiritualism," as it was immediately known, began on 31 March 1848 in the village of Hydesville, near Rochester, New York. The circumstances are so picturesque that every historian of spiritualism has enjoyed retelling the story[1] of how the Fox Sisters acted as mediums for the mysterious raps that occurred in their cottage; how they developed a code for communication with the rapper; how it told them that it was not "Mr. Splitfoot" (the Devil), but the spirit of a peddler who had been murdered in the house; and how the discovery of human remains in the basement seemed to confirm that the dead were indeed able to communicate with the living.

To any reader of the preceding chapters, the question must arise of why spiritualism began as a mass movement when it did. Was no one aware that conversations with the supposed spirits of the dead had been going on for ages? And what was so new about mediumship, after the "lucid somnambulists" of animal magnetism, or the scryers? The Shaker community at Watervliet, New York, had had a rash of communications from the spirit world, beginning in 1837, also given through young women.[2] In France, Alphonse Cahagnet thought he had invented a "celestial telegraph" for communication with the dead via his somnabulists and published in January 1848 *Les Arcanes de la vie future dévoilés*.[3] As for the famous rappings, "bumps in the night" are commonplace in the chronicles of hauntings, and the Fox cottage had already suffered from them some years previously. The only thing that was novel about the 1848 phenomena was the publicity that brought crowds to Hydesville and started the sisters on their careers as professional mediums, first in a Rochester auditorium, then in the broader pastures of New York City.

The credit or blame for this goes to Isaac Post, a repectable Rochester Quaker. Post, drawn to Hydesville out of curiosity, started a systematic conversation with the rapping entity, aimed at establishing what it was and how it worked. As his research proceeded, he learned that it was a question of "the forces of human and spiritual magnetism, in chemical affinity," for which some people had more "medium power" than others. Far from being only the sad shades of murder victims, "the spirits chiefly concerned in the inauguration of this telegraphy were philosophic and scientific minds, many of whom had made the study of electricity and other imponderables a specialty in the earth-life, and prominent among them the name of Dr. Benjamin Franklin was frequently given."[4] Moreover, the spirits recommended the formation of "spirit circles" of family and friends in order to communicate with their beloved dead who still watched over them like guardian angels, and suggested animal magnetism as a way to induce the necessary clairvoyance.

The new religion could have been designed by Madison Avenue. It offered evidence of immortality, direct contact with the departed—even pets—and required nothing in the way of intelligence or moral effort, while providing a new field of activity for the growing number of women in search of emancipation.[5] For gullible intellectuals like Post, there was the supreme thrill of talking with the great ones of the past. For hundreds of thousands who had hitherto doubted the immortality of the soul, the new religion offered a grand vista of eternal progress, combined with loving care for those left on earth. "Modern" Christians far preferred this to the prospect of resting in unconscious limbo until the Last Judgement dispatched them to eternal Heaven or Hell. In this respect, it was an exoteric revelation of attitudes long held among Christian esotericists. Moreover, it was not just a doctrine, but a path to the most moving experience that most people had ever had: the apparent communication with their departed loved ones.

Spiritualism never permeated British society to its roots, as it did that of America. Nevertheless, the impact of the Hydesville rappings was felt throughout the intellectual and esoteric communities in the 1850s, thanks to two American envoys, Mrs. Hayden and D. D. Home.

Mrs. Hayden, the wife of a newspaper editor, came to London in October 1852, and advertized her services in the *Times.*[6] She was a passive medium who would sit, sometimes reading to herself, while raps and table-tiltings went on in her presence. Her clients would use an alphabet-board, running their fingers down it, and the raps would mark the letters of the message. It seems very dull in comparison with later and spookier

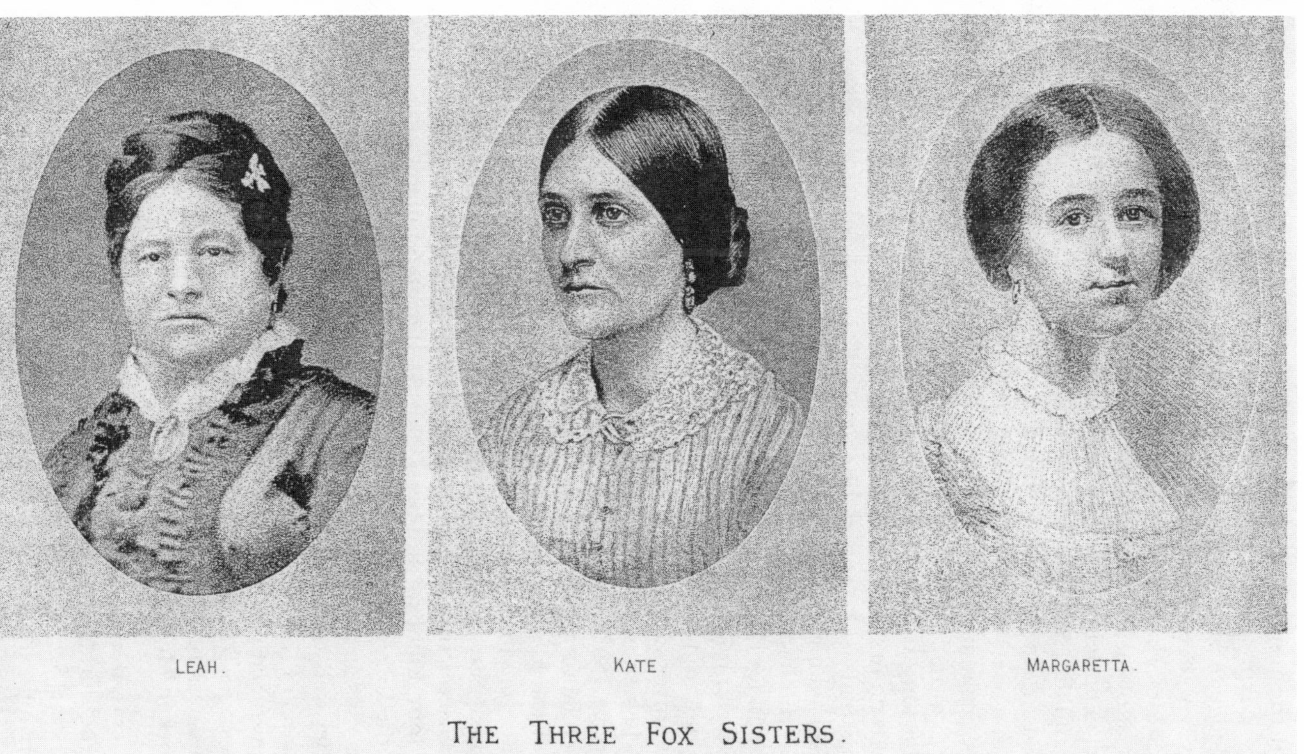

Figure 10.1. *The Three Fox Sisters, from E. H. Britten,* Nineteenth Century Miracles, *1884.*

séances, but the results were often startling enough to convince clients that they were truly communicating with the dead. The messages would show knowledge of private and family matters of which Mrs. Hayden could not possibly have been aware.

One of Mrs. Hayden's converts was Robert Owen, who came to her at the request of his friend Lord Brougham. Owen was more than gratified by the experience. He enjoyed communications with his friends Jefferson, Franklin, Shelley, and especially with the Duke of Kent, whom he consulted in detail about his plans for social renovation. Owen was convinced that the Millenium for which he had been longing all his life would at last begin in 1855. We have already seen the opinion of Frederick Hockley's "Crowned Angel" on the authenticity of these messages, and heard of the long three-cornered debate between Hockley, Owen, and the spirit.[7] Owen in his eighties was as energetic in his profession of spiritualism as he had been for various causes all his life, only now he signed himself "Inspired medium from birth."[8] He still regarded the religions of mankind as "the insane ravings of the undeveloped intellects of humanity," and hoped for their abolition, along with all the professions: priests, lawyers, medical, military, and commercial men. To replace these creatures, who "dare not utter the divinity of truth in their minds," Owen recommended universal science, to be taught to all.[9]

Mrs. Hayden stayed in London for nearly a year, returning to America late in 1853. Another of her converts was Dr. John Ashburner, Elliotson's collaborator on the *Zoist*, who proclaimed himself absolutely convinced of the identity of the spirits.[10] In 1854 Ashburner himself became a writing medium and received messages from his father, who had died in Bombay fifty-six years previously.[11]

This caused a rift between Ashburner and the other members of the *Zoist* circle. John Elliotson and his skeptical colleagues railed in the magazine about the folly and wickedness of the new mediums. The phenomena, such as raps and table-turning, did not worry them in the least: such things, as they well knew, happened all over the world and were doubtless part and parcel of the mysterious energies that they were busy investigating. What outraged these scientists was the claim that the mediums were bringing messages from the dead.[12] One of them, J. W. Jackson, compared the worthlessness of the American craze with the real benefits of Dr. Esdaile's work in Mesmerism. Here is Jackson's analysis of the situation:

> The fact is, the theological mind of Christendom is unsettled; and whether we look to the mysticism of fatherland [Germany], the Scepticism of Paris, the unknown tongues or our own Irvingites, or the recurrent fanaticism of the States, as exhibited in revivalist camps, in Mormon migrations, or in the

> more scientific furor now under consideration, it must be obvious that we have fuel asking for the torch, a mine waiting for the match, a volcano on the eve of an explosion.[13]

Elliotson eventually capitulated. In 1863, he met Home in Dieppe, where the medium reproached the doctor for calling him an impostor without ever having seen him at work. Elliotson was moved by this to begin an investigation of spiritualism, through the mediumship of his friend Dr. Symes's sons. He became convinced of its reality, embraced Christianity, discovered the efficacy of prayer, and henceforth made the Bible his guide. Reconciliation with Ashburner followed, and the former atheist died a pious spiritualist.[14]

Mrs. Hayden's visit to London caused no epidemic of mediumship, no outpouring of information from the distinguished dead, such as was going on in America. The next visitor, David Dunglas Home (1833–1886), came to England in 1855.[15] He had been born in Scotland but raised in America, where he had given a public séance at Mrs. Hayden's house in 1851 and already had a reputation as a remarkable medium. Home is almost unique among those who devoted their lives to displaying mediumistic powers, for he never charged a fee, and he was never caught cheating. His repertoire included not only raps and moving furniture but phantom hands, self-playing musical instruments, levitation, the handling of live coals, and bodily elongation. An effeminate and phthisic man with considerable social graces, Home was patronized by several wealthy women (one of whom he married) and made an unforgettable impression at the courts of Louis Napoléon and of the Tsar.

Home's willingness to cooperate with scientific researchers attracted the attention of some of the hardest heads of his day. Foremost among them were a couple of Scotsmen: Lord Brougham and Vaux (1778–1868), formerly editor of the *Edinburgh Review,* worker for Liberal causes, and Lord Chancellor of England; and Sir David Brewster (1781–1868), a collaborator in Brougham's educational schemes and a physicist who made important discoveries concerning light. Among many weightier works, Brewster's *Letters on Natural Magic* (1832) showed how supposed magic and marvels are all explicable by natural causes. Home's mediumship baffled him, leading to an embarrassing correspondence in the newspapers in which Brewster tried to cover up his initial reaction that "this upsets the philosophy of fifty years."[16] With Brougham (whom the spiritualists would always claim as an ally), Brewster, and Owen, spiritualism joined hands with the progressive, scientific, and educational movement of the Regency period. But the big question remained that of spirit identity. Brougham and Brewster would not commit themselves on that, while Owen committed himself to the point of foolishness. It was the one question raised by spiritualism that would never cease to be debated and never be resolved except in the minds of those for whom it was an article of faith.

Stanhope and Bulwer-Lytton did not hesitate to investigate the new phenomena at first hand, attending séances with Mrs. Hayden.[17] Stanhope seems to have found them convincing. He wrote to Lytton "I could not obtain from [my crystal experiments] any communications with the deceased, and I was told that they forget in another world all that they knew in this. The contrary was however satisfactorily proved by what passed at Mrs. Hayden's."[18] Nor did Stanhope doubt the supernatural nature of the rappings:

> It has been proved, beyond all possibility of doubt, and indeed by my own experience, that the Rappings are not produced by any mechanical means, and I have twice heard them very distinctly when [Mrs. Hayden] was not present. Even if Mrs. H. had the faculty of Thought Reading, of which there is no evidence, and also of influencing the Spirits accordingly, it can hardly be imagined that some person having *both* those powers is present at every Meeting held elsewhere when true answers are returned either by Rappings or by Tiltings.[19]

Later in 1853, Stanhope went to Europe where he continued his researches. He wrote to Lytton from Naples in December, telling him news of table-tilting in Germany, of similar experiments made by French Abbés, of spirit rappings being all the rage in Saint Petersburg, and of a newly invented German instrument called the "psychograph." Here is Stanhope's summary of what it does:

> It points to the Letters of the Alphabet and writes also in Prose or Verse, serious, or humorous, Answers to the Questions of a medium, and sometimes very rapidly, but at other times it will not reply. Its Answers are in German, French, and English, also in ancient, or little known oriental, languages, and it has different orthographies, varying according to the degrees of instruction of those who are present. Sometimes it corrects errors in the Spelling, or in the Style, but is uncertain in the Punctuation. The Questions may be mental or verbal.
>
> It does not predict what ought to remain unknown, or make communications in languages of which the Audience is ignorant, or describe any thing which no one has seen, or reveal secrets which slumber in the Tomb. It does not promote the objects of Stock Jobbers, Diplomatists, or others of that description, or fill up the blanks in History. Its answers refer to

> the individuality of the person who asks the Question, and of those connected with him.[20]

No wonder that Stanhope was planning to revisit Germany to try to acquire this delightful toy, which was later developed into the "planchette" and the "ouija board."

Lytton remained less convinced than Stanhope of the identity of the spirits. When Home came to England in 1855, Lytton had séances with him, both in London and at Knebworth. Home visited the ancestral home of the Bulwers in 1856, in the company of Count Alexander Branicki, a friend of Eliphas Levi.[21] But, like Brewster, Lytton upset the doctrinaire spiritualists by his refusal to come over to their side. He knew that the phenomena occurred, but had no reason to believe them to be caused by the spirits of the dead, rather than by elementaries or by the powers of the mind. Various forms of clairvoyance and telepathy, already manifested by the somnambulists, could account for all the apparent secrets to which the "spirits" seemed privy, while ceremonial magic was able to produce phenomena as yet incomprehensible to science, but not necessarily "supernatural."

Lytton underscored this point in his ghost story *The Haunted and the Haunters,* published in *Blackwood's Magazine* in 1857. The house of the title is haunted by fearful apparitions and noises, in short, by phenomena of the type that the spiritualists attributed to the spirits of the dead. But they turn out to have been caused, instead, by something straight out of the world of the Mercurii:

> Upon a small thin book, or rather tablet, was placed a saucer of crystal; this saucer was filled with a clear liquid—on that liquid floated a kind of compass, with a needle shifting rapidly round, but instead of the usual points of the compass were seven strange characters, not very unlike those used by astrologers to denote the planets . . . Impatient to examine the tablet, I removed the saucer. As I did so the needle of the compass went round and round with exceeding swiftness, and I felt a shock that ran through my whole frame, so that I dropped the saucer on the floor. The liquid was spilt—the saucer was broken—the compass rolled to the end of the room—and at that instant the walls shook to and fro, as if a giant had swayed and rocked them . . .
>
> Meanwhile I had opened the tablet: it was bound in a plain red leather, with a silver clasp; it contained but one sheet of thick vellum, and on that sheet were inscribed, within a double pentacle, words in old monkish Latin, which are

literally to be translated thus:—"On all that it can reach within these walls—sentient or inanimate, living or dead—as moves the needle, so work my will! Accursed be the house, and restless be the dwellers therein."[22]

The *Spiritual Telegraph* was therefore being over-optimistic when it announced in 1853 that Bulwer-Lytton had been converted by Mrs. Hayden's séances to a "larger and more earnest spiritual faith."[23]

Lytton objected to being imposed upon by believers just because he was a public figure and had an interest in these things. In 1850, Elliotson published in the *Zoist* a letter of support he had received from Lytton, but it contained a politely disguised word of caution even against the conclusions of the magnetizers:

I think the manliness of your appeal one of your finest efforts on behalf of the only true mode of following science, viz., experiment of what is before the eyes, with that proper mixture of faith and diffidence which teaches us both the illimitable resources of nature and the little knowledge we have yet acquired of her secrets.[24]

Early in 1853, Morrison/Zadkiel's friend Christopher Cooke tried to get Lytton to put his name to a petition for a giant telescope to be built near the Crystal Palace. This was one of Morrison's many commercial and scientific enterprises, and it had already received the support of that apostle of "Useful Knowledge," Lord Brougham. Although Lytton had attended some of Morrison's crystal-gazing sessions in the early 1850s,[25] he declined to sign the petition, "not being an astronomer."[26] When he was really needed, however, Lytton did not fail: he appeared as a witness on Morrison's behalf when the astrologer sued Admiral Belcher for libel in 1863 and testified that the astrologer had not taken money for displaying his crystal and its powers.[27]

Some years after these events, Lytton spoke and wrote of his conclusions to the Spiritualist Benjamin Coleman, who published them (presumably with Lytton's consent) in the *Spiritual Magazine* for 1867. Coleman had lately returned from a voyage to investigate American Spiritualism at first hand, and Lytton was interested to hear his story of how Judge Edmond's daughter was able to "project her spirit" and appear to friends. This, he said, was the only phase of the subject that was new to him. Challenged by Coleman to say whether he was a believer, Lytton wrote that he had not collected a sufficient number of acknowledged facts for the foundation of a scientific theory:

So far as I have seen or read on the subject, I see no necessity to resort to the machinery of a world of spirits, for the cause of

> effects produced on the senses, which we obtain through material forms, by agencies which originate in another material form (*viz.* the medium) and operate upon or through matter, but not mere matter, than the complicated organism necessary for the utterance of a voice. In all the controversies on this question, I have found no clear definition of what is meant by Spirit; nor does enquiry seem to me to have been directed through the channels demanded by a physiologist or a metaphysician.
>
> All the experiments I have witnessed, if severally probed, go against the notion that the phenomena are produced by the spirits of the dead; and I imagine that no man, who can take care of his goods, would give up his property to a claimant, who could bear cross-examination as little as some alleged spirit, who declares he is your father or friend, and tells you where he died, and then proceeds to talk rubbish, of which he would have been incapable when he was alive. I can conceive no prospect of the future world more melancholy, than that in which Sellaires and Shakespeares are represented as having fallen into boobies—or at best, of intellects below mediocrity.[28]

Lytton would say much the same to the committee of the Dialectical Society in 1869, adding that "The word 'Spiritualism' in itself should not be admitted in rational inquiry. Natural agencies are apparent in all the phenomena (at least as far as I have witnessed them) ascribed to spirits."[29] Such a considered opinion, supported by a lifetime of research and by an ultimate humility in the face of mysteries, was what the *Spiritual Magazine* described in its fractious obituary of Lytton as his "feeble passion for truth."[30]

Bulwer-Lytton, who has loomed so large in these last chapters, is obviously the pivotal figure of nineteenth-century occultism. In Chapter Six, I protested against loose rumors in the less scholarly literature of Lytton being a "Rosicrucian adept," whatever that is supposed to mean. If he was in any sense adept, it was at bringing a rare sanity and balance to subjects that he knew more about than most of their bemused and self-appointed votaries. While acquiring this knowledge, he had reached the top of two difficult professions: that of author—both as novelist and playwright—and that of politician. The talents necessary for these achievements were what saved him from the credulous excesses of a Zadkiel or a Robert Owen, and from the need to boost his ego with fringe-masonic charades. Like W. B. Yeats, the Theosophist and at one time Magus of the Golden Dawn, Lytton knew both the world of the Imagination, from which—aided by magic, drugs, sex, or meditation—the artist in any medium can conjure up "forms more real than living man," and the world of political power and its uses for good or evil. Moreover, if, as seems likely, it was Lytton who led Eliphas Levi into magic, rather than vice versa, that would make him an influence on the French occult revival, which began (by general consent) with Levi's *Dogme et rituel de la haute magie* (1856) and continued through the work of Adrian and Joséphin Péladan, Stanislas de Guaïta, Saint-Yves d'Alveydre, Gérard Encausse ("Papus"), F.-Ch. Barlet, etc.

The most interesting thing about Modern Spiritualism from the point of view of our study is a suggestion found in several sources but little discussed, despite its consequences for cultural and religious history if there be any truth in it. The suggestion is that the Hydesville phenomena were not a spontaneous manifestation, but something provoked by living persons, acting with no lesser intent than that of changing the world view of Western civilization. Reviewing and analyzing this theme will take us far beyond 1848, and introduce characters like Madame Blavatsky who receive their fuller treatment later in the book.

The earliest formulation of the theory seems to have come from Colonel Henry Steel Olcott (1832–1907), co-founder of the Theosophical Society. Olcott had been to London on business in 1870 (during the Dialectical Society's investigation), and had taken the opportunity to visit mediums there. He held conventional spiritualist views, namely that raps, apparitions, moving objects, apports, etc., were all caused by the spirits of the dead. But he began to question this belief when he went to report for the *New York Daily Graphic* on the phenomena produced by the Eddy Brothers in Chittenden, Vermont. It was there, on 14 October 1874, that he met Helena Petrovna Blavatsky and saw how her presence was able to affect the phenomena. Towards the end of the book drawn from his report, *People from the Other World* (1875), Olcott drops a hint:

> After knowing this remarkable lady, and seeing the wonders that occur in her presence so constantly that they actually excited at length but a passing emotion of surprise, I am almost tempted to believe that the stories of Eastern fables are but simple narratives of fact; and that this very American outbreak of spiritualistic phenomena is under the control of an Order, which while depending for its results upon unseen agents, has its existence upon Earth among men.[31]

We can be pretty certain that this idea was planted in Olcott's mind by Blavatsky herself. No one seems to have followed it up seriously for many years, nor tried to define the "order" in question, until early in 1893, when one Charles G. Harrison gave a course of lectures in London. Born in 1855, Harrison was an Anglican and an occultist, but has so far resisted every effort at further identification.[32] One would be tempted to reject his allegations out of hand, were they not set in a discourse of the highest intelligence and the most admirable charity and common sense.

Harrison's story is as follows. By about 1840, modern Europe had reached the "point of physical intellectuality" in its evolutionary cycle, involving it in gross materialism. The various groups of occultists debated as to whether they should counteract this by revealing that there is an unseen world around us as real as the world of sense; and if so, how it could be done safely. Those of the "right wing" were against any profanation of the mysteries; those of the "left," willing to take the risk for the good of humanity. Experiments were made with mediums, first in America, then in France and Britain. "But the whole thing was a failure. The mediums, one and all, declared that they were controlled by spirits who had departed from the earth."[33] Realizing that they had created a Frankenstein's monster, the occultists withdrew from the experiment, but the mischief was done: "The door had been opened to extra-mundane influences, and could not be reclosed." The mediums were thereupon manipulated by the less scrupulous occultists, the "Brothers of the Left," for political or temporal advantage, while the more conservative ones strove to throw discredit on the whole movement.

Almost no one in the esoteric press noticed Harrison's book,[34] but a few of them must have read it; later we will learn of the shocking revelations it contained concerning Blavatsky and her "occult imprisonment." However, corroboration from the side of the Theosophists came the following year, on 21 November 1894, in a lecture given by Alfred Percy Sinnett to the London Lodge of the Theosophical Society.[35] Sinnett says that he has received information from persons whom he believes in a position to know, to the effect that:

> in the beginning the development of modern spiritualism was earnestly promoted by a school of living occultists,—not the school to which the Theosophical development has been due, but a school of which I should never think without great respect [. . .]
>
> I am fully prepared to believe that spiritualism has thus had, from the first, a certain amount of Adept support. Without this, Theosophists will feel pretty sure, a great many of its developments in the beginning would have been impossible. Now, however, the whole system has acquired such momentum, that it has, I venture to think, entirely outrun the original design in one way; though in another—in reference to the effort to show mankind at large, that forces independent of the physical plane are at work around us—it has attained a very imperfect success.[36]

The "persons in a position to know" were probably the Theosophical Mahatmas, Koot Hoomi and Morya, who had corresponded with Sinnett during Blavatsky's lifetime and had not a single good word to say about spiritualists and their beliefs.

When Sinnett came to incorporate this lecture into his book of 1896, *Some Fruits of Occult Teaching*, he explained the status of the school in question as a "subordinate lodge of occultism" acting independently.[37] Evidently Sinnett shared Harrison's belief in maverick lodges of occultists that can work on the superphysical planes, but may make serious mistakes. Koot Hoomi had told Sinnett, in a letter of 1881, of the Adepts' desire to found a new Society as a branch of the "Universal Brotherhood." The Mahatma added:

> The greatest as well as most promising of such schools in Europe, the last attempt in this direction,—failed most signally some 20 years ago in London. It was the secret school for the practical teaching of magick, founded under the name of a club by a dozen of enthusiasts under the leadership of Lord Lytton's father. He had collected together for the purpose the most ardent and enterprising as well as some of the most advanced scholars in mesmerism and "ceremonial magick," such as Eliphas Levi, Regazzoni, and the Kopt Zergvan-Bey. And yet in the pestilent London atmosphere the "Club" came to an untimely end. I visited it about half a dozen of times, and perceived from the first that there was and could be nothing in it.[38]

Twenty years before 1881 would be 1861, the year in which Eliphas Levi performed the evocation of Apollonius in the presence of Bulwer-Lytton. There can be no doubt that a magic circle existed at that time; but did it also exist earlier, and if so, was it involved in the beginnings of Modern Spiritualism? To answer this, we have to turn for a while from England to France.

Harrison and some Theosophists would have us believe that there are adepts who keep watch over the signs of the times, but without divulging their identity. A French Theosophist who wrote as "Jean Léclaireur" in 1895 is not so reticent. Speaking of the Comte de Saint-Germain, Léclaireur says that this enigmatic adept was a disciple of that Fraternity of extraordinarily evolved men who command the forces of nature, and whose goal is ever the material, moral, intellectual and spiritual advancement of the race. Léclaireur, whose name ("enlightener") must have been a pseudonym, adapts a passage from Blavatsky's *Isis Unveiled* in which she mentions the political impact of these *nobles étrangers,*[39] and another on the Druses, a certain "Hermetic Brotherhood of Egypt," and an American

"Brotherhood of Luxor."[40] Of the latter Léclaireur says, in a perfect summary of Harrison's allegation: "It played a capital role in the birth and the propagation of the spiritualist movement, which, despite its mistakes, arrested the flood of materialism which threatened half a century ago to submerge the West." He adds in conclusion that since the Comte de Saint-Germain's seed was spoiled by the French Revolution, another has been planted in the Anglo-American world by Madame Blavatsky.[41]

This theory about the origins of Modern Spiritualism next surfaces in the long series of articles by Narad Mani, published in a French antimasonic journal during 1911–1912. Mani says: ". . . from 1848 onwards, under an impulse given by an occult Centre, the fact of communication with the Invisible had begun to be studied practically everywhere, most often in private circles and by means of individuals of a peculiar psychical organization called mediums."[42] The last phrase is taken verbatim from Harrison.[43]

Many of Narad Mani's facts and opinions were borrowed by René Guénon (1886–1951), a writer of powerful intellect and inside knowledge who, driven by a fierce contempt for both spiritualism and the Theosophical Society, wrote the first of his books against these movements immediately after World War I. In *Le Théosophisme, histoire d'une pseudo-religion* (1921), Guénon amplifies the provocation theory by naming the group in question as the "H.B. of L."—the "Hermetic Brotherhood of Luxor," a later offshoot of the Brotherhood of Luxor or of Light. Guénon alludes to the group as having "played an important role in the production of the first phenomena of 'spiritualism' in America," adding that the H.B. of L. is formally opposed to the theories of the spiritualists, since it teaches that these phenomena are due not to the spirits of the dead, but to certain forces directed by living men.[44]

Guénon is more informative in *L'Erreur Spirite* (1923), saying there that the first spiritualist phenomena were caused by people acting at a distance, by means only known to a few initiates who were members of the "Inner Circle of the H.B. of L."[45] He goes on to give some alternative explanations: either the H.B. of L. provoked the Hydesville phenomena by using the favorable conditions that they found there; or they imparted a certain direction to phenomena which had already begun; or else the H.B. of L., or another agency, profited by what was going on in Hydesville by acting on the inhabitants and visitors through suggestion. Without this minimum contribution, he says, there is no way to explain why Modern Spiritualism began then and there, rather than at the many other places where strange phenomena occurred.

Guénon adds that from the beginning of the nineteenth century there were secret societies in Germany, outside Freemasonry, which worked with magical evocations and magnetism; as a source, he refers us to a book called *Ghost Land* (which will occupy us considerably in later chapters). He says that the H.B. of L., or whatever preceded it, was in contact with certain of these German organizations,[46] which cannot but remind us of the mysterious Frankfurt Lodge mentioned in Chapter Six.

We will leave the provocation theory at this point, but in due course will try to establish what the H.B. of L. was and what it was not.

The present chapter has given no idea of the repercussions of Hydesville on the religious world in general, nor of the conclusions drawn from it by the general run of mediums and spiritualists. That is part of the history of spiritualism, which is at last receiving the attention it deserves from scholars (see note 5) and can in consequence be followed up elsewhere. The rest of this chapter will be devoted to a representative of spiritualist orthodoxy, Emma Hardinge Britten (née Emma Floyd, 1823–1899), whom E. J. Dingwall calls "the most talented and successful propagandist for spiritualism the movement had ever known"[47] and whom Guénon confidently asserted to be a member of the Hermetic Brotherhood of Luxor.[48] Dingwall's biographical sketch remains the main source of information about her.[49]

Born in the East End of London to a sea captain's family, Emma was a sickly, mystical, and musical child. At about eleven she lost her father and was obliged to work as a music teacher to help support her family. At the same time, she was discovered by a group of occultists, which she calls the "Orphic Society," and used by them as a child-medium (see next chapter). It was presumably one of this group who enabled her to go to Paris in her teens to continue her music studies. She worked there in Erard's showroom as a piano demonstrator and hoped to become an opera singer, but that career was blighted by her somnambulism:

> During the progress of her studies at Paris she became impelled to rise from her bed in profound sleep, climb tremendous heights, traverse the wintry streets, preach, recite, and enact fearful scenes; very often the somnambulist would utter wild cries and screams, the result of which was to create so violent an irritation of the vocal chords that she ultimately lost her fine soprano voice . . .[50]

Dingwall mentions a "mystic marriage" that Emma was apparently lured into with a member of the aristocratic Hardinge family, after which she assumed, as in revenge, the surname of the man responsible. Dingwall's further researches, unpublished at his death, uncovered evidence that while working as an adolescent medium Emma had been regularly seduced, or as we would say sexually abused.[51] Her hysterical somnambulism is fully understandable in this light, as are the guarded allusions in her *Autobiography* to a "vicious aristocracy."

Figure 10.2. *Emma Hardinge Britten (1823–1899).*

Returning from France, Emma spent the 1840s and early 1850s as an opera singer, then as an actress at the Adelphi and other London theaters. She does not seem to have been the same "Mrs. Hardinge" who performed as a medium in those years.[52] In 1854 or 1855 she worked for several weeks with an English company in Paris, where she again performed at Erard's. By now, she says, animal magnetism was all the rage, and "my intense susceptibility to occult powers brought me prominently under the notice of the magnetisers, amongst whom were not a few of the highest personages in the land."[53] But her mother prevented her from accepting the offers made by them and instead accompanied her when she was suddenly offered a lucrative contract to go and act in New York.

After one season in America, Emma's theatrical career ended; but a new one began. In 1856 she discovered (or revived) her own mediumistic gifts—much against her will and her Christian principles, she says. A development of her earlier somnambulism, Emma's mediumship now took the form of "inspirational speaking," sometimes accompanied by raps and table-tilting. For several years she worked on the East Coast both as a preacher and as a composer and teacher of music, throwing herself heart and soul into the spiritualist milieu. By 1860 her oratorical powers had made her a famous figure on both Coasts.

Emma's lectures, or sermons, were at first purely inspirational, always unplanned and sometimes based on questions from the audience. She explains them as follows:

> I have never avowed myself a trance speaker, because I am not entirely unconscious; and yet, when questioned what definition I should give to my ability to speak upon any subject committees may choose for me, without a moment's premeditation, I should be absolutely dishonest if I did not acknowledge that the whole of my lectures are obviously, to myself, uttered without thought or volition of my own, and clearly prompted by some attendant intelligences, who, also, to myself as well as to the eyes of many of the most reliable seers, present the unmistakable characteristics of a risen, spiritual, and glorified humanity.[54]

In September 1858, the content of these speeches began to change at the behest of Emma's guides, beginning with a series of eight lectures on "the Origin of All Religious Faiths." Emma writes that there were no novelties there for well-informed students of history, but that her "revelations of Solar, Sex, and Fire worship" and of Messiahs antecedent to Christ were astounding and even frightening to a largely Christian audience. The newspapers protested against her "daring to revive the *theories* of Volney, Dupuis, Robert Taylor, and Abner Kneeland," and some proposed silencing her in the interests of religion.[55] Two years later, Emma's guides permitted her to publish these teachings, as *Six Lectures on Theology and Nature* given in Chicago during October and November 1860. They were taken down in shorthand and published verbatim at her own expense, with any profits to go towards a home for outcast women.

The doctrinal system now given out by Emma was based on exactly the same premises as we examined in the first chapters of this book. She told her audience that the world was not thousands but millions of years old, and that the cradle of civilization was in the East. It was there that the first worship had arisen, that of the powers of nature. This developed into cults of the sun and of its passage through the zodiac, creating an astronomical religion whose vestiges survive throughout the known world,[56] and which is the origin of all known religions, including Christianity.[57] The priests of every nation exploited the mysterious side of religion, encouraging cults of celestial and natural objects without telling the people that these were all subordinate to the one God. It was the priests, too, who in every religion instituted sacrifices in order to sustain their own power and splendor.[58]

Emma, or her guide, praised the founders of religions—Christ, Moses, Osiris, Buddha, and Zoroaster—for breaking the chains of priestcraft; but every time, the priests forged them the stronger. She railed at the dogmas of Nicea and the Thirty-Nine Articles of the Anglicans; she told the Christians that their denial of all other religions was atrocious; and she urged her listeners to go and read the Book of Nature if they wanted to know the true God. As the lecture course proceeded, she expounded the doctrine of the macrocosm and the microcosm (the sun corresponding to the human heart),[59] and the new theory of evolution. She praised death as the necessary transformational agent of nature, without which there could be no development, and refused its identification with sin, which has no part in nature but what humans have given it. She told of how death leads us on to the spirit world, whence we become the guardians of those we loved on earth.[60] Finally, she gave a series of gruesome quotations taken from Christian writers who exulted in the prospect of eternal torment, especially that of unbaptized infants.

It must have been an impressive performance, and it could have come straight from the pages of Robert Taylor, the "Devil's Chaplain." Emma, or her guide, had achieved the marriage of spiritualism with the mythography of the Enlightenment. The "self-sustaining institution for homeless and outcast females," whose prospectus completes the volume of lectures, allied this new religion with the humanitarian and socially progressive movement of its day. In Emma's synthesis, spiritualism becomes a complete religion, with a cosmology and an eschatology, a version of world history able to explain all myths and religions, a devotional practice in the form of a sort of unitarian prayer, and a social or socialist program for this world.

Looking back now to what C. G. Harrison said about the course of spiritualism, I imagine that this alliance is what he interpreted as the manipulation of mediums by "Brothers of the Left" for political and temporal advantage. As an adherent, however esoteric, of doctrinal Christianity, Harrison could not have approved the demotion of his own faith. Emma's system, which soon became the standard one of the "Higher Spiritualism," has a place for Jesus as a sublime moral teacher, but absolutely none for Trinitarian or sacramental Christianity. Nor does it regard the angels of the Western esoteric tradition, whose veneration Harrison wished the church to revive, as anything but advanced and once-human souls.

As for the provocation theory, this exceeds the scholar's brief, for there is no consensus at present on whether such manipulation is possible. The discussion of occult conspiracy at the end of Chapter Eight is relevant here. I can well imagine certain occultists as believing that humanity would be best served by the wider diffusion of such doctrines and attitudes as were outlined in Emma's lectures and taking whatever steps they thought would further this plan. Insofar as the Higher Spiritualism was aimed at taking away the fear of death and at breaking down the barriers that race, class, religion, and sex have erected between human beings, their enterprise can be seen as part of the general philanthropic movement of the mid-nineteenth century. Esotericists of the "left," including most Theosophists, will approve their efforts; those of the "right," including traditionalists of the Guénonian type, will not.

ELEVEN

From the Orphic Circle to the Golden Dawn

In this chapter we continue to worry at the vexed question of the beginnings of spiritualism and its connection with secret groups of occultists. Led by the few clues sown by Emma Hardinge Britten, we will find evidence of a group active in the 1830s, called the "Orphic Circle" or "Orphic Society," and, emerging from that, a line of succession that becomes more and more definite until it culminates in 1888 with the foundation of the "Hermetic Order of the Golden Dawn," probably the most famous of all occult orders.

During the American Civil War, Emma worked indefatigably for the Unionist cause, raising money and lending her speaking talents to Lincoln's campaign in 1864. For the rest of the decade she moved to and fro between England and the United States, collecting material for her great history of the spiritualist movement to date (*Modern American Spiritualism,* 1870). She testified in 1869 before the committee of the London Dialectical Society, confirming Lytton's statement that atmospheric conditions have an effect on spirit manifestations: she said that she had found her own powers much lessened since coming to London and was going to Scotland to recharge them.[1]

Emma published *Modern American Spiritualism* herself, with the financial assistance of a "noble English gentleman" whom she does not name, but who, she says, is known to all the spiritualist community.[2] In October 1870 she married Dr. William Britten, a Mesmeric physician, and settled with him in Boston. In 1872 the Brittens started a spiritualist magazine, *The Western Star.* Emma wrote to her friends asking for contributions. One of these was Robert Fryar, the bookseller of Bath, who submitted a study of "Crystals and Crystal-Seers."[3] But Emma's new life was short-lived: the offices of *The Western Star* were destroyed, along with her property and much of the commercial center of Boston, in the fires of 9–11 November 1872. Left almost without resources, the Brittens moved back to New York. Soon afterwards they were running a joint practice in "electrical therapeutics."[4]

It is not Emma who interests us now, so much as a mysterious friend of hers, who was among the people asked to contribute to the ill-fated *Western Star*. The "autobiographical sketches" he provided under the pseudonym of "Austria" are the most prominent thing in the magazine, appearing in all six numbers.[5] Emma, as editor, reveals that he is a German-speaking gentleman who has moved in public positions with distinction for more than fifty years. The translator of the sketches is an Americanized German who has long known him and has been assured by one of his relatives, a maiden lady who occasionally attended the late Empress of Austria, that everyone thought he had sold his soul to the devil![6]

These sketches were expanded over the next few years into a novel-sized book, published by the Brittens in 1876 as *Ghost Land; or, Researches into the Mysteries of Occultism*. In the same year they also published his treatise *Art Magic, or, Mundane, Sub-Mundane, and Super-Mundane Spiritualism.* The two books, taken together, are the first authoritative statement in English on the distinction between spiritualism and occultism. They are also one of the major mysteries facing the historian of this subject.

Emma Hardinge Britten always stoutly maintained that *Ghost Land* and *Art Magic*'s author was a real person whom she had known for a long time; that *Ghost Land* was only published "on strict condition of suppressing all names, dates, places, and all accessories that would tend to identify him," and that the author never approved or corrected the English version.[7] By 1876 he was living in Havana and going under the alias of "Chevalier Louis de B——," and Emma was showing photographs of him to Lady Caithness, Stainton Moses, and Henry Olcott. These showed a man in his thirties whom the Colonel thought looked like a "sick sensitive," a "fashionable lady-killer" in mutton-chop whiskers.[8] But this may have been part of Emma's plan to conceal his identity through disinformation.

Dr. E. J. Dingwall, the psychical researcher and writer on anomalies, thought that the best candidate for "Louis" was Baron Joseph Henry Louis de Palm (1809–1876).[9] There is no doubt that Palm, who lived a gallant life around the courts of Europe before ending up penniless in New York, fits the persona of "Austria." But whether he was capable of putting two sentences together is another matter. Olcott knew Palm as an early member of the Theosophical Society; he cared for him in his last days and organized his "pagan funeral" and cremation (the first cremation in America).[10] For all his kindness to Palm, Olcott considered the man a decrepit adventurer with no literary or intellectual talent whatever. Others attribute the books to Emma herself, or to William Britten, for no better reason than that the Brittens got them into print.

Given so uncertain an identity, we can only take Louis's autobiography as fiction. But even if it is only a novel, it is a very good one, rivalling *Zanoni* in occult insights and thrills. Louis says that he was born in Hindustan (about 1825[11]), his mother being Italian and his father an exiled Hungarian nobleman who had become a distinguished officer in the British Indian army.[12] At the age of ten (about 1835), Louis was sent to Europe for his education, to be prepared to resume the Hungarian title and estates. At twelve, he came under the tutelage of a German professor of Oriental languages, Felix von Marx, who had also been born and had travelled in the East. Having discovered that Louis was a natural medium, Marx used the boy for the experiments of his circle of researchers. Louis says: "The particular association to which I was first introduced constituted the German branch of a very ancient secret order, the name and distinctive characteristics of which neither I nor any other human being is privileged to mention . . ."[13] For convenience, he calls them the "Berlin Brotherhood." Their purpose was scientific research, and their scientific instruments the young mediums in a state of somnambulism. "This state, they had found, could be induced sometimes by drugs, vapors, and aromal essences; sometimes by spells, as through music, intently staring into crystals, the eyes of snakes, running water, or other glittering substances; occasionally by intoxication caused by dancing, spinning around, or distracting clamors; but the best and most efficacious method of exalting the spirit into the superior world and putting the body to sleep was, as they had proved, through animal magnetism."[14]

Louis's description of his first entry into "lucidity" is one of the best in the literature:

> Like a mountain bearing down upon my shoulders, columns of fiery, cloud-like matter seemed to stream from the professor's fingers, enter my whole being, and finally crush me beneath their terrific force into a state where resistance, appeal, or even speech was impossible. A vague feeling that death was upon me filled my bewildered brain, and a sensation of an undefinable yearning to escape from a certain thraldom in which I believed myself to be held, oppressed me with agonizing force. At length it seemed as if this intense longing for liberation was gratified. I stood, and seemed to myself to stand, free of the professor's crushing hand, free of my body, free of every clog or chain but an invisible and yet tangible cord which connected me with the form I had worn, but which now, like a

> garment I had put off, lay sleeping in an easy-chair beneath me. As for my real self, I stood balanced in air, as I thought at first, about four feet above and a little on one side of my slumbering mortal envelope; presently, however, I perceived that I was treading on a beautiful crystalline form of matter, pure and transparent, and hard as a diamond, but sparkling, bright, luminous and ethereal. There was a wonderful atmosphere, too, surrounding me on all sides. Above and about me, it was discernible as a radiant, sparkling mist, enclosing my form, piercing the walls and ceiling, and permitting my vision to take in an almost illimitable area of space, including the city, fields, plains, mountains, and scenery, together with the firmament above my head, spangled with stars, and irradiated by the soft beams of the tranquil moon. All this vast realm of perception opened up before me in despite of the enclosing walls, ceiling, and other obstacles of matter which surrounded me. These were obstacles no more. I saw through them as if they had been thin air; and what is more I knew I could not only pass through them with perfect ease, but that any piece of ponderable matter in the apartment, the very furniture itself, if it were only brought into the solvent of the radiant fire mist that surrounded me, would dissolve and become, like me and like my atmosphere, *so soluble* that it could pass, just as I could, through everything material. I say, or seemed to see, that I was now *all force*; that I was soul loosed from the body save by the invisible cord which connected me with it; also that I was in the realm of soul, the soul of matter; and that as my soul and the soul-realm in which I had now entered, was the real force which kept matter together, I could just as easily break the atoms apart and pass through them as one can put a solid body into the midst of water or air.[15]

Reports such as this one had convinced the Berlin *Naturphilosophen* that "every fragment of matter in the universe represented a corresponding atom of spiritual existence," and that "this realm of spiritual being was the essence, force, and real substance of the material." One might say that, long before Einstein, they had hit upon the equivalence of matter and energy. They could accept that the human being, too, could exist in spiritual as well as material mode, and that all the physical elements possessed corresponding spiritual beings, some less and others more powerful as one rose from elementals to the spirits of the planets and stars. Among their visitants was a "crowned angel" who categorically denied human survival. Following their tutelary spirits, the Berlin Brothers believed that the human soul or spirit has no permanence, but is absorbed into the general spiritual economy, as the body into the physical. There was for them no absolute immortality, either for man or star.

The Berlin Brotherhood's mediums were not restricted to the role of passive observer, as were Dupotet's somnambulists or Hockley's clairvoyants, but could interact with the material plane. One of their experiments involved the deliberate causing of poltergeist-type disturbances. Louis describes it:

> On one occasion, the society having thrown me into a profound sleep by the aid of vital magnetism, and the vapors of nitrous oxide gas, they directed my "atmospheric spirit" to proceed, in company with two other lucid subjects, to a certain castle in Bohemia, where friends of theirs resided, and then and there to make disturbances by throwing stones, moving ponderable bodies, shrieking, groaning, and tramping heavily, etc., etc. I here state emphatically, and upon the honor of one devoted only to the interests of truth, that these disturbances were made, and made by the spirits of myself and two other yet living beings, a girl and a boy who were subjects of the society; and though we, in our own individualities, remembered nothing whatever of our performance, we were shortly afterwards shown a long and startling newspaper account of the hauntings in the castle of Baron von L——, of which we were the authors.[16]

This is an important passage for the light that it sheds on the topic of the previous chapter. The theory that the Hydesville phenomena were provoked and controlled by living persons rests on the assumption that such things are possible. What *Ghost Land* offers is a philosophic theory to support this hypothesis, and a historical context for such operations. One is then at liberty to regard the book as fact, as fiction, or as a mixture of the two.

Continuing Louis' narrative, he left Germany at about eighteen for a military school in England, to prepare for a career in the Indian Army. He brought with him letters of introduction from Professor Marx to the British occultists, who were nearly all "members of secret societies, and, with one exception, pursued their studies in the direction of magic, deeming they could ultimately resolve the nature and use of all occult powers into a scientific system, analogous to the magical art as practised in the days of antiquity."[17] One naturally wonders whether these British occultists bear any relation to the groups of which at least a little is known. Louis' description could refer equally well to the Mercurii, to the British disciples of Lavater, Mesmer, and von Reichenbach, and to the gentlemanly investigators of occult sciences like Colquhoun, Townshend, Elliotson, Stanhope, and Lytton, all of whom were skeptical about any claims of converse with the dead. Like the Berlin Brotherhood, these men believed themselves to be working with unknown natural forces, which some of them called elementals or elementaries. They were already occultists, as distinct from spiritualists.

In our last quotation from him, Louis mentions "one exception" among these London societies, which he now describes:

> During our residence in London we were constant attendants and welcome visitors at a circle which for distinction I shall name the Orphic Circle. Its president and "Grand Master" was a noble gentleman whom I shall call Lord Vivian.
>
> His methods were inspired by far loftier aims and regulated by much more pious aspirations than those of most other English magians. The seers, of whom Lord Vivian's society numbered several, conducted their experiments through the mirror and crystal, and the young ladies especially who attended these interesting séances, were particularly happy in attracting pure and noble planetary spirits in response to their call.[18]

This sounds very much like the reverent attitude of Hockley or Morrison. Here is a description of what took place at the meetings of the Orphic Circle:

> On the night of March 15 our session commenced at 9 p.m. and our lodge was opened with the usual formalities. Our four neophytes were stationed by the altars, each with the mirror and crystal appropriate to the time. The four lamps which sufficed to dispel the darkness of the lodge were lighted, the braziers duly served, and the fumigations carefully attended to. After the opening hymns had been sung and the invocations commenced, the lamps began to flicker with the usual unsteady motion which indicates responses from the spirits summoned, and in a short time they went out one after another, leaving the room only faintly illuminated by the colored fires from the braziers.[19]

Did they sing Thomas Taylor's translations of the Orphic Hymns, each with its instructions for the proper fumigation? One wonders. Their mirrors were consecrated to angels with Hebrew names, of course—Louis mentions Azrael.[20] But before speculating further, one should ask whether this Orphic Circle ever existed, or whether, with the rest of *Ghost Land*, we are dealing with mere fiction.

The one piece of corroborative evidence comes, as one might expect, from Emma Hardinge Britten herself, who says that the Orphic Circle was none other than the group of London occultists who had employed her as a child-medium. She published the following account in her magazine *The Two Worlds* over the name of "Sirius." But we know that she was the author, because she repeats much of it in her autobiography, also confirming there that this "Orphic Society," as she calls it, was the same as the Orphic Circle of *Ghost Land*, and that it was there that she first met Louis.[21]

> My own claims to be considered as an exponent of true Occultism are founded upon the following grounds: When quite young, in fact, before I had attained my thirteenth year, I became acquainted with certain parties who sought me out and professed a desire to observe the somnambulistic faculties for which I was then remarkable. I found my new associates to be ladies and gentlemen, mostly persons of noble rank, and during a period of several years, I, and many other young persons, assisted at their sessions in the quality of somnambulists, or mesmeric subjects. The persons I thus came into contact with were representatives of many other countries than Great Britain. They formed one of a number of secret societies, and all that I am privileged to relate of them is, that they were students of the two branches of Occultism hereafter to be described [Cabbalistic and Practical]; that they claimed an affiliation with societies derived from the ancient mysteries of Egypt, Greece, and Judaea; that their beliefs and practices had been concealed from the vulgar by cabalistic methods, and that though their real origin and the purpose of their association had at times been almost lost, it had revived, and been restored under many aspects. They claimed that alchemy, mediaeval Rosicrucianism, and modern Freemasonry were off-shoots of the original Cabala, and that during the past 150 years new associations had been formed, and the parties who had introduced me into their arcanum were a society in affiliation with many others then in existence in different countries. [. . .] it was one of their leading regulations never to permit the existence of the society to be known or the members thereof named, until they passed from earth to the higher life. It is in virtue of this last clause that I am at liberty to say that Lord Lytton, the Earl of Stanhope, and Lieut. Morrison (better known as "Zadkiel"), and the author of "Art Magic," belonged to this society.

> I should have known but little of its principles and practices, as I was simply what I should now call a clairvoyant, sought out by the society for my gifts in this direction, had I not, in later years, been instructed in the fundamentals of the society by the author of "Art Magic." When modern spiritualism dawned upon the world, for special reasons of my own, the fellows of my society gave me an honorary release from every obligation I had entered into with them except in the matter of secrecy.[22]

This supplies a connection of the utmost significance, for it shows that Emma received her occult formation among Lytton, Stanhope, Morrison, and their friends in the 1830s. She was working in occultism years before spiritualism appeared on the scene. It was not without cause that she claimed to speak with authority on the difference between the two.

Emma, in the above quotation, mentions the prohibition in the Orphic Circle against revealing members' names until they have died, which conveniently allows for enrolling people no longer in a position to object or to deny their membership! There would be no reason to believe a word of what Emma, or Louis, says, were their accounts not suspiciously close to the few facts that we do know about Lytton, Stanhope, and Morrison, and incidentally to Lytton's "magick" club mentioned by Koot Hoomi (see Chapter Ten). Probably a secret magical group did exist in London between the crystal-gazing craze of the 1830s and the Dialectical Society's investigation of the late 1860s, and Bulwer-Lytton took part in it. Eliphas Levi's evocations of Apollonius of Tyana (see below) might have taken place under its auspices.

In an article of 1888, Emma pushes the origins of this secret society further back in time. She informs her readers that "true occultism," which makes no public demonstration of its pretensions, was organized into secret associations in England more than fifty or sixty years ago. She adds that the experiences related in *Ghost Land* under fictitious names and dates really did occur in an organization established quite three-quarters of a century before even Modern Spiritualism, much less Theosophy or occultism, were publicly talked of.[23] This would take us back to the last quarter of the eighteenth century, in which we know that occult groups were beginning to form. Emma evokes a continuity stretching over more than a century, which is something to be kept in mind when in a later chapter we come to consider the "Hermetic Brotherhood of Luxor" of the 1880s and her possible role therein.

Reserving Louis's further adventures for Chapter Fourteen, the rest of this chapter is devoted to some developments that, if not directly stemming from the Orphic Circle, at least involved some of the same people.

A new generation was now growing up in England to encounter spiritualism during their most impressionable years. The first to enter the arena that we have been exploring in the past few chapters was Kenneth Robert Henderson Mackenzie (1833–1886), an exact contemporary of D. D. Home.[24] (His analysis of crystallomancy appeared in Chapter Nine.) Raised in Vienna, where his father was a physician, the young Mackenzie was a prodigy of erudition. By the age of seventeen he was making frequent contributions to *Notes and Queries*; before he was twenty-one, he had been elected a Fellow of the Society of Antiquaries, in recognition of his annotated translation of a German book on the Middle East; in 1855 he became a Member of the Royal Asiatic Society after publishing a book on Burma.

Mackenzie started his own magazine, *The Biological Review*, in 1858. According to one of the collaborators, it was originally intended to be called *The Pythagorean*, and to take the place of *The Zoist*, which had ceased in 1856, in "connecting and harmonizing practical science with little understood laws governing the mental structure of man."[25]

Mackenzie's chief colleague was Morrison, who probably helped out financially and used the magazine's covers to advertise his household inventions, secondhand books, etc. Hockley contributed messages from a spirit that appeared in a mirror to recommend a Christianity based on the exemplar of Christ, without sacraments, Old Testament, or any church.[26] Mackenzie seems to have been of like persuasion, urging his readers not to reduce the spiritual world, as the *Zoist* group had, to a facet of the material one. "Fearless in a reliance upon the principles of the Christian religion, we display upon our title the Holy Cross of the Egyptians,—the founders of all knowledge upon these subjects—and, confiding in that symbol of Eternal Life [the ankh], we feel assured of ultimate victory."[27]

The use of the ankh as emblem for the magazine was not the only connection with the "unveiling of Isis" by the mythographers with whom we were concerned in the first four chapters. Morrison was evidently well read in that literature. He wrote a learned account of the Hindu yugas and the relation of their numbers to astrology, citing Sir William Drummond on the Book of Joshua. An article on the Hindu gods says that the Indian gods are astrological, as is the Buddhist Wheel of the Law. It attacks the crass ignorance of the Baptist missionaries and approves Francis Wilford's theories. Morrison adds that nearly all the deities of India and, in fact, of the Western world resolve themselves into male or female sun gods, the twin sexes being due to the sun's passing through masculine and feminine signs of the zodiac.[28] This is all familiar ground to us.

Mackenzie's own contributions included the revelations of a certain "S.J." These came through the mediumship of a relative of Mackenzie,

Figure 11.1. *Kenneth R. H. Mackenzie (1833–1886).*

presumably through the crystal; he himself possessed a "very fine globe of rock-beryl."[29] S.J. taught a doctrine of the imitation of Christ, but not the belief that he was sacrificed to a vengeful Father-God. Christ did die for our sins, he added, but only in the sense of giving us an example for life and for the endurance of pain. S.J. spoke of the Inward Light, the Holy

Ghost within us, which, if listened to, will always guide us aright and which is increased by the practice of charity. He then explained the mechanism of his own communication. When man fell from his original state, said S.J., God allowed half of his spirit to wait in an intermediate state, awaiting the release of the other half at death. "During the life of man, these atmospheric spirits hover over and partake, to a great extent, in his worldly affairs; it is difficult to explain, but they are in a manner a portion of the released thoughts of man, and to a seer in the chrystal or mirror if a pure-minded one, they will often appear, and show what may come to pass, provided the man guides his thoughts and actions rightly, and in such a manner as to assimilate with the purer spirit."[30] In the last number of the *Biological Magazine*, Mackenzie tells his readers that he parted from S.J. "with mutual good wishes" on 16 December 1858, adding the surprising information that S.J. had in fact been a living man.[31]

The reader will have to decide whether this could possibly be another instance of a "hidden hand" applied by a living person using occult means. It is certainly unique in its period, when all communications were assumed, and claimed, to come either from the dead or from permanent denizens of the spiritual world. Mackenzie makes no allowance for it in his 1878 paper to the British National Association of Spirituals; perhaps by then he had changed his mind about the spirit's identity. The character of "S.J." carries a flavor of C. G. Harrison, in the sense of being another Christian initiate who seems to stand aloof from the lesser occultists and to speak with a sense of conviction far different from the dogmatic or sentimental messages of the typical "spirit." I take note of S.J. in the same way that Lytton received what Coleman told him about Judge Edmond's daughter and her astral projection: it is a "new phase of the subject."

In 1861 Mackenzie paid a visit to Paris, where his father was now working as a physician, and had two interviews there on 3 and 4 December with Eliphas Levi—otherwise Alphonse Louis Constant (1810–1875). Levi, who spoke no English, had been to England in the spring of 1854, as every student of occult history knows. On that visit, an unknown woman met him and, dropping the name of "Sir B—— L——," persuaded him to perform a ritual of magical evocation, using books that she provided.[32] Levi, who up to then had no known occult experience, nor even much knowledge of magic, performed the ritual alone and obtained the answers to the two questions that were the object of the evocation. He remained skeptical as to the identity of the apparition—supposedly Apollonius of Tyana—that had certainly been visible to him. He repeated the evocation at least twice more, once in 1861 on the roof of the Pantheon, a large store in Regent Street. Bulwer-Lytton was one of the three persons present on that occasion, but while Levi has left a full and circumstantial account of what "Apollonius" looked like, there is no record of what, if anything, Lytton saw.

On Mackenzie's return to England he saw Frederick Hockley, who sat him down then and there to write an account of his interviews. It circulated in manuscript and was published for the delectation of the Societas Rosicruciana in Anglia (see below) in 1873.[33] In his conversations Levi showed a high regard for Bulwer-Lytton and an interest in the state of magical and occult studies in England. He also expressed absolute unbelief that the spirits of the dead can return to communicate with the living. Another interview that Mackenzie had on this visit was with Allan Kardec, founder of the reincarnationist school of French spiritualism, whose views were the absolute contrary of Levi's. Mackenzie told Kardec of the progress that was being made in England, and of why he himself preferred communicating with the spirit world through crystals, mirrors, or vessels of water, rather than through mediums. All that Mackenzie learned in Paris led him to consider the English considerably in advance upon the French.[34]

Mackenzie's particular interest was in the Tarot, and in whether Levi intended to issue a complete set of the cards whose occult significance had been suggested by Court de Gébelin in *Le Monde Primitif* of 1776 (see Chapter One). Levi showed him his own hand-drawn pack, the work of twenty years, and encouraged Mackenzie to publish a set in England. According to the Yeats scholar Roger Parisious, Mackenzie did prepare a book-length manuscript on the subject, but this was never published.[35] There is much to be established about the relation of Mackenzie's and Levi's Tarot interpretations to those of Papus, A. E. Waite, and W. B. Yeats; but this does not enter into our story.

Poor Mackenzie never fulfilled the promise of his brilliant youth. We know from Hockley that he had a drinking problem and a habit of alienating his well-wishers. Mackenzie's next collaboration with his fellow occultists came with the foundation in 1866 of the Societas Rosicruciana in Anglia (S.R.I.A. or "Soc. Ros."). All research into the S.R.I.A. is hampered by the fact that its official history was written by one known inventor of occult orders, William Wynn Westcott (1848–1925), and that Mackenzie, who was not just an inventor but at times a blatant liar,[36] had a hand in its origins. The documents on which the Society was based were supposedly discovered in Freemasons' Hall by the Grand Secretary, William Henry White, and supplemented by the "knowledge and authority" of Mackenzie, who claimed to have been initiated by Rosicrucian adepts in Germany.[37] Given that the nine degrees, and possibly the brief rituals, of the S.R.I.A. are based on those of the defunct *Gold- und Rosenkreuz* (see Chapter Six), the probable truth is that Mackenzie, fluent in German, translated them from old papers of that order, which he may have acquired abroad.[38] An interesting sidelight is that these documents were said by Westcott to have been hidden away since the Grand Mastership of the Duke of Sussex, who, favoring

Figure 11.2. *William Wynn Westcott (1848–1925), in the regalia of Supreme Magus of the S.R.I.A.*

Unitarian doctrines, did all in his power to remove the Christian grades from Freemasonry.[39] As Westcott said unequivocally, "The Order [S.R.I.A.] is essentially a Christian Order."[40] By the time he wrote this, in 1900, the documents were conveniently lost once again.

At a meeting at Freemasons' Tavern on 14 July 1870, Robert Wentworth Little, seconded byWilliam R. Woodman, proposed that Bulwer-Lytton be elected an Honorary Member of the S.R.I.A., and be requested to accept the office of Grand Patron of the Order.[41] The only evidence that he accepted is in *The Rosicrucian* of October 1871, where the "Hon. President" is named as Frater the Lord Lytton, of Knebworth.[42] His formal resignation was recorded in October 1872.[43]

One often reads of Lytton as having been Grand Patron or Hon. President of the S.R.I.A. as if he was an active member and involved in the Order's affairs. I doubt that he attended a single meeting. My reason lies in three letters from John Yarker, preserved in the Lytton archives. In December 1872, Yarker, as head of the Manchester College, sent Lytton a summons to an "Obligatory Meeting" for the 14th of that month. Lytton's reply to Yarker must have been stern, for on 9 December Yarker wrote a most apologetic letter, saying that he had sent the summons in ignorance, but in good faith. He wrote again on 16 December to say that he was passing on the contents of Lytton's letter to Woodman, the Secretary-General of the S.R.I.A., and that "We must require from Metropolitan College some explanation of such an extraordinary proceeding as that of giving your Lordship's name as Grand Patron without consent."[44] Yarker adds, as if Lytton did not even know what the S.R.I.A. was: "It has been started here for the study of the old Rosicrucian literature; and I think really derives from the old Rosicrucian association. The proofs (German) I gave in a small synopsis of the Ancient and Modern History of Freemasonry published this year. . . . "[45] Naturally, Westcott's history of the Order includes Lytton's name without giving any hint of this discord.[46]

The S.R.I.A. was a small and secretive order, full of people who rejoiced in not letting their left hands know what their right hands were doing. Mackenzie, for all his part in its foundation, got around to joining the Order only in 1872, and thereafter made several contributions to *The Rosicrucian.* One of the first was the account of his visit to Levi twelve years before, in which he gives himself the name "Baphometus," either as a result of his masonic interest in the Templars, or else as a tribute to the best-known of Levi's illustrations.[47] Other essays show Mackenzie delving (like the Mercurii) into Dr. Rudd's angel-magic manuscripts in the British Museum and into the mythographers and orientalists. He also made translations from the German, including parts of Goethe's *Faust* and Lessing's *Ernst und Falk.* But he seems to have made no intellectual progress whatever since the days of his *Biological Review.* Ellic Howe remarks amusedly on how, after Eliphas Levi's death in 1875, Mackenzie writes that "he would not be difficult to find" at a spiritualistic séance; "I don't know whether I can get at him through my wife, who is a medium, but I will try." Howe says: "The possibility of contacting Levi was mentioned as casually as if, in a later day and age, Mackenzie hoped to telephone him if he could find the number."[48]

Mackenzie's main projects from now on concerned fringe-masonic orders such as the Sat B'hai and the Rite of Swedenborg, and the compilation of his *Royal Masonic Cyclopaedia*—which, for want of anything better, must remain his memorial. Its compilation was assisted, Westcott tells us, by Fratres Little, Hughan, F. G. Irwin, Woodman, Cox, Yarker, and by Dr. Feason Ranking, M.A.[49] The whole work, with its long articles on Cagliostro, Kabbalah, etc., testifies to Mackenzie's determination not to separate Freemasonry from occultism, which is why it never rivalled the reference works of Albert Mackey (from which it borrowed heavily) or Robert Freke Gould. Another of Mackenzie's objects was to lend authority to fringe-masonic enterprises, both existent and imaginary. Thus the *Cyclopedia* is a compendium of irregular Freemasonry, and as such, not without historical value. It is a period piece, announcing the occult revival of the later nineteenth century.

This revival may be dated from the formation of a very small group within the S.R.I.A., identifiable by their use of the swastika—a symbol quite devoid, at the time, of any evil associations. The group included Mackenzie, Morrison, and their friends Francis and Herbert Irwin, who used the swastika variously on title pages,[50] manuscripts,[51] bookplates,[52] and bindings.[53] Morrison probably started it in 1844, when for the first time he signed the Preface of *Zadkiel's Almanac* "Zadkiel [swastika] Tao Sze, &c." It is surprising to find Morrison using a Chinese title at this early date—presumably a version of *tao shih,* the generic name for a Taoist priest. I have no idea where he picked it up; possibly from some travel book.

Many years later, in his 1870 Almanac (published in the fall of 1869), Morrison announced his intention to "resuscitate in England, and spread throughout Europe, India and America—The Most Ancient Order of the Suastica; or, The Brotherhood of the Mystic Cross," in three degrees of Apprentice Brothers, Tao Sze or Doctors of Reason, and Grand Master. The Order, he said, had first been founded by Foe, "in the confines of Tibet," in about 1027 BCE. Apprentice members were invited to join at the cost of half a guinea. Morrison died in February 1874, but the name of the order, at least, survived him. Mackenzie duly included it in his *Cyclopaedia,* giving its upright moral rules and adding that "This Order was very little encouraged in England."[54]

Another principal actor in this underground drama was Francis George Irwin (1823–1898), a retired army Captain who lived in Bristol and joined every possible Masonic and fringe-masonic order. His correspondence with Frederick Hockley, published by John Hamill, gives much information on his activities, which for years included crystal-gazing with his son Herbert (died 1879) as seer. The Irwins' attitude to scrying was a reverent and Christian one in the style of their friends Morrison and Hockley, full of prayers as safeguards against the appearance of evil entities.

In October and November 1873, Irwin was contacted by an entity that called itself "Count Cagliostro," and given, through the crystal, the history and rituals of an order calling itself the "*Fratres Lucis,*" "Brothers of Light."[55] Cagliostro told him that the *Fratres Lucis* had originated in fourteenth-century Florence (where, he said, they still existed), and had numbered among their members Ficino, Fludd, Thomas Vaughan, Saint-Germain, Martines de Pasqually, Swedenborg, Schüssler, Mesmer, and Cagliostro himself. Other names used for the order were "Brotherhood of the Cross of Light" and "Order of [swastika symbol]." Its objects were the study and practice of "Natural Magic, Mesmerism, the Science of Death and of Life, Immortality, the Cabbala, Alchemy, Necromancy, Astrology and Magic in all its branches."[56]

Although there is an obvious link with Morrison's order, there is nothing Taoist or Tibetan about this Brotherhood of Light: its objects sound like the contents list of Raphael's *Astrologer of the Nineteenth Century*. Neither was its symbol intentionally oriental. One of Irwin's magical manuscripts contains an essay on "Divination by the Crystal and Invocation of Spirits," which shows how to prepare a magic circle of a typical Western type: it is diagrammed with a swastika in the center.[57] There is a manuscript of Irwin's that contains the rituals and traditional history of his "Fratres Lucis or Brethren of the Cross of Light," in which he says of the members that:

> They have made animal magnetism their chief study and have carried it nearly to perfection. It was through being a member of this society that Mesmer practised his healing power and founded his Mesmeric Lodge on the principles of the Order.
>
> Swedenborg derived his Rite from the same source, and from it Count Cagliostro derived the knowledge that enabled him to found the Egyptian Order; those three Rites represent three of the four grades into which this society is divided.[58]

There had of course been an earlier order in Germany called Fratres Lucis, otherwise known as the Asiatic Brethren (see Chapter Six). But that was long extinct, and in any case Cagliostro had had no part in it, alive or dead. Irwin seems rather to have modelled his Fratres Lucis on the English synthesis of the 1780s, the age of Cagliostro, Rainsford, de Loutherbourg, and the London Swedenborgians.

Francis Irwin enrolled a very few friends in his Fratres Lucis. We know that Hockley was a member; also Benjamin Cox (born 1828), another crystal-gazer and addict to fringe-Masonry;[59] and Mackenzie, admitted in 1876 at the earliest.[60] To these we should add Irwin's son Herbert, who was the medium for his father's investigations. Mackenzie's *Cyclopaedia* calls it:

> Light, Brothers of. A mystic order, *Frates* [sic] *Lucis*, established in Florence in 1498. Among the members of this Order were Pasqualis, Cagliostro, Swedenborg, St Martin, Eliphaz Levi, and many other eminent mystics. Its members were much persecuted by the Inquisition. It is a small but compact body, the members being spread all over the world.[61]

Mackenzie has missed by only one year the date of publication (1499) of the *Hypnerotomachia Poliphili*, or the *Dream of Poliphilo*, one of the masterpieces of early printing. Emanuela Kretzulesco-Quaranta[62] has interpreted it as the legacy of a group of esoteric philosophers, sent out in the disguise of a picaresque novel in order to preserve their doctrines of carnal and spiritual love, despite their persecution by the Roman Church. At the very least, we can agree that there is a sympathy across the centuries between the Renaissance Platonists and the later occultists and mystics who are named here.

Like other fringe-masonic groups, Mackenzie's throve on the idea of "Unknown Superiors" of incomparable spiritual attainments as the real power behind the societies that could be joined and the adepts who could be named. The same idea occurs in *Ghost Land*, where Louis says that above and beyond the magical and experimental groups there is one quite different secret society:

> Its actual nature is only recognized, spoken, or thought of as a dream, a memory of the past, evoked like a phantom from the realms of tradition or myth; yet as surely as there is a spirit in man, is there in the world a spiritual, though nameless and almost unknown association of men, drawn together by the bonds of soul, associated by those interior links which never fade or perish, belonging to all times, places and nations alike. Few can attain to the inner light of these spiritually associated brethren, or apprehend the significance of their order; enough that it is, has been, and will be, until all men are spiritualized enough to partake of its exalted dispensations. Some members of this sublime Brotherhood were in session in England, and

> their presence it was which really sent thither my master and myself, at the time of which I write.[63]

Frederick Hockley would also have been familiar with this kind of arrangement, having been advised years before (probably in the mid-1850s) by the Crowned Angel to join "that sacred society of which the Fathers are in Jerusalem [. . .] They are followers of the Rosy Cross." Members of this order "study the occult sciences after an interview with an invisible power, which they have at stated times. The elders travel to Jerusalem." The angel added that Napoleon Bonaparte was a member, and that Jean-Jacques Rousseau was one of its firmest supporters. If Hockley wanted to join, he would have to go to France and be installed as a Brother there.[64]

We must remember that all this came through crystal-gazing and has no possible claim on the scholar as true information. Hockley's letters show that he did visit Paris, but nobody knows what happened to him there. Given his interest in Mackenzie's visit, I imagine that he made a beeline for 19, avenue de Maine, and gave a masonic knock upon Eliphas Levi's door. A slightly firmer fact is that Francis Irwin was in Paris early in 1874 and told Benjamin Cox that he had met with a warm reception there from members of the Fratres Lucis.[65] We know that he also met Levi (see Chapter Thirteen). But since he was stringing Cox out for over a year with promises that he might be admitted to this very select and secret order, nothing that Irwin said to Cox can be trusted, either.

The Brotherhood of Light, slight as it may seem, was the breeding-ground for a much more important esoteric and cultural movement, the Hermetic Order of the Golden Dawn, about which there is no lack of published information. The Brotherhood of Light, as we have seen, included Francis Irwin, Frederick Hockley, Kenneth Mackenzie, and Benjamin Cox. In 1883, the chemist and metallurgist Frederick Holland started another secretive order called the "Society of Eight," whose primary pursuit was to be alchemy. Four of the eight members were again Irwin, Hockley, Mackenzie, and Cox. The others were John Yarker, the universal purveyor of fringe-masonic grades; Westcott, a London coroner who headed the Metropolitan College of the S.R.I.A.; and possibly William Alexander Ayton, a clergyman and practicing alchemist.[66] Hockley died on 10 November 1885, leaving a place vacant. On 20 November, Mackenzie wrote to Francis Irwin that he had met a certain Mathers, whom he calls: "a highly intelligent and earnest seeker into our favourite studies. I hope to see more of him."[67] It was Frederick Holland who had discovered Samuel Liddell MacGregor Mathers (1854–1918) as a fellow-member of the S.R.I.A., and encouraged the younger man in his occult studies.[68] Mathers duly took his place among the Eight.

The last gathering of the Society of Eight was on the Tarot,[69] a subject that we know Mackenzie had discussed with Eliphas Levi. According to Mr. Parisious's researches, it was Holland's interpretation of the Tarot that went back to France, to be publicized by Papus in his best-selling books. In England, its most profound students were A. E. Waite and W. B. Yeats, who made Tarot symbolism central to their own researches and systems.

This was only one of the ways in which the Society of Eight served as a pivot or a relay between two generations-even two centuries-of British occultists. In Hockley (born 1808) there was a connection with the age of the Siblys and the Mercurii, while in Westcott and Mathers there were two of the three founders of the Golden Dawn, the order that would virtually redefine the British occult world for the twentieth century.

The history of the Golden Dawn is best learned from the scholarly and entertaining works of Ellic Howe and R. A. Gilbert. According to the latter, the order pretended on its first, discreet appearance to be the continuation of Dr. Falk's Kabbalistic school (see Chapter Five). Westcott insinuated the news of its existence in December 1888 by placing a query in *Notes and Queries*, the vehicle for literary and cultural curiosities. Writing as "Gustav Mommsen," he mentioned that "Johann F. Falk succeeded to the directorate of a secret society of students of the Kabbalah about 1810, in London I believe," and asked if it was still in existence. In February 1889, Westcott answered the query in his own name, saying that "the Order of mystics which gave Eliphaz Lévi (Abbé Constant) his occult knowledge, and of which Johann Falk was at one time the Lecturer on the Kabbalah in London, is still at work in England. . . ." He says that it is not masonic, open to men and women, and called "The Hermetic students of the G.D.," then, in a transparent invitation to neophytes, adds his own address.[70] Mackenzie's *Cyclopaedia* had named two London Falks: Caïn Chenul, "known as Doctor Falcon," aged about seventy in 1788, and his son Johann Friedrich Falk, born in Hamburg, a jeweller and diamond merchant by trade. The latter "is reported to have died about 1824, and he was the head of a Kabbalistic College in London," says Mackenzie.[71] Granted, it is possible that the Kabbalistic school founded in London by Samuel Falk in the 1740s passed to a collateral line (Samuel, to judge from his will, had no children), and that it continued after Johann Friedrich's death in 1824. But there is no evidence for this apart from Westcott's statement.

The tangible foundations of the Golden Dawn are the famous cipher manuscripts, which still exist in a private collection in England. Easily deciphered, since they are written (in English) in an alphabetic code published by Trithemius, they contain outlines and brief rituals for the hierarchical grades of an occult order. Westcott always maintained that his masonic colleague, the Rev. Adolphus A. F. Woodford, had found the manuscripts by chance at a London bookstall, and that an address included in them had led Westcott to contact a lady in Nuremberg, Anna Sprengel. She had revealed to him the existence of the order, and, on her authority as a seventh-grade "Adeptus Exemptus," given Westcott the fifth grade of "Adeptus Minor" and authorized him to initiate others. Before anyone could track Fräulein Sprengel down, she was reported to have died, leaving Westcott and his two S.R.I.A. colleagues, Mathers and Dr. William R. Woodman, in sole control of the order.

No Golden Dawn scholar believes Westcott's story. According to Mr. Gilbert, the cipher manuscripts are in the handwriting of Kenneth Mackenzie,[72] the colleague of Westcott and Mathers in the Society of Eight. Mr. Parisious has found that after Mackenzie's death in 1886, his widow gave his masonic papers to Westcott. These included the cipher manuscripts, which Westcott decided to use for the foundation of his intended Order. Mrs. Mackenzie was among the first people enrolled in the Golden Dawn, effectively binding her to secrecy about the origin of the rituals. But where did Mackenzie get them from? There are rumors that they had passed through the hands of Eliphas Levi,[73] and that there are manuscripts in the Grand Orient Library (the headquarters of Freemasonry in France), which show their origins in the "Jewish Lodge."[74] Thus we come back again to that offshoot of the Asiatic Brethren and the Fratres Lucis of the early nineteenth century, in which Bulwer-Lytton is said to have been initiated.

The Golden Dawn's position in the history of British occultism will become clearer after we have treated its contemporaries, the Theosophical Society and the Hermetic Brotherhood of Luxor. Then we will see how it answered the need for instruction in practical occultism in the Western tradition, which the Theosophical Society had failed to provide; and how it found a ready-made clientele among those recently disillusioned by the "H.B. of L."

It was the elaboration of the Golden Dawn's simple rituals after 1892 that transformed it from a society teaching practical occultism into a vehicle for effective magical initiations.[75] This enhancement was provided by Mather's wife, Moïna Bergson Mathers, while the Mathers' were living in the Sixteenth Arrondissement of Paris. Moïna, sister of the philosopher Henri Bergson, was a scryer, and it was by this method that she contacted the "Secret Chiefs" of the Order on the inner planes.[76] This circumstance places the real origins of the Golden Dawn beyond the reach of the historian. What is most essential, and most precious, derives not from books, manuscripts, or earthly meetings, but from contacts with other levels of reality. When these are present, as in the cases of the Golden Dawn, the Theosophical Society, and a certain number of other orders, the scholarly investigator is doomed to frustration. But the order possesses the one thing needful: the access to energies that will make it more than an interesting charade.

TWELVE

The Way to Christ

Much of this book has been about people whose philosophical and spiritual lives were incompatible with Christianity as it existed in the nineteenth century. Some of the obstacles were the theology superimposed on Jesus' teachings by the Apostles, Fathers, and Doctors of the Church; the establishment of Christianity as the state religion by the Emperor Constantine; the atrocities of the Crusades, the Inquisition, and the Wars of Religion; the oppression of the common folk by a privileged clergy; and the literal acceptance of the Bible, especially the Old Testament.

As we have seen from the example of C. G. Harrison, there is also a Christian esotericism that has negotiated these obstacles with more or less success. To the blustering of the theologians, it prefers the certainty of the mystics. It deplores the misalliance of the Church with worldly power, and the actions that owe more to the example of terrible Jahweh than to that of Jesus of Nazareth. Its reading of the Scriptures is symbolic rather than literal, just as the Kabbalists' reading of the Torah or the Sufis' reading of the Quran. It is more tolerant of other religions, because it has to be tolerant of the exoteric part of its own. At the same time, it never abandons the claims of uniqueness and (however tactfully phrased) of superiority to all other religions.

We turn in this chapter to a group of Christian esotericists. All of them felt the thirst for direct spiritual experience which, as I said at the end of Chapter Four, was lacking in the men of the Enlightenment. But unlike the occultists, whom we have seen running after all manner of strange gods, these people were able to satisfy it within their native Christianity—even, in most cases, without abandoning the exoteric religion of their Anglican or Methodist churches.

The reason for this was that they had entered a spiritual current that has been alluded to, but not yet emphasized: the one set in motion by

Jacob Boehme (1575–1624), the shoemaker of Görlitz. Boehme was an allegorist in biblical matters, thus freeing his followers from obedience to the literal text that had become so vexatious to a scientific era. He was also a mystic, or to be precise a theosopher. (I follow the convention of calling the followers of Boehme theosophers and his doctrine theosophy—"wisdom of the divine"—whereas the members of Blavatsky's society are called Theosophists, this being their chosen title and not a generic term.)

Boehme's theosophy comprised both a theoretical system of metaphysics and cosmology, and a practical one of mysticism couched in alchemical language. In Chapter Seven I mentioned the interest of the London Swedenborgians and of the Mercurii in the documents of Boehme's English followers. During the hundred years around 1700 there were his translators Sparrow, Ellistone, and Blunden; his commentator Freher and his illustrator Gichtel; the "Philadelphian Society" of John Pordage, Jane Lead, and Francis Lee, who published their *Theosophical Transactions* during 1697; and lastly the Rev. William Law, who oversaw the publication of the four-volume English edition of Boehme in 1764–1781, with its famous folding plates. Richard Cosway and J. P. de Loutherbourg collected Behmenist books and manuscripts, while the enthusiasm of the Romantic poets, especially Coleridge and Blake, was still keener. Yet for more than a century, between "Law's Boehme" and the Glasgow edition of the *Epistles* in 1886, only one small book of his was published in England.[1]

Perhaps Boehme's trumpet voice was too strident, his imagery too baroque, to appeal to an era both rational and sentimental. His name was only mentioned by the treaders of literary byways, as one of the queer sages of the past: half crazy, no doubt, like Paracelsus or the unfortunate Giordano Bruno. Only by a handful of earnest souls were Boehme and his followers still admired and their example cultivated.[2]

This Behmenist circle was a loosely knit group of friends and relatives comprising a founder, James Pierrepont Greaves; a man and his daughter, Thomas South and Mary Ann South (who later became Mrs. Atwood); a central figure, Christopher Walton; and another man and his wife, Mr. and Mrs. Penny (née Anne Judith Brown).

James Pierrepont Greaves (1777–1842) was a London merchant whose inherited business was ruined in 1806 when the Napoleonic Wars cut off foreign trade. Accepting bankruptcy, he turned over his property to his creditors, and thereafter lived on the income allowed by them. The turning point of his life came when he read about Johann Heinrich Pestalozzi (1745–1827), the Swiss pioneer of humane education for the very young. Greaves was so excited that he packed up then and there and

***Figure 12.1.** James Pierrepont Greaves (1777–1842) from Greaves's* Letters and Extracts, *1845.*

moved to Switzerland. He arrived at Pestalozzi's establishment in Yverdun in 1817 and stayed for eight years, until family matters necessitated his return to England.

At Pestalozzi's, Greaves met Robert Owen,[3] many of whose ideals he shared. They were both against the aloof paternalism of the established Church, the selfishness of the rich and the dog-eat-dog mentality of the poor, and all that made people strive against each other rather than live in fellowship. But there the resemblance ended, for the two pupils diverged from Pestalozzi's principles in diametrically opposite ways. Pestalozzi, in a letter to Greaves, had described the end of education as: "to render man conscientiously active in the service of his Maker; to render him useful, by rendering him independent, with relation to society; and, as an individual, to render him happy within himself."[4] The Swiss educator believed in the essential goodness of the human creature, and that "the ultimate destination of Christianity is to accomplish the education of mankind."[5] But for Robert Owen, as we saw in Chapter Three, Christianity had already done its best to corrupt and malform the natural man. For Greaves, on the contrary, mankind existed solely in order to realize the goal of Christianity.

Everything in Greaves's writing directs attention to the inner voice, the divine nature within man, which is our common birthright but which we need to rediscover and submit to. Socialists such as Owen and Charles Fourier had much to say about Love, but to Greaves they lacked the essential "Love-nature." In other words, theirs was a social and sexual love, profane rather than sacred. Far from the free and joyful indulgence of the passions that was the raison d'être of Fourier's utopia, Greaves believed that "every abstinence is good."[6]

This "Sacred Socialist" was as good as his word. Freed, for all his business failure, from the necessity to earn a living, Greaves lived a life of philanthropy, asceticism, and voluntary poverty. He organized a large-scale scheme of public works in 1832, in Randwick, Gloucestershire, paying his workers not with money but with credits redeemable for basic foodstuffs, clothes, and household goods, thus preventing them from spending their wages on drink.[7] Not only was Greaves a vegetarian and teetotaller, but he considered that there was no need in the human diet for tea, coffee, sugar, butter, cheese, salt, mustard, pepper, or vinegar.[8] Uncooked food from the fruit garden was his ideal, eaten so slowly that a five-minute snack would take as many hours. For variety, he urged adoption of what he called the "Boil'd Bread Diet."[9]

Diet was only one level of Greaves's triple program for the rescue of mankind from its predicament, which he describes as follows:

> Man is a being in a three-fold confusion; he is made of substances which are in confusion, in his stomach, in his head, in his heart. His cookery is as erroneous as his philosophy and his religion. He is as much without a rule in his head as he is without a rule in his religion, and in his food, and he will remain so while the natures are so confused within him. No animal can be so sadly disorganized as man.[10]

To remedy the situation, Greaves proposed nothing less than a movement of "pennyless, moneyless missionaries, who being filled with love can go forth, and deliver the Love message, and demand what they need of those who have the same."[11] Though there were few in England willing to take on the life of a Buddhist monk, Franciscan friar, or Hindu sannyasin, Greaves's personal qualities did attract a few kindred souls. One, Alexander Campbell, was working for Robert Owen's movement in Cheltenham, as a missionary of the "Association of all Classes of all Nations," when he met Greaves and was converted to his principles of theosophy.[12] Campbell's contribution was to edit and publish his master's letters after Greaves's death.

Greaves did not see the infant as a pure spirit whom "civilized" education warps and depraves: the trouble began earlier. "I affirm that Education can never repair the defects of Birth," was the quotation chosen by Campbell for the title page of Greaves's *Letters and Extracts.* And what causes these birth defects? The abuse of sexuality on the part of the parents. Greaves urges repeatedly the deferral of marriage until both partners have reached a degree of spiritual maturity; and then, he says, consummation should occur when the woman, not the man, demands it. "The woman, with the love in her feelings, must win the man's affection, and the man, with his wisdom, must exercise and direct the woman's understanding."[13]

Just as he was out of sympathy with the free-love movement and with materialistic, "physical" socialism, so Greaves also rejected the popular and sectarian Christianity that seemed to him on the same low level of aspiration. The complacency, the blind trust in Church and Bible, and above all the exclusivity of such Christians were as far as possible from the inward path of his theosophy. In the curious *Contrasting Magazine of errors and truths,* which he produced for four months in 1827, Greaves would contrast texts by others with what, in his view, they should have said, printing the two versions in double columns, side by side. One example will show how Greaves dealt with an exoteric Christian of the type who boasted of his own tolerance of unbelievers. The latter, "C.A.W.," writes:

> Nay, I could live upon good terms even with a Deist, provided he keeps within the bounds of decency, and does not carry with him through life, that juvenile vanity, which will not suffer him to be quiet, till he has told all the world that he laughs at those things which they consider as the most sacred and inviolable.

Greaves offers as a contrasting statement:

> Nay, we shall live upon good terms with every human being, and not oppose their professions, unless, instead of keeping them for themselves, they be animated by that selfish spirit of bigotry, which will not suffer them to be quiet till they have told all the world that all that is sacred and inviolable is contained in their articles of belief, and all the remainder is doomed to eternal damnation.[14]

Greaves's religion did not need Thirty-Nine Articles, nor the church, nor even Jesus Christ as the vicarious sacrifice for mankind's salvation. Jesus was for him simply the highest possible exemplar of the union with God, to which every human being can and should aspire. The desire of the soul for union, he writes, is the strongest possible prayer, and must not be lost sight of at any moment.[15]

Greaves was a Behmenist in the sense of his devotion to the inner church and the inner way; in his acceptance of Boehme's explanation of the roots of sin and suffering; and in his refusal to countenance a mystic path that was not suffused through and through with love. But unlike most of Boehme's disciples, and certainly unlike the master himself, Greaves seems to have had little interest in the intermediate domains of spirits, spheres, and cosmogonic systems that make Boehme's works so compelling to a certain mentality. In comparison to the Behmenists, Greaves's letters and diaries make monotonous reading. He was uninterested in occultism and cosmology, indifferent to the current craze for animal magnetism and Mesmerism, and seemingly ignorant of the historical context of his quest. His was the short path to regeneration and union, and his influence was less as a writer or persuader than through the power of his own presence—which, as the twinkling eyes of his portrait show, was anything but solemn and sanctimonious.

Towards the end of his life, in the 1840s, Greaves led a theosophical circle that met in a country house in Kent.[16] His influence thus passed to two remarkable women, Mary Ann South and Anne Judith Brown. Mary Ann South (1817–1910) was one of the daughters of Thomas South (c. 1785–c. 1855), a gentleman, of Bury House, Gosport, Hampshire. In conformity with her era and class, she had only the education deemed suitable for a lady; she later deplored her lack of a proper grounding in classics and philosophy, to say nothing of chemistry, astrology, and geology. However, to her friend Isabel de Steiger (1836–1927), who was under the same disadvantage, Mary Ann's self-earned knowledge of classics was extraordinary.[17] Some scientific gaps must have been filled, too, by Mary Ann's study of what she called her chief guide: Lorenz Oken's *Elements of Physiophilosophy*. This book of 1810, of which an English translation appeared in 1847, was a universal manual of knowledge, covering nature, science, and

Figure 12.2. *Bookplate of Thomas South (c. 1785–c. 1855).*

the arts: a product of the German Romantic *Naturphilosophie.* Oken's central idea was the correspondence of every domain of nature with the human body and its senses. In a way, this was a version of the Renaissance doctrine of correspondence between the macrocosm and the microcosm, adapted to the new discoveries of science and the categorizing zeal of German scholarship. It was a "Philosophy of Nature" in the spirit of Novalis or of Goethe's *Pflanzenlehre,* and thus inspired at second remove by Paracelsus, Boehme, and the seventeenth-century alchemists.

The 1840s, as we know from Chapter Eight, were the era of Elliotson's *Zoist* magazine, in which Mesmerism and magnetism, trance states and clairvoyance, were investigated by physicians, clerics, and natural philosophers, while also being the talk of London's drawing rooms and fodder for popular novelists. Thomas South's daughters plunged into this world and into practical experimentation of a type that Greaves would never have condoned.

We can discover something of their activities from Thomas South's *Early Magnetism* (1846).[18] In view of future developments, it seems likely that Mary Ann collaborated on the work,[19] and that the following description of the trance state as a short cut to mystical experience may be hers:

> Now it is believed, and on no light evidence, that the magnetic trance affords, nay, is itself, when justly and perseveringly ordered for that end, THE METAPHYSICAL CONDITION, pre-eminently perfect. It removes the sensible obscuration, and presents a clearer glass before the mind than it can ever regard in the natural state.[20]

Thomas South believed that this trance experience and the "magnetic" means of inducing it were the great secrets of antiquity. The statues of Egypt and India seemed to demonstrate "magnetic postures" such as Mesmer and his pupils had rediscovered; from Egypt, these mysteries must have spread to the Hebrews and later to the Greeks.[21] While he quotes the Scriptures whenever he sees in them a hint of ancient knowledge and practice of this secret art, South's heart was more with the Neoplatonists, whom he cites in Thomas Taylor's translations. With Proclus, he believed that the Absolute can only be known by becoming it.[22]

Mesmerism here reaches a third stage of development. At first, under Mesmer, it was a cure for the sick. Second, under the Puységurs, it was a way to mediumship. Now it is regarded wholly from the point of view of the entranced subject, as a short cut to mystical experience.

By 1849, Mary Ann and her father (one never hears of her mother) were collaborating on a larger project: an exposition of how this kind of mysticism had been concealed in the writings of the alchemists and Hermetic philosophers. Thomas was going to treat the subject in verse, Mary

Ann in prose. His poem was not published until 1919,[23] but her treatise was duly printed in 1850 as *A Suggestive Inquiry into the Hermetic Mystery*.[24] No sooner did they see the book in print than the Souths got cold feet: was it for nothing that these mysteries had been concealed so long, and was it for them to violate the discretion of the ages? The story goes that they collected and bought back all the copies of the *Suggestive Inquiry* that they could lay their hands on and burnt them on the lawn of Bury House.[25] However, for all their scruples Mary Ann was not unwilling to lend the odd surviving copy (booksellers speak of a couple of dozen) to friends and confidants.

For Thomas South, the revelations of animal magnetism were a godsend, supplying what a moribund Christianity could no longer provide. He wrote to Walton circa 1853 that:

> now when the light of Christian Truth is so intirely eclipsed amongst us, the natural magic ought to be again developed and must be, before we can hope for a restitution of the Divine.
>
> It was chiefly with this view that the Hermetic Inquiry was written, to promote the investigation and open all initiatory means to the great End, but I had no inclination to systematize prematurely or accommodate reviewers with propositions which can only be appreciated by following the progressive evidence throughout.
>
> The whole Edition of the Book is now withdrawn into my own hands for private circulation only, having had reasons to fear the consequence of indiscriminate publication.[26]

Thomas South himself may have gone further into forbidden zones than is implied in Mary Ann's *Suggestive Inquiry*. The evidence for this is also in his letters to Walton, in which he repeatedly urges his friend to abandon his slow path of studying Boehme, Freher, and Law. South wrote early on in their relationship: "We are evidently in different spheres of mind, I cannot help viewing it as though you travel by rail, and that our school passes you in the electric telegraph—what this means can only in any way be explained personally."[27] Now the Souths were, as we have seen, willing to share the *Suggestive Inquiry*, with its dangerous revelations, with selected friends—Walton among them. So it cannot be simply of these that Thomas South is speaking in the following letters. I can only interpret what follows as a hint at the practice of sexual alchemy:

> I had hoped to find in you an ardent enthusiastic enquirer in the road I put you on, but dared not venture farther unless, at your own instinctive suggestion. Business I fear has intervened and drawn you away from the pursuit, be

> assured it is the only clue to thread the labyrinth of this life's mystery, the only saving passage for Regeneration. The little you have seen of Magnetism, the unprepared subjects, both agents and patients have probably afforded you but little light. Mrs. Walton is likely to be far the best vessel you have ever seen or heard of for enlightening you, and I was in hopes ere this to have heard of some result in that quarter, I have never seen any one more apparently fitted for the experience. Pray remember me and all of us most kindly to her—remember this, the secret is most awful and to those who have by any means intellectually or spiritually ever attained a knowledge of it, conscience has at once hermetically sealed and discretionary revealment [sic], the recipient of such sacred science must first be deeply moved with a desire (this longing after Immortality) for the Attainment when his spirit is quickened and duly craving for the flame the light assuredly will from without kindle the fire within, and he will at once see and believe and know the way of regeneration, and that there are indeed no other . . .[28]
>
> * * *
>
> . . . of this be assured, Freher as well as others had knowledge of a practice in common with Behmen, which and which only raised them when they were not regenerate but on the road to be so. In one generation there is but one, one only way, no one ever dared to reveal it openly, never in print never in writing and never personally but after long experience of character, particularly as to one point, reticence—tis true it was never discovered to me in this way, I am under no oath but those which conscience sealed my lips with as the light burst on me as it has rarely burst on others. I tell you as my honest friend this holy light, has surely beamed on my unworthy self, after a long course of intense worldly suffering mental and bodily, that beam that kindled Behmen [and] Freher also fell on the humble head that now directs this pen.[29]

I may be wrong in my surmise, but I can think of nothing else that would have evoked from a liberal-minded early Victorian such awed discretion. The mesmeric trance was one thing, and perhaps from Thomas's point of view a spectator's phenomenon only. But here he is speaking of a personal experience. Possibly he attained by this means, well known in the Tantric traditions of the East and in certain Kabbalist schools, the certainty of other modes of being that had been denied him, not being a good mesmeric subject. But even if I am right about this, I have no reason to believe that Mary Ann South was a party to it.

We will return later to Mary Ann South's history, after she became Mary Ann Atwood in 1859. But the reader may already have wondered who this Walton was, who in Thomas South's words never got sufficiently out of his "Behmenist straitjacket" to learn these awful secrets.

Christopher Walton (1809–1877) was the scion of a prominent Northern Methodist family on his father's side, and of a Bristol one on that of his mother, Anna Maria Pickford. Walton came to London as a silk mercer in 1830, and subsequently set up as a "Goldsmith, Dealer in Diamonds, Pearls, etc." at 24 Ludgate Street (later at 8 Ludgate Hill). His route to Jacob Boehme is easier to trace than his road to riches. As a Methodist, he happened upon John Wesley's *Some Extracts from Mr. Law's Writings.* This led him to read all of William Law's works in order of publication, thus moving from the devotional tracts to the great illustrated edition of Boehme, and to collect a magnificent theosophic library.

Walton had decided by 1845 to devote all his energies outside his business to the Behmenist cause, and in particular to gathering and presenting to the world the materials for a proper appreciation of William Law. During 1845–46 he was paying the Rev. Robert Payne Smith of Pembroke College, Oxford (a future Dean of Canterbury) for editing and perhaps translating. Samuel Jackson, the translator of Jung-Stilling and other German religious books, called Walton's attention to the Freher manuscripts in the British Museum and offered to translate for him. But the bulk of the work was done by Walton himself, who worked diligently to understand Boehme's ideas and make them comprehensible to others through extracts and quotations.

The result of his labors was an edition of 500 copies, not sold but distributed to libraries and individuals, of a stout octavo entitled *Notes and Materials for an adequate biography of the celebrated divine and theosopher William Law. Comprising an elucidation of the scope and contents of the writings of Jacob Bohme, and of his great commentator, Dionysius Andreas Freher; with a notice of the mystical divinity and most curious and solid science of all ages of the world. Also an indication of the true means for the induction of the intellectual "heathen," Jewish, and Mahomedan nations into the Christian faith.*

The title page of this anonymous work is dated London, AD 1854, but the Preface is signed Midsummer 1856. Evidently Walton had trouble bringing his work to a conclusion, and no wonder: it is the most chaotic presentation imaginable. Certainly there are riches in abundance: an ample exposition of Boehme's system; a biography of William Law; extracts from Freher's manuscripts, both those in the British Museum and in Walton's own possession; an introduction to Boehme's French translator, the "Unknown Philosopher" Louis-Claude de Saint-Martin . . . But it is all piled higgledy-piggledy, stuffed into immense footnotes, and, worst of all, printed in microscopic type. It is not the work of a scholar, but of a man who spent his days peering at pearls and gemstones. When Thomas South thanked Walton for the book, he complained that the "small type debarred me from deep perusal," and he was not the only one. Twenty years later, with a certain impatience, Walton was telling Mrs. Penny that his magnum opus was perfectly legible if one would just obtain a pair of "common spectacles," and gave her the address of where to get them.[30]

If Walton had not penetrated to the Souths' deepest alchemical arcanum, he had at least learned from the father and daughter of the fashionable context within which to present his magnum opus. He calls Boehme "a perfect clairvoyant," though (he adds) not as the current scientists define this, nor as the seers and "lucides" explore inferior astral or "phantasaic nature." No: Boehme penetrated to the centre of the divine majesty itself, "for being a highly regenerated gospel christian," (there speaks the Methodist!) "therefore the divine eye found in him a proper medium of understanding."[31] While putting Boehme on a higher level entirely than the Magnetists, Walton does allow that the student, besides reading, will do well "to witness some really good cases of magical sleep or trance, with lucid clairvoyance."[32] At the very opening of his Preface, Walton confesses that his understanding was "much enlarged and perfectionated" recently when he "obtained a true and philosophic insight into the arcanum of 'Animal' or 'Vital Magnetism'."[33]

For all his enthusiam for the theosophers, Walton was a typical example of the would-be esotericist trapped within his exoteric tradition. Far from giving him a broad, detached, and serene view of the universe, his following of Boehme's footsteps left him a literalistic worshipper at the letter of both Old and New Testament, and a missionary intent (expressed in his long title) to convert the heathen to "pure gospel christianity." This Gospel Christian ended up by quarreling with all of his family and instigating lawsuits against his own son.

Like Bulwer-Lytton and Stanhope, Walton never lost his fascination with mediums. He had business correspondence with the French clairvoyant Alphonse Didier, with the famous American mediums Mrs. Hayden and D. D. Home, and, as late as 1876, with Mr. Williams, a "physical medium." At Mrs. Marshall's, in 1861 or 1862, he got a written message that purported to be from the spirit of Freher himself; and in 1865, he had a long psychic reading of his character by J. Murray Spear, positively dripping with praise—thus tending to confirm the theory that psychics, and even "spirits," tend to reflect what is in the querent's own head!

Figure 12.3. *Anne Judith Penny, née Brown (1825–1893), from* Essays on Jacob Böhme, *1909.*

Although Walton's presence will continue to brood in the background, I turn now to the other members of this Behmenist circle: Anne Judith Brown (1825–1893) and her husband Edward Burton Penny (1804/5–1872). Anne was one of thirteen children of an Oxfordshire vicar.

Orphaned at six, she was raised by an older sister; then a spinal disease left her crippled for life, and often in pain.[34] She must have had little to look forward to in life, but as it turned out she had a happy marriage and a career of vigorous intellectual activity and writing, first as a moralist and novelist, then as one of the deepest thinkers of the spiritualist movement.

According to Isabel de Steiger, Anne Brown was a friend of Mary Ann South and a member of Greaves's study-group in Kent, though she could only have been in her teens at the time.[35] C. C. Massey, on the other hand, says that she was introduced to Boehme by the Rev. Enoch Warriner, Rector of Foots Cray, Kent, in 1854, and thereafter to Saint-Martin. Whichever is the case, she remained a firmly committed Behmenist to the end of her days.

The modern reader is not going to have much interest in a writer who could produce a *Romance of the dull life* (1861), dedicated "To those who know the weight and worth of dullness." Anne Brown wrote for people like herself, with time on their hands to ramble and muse through "three-decker" novels and moralities, interspersed with good works. Even her later philosophical writing is extremely wordy and often unclear. But there is something noble in the way she accepted her dullness, her spinsterhood, her aches and pains, and boredom as she watched men busily running the world for her and other women running after the men. It did not worry her because she had found an inner sense of worth, an inner light metaphorically and perhaps actually. It is this that she was trying to convey to her readers.

When Anne married the Rev. Edward Burton Penny, Rector of Topham, Devon, on 3 October 1865, her life must have become a lot less dull. Mr. Penny had long been familiar with the theosophic and mystical tradition. Many years before, he had followed William Law's advice of taking a month's retreat for prayer; he said he was far from attaining the degree of concentration that Law recommended, but that it had had a permanent influence on him.[36] By 1863 Penny was corresponding with Christopher Walton, having responded to the latter's recent entries in *Notes and Queries,* and inviting him to visit him and his (first) wife in Devon. Penny was thrilled by the discovery of Saint-Martin's letters to Kirchberger, and said that he felt like translating them—which he duly did.[37] But he was not self-restricted, as Walton was, to the Behmenist school. Penny read the French esotericists Fabre d'Olivet and Eliphas Levi, and even Paschal Beverly Randolph's *Dealings with the Dead,* in which he was struck by the parallel with an experience of Gichtel's: the discovery of his friend's soul in the form of a globe. Feeling that he had to excuse himself for this slumming in disreputable literature, he asked Walton:

> Is it not lawful to look for jewels, even under the swines' feet? If the smell of the sty does not offend you too much, I should like to know whether you can not find something worth picking up in Randolph's Dealings with the Dead, 1862 . . . This Randolph is a colored man, and was a medium and trance-speaker in England, a few years, ago;—but he repudiates such practice now.[38]

Penny was the sort of clergymen who could say that "to me all days are Sabbaths," and that "even the Devil is a useful idiot in a way."[39] But Walton was having none of this. Although his replies have not survived, it is easy to tell from Penny's reactions that the pious goldsmith considered Fabre d'Olivet "almost as bad as Swedenborg,"[40] and declined all comment on the egregious Randolph.

Anne Judith Brown, as the second Mrs. Penny, made an excellent team with her husband. To his French she added her knowledge of German and Italian, and introduced him to the works of Franz von Baader, Boehme's German editor and commentator.[41] The two of them were close friends of the Atwoods, visiting each other's houses and, as Steiger says, "all four being much connected with Church dignitaries."[42]

This cosy life of teas in vicarage gardens did not prevent Edward Penny from going to Paris in Spring 1867 and paying a visit to the ever-hospitable Eliphas Levi.[43] Six years earlier, Kenneth Mackenzie had visited the French magus and written down an account of his conversations (see Chapter Eleven). I give here the narrative that Penny sent to Walton, so that it can compared with Mackenzie's.[44]

> I called upon him in Paris, and told him I believed Boehme got his wisdom from the original source of the Kabbala itself. I questioned him about his ideas of miracles—the increase of loaves and fishes—the evil spirits sent into swine &c, he considers purely figurative. I told him Boehme would explain it more satisfactorily to him.—He professes to be ready to learn–but he does not read either German or English.—The point where his science seems to me to be truncated, or shortened abruptly, is his dogma that—"A thing is not just because God wills it, but God wills it because it is just"—His conception of God being restricted to what He is in His Works—he seems unable to ask the question what He is in Himself—Which, though we cannot comprehend it, we may apprehend.—and if a thing is not just because God wills it, but God wills it because it is just—it follows that justice is greater or prior to God and that there must be another God besides God.—I had not read

this passage when I saw him, so I had not an opportunity to get him to explain;—I mean however to write to him.

With these exceptions you will find what a wonderful analogy there is between what he claims for the Kabbala and we claim for Theosophy!

The "Grand Oeuvre"—the Magical Science—Magnetic Power—all having for object to control, cut off, overcome the Astral Light, which is the same as the "Old Serpent," the "Spirit of the World," "Satan"—he approaches very nearly to Boehme's teaching,—though Boehme distinguishes between three forms or powers. It provides the fulcrum for Archimedes' lever whereby to move the world.

Levi's great aim is to bring his science into practical, positive form.—he is eminently synthetical—while Boehme is more eminently analytical.—There appears to me in Levi a great waste of words about Magical Rites, and the superstitions of antient astrologers and professors of Magic and in the description of disgusting works of witchcraft and sorcery—and I should have thought his book would have been much better without it.—I should like to ask him why he has reproduced all this forgotten trash;—possibly it may be merely to gibbet the arms of the enemy—and hold them up to public contempt?

I hope you will see this remarkable man when you go to Paris. His real name is Constant—Levi being a nom de plume, as I found out by his books,—since I saw him (for he allowed me to call him Levi)—He is about sixty. A man in his position, Cabbalistic I mean, who finds himself so much higher than all others of the school—or any other school he knows of—must necessarily feel strongly fortified in his own conclusions and dogmas;—but he professes not to be above being taught;—and I am sure you will say that there are many things he may learn from Boehme—if he will but examine them patiently, and with an unfettered mind—and certainly nobody is more able to open Boehme to him than you are—provided you also are willing to exercise much patience, and lose your time with him;—(and supposing also you can converse in French which is his only language)—I should like very much to be the means of bringing you together—for I believe you may do each other good—his studies and experiments in Magic I conceive to have gone much farther than those of any man I know of—and, on the other hand, he knows nothing of the "zero" or the "little door within"—nor of the beauties of your Theosophic Problems.

> I have still to read his Histoire de la Magie and his Clef des Grands Mysteres—perhaps they may tell me more about the man and his attainments.[45]

Penny had a basis of theosophic experience that made him rather condescending to the French magus, who seemed to him to lack "the one thing needful." Mackenzie, on the other hand, was fascinated by Levi's cluttered apartment, with its grimoires, magical apparatus, and general atmosphere of sorcery. This is probably why Levi did not respond to Penny's subsequent letters, while he kept in touch with Mackenzie and his circle.

After Edward Penny's death, Mrs. Penny began a second career as a writer for the spiritualist journals. Her many contributions to *Light* show her horizons in a continual state of expansion. In 1881 she praised Swedenborg, not ready to class him with Boehme but no longer dismissing him, as she said Saint-Martin and Walton had done.[46] She recommended the revival of respect for the science of astrology, as an element in the doctrine of the World-Souls of this and other planets.[47] On another front, she outgrew her skepticism of thirty years earlier concerning the Bible as an authority[48] and was no longer willing entirely to dismiss the Church's doctrines of prayer for the dead[49] and vicarious suffering.[50] Although she saw no hope for the near future that the esoteric and exoteric might unite within Christendom, she could now forgive the Church for teaching at the "child level," as many spirits were also doing—and being blamed for it.[51]

Spiritualism was a fact that had to be faced, especially if one was writing for spiritualist magazines, and Mrs. Penny took part in the endless debate about what entities were actually communicating through the mediums: were they the souls of the dead, as most spiritualists believed, or were they mindless discarnate "shells" and elementaries, as Madame Blavatsky was now proclaiming? Mrs. Penny was inclined to believe that human personality does survive bodily death, as Swedenborg taught, and that consequently the dead can on occasion communicate with us and benefit from our prayers. Her study of Boehme led her to agree that the average souls, which retain an attachment to earth, are eager to embody and speak, and that the medium may serve to awaken their memories. But she was very doubtful that apparitions are who they say they are; the more so since the most blessed souls, in Boehme's system, go at death to the purely spiritual state.[52]

After contributing little during 1884–1886, Mrs. Penny returned to the pages of *Light* in 1887. Now one of the chief themes of debate was over reincarnation, which the French *spirites* generally believed in, the

American and British spiritualists not (though there were counter-schools on both sides). "I am almost a convert . . . and a very reluctant one," was Mrs. Penny's position: reluctant because the doctrine was not in Boehme, and because the idea of a return to the earthly arena was repulsive to her. She could not believe that "enfleshed life" was the only possible vehicle for spiritual progress, but preferred to reserve judgment on the question.[53] Entering another popular debate, on the question of whether animals (especially pets) have souls, she was sure that they do. Dogs are potentially the younger brothers of humans, and conversely (says Boehme), depraved humans appear in the next world as dogs. [54] She cites Pierrepont Greaves in support of the idea of universal spiral evolution, with its consequent phases of spiritual life and the inevitable death of old religious systems.[55] Thus she could allow that the new "revelation" of spiritualism was God-sent: a view diametrically opposed to that of the Archbishop of Canterbury and of most churchmen, Anglican, Roman Catholic, or Dissenting. "I disbelieved twenty-five years ago," she confesses, but "God offers new truth in every age that lights up, but can never contradict, the old."[56]

In 1889 Mrs. Penny published a series of articles about Blood Sacrifice: one of the stumbling-blocks for those who wanted to accept ancient and pagan religions as valid and sacred, not to mention those spiritualists who felt uneasy with one of the central dogmas of Christian theology. She calls on Thomas Lake Harris, Baader, Saint-Martin, Joseph de Maistre, Eliphas Levi, and Greaves in these erudite articles, whose burden is (1) that the animal sacrifices of ancient times were necessary to demonstrate the efficacy of blood in attracting good invisible agents, and repelling bad ones (this from Baader); (2) that in sudden and violent death, a multitude of subordinate soul-entities are released from control, and thus made available for use by higher, spiritual influences (this based on Greaves); and (3) that the Pentecostal outpouring was conditional on the shedding of Christ's blood.[57] Mrs. Penny kept up her writing throughout the three-year illness that ended with her death on 18 December 1893.[58]

The Behmenist revival had few contributors outside this circle, but one of them should be mentioned, if only to illustrate the synchronicity of ideas. In 1856, the same year as Walton completed his book on William Law, Robert Alfred Vaughan (1823-1857) published his two-volume *Hours with the Mystics*, in which fifty pages are devoted to Boehme and a few more to Pordage and Jane Lead. Vaughan had studied in Germany, been ordained, then retired to devote himself to writing, but did not live long enough to pursue any further his researches on this untrodden ground. In the same work, he introduced Meister Eckhart, but warned that this greatest of mystics was "not acquittable of pantheistic errors."[59] In the following year, 1857, appeared Catherine Winkworth's translation of another

German mystic, Johannes Tauler. Both of these books were praised by Charles Kingsley and did much to kindle an interest in mysticism among such of the clergy as were not mired in the High versus Low Church or the evolution debates. But Boehme, with his titanic imagery, his earthiness of diction and his frightening revelations about God's inner conflicts, was too strong stuff for them.

The last survivor of Greaves's circle was Mary Ann South. In 1859 she married the Rev. Alban Thomas Atwood (1813/14-1883) Vicar of Knayton-in-Leake, near Thirsk, Yorkshire.[60] In this remote village the Vicar built a house, Knayton Lodge, out of his own money, leaving the funds for a vicarage to accumulate for the benefit of the future incumbent. Mrs. Atwood became a great gardener, but was more respected than beloved by the locals. Like the Pennys, the Atwoods had no children. Mr. Atwood "appreciated but did not share his wife's mystical views; and respected but did not understand her great book," says Steiger.[61] Isabel de Steiger (1836–1927) had contacted Mrs. Penny after reading her articles in *Light,* and was introduced by her to Mrs. Atwood, whom she then visited in Yorkshire each year until her death at the age of 92.

Steiger was now a keen member of the Theosophical Society, which had become popular in London's artistic and freethinking upper-class circles after A. P. Sinnett settled there in 1883. Mrs. Atwood was delighted on hearing that the young woman was involved in this new society, for "theosophy" to her meant Jacob Boehme and his followers. This impression cannot have lasted after Steiger had given her Sinnett's *The Occult World* and *Esoteric Buddhism,* and Anna Kingsford's *The Perfect Way, or the Finding of Christ.* But the old lady still felt a kinship with the new Theosophists, especially as Kingsford was a powerful voice in the antivivisectionist cause, which Mrs. Atwood and Mrs. Penny (and no doubt Greaves) had long supported. After visiting London for the last time in 1886, Mrs. Atwood wrote to Sinnett offering the gift of her father Thomas South's rich library of alchemy and esotericism. Although it was accepted, few of the London Theosophists were interested in its arcane lore. For them it was a time of present revelation, especially when Madame Blavatsky herself settled in London in 1887. Only Blavatsky's young secretary G. R. S. Mead profited by Mrs. Atwood's generosity, thereby becoming the best scholar that the Theosophical Society ever produced. Bits and pieces of the library were given away or sold, and after Patience Sinnett's death in 1908, the residue passed to the Scott-Elliotts, a Theosophical couple who lived in Ayrshire.[62]

Another Theosophist friend of Mrs. Atwood was Charles Carleton Massey (1838–1905).[63] Their correspondence began when he was quite young and continued faithfully until his death. Massey, who will reappear in later chapters, was a prosperous barrister who gave up his practice around 1870 for a bachelor's life of writing, traveling, translating, lecturing, and brige-building in the service of the various spiritual movements to which he belonged: Behmenism, spiritualism, the Theosophical Society, and finally mystical Christianity. He became early on a convinced theosophist in the Behmenist sense, and, since he read German, an admirer of Franz von Baader as Boehme's best modern exponent.[64] He admired Lorenz Oken's book (the *vade mecum* of Mrs. Atwood's youth), and studied her own *Suggestive Inquiry*. He came to believe that reincarnation is inevitable for most of mankind, but that Christianity alone offers a means of escape from it. All of this esoteric study left him perplexed at the insistence of William Law and Saint-Martin on the necessity for an exoteric Christianity.[65]

Steiger's enthusiasm for Theosophy, which would last for the rest of her long life, was countered by Massey's increasing disillusionment with Blavatsky and her Buddhist masters. Since Massey and Mrs. Atwood seem to have corresponded on the most intimate level, it was probably his influence that disenchanted her not just with Theosophy, but with the whole revival of occultism. By 1903, as Steiger says, "age and other circumstances had closed all mystic doors" to the old lady.[66] She now regarded occultism as a large-scale operation of evil magic.[67] She could look back over more than half a century since she had burned her books and voluntarily entered the silence: whatever had happened, it was not her fault.

Mrs. Atwood, the key figure of this chapter, links five important movements. First there was her introduction to the English Behmenist tradition through Greaves's study-group. Next came her immersal in the exciting world of Mesmerism during the 1840s. Her attempt to gather her experiences into some sort of cogent whole led to the creation of one of the monuments of alchemical literature, the *Suggestive Inquiry*. After a long period of obscurity, Massey and Isabel de Steiger aroused her interest in the Theosophical Society, which she endowed with her father's library. Lastly, she returned with Massey to the fold of Christian esotericists, having visited the occult world, felt the breath of the Orient, and found them wanting.

THIRTEEN

Rosicrucian Pretenders

Several chapters of this book center around the period between the beginning of Modern Spiritualism (1848) and the founding of the Theosophical Society (1875): a period so rich and complex, even considering the English-speaking world alone, that it cannot be treated as a mere sequence of events. We have seen how the currents of Mesmerism, crystal-gazing, spiritualism, and Behmenist theosophy flowed around each other, forming vortices of energy wherever some person was caught in one or more of them. This chapter and the next scarcely stray outside the same period, but instead of currents of themes they present three individals, chosen because they acted as just such vortices or foci of energy. Madame Blavatsky, who is the subject of Chapter Fourteen, is entirely *sui generis*, and one may wonder whether there is anything left unsaid about her. But the two subjects of the present chapter, P. B. Randolph and Hargrave Jennings, are anything but exhausted. They have been neglected by historians of esoteric movements, despite their demonstrable influence on the early Theosophical Society and their anticipation of its blend of the Western Hermetic tradition with the wisdom of the modern East. The work of both of them was integral to Theosophy's rival, the Hermetic Brotherhood of Luxor (see Chapter Sixteen).

Both these men called themselves "Rosicrucians" and claimed to be authorities on the vexed subject of the brotherhood. They knew many of the people mentioned hitherto, yet each one worked largely alone, making his own synthesis of the esoteric teachings that had come his way. They wrote much on the subject of sex and incorporated it into their philosophic and occult systems with a boldness uncharacteristic of their era. In this respect, they provide continuity with the people mentioned in Chapter One, who saw in sexuality the mainspring of all mythologies. But Randolph, at least, went much further than D'Hancarville, Knight, or O'Brien in drawing practical results from the sexual philosophy.

Paschal Beverly Randolph (1825–1875)[1] was born in New York. He is included in lists of black authors, and was referred to in his lifetime as an octoroon (one-eighth Negro ancestry). It is best to let him define the racial blend which he regarded as both his handicap and the source of his uniqueness:

> Flora, his mother, was said to have been, as is likely, a woman of extraordinary mental activity and physical beauty, nervous, "high-strung," and wilful; a native of Vermont, of mingled Indian, French, English, German and Madagascan blood,—she had not a single drop of negro in her veins, nor consequently has her son, the subject of this memoir. The tawny complexion of both mother and son came from her grandmother, a born queen of the Island of Madagascar. It is not necessary to trace events minutely. Suffice it to say, that the father of *the* Randolph was William Beverly Randolph of Virginia; Flora died in 1832, leaving her son practically an orphan.[2]

Forced into a life of beggary by his foster parents, Randolph ran away to sea and worked as a sailor from adolescence to the age of twenty. He received only one winter's proper schooling during this time, in Portland, Maine.[3] After an injury received while chopping wood, he gave up the sea and learned the dyer's and barber's trades.[4] In his spare time, he studied voraciously, especially medicine—though he surely never earned the M.D. that graced his name from the 1860s onwards. The phenomena of Modern Spiritualism interested him, and he gravitated to spiritualist circles around 1849.[5] By 1852 he was working in Upstate New York both as a barber and as a physician and giving Sunday orations, probably on behalf of the "free speech" Reformatory Party.[6]

It was from Utica, New York, a prosperous canal-servicing and manufacturing city near the center of the state, that Randolph began writing in June 1853 to the *Spiritual Telegraph,* a New York City magazine, about messages he was receiving from the spirits. The first communication was from his "Angel Mother," given in automatic writing. Randolph introduced it by saying that he "had been disappointed grievously and yielded to influences thence derived." His mother had warned him that if he wanted to consort with angels, he had better become more angelic himself. It seemed worthwhile, he said, to pass this message on to others.[7]

The next message Randolph sent to the magazine was from an entity that signed as "Zoroaster," adding that he had been the first of that name. (Since the Renaissance it had been known that there were three Zoroasters.) This august being confessed that, contrary to what he had believed when the hosts of Persia were hearkening to him, wisdom was given not to one sect alone but to the whole family of man, on this and

Figure 13.1. *Paschal Beverly Randolph (1825–1875).*

other earths. Zoroaster advised Randolph to "listen to every voice that whispers 'God is love'," and promised to make the young man a channel, giving him light that he might illumine others.[8]

Shortly after, in July 1853, Randolph's spirit visitors appeared to him, and he was influenced by them to speak as well as to write. Besides Zoroaster, they now represented themselves as "Blaise Pascal" and "Eben el Teleki," and congratulated Randolph on his recent victory over temptation. Here is an extract from their teachings on this occasion, which anticipate the Theosophical systems of seven rays and sevenfold world-epochs:

> God manifested himself first, by rays of love, in seven modes, forms, or degrees; and when it had performed its first office (for there are still six more), matter was ushered into being; man, the *animus*, was born, and love manifested itself in him in the form of desire, which is the first of all actions.[9]

The trio of spirits promised that they would shortly use Randolph's lips to speak to the multitude, in different parts of the state. They were as good as their word. On 15 January 1854, he spoke publicly in Auburn, another upstate town that was already notorious for its number of spiritualists. The occasion was the Harmonial Convention, a meeting of followers of Andrew Jackson Davis, the "Seer of Poughkeepsie" whose teaching was a blend of Spiritualism with the ideas of Swedenborg. Randolph later said that he had been a very keen reader of Davis's works,[10] which supplied all the occult cosmology one could desire. Once Randolph got on stage at the Convention, he "became clairvoyant," as the report says, and so held the audience's attention that he continued his speech after lunch. He announced that he did not believe in evil, or in any evil principle, and that there were no negative currents in Nature, which was the book and image of God. The Bible had been true in its own way, but now the door of progress had been opened through which man could advance on the planes of truth. Randolph urged his listeners to examine the laws of Nature and of man's own being, and enjoined them to look forward to an age of gold in which peace on earth would prevail, and all men could meet, as they were doing at the Auburn Convention, without distinction of color, sex, or money.[11]

In these early communications we can recognize a number of favorite themes of Modern Spiritualism, such as the validity of all religions, faith in social progress, and spiritualism as the new revelation that superseded the Jewish and Christian ones.

Randolph's own role in this revelation required a broader field to till than Upstate New York. Consequently, in the summer of 1854 he moved 250 miles south to New York City, describing himself as a "Clairvoyant and Psychometric" and "intending to devote himself to the examination of disease, and to giving delineations of character."[12] In July 1854 and on several further occasions, he called in at the office of the *Spiritual Telegraph.* The young medium must have been quite a distraction to the staff. On one occasion, the editor mentions coming in to find "Robespierre" holding forth through the vocal organs of Randolph and speaking (as one might imagine) with great force and impetuosity.

A certain Dr. Thomas who was present on this occasion observed that when Randolph spoke in his own person, his philosophy and eloquence were far superior to those of his guides. Randolph apologized for yielding to the influence, and promised to work henceforth in this direction.[13] He now began to be magnetized by Dr. Bergevin, of Paris, whom the *Spiritual Telegraph* describes in the following terms:

> one of the most skillful and scientific physicians in the country, being a graduate of the Medical School of Paris, Member of the Philosophic Institute of France, Director of the Société Magnétique, and assistant of the Baron Dupotet and M. Cahagnet. At a recent trial of Mr. Randolph's powers, Prof. Toutain,[14] of France, expressed his belief that as a seer Mr. Randolph is superior to Alexis [Didier], of Paris, the world-renowned somnambulist. This is a high recommendation, coming, as it does, from such a source.[15]

The *Spiritual Telegraph*'s reports from Randolph's early years as a medium depict a young man discovering his psychic gifts and searching for the best way to master and use them. The New York physicians were keen to use his gifts for the trance diagnosis of diseases, and he prescribed some hundreds of cures in this way, as the famous Edgar Cayce was to do a century later. But Randolph needed more independence than passive mediumship would allow: he had ideas of his own. Over the next two years he developed in a similar direction to that taken by Emma Hardinge Britten, namely as a lecturer, sometimes in trance but usually conscious. There is no doubt, since disinterested newspaper reports are there by the dozen to prove it,[16] that he became one of the most powerful orators in America. Emma followed in his footsteps in more ways than one, becoming a medium in 1855, first in Upstate New York (Troy) and then in New York City; crossing the country and visiting Canada on a lecture tour (Randolph's tour was in 1856, Emma's in 1857); meeting the London spiritualists; working for the Union side in the Civil War (1861–1865) and for Abraham Lincoln's presidential campaign. They can hardly have avoided meeting each other, especially during the political phase of their work.

Among the accomplishments that interested the French physicians was Randolph's ability, when in magnetic trance, to read and play excellent chess while blindfolded. These were also specialties of the brothers Alexis and Alphonse Didier, currently at the height of their fame. In consequence, Randolph received an invitation to display his powers in Paris, the center of the magnetic movement.[17] Dr. Bergevin was in touch with Baron Dupotet (see Chapter Eight), who was now editing the *Journal du magnétisme* in an effort to persuade the scientific world to take notice of new phases of the phenomenon.

At this point of my biographical sketch, a digression is unavoidable because the facts of Randolph's life become harder and harder to establish. The richest fund of biographical information is in the publications of R. Swinburne Clymer (1878–1966), who was head of one of the several American orders calling themselves "Rosicrucians." Clymer had no hesitation in misquoting Randolph's rare works[18] in order to support his own claim to the coveted mantle of "Supreme Grand Master" of the *Fraternitas Rosae Crucis,* as against his rival Spencer Lewis who headed the Ancient and Mystical Order of the Rose-Cross (A.M.O.R.C.). The large number of contradictions and falsifications disqualifies Clymer's writings as a reliable source—which is unfortunate, since Clymer had, without a doubt, access to lost documents and to people who had known Randolph and his close associates.

Clymer's main claims concern Randolph's travels outside the US, which he summarizes thus:

> In 1850 he was in Germany and was admitted to the meeting held by the *Fraternitas Rosae Crucis* at Frankfort on Main as a member of the First degree. There he met General Hitchcock, who quickly recognized in him the person to become Supreme Grand Master of the Western World. He was there introduced to Charles Trinius and *Count Guinotti.*
>
> In Paris during 1854 he finished his studies in the practice of *skrying* by means of water, ink and the magic Mirrors, as followed by Count Cagliostro and Saint Germain, and laid plans for the publication of his work on *Seership.*
>
> In England, then in France in 1856, in preparation for induction as Supreme Grand Master of the Western World of the *Fraternitas Rosae Crucis.*
>
> In Paris 1858, inducted as Supreme Grand Master of the *Fraternitas Rosae Crucis* of the Western World and the Isles of the Sea, and created a Knight of *L'Ordre du Lis.*
>
> In London 1861, where he was made a member of the Order of the Rose and received with honors by the Supreme Grand Master Jennings of England. Thence to the Orient, where he received final *Initiation* into the Ansaireh of Syria and

> was inducted as Hierarch of the Ansaireh; then travelled through other countries of the Orient and back to America, *via* France, in 1863, as Hierarch of the Ansaireh or Imperial *Eulis.*[19]

Some of this may be true, but one should not believe a single word without proof or corroboration from a disinterested source. To give one example of Clymer's quality as witness, he cannot even make up his mind about so important a matter as Randolph's installation as Supreme Grand Master, for in another place[20] he dates it not 1858 but 1861, and assembles an all-star congregation comprising Eliphas Levi, Bulwer-Lytton, Kenneth Mackenzie, Charles Mackay, Count Guinotti, Count Brasynsky, Emperor Napoleon III, Alexis and Adolph [sic] Didier, Count Tsovinski, General Pellister, the Duke de Malakoff, Ethan Allen Hitchcock, and Albert Pike, plus representatives from France, Germany, England, Poland, Russia, and Egypt.

Randolph's own works overflow with biographical details, but these, too, can seldom be taken as hard evidence. The fact that the main character of *Ravalette* is called Beverly, or the "Rosicrucian" of *Tom Clark and His Wife* Paschal, and that much of their life-stories is ascertainably Randolph's own, does not change the fact that these are novels, in which the author has every right to invent as he pleases. Moreover, like *Ghost Land* they are occult novels about secret societies, in which vows of secrecy compel the disguising of times, places, and persons. The same caveat must apply to his nonfictional works: Randolph had a self-image to project and a mission to perform that were more important than gratifying the curiosity of future scholars.

Returning to the world of facts, there is no doubt that Randolph was in London in May 1855 for the World's Convention of Robert Owen's disciples, held "to inaugurate the commencement of the millenium."[21] It may be remembered that the elderly Owen was now a believer in spiritualism. Randolph had come on behalf of the American spirits and was supposed to read a message that they had sent through John Murray Spear, who had been in his day, like Owen, a red-hot social reformer. Owing to the stress of other business, this message was never read out—which Owen, in retrospect, thought just as well, as it might have prejudiced his nonspiritualistic plans. To the sensitive Randolph, his failure to be invited onto the platform must have seemed one more racial and social slight. Nor did he admire the "pretended adepts" whom he met in the London spiritualist world: he names "Bulwer, Jennings, Wilson, Belfedt, Archer, Socher, Corvaja."[22]

Randolph was now able to accept the invitation of Dupotet to visit Paris, where he gained such a reputation from a mesmeric séance in which he took part that within days he was summoned to perform at the Tuiléries Palace, before the Emperor Napoleon III—just as D. D. Home would do the following year.[23] The reader of Randolph's autobiographical novel *Ravalette* will have to decide how far to believe the descriptions he gives there of his Paris adventures. He witnessed the willed materialization and disappearance of animal and human forms, due to powers that their adepts had learned in the East. His own talent was called upon because he was able to enter an unusually profound state of trance. In this state, called the Sleep of Sialam, he uttered prophecies concerning the fate of Europe and its crowned heads over the coming seventy years.[24] Like most prophecies, they lend themselves to multiple interpretations, but they missed most of the important events that actually transpired.

On returning to the United States, Randolph became a successful professional medium, touring the country and Canada from coast to coast.[25] He was back in England in the autumn of 1856,[26] and made a great impression in private groups such as the "Charing Cross Spirit Circle," for whom he gave several sittings early in 1857.[27] It may have been on this visit, rather than in 1855, that he met Hargrave Jennings and Bulwer-Lytton. An anonymous witness later recalled that Randolph had given amazing trance discourses, equal to any speaker in the normal or abnormal state, and that, like many mediums, he "was impulsive and eccentric, but kind-hearted, social, and grateful for any little kindness that might be shown him."[28] No one could ever claim that Randolph was mean, inflated, or lacking a sense of humor.

He now revisited Paris, if *Ravalette* is to be believed, and gave further sessions before the Emperor. One of Randolph's discoveries in this city was the drug hashish, in a particularly powerful form that he calls "Dowam Meskh." Apparently hashish was regularly used in the French magnetic world to enhance the sensitivity of mediums.[29] Randolph wrote in 1867 that he had taken it twice deliberately and twice accidentally, then left it alone for the rest of his life.[30] But his biographer, John Patrick Deveney, shows that this was by no means the extent of his drug use.[31] In an age that has seen the "acid enlightenments" of the 1960s, it is interesting to read the following account of the results of taking 18 grains of Dowam Meskh:

> It may astonish those who knew me some years ago as a blank atheist, and believer in the accursed individual sovereignty sophistry, when I tell them, that when in the deepest gloom of soul after trying to believe in Jehovah, with only partial success, I was at last perfectly convinced through the agency of this wonderful conserve. I took a portion of Dowam Meskh; it perfectly illuminated me, but the lucidity infinitely exceeded anything

> that I had ever known before, either spiritual, self-induced, or mesmeric. In this illumination there was no loss of will or self. When fully clear, I asked the question, "Is there a God?" *The answer came, or I went to it;* but the mysteries revealed to my astonished soul on that eventful night, will never be disclosed to mortal ears. One thing only shall be said, namely—*Never! no, not for an instant have I since doubted the existence of a God.*[32]

From England and France, Randolph appears to have gone to Egypt,[33] where he succeeded in learning the secret of how to concoct this Dowam Meskh. Hashish was henceforth the crown jewel of his pharmacopoiea, being an ingredient of all the "elixirs" that he peddled in person and by mail order.

In 1858 Randolph returned to America, where he made a temporary ripple in the Spiritualist pond with a public renunciation of Spiritualism in favor of Christianity.[34] As Emma Hardinge Britten callously observed, "he was most cordially received, formally baptized, and greatly patronized and prayed over" by a sect of Bostonian Christians; but "after having made some rambling and utterly inapplicable remarks about Spiritualism, interspersed with evidently sensational attempts to show that he was still 'under the influence' and compelled occasionally to break off from his written lecture and return to his old style of improvisation, the whole affair concluded by the said Dr. Randolph's speedy return to the ranks of Spiritualism, in which he has been practicing on and off ever since."[35]

The most signal contribution of Randolph to occultism concerned sex. In his medical practice, he specialized in curing sexual complaints, both physical and psychological. But he did not stop at this level: he was not a Kraft-Ebbing or a proto-Freudian, but an occultist and a spiritualist, for whom sex had also, and most significantly, a spiritual dimension. Consequently, Randolph's writings treat sex in a more comprehensive fashion than any writer of his time. It is quite surprising that they have been overlooked by social historians.

On a practical level Randolph's doctrine, in brief, was that the "normal" sex of nineteenth-century couples ignored the woman's capacity and need for satisfaction; but that if the man understood this and acted accordingly, unsuspected depths of pleasure and spirituality lay open to both partners, with a consequent strengthening of the marriage bond and avoidance of numerous physical, psychological, and social ills. Works such as *The Ansairetic Mystery*, *Physical Love*, *The Golden Secret*, and *Eulis* teach this without embarrassment and almost without reserve, which is why they were at first circulated in manuscript copies or private prints.[36] As regards its higher level, sex, for Randolph, was a sacrament and nothing less than a means to a "holy communion" of souls. Consequently he hedges it round with taboos: it should not be enjoyed frequently nor promiscuously, never with any form of contraception, and absolutely never alone or with the same sex. Nothing could be further from the sexual magic later developed by the Ordo Templi Orientalis (O.T.O.), still less that of Aleister Crowley and his followers.

When Randolph was arrested in 1872 on suspicion of distributing immoral "free love" literature, the case was never brought to court. Randolph capitalized on his arrest and on the weekend he had spent in jail by publishing a fictional transcript of a trial and acquittal, *P. B. Randolph: His Curious Life, Works, and Career. The Great Free-Love Trial . . .* He depicts a prosecuting attorney as finding nothing worse to say than that Randolph encouraged women to think of themselves as equals to men. He was indeed one of the century's great feminists.

To resume this biographical sketch: we find Randolph in 1860–61 moving from Boston back to Utica and working as a physician and writer. His wife or companion, Mary Jane Randolph, was called an "Indian Doctress" who had had her own practice in Boston, specializing in women's problems and using the traditional remedies of her Native American ancestors. It was she who registered Randolph's works for copyright and urged him to write his recantation, *What I think of Spiritualism* (1860). The Randolphs had three children, including a daughter, Cora, born about 1855,[37] and a young son, Winnie, who died of neglect and poverty during Randolph's long absence from home in 1861–62.[38] There is little doubt that this tormented man was a great lover, an unreliable husband, and a wretched father.

In the summer of 1861, Randolph spent ten weeks lecturing in California, then traveled in turn to Britain, France, Malta, Greece, Turkey, Syria, Egypt, and Arabia. One object of the journey was to investigate the origins of mankind, which Randolph had long suspected to be older than the 6,000 years allowed by the Bible. As mentioned in Chapter Two, the biblical dating had been doubted for a century by freethinking Frenchmen like Boulanger and Voltaire and had long become an open question among the British intelligentsia. Randolph contributed to its questioning by an American public that was, and is, more prone to fundamentalism than its European contemporaries. On his return to America, he compiled a book on the subject, *Pre-Adamite Man* (1863), which presented the latest theories of geologists and paleontologists. The book, ascribed in early editions not to Randolph but to "Griffin Lee," was dedicated with permission to Abraham Lincoln.

In *Pre-Adamite Man,* Randolph concluded that the various races of mankind had arisen separately, though whether evolved from apes or separately created, he could not say.[39] Because of recent discoveries of human fossils in Europe that were far earlier than any monuments of India and Egypt, he concluded that Europe had been in prehistoric times, as in historic ones, the spearhead of human development, and this owing to an innate "superiority of blood and race."[40] As for the Negro race, he regarded it as the purest survival from primordial times, whereas all the other races had become intermingled. He added: "It is doubtful if the Negro, since the world began, ever even approximated to such a high state of civiliation as he has attained on Northern American soil; but that he will achieve great things in the future, is, of course, but a mere question of time."[41]

Although he denied having any continental African ancestry, Randolph had felt the bitter weight of racial prejudice. When he returned from his long voyage to find the nation in full civil war, he determined to throw his weight behind the cause of the Southern slaves and to accept identification as one with them. While resuming residence in Utica, he worked to enlist Black soldiers for the Unionist cause and put his oratorical powers to work. In nearby Syracuse, N.Y., October 1864, Randolph saluted the battle flag stained with Louisianian blood and said: "We are here to ring the bells at the door of the world, proclaiming to nations, white men, slaves, kings, and the universe, 'We are coming up . . . and going to stay'."[42] At the end of the year, on Lincoln's suggestion, he moved to New Orleans to work for the President's cause.

After Lincoln's assassination (15 April 1865), Randolph stayed on in the South. By October, he was Principal of "Lloyd Garrison Grammar School—Colored" in New Orleans, and writing to William Lloyd Garrison, the antislavery leader, to ask for support. In particular, he asked for "apparatus to illustrate Astronomy (tellurian)—a Gyroscope, Microscope, a numerical frame, Conic Sections, Cube root blocks, a Magnet and such other instruments as will enable us to fight the battle for my race against ignorance."[43] In 1866 he came north to raise money for his school; General Ulysses Grant gave him $200.[44] In September he was a delegate from Louisiana to the Southern Loyal Convention in Philadelphia, and made a speech acclaimed in the newpapers as the high point of the convention. But this, and the associated pilgrimage through the Northern states to Lincoln's tomb in Illinois, were a disillusioning experience owing to infighting and racial prejudice even within his own party.

Randolph now abandoned politics and settled in Boston to make his living as a physician, medium, and writer. He adopted the persona of a "Rosicrucian," collaborating with a Mrs. Mary P. Crook in setting up the "Rosicrucian Rooms" at 27 Boylston Street. According to Mrs. Crook's prospectus of May 1867:

> At the Rooms, Clairvoyant Examinations are daily made, Circles for Development in Clairvoyance, Psychometry and Mediumship are held. GRAND LEVEES, on Wednesday Evenings, for the cultured and refined only. Admission by card. I have employed Mr. Randolph as Clairvoyant in *five specialties*, and have others equally good in their line. I can also procure SYMPATHETIC RINGS, LOCKETS and STELAE, ROSICRUCIAN MIRRORS, (for seeing the dead, etc.,) and all things pertaining to the Grand but Mysterious Science of the Soul.[45]

For all his independence of thought, Randolph could still act (and perhaps "act" is the word) as medium for the famous dead: in the same Prospectus, Mrs. Crook describes how at one séance he suddenly announced that Raymond Lully would now dictate an oracle to him, which was duly published.

Randolph tells us little about his personal life at this period, but there is one clue: by 1868, Mary Jane Randolph, still in Utica, was calling herself a "widow,"[46] perhaps to save face after being abandoned by him. Advertisements in his publications show that he was energetically peddling his patent remedies, giving consultations on sexual troubles both in person and by mail, and selling privately his more sensitive books and pamphlets, which he was constantly revising and reprinting. To trace them all would be a bibliographer's delight, or nightmare.

In 1870, Randolph sold out his medical practice to a Dr. Smith,[47] and became embroiled with a pair of swindlers who attempted to divest him of his copyrights. His side of the story is told in his *Curious Life*. Ruined by the swindlers, the trial, and by the Boston Fire later that year, his misfortunes were crowned in May 1873 when he fell from a elevated railroad near Toledo, Ohio.[48] He stayed there as a half-paralyzed invalid, and made Toledo his home—if one can call it that—for the rest of his life. But despite injuries that left him unable to speak for more than five minutes on end, he was still able to give discourses when in trance that were fully equal to his old style and to make spirits visibly and tangibly present in the room.[49]

Randolph's accident did not interfere with any of his activities. Before the end of 1873 he was married again, to Kate Corson, a woman of nineteen. She remained at home, caring for their infant son Osiris Budh Randolph (born 1874 and later a successful—and genuine—M.D.[50]), while her husband crossed the Atlantic once more. This was probably the occasion for the initiation of Peter Davidson, who would later incorporate Randolph's teachings into the Hermetic Brotherhood of Luxor.[51] Randolph was in California from September 1874 to May 1875, organizing societies on a regular ritualistic basis.[52] On his return to Toledo, he seems to have become disenchanted with his new wife, accusing her of betraying him. Always unstable, and often intoxicated, he shot himself on 29 July 1875 after announcing his intention to an incredulous neighbor, whose eyewitness account of the Rosicrucian's sad end is preserved in the local newspaper.

How long Randolph had called himself a Rosicrucian and directed any sort of fraternity is hard to determine. Clymer makes him out to have obtained his Rosicrucian credentials in Frankfurt and Paris as early as 1850. Certainly the mention of Frankfurt is alluring, in the light of its importance to other figures in our story. In the mock trial, the prosecuting attorney says:

> Over twenty years ago, Mr. Randolph was known to be a Rosicrucian, and in that period he ascended the steps of that mystical brotherhood, outstripping thousands and rushing past hundreds of gray-beards in the mental race, until he attained the chieftainship of the true Rosicrucians in America and the Isles of the Seas, and finally to the supreme High Priesthood of the Order and Grand-Mastership of the combined Lodges of the earth likewise, reaching the double office through his absolute defiance of poverty and wealth, and persistent pursuit of ideas alone![53]

But until there is some (unforged) evidence of this from the early 1850s, it is imprudent to take it as anything more than the story Randolph told to the Bostonians after the public establishment of the "Rosicrucian Rooms." In *Eulis*, first published June 1874, he makes a confession that has more of a ring of truth about it:

> Early in life I discovered that the fact of my ancestry on one side, being what they [sic] were, was an effectual estoppal on my preferment and advancement, usefulness and influence.[54] I became famous, but never popular. I studied Rosicrucianism, found it suggestive, and loved its mysticism. So I called myself The Rosicrucian, and gave my thought to the world as Rosicrucian thought; and lo! the world greeted with loud applause what it supposed had its origin and birth elsewhere than in the soul of P. B. Randolph.
>
> Very nearly *all* that I have given as Rosicrucianism originated in my soul; and scarce a single thought, only suggestions, have I borrowed from those who, in ages past, called themselve by that name—one which served me well as vehicle wherein to take *my* mental treasures to a market, which gladly opened its doors to that name, but would, and did, slam to its portals in

> the face of the tawny student of Esoterics. [. . .] the world is challenged to find a line of my thought in the whole 4,000 books on Rosicrucianism; among the brethren of that Fraternity—and I know many such in various lands, and was, till I resigned the office, Grand Master of the only Temple of the Order on the globe . . .[55]

It looks as though the Rosicrucianism of his Boston years was his own invention—though he may have started it in a private way before the opening of the Boylston Street Temple—and the Grand Mastership a self-assumed office. At the time of the above confession, Randolph considered himself entitled, as the last Grand Master of Rosicrucianism, to dissolve the order altogether, on the grounds that "the Rosicrucian system is, and never was other else than a door to the ineffable Grand Temple of Eulis."[56]

Randolph started a "Provisional Grand Lodge of Eulis" in Tennessee in March 1874, in order to "teach all the occult branches of esoteric knowledge [and] constitute it my literary heir"; but he also dissolved this on 13 June because of personal incompatibilities.[57] The subsequent months in California were evidently spent in a renewed attempt to propagate it as a school of practical magic. As for the name, he says, "Many will suspect from our true name—BROTHERHOOD OF EULIS—that we really mean 'Eleusis,' and they are not far wrong. The Eleusinian Philosophers (with whom Jesus is reputed to have studied) were philosophers of Sex; and the Eleusinian Mysteries were mysteries thereof . . ."[58]

Eulis also contains Randolph's confession of how he learned one, at least, of his secrets:

> One night—it was in far-off Jerusalem or Bethelehem, I really forget which—I made love to, and was loved by, a dusky maiden of Arabic blood. I of her, and that experience, learned—not directly, but by suggestion—the fundamental principle of the White Magic of Love; subsequently I became affiliated with some dervishes and fakirs of whom, by suggestion still, I found the road to other knowledges; and of these devout practicers of a simple, but sublime and holy magic, I obtained additional clues—little threads of suggestion, which, being persistently followed, led my soul into labyrinths of knowledge themselves did not even suspect the existence of. I became practically, what I was naturally—a mystic, and in time chief of the lofty brethren; taking the clues left by the masters, and pursuing them farther than they had ever been before; actually discovering the ELIXIR of LIFE; the universal Solvent,

> or celestial Alkahest; the water of beauty and perpetual youth, and the philosopher's stone,—all of which this book contains; but only findable by him or her who searches well.[59]

My conclusions, helped by Randolph's other writings, are that the "elixir of life" in question was a medicinal preparation that Randolph called "Protogene," a tonic for nerves, sex, and brain.[60] The "universal Solvent, or celestial Alkahest" was probably another of his patent medicines, laced with hashish-if indeed it was not the drug itself. The "water of beauty and perpetual youth" probably referred to his theory of the mingling of male and female fluids during sexual excitement, but before male orgasm.[61] The "philosopher's stone" was the magic mirror.[62]

Randolph's books, taken as a whole, contain the nineteenth century's fullest compendium of practical magic: not the ceremonial kind found in Barrett's *Magus,* nor the Ficinian and Kabbalistic kind compiled by Eliphas Levi, but magic presented without antique jargon as a way for modern men and women to increase their happiness and to control their lives. The essentials of his practical teaching are contained in *Seership,* which is on the use of magic mirrors to develop clairvoyance and other psychic powers, and in *The Ansairetic Mystery*[63] and *Eulis,* which is the longest of his sexual treatises. Both books would become fundamental documents of the Hermetic Brotherhood of Luxor, the school of practical occultism that is the subject of Chapter Sixteen.

As early as 1860, Randolph had adopted as his motto the word "TRY." It appears frequently in his texts and in emblematic figures. On first sight a banal motto, the word embodies the doctrine of the occultist and magician for whom the primary task is the development of the will, and for whom countless obstacles can be predicted that can only be overcome by repeated and patient effort. We will find it used among the early Theosophists as a codeword for the essential difference between occultism and spiritualism. Until his tragic suicide, Randolph's own life and works exemplify the motto, as he repeatedly rose above the adversities that race, poverty, vice, lack of education, betrayal, the law, fire, and accident put in his way.

Few such hazards seem to have sown the path of Hargrave Jennings (1817?–1890), whose biographer has even less to go on than Randolph's, but enough to know that the life of the English writer contrasted in every way with that of the American seer.

Jennings tells us that his family circumstances were "not poor, though not overwhelmingly rich." He grew up in the West End of London, and as a child would accompany his mother to church at St. James's, Picadilly. Here is his own character-sketch:[64]

> I was always a strange, moody, unaccountable child; fond of solitude—drawing all my mental nutriment from reading—setting with indomitable perseverance to the perusal of every book which fell in my way; and studying and restudying my favourite authors with loving pertinacity. I grew very superstitious, contemplative, and fanciful. The faculty of 'marvellousness' was largely developed in me very early. I read works of imagination with avidity. The town became filled to me with phantom romance-pictures. I led a life quite out of my real life.

As a result, Jennings would later claim than from his childhood he had been fully acquainted with everything about Spiritualism that was "reliable and philosophical."[65] A precocious writer, at the age of fifteen he contributed a series of sea-sketches to the *Metropolitan Magazine,* whose editor, the novelist Captain Marryat, was amazed when he learned how young their author was.[66] In 1842, Bulwer-Lytton wrote Jennings a kindly note acknowledging receipt of the latter's poem *Astolfo.* But the praise of famous authors did not bring success in its wake. For many years, Jennings worked as the secretary of an opera company,[67] then was thrown on his own meager resources. In a sad letter of 1870 (see Appendix B), he wrote to Lytton that he had never been treated decently by publishers or enabled to make any money from his work.[68] He probably survived on a miniscule private income, eked out by hack writing. His brother lived at Ambassador's Court, St. James's Palace, and Hargrave Jennings used this address in later life.[69] Whether or not he actually lived in such a desirable locale, he died there on 11 March 1890. There is no sign of the reminiscences he is supposed to have completed shortly before his death.

Although his early publications were fictional and topical,[70] Jennings was claiming as early as 1858 a "lifelong devotion to metaphysics" and "years of research and reading" in preparation for his first philosophical book, *The Indian Religions.* Stated to be "by an Indian missionary," it was written to criticize and correct the lack of understanding of the Orient, especially as shown in an essay on Buddhism published in the London *Times* in the Spring of 1857, and, more generally, in the climate following the First War of Indian Independence of May–September 1857. Among the books Jennings lists as having consulted "in the attainment of the following philosophical results"[71] are the works of Cornelius Agrippa, Paracelsus, J. B. van Helmont, and Swedenborg (all in English); Thomas Taylor's translation of Plato; recent books on magnetism and spiritualism; Catherine Crowe's *The Night Side of Nature* and Ennemoser's *History of Magic*; the *Asiatic Journal* and *Asiatic Researches,* and Ward's *The Religion of the Hindoos.* This list already serves to place him at the center of our intersecting circles of interest.

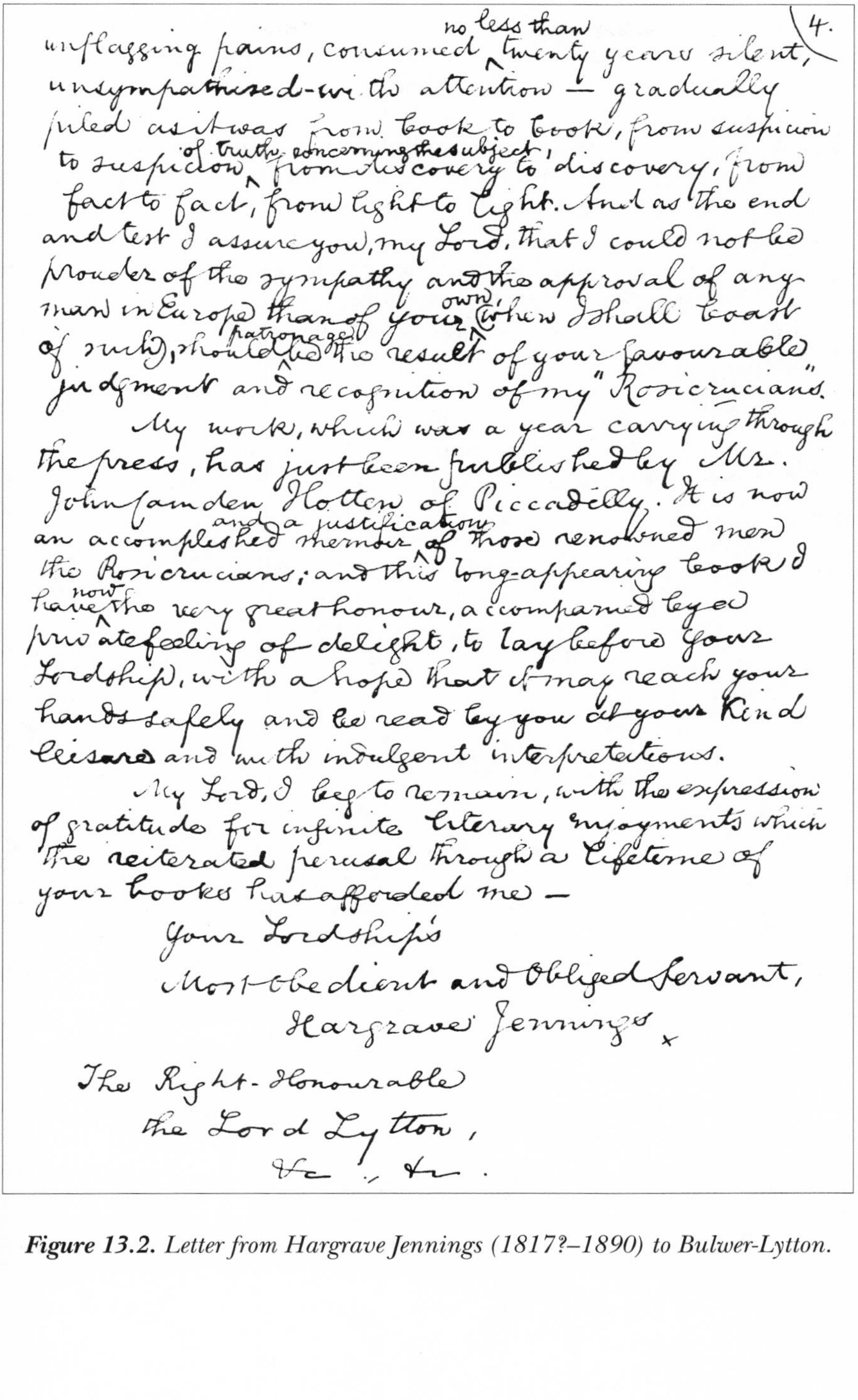

4.

unflagging pains, consumed no less than twenty years silent, unsympathised-with attention — gradually piled as it was from book to book, from suspicion to suspicion of truths concerning the subject, from discovery to discovery, from fact to fact, from light to light. And as the end and test I assure you, my Lord, that I could not be prouder of the sympathy and the approval of any man in Europe than of your own, when I shall boast of such, should patronage be the result of your favourable judgment and recognition of my "Rosicrucians."

My work, which was a year carrying through the press, has just been published by Mr. John Camden Hotten of Piccadilly. It is now an accomplished and a justification memoir of those renowned men the Rosicrucians; and this long-appearing book I have now the very great honour, accompanied by a private feeling of delight, to lay before Your Lordship, with a hope that it may reach your hands safely and be read by you at your kind leisure and with indulgent interpretations.

My Lord, I beg to remain, with the expression of gratitude for infinite literary enjoyments which the reiterated perusal through a lifetime of your books has afforded me —

Your Lordship's
Most Obedient and Obliged Servant,
Hargrave Jennings

The Right-Honourable
the Lord Lytton,
&c., &c.

Figure 13.2. *Letter from Hargrave Jennings (1817?–1890) to Bulwer-Lytton.*

The author of these *Times* articles, published on April 17 and 20, was in fact F. Max Müller, future Professor at Oxford and editor of the *Sacred Books of the East* series. In this early venture into Buddhist studies, Müller called the aspiration to a Nirvana of utter annihilation little short of insane, but allowed that individual Buddhists, through not understanding it properly, had triumphed over the "madness of its metaphysics." Jennings thought the anonymous author woefully ignorant in thinking Buddhism atheistic, whereas in point of fact: "We, in this religion, stand face to face with an Antiquity when men, even in our own suspicion—in our own granting—were very greatly more near God."[72] (The awkwardness of style always appears when Jennings is speaking of matters close to his heart.) He goes on: "Brahminism may be considered to be the starred and decorated, and the human-marked child of its inexpressibly sublimely descended parent, Buddhism."[73]

So little was known about Buddhism in the earlier nineteenth century that it was widely thought to be older than the Brahmanism of the Hindus. Among the reasons for this conclusion was the Enlightenment idea that the simple precedes the complex, so that a Buddhism supposedly atheistic and nihilistic had to be more primitive than the luxuriant polytheism of India.[74] In the 1840s, mainly thanks to the work of Eugène Burnouf, a clearer picture was beginning to emerge of Buddhism's origin in India (not from the Black race or from Tartary) and of its founding by a single man in historical times. But Jennings was not familiar with the latest continental scholarship: he probably learned all he knew from those weighty and wordy Victorian periodicals such as the *Edinburgh Review* and the *Quarterly Review*.[75]

Jennings was incited by Müller's article to defend Buddhism from the oft-laid charge of atheism (to which we will return in Chapters Fifteen and Seventeen), and to point out that the original, pre-Gautama Buddhism was the primordial wisdom of mankind. It stretched his powers of expression to the utmost as he strove to explain this wisdom to his audience of 1858:

> In the theory of the Buddhist philosophers, life being an accident, *something* has passed on and is passing on, behind to make it so. And this unknown, moveless, passionless REST, in which life should be impossible, being *form* or the Pythagorean number, is their *Nirvanâ,* or non-existence.[76]

This, he says, is the Buddhists' "much-belied abyss of atheism," misunderstood because the West can only conceive of God as a being; whereas the ultimate, in Buddhism, is beyond being or, as Jennings elsewhere calls it, "sublime 'Non-Being'."[77]

There were few Western minds in the mid-nineteenth century capable of entertaining the conception of God as a "spiritual gulf of nothingness,"[78] or of Non-Being as metaphysically prior to Being. Nor were there many who would agree with Jennings that

> the mistake that is made, in the objections to Buddhism, is just this, that the objectors will insist upon starting upon the premiss that life is real. Ideas, by which we converse with that outside, are all which we are. And these are not real things, but mere delusive lights of the master phantom-light of intelligence.[79]

Given the nullity of the universe in the face of Nirvana, there are still certain laws, or habits, to which the great illusion is obedient. What Jennings calls "the master phantom-light of intelligence," he elsewhere calls Nature, "the soul of the world, or final conceivable mechanical intelligence,"[80] which works through the opposites, or complementaries, such as Light and Darkness, Life and Death. This idea is of course more Hermetic than Buddhist.

If God is nothingness, any notion we form of "him" is bound to be wrong. Jennings blames human reason as the great deceiver, because it makes us form ideas about the formless, and erects itself as a substitute for direct intuition. If there is a devil in his theology, it is Reason.

> Divinity must be complete and clear (out of idea), and therefore nothing . . . Thus the human *reason* infallibly, under all its various heavenly deceits and just the more successfully according to its perfection, leads FROM God, and the idea of God (which is not God) is the very opposite of God, and being the very opposite of God, it must be the Evil-Principle.[81]

So how are we to know the unknowable, nonexistent Absolute? Only, it seems, through the direct replacement of our consciousness by the inconceivable:

> [God] is only ultimately and really possible in the divine immediate possession, or in the supernatural *trampling* on Idea, and (to the world) madness or ecstasy. We can never rise to Him. He must descend to us . . . He is only possible in thus snatching us out of the world, or out of ourselves.[82]

Failing the mystical assimilation to the Absolute which he struggles to describe here, Jennings seems to have nothing better to offer than to seek God in "miracle." He understands miracles not as God's occasional contravention of the laws of nature, but as the multifarious phenomena that contradict the petty reasoned order of the illusory thought-world. He evidently saw the breaking-down of the over-rational mind as the necessary first step towards the assimilation of the Buddhist world view, and to the experiences that may follow.

In the remainder of *The Indian Religions,* Jennings is unsparing in his tirades against the British in India and their "hundred years of inexpressible misrule," which he holds responsible for the Mutiny.[83] He castigates the "proselytizing colonels" who bully the natives into conversion and the general insensitivity to the religious rites of the Hindus, asking how the British would like their own religion to be treated like that.

It would be difficult to exaggerate the boldness and originality of *The Indian Religions,* coming as it did twenty years before Sir Edwin Arnold's *The Light of Asia* (1879) presented Buddhism to the public in a glow of admiration. At mid-century, knowledge of Buddhism in Europe and America was slight, and enthusiam for it nil. The American Transcendentalists, whose admiration for Hindu doctrines was based on the ample source material of the *Asiatic Researches,* found Buddhism chilly and negative by comparison.[84] Academic experts such as Burnouf, Müller, and Barthélemy Saint-Hilaire painted Buddhism as a gloomy religion of negation, and Nirvana as nothing more or less than extinction, then exclaimed with astonishment that a third of the world's population could be so stupid as to embrace such a faith. Jennings stands alone in his realization that, in order to understand Buddhism as a reality, one's mind must be disburdened from every prejudice of rationality.

Jennings's next book, *Curious Things of the Outside World* (1863), attacked the foundations of rationalism by forcing attention on the inexplicable and the supernatural. Its two volumes contain a philosophical treatise prefaced by a collection of ghost stories and tales of the supernatural such as were popular at the time, as witness the better-known works of Catharine Crowe, Henry Christmas, Joseph Ennemoser, and Robert Dale Owen.[85] Jennings says that his purpose in presenting these instances of miracle and anomaly is to show:

> That there is an universal connection in nature, and a mutual reciprocity in sympathetical and anti-pathetical contrasts, but which cannot be perceived by the waking senses . . . That a spiritual communion exists between man and man, and therefore also between man and superior beings . . . That in science nothing yet is certain, or fixed, respecting nature and spirit, the soul or body, or the possibility, or probability, of reciprocal influence.[86]

Evidently we have moved from the metaphysics of *The Indian Religions* to cosmological theory; Jennings is already writing like a Rosicrucian, with the characteristic world view based on Hermetic correspondences. His own enthusiasm is evident when he summarizes the doctrines of the Gnostics:

> Those souls, or divine possibilities, which, in their reception of the Light, are enabled to clear themselves of the fogs of the worlds of being, will, at the dissolution of their sense-bodies, transcend into the Pleroma. The souls that are unable to *illuminate* themselves out of it, continue in the deceits, and therefore thraldom, of Matter—however beautiful or grand be it:—and they remain under the sceptre of the King of the Visible, and will, at death, transmigrate into other bodies, losing all trace of their previous stages—the nature of which are alone known to God—until, in purification, they really AWAKE. At last—in their escape into the *Pleromae,* or state of the eternal Matterless Light—they triumph over *its imitation* and over *its* master, this King of Bright Shadows, Devil, or Great Demiurgus. This is the pure Transmigration of Pythagoras, and the Bhuddism [sic] which, in its truer or falser forms, prevails over all the East. And will be found, indeed to be the foundation and parent of all religions.[87]

Hargrave Jennings envisages the destiny of the human being as a dual path, leading either to the dissolution of self in the Pleroma (the Nirvana of *The Indian Religions*), or else to a purifying series of reincarnations in the world of the diabolical Demiurge, which have the same end result.

Nothing could be more different from the sentimentality of the Spiritualists, obsessed as they were by the apparent proof of personal survival. Indeed, the "presumed Spiritual Disclosures" that followed the Hydesville rappings of 1848 were, in Jennings's view, nothing more than a reflection from the minds of the living and had done much harm in discrediting the general subject of supernaturalism.[88]

Soon after publishing *The Indian Religions,* a new world of erudition opened for Jennings. In Volume II of *Curious Things of the Outside World* he cited Robert Fludd's *Mosaical Philosophy*; he now knew the history of the Rosicrucian manifestoes and the importance of Johann Valentin Andreae; he could cite the Rosicrucian manuscripts of Dr. Rudd, "who appears to have been an adept," in the British Museum. He gives much rambling information on these and on the "Fire-Philosophers," whom he calls a fanatical late-sixteenth century sect, active in almost all the countries of Europe.[89] It looks as if he had contacted the survivors of the Mercurii, at least on paper.

This "Philosophy of Fire" was central to Jennings's thinking, if contradictory in its meaning. In *The Indian Religions,* Fire was the Non-Being or Nirvana in which all things are annihilated. In *Curious Things* and later works, Fire meant the first creative impulse that brings a universe out of nothingness—which one may as well call God.

Having once posited Fire (or its companion, Light) as the first principle of all religions and mythologies, a vast field for comparative study opened up before our philosopher, as the relevant symbols could be found everywhere.[90] Near the end of *Curious Things,* Jennings recommended a "special group of books" that shared his approach: Godfrey Higgins's *The Celtic Druids* and *Anacalypsis,* and Sir William Drummond's *Oedipus Judaicus.* He had been as unaware of these sources as he was of the Rosicrucian literature when drawing up his booklist at the start of *The Indian Religions,* but in his subsequent books he never failed to mention them with great respect. Naturally they confirmed his belief in the antiquity and universality of Buddhism. The "keynote" of the second volume of *Curious Things* is taken verbatim from Higgins:[91]

> That extraordinary race, the Buddhists of Upper India (of whom the Phoenician Canaanite, Melchizedek, was a priest), *who built the Pyramids, Stonehenge, Carnac,* etc., can be shewn to have founded all the ancient mythologies of the World, which, however varied and corrupted in recent times, were originally ONE, and that ONE founded on principles sublime, beautiful, and true![92]

This statement was among the many extracts from *Curious Things* that Randolph included in his own book, *Seership, Guide to Soul Sight.*[93] Jennings, whose writings are a mass of afterthoughts, says at the end of *Curious Things* that the title really ought to have read as follows:

> "Curious Things of the Outside World. Concerning that, also, which is to be understood in the Divinity of Fire. By Hargrave Jennings, F.R.C. (Rosicrucian); Author of *The Indian Religions.* Towards the Philosophical Substantiation of their Sublime groundwork, Buddhism."[94]

Hargrave Jennings could certainly call himself a "Rosicrucian" if he wanted to after October 1870, in which month he was admitted to the Societas Rosicruciana in Anglia (founded 1866).[95] But whatever sort of *Frater Rosae Crucis* are we to suppose him to have been in 1860? There are a couple of hints towards the end of *Curious Things.* First, Jennings assures the "guardians of the more recondite and secret philosophical knowledge, of whom, in the societies—abroad and at home—there are a greater number, even in these days, that the uninitiated might suppose,"[96] that he has not made unguarded disclosures. This is evidently meant to convey the impression that Jennings himself is initiated and possesses knowledge that he is sworn not to reveal.

Second, Jennings suggest a novel interpretation of what the old alchemists meant by the "Philosophers' Stone," namely that it might have signified the "magic mirror, or translucent spirit-seeing crystal, in which impossible-seeming things are disclosed."[97] As we have seen, this is precisely how Randolph understood the term.

I can suggest two possible reasons for Jennings's claim to be a brother of the Rosy Cross in 1860. The first is that he had met Kenneth Mackenzie. Mackenzie was active in London in the late 1850s as a Member of the Royal Asiatic Society and a Fellow of the Society of Antiquaries. He was familiar with the Renaissance "fire-philosophers," and would later write a report on Dr. Rudd's manuscripts.[98] He knew all about magic mirrors and crystal gazing, and he gloried in the creation of secret esoteric orders, of more or less tenuous existence. Mackenzie would have been the natural person to plant in Jennings's mind the idea that would obsess him to the end of his days: that of the Brotherhood of the Rosy Cross as an invisible coterie of adepts whom one might hope, but never expect, to meet.

A second possible source for Jennings's "F.R.C." is none other than Randolph. In a letter of 10 August 1887, written to his publisher Fryar, Jennings says (à propos of nothing): "I first knew Randolph the American 35 years ago, he was, physically, a very remarkable man."[99] If Jennings were accurate, that would place their meeting in 1852. Alas, in the same letter he dates the publication of Blavatsky's *Isis Unveiled* to early 1871 (instead of 1877) and calls A. E. Waite the author of *Art Magic,* so we cannot take his statement unqualified. But I suspect that Randolph and Jennings met in 1857, when Randolph was giving séances in London. We know from the confession in *Eulis* that Randolph would habitually give himself out to be a Rosicrucian. Perhaps the American was already claiming high rank in the Brotherhood and gave Jennings some form of initiation under oath of secrecy. We will return at the end of this chapter to the question of the connection between the two men.

Jennings's next major book was *The Rosicrucians, Their Rites and Mysteries,* published in 1870 after having purportedly been twenty years in the writing.[100] It is impossible to summarize or describe except by saying that the one thing it is definitely not, is the history of the Rosicrucians promised in the Preface. Nor are any rites or mysteries described within its pages. Its torrent of information serves primarily to frame the theory of sexual symbolism that Hargrave Jennings had derived from reading Knight and Higgins, and hinted at in *Curious Things.*[101] This now becomes the point at which all religions and mythologies meet. But there is also a practical dimension to this teaching. Here is a passage from the earlier work, taken over verbatim into *The Rosicrucians,* in which Jennings seems to be fumbling towards a description of sexual intercourse practised as a mystical exercise:[102]

> The hollow world in which that essence of things, called Fire, plays, in its escape, in violent agitation,—to us, combustion,—is deep down inside of us: that is, deep-sunk inside of the time-stages; of which rings of being (subsidences of spirit) we are, in the flesh,—that is, in the human show of things,—in the OUTER. It is exceedingly difficult, through language, to make this idea intelligible; but it is the real mystic dogma of the ancient Guebres, or the Fire-Believers, the successors of the Buddhists, or, more properly, Bhuddists.
>
> What is explosion? It is the lancing into the layers of worlds, whereinto we force, through turning the edges out and driving through; in surprisal of the reluctant, lazy, and secret nature, exposing the hidden, magically microscopical stores of things, passed inwards out of the accumulated rings of worlds, out of the (within) supernaturally buried wealth, rolled in, of the past, in the procession of Being. What is smoke but the disrupted vapour-world to the started soul-fire? The truth is, say the Fire-Philosophers, in the rousing of fire we suddenly come upon Nature, and start her violently out of her ambush of things, evoking her secretest and immortal face to us. Therefore is this knowledge not to be known generally of man; and it is to be assumed as the safest in the disbelief of it: that disbelief being as the magic casket in which it is locked. The keys are only for the Gods, or for godlike spirits.
>
> This is the true view of the religion of the leaders of the ancient Fire-Believers, and of the modern *Illuminati.*

By 1870, Jennings had discovered the other work of phallic scholarship from the 1830s, written synchronously with *Anacalypsis* but independently of it: Henry O'Brien's *The Round Towers of Ireland.* O'Brien, as explained in Chapter One, had interpreted the enigmatic towers as being phallic symbols, and the religion of the ancient Irish as Buddhism, "*Budh* signifying, indiscriminately, Sun and Lingam."[103] No matter: it was all Rosicrucianism to Jennings, and it clarified the equations he had been trying to enunciate, namely that all religions derive from the original worship of mankind, which was of the one primordial energy that brings the universe out of Nirvana. This had been symbolized variously as Light, as Fire, as the Sun, and as the procreative power of the male, hence by the phallus or (since these writers preferred the Sanskrit term) lingam. Phallic worship, in short, is offered to God the Creator of Heaven and Earth, and only in our so-called civilization does it seem indecent. This, through many circumlocutions, is the theme of *The Rosicrucians.*

His next book, *Live Lights and Dead Lights* (1873), was written "in conjunction with two members of the Church of England," and ostensibly treats the question of whether there should be candles on the altar of a church, or whether that object is merely to be treated as a table commemorative of the Last Supper. Jennings's "fire-philosophy" comes into its own here, as the altar candles "typify Immortal Light, the great fiery 'Idea' which annihilates matter and crushes it to light."[104] *Live Lights* develops many of the ideas of *The Rosicrucians* on Christian symbolism, particularly that of church architecture in East and West. Sexual symbolism is there, too (the twin candles being, for example, the "cleft" through which the Sun of Righteousness appears), but put in such a way that the innocent reader could easily miss it. But the conclusions of the book are nothing less than a defence of the Personal God, which one would have thought as far as possible from the ideas of divinity that have filled Jennings's work so far. A similar drift towards Christian piety appears in *One of the Thirty* (1873), a novel about the adventures of one of the pieces of silver for which Jesus was sold. Here he proclaims his belief in "a real, personal God who can both see me on my knees and hear me," admitting that this is "childlike and therefore ridiculous in this Neo-Platonic and Neo-Christianised (or non-Christianised) age."[105] The squib against Neoplatonism is telling; was it aimed at the S.R.I.A. members who were beginning to take an interest in Thomas Taylor? Jennings has evidently shelved, for the present, the philosophical attitudes of *The Indian Religions,* while his antirationalism now takes the elementary form of Christian pietism.

Jennings's lively sense of London and its life, and his emotional involvement with the capital, come out in the mixture of "serious sermons" and "interesting narratives" that he published in 1883 under the title *The Childishness and Brutality of the Time.* Chapters on newspapers, life insurance, advertising, drama, opera, lawyers, fashion, and the American penchant for novel machines show that he was anything but an unworldly scholar, while the bitter title indicates his general attitude to an England which, he says, "is governed by the three selfish classes: the Jews, Lawyers, and Publicans."[106] He fills up this book of over 300 pages with a long narrative of a supernatural experience at sea, and a philosophical Appendix on the "strange Buddhistic idea of the nonexistence of everything," in which he reiterates the findings of *The Indian Religions*:

> The deeply metaphysical Buddhists, too, have originated in their humiliating, although very profound, reveries the idea

> the *Man is asleep*; by which we mean . . . that the Human Race is buried in a dream of many thousand years' duration—that nothing is real, because there is nothing really real at the back of anything to make it real.[107]

In 1880 there appeared, to a very select audience, the first of a number of books acknowledged by or attributed to Jennings, forming part of what was called by the reticent publisher (George Redway) the "Nature Worship and Mystical Series"; otherwise the "Phallic Series," issued in editions of about 200 copies. The titles include *Phallic Worship, Phallic Miscellanies, The Masculine Cross, Nature Worship,* etc.[108] The most noteworthy thing about this series of short, elegantly produced, and semischolarly studies is their cold and sober nature. If any of their subscribers were in search of pornographic stimulation, they must have been sorely disappointed.

Jennings's last major work, which grew out of this series, was entitled *Phallicism, Celestial and Terrestrial, Heathen and Christian; its connexion with the Rosicrucians and the Gnostics and its foundation in Buddhism. With an Essay on Mystic Anatomy* (1884). It is his best book, gathering most of what was of value in his preceding ones. He claims, a little ingenuously, that all the facts and theories in it were first brought forward in *The Indian Religions*; also that other writers on the subject (not excepting his revered Godfrey Higgins) are destructive to faith and religion,[109] whereas he, Jennings, regards religion as true and the present book as constructive of Christian belief.[110]

His theory of sexual symbolism as the place where all religions and mythologies unite has the natural corollary that human sexual intercourse, along with the parts of the body concerned, is nothing shameful or indecent, but a replication in the microcosm of the macrocosmic act. The universality of sexual symbolism in art and architecture is a recognition of this. But something has also imposed on the human race a guilt or at least an embarrassment about sex. Most people live in a state of perpetual tension between the forces of desire and prohibition. Monks, ascetics, and also, in Jennings's opinion, the Brothers of the Rosy Cross seek to obey only the latter, mastering their passions; and their way of life, though contrary to nature, has always been esteemed the holiest.[111]

In these "strange contradictory theosophic speculations," as he himself calls them,[112] Hargrave Jennings is striving to express the paradoxical existence of two paths of Gnosis, the negative and the positive. The first rejects creation, seeing everything manifested as a sham and an evil and finds its goal exclusively in the Non-Being of Nirvana. The second accepts creation as holy and aims at unity with its Creator.

Since Jennings repeatedly invokes the names of Robert Fludd and Jacob Boehme when trying to explain his philosophy, it is possible that he got his ideas from these great metaphysical writers and exponents of a theology in which God is both negative and positive, both dark and light. To sum it up in a few words, God's darkness, or noncreative aspect, in which the Deity is enwrapped in itself, spells extinction to all creation. This is Nirvana. God's light, on the other hand, is the first emanated or ejaculated substance, from which the universe is made. This is the origin of phallicism. Each point of view has its devotees.[113]

Jennings deserves credit for wrestling with these ultimate questions of metaphysics, in comparison to which the concerns of many nineteenth-century philosophers seem rather trivial. He also did more than anyone of his time to remove sexual taboos and to restore the worship of Priapus, the god of joyful creation, to its rightful and by no means un-Christian place.

Perhaps because of his own poor and unmarried life, Jennings also manifested the shadow side of the inspired philosopher, in the common form of a curmudgeonly rejection of everyone else. One can see this in the series of letters that he wrote to Robert H. Fryar, the Bath publisher whom we have already mentioned in connection with the phallic theorists (see Chapter One), between 1879 and 1887. Here is a list of those whom Jennings mentions specifically with contempt, disapproval or mistrust:

The American advertisers of Magic Mirrors, and American mediums in general (letter of 12 August 1881)
P. B. Randolph (7 December 1883)
Modern Theosophy and Spiritualism; Moncure S. Conway; W. Oxley; Henry Melville; Gerald Massey (26 April 1884)
Women in general; Anna Kingsford and Edward Maitland (18 August 1885)
A. E. Waite; A. P. Sinnett; H. S. Olcott; H. P. Blavatsky; Eliphas Levi; Emma Hardinge Britten; Richard Proctor; Petrie and all the "Anglo-Israel" tribe; Major-General Forlong; Rev. George Ouseley (10 August 1887)

If all these were worthless, who was left? Only Hargrave Jennings, apparently. It is embarrassing to read the many passages in the letters in which he praises his own works, particularly *The Rosicrucians* ("the only book of real authority in English, upon this surpassing sect"[114]); or makes claims such as: "I think you will admit that I am entitled to be considered by every one as the first authority in England on the Cabala, &c."[115]

With the introduction of Robert Fryar, the twin threads of this chapter begin to twine together. Fryar was a friend of the astrologer Morrison/

Zadkiel[116] and shared his interest in crystal gazing. In 1870, Fryar published a pamphlet, "History and Mystery of the Magic Crystal,"[117] in which he tried to popularize "conscious clairvoyance" as a faculty available to many men and women who had no other psychic sensitivity. The manuscript of this work was with the papers of Emma Hardinge Britten when they were destroyed in the great Boston Fire of 1872.[118] Fryar was probably one of the friends from whom she had begged for material for her new magazine, *The Western Star.*

In 1878 Fryar wrote to the *Spiritualist* magazine, under a pseudonym, to supplement Kenneth Mackenzie's article on "Crystallomancy." Here he said of scrying that "The only way to ascertain individual capacity for development is to 'try'"—a use of Randolph's motto that would not have been lost on those familiar with the American's works on the same subject. By now he was acting as the British agent for the sale for Randolph's sex-magic manuscripts.[119]

Fryar's correspondence with Jennings began the next year, 1879, when the publisher wrote to him from Bath with questions on subjects treated in *The Rosicrucians.*[120] The men had not met previously. The correspondence developed in 1881 as Fryar asked for an opinion of an American advertisement for magic mirrors: Jennings snorted his disdain for this marketing enterprise, and for Americans in general.[121] Undeterred, Fryar continued his business, as shown by the following advertisement that appeared in the spiritualist press:

> Robt. H. Fryar, the Inventor of the almost human "Automatic Insulator" on Crystal Balls, the Planchette of the future—still supplies the Black, Concave, Ovoid Mirror for developing "Clairvoyant Faculties," (his original *specialite*) by which untold numbers have been awakened to Lucidity of Soul-Sight.[122]

Both Randolph and Fryar respected Jennings's Rosicrucian pretentions. In *Seership,* Randolph calls him "one of the master Rosicrucians of England,—a man whose writings on 'Fire' rank him high among the true genii of the world of letters . . ."[123] In *Mental Magic* (1884), which Fryar edited and partly wrote, a quotation from Jennings is ascribed to the "Chief Rosicrucian of all England."[124] The same book praises Randolph fulsomely and advertizes Fryar as a source for obtaining *Eulis* and *The Ansairetic Mystery,*[125] of which Jennings also disapproved:

> I do not approve of Randolph's Book nor do I look with favour upon his "Eulis," or upon anything which refers in any way to this coarse and rough—even vulgarly mischievous and most mistaken way of dealing with these—in truth—sublime and exquisitely learned subjects.[126]

After a few more letters, Fryar asked Jennings to write a preface to a new edition of the *Corpus Hermeticum* in John Everard's translation of 1650, a proposal that was accepted on 25 February 1884 after a suitable fee had been agreed upon. This was the first reprint of Everard's translation since Randolph had published the work, with much supplementary material, in 1871. Jennings was upset the following year to learn that Fryar was issuing a companion volume containing the remaining Hermetic texts under the care of Anna Kingsford and Edward Maitland, entitled *The Virgin of the World*. He wrote: "I do not approve of women having anything whatever to do with these extraordinary and exclusively profound subjects—quite beyond their hope of comprehension in the correct way . . ."[127] Fryar's poor judgment made Jennings hesitate about collaborating on an edition of the *Comte de Gabalis*, attributed to the Abbé Montfaucon de Villars; he wrote that he, Jennings, was the "only man in England who knows how to use" this book, and paired it with another, whose apparently unique copy was in his possession: *Disputatis Nova contra Mulieres, qua probatur, eas Homines, non esse* (1595).[128] He considered these texts precious "for various reasons which no one in England (nor in any other country either, for the matter of that) probably can understand except myself."[129]

One can see why Robert Fryar never seems to have accepted Jennings's repeated invitations to come up from Bath for a face-to-face meeting in London. In his old age, at least, our Rosicrucian must have been a cantankerous person to deal with.

Fryar's reprints of the Hermetic texts were followed in 1885–89 by a series of "Bath Occult Reprints" which included works on alchemy (edited by John Yarker), the magic crystal, elementals, hieroglyphics, Kabbalah, the Tarot (edited by Wynn Westcott), and—last but not least, the "Esoteric Physiology Series" that was suppressed in 1889 (see p. 24).

Fryar is thus one link between these two authorities on the "generative principle," these two Rosicrucian "Grand Masters," these uneasy collaborators in the revival of the ancient, secret wisdom. In Chapter Sixteen we will see how their work was synthesized with that of Samson Mackey and a few others, to make the "secret documents" of an initiatic order dedicated to practical occultism: the Hermetic Brotherhood of Luxor.

FOURTEEN

Enter Madame Blavatsky

Although the life of Helena Petrovna Blavatsky (1831–1891) is much more accessible (in multiple versions) than those of P. B. Randolph or Hargrave Jennings, it may help the reader to give here Paul Johnson's useful summary of her earlier life:

> HPB was born Helena Petrovna von Hahn in Ekaterinoslav, Ukraine, on August 12, 1831. Her father, Peter Alexeyevitch, was an army colonel descended from German minor nobility. Helena Andreyevna de Fadeyev, her mother, became known as a novelist before an early death. From her eighth year, Helena Petrovna was reared by her maternal grandparents, Privy Councillor Andrei de Fadeyev and Princess Helena Dolgoroukov. In 1849 she married Nikifor Blavatsky, Vice-Governor of Erivan province in Armenia, but left him soon thereafter. For the next nine years she traveled widely, but her itinerary is uncertain. She was definitely in Cairo as companion to a Russian princess in the early 1850s; thereafter her whereabouts are disputed by biographers. In 1858, she returned to her family in Russia, having acquired remarkable mediumistic skills. She spent the early and mid-1860s in the Caucasus, where she was briefly reunited with her husband in Tiflis. During the rest of the decade, she traveled extensively in Eastern and Southern Europe. In 1871 she survived a shipwreck in the Eastern Mediterranean en route to Egypt where she remained through the following year. Traveling via Odessa and Eastern Europe, she arrived in Paris in the spring of 1873, and went to New York the following July.[1]

Broadly speaking, Blavatsky's public life can be divided into an "Egyptian" or Hermetic period, beginning with her attempt to form a magic club or "*société spirite*" in Cairo in 1872, and an "Indian" or Oriental

Figure 14.1. *Helena Petrovna Blavatsky (1831–1891), with James Pryse and G. R. S. Mead.*

period, beginning with her arrival in Bombay at the beginning of 1879. The first period is treated in this chapter, the second in the next one, concentrating on those aspects of her activity that most connect her with the other characters and currents of this book. My primary concern is to identify what she called the "Brotherhood of Luxor," for which we must begin by scrutinizing her Egyptian activities.

Unlike many of her travels, Blavatsky's presence in Egypt in 1851 is corroborated by independent testimony. The witness is her longtime friend Albert Leighton Rawson (1828–1902), a prolific American writer and illustrator who claimed doctorates in medicine, divinity, and letters.[2] On this first of his many voyages to the East, he succeeded in visiting Mecca in disguise, shortly before Richard Burton went there equipped with Hockley's crystals (see Chapter Nine). Rawson and Blavatsky disguised themselves as young Muslim men so as to circulate more safely in

Old Cairo, where they learned the techniques of the snake-charmers. In a rather haphazard memoir, Rawson later recalled:

> A fortunate acquaintance was made with Paulos Metamon, a celebrated Coptic magician, who had several very curious books full of diagrams, astrological formulas, magical incantations and horoscopes, which he delighted in showing to his visitors, after a proper introduction.[. . .]
>
> An attempt to form a society for occult research at Cairo failed, and Metamon advised delay.[3]

The attempt was in fact delayed almost twenty years, until Blavatsky was in Cairo again after surviving a shipwreck in 1871. This time she started a "*Société Spirite* for the investigation of mediums and phenomena according to Allen Kardec's theories and philosophy . . . " with the intention of showing the difference between what these "passive mediums" could produce and what she herself could achieve as an "active doer."[4] As she told her collaborator A. P. Sinnett, the *Société* foundered within two weeks, as the hired mediums drank and cheated, and a madman with a gun disrupted the proceedings. In consequence,

> She broke off all connection with the "mediums," shut up her *Société,* and went to live in Boulak near the Museum. Then it seems, she came again in contact with her old friend the Copt of mysterious fame, of whom mention has been made in connection with her earliest visit to Egypt, at the outset of her travels. For several weeks he was her only visitor. He had a strange reputation in Egypt, and the masses regarded him as a magician. [. . .] The Egyptian high officials pretending to laugh at him behind his back, dreaded and visited him secretly. Ismail Pasha, the Khedive, had consulted him more than once, and later on would not consent to follow his advice to resign.[5]

Another version of the story shows that the *Société Spirite* outlasted Blavatsky's disillusionment. The diplomat, traveler, and spiritualist James M. Peebles (1822–1922), writing from Egypt early in 1874, mentioned that

> Mme Blavatsky, assisted by other brave souls, formed a society of Spiritualists in Cairo about two years since. They have fine writing mediums, and other forms of the manifestations. They hold weekly *séances* during the winter months. Mme Blavatsky is at present in Odessa, Russia. The lady whose husband keeps the Oriental Hotel, is a firm Spiritualist.[6]

The lady in question was surely Emma Coulomb, who took Blavatsky in after her shipwreck.[7] She would become Blavatsky's housekeeper in

India in 1880, and later one of her bitterest enemies. Evidently Madame Coulomb and the continuing membership of the *Société Spirite* were on one level—that of conventional spiritualists and their mediums—while Blavatsky and Metamon were involved in practical occultism that had nothing to do with the putative spirits of the dead. By the time Peebles was in Cairo, where he was treated to a séance on top of the Great Pyramid, the two levels had gone their separate ways.

Thanks to Paul Johnson's research, it is possible to say a little more about Blavatsky's Egyptian connections. She was in Cairo at the same time as two men known to have been involved in Freemasonry, Middle Eastern politics, and esotericism: the Jewish-Egyptian playwright James Sanua, and the cosmopolitan Sufi Jamal ad-Din al Afghani. Mr. Johnson shows that Blavatsky shared with these men common ideals, common friends, and, in the case of Jamal ad-Din, no fewer than five nearly simultaneous arrivals in vastly separated places: India, in the late 1850s, Tiflis in the early 1860s, Cairo in 1871, India in 1879, and Paris in 1884.[8] If we interpret the "Brotherhood of Luxor" to refer to the coterie of esotericists and magicians that Blavatsky knew and worked with in Egypt, then we should probably count Sanua and Jamal ad-Din as members.

Peebles was correct in saying that Blavatsky had left Egypt to go to Odessa, where her family were; but she had already left there in the spring of 1873 to stay with one of her von Hahn cousins in Paris. She had been in Paris long before, as Rawson testifies in his memoir of their travels:

> Madame visited Paris on her way to New York, and compared notes with Thevenot, Grand Secretary of the Grand Orient of France, and astonished that very learned and highly advanced Freemason by her knowledge of all the secrets of the degrees in one branch to the Thirty-third, and in another to the Ninety-fifth. In 1853 she came to New York and made a few acquaintances, nearly all of whom continued her friends to the last.[9]

The branch of Freemasonry that has thirty-three degrees is the "Ancient and Accepted Scottish Rite." The one that has ninety-five is the "Rite of Memphis," reputedly brought from Egypt to France in 1814 by Samuel Honis and Gabriel-Mathieu Marconis de Nègre. Following the 1848 revolution, Marconis had propagated this rite in Britain, Egypt, and the United States.[10] Since women were not admitted, Blavatsky probably learned the necessary secrets in Cairo, possibly from Rawson himself. An enthusiast for fringe-masonry, Rawson is mainly celebrated as the founder of an order called "The Guardians of the Mystic Shrine,"[11] which uses the symbolism of Islam and of Egypt. As one might imagine of a man who could penetrate Mecca in disguise, Rawson moved in Arab secret societies.

He had been adopted as a "brother" by the Adwan Bedouins of Moab, and initiated by Druses in Lebanon, about whom he contributed an account to Blavatsky's first book, *Isis Unveiled*.[12] His seriousness and persistence in trying to orientalize American Freemasonry show that he believed in the validity of some initiatic transmission from the Near East.

Blavatsky also spent time in the Druse country on her way from Cairo to Odessa in 1872, treading in the footsteps of Lady Hester Stanhope (half-sister of the Fourth Earl), whose name, Blavatsky wrote in *Isis Unveiled*, "was for many years a power among the masonic fraternities of the East."[13]

To summarize so far: Blavatsky, Rawson, and Metamon were working on occultism in Cairo in about 1851, after which Blavatsky went to Paris and astonished the Freemasons there with her knowledge. In 1853 she proceeded to New York where she made lifelong friends, presumably through the same network of fringe and Oriental masonry. Twenty years later she repeated the itinerary: she again contacted Metamon in Cairo, then went by a roundabout route to Paris, and shortly after sailed to New York, where she arrived on 7 July 1873 and founded the Theosophical Society in 1875. Everywhere she was involved with Freemasonry, Oriental secret societies, occult fraternities, and with the spiritualists who constituted, as it were, the exoteric "church" from which doors opened to the more esoteric circles.

I turn now to her involvement with spiritualism. When Blavatsky was in Paris in 1851, she kept other company than that of Freemasons. There was a magnetizer called Victor Michal (1824–1889), who was familiar with crystal-gazing, with hashish, astral projection, table-turning, and a certain "theory of Séidism" as taught by the Old Man of the Mountain, i.e., the chief of the "Assassins" of Lebanon.

Michal is said to have magnetized Blavatsky, finding her a marvelous subject who in trance would take on a completely different character from her normal one, but whose fits of anger on returning to herself became too much for him.[14] Michal wrote in 1854 of how the "aromal body" occupies the position between the physical body and the spiritual soul, and of how, "without one's knowledge, it can be *physically* transported from one place to another, and penetrate opaque bodies . . ."[15] This is the same procedure as was attributed to the "Berlin Brotherhood" in *Ghost Land* (see Chapter Eleven). Later it would be known as "astral travel."

During Blavatsky's curtailed stay in Paris, she was close to the Leymarie family, who were followers of the Allan Kardec (reincarnationist) school of spiritualism. But she was far from being a believer. This is how she explained her sudden move from Paris to New York:

> I was sent from Paris on purpose to America to *prove* the phenomena and their reality and—show the fallacy of the Spiri-

> tualistic theories of "Spirits." But how could I do it best? I did not want people at large to know that I could *produce the same thing at will.* I had received ORDERS to the contrary, and yet, I had to keep alive the reality, the genuineness and *possibility* of such phenomena in the hearts of those who from *Materialists* had turned *Spiritualists* and now, owing to the exposure of several mediums fell back again, returned to their skepticism.[16]

And:

> I am here, in this country sent by my Lodge, on behalf of *Truth* in modern Spiritualism, and it is my most sacred duty to *unveil what is,* and expose *what is not.*[17]

Her exposure hinged on the revelation that what was communicating in spiritualism was not the spirits of the dead, but either elementals or "shells." The former were the spirits of earth, water, air, and fire, whose mastery is an essential part of ceremonial magic. The shells were psychic detritus left behind by human beings who had passed beyond the possibility of communication. Just as a corpse looks for a while like a living body, so the shells could supposedly imitate, up to a point, the individual who had sloughed them off. Thus the spiritualists who thought that they were talking to Socrates, Ben Franklin, or their grandmothers, were told bluntly that they were being bamboozled. As an alternative to this profitable farce, Blavatsky urged the study of Hermeticism and the occult sciences.

The mention of Hermeticism echoes the Egyptian theme that was so important at the early stages of Blavatsky's public work, for no one had known more about occultism and the science of life and death than the ancient Egyptians, while it was in modern Egypt, apparently, that she had served her apprenticeship.

The first formal announcement of Blavatsky's mission was an advertisement addressed to spiritualists and placed by Henry Olcott on 17 April 1875 in *The Spiritual Scientist.* After he had written it, Blavatsky told Olcott to sign it: "For the Committee of Seven, Brotherhood of Luxor."[18] He was given to understand that this was "a group of seven Adepts belonging to the Egyptian group of the Universal Mystic Brotherhood."[19] The Theosophical historian David Board argues from various allusions in Blavatsky's and Mackenzie's works that this American Brotherhood of Luxor was inspired by the English Brotherhood of Light, i.e., the Fratres Lucis founded by Francis Irwin in 1873 at the behest of "Cagliostro" (see Chapter Eleven). Mackenzie defines the Brotherhood of Luxor in his *Royal Masonic Cyclopaedia* as "A fraternity in America having a Rosicrucian basis, and numbering many members."[20] In *Isis Unveiled,* Blavatsky amplifies this:

> What will, perhaps, still more astonish American readers, is the fact that, in the United States, a mystical fraternity now exists, which claims an intimate relationship with one of the oldest and most powerful of Eastern Brotherhoods. It is known as the Brotherhood of Luxor, and its faithful members have the custody of very important secrets of science. Its ramifications extend widely throughout the great Republic of the West. Though this brotherhood has been long and hard at work, the secret of its existence has been jealously guarded. Mackenzie describes it as having "a Rosicrucian basis, and numbering many members" ("Royal Masonic Cyclopaedia," p. 461). But, in this, the author is mistaken; it has no Rosicrucian basis. The name Luxor is primarily derived from the ancient Baloochistan city of Looksur, which lies between Bela and Kedgee, and also gave its name to the Egyptian city.[21]

Almost in the same breath, she quotes Mackenzie's "recent and very valuable" *Cyclopaedia* on the subject of the "Hermetic Brothers of Egypt," whose secrets include "the philosopher's stone, the elixir of life, the art of invisibility, and the power of communication directly with the ultramundane life."[22] Mackenzie had first mentioned this order as the "Hermetic Order of Egypt" in *The Rosicrucian* of May 1874, where he said that he had met six members of it: two Germans, two Frenchmen, and two of other nations.[23] In the *Cyclopaedia* he reduced the known members to three. Thanks to Ellic Howe, we know that this order intrigued Francis Irwin, who was at this very moment disclosing his Fratres Lucis to a few friends. On Irwin's return from Paris in autumn 1874, where he had seen Eliphas Levi but forgotten to ask about the order, he asked Mackenzie for more information. Mackenzie replied evasively: "I can give you very little information about the Hermetic Order of Egypt. Constant [i.e., Levi] could have given you far more than I could—he was one of my preceptors."[24]

We have here the situation in which Mackenzie introduces his readership to one order, the Hermetic Brothers of Egypt, to which Blavatsky gives her stamp of approval; while Blavatsky introduces another one, the Brotherhood of Luxor, which Mackenzie confirms by including it in his encyclopedia. Neither person is completely open about their order even to their closest associates: Mackenzie to Irwin, Blavatsky to Olcott.

Years later, Blavatsky tried to disassociate her Brotherhood of Luxor from Mackenzie's, saying that she had learned after the publication of *Isis Unveiled* that they were not the same.[25] Be that as it may, in the mid-1870s she was closely linked to Mackenzie's fringe-masonic world through Charles Sotheran (1847–1902), an English man of letters and socialist who had moved to New York in 1874, just after Blavatsky arrived. When he was only nineteen, Sotheran had spent a year in Paris, supporting himself by sending articles to a Manchester newspaper. These included "brilliant reviews on the traditions which form the basis for the foundations for exoteric [sic—meaning esoteric?] or high grade Masonry. These essays made it patent to the initiates that when Mr. Sotheran took the first degree all the arcana required for the last were in his possession . . ."[26] Back in England, Sotheran attained the 32nd degree of the Ancient and Accepted Scottish Rite and the 94th degree of the Rite of Memphis, and joined the S.R.I.A. (of which Rawson, Irwin, and Mackenzie were also members [27]). It was Sotheran who in 1875 suggested the name of "Theosophy" for the new society, of which he became a founding member and the first librarian. In 1876 he published a book in defence of Cagliostro, founder of Egyptian Masonry and inspirer of Irwin's Brotherhood of Light. He was the New York representative of the Swedenborgian Rite, and was twice leader of Rawson's Guardians of the Mystic Shrine.[28] In sum, Sotheran knew both the English fringe-masonic milieu, and the Franco-Egyptian masonry with which Blavatsky had shown such startling familiarity; and he was hand-in-glove with Albert Rawson.

Sotheran is said to have known Blavatsky before they both came to New York, and to have been aware of the nature of her mission.[29] Possibly he had met her in Paris in 1873. His uncle and patron, head of the London bookselling firm of Henry Sotheran, had a Paris branch, and there was every reason for Charles to go to and fro. Masonic contacts could easily have brought him and Blavatsky into each other's orbit. On the political front, they were both passionate admirers of the Italian revolutionary Giuseppe Mazzini (1805–1872), whom Sotheran and perhaps Blavatsky had met. Paul Johnson writes that Sotheran's book on Cagliostro "makes it clear that he regarded the work of Mazzini and the Carbonari to be [the] direct continuation of Cagliostro's mission."[30]

Once their association resumed in New York, Sotheran became one of Blavatsky's most useful helpers, through his network of contacts in every field that had to do with secret societies, left-wing politics, books, and the printed word. But he was vigorously opposed to the exploitation of any occult powers she may have had, and to spiritualistic séances. What he admired in Blavatsky was her intellect, and when he felt that she was not doing it justice by her other dabblings, he did not hesitate to say so. This led to more than one break and reconciliation between the two volatile characters.

Outside the book world, Sotheran busied himself with radical politics, whipping up the working classes to demand their rights, much as Charles Bradlaugh and Annie Besant (future head of the Theosophical Society) were doing in England. Paul Johnson links Sotheran with Rawson

Figure 14.2. *Albert Leighton Rawson (1828–1907), self-portrait, from* Freemasonry in the Holy Land, *1870.*

and other close friends of Blavatsky's American period as "committed to an international effort to combat religious dogmatism, extend the range of democratic government, and direct public attention to the values of liberty, equality and fraternity."[31]

Rawson also joined the early Theosophical Society, but did not go to meetings as his health kept him at home in the evenings.[32] It did not prevent him, however, from attending the Freethinkers' Convention of 1878, held at Watkins Glen in Upstate New York. Here, seven or eight years before Nietzsche announced the death of God in *Also sprach Zarathustra,* Rawson said to an audience of a thousand:

> It is proposed that I say a few words by way of an appetizer for your dinner. I wish to call your attention to the fact that the

great Jehovah of the Jews is dead. Just when he lived or died is a matter of history not easily determined.[33]

The next day, like another "Devil's Chaplain," Rawson gave a long address contrasting the evils of Christianity with the promises held out by Liberalism, Positivism, science, and altruism.[34] I cannot imagine that this exercise in "therapeutic blasphemy" would have gone down very well with his brothers in the S.R.I.A., or with the readers of his many books on the "Bible Lands," but one side of Blavatsky's personality would have loved it. They both found blasphemy a liberating gesture.

An Egyptian atmosphere prevailed in the Theosophical Society up to the publication of the significantly titled *Isis Unveiled.* The very meeting at which the Society was first mooted, on 7 September 1875, was a lecture given in Blavatsky's apartment by George Felt on "The Lost Canon of Proportion of the Egyptians." The researches of Professor Santucci have revealed George Felt (1831–?) as a Civil War officer and an inventor of telegraph devices and rockets.[35] Already in 1872 he was working on a magnum opus expounding the ancient Egyptian canon of proportion and its connections with the Kaballah. His work apparently involved the copying of the Egyptian Zodiacs, which had so interested Dupuis, Drummond, Landseer, and other mythographers. While he was doing this, he noticed that his dog and cat began behaving as if something unseen was present in the room.[36] Intrigued, Felt experimented on making the presences visible "by chemical means." He continues:

> I then began to understand and appreciate many things in my Egyptian researches that had been incomprehensible before. As a result I have become satisfied that these zodiacal and other drawings are representations of types in this invisible creation delineated in a more or less precise manner, and interspersed with images of natural objects more or less conventionally drawn. I discovered that these appearances were intelligences [. . .]
>
> I satisfied myself that the Egyptians had used these appearances in their initiations; in fact, I think I have established this beyond question. My original idea was to introduce into the Masonic fraternity a form of initiations such as prevailed among the ancient Egyptians, and tried to do so, but finding that only men pure in mind and body could control these appearances, I decided that I would have to find others than my whisky-soaked and tobacco-sodden countrymen, living in an atmosphere of fraud and trickery, to act in that direction.

Felt's desire to make Freemasonry better resemble the Egyptian mysteries—one of its supposed ancestors—brings him into the same ambit as Rawson, the propagator of the Rite of Memphis and other orientalizing orders. What "chemical means" did he use to make the elemental spirits visible? One possibility that leaps to mind is the controlled use of a drug such as hashish, with which the French magnetists often enhanced the perceptions of their somnambulists, which had brought Randolph such unforgettable experiences, and with which Blavatsky herself had experimented both in Cairo and New York.[37] But Felt's harsh words against tobacco and alcohol hardly seem compatible with drug use. Another means is hinted at in *Isis Unveiled*, where Blavatsky mentions a chemical experiment performed by Professor John Tyndall. This arch-skeptic showed that illuminating the vapors of volatile liquids could produce gorgeously colored clouds, shells, flowers, leaves, and scrolls; even a serpent's head darting out its tongue, and a marvelously lifelike fish.[38] There is no doubt that a suitably prepared believer, looking into Tyndall's tube, would believe himself to be seeing elementals. But the third and most likely possibility is that Felt was referring to some form of scrying, perhaps with chemically treated mirrors such as the French magnetists had been experimenting with, and Randolph described in *Seership*. These mirrors would become the primary magical tool of the Hermetic Brotherhood of Luxor, to which many early Theosophists belonged (see Chapter Sixteen).

Felt also did experiments in telepathy, based on those of Agrippa and Trithemius, with another Theosophical Society member, "a legal gentleman with a mathematical turn of mind." This friend of Felt's once came to his house in the suburbs to examine some of Felt's Kabbalistic drawings, and while returning to the city by public transport, saw in broad daylight a "curious kind of animal," which he sketched from memory. He immediately consulted "one of the *illuminati* of the Society," who told him that this was an elemental spirit represented by the Egyptians in their zodiacs and initiations. (It sounds very much as if the legal gentleman was Olcott, and the illuminatus Blavatsky.) Later, when Felt showed his drawings at a Theosophical Society meeting, many of the lower-degree members felt fearful, uncomfortable, or became abusive, until "Mme Blavatsky, who had seen unpleasant effects follow somewhat similar phenomena in the East, requested me to turn the drawings and change the subject."[39]

After this, Felt says, it became plain that the Society could no longer continue as a public one, but must be organized like a secret society, with different degrees. This was duly done. On 8 March 1876 the Theosophical Society became a secret body, with signs of recognition and an appropriate seal. This brought it closer still to the world of fringe-masonry in which several of its members were involved. But Felt, who entered this phase as one of the Vice-Presidents, disappointed the other members because he was never able or willing to fulfil his promise to demonstrate the elementals to them. He remained sufficiently in touch to request permission to publish the above account in *The Spiritualist* in 1878, respecting the vows of secrecy that he had taken regarding the Society's affairs. Thereafter, Professor Santucci's researches have shown no trace of him.

The London members of the S.R.I.A. were kept up to date with some of these events by their magazine, *The Rosicrucian*. They learned in 1872 of Felt's discovery that the Egyptian, Greek, and Hebrew "Kabbalahs" (here meaning esoteric numerical systems) were identical with each other and with the system of proportion found in nature.[40] In May 1874, Kenneth Mackenzie wrote about "The Hermetic Order of Egypt," as mentioned earlier in this chapter. In April 1879, John Yarker, who was by now exchanging masonic certificates with Blavatsky, wrote of the Rosicrucians as having "knowledge of elemental and elementary spirits, which an American mathematician claims to have rendered palpably visible by chemical means."[41]

Blavatsky herself wrote an essay on elementary spirits, partly adapted from Eliphas Levi, which circulated among the early Theosophical Society members.[42] A copy of it reached Stainton Moses (see below), as a result of which Blavatsky wrote to him on 16 November 1875 (the eve of the Society's inauguration) to clarify several points.[43] Questioned as to which lodge she belonged to, she told him: "it is certainly not to the Rosicrucians—as I said to every one in the Article to Hiram—It is a secret Lodge in the East; perhaps they are the Brotherhood Mejnour speaks about in Zanoni."

One turns to Lytton's novel and finds that Mejnour's brotherhood, which is anterior to the Rosicrucians, comprises only two members: himself and Zanoni.[44] What is more to the point is that after revealing this, and after giving Glyndon a lecture about the elementals, Mejnour seems to have succeeded where Felt would fail:

> With that, Mejnour led [Glyndon] into the interior chamber, and proceeded to explain to him certain chemical operations, which, though extremely simple in themselves, Glyndon soon perceived were capable of very extraordinary results.
>
> "In the remoter times," said Mejnour, smiling, "our brotherhood were often compelled to recur to delusions to protect realities; and as dexterous mechanicians or expert chemists, they obtained the name of sorcerers. Observe how easy to construct is the Spectre Lion that attended the renowned Leonardo da Vinci!"

> And Glyndon beheld with delighted surprise the simple means by which the wildest cheats of the imagination can be formed.[45]

Later in this chapter, the reader may decide that Colonel Olcott was the witness to "cheats" of this kind.

On 20 September 1875, Blavatsky wrote to the Russian psychical researcher Aksakov that Olcott was now organising the Theosophical Society in New York:

> It will be composed of learned occultists and cabbalists, of *philosophes Hermétiques* of the nineteenth century, and of passionate antiquaries and Egyptologists generally. We want to make an experimental comparison between Spiritualism and the magic of the ancients by following literally the instructions of the old Cabbalas, both Jewish and Egyptian.[46]

Note here the allusion to Felt's revival of ancient magic and his discovery of an "Egyptian Kabbalah," and the placing of the new society in the ambit of the Hermetic tradition and the occultism of Egypt. I suspect that the "Brotherhood of Luxor" was Blavatsky's way of referring to all this.

Early in 1875, Olcott started studying occultism under the orders of an Egyptian adept he knew as "Tuitit Bey."[47] His new-found friend Blavatsky was the vehicle for the teachings in question, which dwelt on the various kinds of elementaries and nature-spirits that were henceforth to be held responsible for the "spiritualist" phenomena, rather than the spirits of the dead.[48] In about May 1875, Blavatsky noted in her scrapbook that the "Miracle Club" she and Olcott were attempting to launch was in consequence of orders received from Tuitit Bey. Now, she added, her martyrdom would begin, as to tell the truth about the spiritualist phenomena would turn spiritualists, skeptics, and Christians alike against her. She concluded: "Thy will, oh M., be done."[49] Theosophists have interpreted the "M" as her later master, the Tibetan Mahatma Morya, but at this stage it could equally well have signified Paulos Metamon, while Tuitit could have been another Egyptian adept with whom she was in communication.

Olcott was dumbstruck when he discovered that the advertisement for the *Spiritual Scientist*, composed by himself alone, turned out to spell as an acrostic the name TUITIT: the name he already knew as that of the master under whom he was studying. Not long after, Olcott received at his law office an impressive document written in gold ink upon thick green paper, signed by Tuitit Bey.[50] This informed him that three other masters were also interested in him: Serapis Bey, Polydorus Isurenus, and Robert More. Moreover, the brief letter thrice urged Olcott to "TRY."

Figure 14.3. *Henry Steel Olcott (1832–1907), by H. P. Blavatsky, from* The Theosophist, *1931.*

A number of letters followed, delivered to Olcott in various odd ways and generally signed by Serapis Bey. C. Jinarajadasa, the editor of the Serapis and Tuitit letters, suspected that Tuitit had traveled with Blavatsky in Egypt during her early wanderings, and says that when she and Olcott were passing through the Suez Canal on their way to India in 1879, "the venerable" Tuitit sent the Colonel his greetings.[51]

During the same period in 1875, Olcott was also receiving copious letters (now lost) from "John King," a well-known spirit who had been figuring for years at séances on both sides of the Atlantic; Olcott had encountered him in London in 1870. Although John King always pretended to have been a pirate, and certainly spoke and looked like one, Blavatsky was bringing Olcott round to the idea that King, too, masked one of the living adepts. This was a third explanation for the phenomena of spiritualism, following the commonplace one (that they were caused by the spirits of the dead) and their attribution to elementals. The new explanation presupposed the existence of adepts who had mastered the occult powers needed to cause physical events at a distance, and begged the question of what motives might underlie such interference with the normal course of events. Knowing what we do, we would associate this explanation with the Hydesville provocation theory of Chapter Nine, and with the various brotherhoods of adepts described in *Ghost Land* (Chapter Eleven).

Viewed in such a context, Serapis's letters to Olcott have little of the reverence and the high moral tone one might expect of an adept, and virtually no indication of how the disciple might proceed on the quest to perfection, beyond indulging a fascination with occult phenomena. They read more as the advice of a Machiavellian schemer than as the words of a "Master of Wisdom." Serapis, who calls himself "not a disembodied spirit [but] a living man, gifted with such powers by our Lodge as are in store for thyself someday,"[52] seems mainly concerned to bind Olcott to his cause by way of occult promises and financial ties. He urges the credulous Colonel to involve his in-laws in dubious business ventures with Blavatsky's temporary husband Michael Betanelly, for whom "there are millions in the future in store."[53] He has Olcott trick his colleague by telling her that they are going from Boston to Philadelphia, but only buying tickets as far as New York City.[54] With deplorable lack of prophetic vision, he tells him: "Your distant future is at Boston."[55] Brother Henry is obliged to report every night, by mail sent to the address of "our good Brother John"—for evidently Serapis' plans were at one with those of "John King." They also involved Emma Hardinge Britten, still an ally of the Theosophists, whom Serapis praised and urged Olcott to be friendly to.[56]

A feature of Serapis's letters is that they frequently and emphatically use Randolph's motto "*try*." So does Blavatsky in her first doctrinal article, "A Few Questions to 'Hiraf',"[57] associating it specifically with Rosicrucian initiations. The one time she mentioned Randolph in her early writings, it was with respect for his efforts to enlighten the Spiritualists.[58] Only later, when she became aware of the sexual teachings of *Eulis*, did she shun his work.[59] According to John Patrick Deveney, Randolph himself contacted Olcott after the publication of *People of the Other World*, saying in effect that although Olcott might not have heard about him, they might have things in common.[60] I conclude that there was no direct influence, much less the magical battle that some have imagined between Randolph and Blavatsky, but that the latter's omnivorous mind had somewhere picked up the association of Rosicrucianism with the motto "TRY." Her reliance on, and guarded praise of Hargrave Jennings's *The Rosicrucians* makes one wonder how much historical knowledge she really had on that subject.[61]

To summarize, it looks as though in 1875 "Serapis," Blavatsky, Sotheran, and probably Rawson knew of things that Olcott did not, and that the Colonel was being manipulated in order to enroll him in the program that she and her "Brothers of Luxor" were promoting. One wing of this program was the replacement of the illusions of spiritualism by the higher knowledge of occultism. This it shared with the English Brotherhood of Light and their French mentor Eliphas Levi, as well as with Randolph. Occultism taught one not just to sit back and exchange sentimentalities with the "spirits," but to *try*: that is, to cultivate one's will, increase one's knowledge, and eventually to master the higher powers and faculties that lie latent in everyone.

The other wing of their program was not shared with the occultists of this or any other time. It was nothing more nor less than the abolition of Christianity in favor of freethinking humanism. This was the particular animus of Sotheran and Rawson, and was eagerly embraced by Blavatsky, as by the social reformer Emma Hardinge Britten. Like most nineteenth-century radicals, they had no quarrel with Jesus the Nazarene, whom Blavatsky calls "the great Socialist and Adept, the divine man who was changed into an anthropomorphic god."[62] But they could see no common measure between Jesus and the disagreable, racist god of the Hebrew scriptures whom Christians supposed to be his father. An absurd theology, supporting a corrupt priesthood and an unintelligent bibliolatry: that was what Blavatsky saw, and loathed, when she surveyed the history of Christianity.

With the entry of this redoubtable woman, the two major themes of this book at last coincide: the anti-Christianity of the Enlightenment, and the nineteenth-century revival of the occult sciences.

While Blavatsky was in Paris and New York, a body of doctrine very similar to hers was appearing in England, in such a way as to make one suspect that a common intention lay behind it, through the mediumship

Figure 14.4. *William Stainton Moses (1839–1892), from* Spirit Teachings, *1904.*

of the Rev. William Stainton Moses (1839–1892). Moses was a headmaster's son whose academic career was interrupted by a year's wandering in Europe: he went as far as Saint Petersburg and spent six months on Mount Athos. On graduating from Oxford, he was ordained and worked as a curate on the Isle of Man.

Moses was a Freemason, and a member of the S.R.I.A. from 1867, the year after its foundation. Later he also joined the Swedenborgian Rite. Forced by persistent throat infections to give up preaching and public speaking, he spent a year as private tutor in the family of Dr. and Mrs. Stanhope Speer. In 1870 he moved to London, where until 1889 he taught English at University College School.

In London, Moses met the Speers again and found that they, like him, were now verging towards unorthodoxy, even to agnosticism, concerning the immortality of the soul. Mrs. Speer urged Moses to read *The Debatable Land* by Robert Dale Owen, the diplomat son of Robert Owen and a spiritualist like his father. No sooner had the friends taken the further step of visiting a medium, than Moses himself started to manifest extraordinary mediumistic powers. Raps, lights, scents, musical sounds, table tiltings, and written messages occurred in his presence, but the chief and most lasting phenomenon was automatic writing. All of this started in 1872. By the following year, the well-connected Moses was one of the foremost figures in London's more serious spiritualist circles. An enthusiastic clubman, he was involved in founding the British National Association of Spiritualists in 1873, the Psychological Society of Great Britain in 1875, the Society for Psychical Research in 1882, and the London Spiritualist Alliance in 1884.[63]

Moses was a most atypical medium. He was male, devoid of any financial ambition, scientifically curious, and shy of publicity. He wrote under the pseudonym of "M.A. (Oxon.)," an academic conceit which was understandable: what other medium could boast such a degree? He did not go into trance, but conversed with his spirit controls by writing down his questions, then entering a state of abstraction, thinking of something else, or even reading, while his hand wrote the answers in another handwriting.

A consistent body of "spirit teachings" started to come through Moses' automatic writing in 1873. His chief control signed itself as "Imperator +." This spirit said that he had lived on earth and studied in Paris (the only piece of biography he disclosed[64]), and that now he was inhabiting spheres of such light, purity, and beauty that it was positively painful to descend to earth to work among living men. He told Moses that the latter had been sent to Mount Athos in his youth to prepare him for his life's task. Here are some of the key ideas that Imperator and another control called Prudens gave their pupil:

A new revelation is coming now [131][65]
We are doing for Christianity what Jesus did for Judaism [148]
The Bible is a compilation, not literally true [184]
Much of Jesus's life is to be understood symbolically [256]
Modern Christianity is a degenerate offspring of the original [233]
Each religion is a ray of truth from the Central Sun [131]
There have been many Messiahs [212]
India is the source of all religions, and deserves to be studied [212]
The ancient Egyptians were wise and erudite philosophers [217]; Jesus was educated by them [262]
Man makes his own future, stamps his own character, suffers for his own sins, and must work out his own salvation [277]
The only devils are the ones you create yourself [98]
The spirit is a temporarily separated portion of divinity, which grows more and more like God [228]
The doctrine of transmigration is an error [218]
In America, many have developed so as to speak to "us" directly [239]

Some of these thoughts were strong stuff for a rather stubborn Church of England curate (just how stubborn can be seen from Moses' written objections). Imperator was trying patiently to give him a broader view of religion and of reality, while at the same time playing down the vulgar spiritualist themes of communication with the dead and physical phenomena, with which so many in the movement were obsessed. Whoever Imperator was—and Blavatsky thought he might simply be Moses' own Higher Self[66]—his teaching was perfectly adjusted to the needs of this pupil. Through publication in *The Spiritualist* from January 1875 onwards, Imperator's dicta also reached all the more intellectual and socially prominent English spiritualists.

In early 1874 that magazine had carried James Peebles's account of his Great Pyramid séance, and his news of Blavatsky's *Société Spirite*. On Christmas Eve, 1874, it reprinted the letter to the *New York Graphic* in which Blavatsky defended the Eddy Brothers (the mediums of Chittenden, Vermont) from charges of fraud. On New Year's Day 1875 the *Spiritualist's* American correspondent mentioned her (as "Countess Helen P. de Blavatsky") and the surprising manifestations that she provoked, saying that there had been nothing like it since Hydesville. By now the English spiritualists' antennae must have begun to twitch at the news of this intriguing woman.

One of the most respectable of them was Charles Carleton Massey, whom we met at the end of Chapter Twelve as a friend of Mrs. Atwood.

Massey was an intimate friend of Stainton Moses and the other "Higher Spiritualists" of London. He may already have met Olcott during the latter's business trip to England in 1870, when Olcott took time off to visit mediums and to mix with people involved in the Dialectical Society's investigation. In any case, the two men became good friends when Massey went to America in 1875 to investigate American spiritualism at first hand. He and Olcott toured New York together and visited Henry Slade, the slate-writing medium, then Massey went alone to Chittenden to see the Eddy Brothers operate. On the eve of his departure from America, he attended the meeting of the new Theosophical Society on 13 October and was elected a Fellow. Returning to England, he became the first President of the London Branch of the Theosophical Society, wrote about his experiences in *The Spiritualist*, and shared his more private thoughts with Stainton Moses. For a few years, Massey united English spiritualism with the new movement from America, while reserving an inner spiritual life on Behmenist Christian principles.

Just before Massey's arrival in New York, Blavatsky had published her earliest doctrinal article, "A Few Questions to 'Hiraf',"[67] in which she aired the key ideas of her program. These bore a remarkable similarity to those of Stainton Moses' controls. For example:

> This planet is a place of transition where we prepare for eternity [112][68]
> There is eternal progress for every living being [112]
> Elementary spirits are often mistaken for those of the dead [112]
> Reincarnation is a modern misunderstanding [112]
> Oriental philosophy denies the existence of Satan [111]
> The Jewish religion is derived from the pagan Mysteries [118]
> Ancient Cabalists knew as much as modern scientists [115]
> Egyptian initiation took away the fear of death [115]
> The Scriptures are full of secret meanings [114–115]
> With the Hydesville rappings, the door is ajar [117]
> Now occultism needs to explain and alter much of spiritualism [117]

For all their common ground, Olcott, Moses, and Massey were shocked by Blavatsky's attack on the spiritualism that they felt had given them evidence of the immortality of the soul. But the new theory was something to be reckoned with, especially when it came aureoled with Blavatsky's undeniable psychic powers, her apparent erudition in every sort of occultism, and her assurance that she brought secret knowledge from Egypt and the East.

Stainton Moses, as soon as he heard of Olcott's intention to publish a book about his experiences with the Eddy Brothers and with Blavatsky, wrote to his friend Epes Sargent in Boston, offering to introduce the book (*People of the Other World,* published April 1875) to English Spiritualists. As a result, he heard from Olcott himself on 10 April 1875. A long correspondence followed, in which Olcott was aware that his letters were shared by Moses and Massey. They were full of enthusiasm for the new explanation of spiritualist phenomena as the work of elemental spirits, and for the books that Blavatsky was introducing him to, as the key to them.[69] More than that, Olcott told his English friends of his meetings in the flesh with some of Blavatsky's "Brothers," and of the almost incredible phenomena that accompanied them.[70]

One of these Brothers, who visited Olcott in New York at the end of 1875 or early in 1876, was a man of about fifty with dark skin and a gray beard, who spoke French and showed Olcott visions in a crystal. Another was a younger man whom Olcott had already met in August 1875: he resembled an Indian but was actually a Cypriot called Ooton Liatto; he spoke English and produced the phenomena of flowers and rain. This may have been the Greek well known in Theosophical history as Hilarion Smerdis, or the Master Hilarion, whom Blavatsky says she knew from 1860, and whose astral body she says was mistaken for "John King."[71] Equally, he may have been the "monk of Mount Athos who, from 1869 onwards, taught her a lot of what she knew."[72]

In *Old Diary Leaves,* the Colonel describes how Liatto/Hilarion visited his apartment and made his bedroom disappear into a cube of empty space, into which came bizarre landscapes and elementary forms, some "as horrid to see as the pictures in Barrett's *Magus.*"[73] The phenomena that occurred on a subsequent visit were so extraordinary that Olcott never published an account of them, but did describe them to his London friends.[74] Liatto came tapping on Olcott's door one Sunday, accompanied by a dark-skinned gentleman of about fifty with a bushy gray beard. Telling Olcott to ask no questions, Liatto produced a vast bouquet of perfumed flowers in mid-air, which floated to the floor. Next he caused a shower that soaked Olcott to the skin, as well as his cigar, books, clock, and carpet, but left the Brothers (and their cigars) perfectly dry. The older man now offered Olcott visions in a small crystal, which were so intense that for an hour Olcott quite forgot where he was.

Olcott had several times mentioned Blavatsky to his visitors, and now he prevailed on them to let him introduce them to her. Going downstairs to her apartment, which was directly beneath his own, Olcott was flabbergasted to find the two men already there, chatting with her like old friends. He rushed upstairs and found his own room empty; looking out of the window, he saw the men disappearing around the street corner. But the wet clothes and the flowers remained as evidence that it had not all been a hallucination.

The infuriating Madame, Olcott complained to his London friends, would do nothing to satisfy his curiosity about these men, she being furious at him for having given her publicity in his *People from the Other World.* He told them:

> When I saw Liatto before I tried my best to pump Madam B about him—I might as well have tried to draw milk out of a stone—the infernally tantalizing woman would not tell me a word—but just looked blank.
>
> She has sworn that she will not show me a thing, or tell me a thing except about the book [*Isis Unveiled*]—and when that is done she is going to India to stay I fear for ever—if you are vexed to get so little at the distance of 3000 miles—what do you think of my state? when I am with her every evening and can't get a word even about things like these that were shewn to me, and then on top of that be abused like a pickpocket for printing her name in my book which she says has caused all her suffering and mortification.

Olcott feared that Blavatsky would accept an offer from two American ladies to pay her expenses to go to India for two years. He told his friends in the same letter: "Two Theosophs [sic] have been this morning to ask me what we'll do if the Madam accepts the offer of Miss A and Mrs. S—she'd be a great loss but perhaps the lodge might send some one to take her place." By March or April 1876, Olcott's worry had increased. He wrote to Moses:

> I wish you would ask Imperator, with my compliments, if he can't do *something*, in the psychological way, to prevent Madame Blavatsky from going to India. [. . .] she so longs for her sacred Ganges, and the society of her Brethren, that I am afraid we will lose her. It may be a small matter to Spiritualists, but it is a great one for us three.[75]

These remarks show that Olcott, Massey, and Moses shared the idea of some "lodge" that might send a replacement for Blavatsky, so that the Theosophical Society could carry on if she disappeared to India. She reciprocated his unkind suggestion of working on her psychologically when, two years later, she herself wrote to Hurrychund Chintamon in India that in her hands the Colonel was a "psychologized baby."[76]

In July 1876 there occurred the strange episode of the thirteen shipwrecked Arabs for whom Olcott raised the money to buy their passage home, as a gesture of friendship to his "fellow Heathens." They were accompanied to Tunis by Edward S. Spaulding, a member of the Theosophical Society. The reason I mention this here is that in Olcott's letter to the *New York Daily Graphic*, he says that he has told Spaulding to seek in Africa for magic and necromantic phenomena, and to find a "real magician or sorcerer" to come to America. Olcott advised Spaulding on how to tell black magic from white and assured him that the Society would pay all expenses.[77] The idea of high magic surviving among the Arabs of North Africa must have become firmly fixed in Olcott's mind.

When Olcott wrote privately to Massey and Stainton Moses, it was with a slightly conspiratorial male fellowship. Here is an extract from his letter of Christmas 1876:

> Dear Oxon,
> Merry Christmas to you and yours, to Massey and his, and all the decent people in England who are studying Spiritualism for the instruction of their minds, and the purification of their souls, and not for the filling of their pockets or bellies, the nutrition of their vanity, or the exercise of their phallus.[78]

The survival of this letter in a copy by Francis Irwin shows that the comradeship went further than "us three." All these men—Irwin with his Fratres Lucis inspired by Cagliostro's spirit and his contacts in Paris, Mackenzie with his *Cyclopaedia* full of hints about Unknown Superiors, Moses with his Imperator and other controls, Hockley with his Crowned Angel, Olcott with his Brotherhood of Luxor—felt part of a small elite under spiritual guidance, able to look down benignly on the naive and credulous spiritualists. A certain one-upmanship among them appears, as in the same Christmas letter to Moses:

> I can't answer your questions as to when, where or how the B of L will manifest itself to you. I think they have already in your inner experience, and that the engagement of your ideas as to occultism is an evidence of the fact. I am satisfied that you are helped by them without your knowing who the persons are, keep cool, and you will see all in good time . . .[79]

The Colonel adds that he wants Moses to become a Fellow of the Theosophical Society, as Massey already is, and tells him not to let the expense be a consideration. Olcott promises that all his friend's obscurities will be cleared up by the book that Blavatsky and he are writing, "or rather she is preparing and I polishing"—referring to *Isis Unveiled*, which was now occupying Blavatsky full-time.

Moses, for his part, was converted even before meeting her. On 7 October 1876 he wrote to her: "It is because I dimly see—and far more because he [Imperator] tells me that in Occultism I shall find a phase of Truth not yet known to me that I look to it and you."[80] In an undated letter of the same period he says: "Certainly all doubt as to the Brotherhood and their work is gone."[81] Olcott would later surmise that both Blavatsky and Moses were inspired by the same Intelligence, and would be "almost certain" that another of Moses' guides, called "Magus," was "a living adept; not only that, but one that had to do with us."[82] The Colonel suspected, in fact, that all of Moses' "band" were adepts, not the departed spirits that Moses, still an unshaken spiritualist, believed them to be.[83]

Olcott must have felt that his own contact with Serapis and the Brotherhood of Luxor united him with his English friends, whereas a foreign influence was coming to bear on his colleague, which at this stage (in 1875–76) he did not like. This is why he appealed to Imperator behind Blavatsky's back. Yet India had been present from the start as a subsidiary theme of the Brotherhood of Luxor. In the first letter of a Master, addressed to Olcott by Tuitit Bey, Serapis is assigned not to Luxor, as his Egyptian name would lead one to expect, but to the "Ellora Section" of the Brotherhood.

Ellora, the site of great caves and temples near Arungabad, India, must have had some peculiar significance to these early Theosophists. In his letters to the Colonel, Serapis twice refers to Blavatsky as an "Ellorian."[84] Also, it was in India, upon joining the "Ellora Brotherhood," that the Chevalier Louis of *Ghost Land* attained the degree of adeptship to which the Berlin Brotherhood and the London Circle could not raise him.

I return for a moment to Louis's story, which left off in Chapter Eleven at the point where he was in his early twenties, acting as medium for the Orphic Circle in London. Shortly after this, his mentor and adopted father Professor Marx died, causing an acute crisis in his pupil. As Marx had believed in nothing but the elementals, he found himself after death abandoned in their realm, and it was now Louis's task, through a "blending" of their personalities, to raise his teacher to higher realizations. (Blending of this kind had been previously described in Randolph's *Dealings with the Dead*.) At the same time, the news that came to the Orphic Circle of the Hydesville phenomena forced them to reconsider the question of survival. While the circle broke up under this new challenge to its members' assumptions, Louis left for his army commission in India.

His family connections there led to rapid promotion, and he spent eight or ten years in active public service as a soldier and a statesman. Whenever his duties allowed, he pursued his occult interests among the fakirs and magicians. These confirmed his new-found faith in immortality by asserting that they owed their powers to their living ancestral spirits (*pitris*). Eventually Louis encountered a third occult group, called the "Ellora Brotherhood," which met in secret conclave in an underground temple. Here they did experiments with electricity, communicated with gods and angels, and radiated forces to change public opinion in anticipation of the Apocalypse. Louis was accepted into the group, and made

Figure 14.5. *"Chevalier Louis de B——," reputed author of* Ghost Land *and* Art Magic, *from H. S. Olcott,* Old Diary Leaves, *1895.*

an adept or hierophant. The remainder of *Ghost Land* tells of personal and romantic events, concluding with Louis's return to England after the First War of Indian Independence (the "Indian Mutiny" of 1857). Now "nearly twenty" years remained, during which this elusive character shared many adventures (otherwise unrecorded) with Emma Hardinge Britten. At the time of publication, he was conveniently inaccessible, in Cuba.

In another book I have quoted the description of the underground temple at Ellora which Louis attended at first in the flesh, then, as an initiate, in the astral body and compared it to other rumors of such places.[85] What is interesting here is that, according to *Ghost Land*, the first principles of the Ellora Brotherhood are the sentiment of brotherhood to humanity at large, and the discovery of occultism.[86] Since these would become two of the three principles of the Theosophical Society (the third one being the study of world religions), it seems that the Ellora Brotherhood, headed by nameless Oriental adepts, was a remarkable anticipation of the Society's developments after it moved its headquarters to India.

Two days before the Theosophical Society met at Emma Hardinge Britten's residence to organize and elect officers, Blavatsky had confessed in print that "The BROTHERHOOD OF LUXOR is one of the sections of the Grand Lodge of which *I am a member*," and challenged her critic to write to Lahore for information.[87] Blavatsky, by her own account, had been in Lahore in late 1855 or 1856. It was there that she met a German acquaintance of her father (who alone knew where she was), who was also traveling "with a mystic purpose in view."[88] With two other companions, they planned a journey to Tibet, which may or may not have taken place, depending on whose authority one believes. Blavatsky certainly went from Lahore to Leh, bringing her into the domains of Ranbir Singh, Maharajah of Jammu and Kashmir. In his study of the identities of Blavatsky's masters, Paul Johnson proposes that Ranbir was a model for the Mahatma Morya. He also produces evidence to suggest that Blavatsky met both Ranbir and Jamal ad-Din in that region around 1857, and that on a subsequent meeting around 1869, she may have been enabled by Ranbir Singh at last to enter Tibet.[89] Such connections in her past could account for her references to a "Grand Lodge" at Lahore. Another consideration is that Dayananda Saraswati moved the headquarters of his Arya Samaj there in 1876–77. All of this indicates that Blavatsky's turning to India in 1876 or 1877 was not a new whim, but the reactivation of old ties.

There seems to have been a concerted effort in the early 1870s to give out fresh doctrines to a world already familiar with spiritualistic ideas of occult phenomena and the afterlife. The new doctrines would be known collectively as "occultism," and for some years the relative merits and meanings of occultism and spiritualism would be debated. The two sects looked to different authorities and held out different goals to the aspirant. The authorities of spiritualism were the conscious spirits of the dead, and the goal was to continue one's spiritual development in the afterlife so as to become more like them. The authorities of occultism were adepts of the past, contacted mainly through their books, and living adepts who were inaccessible unless one was contacted by them. The highest goal was to attain adeptship oneself, in this life.

As we know from earlier chapters, there had long been a European tradition of the occult sciences to which spiritualism, when it arrived from America, was largely an irrelevance. This was one tradition to which Blavatsky introduced Olcott, having him read Thomas Vaughan's *Magia Adamica* and French texts such as Baron Tschoudy's magical-masonic *L'Etoile Flamboyante* and the works of Eliphas Levi. Occultism had always been there, but one had to collect rare books and read foreign languages in order to make much headway in it. Few spiritualists had either the temperament or the opportunity to do so.

Three books, by three women, spearheaded this effort in the literary world. The first to appear was *Art Magic*, by the same author as *Ghost Land*, edited by Emma Hardinge Britten and published by her husband Dr. William Britten early in 1876. The title suggests a contrast with "Natural Magic"; the book is a compilation of every sort of occult and mythographic chit-chat.[90] Yet it contained the same key ideas as we have already noticed in Imperator's teachings and in Blavatsky's first article:

> One God can be traced through all ancient faiths. [35][91]
> Jesus's life is an allegory. [50]
> Much of ancient religion concealed solar or phallic worship. [63–7]
> India is the oldest source of wisdom. [23]
> Besides the Jewish Cabbala there is an Oriental Cabbala, but its key is found only in Oriental fraternities. [81]
> The Egyptian priests were masters of occult arts. [187]
> The human being is triple: Body, Astral Spirit, and the deific Soul. [124]
> Spirits have come from a heavenly, sexless state (this from a Hindu source) and lived on many earths before this one. [29]
> Modern reincarnationism is a fantasy. [83]
> There is evolution from elementals to humans, and from humans to angels and planetary spirits. [93]

One can contact spirits on all three levels. [87–92]
Modern American Spiritualism marks a great spiritual outpouring. [347]
Spiritualism needs scientific investigation. [362]

Louis was encouraging the study of the Western magical tradition and of Oriental religions and teaching that spiritualism could include commerce with submundane elementals and supermundane angels, as well as with the "mundane" spirits of the unprogressed human dead. This commerce was one thing that distinguished occultism from spiritualism; the other was the development of the will and a practical, conscious attitude to supernatural contacts.

Many of the themes and arguments of *Art Magic* had already arisen in Emma's inspired discourses from the new period that began for her in 1858 (see Chapter Ten), and they show how close she came to throwing in her lot with the occultists. But her occultism came from outside herself: that of the 1860 lectures came from her "spirit guide," and that of *Art Magic* from her friend Louis. When she was writing as herself, as in her long histories of the spiritualist movement, she emphasized the difference between occultism and spiritualism, but indulged her sentimentality in favor of the latter. Here are her words after Blavatsky's death:

> For my own part, I affirm that as long as the victims or hypnotized subjects of Blavatskism insist upon trying to build up their sect by abuse of ours (the spiritualists)—calling our loved and loving spirit friends "spooks" and "shells," and those who have tested and proved them "lost, deceived, and degraded men and women"—just so long shall I continue to show the utter worthlessness of the authority from which they speak and write.[92]

The second book of this trio was *Old Truths in a New Light,* by the Countess of Caithness. I shall have more to say about Lady Caithness in Chapter Seventeen. For the time being, it will be enough to show how some of the themes tabulated above permeate her work, too:

The Devil is only ignorance and opposition to the Divine plan. [51][93]
Ancient revelations correspond all through the East. [169]
The Bible speaks by emblems. [221]
The Hindu and Egyptian zodiacs show the Virgin and Child. [223]
Mankind, with the whole universe, is in eternal progress. [240]
Elementary spirits are all around us, but on a different plane. [276]

There is a New Dispensation dawning. [297]
The Mysteries of all ancient religions taught the same. [353]
Man is tripartite: body, spirit-body, and the immortal principle (soul). [444]
The Church has ignored all this truth. [448–9]

What makes Lady Caithness different from these other writers and mediums is that she believed firmly in reincarnation and devoted much of her book to arguing in favor of this doctrine.

The third book, and the real testament of the Brotherhood of Luxor, was *Isis Unveiled*, mainly written in 1876 and published in 1877. Blavatsky never claimed to have written every word of the two volumes herself: it included contributions from Sotheran, Rawson, Alexander Wilder, and especially from Olcott, beside the innumerable quotations from about a hundred books on comparative religion, occultism, and contemporary science. Olcott describes her—and there is no reason to disbelieve him—as writing much of it in a state of semi-trance, as if taking dictation from invisible beings or copying from invisible books, or else being temporarily possessed by other personalities. It remained for Emma Hardinge Britten to put about the rumor that the whole thing came from the manuscripts of Baron de Palm (see Chapter Eleven). Perhaps this explanation satisfied those who could not bear the idea that a woman should have written such a formidable book. Alexander Wilder, who helped Blavatsky cut out hundreds of pages from *Isis*, wondered about this theory and guessed that at least *Art Magic* and *Isis* had come from the same source.[94]

Isis Unveiled was a clarion summons to humanity to awaken from the charmed sleep into which it had been plunged by the deceptions of Christianity and the illusions of science. In a way, it did come from the same source as *Art Magic* (and *Ghost Land*), if the definition of "source" is taken as something far larger and more mysterious than a sheaf of papers found in Palm's old trunk. Admittedly, the book is almost impossible to read from cover to cover, being twelve hundred pages of anecdotes, diatribes, and quotations. Its importance comes clear if one compares it to another compendium, *The Warfare of Science with Theology in Christendom* (1896, but based on an essay predating *Isis*), by Andrew Dickson White, the first president of Cornell University.[95] White's work does half the job of *Isis Unveiled*: the exoteric half of demolishing religious superstition, obscurantism, and persecution in the clear light of science. What its rationalist author could not possibly imagine was the esoteric half of Blavatsky's work, which in turn demolishes the pretensions of science by adducing a mass of evidence against the premises of materialism.

All of the themes I have listed in this chapter receive their fullest expansion in *Isis*: the solar and phallic origin of religions; the superiority of Eastern and Egyptian wisdom to modern science; the existence of an esoteric tradition handed down by adepts; the validity of all the world's religions; the errors of Christianity and the crimes of the Church; the pre-existence and future evolution of the human soul; the rejection of the doctrine of reincarnation; the elementals as causes of phenomena; the existence of adepts; and the significance of Modern Spiritualism to the destiny of humanity.

FIFTEEN

Wisdom from the East

In the previous chapter the work of Blavatsky and Olcott in founding the Theosophical Society in 1875 was presented as a mission to correct the misapprehensions of spiritualism, to expand the horizons of science, and to oppose dogmatic Christianity. The means to do this were drawn from Egyptian occultism, both ancient and modern, and from the Western esoteric tradition. At the same time, there was the brooding presence in the background of India and of an Oriental wisdom that surpassed that of the West. As Blavatsky's allies and masters in this work there were the mysterious "adepts" who appeared to have both Egyptian and Indian connections. I then explained how Colonel Olcott became increasingly uneasy about Blavatsky's leanings towards India, and how he asked his London spiritualist friends to help him dissuade her from going there.

This chapter is devoted to the other side of the story. We will see that, for all his protests, Olcott had already made contact with Indians involved in movements for religious and political reform that paralleled those of the early Theosophists. Within a year of his complaints to Stainton Moses ("Do not forget Imperator . . ."), he was corresponding both with Hindus in India and Buddhists in Ceylon (modern Sri Lanka). In the course of 1878 it became plain that the founders were going to follow the instructions of Blavatsky's masters and leave America for India. This they did on 18 December 1878, arriving in Bombay on 16 February 1879.

On their way, the founders spent two weeks in England more or less incognito.[1] There were sources in the British Museum that Blavatsky wanted to consult, and people whom it was important to meet face to face. Their hosts, in Norwood, Middlesex, were Dr. Billing, who had been present at the founding in New York, and his wife, Mrs. Hollis-Billing, a well-known medium for a spirit called "Ski." They met Olcott's friends Stainton Moses and Charles Massey; George Wyld, a homeopathic and mesmeric doctor who became President of the British Branch of the Society; Kenneth Mackenzie and the alchemist-vicar William Ayton and his wife; and various Hindus, both students and masters.[2]

In order to appreciate the world which Blavatsky and Olcott were entering as they sailed out of Liverpool, we need to go back several decades and trace two lines of influence. One of these is the reform of Hinduism started by Rammohun Roy in the early years of the nineteenth century under the influence of the European Enlightenment. The other is the Western discovery of Buddhism. Chapters One and Thirteen have already touched on some of these matters. This chapter focuses on the transformation that occurred between the period of the *Asiatic Researches*, when India and the Far East were studied out of intellectual curiosity and a thirst for new sensations, and that of the Theosophical Society a century later, when a substantial body of Westerners transferred their spiritual allegiance to the East.

The curiosity of the early orientalists was practical, for the process of colonization went more smoothly when the colonizers could understand the language, culture, and world views of their subject peoples. This is why, for example, the East India Company and the Crown encouraged the scholarly interests of their respective employees Charles Wilkins and Sir William Jones. The *Asiatic Researches*, discussed in Chapter One, were the first fruits of this policy, setting a standard for orientalists that was at first emulated by the French, then outdone by the heavy armor of German scholarship.

Since the later seventeenth century, Europeans had enjoyed the oriental ambience through the decorative arts and literature. China was the first enthusiasm, thanks partly to the Jesuit missionaries who established themselves in the imperial court, and partly to the business sense of the Chinese who perceived a growing appetite in Europe for silks and porcelain. Philosophers such as Leibniz and Voltaire were fascinated by the orderliness and stability of Confucian civilization, so secure and in its way so moral, for all its ignorance of the Judeo-Christian scriptures. A second enthusiasm was for Persia and, in general, for the more sensuous aspects of Islamic civilization. The harem of the Ottoman sultans, the scented gardens of Isfahan, the *Arabian Nights*, the visions induced by hashish: these appealed to the Romantic imagination in a way that China, distant, odd, and rather cold, could never do. Napoleon's Egyptian campaign of 1797 started a brief fashion for decorative motifs from Pharaonic Egypt, but its more lasting result was to open up the modern Islamic countries of North Africa and the Near East, where this sensuous aestheticism could be enjoyed by thousands of Europeans who went there for administration, trade, health, or exploration. Yet none of these visitors felt inclined to abandon

Christianity for its old enemy, Islam, nor were they led to the feet of those Sufi masters who, we are told, care little for religious differences.

In between the extremes of the Mahgreb and the Far East lay India, seething with incomprehensible forms of human life as the Hindu heavens seethed with their crores of gods and goddesses, and waiting like a ripe fruit for colonization. It was the extreme religiousness of the Indians that most struck the first imperialists. The innumerable temples, the festivals, the sacred cows, the holy men and their horrid self-tortures: these had no resemblance to the Islamic world, where the Koran, however unappealing to Christians, could be read and understood, and where there was no mystery about what went on in the mosques. True, we have seen instances of Arab magic witnessed by Westerners, but it had to be sought out, whereas in India any number of yogis, fakirs, and magicians were eager to display their wares to a new audience.

The Brahmins regarded the uninvited visitors with disdain. For a start, any European was a *mleccha*, an untouchable with no rank in the caste system. Besides, most of the visitors were merchants, common seamen and soldiers, or equally aggressive missionaries, to whom no sacred text was going to be opened. The first successful breach of Brahmanical reserve was made by Charles Wilkins, a senior merchant of the East India Company. He was aided diplomatically by Warren Hastings, the first Governor General of India, who persuaded one or more Brahmin *pandits* (scholars) to help Wilkins with his great project, a translation into English of the *Bhagavad Gita*. Its appearance in 1785 marks the beginning of serious Anglo-Indian relations on the intellectual plane and the beginning of the responsible presentation of Hindu texts to a European readership.

Wilkins' *Gita* was dedicated to Warren Hastings and prefaced by a letter from the Governor to the head of the East India Company, Nathaniel Smith, who had granted Wilkins a leave of absence for his project. In this letter Hastings remarks on the capacity of the Brahmins for concentrated devotion, whereas, he says, "even the most studious men of our hemisphere will find it difficult to restrain their attention but that it will wander to some object of present sense or recollection . . ."[3] He concludes that in the case of the Brahmins, after years of training, "their collective studies may have led them to the discovery of new tracks and combinations of sentiment, totally different from the doctrines with which the learned of other nations are acquainted . . . [which] may be equally founded in truth with the most simple of our own."[4] This must have been the first time that a European had given credit, in print, to the fruits of yoga.

Warren Hastings was not only the first, but arguably the greatest of India's governors-general. Besides overcoming the Brahmins' reluctance to make their Sanskrit texts available, he helped to establish the Asiatic

Society of Bengal and its *Asiatic Researches,* instituted the first land survey of Bengal, and sent an embassy to the Panchen Lama to try to open a trade route to Tibet. Far from despising the native religions, he provided from his own funds for the founding of a Moslem college in Calcutta. Of the *Bhagavad Gita,* Hastings wrote:

> I do not hesitate to pronounce the Geeta a performance of great originality; of a sublimity of conception, reasoning, and diction, almost unequalled; and a single exception, among all the known religions of mankind, of a theology accurately corresponding with that of the Christian dispensation, and most powerfully illustrating its fundamental doctrines.[5]

Charles Wilkins shared Hastings' approval, both of the literary quality of the *Mahabharata* (from which the *Gita* comes), which both men compared favorably with Milton, and of its theology. But Wilkins makes it clear that the doctrines of the *Gita* are not representative of Hinduism in practice, and that the Brahmins are not just unworldly, monotheistic contemplatives:

> The most learned *Brahmans* of the present times are Unitarians according to the doctrine of *Kreeshna*; but at the same time that they believe but in one God, an universal spirit, they so far comply with the prejudices of the vulgar, as outwardly to perform all the ceremonies inculcated by the *Vedas,* such as sacrifices, ablutions, etc. They do this, probably, more for the support of their own consequence, which could only arise from the great ignorance of the people, than in compliance with the dictates of *Kreeshna:* indeed, this ignorance, and these ceremonies, are as much the bread of the *Brahmans,* as the superstition of the vulgar is the support of the priesthood in many other countries.[6]

I do not know whether Wilkins had in mind his own country, with its established Anglican church, or whether this was merely a dig at the Roman Catholics. But it is a remark of a kind with which we are familiar, the hypocrisies and exploitations of exoteric religion being a *leitmotif* of so many of our authors.

After 1785, any English speaker able to buy this beautiful quarto volume could read the *Bhagavad Gita* for himself. But outside the intellectual world, the influence of the *Gita* and of the *Asiatic Researches* was negligible, as Sir William Jones's biographer S. H. Mukherjee has sadly observed.[7] The more the British in India learned about Hinduism, the less they liked it and the more unfavorable reports they sent home. As colonial administrators, what they came up against was not the sublime universality of the

Gita or the monism of the Vedanta, but a people led by the example of petty monarchs who fought and squabbled in the most unspiritual way. When they were not squabbling, they were given to very uncivilized practices in the name of that same religion. The caste system was the most obvious of these. A cynic might observe that it offended the British because it so resembled their own class-ridden society, while committing the unforgivable sin of making explicit the social distinctions that should remain politely unspoken. An easier target, and one whose suppression lay within the bounds of possibility, was the practice of *suttee*, named after Sati, the wife of Rama who willingly ended her life on her husband's funeral pyre. Whatever its origins, the custom of burning Hindu widows had become a matter of social and even physical pressure from in-laws who did not want the burden of supporting them, because—and here was a second target for reform—widows were not allowed to remarry. The situation was made still worse by the custom of child brides, by which a girl would be taken even before puberty into her husband's house, and, as the Europeans imagined, his bed. If he died without leaving his wife a fortune, no matter how young she was, her fate was either suttee or a life on the charity of her in-laws. One sympathizes with the administrators who, anxious not to upset the natives, saw these things going on in their territories and had to decide whether or not to act. Lastly there was the temple worship, which seemed to the Protestant British to be directed to "idols" in a way that made Rome's worst excesses pale by comparison, its most shocking feature being that the most sacred idol of the Shaivite temples was revealed as nothing other than a phallus. To any but the most open-minded scholar, Hinduism appeared to be a cruel, foolish, and obscene religion.

In her book on *Sir William Jones and the Romantics,* Fatma Moussa-Mahmoud contrasts the British experience of India with that of the French and German Sanskritists who began to appear after 1800. Not only were the Continental scholars insulated from the ugly spectacle of Hinduism in practice, but they were spared the incessant tirades of the British missionaries, in whose interest it was to point out the worst aspects of the rival faith.[8] Thus the field of Sanskrit and Buddhist studies came to be dominated by continental philologists such as the brothers Schlegel, Csoma Körösi, Eugène Burnouf, Barthélémy Saint-Hilaire, and Max Müller.

One result of British disillusionment was that when the *Asiatic Researches* resumed publication in 1816 under H. T. Colebrooke's presidency, there were no more of the delightful, speculative articles such as Jones had written on the Greek and Hindu gods, or Wilford on the Sacred Isles of the West, which brought India, via comparative mythography, into the family of nations. The time of the gentleman amateur was passing.

Whereas formerly an educated man could read the whole journal with pleasure and understand most of it, now it was a vehicle for conversations among a handful of scholars. By 1833, it had divided into a literary and a scientific section, and its cultural influence was nil.

A similar change was taking place in the field of mythography. No longer could one man pretend to take all the world's myths and religions as his topic, and propose some all-embracing theory to explain them, but the work had to be done piecemeal by specialists. Consequently, the only people who persisted with universal theories were the occultists or esotericists who felt themselves exempted, by the possession of special knowledge, from the impossible burden of becoming adept in a dozen Western and Eastern languages. Godfrey Higgins's *Anacalypsis* marks the end of the old era of mythography; Madame Blavatsky's *Isis Unveiled*, the bravest attempt of the latter type.

In sum, there was nothing to kindle any religious warmth towards Hinduism on the part of Europeans, nor did the Brahmins do anything to encourage it. Some of the lower castes or outcasts sought to improve their status by converting to the Christianity of their conquerors. The higher castes either ignored the missionaries' efforts or tried to subvert them.

Against this background there appears the solitary figure of Rammohun Roy (or Ram Mohan Rai, 1772–1833), the first Brahmin to fall under the spell of Enlightenment ideas, and the first emissary from India to the West.[9] The rebellious son of a wealthy Bengali Brahmin, Rammohun early developed a distaste for Hinduism as it was practiced. When he was sixteen, he wrote a work against idolatry, which offended his family and caused him to spend several years in wandering. No one has yet disproved the claim that two or three of those years (1788–1790) were spent in Tibet, but there is no sign whatever that Rammohun was influenced by Mahayana Buddhism.

On returning to India, Rammohun settled into family life and a high position in the Bengal Civil Service. In 1803 he published a work in Persian and Arabic entitled *A Gift to Monotheists*, being a plea for the reconciliation of all religions on a monotheistic basis. Rammohun's theology was closer to Islam than to Hinduism, but the Islamic hostility to other faiths seemed to him as regrettable as the polytheism and idolatry of his native faith. He was to see the latter at its worst in 1811, when the widow of one of his brothers became a suttee. Undeterred before the event by Rammohun's remonstrances, her nerve failed her as she felt the flames, but the priests held her down with poles and a band played loudly to drown her cries. Suttee claimed several hundred lives each year, and Rammohun vowed never to rest until it was abolished. His efforts succeeded in 1829, when the Governor General, Lord William Bentinck, approved a law that defined suttee as murder.

Rammohun now set out to balance his erudition in oriental languages and literature with its Western complement. Settling in a grand house in Calcutta, he became the center of a group of progressive Hindus, with whom he initiated the study of what would now be called comparative religion. Always the theme was to do away with corruptions and complications and to go straight to the moral and devotional heart of each faith. This upset the Christian missionaries because while Rammohun expressed admiration for Jesus and the Gospel teachings, he refused to discard the truths he found in Islam and Hinduism. He was, in fact, a Unitarian, and open to any expression of faith in the "Fatherhood of God and the Brotherhood of Mankind."

From 1816 to 1819, Rammohun published English translations of the basic texts of Vedanta and of several Upanishads, annotating them from the point of view of Sankaracharya's monism. His object was to show that Hinduism at its purest is monotheistic, and gives no warrant to the superstitions and abuses of the Brahmins. As Mukherjee points out, the foundations of Rammohun's approach were laid in the 1780s, when Sir William Jones recognized in India a civilization second to none in the ancient world, and in Vedanta a doctrine of the purest monotheism quite free from the accretions of priestcraft.[10] It was Rammohun's translations and Wilkins's *Gita* that were read by the American Transcendentalists and gave them an appreciation for Hinduism, or at least for Vedanta, for which there was as yet no parallel in other countries.[11]

In 1828, Rammohun founded the Brahmo (or Brahma) Samaj, "for the worship and adoration of the Eternal Unsearchable Immutable Being who is the Author and Preserver of the Universe" (without giving this being any title), and "to promote charity, morality, piety, benevolence, virtue and the strengthening of the bond of union between men of all religious persuasions and creeds."[12] One can imagine a chorus of assent from every contemporary of Rammohun's treated in this book. More details emerge from the analysis of Rammohun's religious thought by Sisir Kumar Das, who explains that Rammohun chose Vedanta because he had to allow a national, tolerant, and monotheistic religion: not because he really accepted its doctrines, which are so monistic as to be socially quite useless. One cannot organize or reform a society on the basis of the unity of all existence and the deceptive nature of all phenomena! Nor did Rammohun have anything to say about salvation, a topic on which the different religions and sects have no agreement. Regarding religious practices, he favored worship through contemplation rather than prayer. The songs he wrote for his Samaj have no reference to religious experience, but are about selflessness and the unity of God. He seems to have been unconcerned with the question of life after death, saying that although we die, mankind lives on, and that our duty is consequently to serve it.[13]

This should make it plain that Rammohun was a thoroughgoing exotericist, seeking religious agreement on humanistic principles rather than through esoteric and metaphysical knowledge.

Rammohun had by now perfected his English and learned a good deal of Greek and Hebrew, the latter in six months' study under a Jewish teacher, so that he could apply himself to the Bible with the same respect for its original sources as he brought to Hindu and Muslim texts. The first fruits of his studies was *The Precepts of Jesus,* a collection of extracts from the four Gospels that did away with what he considered the extraneous matter of miracles, the Trinity, etc. Rammohun's fellow deist and social reformer, Thomas Jefferson, had made a similar compilation in his student days, in the attempt to disburden the teachings of Jesus from even the earliest accretions. Naturally this selectivity offended the missionaries for whom every word of the Bible was to be accepted as the word of God, and Rammohun had to answer them in a series of *Appeals to the Christian Public* (1820–1823). From this time onwards, Rammohun became increasingly Christian in the sense of accepting Jesus's teachings as the best guide ever offered for human life. But he never renounced the sacred thread of the Brahmin nor transgressed the dietary laws of his caste, since that would have discredited him with his own people; in addition, he always kept his head covered, in Muslim fashion.

Rammohun's reputation had spread long before he left India. The Spanish Constitution, drawn up in 1812 after freedom had been granted to the South American countries, was dedicated to him. He had correspondents in the United States and in France, a country which honored him as Britain and India never did by making him an honorary member of the Société Asiatique. With this went a lively interest in European politics. Like Godfrey Higgins, he rejoiced in 1830 when he heard the news of the July Revolution in France which had deposed the rigid Charles X in favor of Louis-Philippe. While in London, one of Rammohun's chief concerns was the passage of the Reform Bill. If it were to fail, he had decided to move to America.

In 1830 Rammohun accepted a commission from the Muslim Emperor at Delhi to make representations to the British Government concerning the Emperor's allowance. To ensure him a proper reception, the Emperor made him a Raja or petty "king." Rammohun reached England in 1831 and was immediately lionized by three distinct parties. The Unitarians wanted him for their own, and it was in their care that he died in Bristol in 1833. The leading society ladies wanted this elegant and well-spoken Indian as an ornament to their parties. The politicians did not so much want him, as feel obliged to treat him with the respect due to a raja and an ambassador, and as a result his commission for the Emperor was fulfilled through representations to the Houses of Commons and Lords.

Society life seems to have agreed with Rammohun, with visits to the theater, receptions, and banquets at which his prestige was, if anything, increased by his taking only rice and water. A rich man by Indian standards, he kept his end up with liveried servants, a carriage, and a succession of smart London addresses, but he practically beggared himself in the attempt to maintain the prestige of his nation. Among the personalities he met were several who have already appeared in this book. He had much in common with Robert Owen, and admired the latter's socialism, but they differed in that Rammohun could not share Owen's determined opposition to religion of any kind (see his letter to Owen's son, Appendix A). A more congenial acquaintance was Lord Brougham, with whom Rammohun shared a concern for popular education (he had founded schools and colleges in India) and an open mind in matters of religion. He met and liked Spurzheim, but having not the slightest leaning towards the occult sciences, Rammohun could not take phrenology seriously.

In his English years, Rammohun kept company in Unitarian and Anglican circles and went regularly to services of both kinds. This in itself was puzzling to those for whom the choice was "Church or Chapel." But what his Christian friends wanted most of all, he refused: namely, to declare himself a convert to Christianity and hence an object of triumph for them. What he valued was the morality and simple unitarianism of Jesus, not the polytheism of the Trinity, and least of all the doctrines of original sin, atonement, and salvation by faith, which were responsible, in his view, for the most deplorable feature of Christianity, its rejection of every other religion.

Rammohun Roy's gift to India was the combination of deism, religious tolerance, and social justice, which was the legacy of the eighteenth-century Enlightenment, and which would act as a ferment through the continuing educational and social work of the Brahmo Samaj. He set in motion the process that makes India today, for all its difficulties, the world's largest democracy.

By now the reader will have realized that Rammohun belongs, in sentiment as well as in chronology, with the mythographers of the first four chapters of this book, and especially with Godfrey Higgins, who did not find it necessary to blaspheme in order to wish Christianity free of its dogmas and priestcraft. Both Rammohun and Higgins were landed gentlemen and scholars, who used their privileged positions for gaining universal knowledge about religions and for social reform. Higgins's cause was the plight of the insane and of the agricultural laborer; Rammohun's, that of the widow and outcast. Both admired Islam, yet would at the end of their lives call themselves followers of Jesus Christ.

It goes without saying that modern opponents of the Enlightenment such as René Guénon regard the Brahmo Samaj as despicable, and

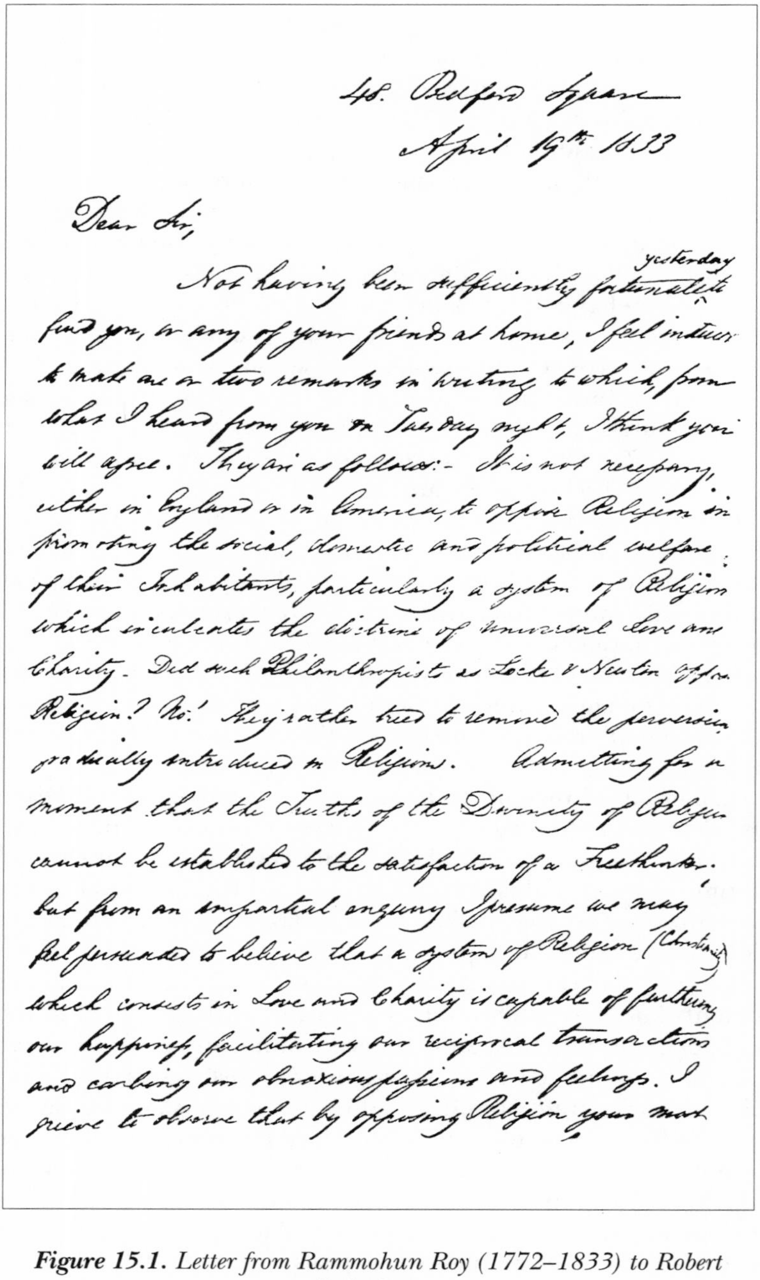

48. Bedford Square
April 19th 1833

Dear Sir,

Not having been sufficiently fortunate yesterday to find you, or any of your friends at home, I feel induced to make one or two remarks in writing to which, from what I heard from you on Tuesday night, I think you will agree. They are as follows:- It is not necessary, either in England or in America, to oppose Religion in promoting the social, domestic and political welfare of their Inhabitants, particularly a system of Religion which inculcates the doctrine of universal Love and Charity. Did such Philanthropists as Locke & Newton oppose Religion? No! They rather tried to remove the perversion gradually introduced in Religion. Admitting for a moment that the Truths of the Divinity of Religion cannot be established to the satisfaction of a Freethinker, but from an impartial enquiry I presume we may feel persuaded to believe that a system of Religion (Christianity) which consists in Love and Charity is capable of furthering our happiness, facilitating our reciprocal transactions and curbing our obnoxious passions and feelings. I grieve to observe that by opposing Religion, you must

Figure 15.1. *Letter from Rammohun Roy (1772–1833) to Robert Dale Owen.*

Rammohun as one of the worst traducers of the Hindu tradition.[14] This is partly because his religion was purely exoteric, adapting Vedanta to deism rather than pursuing the esoteric goal of a spiritual enlightenment, and partly because of Rammohun's detestation of "traditional" doctrines and practices. H. P. Blavatsky, on the other hand, who also knew the difference between exoteric and esoteric religion, wrote a stirring tribute in which she called Rammohun "one of the purest, most philanthropic, and enlightened men India ever produced."[15] Like Rammohun, Blavatsky was of the religious "Left": she had no regard for formalism nor for age-hallowed customs, especially those that appeared to her rooted in priestcraft and the cynical exploitation of the populace.

After a few years of somnolence following Rammohun's unexpected death, the Brahmo Samaj was led by Devendranath Tagore (Debendra Nath Thakur, 1817–1905), son of Rammohun's friend Prince Dwarkanath Tagore and father of the Nobel prizewinner Rabindranath. The Tagores were among the numerous Calcutta dignitaries who supported Dr. Esdaile's Mesmeric Hospital in the 1840s.[16] Under Devendranath's leadership, the Samaj reversed Rammohun's Christian tendencies and concentrated on a reform within Hinduism. After a flirtation with revealed religion in the form of the Vedas, the Samaj decided around 1850 to do away with scriptures altogether. It now defined itself as a theism, whereas Rammohun, for all his hymns to the nameless One, had been closer to deism. The Samaj now acknowledged a personal God who answers the prayers of the individual, but who is only revealed through "nature and intuition." This vague and sentimental religion, of a type common enough in the West, lived in an uneasy symbiosis with Hindu society. On the one hand, the Brahmo Samaj utterly rejected "idolatry," thus excluding its members from the domestic rites that are so much a part of Brahmin family life. On the other hand, Devendranath was a sufficiently unreformed Brahmin to remain strongly against intercaste marriage and the remarriage of widows. Only Brahmins, moreover, could officiate at the Samaj's services.

The rising star of the Samaj in the 1860s was Keshub Chunder Sen (Keshava Chandra Sen, 1838–1884), a middle-class recipient of a British education, ignorant of Sanskrit and enthralled by Christianity. Keshub was not of the Brahmin caste, so it is not surprising that he called for the discarding of the sacred thread worn by all Brahmins, and broke other taboos, e.g., by bringing his wife into the services. Devendranath was fond of him and for some time tried to keep up with Keshub's idea of progress. But by 1865 their styles had diverged so far that the Samaj split in two, the greater part following the "Brahmo Samaj of India," founded by Keshub in 1868.

Keshub was a *bhakta*—a follower of the path of love—who had no sympathy with traditional Hinduism, but was enthralled by the personality of the great *bhakta* of Galilee. Throughout his life he teetered on the brink of Christianity, but like his predecessors could not stomach its claim of supremacy over every other religion. He soon determined to follow in the steps of Rammohun Roy, and make his synthesis known to the West. His visit to England in 1870 was a triumph: the President of the Brahmo Samaj was received by numerous dignitaries from Queen Victoria downwards, and welcomed by the Unitarians as if he were a reincarnation of Rammohun himself. But for his part, he was appalled to discover what a nation of "Christians" was really like: the British seemed more alienated from Jesus' teachings than even the Brahmins.

Keshub's admiration for Jesus had brought him round to a belief that God had actually been revealed in certain men. The next step, perhaps an inevitable one for a charismatic leader lacking in any philosophical subtlety, was to class himself as one such man. This was his first major mistake. Struggling to define the prophetic status of which he had become convinced, Keshub said that he had no creed or doctrine to reveal, but was under a "perennial and perpetual inspiration from heaven."[17]

Some of the Brahmo Samaj members were dismayed by this kind of claim. But not far away from the headquarters in Calcutta, in the temple precincts of Dakshineswar, there was a man who left most visitors in no doubt that he was a recipient of such inspiration. It is to Keshub's credit that, towards 1875, he did not hesitate to go and see Ramakrishna Paramahamsa (1836–1886). The two *bhaktas* fell in love with one another, in a spiritual sense, but it was Ramakrishna who was evidently the senior partner. With great delicacy and humility he tried to lead his more famous friend on to the realization that God and the devotee are one and the same; but this was going too far for the church leader. Nor was Keshub happy with Ramakrishna's easy acceptance of "idols," or with his seeming indifference to social reform. Enough that Ramakrishna succeeded in bringing Keshub round to worshiping God as Mother as well as Father, and that they spent many hours in ecstatic singing and dancing.[18] More significant historically is the fact that some Brahmo Samajists gravitated permanently to Ramakrishna's circle, finding there a level of spiritual awareness and presence that their own services lacked. It was they who brought Narendranath Datta into the sage's influence, initiating his transformation into Swami Vivekananda (1863–1902), founder of the Ramakrishna Mission and Order and envoy to the Chicago Parliament of Religions in 1893. Mysticism apart, one can say that whereas the Brahmo Samaj was founded on rejection (albeit of social abuses and religious nonsense), Ramakrishna was an accepter. He adored Jesus with the Christians, not worrying that some of them were Trinitarians; worshiped Allah with the Muslims, agreeing that there was One God and that Mohammed was his prophet; and joyfully accepted the whole pantheon of Hindu gods and goddesses in all their idolatrous imagery. Every one of them spoke to him with the voice of his elected deity, the Mother Kali, and he knew that she was ready to speak to everyone who would listen to her.

It is one of the ironies of history that Blavatsky and Olcott failed to make contact with Ramakrishna, their one contemporary in India to whom no one can deny the title of spiritual master. That they did not was probably the fault of Keshub Chunder Sen, whose reputation reached them as one of "personal leadership and reckless egotism" diametrically opposed to the ideals of Rammohun Roy.[19] In 1881 it seemed to Blavatsky that the Brahmo Samaj, fifty years after its foundation, was developing in exactly the same way as Christianity and Buddhism, with "the approach of a pompous ritualism, which in the progress of time will stifle what there is of spirit in the new church and leave only a gorgeous formalism in its place."[20] She warned her readers that whereas Rammohun had always been humility itself, the Samaj's new leader, Keshub Chunder Sen, was claiming the church as a new dispensation and himself as an avatar.

In 1870, the same year that Keshub visited England, two other Indians took ship from England to America. They were a Bombay textile magnate called Moolji Thackersey (Seth Damodar Thackersey Mulji, died 1880[21]) and a Mr. Tulsidas. Josephine Ransom, an early historian of the Theosophical Society, writes that they were "on a mission to the West to see what could be done to introduce Eastern spiritual and philosophic ideas."[22] Traveling on the same boat was Henry Olcott, fresh from his experiences in London's spiritualist circles. Olcott was sufficiently impressed by this shipboard meeting to keep a framed photograph of the two Indians on the wall of the apartment he was sharing with Blavatsky in 1877. It was one evening in that year that a visitor who had traveled in India (sometimes identified as James Peebles[23]) remarked on the photograph. Olcott writes in his memoirs of the consequences of this extraordinary series of coincidences:

> I took it down, showed it to him, and asked if he knew either of the two. He did know Moolji Thackersey and had quite recently met him in Bombay. I got the address, and by the next mail wrote to Moolji about our Society, our love for India and what caused it. In due course he replied in quite enthusiastic terms, accepted the offered diploma of membership, and told me about a great Hindu pandit and reformer, who had begun a powerful movement for the resuscitation of pure Vedic religion.[24]

This reformer was Swami Dayananda Saraswati (1824–1882). In 1870 he was still an eccentric traveling preacher with no aspirations to international influence: something that grew on him precisely after meeting the Brahmo Samajists. He met Devandranath Tagore in 1870; in 1873 Keshub Chunder Sen gave him the advice (which he took) to stop wearing only a loincloth and speaking only Sanskrit. Indefatigably stumping round the subcontinent, Dayananda founded his "powerful movement," the Arya Samaj, in 1875. This chronology suggests that in 1870 Thackersey was probably coming to America as a representative of the Brahmo Samaj, but that by the time Olcott got in touch with him again, he had transferred his allegiance to the Arya Samaj.

The Arya Samaj was more radical than any wing of the Brahmo Samaj, on which it was partially modeled. Dayananda was a monotheist who believed in the Vedas as the sole revealed scripture and the basis for a universal religion. The various gods addressed in the Vedic hymns (Agni, Indra, etc.), he explained as aspects of the One, and he was prepared to demonstrate how these ancient texts contained all possible knowledge of man, nature, and the means of salvation and happiness. Of the quarrels between the various religions, he wrote: "My purpose and aim is to help in putting an end to this mutual wrangling, to preach universal truth, to bring all men under one religion so that they may, by ceasing to hate each other and firmly loving each other, life in peace and work for their common welfare."[25] He had no respect whatever for Brahmanism: for their scriptures, rituals, polytheism, caste system, and discrimination against women. Unfortunately for his opponents, he was immensely learned and articulate, could out-argue most pandits, and had, in the last resort (which often seems to have occurred) the advantage of being 6'9" tall and broad to match.[26]

From Dayananda's point of view, the Brahmo Samajists had erred both in their failure to recognize the supremacy of the Vedas, and in their too-ready embrace of the errors of other religions. They were moreover too addicted to Brahmanic customs and privileges. Here is a contemporary summary of his social principles:

> He says that no inhabitant of India should be called a Hindu, that an ignorant Brahmin should be made a Shudra, and a Shudra, who is learned, well-behaved and religious should be made a Brahmin. Both men and women should be taught Language, Grammar, Dharmashastras, Vedas, Science and Philosophy. Women should receive special education in Chemistry, Music and Medical Science; they should know what foods promote health, strength and vigour. He condemns child marriage as the root of the most of the evils. A girl should be educated and married at the age of twenty. If a widow wants to remarry,

she should be allowed to do so. According to his opinion, there is no particular difference between the householder and the sannyasi.[27]

It is not surprising that the Theosophists in New York took kindly to the Arya Samaj, at first through correspondence with Thackersey, then through the Bombay branch head, Hurrychund Chintamon, and lastly through Dayananda himself. The two societies were united for a time, though the Theosophists were disillusioned as soon as they discovered the strength of Dayananda's Vedic fundamentalism and his hostility to all other religions. On Dayananda's unexpected death, Blavatsky wrote a generous obituary in *The Theosophist* for December 1883.[28] She appreciated him for defending what he saw as the best of his native heritage against the priestcraft of Brahmins and Christians alike, and for his leadership in an enlightened social policy of which she could only have approved.

As the Arya Samaj continued to flourish after Dayananda's death, it became a rallying point for that movement of Hindu nationalism that wanted neither to turn back the clock to Brahmanic theocracy, nor to embrace Western materialism along with the benefits of science and technology. What Rammohun Roy had set in motion, the Arya Samaj carried forward into the era of the Indian National Congress and the independence movement of the twentieth century. Dayananda himself died—some said poisoned—at the time when his mission was beginning to have real success among the North Indian rulers, but he had done enough to be celebrated as a father-figure by leaders of Indian independence such as Jawaharlal Nehru, Mahatma Gandhi, Indira Gandhi, and Aurobindo Ghose.[29]

This in itself defines the limits of Dayananda's mission, which was, as it turned out, for India alone.[30] Likewise, the mission of the Brahmo Samajists was a one-way street, bringing liberal Christian principles to India but making only the slightest inroads on the West through Emerson and his friends. The purpose of the foregoing survey has been to show how these Indian movements form another link between Enlightenment ideals and the Theosophical Society, which after its move to India took on the role of a mouthpiece for Eastern wisdom to address the West.

Madame Blavatsky and Colonel Olcott were not converts to Hinduism. One cannot convert to a religion which is entered only by birth into one of its castes. Western followers of the liberal, bhaktic Hinduism of the Ramakrishna Mission may well regard themselves as converts (Christopher Isherwood being perhaps the most eminent of these), but they are Vedantists, not Hindus. What Blavatsky and Olcott were was Buddhist.

Having arrived in India early in 1879, the founders of the Theosophical Society took the Five Vows of Buddhism, known as *Pansil,* during a visit to Ceylon on 25 May 1880, which made them formally Buddhists. But Blavatsky already considered herself a Buddhist in her New York days, as witness these quotations:

> I am, Sir, your obedient servant,
> H. P. Blavatsky,
> A benighted Buddhist, and the Corresponding
> Secretary of the Theosophical Society.
> New York, January 23rd [1877].[31]

> Let us settle, once and for all if you please, as to the word 'Spiritualist.' I am not one—not at least in the modern and American sense of the word. I am a Svabhavika, a Buddhist pantheist, if anything at all. I do not believe in a *personal* God, in a direct Creator, or a 'Supreme'; neither do I confess to a *First* cause, which implies the possibility of a *Last* one—and if so, then what comes next? I believe in but one eternal, indestructible substance, the Svabhavat, or invisible, all pervading matter, whether you call it God, or many Gods in partnership.[32]

> . . . if the reporter—the author of the article in question—had simply said that I belonged to the religion that had inspired the Buddha, instead of presenting me to the public as a Buddhist turning the *Wheel of the Law*—he would have spoken nothing but the truth.[33]

By the time Blavatsky was speaking thus, there had been nearly a century of debate as to what Buddhism was.[34] Some of this was touched on in Chapter Thirteen, when Hargrave Jennings's remarkable *Indian Religions* of 1857 was discussed. Now we have to go back to the late eighteenth century, in order to see why Buddhism was so much more difficult for Westerners to understand than Hinduism, and why in the end it was to have a greater influence on the West than any other oriental religion.

Buddhism, although founded in India by Prince Gautama Siddartha in the sixth century BCE, was all but extinct in that country by the time the modern colonists arrived. The Brahmins who informed the early *Asiatic Researches* scholars had no good word to say for the heretic philosophy, though they would grudgingly admit that Buddha was the Ninth Avatar of Vishnu, sent to tempt evil men away from the truth. Outside India, Buddhism flourished in two main forms or schools: the earlier, southern one, called Hinayana or Theravada, in Ceylon, Siam, Cambodia, and Burma, and the later, northern one, Mahayana, in Mongolia, Tibet, Nepal, China, Korea, and Japan.

In 1799, the *Researches* carried a first report on southern Buddhism from a physician, Francis Buchanan, who had obtained some treatises from an Italian priest in Rangoon. From these he gathered that in the Buddhist cosmology, the universe is periodically destroyed by fire, water, or wind, and then restored. The soul of every being dies with the body, whereupon another soul arises out of the same materials according to the good or bad actions of that being. All beings continually revolve through these changes until their perfected actions entitle them to "*Nieban,* the most perfect of all states, consisting in a kind of annihilation, in which beings are free from change, misery, death, sickness, or old age."[35] Buchanan agreed with the mythographers who identified Buddha with some deified man of the past, like the Egyptian gods. "His followers are strictly speaking atheists, as they suppose everything to arise from fate: and their gods are merely men, who by their virtue acquire supreme happiness, and by their wisdom become entitled to impose a law on all living beings."[36] Sir William Jones, in a postscript to the article, gave a variety of dates for Buddha, ranging from the Chinese (1028 BCE) to the Cingalese (542 BCE), and thought the last date the most likely one. He adds cynically that while the Buddhist laws of Burma have contributed little to the happiness of the people, at least they have not provided obstacles to happiness, like the laws of the Brahmins.

Buchanan's account, apart from its attempt to explain Nirvana ("Nieban"), made Buddhism seem not unlike Hinduism. But it soon became plain that the "gods" of Buddhism, whether or not they included Gautama himself, could not be fitted into any of the current mythographic theories.

In 1801 there came a further report from Ceylon, by Captain (later Major) Mahony.[37] This was more like a sea-captain's yarns than a scholar's. Mahony tried to explain the dual status of Buddha: as a man who had attained his position by his own efforts, and as one of a series of divine incarnations. But the subtlety of the matter was beyond him. The same volume of the *Asiatic Researches* carried a parallel effort by Mr. Joinville, Surveyor General, "On the Religion and Manners of the People of Ceylon." Joinville wrote that Buddha seemed to be superior to all the Gods, yet not what we mean by a God. He thought Buddhism more ancient than Brahmanism, for the following reasons that are the epitome of early nineteenth-century rationalism: "An uncreated world and mortal souls, are ideas to be held only in an infant state of society, and as society advances such ideas must vanish"; and "Ideas in opposition to all religion cannot gain ground, at least cannot make head, when there is already an established faith."[38]

The readers of the *Asiatic Researches* must by now have been left in a state of utter confusion as to what Buddhists believed. Edward Moor, author of *The Hindu Pantheon* (1810), was humble enough to admit as much, saying: "I am not sufficiently informed of the tenets or usages of the

Buddhists, to say in what particulars especially consist the differences between them and the tenets and usages of the *Brahmans.*"[39] Basing himself largely on the articles cited, Moor does his best to explain the Buddhist sculptures in the temples of Ellora and Elephanta, concluding that on the whole Buddhism seems to have been a reformation within Brahmanism.[40] He comments on the apparently negroid features of certain statues of Buddha, which would persuade Godfrey Higgins that they were the pointers to a primordial Black race, hence to the anteriority of Buddhism to Brahmanism.[41]

The Western knowledge of Buddhism was only confused further when news of Mahayana doctrines began to come in from the northern countries. The *Asiatic Researches* of 1828 carried a comprehensive "Notice of the languages, literature, and religion of the Bauddhas of Nepal and Bhot," by a civil servant, B. H. Hodgson. This explained the speculative systems, especially the Swabhavika school. Hodgson wrote of the northern Buddhists:

> In regard to the destiny of the soul, I can find no moral difference between them and the Brahminical Sages. By all, metempsychosis and absorption are accepted. But absorbed into what? into BRAHME, say the *Brahmans*—into *Sunyata,* or *Swabhava,* or *Prajna,* or *Adi Buddha,* say the various sects of the *Bauddhas*; and I should add, that by their doubtful *Sunyata* I do *not,* in general, understand annihilation, nothingness, but rather that extreme and almost infinite attenuation which they ascribe to their material powers or forces in the state of *Nirvritti,* or of abstraction from all particular palpable forms, such as compose the sensible world of *Pravritti.*[42]

The notion of Nirvana tormented the nineteenth-century mind. How could a religion have "nothingness" or "annihilation" as its *summum bonum*? Barthélémy Saint-Hilaire and Max Müller, the two principal orientalists of the 1850s, thought it a kind of collective madness, which was a convenient way of disposing of things for which their immense learning had no pigeon-hole. Hargrave Jennings, with an amateur's zeal, rightly attacked Müller for this. No less taxing were the paradoxes concerning God and the soul. Mahayana Buddhism was full of godlike beings such as the five Dhyani-Buddhas, to whom prayers were addressed, but Hinayana Buddhism taught self-reliance alone and appeared to be atheistic. Christians trembled and skeptics sneered at the blasphemy of a religion without a god. As far as the soul was concerned, it was easy enough to grasp the idea of its reembodiment: half the spiritualists believed in this. Less appealing was the belief of many Buddhists and Brahmins that human beings, if they are not careful, may reincarnate as animals. But deeper acquaintance with the Buddhist scriptures revealed that one of its foundations is the *anatta* doctrine, which teaches that the immortal soul (*atma*) beloved of Brahmins and Christians alike is nonexistent. So what can it be that transmigrates?

I am obviously not going to attempt an answer to such questions in this historical study, but they form the essential background to the debates and schisms that are the subject of these closing chapters.

More accessible than the metaphysical was the social side of Buddhism, which the British were inclined to approve, seeing in it both a protest against the abuses of the Brahmins and a parallel to their own Protestantism vis-à-vis Rome.[43] As more documents emerged, Gautama seemed to be an admirable character: upright, truthful, courageous, and compassionate—like Jesus himself. These were the aspects highlighted in Edwin Arnold's epic poem, *The Light of Asia* (1879), which first brought a positive vision of Gautama and of Buddhism before the eyes of the multitude.

Before *The Light of Asia*, and before the public "conversion" of the founders of the Theosophical Society in 1880, there had been several direct or indirect oriental envoys to the West. The first of these was a Siamese nobleman, Chao Phya Thipakon, who had conducted foreign affairs for Siam from 1856 until prevented by blindness in 1869. Chao's account was presented by Henry Alabaster, interpreter to the Siamese Consul General, in *The Wheel of the Law* (1871). The object of both authors was to sift the authentic Buddhist teachings from the superstitions that were rife among Chao's countrymen. Chao ridiculed the elaborate cosmology which the West had learned of through Buchanan's work;[44] as a "modern Buddhist," he laughed at the legends of magic powers;[45] he had no place for prayer, because in Buddhism there is no divine being to pray to;[46] and he discriminated carefully between the indefinable Nirvana and the common Buddhists' aspiration to "heaven."[47] Alabaster's own sympathies were with Buddhism, for he praises Buddhist tolerance and morality and ridicules the futility and expense of Protestant missionary efforts. A book like *The Wheel of the Law* probably did much to clarify what the publication of original texts had only obfuscated.

California was an early Buddhist center on account of the migrant workers who came there from across the Pacific. The priest of one Californian temple, Wong Chin Foo, appeared in New York in April 1877, lecturing in fluent English. He was introduced at a reception given by Blavatsky at her apartment.[48] In *Isis Unveiled* she quotes a conversation with him in which he says of Nirvana: "This condition we all understand to mean a final reunion with God, coincident with the perfection of the human spirit by its ultimate disembarrassment of matter. It is the very opposite of personal annihilation."[49] The ideas of reunion with God, spirit-matter duality, and personal survival have no place in original

Buddhist doctrine, but occur in the bhaktic "Pure Land" school of China and Japan, to which one presumes Wong Chin Foo belonged. Blavatsky probably used Wong Chin Foo as the basis for a series of tall tales she told her friends concerning Morya and Krishnavarma being Buddhist missionaries, and about travels to California by various figures, including Krishnavarma, Hilarion, and Blavatsky herself.[50]

Sympathy with oriental religion in American spiritualist circles went along with contempt for what Dr. Peebles called "the revengeful, repenting, personal God of Judaism."[51] While traveling in Ceylon, Peebles had witnessed in 1873 a two-day debate, before an audience of over 5,000 people, between the Reverends Mohottiwatte Gunananda (for Buddhism) and David da Silva (for Christianity), both of them learned in Sanskrit, Pali, and the Buddhist and Christian scriptures. Most of the debate focused on the "soul," which the Christian saw as an entity originating in the body, while the Buddhist saw it as an immortal essence, existing independently of its manifestation.[52] The importance of this debate is that Henry Olcott saw the original report of it,[53] which became his first link with Ceylon and led him, even before leaving New York, to establish contact with Gunananda and other Buddhist dignitaries in that island. Peebles continued active in the same cause: in the summer of 1878, he conveyed to the spiritualists of Boston a letter from Ceylon outlining the terms on which a Buddhist priest would consent to come for a year as missionary to "the corrupt and war-practising Christians of America," adding that there were already two Buddhist priests active in France: one teaching Pali to university linguists, the other as a missionary among the Catholics.[54]

Blavatsky let it be known as soon as she arrived in America that she had been in Tibet, and Theosophical orthodoxy has it that she studied there for several years under her masters before her mission to the West. However, there is nothing in the many passages on Buddhism in *Isis Unveiled* that could not have been drawn from Western publications, except the skill with which Blavatsky negotiated the pitfalls inherent in the subject. As she says, "Beginning with Godfrey Higgins and ending with Max Müller, every archaeologist and philologist who has fairly and seriously studied the old religion, has perceived that taken literally they could only lead them on a false track." And she goes on to give this explanation of Nirvana, which is like a clarification of Hodgson's statement above: "The *pravritti,* or the existence of nature when alive, in activity, and the *nirvritti,* or the rest, the state of non-living, is the Buddhistic esoteric doctrine. The 'pure nothing,' or non-existence, if translated according to the esoteric sense, would mean the 'pure spirit,' the NAMELESS or something our intellect is unable to grasp, hence nothing.[55]

Even among the scholars who had "seriously studied the old religion" there were few who felt secure writing about things that their "intellects were unable to grasp." We have seen that Hargrave Jennings made a brave attempt at this in 1857 and ended in virtual incoherence.

It was probably again through Peebles that Blavatsky and Olcott contacted Peary Chand Mittra (Piari Chand Mitra, 1814–1883). This Calcutta businessman stands at the intersection of Buddhism with spiritualism (he belonged to the British National Association of Spiritualists), the Brahmo Samaj (he had been educated at the Hindu College), and the Theosophical Society (he joined in 1877, and later became President of the Bengal Theosophical Society).[56] A frequent contributor to the London *Spiritualist* magazine, in July 1877 he wrote on "The Psychology of the Buddhists." Here he explained that in the beginning, Buddhism had been a protest against Brahmanism and had no belief in God, only in Karma. It grew, he said, from the Samkhya philosophy, and both were originally atheistic. They used intense yoga and contemplation to rise from the personal to the impersonal state, from the finite to the infinite, aiming to arrive on the other shore of Nirvana "in the attainment of the void or nothingness of the mundane." He then calls this the "absorption of the brain into the soul," and says that thereby the spiritual life is attained, exactly as it is by the Christian mystics. As time went on, Mittra explains, Buddhism became Vedantic in its conception of God and the soul, and in the means of attaining Nirvana or soul life.[57]

Mittra was primarily a spiritualist and a medium, very much influenced by the West.[58] For example, he compares the Vedic use of *soma* for attaining clairvoyance to Sir Humphrey Davy's experiments with nitrous oxide, and equates the effects of the latter with Nirvana.[59] He confesses that for sixteen years he has not been away from the spirits for a moment, and that he talks to them as to living people.[60] The London spiritualists presumably found him agreable as their "token oriental," with his not-too-threatening version of Buddhism.

Just as Blavatsky alienated many of the spiritualists by her unfavorable comparison of spiritualism with occultism, so her religious views became more uncompromising after she severed the connection of the Theosophical Society with the Arya Samaj. Dayananda's rigid theism and his intolerance of Buddhism and all other religions had been one of the chief disappointments of her meeting with him. At first her Buddhist contact was mainly in the Theravadin world, through H. Sumangala Unnanse (1827–1911), high priest of the temple of Adam's Peak in Ceylon, whom Olcott had contacted from New York. It was under the high priest's patronage that she and Olcott took *Pansil* (declared themselves Buddhists) in 1880. Olcott would repay Sumangala's hospitality and friendship with heroic efforts on behalf of the Buddhists of Ceylon, who to this day celebrate "Olcott Day" in memory of the man who encouraged them to assert their own religion against the pressure of their colonizers and missionaries. From now on, although the Theosophical Society was open to those of any faith or of none, the founders made it plain to which they belonged, though Olcott emphasized that their Buddhism was identical to the "Wisdom Religion of the Aryan Upanishads, and the soul of all the ancient world-faiths. Our Buddhism was, in a word, a philosophy, not a creed."[61]

As the Theosophical Society began to define itself as a public body, Blavatsky faced up to the charge of atheism that came both from the Arya Samajists and from the Christians.[62] First and foremost she placed what she called the "old Buddhist axiom": "Honour thine own faith, and do not slander that of others," comparing it to the noble principle of the Brahmo Samaj: "no sect shall be vilified, ridiculed, or hated." It was in this spirit that she would later comment on the failure of Parliament to repeal the law against blasphemy: "Why should [Christian missionaries] be allowed to break the law against Vishnu, Durga, or any fetish; against Buddha, Mohammed, or even a spook, in whom a spiritualist sincerely recognizes his dead mother, any more than an 'infidel' against Jehovah?"[63] But her particular animus against Judeo-Christianity made her prefer to be seen as an atheist than as a believer in the hated "P.G." or Personal God. In the first number of the Society's magazine (October 1879), she said that those Theosophists who happened to be Buddhists "can be considered as atheists only in respect to a personal God, and not to the Universal Soul of the Pantheist."[64] Ten years later, she virtually excluded "P.G.-ers" by writing that:

> *real* Theosophy—*i.e.*, the Theosophy that comes to us *from the East*—is assuredly Pantheism and by no means Theism. Theosophy is a word of the widest possible meaning which differs greatly in Eastern and Western literature. Moreover, the Theosophical Society being of Eastern origin, therefore goes beyond the narrow limits of the mediaeval Theosophy of the West. Members of the T.S. can, therefore, subscribe to this Western idea of Theosophy. But as the vast majority of these members accept the Eastern ideas, this majority has given us the right of applying the term *Theosophist* only to those members who do not believe in a 'personal' God."[65]

This was a far cry from the "occultism" of the 1870s and the Brotherhood of Luxor. Blavatsky had truly transferred her allegiance from the Nile to the Ganges, resulting in the process that I describe in Chapter Seventeen as the "parting of East and West."

The factor of Theosophical "atheism" is of such importance in this schism that a few more clarifications are necessary. One of its plainest and most uncompromising formulations comes from Blavatsky's master Koot Hoomi. I am not going to enter here into the question of Koot Hoomi's identity: Mr. Johnson has tentatively identified him as Thakar Singh, a prominent Sikh, but nowhere suggests that Thakar wrote what are known as the "Mahatma Letters" to A. P. Sinnett and A. O. Hume. In 1882 K.H. wrote to Hume: "We deny God both as philosophers and Buddhists. We know that there are planetary and other spiritual lives, and we know there is in our system no such thing as God, either personal or impersonal."[66]

Much of Blavatsky's later work, in particular *The Secret Doctrine* (1888), is based on information first given out in the "Mahatma Letters," supposedly from an esoteric Buddhist source, and on esoteric Hindu teachings for which one of her known informants was T. Subba Row (1856–1890). A brilliant Brahmin lawyer, Subba Row was the one person known to have conversed with Blavatsky as an equal. Despite his youth, and the fact that he spent more time playing tennis than studying philosophy, he demonstrated a matchless command of esoteric Hindu doctrines. Blavatsky wanted him to correct her *Secret Doctrine*, but he refused because he felt that in that book she had revealed too much.

Subba Row treats the question of God from the standpoint of an Advaitin (non-dualist). He explains that a personal god is as much to be doubted as any other phenomenon in the universe—all phenomena being, from the Advaitin point of view, devoid of ultimate reality. Even an impersonal god, if he were in any way conscious, would have to participate in the illusory split between ego and non-ego, and hence be traceable to a prior cause. The pantheist position, in which God is the sum of all beings, is also untenable because in Advaita beings are but states of consciousness, and these are constantly changing and becoming extinguished. That leaves one and only one permanent condition in the universe: perfect Unconsciousness. Subba Row sums up:

> When my readers once realize the fact that this grand universe is in reality but a huge aggregation of various states of consciousness, they will not be surprised to find that the ultimate state of unconsciousness is considered as Parabrahmam by the Advaitins.[67]

Although Subba Row did not like the word "atheist," so much thrown around as a term of abuse, the ultimate reality as he defines it bears no resemblance to any god, personal or impersonal, and one can conclude that his convictions on this subject were the same as Koot Hoomi's.

Blavatsky welcomed those of any time or place whose theology (or a-theology) could rise to this level. She wrote in a posthumously published essay:

Figure 15.2. *T. Subba Row (1856–1890), from* Esoteric Writings, *1895.*

> "Nihil" therefore stands—even with some Christian theologians and thinkers, especially with the earlier ones who lived but a few removes from the profound Philosophy of the initiated Pagans—as a synonym for the impersonal, divine Principle, the Infinite All, which is no Being or thing—the Ain-Soph, the Parabrahman of the Vedanta. [. . .] Union with That is not annihilation as understood in Europe.[68]

Thus she shared her so-called atheism with Dionysius the Areopagite and with the Kabbalists, as well as with Advaitins and Buddhists. But how did she fill the gap between the "Nihil" and everyday life—the gap that even the most metaphysical Christians, Jews, and Muslims fill with a god who reveals himself and listens to prayer? Setting aside the titanic vista of cosmic and human evolution described in *The Secret Doctrine*, she filled it with the ideals of a Mahayana Buddhist. One of her last works, a short manual called *The Voice of the Silence* (1889), is a distillation of Mahayana Buddhist doctrines which was later given the stamp of approval by the Panchen Lama himself.

The main theme of *The Voice of the Silence* is that two paths are open to the initiate upon attainment of Nirvana. One option is to remain there for ever, in the human equivalent of the blissful unconsciousness of Parabrahman. That is the end of his or her participation in the universe, at least in this inconceivably long cosmic cycle. The second option is to renounce Nirvana and consent to be reincarnated again and again until the end of the cycle, in order to benefit all beings. The latter choice—the great sacrifice of the Bodhisattva—is regarded as the more compassionate one, and far more praiseworthy from the point of view of the beings thus benefited. There seems little doubt that Blavatsky saw her own life's work as a minor version of the sacrificial path, and her ultimate mission as that of offering Eastern wisdom to supplant Western ignorance.

SIXTEEN

The Hermetic Reaction

As we have seen in the preceding chapters, the establishment of the Theosophical Society in India from 1879 onwards discomfited many of its Western members. In this chapter we follow the fortunes of two counter-movements whose allegiance was to a Western esoteric tradition that was friendly to the East, but not subservient to it. They are the Hermetic Society, founded in 1884 by Anna Kingsford and Edward Maitland, and the Hermetic Brotherhood of Luxor, which started public work later the same year under the auspices of Max Theon, Peter Davidson, and Thomas H. Burgoyne. A third movement with ties to both of these has already been discussed at the end of Chapter Eleven. It is the Hermetic Order of the Golden Dawn, founded in 1888 by William Wynn Westcott, William R. Woodman, and Samuel L. McGregor Mathers.

It is remarkable in how many respects the life of Anna Kingsford (1846–1888) resembled that of Annie Besant, Blavatsky's heir-apparent and future President of the Theosophical Society. Intensely pious as children, they both moved on to freethought; married clergymen, found marriage physically unsatisfying and separated from their husbands; were good at French, edited journals, worked for women's enfranchisement, and with great difficulty earned a scientific degree; led a life of vigorous political activism; had an intense but sexless relationship with an older man (in Besant's case, Charles Bradlaugh); rose quickly to the top of the Theosophical Society; cooperated with a man in occult researches (Besant and Charles W. Leadbeater; Kingsford and Maitland); wrote on esoteric Christianity, and nurtured messianic ambitions (projected, in Besant's case, onto Krishnamurti).

When Henry Olcott met Anna Kingsford in 1884, she laid bare the heart of her problems. The Colonel writes:

Figure 16.1. *Anna Kingsford (1846–1888), from E. Maitland,* Life of Anna Kingsford, *1913.*

I cannot say I altogether liked her, although it did not take many minutes for me to gauge her intellectual power and the breadth of her culture. There was something uncanny to me in her views about human affection. She said she had never felt love for a human being; that people had told her, before

> her child was born, to wait its appearance and she would feel the great gush of mother-love and the fountains of her affection would be unsealed; she had waited, the child had been shown her, but her only feeling was the wish that they should take it away out of her sight! Yet she lavished excessive love on a guinea-pig, and, in his *Life of Anna Kingsford,* Mr. Maitland's splendid pen has made us all see, as in a mental Kinematograph, his great colleague carrying the little beast around with her in her travels, lavishing on it her caresses, and keeping the anniversary of its death as one does that of a near relative.[1]

Kingsford had brooded much on the cruelty of a world where creatures are killed and eaten, or, worse, dissected alive in the name of science, and had taken up the causes of vegetarianism and vivisection. To the further humiliation of her husband, she became a Roman Catholic in 1870, and edited a women's rights magazine. In order to give more authority to her crusade against these evils, she decided to become a medical doctor, but, living in a Shropshire vicarage with a small daughter, could see no way of achieving this. At the time of her meeting with Maitland she was writing fiction and biding her time by studying medicine on her own.

Edward Maitland (1824–1897) had graduated from Cambridge in preparation for the church, but his vocation had failed him and instead he went out to California with the "Forty-Niners." From there he had gone on to Sydney, married, been widowed after one year, and come back to London. He would have remarried, were it not for a series of financial losses, "reducing my means to the minimum compatible with existence at all in my own station,"[2] i.e., that of a man not obliged to work, but not averse to earning a little by writing. It was in the summer of 1873 that this poor but independent gentleman received a letter from "Mrs. Algernon Kingsford." She introduced herself by pointing out that she and Maitland had had stories reviewed in the same magazine, and that it seemed that they had interests in common. Might they meet?[3]

Maitland turned out to be the key to Kingsford's predicament. The British medical schools were still closed to women, to protect the fair sex from the gruesome experiences of dissection. But the French were a little ahead of them, and the school in Paris had just opened its doors. He could be her chaperon! If people assumed that they were uncle and niece, they would not be undeceived.[4] In 1874, then, Kingsford and Maitland took an apartment in Paris with the consent (and perhaps to the relief) of the Rev. Algernon.[5]

Until the granting of Kingsford's M.D. in 1880, the two spiritual companions fought a hard battle against male chauvinism, and against the

***Figure 16.2.** Edward Maitland (1824–1897), from* Life of Anna Kingsford, *1913.*

vivisection of animals that was normally required of students. A Pythagorean to the core, she wrote her dissertation on vegetarianism, and made that and antivivisection the public cause of the rest of her short life. She herself suffered constantly from asthma and other ailments, through which Maitland often nursed her; she eventually died of tuberculosis, with her head on his shoulder. There is not the slightest suspicion that they were physical lovers. But the immediate bond between them led them to form a unit on a higher plane, in a rare instance of double mediumship.

Stainton Moses was not quite the only Oxbridge-educated medium of the nineteenth century. In 1875, while writing a book about politics, Maitland had found himself being taken over by another intelligence. Gradually submitting to its guidance, he completed *England and Islam* (1876) and *The Soul and How It Found Me* (1877). The first book urged the British government to support the Turkish Muslims against the imperial ambitions of sacerdotal and materialistic Russia; part of it, Maitland believed, was dictated to him by the late Prince Albert.[6] The second told of his mediumistic experiences and of the new view of spiritual realities that they gave him. Like that of Stainton Moses, Maitland's automatism was entirely conscious: it was in fact "automatic typing." He supplemented it by researches in the British Museum on ancient religious systems and the old Hermetic philosophers[7]—exactly the topics that Henry Olcott was being led to study during these same years.

Anna Kingsford had had psychical experiences as a child. Now she also began to receive inspired messages, which she usually dreamed during the night and wrote down upon waking. Sometimes the two mediums used a planchette together, made according to a design given them by elemental spirits. But they were careful to distinguish the messages that came from that source from the dream "illuminations," which seemed to be of far higher origin. These spiritual researches, sustained alongside a rigorous medical training and Kingsford's constant battles with the authorities and with ill-health, gradually took on the proportions, or the pretensions, of a new revelation. Kingsford and Maitland convinced themselves that their work corresponded with the much-prophesied "end of the world," due in 1881, and with the inauguration of the Age of Michael in that year, as specified by Trithemius in his treatise *De Septem Secundeis.* But for the time being they kept their convictions to themselves.

Both mediums were Christian at heart, but unable to swallow the literalistic reading of the Bible or the dogmas of the churches. Kingsford's illuminations solved all their difficulties. They showed how the Bible is to be read allegorically from beginning to end, as a description of the destiny of the soul. In particular, the crucifixion of Christ and of other solar saviors (Maitland was a good student of the "solar myth"[8]) was explained as a spiritual experience through which we all have to pass on the way to regeneration. The Christ is not a person, but the state of the regenerated man, in whom the soul has become united with the Divine Spirit. At the same time, they were told that Jesus had really lived, as a man who realized the Christ-state in himself. Kingsford was shown episodes from his life which she described as if she were an eye-witness.

Charles Carleton Massey wrote a congratulatory letter to Maitland when he read *The Soul and How It Found Me* in 1877, and reviewed it for *The Spiritualist.*[9] Thus began a connection that would inevitably lead Kingsford and Maitland into the Theosophical Society—and out of it. Another Christian spiritualist, if one can sum up in two words so complex a person, was Lady Caithness (1830–1895), with whom Maitland was in correspondence at least by the summer of 1878.[10] In Chapter Fourteen I mentioned that her *Old Truths in a New Light* taught a doctrine not far different from that of *Art Magic* or *Isis Unveiled,* except for her insistence on the reincarnation doctrine. This remarkable woman who quarreled with no one, not even the Roman Catholic Church, who fraternized with French socialists and English peers, believed in esoteric Buddhism and in esoteric Christianity, entertained mediums and cardinals, was loyal to the death both to Anna Kingsford and to H. P. Blavatsky.

It was Lady Caithness who broadened the horizons of her protégés by acquainting them with Levi's and Boehme's works; before that, the only Christian esotericist they had known of was Swedenborg.[11] By special permission of the spirits, Lady Caithness was the first to be favored with a reading of what Maitland and Kingsford now regarded as holy scriptures,[12] and she immediately accepted them as the gospel for the new age of the world. Among the doctrines that appealed to Lady Caithness were the firm denial of the Vicarious Atonement and the equally firm assertion of the necessity for reincarnation.[13] The two doctrines were mutually supportive, for just as "no man may deliver his brother," but all have to suffer or enjoy the consequences of their own acts, so a series of repeated human lives gives the soul the opportunity for refinement, and eventually for the regeneration exemplified by the various Christs.

Not all of the illuminations were couched in Christian terms: far from it. Beside the many reminders of the utter corruption of Christianity (beginning with Saint Paul's antifeminism and his atonement doctrine), Kingsford had visions of the Greek gods, naked and shining like silver, who dictated ecstatic hymns to her.[14] One of the most impressive of these, the "Hymn to the Planet-God, Iacchos, and the Elemental Divinities," was learned by her as she processed with a band of initiates through a vast Egyptian temple: it revealed the allegorical meaning of the Exodus, and the essential identity of the Hebrew, Egyptian, and Greek theogonies.[15] She was left in no doubt that Christianity was only one of the religions of antiquity, whose mysteries had all taught the same truths of the soul's destiny. "My intiation was Greco-Egyptian," she wrote to Lady Caithness, "and therefore I recall the truth primarily in the language and after the method of the Bacchic mysteries, which are indeed, as you know, the immediate source and pattern of the mysteries of the Catholic Christian Church."[16]

Some of Kingsford's visitants were more recent, and less solemn. There was Emanuel Swedenborg, who took a considerable interest in the new gospel; he had, it seemed, abandoned several of his old ideas in favor of hers. She spent many hours (in trance or lucid dream) reading the books in his library, and even eating tea, toast, and eggs with him. "Do not be too kind to the Christians," he told her.[17] Another celebrity was Apollonius of Tyana, known to all occultists from the account of his evocation in London given in Eliphas Levi's *Dogme et rituel de la haute magie.* But Maitland was certain that whereas Levi had seen only Apollonius's astral phantom, if not a figment of his own heightened imagination, Kingsford had met his true self.[18]

By the end of her degree course in France, Kingsford's illuminations had produced a large and coherent body of esoteric Christianity. Much of it was theoretical teaching concerning the four parts of the human being and their respective destinies, the classing of intermediate entities ranging from spooks to gods, and the allegorical meaning of the scriptures. The practical teaching that went along with it was more moral than magical, and emphasized again and again the necessity to give up eating flesh food, the preeminence of the feminine, and the universal solvent of Love. Although there was much about the need to free the soul from bondage to the body, sexuality did not enter into it in either a positive or a negative way: the bondage in question showed itself in materialism and unthinking cruelty.

Shortly before leaving Paris, the seers discovered *Isis Unveiled* and learned about the Theosophical Society's existence. Although they found *Isis* disorganized and unnecessarily truculent, they were astonished and delighted to find that another pair of collaborators had been engaged on a parallel course during exactly the same period.[19] Coming to London, they moved immediately into the circle of highbrow spiritualists, psychical researchers, and members of the British Theosophical Society, a body founded under Massey's presidency in 1878. A select audience was assembled to hear the first announcement of the "new gospel," in a series of lectures read by Maitland and Kingsford during May and June of 1881. Thanks to Lady Caithness's financial support, the lectures were published early the next year as *The Perfect Way; or, the Finding of Christ.*

The year of destiny, 1881, saw the foundation of Stainton Moses' weekly spiritualist magazine *Light,* which from the start maintained a far higher standard of intellectual discourse than its rivals. Its pages record every nuance of the British spiritualists' reactions to the twin revelations of *The Perfect Way* and A. P. Sinnett's *The Occult World* (1881). Sinnett's work, which included the first "Mahatma Letters" from Koot Hoomi, challenged the complacency of Western spiritualists with the claim—if not the proof—that there were living adepts in the East whose mastery of psychic powers and knowledge of occultism far exceeded anything yet demonstrated in the West. Moreover, since the living were apparently able to produce messages phenomenally, it dealt another blow to the spiritualist belief that all communications come from the dead.

The Perfect Way was most troubling in its strong assertion of the reincarnation doctrine and secondarily in its passionate but entirely ahistorical Christianity. The reincarnation debate was a hardy perennial of spiritualism, rising and falling every decade or so. The doctrine's strongest proponents up to now had been the French school of "*spirites*" founded by Allan Kardec, whose mediums uniformly taught reincarnation to be a fact. Beside Lady Caithness, their chief envoy to the English-speaking world was Anna Blackwell, for forty years a newspaper correspondent in Paris. Adherents included Francesca Arundale, Isabel de Steiger, and the spirit "Ski" who spoke through Mrs. Hollis-Billing.[20] Ranged against them were the majority of the English and American mediums, including P. B. Randolph, Emma Hardinge-Britten, and Stainton Moses. The British National Association of Spiritualists staged what must have been an entertaining debate in March 1882, in which Francesca Arundale, speaking in favor of the reincarnation doctrine, was pitted against a sixteenth-century Chinese Mandarin called Tien-Sien-Tie, who spoke through the medium Mrs. Morse.[21]

Feelings against the reincarnation theory ran amazingly high. In *Light* of 1881, S. C. Hall called it a "repulsive and unnatural doctrine" put about by "missionaries of Satan." William Howitt called it a "loathsome dogma" that all Christians must reject as an abomination.[22] George Wyld, a homeopathic physician who had suceeded Massey as President of the British Theosophical Society, said that the Orientals held many repulsive ideas, such as slavery, but that that was no reason to adopt them. Man is on earth, he went on, to multiply the human race and increase the number of souls, which is the justification for marriage.[23] Stainton Moses was quite attracted by the *Perfect Way* material, and at the B.N.A.S. debate he urged that the new teaching be given a fair hearing.[24] In March 1882, however, he called a halt to the reincarnation debate, which had flooded his editorial office with more letters than he could ever print.[25]

We noted earlier that *Isis Unveiled* and *Art Magic* also gave the impression of rejecting reincarnation, and that the idea was not current in the early Theosophical Society. Nor did it appear in Sinnett's *Occult World,* for all that this was supposed to be "esoteric Buddhism." In the course of

1882, another attitude began to be heard in the pages of *The Theosophist.* The publication of further Mahatma Letters as "Fragments of Occult Truth," a review of *The Perfect Way*, and an editorial note which Blavatsky privately attributed to Koot Hoomi[26] revealed that the Tibetan Mahatmas did, after all, teach the doctrine of reincarnation, despite Blavatsky's denial of it in *Isis.*[27] C. C. Massey, who took all these matters with the greatest seriousness and read everything with a barrister's eagle eye, asked politely for a clarification. Blavatsky's explanation,[28] in brief, was that there are two ways of talking about the destiny of the individual. From the more exoteric point of view given in *Isis Unveiled*, it was correct to say that a *person* is never reincarnated. Yet from a higher point of view, an *individuality* is. To illustrate this, she set out the esoteric scheme of the seven principles of the human being. Of these, the three lower ones invariably die. They are:

1. physical body (*sthula-sarira*)
2. life-principle (*jiva*)
3. astral or vital body (*linga-sarira*)

Two more principles survive for a time, then disappear, reincarnating only in the exceptional circumstances of abortion, death in infancy, and congenital or incurable idiocy. Together these constitute the "Astral Monad" mentioned in *Isis*, or the "personal Ego":

4. body of desire (*kama-rupa*)
5. mind or animal soul (*manas*)

The remaining principles constitute the "Spiritual Monad" or "Individuality," and are eternal and indestructible:

6. spiritual soul or intelligence (*buddhi*)
7. pure spirit (*atman*)

It is they that return to earth as long as their evolution demands, presiding over many utterly distinct egos, each made from a new set of principles 1–5.

The reader may wonder why the whole situation was not made plain in *Isis Unveiled*, which Blavatsky said proceeded from the same source as the later teachings—"the Adept Brothers."[29] Moreover, since one of the cornerstones of the Buddhist philosophy is the *anatta* doctrine (meaning the non-existence of *atman*), the non-Theosophist will have to look tolerantly on the efforts of Blavatsky and her successors to reconcile this contradiction with her adopted religion. Finally, it seems that the writers of *The Perfect Way*, despite their division of the human being into only four principles, were not so much at variance with the Oriental Theosophists as the latter claimed.

The four principles of the Kingsford–Maitland system were as follows:

1. material body [includes Theosophic 1 and 2][30]
2. astral body [Theosophic 3, 4, 5]
3. soul [Theosophic 6]
4. divine spirit [Theosophic 7]

It was within this scheme that the *Perfect Way* taught the reincarnation of the individual soul in many different "bodies" or personalities, to learn the lessons that culminate in its union with the divine spirit, "the Christ within."

The reincarnation debate aside, there was still the problem of the *Perfect Way*'s claim to be a new, revealed gospel. Mrs. Penny, whom we met in Chapter Twelve, was one of those Christian esotericists who did not see the necessity for a new revelation. "Can two gospels differ so widely if they come from the same source?" she asked her ally George Wyld,[31] who shared her devotion to Jacob Boehme. The *Perfect Way*'s "writers" (not, they emphasized, its "authors") defended themselves in the pages of *Light,* amply supported by Lady Caithness, Isabel de Steiger, and Francesca Arundale, until once more the editor closed the debate.

In 1883 the London spiritualists received a further stimulus to their inner and outer debates in the form of Sinnett's *Esoteric Buddhism,* a work closely based on the Mahatma's letters. Now the Theosophical system became clearer, with its sevenfold division of the human being, its planetary chains of evolution, its seven Root-Races of mankind (including Lemuria and Atlantis), its analysis of reincarnation and other after-death states, its explanations of karma and Nirvana ("a sublime state of conscious rest in omniscience"[32]), and its denial of the personal God.

The last point was too much for Wyld, who resigned his Presidency of the British Theosophical Society. Who was to succeed him? C. C. Massey proposed Anna Kingsford. Although she was now back living with her husband in Atcham Vicarage, near Shrewsbury, and was not even a member of the Society, she accepted, and duly became President at the end of May 1883.[33] Maitland became a Vice-President. Kingsford's first act was to change the name of the group to the "London Lodge of the Theosophical Society," by analogy with the single Society of Freemasons with its various Lodges. She wrote to Lady Caithness: "I am going to do my utmost to make our London Lodge a really influential and scientific body. . . . Besides, we do not want to pledge ourselves to Orientalism only, but to the study of all religions esoterically, and especially to that of our Western Catholic Church."[34]

Now there came a clash of egos. A. P. Sinnett had arrived in London in April 1883, having lost his newspaper editorship in India. He was promoting his new book, *Esoteric Buddhism,* as well as enjoying the status due to a correspondent with the Mahatmas of the snowy range. He found, in his own words, that Anna Kingsford "had a very high opinion of the importance of her own 'Hermetic' movement and of her own book 'The Perfect Way' and aimed rather at annexing The Theosophical Society to that undertaking than at working in it as the predominant organisation. This attitude on her part alienated the sympathies of the theosophists who had been drawn into the movement by the new teaching from India embodied in my own books . . ."[35] Kingsford had no better opinion of him, or his book. She wrote to Isabel de Steiger that "First, the system expounded by Mr Sinnett is not—so far as I can see—*esoteric* at all, being simply a scheme of transcendental physics; and, secondly, he is deliberately seeking to *silence* every other voice but that of the 'Mahatmas.' "[36]

One can imagine the atmosphere that this kind of rivalry created in the London Lodge during 1883. Blavatsky, although furious with Sinnett for having said too much about the Mahatmas in *Esoteric Buddhism* and letting Koot Hoomi "be now reviled and so abused by every old ass in *Light,*"[37] had no friendly feelings towards the elegant Kingsford, whom she had been shown in a vision dressed in zebra-striped silk and dripping with gems. With perhaps a certain feminine jealousy, she burst out to Sinnett: "why had *she* 'the mystic of the century' so much jewellery on her! How can she confabulate with the unseen Gods when she looks like a Delhi English Jeweller's front window."[38]

Koot Hoomi was more disposed to see Kingsford's good points. He wrote to Sinnett in London:

> Well may you admire and more should you wonder at the marvellous lucidity of that remarkable seeress, who ignorant of Sanskrit or Pali, and thus shut out from their metaphysical treasures, has yet seen a great light shining from behind the dark hills of exoteric religions. How, think you, did the 'Writers of the Perfect Way' come to know that Adonai was the Son and not the Father; or that the third person of the Christian Trinity is—female? Verily, they lay in that work several times their hands upon the keystone of Occultism.[39]

By the end of the year, the situation in London was so tense that Koot Hoomi had to intervene. He took the unprecedented step of writing to the London Lodge members from Mysore on 7 December 1883, directing that Mrs. Kingsford should continue to be President. This, he said, was at the express wish of the Chohan (the chief of the Mahatmas), who was moved in her favor by her campaign against vivisection and her strict vegetarianism.[40] Whereas the Sinnett party regarded Kingsford's skepticism about the Mahatmas as no better than blasphemy, Koot Hoomi told the Londoners that it was immaterial whether Kingsford had any respect for them or not. He reminded them that "*Hermetic* Philosophy is universal and unsectarian, while the Tibetan School will ever be regarded by those who know little, if anything of it, as coloured more or less with sectarianism." And he ended with a threat: if Mr. Sinnett and Mrs. Kingsford could not "agree to *disagree* in details and work in strict unison" for the Society's objects, the Mahatmas would have nothing more to do with the London Lodge.[41]

Even this Solomonic judgement did not set matters to rest. It appears that Kingsford was making trouble for her opponents by pointing out that *The Theosophist* carried advertisements for *The Fruits of Philosophy*, the birth-control manual of Bradlaugh and Besant. The prudish Koot Hoomi could not bear to read the book: its "unclean spirit [and] pernicious aura" were enough to tell him that the advice in the book was the "fruits of Sodom and Gomorrah."[42] and made Blavatsky stop advertising it.[43] Trouble was brewing in France, too, where Lady Caithness's Société Théosophique d'Orient et d'Occident was at odds with the spiritualists.[44] It was time for the Society's visible chiefs to step in.

By the spring of 1884, Olcott and Blavatsky were both in France as guests of Lady Caithness. Olcott, as President of the Society, decided to come to London in time for the elections for the London Presidency; on the train from Paris, he received a letter from Koot Hoomi advising him how to act. Olcott immediately called on Anna Kingsford, recording the impression quoted at the beginning of this chapter. Then he went to see his old pal Massey. Following the latter's advice, Olcott cannily offered Kingsford a charter for her own, separate branch of the Society, to be called "The Hermetic Lodge of the Theosophical Society." The election then went forward in peace, with the Presidency of the London Lodge going to Sinnett's puppet candidate Gerard B. Finch. The occasion was enlivened by the dramatic and totally unexpected entry of Madame Blavatsky, after which the proceedings broke up in happy disorder.

The London Theosophists could now turn East or West as they preferred. They could even turn both ways at once, for the Kingsford group immediately renamed itself "The Hermetic Society," to circumvent a rule that no Theosophist could belong to more than one Lodge. Olcott and Mohini Chatterjee brought the blessing of the oriental contingent to the inaugural meeting on 9 May 1884. Oscar Wilde was also there, with his mother Lady Wilde and his brother Willie. The new Hermetic Society, in short, was a social success. Kingsford's lectures filled the large rooms of the Royal Asiatic Society,[45] where instead of the esoteric Buddhists, she and Maitland now only had to contend with prolix defenders of the historical Jesus, such as George Wyld and the Honorable Roden Noel.

The Hermetic Society's activities brought out fresh interests in Kingsford and Maitland. In 1885 they prepared two works for Robert Fryar's series of "Bath Occult Reprints." One of these was a translation of *The Virgin of the World,* which contained those writings of "Hermes Trismegistus" not already published in Hargrave Jennings's *The Divine Pymander* (1884). We heard in Chapter Thirteen of Jennings's berating of Fryar for entrusting such a work to a woman. The second was a reissue of Valentin Weigel's *Astrology Theologized* (originally published in English in 1649). Both works had extensive introductions that placed them in the *Perfect Way* world-view, but the translation and notes of *The Virgin of the World* were not original, being taken from Louis Ménard's French version.[46]

Their allegorical reading of the Hebrew scriptures naturally led Kingsford and Maitland to interest themselves in Kabbalah. When they went to the British Museum and leafed through Knorr von Rosenroth's *Kabballah Denudata,* they were amazed by the coincidences they found there with Kingsford's dream-visions. These were further confirmed when the Kabbalistic scholar Christian Ginsburg paid them the compliment of admiring their knowledge. It appeared that they already knew what the Kabbalah had to teach. After the publication of *The Perfect Way* a letter came from Baron Giuseppe Spedalieri, the disciple and literary executor of Eliphas Levi, congratulating them on restoring the Kabbalistic doctrine in its original purity.[47]

Earlier in the year, Spedalieri had been on the quai-side at Marseille to welcome Blavatsky and Olcott as they arrived in Europe from India. Now he became not only a firm friend of our pair, but a disciple of the new gospel. He wrote an introduction to the French edition of *The Perfect Way* in which he hailed it as the fulfilment of the prophecies of Postel and Trithemius.[48] Levi had reckoned 1879 to be the year when the Archangel Michael's reign would begin, whereas most others interpreted Trithemius's system to point to the year 1881.[49] But the difference was slight: the Baron had no doubt that this was the "New Illumination" that initiated the Michael Age.[50] In 1887, when Maitland was visiting France, Spedalieri gave him some of Levi's manuscripts and his annotated copy of Trithemius's *De Septem Secundeis.* Maitland later gave this material to Wynn Westcott, who published it as *The Magical Ritual of the Sanctum Regnum* (1896).[51]

The Perfect Way laid the basis for a new Christian esotericism, radically different from that of Boehme, Saint-Martin, and their disciples who were treated in Chapter Twelve. The Christianity of Kingsford's illuminations was not historically based, did not regard Jesus as the only Son of God or as a personal savior, and did not pretend that the Christian revelation was unique or superior to all other religions. Thus it removed the "stumbling-block" that Christianity presents to the Jews (or Kabbalists), and the "foolishness" that it otherwise seems to the Greeks (or Platonists).[52] The teaching of reincarnation also eliminated one of the major disagreements between Christianity and the oriental religions. Once the conflict of personalities was out of the way, this became the sort of Christianity with which the Theosophists could live. The principles of *The Perfect Way* were appropriated by Annie Besant (*Esoteric Christianity*, 1901), and by her colleague the Rev. C. W. Leadbeater in his many works. The Christian parts of Alice A. Bailey's writings (especially *From Bethlehem to Calvary*) are in the same allegorizing tradition.

Had it not been for Kingsford's premature death, she might have tried to embrace the entire Western esoteric tradition—alchemy, astrology, angelic magic, Kabbalah—within the philosophic framework of her illuminations. As it was, the work was done by the two most prolific scholars to emerge from the Theosophical Society, G. R. S. Mead and A. E. Waite. Mead, as Blavatsky's private secretary and a leader in the Theosophical Society until his disaffection by Leadbeater, could not and did not give any credit to "the divine Anna." But his lifelong program of research into Hermetism, Gnosticism, Orphism, and Christian origins gave substance to Kingsford's intuition: that Christianity belongs to the great family of mystery religions that spread around the Mediterranean in the early centuries before and after the Common Era. Waite joined the Hermetic Society at its inception,[53] and was never attracted to the Tibetan Mahatmas' teachings as the young Mead was. Like his friend C. C. Massey, he became a more exclusively Christian mystic as he grew older, leaving behind a whole library of works that, for better or worse, define the Western esoteric tradition for the general readership to this day.

For all its virtues, Anna Kingsford's movement still did not supply the thing that many Theosophists had come to find most signally wanting in their society: instruction in practical occultism. For nearly ten years, promises had been made, beginning with George Felt's plan to make the elementals visible. But they had come to nothing: the powers of the practical adept seemed to be limited to Madame Blavatsky. And now there were the tantalizing accounts in Sinnett's books of the still greater powers of the Himalayan Mahatmas, which were held out as the ultimate goal of everyone. But how was one even to put one's first step on the ladder that led to these heights? Those close to Blavatsky hoped deperately to be taken on as chelas (disciples) by one of these "great souls" (which is what *maha atma* means), but it was made clear that this privilege was almost beyond hoping for.

The discomfort of the Theosophists—for at first it was nothing more—was fanned into disillusion and finally into desperation by a series of unfortunate incidents. First was the discovery in 1883 that one of

Mahatma Koot Hoomi's letters in *Esoteric Buddhism* had borrowed verbatim from a lecture by Henry Kiddle, one of the chief American spiritualists. It was a trivial matter, perhaps, but to Theosophy's opponents it showed up the Tibetan Mahatma as a common plagiarist. Second was the investigation of the phenomena reputed to have taken place in Adyar (the Theosophical Society's headquarters near Madras) by Dr. Richard Hodgson, on commission from the Society for Psychical Research. In the course of this investigation, Emma Coulomb, whom we encountered briefly in Egypt in 1871, gave a series of letters to the local missionaries, supposedly written by Blavatsky, which indicated that phenomena such as the appearance of Mahatmas' letters in the Adyar "shrine" had been faked. The year 1886 saw the publication of Hodgson's report to the S.P.R., which was a wholesale condemnation of Blavatsky as an impostor, and of her Mahatmas as a fiction. A mass exodus from the Society followed.

Even before the catastrophe, a number of Theosophists had made good the Society's shortcomings by joining the Hermetic Brotherhood of Luxor, known as the "H.B. of L." This was a school of practical occultism that first became public late in 1884. Its appearance was discreet enough, coming on the last page of *The Divine Pymander* of Hermes Trismegistus, published by Robert Fryar of Bath with a Preface by Hargrave Jennings. But the wording of the advertisement was guaranteed to get the message passed around:

> TO WHOM IT MAY CONCERN.
>
> Students of the Occult Science, searchers after truth and Theosophists who may have been disappointed in their expectations of Sublime Wisdom being freely dispensed by HINDOO MAHATMAS, are cordially invited to send in their names to the Editor of this Work, when, if found suitable, [sic] can be admitted, after a short probationary term, as members of an Occult Brotherhood, who do not boast of their knowledge or attainments, but teach freely and without reserve all they find worthy to receive.
>
> N.B. All communications should be addressed 'Theosi' c/o Robt. H. Fryar, Bath.
>
> CORRECTION.
>
> "Correspondents" will please read and address "Theosi" as "THEON."

What the H.B. of L. had to offer disenchanted Theosophists was a course of very specific instructions in practical occultism, issued in the form of "secret" documents that were rented out, copied, and (needless to say) leaked outside the membership. Secondarily, it held a number of theoretical or doctrinal positions that differed from those of the Mahatmas, especially on questions of East versus West and the destiny of the soul. The most striking difference between the two groups was that the H.B. of L.'s teachings were much concerned with sexual matters, whereas Blavatsky and her masters were quite puritanical on the subject. Theosophists were led to believe that the ideal, "adeptic" life excludes this area of human experience, and encouraged to aspire to a chastity even within marriage that many of them found very trying. The H.B. of L., on the contrary, showed how to cultivate the physical, psychological, and spiritual benefits of an active sexual life. And to do this, it circulated the teachings of Paschal Beverly Randolph.

While preparing our edition of the H.B of L.'s teachings and historical documents,[54] I and my collaborators Christian Chanel and John Patrick Deveney have had to admit that there are enigmas concerning the H.B. of L. that may never be solved. The chief of these are the connection, if any, with the Brotherhood of Luxor of the 1870s; and the role of Max Theon, called "Grand Master of the Exterior Circle."

The name of the H.B. of L. is very close to that of the "Brotherhood of Luxor" that contacted Henry Olcott in New York in 1875 and seemed to be guiding the fledgling Theosophical Society from behind the scenes. The similarity, so obvious to us, was not so at the time. Olcott's account of his relations with the Brotherhood of Luxor in *Old Diary Leaves* was not yet published, and the H.B. of L. was known by its initials alone. The actual name was a deep secret, being divulged only to initiates on a piece of paper that was immediately burned. In Chapter Fourteen, I surmised that the "Brotherhood of Luxor" was Blavatsky's way of referring to the occultists she had known in Egypt and to Westerners like Rawson and Sotheran who were committed to Egyptian Freemasonry. One possibility is that after the Theosophists had departed for India, this Brotherhood of Luxor went about its business without Blavatsky and Olcott, and resurfaced five years later as the semisecret "Hermetic Brotherhood of Luxor." But the evidence of an actual link is wanting.

When the H.B. of L. began to solicit membership in 1884, it claimed to be "very ancient," in contrast to the Theosophical Society which, as everyone knew, had been founded in 1875. Trivial as the quarrel about priority may seem today, it was essential to the idea of an intervention in modern society on the part of adepts, which we have met in the Hydesville provocation theory and in the early Theosophical masters. To the aspirant for esoteric knowledge and occult experience, it was important to know which group was the original and genuine vehicle of the age-old work of adepts to enlighten the world. Both orders claimed to be this.

Figure 16.3. *Max Theon (1850?–1927).*

The impetus for the H.B. of L. appears to have come in the first instance from a Polish Jew, probably an initiate in Hassidism, who had wandered in many countries before settling in London in 1873. No one knows his original name or date of birth, but we will call him by the alias he used during the 1880s: Max Theon, and give his dates as they stand in his obituary: 1850–1927. Much later, Theon was the teacher of Mirra Alfassa (1878–1973), later to become the companion of Aurobindo Ghose and the ruler, as "The Mother," of the Sri Aurobindo Ashram in Pondicherry, India. Most of the biographical information on Theon comes from Mirra's reminiscences, told to her disciples fifty years after the fact and sometimes embroidered by the listeners before being written down.[55] Therefore we cannot rely on it here, beyond pointing out the close connection between Theon's philosophy of the period around 1900, and the teachings of Aurobindo and the Mother.

When the H.B. of L. was founded, Theon was going privately under the name of Louis-Maximilian Bimstein, and professionally under that of "Theosi" or "M. Theon." He lived in Saint John's Wood, in the north of London, and advertised as follows in the spiritualist press: "Theon, the Eastern Psychic Healer, cures all diseases [. . .] sure preventive of Cholera." He allowed himself to be named as the Grand Master and as an "exalted adept" in the publications of the H.B. of L., but did not write any of their teaching documents or have anything to do with the members. Nor, at this point, did he divulge his own occult teachings, which would be published later as the "Cosmic Philosophy." This system, which is of considerable originality and combines Kabbalistic with Vedic elements, was developed by Theon in collaboration with his English wife, who was an automatic writing medium. By the time it was complete and beginning to be published (in French), Theon had severed all connection with the H.B. of L. and settled permanently in Algeria.

Theon always used a collaborator for his occult researches, for he found that the best results came from having one person as controller, and the other as seer. Ideally they should be male and female respectively, and such was the case once Theon was married to a powerfully mediumistic woman in 1885. Before that, he had to make do with what he could find. In 1882 he worked for a long period in daily sessions with a young Scotsman, Thomas Dalton (1855–1895), whom I will call by his later alias of Thomas H. Burgoyne. In awakening Burgoyne's spiritual vision, Theon put him in touch with "entities"—I can be no more specific than that—who must be regarded as the true founders of the H.B. of L. From then onwards, Theon could retire into the background, having discharged his office as "Grand Master of the Exterior Circle," and leave matters to the "Interior Circle" and their human agents.

Beside Theon as the opener of a channel to the Interior Circle, and Burgoyne as medium, it needed another person more willing that Theon to undertake public work, and more *persona grata* in occult circles than Burgoyne. This was Peter Davidson (1842–1916), another Scotsman who lived near Findhorn and worked, when he could, as a violin maker. Neophytes who joined the H.B. of L. in the late 1880s and 1890s received the following history of the Order, signed by Davidson, which said that in 1870,

> an adept of the serene, eternal, and ancient Order of the original H. B. of L., after having obtained the consent of his Brother Initiates, resolved to choose a neophyte in Great Britain who would answer to his purposes.
>
> After having completed an important and secret mission on the European Continent, he arrived in Great Britain in 1873 and discovered by chance a neophyte who satisfied his plans, and after having tested him thoroughly and had his letters of recommendation authenticated, he gradually instructed this neophyte. [. . .]
>
> The neophyte in question obtained permission to establish an Exterior Circle of the H.B. of L., and thus to prepare all deserving persons for the form of initiation for which they were suited . . .[56]

The "neophyte" here was Theon. But Davidson wrote to Ayton in 1887 that the same adept had appeared to him, in astral form, in connection with the launching of the Order. On a more mundane level, it is possible that Davidson was initiated by Randolph. As we saw in Chapter Thirteen, Randolph probably visited England in 1874, and, if he did so, would certainly have initiated people into his Brotherhood of Eulis. Davidson clearly valued Randolph's teachings, but not the personality of the teacher. In the *Occult Magazine,* he took care to report the fact of Randolph's suicide, which was suppressed or modified in other sources. And when he and Burgoyne adapted Randolph's writings for the H.B. of L.'s members, the authorship was suppressed.

Davidson, who was struggling to support a wife and five children by working, when necessary, in a distillery, prepared for his public work by gradual stages. He first came to public notice in 1871 with a book not on occultism but on *The Violin,* which was widely reviewed and eventually ran to five editions. The third edition, published in 1881, was enlivened with remarks on the symbolism of color and of number and on the marvelous powers of music, with reference to Hargrave Jennings's *The Rosicrucians.*[57] Davidson suggests that the claims of the Rosicrucians concerning music may not be so far-fetched as they seem[58] and speaks of the Astral Body that is set free in sleep, and the imperishable tablets of the Astral Light on which all things are recorded.[59] An appendix of musical anecdotes brings in trance and spiritualistic phenomena, and also prints the entire story "The Ensouled Violin," taken from *The Theosophist.* (Blavatsky attributed it to Hilarion Smerdis.) Praising India as the cradle of music, as of all arts and sciences, Davidson cites the *Surya Siddantha,* a Hindu astronomical work much used by Blavatsky, and the *Agroushada Parikshai,* another Hindu work quoted in *Isis Unveiled.* At the end of the book he takes the opportunity to mention the ghastly crimes of Constantine, the first Christian emperor, and the greed of the Church.

If one mentions such things in a book that is supposed to be about the violin, it must be for a reason. These digressions alone would place Peter Davidson unambiguously among those whose doctrines I have outlined in Chapter Fourteen. Like Stainton Moses' "Imperator," like the "Chevalier Louis" of *Art Magic,* and like the author of *Isis Unveiled,* Davidson has called attention to astral travel, occult phenomena, the superior science of the ancients, the primacy of Indian wisdom, and the shortcomings of official Christianity. Moreover, in printing his own address, he was not only soliciting trade for his violin business but inviting communications from those who were intrigued by these hints of another sort. It may be that the first members of the H. B. of L. were enrolled in this surreptitious way, at the beginning of the 1880s.

Davidson joined the Theosophical Society around this time, contributing to its magazine *The Theosophist* and receiving complimentary editorial remarks from Blavatsky. His main offering, significantly enough, was an account of a ceremony in India in which magic mirrors were consecrated through a sexual orgy.[60] This already united the two main themes of the H.B. of L.'s practical occultism. He also met Theon and Burgoyne.

Burgoyne was a man of obscure origins, whose only known trade (aside from astrology and mediumship) was the repectable but humble one of a grocer in Leeds. He claimed to have been a student of occultism from his boyhood, but his first documented appearance is in 1882, when he took the initiative of contacting other occultists. One of these was the Rev. William Ayton, who was an alchemist, a Theosophist, and a familiar of Irwin, Hockley, Mackenzie, and their circle. Ayton later recalled the young man as making a horrible confession of Black Magic.

It is very probable that Burgoyne also met Hurrychund Chintamon, the agent of the Arya Samaj who had been Blavatsky's main Indian correspondent when she was in New York. Chintamon had "welcomed" the Theosophists when they arrived in Bombay early in 1879, then embezzled both them

Figure 16.4. *Peter Davidson (1842–1916), from* The Violin, *1881.*

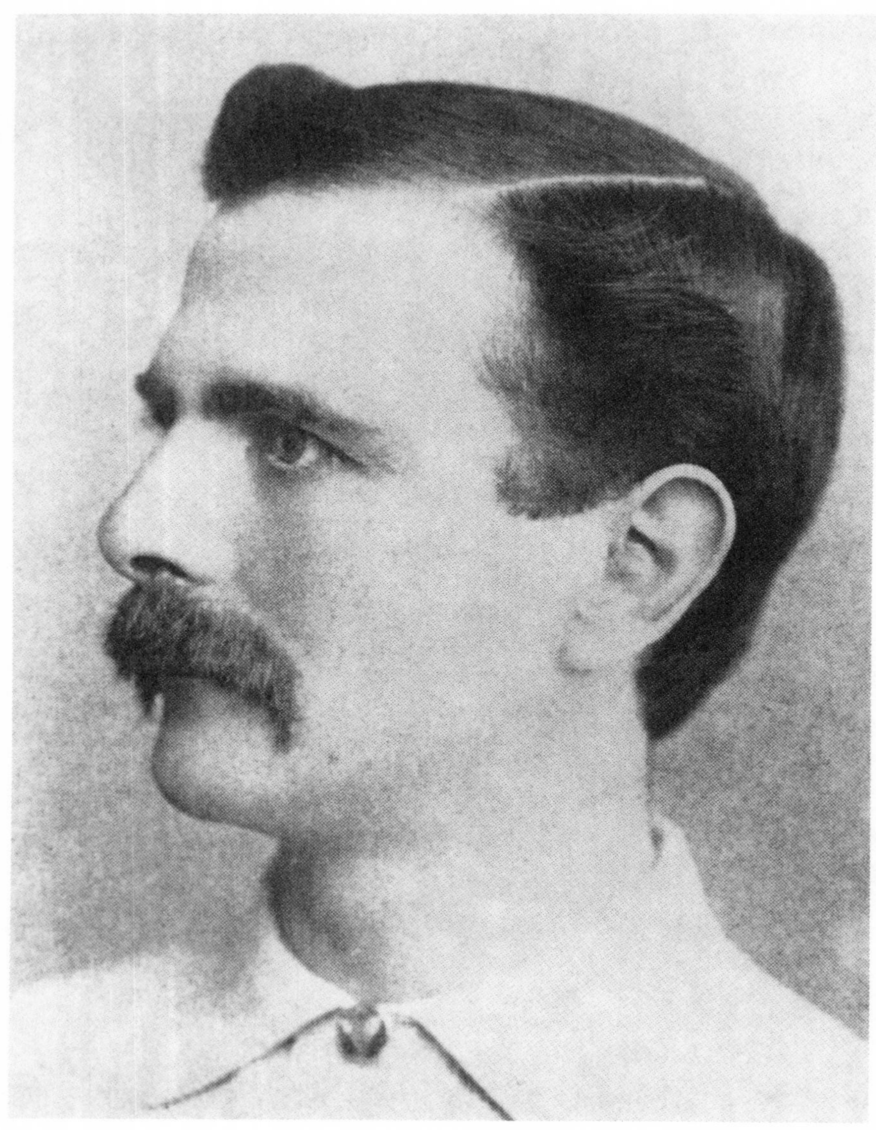

Figure 16.5. *Thomas H. Burgoyne (1855–1895), from* The Light of Egypt, *1897.*

and his own chief, Dayananda Saraswati. He was expelled from the Society, and spent the next four years in England. The London Theosophists had been led by Blavatsky to believe that Hurrychund was a great adept, and were quite taken aback by the evil things he told them about her.

Meanwhile, Burgoyne's esoteric aspirations were interrupted when in January 1883 he and an accomplice were sentenced at Leeds to seven months' imprisonment for mail fraud. Poor Burgoyne's swindle was of the most timid and pathetic kind. It consisted of advertising a nonexistent job and collecting payments of half-a-crown from those who applied for it.

After his release from jail, Burgoyne again contacted Peter Davidson and was secretary of the H.B. of L. when it began public work in 1884. In this capacity, he solicited membership from likely people, including Ayton, who only later discovered that Burgoyne was the same person as the black magician Dalton. From January 1885 to December 1886, the two Scotsmen published a monthy, the *Occult Magazine.* Most of it was written pseudonymously by "Mejnour" (presumably Davidson himself), with help from "Zanoni" (Burgoyne), later joined by "Glyndon," a French occultist (probably F.-Ch. Barlet) and by two persons who signed respectively with a star of David and a swastika. There was also one incomplete article by "Eos," which bears some resemblance to Theon's later doctrines. Together with the frequent mention of Theon as Grand Master, this is the extent of the reclusive adept's contribution.

The *Occult Magazine* is very much in the tradition of British occultism as it had developed in the preceding hundred years. The pseudonyms, of course, came from Bulwer-Lytton, and had no more significance than any other attempt made in the later nineteenth century to enrol the enigmatic novelist to one's cause. As for the swastika, Burgoyne used it to sign his works (such as *Celestial Dynamics* and *The Light of Egypt*) even after breaking with Davidson. I mentioned in Chapter Ten the use of the swastika by Morrison/Zadkiel and his circle. In particular, it was the signature of Irving's Fratres Lucis, otherwise known as the "Order of the Swastika." As David Board has pointed out, the titles of "Brotherhood of Light" and "Brotherhood of Luxor" are also not far apart. Informed readers of the *Occult Magazine* can only have concluded that the H.B. of L.'s directors belonged to the same august group.

The magazine also pays its dues to the mythographers of our early chapters. It praises Samson Arnold Mackey and calls him "the Neophyte of an Initiate of the H. B. of L., whence he got his information."[61] It accepts the solar theory of religions, and shows an interest in Godfrey Higgins and the 600-year Naros cycle. Morrison is praised and his crystal visions of 1848 reprinted. Few recent books are recommended aside from

Figure 16.6. *Seal of the Hermetic Brotherhood of Luxor.*

Davidson's own, but the ones that receive favorable mention include *Ghost Land*, *Art Magic*, and *The Temple of the Rosy Cross* by Freeman Benjamin Dowd, who was the successor of P. B. Randolph as head of the Brotherhood of Eulis.

As far as doctrine is concerned, the *Occult Magazine* is rather vague. It has a strongly anti-ecclesiastical tone, tending towards the christology of Dupuis and his English disciple Robert Taylor: that Jesus is just another solar symbol, his cross solely that of the vernal point in the celestial zodiac. Someone—probably "Glyndon," the French occultist—seems to have read Jean Sylvain Bailly (the historian of astronomy), Fabre d'Olivet, and Louis Figuier. A new translation of the Hermetic treatises *Asclepius* and *The Virgin of the World* is published in parts. But above all, the H.B. of L. stood not for theoretical research and scholarship, but for the practical instruction in occultism that the Theosophical Society was failing to provide for its members: hence the H.B. of L.'s contention that the two movements were not competitive but complementary.

People joined the H.B. of L. by writing to Peter Davidson and sending him their photograph, the details of their birth, and a five-shilling fee. He then drew up and interpreted the horoscope of the postulant. If accepted, one filled out a pledge of secrecy and sent Davidson the admission fee of one guinea. One was then permitted to borrow and copy a series of manuscript essays and instructions, for an annual fee of five shillings. The idea was that members should work as far as possible by themselves. Davidson provided personal guidance and answered queries by letter when these could not be handled by the "Provincial Grand Masters" (Davidson for the North, Ayton for the South, and Barlet for Europe). There was an initiation ceremony, but it was usually performed alone. The whole thing could be done, as it were, by mail-order. The H.B. of L. made no appeal to those who enjoyed fancy rituals, costumes, and titles. Finally, it allowed its members complete liberty of thought; they might belong to anything else they liked.

The "secret documents" that were sent, one by one, to members, were as follows:

The Hermetic Ritual for Private Initiation of Neophytes is to be performed after seven days' continence and abstinence from animal food and alcohol. It involves candles, incense, the reading of sections from the *Corpus Hermeticum,* and invocations of the spirits of the four elements from Eliphas Levi. *The Rites and Ceremony for Exterior Initiation* is similar but more elaborate, with a homily on the Fall of Man. It also has invocations of the elementals, that of the Salamanders being drawn from the *Comte de Gabalis* of the Abbé Villars. Robert Fryar's publication of the *Divine Pymander* (i.e., the *Corpus Hermeticum*) in 1884, and of the *Comte de Gabalis* in 1886, thus relate closely to the H.B. of L.'s rituals.

An essential part of the initiation ceremony seems to have been the taking of a pill that was sent along with the instructions. Probably this contained a concentrated dose of hashish and/or opium, to ensure a memorable experience and perhaps even a communication with the entities of the "Interior Circle."

Symbolic Notes for the First Degree is largely adapted from Hargrave Jennings' *The Rosicrucians* and from Thomas Inman's *Ancient Faiths Embodied in Ancient Names* (1868), both of which, with the works of Eliphas Levi, it recommends for further reading. The purpose of this document is to impress the student with the ubiquity of sexual symbols, and with the divinely sanctioned nature of sexual intercourse.

La Clef Hermétique, written in English but titled in French, is an ambitious attempt to reconcile several systems of cyclical time: the earth's axial motion according to Mackey (whose poem was reprinted in the *Occult Magazine*); the Hindu Yugas; the septenary system of Sinnett's *Esoteric Buddhism;* the Four Ages of the Greeks; and nineteenth-century theories of evolution. Connected to this is *La Clef,* subtitled "A Key to the Work of Abbot Trithemius, entitled *The Secondaries, or Ruling Intelligences Who, After*

God, Actuate the Universe." I have several times had cause to mention this treatise of Trithemius (1462–1516), which lists the successive rulerships of the earth by the seven planetary archangels, each one lasting about 308 1/2 years (one-seventh of an astrological "age"). The translation used was probably that of the Rev. William Ayton, which was being read by the Theosophists in the 1870s.[62]

The H.B. of L.'s commentator calculates that the beginning of the Age of Michael was 21 December 1880, and that of the Age of Aquarius, February 1881. Of Michael's reign, he says:

> This will be a period of Imperial Greatness. Empires will shine full of glory, the Human intellect will have full play and all Churches, Religious Creeds and Ecclesiastical Dogmas will fall to the ground and become things of the past. Parsons, Vicars and Bishops will have to work in different fields if they mean to obtain an honest livelihood. Yes, I repeat this prophecy. The Churches and Chapels will fall with a terrible crash, and be destroyed. But from their ashes, Phoenix-like, shall arise a new Religion, whose shining Motto will be: Veritas Excelsior, Truth Above. This era shall proclaim the rights of man. It is essentially the age of reason dreamed of by Bruno and Thomas Paine.

Here the occult prophecies of Renaissance Hermetism join with the anticlericalism of the Enlightenment, in as perfect an illustration as I could want of the major thesis of this book.

A short document on Reincarnation also circulated around the H.B. of L.'s members. It is lost in that form, but has been reconstructed by Mr. Deveney from long quotations in Burgoyne's *Light of Egypt* and in Guénon's *L'Erreur Spirite.* The essential point is that although every being passes through multiple lives, it only incarnates once on earth as a human. This was also the doctrine of *Ghost Land* (which is cited in the document), of Emma Hardinge Britten, and of Blavatsky's "Hermetic" phase.

The practical occultism of the H.B. of L. was taught through several separate manuscripts, as well as through a large and comprehensive one called *The Mysteries of Eros.* Peter Davidson's contributions have a highly moral and devotional air, as do his letters. While he makes ample use of Randolph's work, in *Psychic Culture* he warns the aspirant against the sexual doctrines which misled Randolph and ruined many others, namely the idea that through concentration during sexual intercourse, one can obtain anything one wants. Davidson's adaptation of these doctrines and mental techniques is always with the intention to raise and refine the brute instincts, especially of the male. He says categorically that the sexual magic of the H.B. of L. has only two purposes: the spiritual elevation of the partners, and the benefit that this confers on any child conceived. Beside this, *Psychical Culture* urges a wholesome way of life free from meat, alcohol, and tobacco; the cultivation of self-awareness; and exercises with a magic mirror designed to develop clairvoyance.

Clairvoyance is treated at greater length in *Laws of Magic Mirrors*, being extracts from Randolph's *Seership* on the construction and use of mirrors and crystals, combined with rites of consecration that seem to be adapted from Barrett's *Magus*.[63] In Davidson's version the name of Christ is removed, the "blessed and holy Trinity" becomes "the Eternal and Omnipresent Creator," etc.

The magic mirror was the primary tool of the H.B. of L.'s members, particularly the unmarried ones who could not follow the sexual path. Whereas in Hockley's and Mackenzie's circles the scrying had been done by young mediums, because these men believed themselves to lack the gift, the H.B. of L. insisted that nearly everyone possesses the capacity to scry. It just takes a concentrated course of study, like learning a musical instrument. The idea was that once it is mastered, scrying serves as a gateway to other levels of being, and as a means to establish one's own contact with the Interior Circle, making further instruction from the earthly plane redundant.

The sexual teachings of the H.B. of L. would have been nothing without Randolph's published and privately circulated writings. They were contained, first, in *A Brief Key to the Eulian Mysteries*, which is on the direction of the will during sexual intercourse. From Randolph also came the *Mysteries of Eulis*, on the threefold development of the magical will through "Volantia," "Decretism," "Posism," the power of the breath, and ritual sexual intercourse; and *The Ansairetic Mystery*, a privately circulated pamphlet on "sexual science." The foregoing documents circulated separately before being gathered, in edited form, into *The Mysteries of Eros*, "expressly arranged for the Exterior Circle of the H.B. of L. by T. H. Burgoyne, Private Secretary."

Quite obviously, there was nothing original about the H.B. of L.'s documents except the eclectic choice: the *Corpus Hermeticum*, the *Comte de Gabalis*, Mackey, Levi, Jennings, Inman, Randolph, *Isis Unveiled*, *Esoteric Buddhism*, perhaps *Ghost Land*. It is just the kind of reading evidenced by Davidson's violin book of 1881, plus a large contribution from Randolph. There is no sign whatever of Max Theon's involvement or superior knowledge; he seems to have left Davidson and Burgoyne to run the show as best they could. But for all its unoriginality, the H.B. of L. brought novel ideas into currency, providing, at long last, the practical complement to all the theorizing about "the worship of the generative powers" that had been going on since Payne Knight. Its teaching on cosmic cycles similarly supplied the essential element, missing in Higgins and Mackey, of precise dating, to which all the cyclical systems could now be related. René Guénon writes that the doctrine of cycles is one of the most closely guarded secrets of initiation, because of the political and social dangers of knowing too much about them.[64] The techniques for developing clairvoyance and developing the magical will would became part and parcel of the modern occult orders, while the anti-reincarnation teaching became a pivot of opposition to the Theosophists in particular, and to the East in general. The H.B. of L. remained aggressively Western—so long as the West is understood to start with Egypt and Israel.

I will now complete the tale of the H.B. of L.'s founders.[65] Davidson settled with his family in Loudsville, White County, in the northwest of Georgia. Burgoyne left him and moved to Carmel, California. Here Burgoyne met Norman Astley, a retired British Army officer who had studied occultism in India and received from Astley and some other members a commission to write a series of lessons for the H.B. of L.'s teachings. These lessons were at first privately circulated to members, but in 1889 Burgoyne published them as *The Light of Egypt,* by "Zanoni [swastika symbol]".[66]

The title of the book of course puts it in the Egyptian, rather than the Indian current, yet though it gives historical precedence to Egyptian wisdom over Indian, it is not anti-Oriental. The author praises the true Hindu and Buddhist religions, which apparently do not teach the "poisonous doctrines of karma and reincarnation," and speaks favorably of the scheme of world-ages given in Sinnett's *Esoteric Buddhism.* More predictable is Burgoyne's friendliness to the author of *Art Magic,* and even to *Isis Unveiled* as a work from before the time of Blavatsky's defection to the East. Emma Hardinge Britten would return the compliment by heralding *The Light of Egypt* as "one of the masterpieces of the age we live in [. . .] Nothing comparable to it in the English language [. . .] Surpassing powers of delineation possessed by writer."[67] But Burgoyne did not live long enough to bask in these compliments.

In 1892 Davidson started a new journal, *The Morning Star,* which resembled his *Occult Magazine,* but with a more Christian outlook. Early in the new century he renewed his contact with Max Theon, now settled in Tlemcen, Algeria and publishing the "Cosmic Philosophy" which was channeled through his wife. Barlet, the H.B. of L.'s agent in France, worked on the French publication of the Theons' doctrines, while Davidson published English extracts from them in his magazine. Thus the two men who had done most to keep the H.B. of L. going in the 1880s ended by coming back to the man who had started it all.

The influence of the H.B. of L. was out of all proportion to its obscurity. In France, its practices permeated the occult revival of the *fin de siècle,* thanks to the Grand Master Barlet and his wide web of connections.

All the chief French Theosophists belonged to the Order. Papus, the best publicist that occultism ever had, used the many ceremonial and study-groups that he founded or headed as recruiting grounds for the H.B. of L.[68] It was the inmost group, differing from the Martinists, the Gnostic Church, the French Theosophical Society, the Kabbalistic Order of the Rose-Cross, etc., in the respect I have constantly underlined: it *worked.* People had amazing experiences from following its instructions.

In the German-speaking world, the most notable member of the H.B. of L. was the Austrian industrialist Karl Kellner (1850–1905). In 1895, Kellner met the Theosophist Theodor Reuss (1855–1923), and the two of them conceived the idea of a "masonic academy" which was later to materialize as the OTO (Ordo Templi Orientis).[69] Based on the Rite of Memphis and Misraïm, which had been obtained from John Yarker, the OTO was supposedly the more exoteric part of Kellner and Reuss's enterprise, while, in the latter's own words, "the teachings of the Hermetic Brotherhood of Light were reserved for the few initiates of the occult inner circle."[70] This must refer to sexual teachings, though it is important to distinguish between those of Randolph and Davidson, and the sexual magic developed by the OTO and later made notorious by Aleister Crowley. Randolph had a typical nineteenth-century horror of masturbation, and neither he nor Davidson had the slightest tolerance for homosexuality—both integral parts of Crowley's practice.

Continuing the list of those influenced by the H.B. of L., Rudolf Steiner joined the OTO in 1906 and was immediately delegated Grand Master to found a Berlin Lodge. He must have known of these inner circle teachings. By 1917 the distinction in the OTO of inner and outer circles appears to have broken down, for in that year a manifesto published from Monte Verità, Ascona, openly named "the Hermetic Brotherhood of Light, known as the O.T.O." as the pioneering organization for world-reform.[71] Another OTO initiate was H. Spencer Lewis,[72] founder of the AMORC. He, too, would have known of the H.B. of L.'s teachings, as would his rival, R. Swinburne Clymer. Clymer's Rosicrucian Fraternity, based in Quakertown, Pennsylvania, acknowledged both Randolph and Davidson as great initiates, and republished Randolph's *Eulis* as *The Immortality of Love.* Some relics of the H.B. of L. are probably among the "secrets" still offered to initiates by these Rosicrucian groups.

It remains to make the link with the third "Hermetic" order of the decade, the Golden Dawn. The Burgoyne scandal coming to light in 1886 and the emigration of both the culprit and Davidson reflected so badly on the H.B. of L. that most of the respectable British members abandoned the Order. This does not mean that they abandoned the practices it had taught them. But it left a void, which both the Eastern and Western factions hastened to fill: the former with the Esoteric Section of the Theosophical Society, and the latter with the Golden Dawn, both founded in 1888.

The two principal founders of the Golden Dawn, Westcott and Mathers, were both previously active in Kingsford's Hermetic Society. Mathers made his first public appearance there on 3 June 1886, when he lectured very knowledgeably on the Kabbalah.[73] On 8 July he gave another lecture, on "Physical Alchemy": [74] not a subject that Mathers is usually associated with, but the very one for which the Society of Eight had been founded by the chemist Frederick Holland (see Chapter Eleven). During this year, Mathers was working on a translation of the book that Kingsford and Maitland had consulted in the British Museum, and when it appeared in 1887 as *The Kabbalah Unveiled* he dedicated it to them. According to Ithell Colquhoun, Mathers's biographer, it was probably due to Anna Kingsford's influence that Mathers became a feminist, at least in occult matters, and insisted on women being admitted to the Golden Dawn on equal terms to men.[75] A further reason is that there was no sexual discrimination either in the H.B. of L. or in the Theosophical Society.

Westcott lectured at the last meeting of the Hermetic Society before Kingsford's fatal illness brought its activities to a close. His subject was the *Sepher Jetzirah*,[76] of which he also prepared an edition for Robert Fryar's "Bath Occult Reprints." Given such associates, it is almost unthinkable that this extremely "clubbable" man was not also enrolled by Ayton into the H.B. of L.

One can understand the Golden Dawn much better after knowing Kingsford's and Maitland's work. Its rituals evoked the same initiatic universe as Kingsford's illuminations had described: one whose mythology was Egyptian, Kabbalistic, Eleusinian, and Christian (Rosicrucian): it was a practical complement to the theoretical and moral teachings of *The Perfect Way*. With its rituals derived, at least to some degree, from the Golden and Rosy Cross, it also offered an alternative to the Orientalism of the Theosophical Society, whose Esoteric Section, Mr. Gilbert suggests, "was created specifically to avert the loss of would-be practical occultists to the ranks of the Golden Dawn and to prevent a complete split between the followers of the Eastern and those of the Western Path."[77] In comparison to the H.B. of L.'s correspondence course for lonely occultists, the Golden Dawn was sociable, theatrical, and generally exciting. It was also non-polemical, whereas the documents of the H.B. of L. had material to offend Christians, Theosophists, and those who preferred not to read about sex. This is some measure of the Golden Dawn's success.

SEVENTEEN

The Parting of East and West

The departure of Olcott and Blavatsky from New York at the end of 1878 was the crucial moment of the nineteenth-century occult revival, marking an apparent parting of the Eastern and Western ways. Those who followed them, in whatever sense, seemed to be admitting that the traditions of the West had failed them. Those who stayed behind contributed to a Hermetic renaissance which wanted nothing from the East.

For a contemporary view of the East-West schism I call once more on C. G. Harrison, whose 1893 lectures on *The Transcendental Universe* were cited in Chapter Ten. It may be remembered that Harrison was recounting what he had been told by an unnamed informant about the nature of Blavatsky and her work. Here is his summary:

> That the "aspect of the heavens" at the time of the birth of Madame Blavatsky frightened the "Conservatives," [i.e., the Conservative party among occultists] and resulted in a kind of "coalition ministry," which gave place to a Liberal one in the year 1841.
>
> That a "Brother of the Left" revealed this fact to Madame Blavatsky in Egypt about twenty years ago, that she returned to Europe immediately, and imposed certain terms as a condition of reception into an occult brotherhood in Paris, which were indignantly refused; that she was subsequently received in America and expelled very shortly afterwards.
>
> That in consequence of a threat from Madame Blavatsky that she would soon make the American brotherhood "shut up shop," a conference of American and European occultists was held at Vienna,[1] and a particular course of action decided upon.

> That during the time Madame Blavatsky imagined herself to be in Thibet, she was, in reality, at Khatmandhu in the state known to occultists as "in prison."
>
> That certain Hindu occultists who, for patriotic reasons, having sided with her against the American brotherhood, had nearly succeeded in procuring her release from "prison" by their own efforts, consented to a compromise whereby she was to be set free on condition of their non-interference with anything that had been already accomplished.[2]

This was certainly a novel way of explaining Blavatsky's apparent change of allegiance, as the result of her capture by a group of Hindu patriots. After this astonishing report, Harrison gives his own explanation of what "occult imprisonment" is:

> There is a certain operation of ceremonial magic by means of which a wall of psychic influences may be built up around an individual who has become dangerous, which has the effect of paralyzing the higher activities, and producing what is called the "repercussion of effort," and the result is a kind of spiritual sleep characterised by fantastic visions. It is an operation seldom resorted to even by Brothers of the Left, and in the case of Madame Blavatsky *was disapproved of by almost all European occultists.* On the American brotherhood alone rests the responsibility for what has since happened. The late Mr. Oliphant, I believe, knew more about the affair than any Englishman.[3]

Laurence Oliphant (1829–1888) was one of those supremely accomplished Victorians who appeared to have the world at his feet. He had a brilliant career in gunboat diplomacy, war reporting, and London society, then suddenly abandoned it to become a disciple of Thomas Lake Harris, one of the earliest American cult leaders. Oliphant spent the years 1873–1877 in America, alternately subjecting himself to humiliations at the tyrannical Harris's commune in Brocton, New York and directing a telegraph cable company in New York City. Here he had ample opportunity to meet the early Theosophists and their rivals. He knew Blavatsky and Olcott well, he said later, but declined the invitation to join the Theosophical Society because he "believe[d] the whole thing to be a delusion and a snare."[4] Certainly if there were disappointed American occultists, Oliphant was in a position to know of them.

Until a better explanation appears, I suspect that Harrison's unnamed informant was none other than Charles Carleton Massey, former President of the London Branch of the Theosophical Society. Massey was close to Oliphant, both socially (Oliphant belonged to the Athenaeum Club, where Massey virtually lived[5]) and spiritually. In 1888, Massey was even considering joining Oliphant's own projected commune in Haifa, Palestine, and was close to Oliphant up to the week of his death.[6] Massey had also known all the actors in this plot, ever since he went to America in 1875. His loyalty to the Society gave way when he learned that a letter from Koot Hoomi with which he had been honored had been planted on him by Mrs. Hollis-Billing, on Blavatsky's instructions.

Blavatsky's militant anti-Christianity had always hurt Massey, who was a theosopher long before he was a Theosophist, and long afterwards, too. Something of his attitude can be understood from a letter he wrote to Mrs. Atwood in 1888. He told his old friend and guide that he had long been averse to historical Christianity, but that lately:

> I have felt so deep a need of Christ, and have been so vehemently drawn to personify Him as the object of devotion, that I welcome any conception of natural processes which facilitated belief in the historical descent of a Divine Humanity on earth, as manifested in an individual germ of our regeneration, an external Personality as a fulcrum so to speak, from which spiritual thought and love can spring upwards. I don't think one need be a worse philosopher for being also a devotee, and after all, we cannot dwell in the purely occult and impersonal, or pass at once behind all manifestation into the subjective adytun of the Atma.[7]

Blavatsky's death in 1891 would have released Massey from a gentleman's obligation not to "bandy a woman's name about." I see the "occult imprisonment" story as Massey's effort to understand, in retrospect, the movement he had become entangled in, as told to his fellow Christian esotericist, permitting Harrison to disclose part, but not all of it in his lectures.

This does not mean that I dismiss Harrison's bizarre account as an invention, whether by T. L. Harris, Oliphant, Massey, or anyone else. Occultists, as we well know, do very odd things, and as a result they develop very odd perceptions and convictions. Historians cannot allow that something like this occult imprisonment can have any effect in the world of facts. But they can accept that to perform such magic may have a psychological effect on those who do it, and that subsequent events can be interpreted by them as proof that they have succeeded. And we are aware that self-deception, coupled with spiritual fanaticism, has been known to cause historical effects of the most concrete and painful kind.

Seen in this light, the occultists' interest in Blavatsky's horoscope has a ring of truth about it, when we recall the expectations of an avatar to inaugurate the Naros cycle early in the nineteenth century (see Chapter Four).[8] These expectations *may* have reached Blavatsky's ears while she was in Egypt, and she *may* have contacted people in Paris who entertained such beliefs, and been rebuffed by them. The "American brotherhood" probably included Emma Hardinge Britten and her friends, who had already published part of *Ghost Land* with its eyewitness accounts of unpleasant occult machinations. As Blavatsky turned her face to the East, certain people (though surely not Emma herself) may have tried to influence her by magical means and attributed subsequent events to the counter-operations of her Indian masters. There was no one better equipped to supply that detail of the plot than Hurrychund Chintamon, the malevolent "adept" who had come to London in 1879 and begun to turn Massey against Blavatsky.

At the conclusion of his ground-breaking study of Blavatsky and the Mahatmas, *Madame Blavatsky and the Myth of the Great White Lodge,* Paul Johnson suggests two other possible sources for the "occult imprisonment" story: A. O. Hume and Franz Hartmann. After an analysis in which he demonstrates that, stripped of its sensational elements, Harrison's story lies very close to the psychological truth, this scholar concludes: "HPB's real occult imprisonment was the continual need to keep the truth hidden in order to protect her Masters and herself."[9] He adds that she was, of course, never in Katmandu.

The Mahatmas of Theosophy, most of whom Mr. Johnson has shown to have been identifiable historical persons, took on an ever more mythic status in the neo-Theosophy of Annie Besant and Charles W. Leadbeater, who controlled the parent (Adyar) branch of the Society until 1933. It was the clairvoyant Leadbeater who established the canonical figures of this celestial bureaucracy and filled in the details of their past lives and present habits.[10] Some of them obliged by dictating "channeled" works to various recipients. Alice A. Bailey worked with "The Tibetan," Djwhal Kul, to produce her voluminous writings. Helena Roerich, wife of the painter Nicholas, received a body of teaching from Morya. Cyril Scott, the composer and anonymous author of *The Initiate* series, wrote some of his later music from the direct inspiration of Koot Hoomi. The "Summit Lighthouse" movement, led by Elizabeth Clare Prophet, publishes a book on alchemy by the Master Racokzy, formerly the Count of Saint-Germain, and other teachings of the "Ascended Masters." The phenomenon of the survival of the Theosophical Mahatmas into our own time would make a fascinating study.

In the years before World War I, there was an unfriendly parting within the Theosophical Society between those who traveled at least part of the way with Besant and Leadbeater and those who were repelled by them. One of the main reasons for the schism was the new leaders' adoption of the young Brahmin boy Jiddu Krishnamurti. Their intention was to train him to become a Mahatma himself, and eventually to assume the office of "World Teacher." It was on account of this that Rudolf Steiner left the Society in 1909, taking the majority of the German Theosophists with him into his new movement of Anthroposophy. When the long-awaited moment came for the World Teacher to manifest, on 3 August 1929, Krishnamurti declined the office with the memorable words:

> I maintain that Truth is a pathless land, and you cannot approach it by any path whatsoever, by any religion, by any sect. That is my point of view, and I adhere to that absolutely and unconditionally. Truth, being limitless, unconditioned, unapproachable by any path whatsoever, cannot be organized; nor should any organization be formed to lead or coerce people along any particular path. If you first understand that, then you will see how impossible it is to organize a belief. A belief is purely an individual matter, and you cannot and must not organize it. If you do, it becomes dead, crystallised; it becomes a creed, a sect, a religion, to be imposed on others.[11]

Krishnamurti demonstrated in his own person an extreme form of the Theosophical Enlightenment, consisting in the utter rejection of all gods, religions, faiths, scriptures, doctrines, Mahatmas, and gurus.[12] All that was left was a "state," which he radiated so powerfully that this teacher without a teaching never lacked for audiences—or wealthy devotees. Krishnamurti's deconstruction of spirituality marks one endpoint of the developments outlined in this book. Some would class him with those paradoxical masters of Zen Buddhism, the very absurdity of whose words and conduct is supposed to shock the disciple out of the sleeping state of ordinary consciousness. If every concept is rejected, if truth is a pathless land, it must be present here and now as the ultimate reality, void of all distinction. Nothing could be further East, geographically or spiritually, than this.

At the other extreme, an increasingly prominent feature of the Theosophical Society during the years of Krishnamurti's preparation was the Liberal Catholic Church. Leadbeater had been an ordained clergyman of the Church of England before entering Theosophy and, like the Society's founders, took the formal vows of Buddhism in Ceylon. This did not prevent him later from reactivating his priesthood within the freer climate of the "Old Catholics," who claim the apostolic succession but do not acknowledge the authority of the Pope. In this subculture, where the bishops outnumber the simple priests and deacons, Bishop Leadbeater could indulge his love of dressing up and celebrating Mass, in which he convinced his congregation that he, at least, could see with his astral vision the angelic host present at the Eucharist. Leadbeater was anything but a Christian supremacist or literalist: he revered the "Master Jesus" as one among other masters, after the Hindu pattern of multiple avatars. At heart he was a magician, and the Mass was his preferred rite of ceremonial magic.

After reading Krishnamurti's speech above, one can see what agonies he must have suffered when he was obliged to attend Leadbeater's services. Blavatsky, too, must have turned in Devaloka to see the religion she detested taking over her Society. But would Anna Kingsford have objected? Certainly not. Like Lady Caithness, she remained a "Catholic" by her own definition, because she believed that the Catholic myths, symbols, and rituals preserved a valid and living stream of the universal Gnosis. Leadbeater's Liberal Catholicism was the logical consequence of *The Perfect Way.* It preserved all the glory of Catholic ritual for those whose tastes ran in that direction, minus the discomforts of papal authority and dogma.

Harrison's lectures about Theosophy and esoteric Christianity make no mention of Kingsford and Maitland. He could not have approved of their rejection of historicism and of the "Word made Flesh," so central to his own beliefs. Nor did he share their conviction of the doctrine of reincarnation. In the last of his three books, *"The Fourth Mystery"; Birth and Death* (1929), Harrison remarks that reincarnation may or may not be true, but that it is merely philosophical speculation and not part of the Christian faith.[13] He was probably alluding to *The Perfect Way* at the end of *The Transcendental Universe,* where he mentions "a revival of gnosticism in one of its most dangerous forms."[14]

Harrison's Christian esotericism was a very different thing from Kingsford's esoteric Christianity, or Leadbeater's. In *The Perfect Way* it is the Hermetic tradition that provides the esoteric key to understanding and revivifying Christianity: a key that is equally applicable to other religions. In Christian esotericism, on the contrary, it is Christianity that comes first and justifies esotericism. In the English-speaking world today, its representatives include groups as different as the Anthroposophists, the school of Qabalistic magic headed by Gareth Knight, and the admirers of Valentin Tomberg's teachings (notably his once-anonymous *Meditations on the Tarot*). For them, the historical Jesus is a unique vessel of divine incarnation, differing in essence from all other teachers or avatars. With the best will in the world, they cannot reconcile the "revealed" religions of the Abrahamic family with the "natural" religions of Buddhism and Hinduism, any more than with the deism of the Enlightenment. In Buddhism, there is no god to do the revealing; in Hinduism, there are too many, so that no people or group can claim an exclusive relationship or a unique incarnation. None of the Christian esotericists denigrate the oriental religions after the fashion of Victorian missionaries. They convey the message more subtly, by saying that oriental religions are all very fine for Orientals, but that Westerners do much better to follow a Western way. When coupled with the doctrine of Christ's uniqueness, this implies that Hindus, Buddhists, and pagans are still stuck in an earlier stage of humanity's religious evolution. The coincidence with general European attitudes to the East in the colonizing period is too obvious to overlook.

I turn now to a figure whose whole life illustrates the title of this chapter. He is Allan Bennett (1872–1923), otherwise the Bhikku Ananda Metteya (or Maitreya). Bennett lost his father when he was a boy and was already earning a living in his teens as a skilled chemist and laboratory technician. At some point, he was "adopted" by S.L.McGregor Mathers,[15] and added the clan name "McGregor" after his own.[16] Given Mathers' circumstances during Bennett's youth,[17] it cannot have been an adoption as normally understood, but was probably a case of the older man taking the youth under his wing. This included bringing him into the Golden Dawn, as one of its earliest and most precocious members.

Another man who assumed the name McGregor as a tribute to Mathers was Aleister Crowley (1875–1947). When he joined the Golden Dawn in 1898, he sensed immediately that Bennett was the most advanced magician of the Order. Crowley installed him in a room next to his own flat in Chancery Lane, and together "they regularly evoked spirits to visible and even tangible appearance," writes Kenneth Grant.[18] The two magicians also experimented with drugs. Bennett was already a connoisseur of these, and not just as a research chemist, for to alleviate his asthma he used to take, in rotation, opium, morphine, and cocaine (all legal at that time). He also made use of Anna Kingsford's chosen vehicle for illuminated dreams, chloroform.[19] Brunton adds that "he went on to experiment with poisons until once he took a tremendous overdose which would have instantly killed another man but which left him quite unharmed."[20]

There were two other elements in Bennett's makeup that kept him from the destiny that the last paragraph might lead one to predict. First, there was the deterioration of his health, which by 1900 was so bad that his only hope was to leave England for a warmer climate. Second, he had been a Buddhist since the age of eighteen. His enthusiasm began with the reading of Edwin Arnold's *The Light of Asia*, then, "deeply moved by the pure and rational Faith,"[21] he studied all the English translations of Buddhist scriptures that he could find. Now he was eager to see the lands where, he believed, a third of humanity lived under this benign philosophy. Crowley gave him a hundred pounds,[22] and he took ship for Ceylon.

In this country, where Blavatsky and Olcott had formally entered Buddhism twenty years earlier, Bennett spent his time studying Pali under Buddhist monks and yoga under an Indian adept. Crowley, who was

Figure 17.1. *S. L. MacGregor Mathers (1854–1918).*

by now on a mountain-climbing expedition around the world, visited him and stayed for some months of "magical retirement" and yoga study.[23] That was the end of Crowley's apprenticeship, and the end of Bennett's magical life, for he had decided to enter the Buddhist monastic order (the Sangha). For this purpose he moved to Burma, and was ordained with splendid ceremony on 21 May 1902, being only the second white man ever to have become a Bhikku or Buddhist monk.[24]

Bennett's ambition was to take Buddhism back to the West, because he was convinced that it was the only solution to the problems of modern mankind. Under his religious name of Ananda Metteya, he edited a magazine, *Buddhism,* intended to reach libraries and readers in England and prepare for the appearance of missionaries in person. Here he established his position as an uncompromising Theravadist or Hinayanist, i.e., a follower of the ancient Southern School of Buddhism that denies the existence of any god or any soul. He wrote that he regarded the Dalai Lama, spiritual head of the Mahayana school, with absolute indifference.[25] Bennett's first lectures in Ceylon had been given at the Theosophical Society. While he praised Theosophy as the first opener of the Western mentality to Buddhist truths, he held that so-called "esoteric" Buddhism was presumptuous and misleading, especially in re-imposing the soul-doctrine.[26] As for other religions, he considered them as stemming merely from someone's experiences of one of the stages of Nibbana,[27] interpreted according to their own psychology, religious prejudices, and the needs of their audience for gods, etc. In short, they were delusions.

Like the Theosophists, it hurt Bennett to see the efforts made to export these infantile religions to the East. But while the blasphemers of Chapter Three were content to abuse Christianity while admiring Jesus Christ, Bennett was not. In an article on "The Training of the Mind," he wrote:

> who can estimate the power of one human mind, whether for good or for evil? One such mind, the mind of a man like Jesus Christ, may bring about the tortured death of many million men, may wreck states and religions and dynasties, and cause untold misery and suffering; another mind, employing the same manner of energy, but rightly using that energy for the benefit of others, may, like the Buddha, bring hope into the hopeless lives of crores upon crores of human beings, may increase by a thousandfold the pity and love of that third of humanity, may aid innumerable lakhs of beings to come to that Peace for which we all crave—that Peace the way to which is so difficult to find.[28]

It is not surprising to learn that these words were published in Crowley's private magazine *The Equinox.* No other editor in the occult, spiritualist, or esoteric field would have allowed them.

Bennett's formation as a scientist was crucial to his religious attitude. In the pages of *Buddhism* he continually mentions the latest discoveries in

Figure 17.2. *Allan Bennett (1872–1923).*

the physical sciences and draws many parallels from machinery, chemistry, and physics in order to illustrate Buddhist teachings. He had a touching faith that the application of reason would ensure the progress of humanity:

> Humanity will surely advance during this coming century beyond our highest dreams. As the great teachings of science come home to the masses of the people; as education progresses; as the conditions of the striving proletariat are constantly improved, alike by new discoveries and by the out-growth of the spirit of humanity; the old barbarous race-hatreds will swiftly perish, till the whole folly and fanfarronade of militarism and its evil fruits of warfare are swept away for ever.[29]

Bennett contributed to this happy prospect by working on useful inventions—novel types of motors, refrigerators, etc.—with the hope that, if developed, they might provide the financial backing for a Buddhist mission to the West. In 1908 he came to London with the shaven head and yellow robe of his Order and made his headquarters at the Buddhist Society of Great Britain and Ireland, founded the previous year. During his mission he gave an interview to the spiritualist magazine *Light,*[30] in which he said that Buddhism and spiritualism are not in conflict: that Buddhism has a ghost world, too, which is one of six kingdoms into which one is immediately reborn on death. If some spiritualists bridled at this parallel with their "Summer Land," few can have liked what the Bhikku said next:

> Buddhism has no God, either in the anthropomorphic or spiritistic sense. There are the Brahmaloka beings, and Mahabrahma is the greatest of them all, because of the vast realm of consciousness open to him; but any human being, by interior development, can rise to any particular plane whilst in this life. From the Buddhist point of view this Brahma, devoid of characteristics and limitations, imagines that he is God, imagines he is eternal, that all this universe emanated from him.[31]

We will return to this theme below. For all his scientism and rationalism, Bennett was a deeply devotional man. Nibbana was not a pessimistic doctrine for him, not annihilation or oblivion, but

> It is the apotheosis of sanity:—no vain longing after future states of bliss, but the attainment even in this life, of that Goal of Happiness after which humanity has craved, since first speech became articulate—the bliss that comes to him who has put aside the causes of woe—who lives freed from the passions, hatreds, and illusions that enchain us,—his life filled with the

> unutterable Peace, his heart filled with love and helpfulness to all living things.[32]

The writers Clifford Bax and Paul Brunton, who left separate accounts of Bennett's last years, both remarked on the equanimity and serenity of mind, and the love for all beings, that he sustained—or that sustained him—through his poverty and excruciating illnesses.[33] His body finally failed him in 1923.

Allan Bennett embodies the "enlightenment" of my title in both its meanings. He was a thoroughly modern man: converted to atheism by science; believing in evolution and progress; trusting in human reason and technology to bring about a Golden Age of peace and plenty. At the same time, he was a magician who commanded awed respect from his colleagues in the occult sciences, even the most ambitious and egotistic of them. Like his friend Crowley, he illustrates the seeming paradox that extreme rationalism can coexist with a belief in magic. The only possible explanation of this paradox is that for occultists of their caliber, magic was not a belief but an experience so concrete as to demand a scientific rather than a superstitious explanation.

This was also the reason that Bennett could drop the Golden Dawn and all that it stood for: he had traversed it and understood it, and it no longer satisfied him. Crowley explains why this was so. He tells of how at the age of eighteen, without any training or preparation, Bennett had an "accidental" experience of *Shivadarshana,* in which "the *whole* Universe, grasped firmly as a homogenous Unity, and deprived of all its conditions and categories, is united with the pure Self of the Yogi—equally purged of its conditions—in a single supreme Act"—and annihilated. It was a marvel that Allan survived and kept his reason, Crowley adds.[34] This glimpse of Enlightenment in the Buddhist sense remained the lodestar of Bennett's career, for he was determined at all costs to regain it. All his writing on Buddhism, especially on Nibbana, bears the stamp of authentic experience, not merely book-learning. And given the nature of his glimpse, it is not surprising that he remained as far outside conventional religion as he had ever been. His was no vision of the Mystery of Golgotha, no union with a loving God, not even a merging with the Cosmic All that are familiar from the literature of theistic and pantheistic mysticism. Bennett's description of it dismisses in a few precise words the whole cosmology of the Golden Dawn:

> Beyond the radiance of Sun and Moon and Star, further than the Dark Void beyond, far past the Gates of Birth and Death, It reigns, Immutable, Supreme. Beyond the inner consciousness of man, wherein these worlds and systems and the far-reaching Aether that includes them float like a grain of dust in the abyss

of space;—beyond that vaster sphere where Thought and Non-thought co-existent dwell, where the last faint passing echoes of act and speech and thought blend with the Silence and are heard no more:—beyond all these It is; yet here, here in our hearts this day, albeit uncomprehended and unperceived; to be gained in this our human life alone, to be attained here on earth by him who follows on the Eightfold Way our Master taught.[35]

This eloquent passage illustrates the central difference between the spiritual aspirations of East and West, as they had developed in the esoteric movements of the later nineteenth century. It hinges on two contrary philosophic views of the ultimate destiny of the human being and the purpose of life on earth. For Randolph, Emma Hardinge Britten, the H.B. of L., and the "Higher Spiritualism" in general, the destiny of the soul was to leave this earth after a single lifetime and then, either alone or with its beloved partner, to travel ever finer, grander spheres, leading ever more marvelous angelic and cosmic existences in universes beyond universes, finally being reabsorbed into God. Buddhism and Advaita Vedanta, on the contrary, see the ultimate goal as being attainable here on earth, in a human body that is the fruit of many incarnations. The Bodhisattva or Jivan-mukti (liberated sage) who achieves this goal is simultaneously in the world of existence and in that of Non-Being or Nirvana, which is the support of all universes, no matter how spectacular or how sordid.

G. R. S. Mead (1863–1933), already independent from the neo-Theosophists, read Allan Bennett's articles with great interest and compared them with evidences of the Mahayana school. He was struck at first by the discovery that the ideal of the latter was fundamentally the same as that of Christianity: self-renouncing love. "But," he added, "the doctrine of Hell, though not of the eternal type that disfigures Western theology, is very conspicuous, and of course extreme ascetic dualism with its unhealthy and unjust hatred of the body, is very prominent [. . .] That body should be excluded in a doctrine of love for all creatures is, we should imagine, as great a hindrance as love of body in the general sense is to the life of the spirit."[36]

A year later, Mead had discovered the *Outlines of Mahayana Buddhism* by the Japanese scholar and Zen Buddhist, D. T. Suzuki. The Zen idea that Samsara *is* Nirvana completely baffled him: it was a challenge, Mead said, to all our former ideas about Nirvana. But other things had become clearer to him, notably the rift within Buddhism itself. He likened the difference between "stagnant and reactionary" Hinayana and "Catholic and Progressive" Mahayana to the difference, in the West, between the liberal and rationalistic view of the historic Jesus, and the "Catholic" view of a world-religion of the Christ Principle and the Living Logos.[37] The *anatta* (no-soul) controversy appeared to him nothing but a quarrel over the meaning of words: the *atma* denied in Buddhism is the false and separative ego, not the *Atman* of the Hindu Upanishads, which is the Self, the true wholeness of the being.[38]

While Bennett was planning his Buddhist mission to England, the author of those *Outlines*, Daisetz Teitaro Suzuki (1870–1966), was living in America (from 1897 to 1909) and preparing to introduce the West to the Zen Buddhism of his native land. In 1909 he contributed an article to *The Buddhist Review* that seems deliberately aimed at countering the narrowness of Bennett's views. Suzuki writes on the broader outlook of Mahayana Buddhism, explaining that the Northern school does not stop, like the Hinayana of the South, with the negation of God and the *atman* or ego-soul. It goes beyond them to the higher affirmation of the "suchness" beyond intellect, which is felt as love and wisdom, with the desire to awaken it in all. He calls it "Eternal Motherhood," the source of infinite love, and evokes a universe that is "a grand spiritual system composed of moral beings, who are so many fragmentary reflexes of the Dharmâkaya."[39]

Suzuki single-handedly brought Zen to the West, with all its cultural consequences. Thanks to his efforts, and to the more recent ones of the Dalai Lama XIV and other Tibetans, Buddhism as known in the West today is almost exclusively of the Mahayana school. Bennett's combination of the strict and monastic Hinayana with Western scientism could never have succeeded. Although in his person he was the embodiment of compassionate wisdom, in his writing he was too harsh on the native faith of the West, and too sanguine in his confidence in scientific rationalism. In a way, he turned back the clock, to the point at which "Buddhist atheism" had appalled Max Müller, Eugène Burnouf, Barthélémy de Saint-Hilaire, and other Orientalists of the mid-nineteenth century. The West needed a warmer Buddhism, such as Blavatsky had already offered in *The Voice of the Silence*, that paean to the Bodhisattva ideal.

Bennett's cloak as the bringer of the Dharma to England fell on Christmas Humphreys (1901–1983).[40] Born to a patrician legal family, he discovered Buddhism at sixteen through reading *Buddha and the Gospel of Buddhism* by Ananda K. Coomaraswamy, and Theosophy while he was an undergraduate at Trinity Hall, Cambridge. In 1923 he met Krishnamurti at the Theosophical Congress in Vienna, and persuaded him to be President of an International Federation of Young Theosophists. The next year, excited by the first publication of the complete *Mahatma Letters to A. P. Sinnett*, Humphreys started a Buddhist Lodge within the London Theosophical Society, which soon separated from the splintering Theosophists to become The Buddhist Society. He rose in his profession of criminal law to become the senior Judge at the Old Bailey, while writing a whole shelf of books about Buddhism. Humphreys showed how an active life in the West was fully compatible with an Eastern philosophy, and also how the severest of professions could be ruled by the doctrine of compassion. Unlike Bennett, who left Theosophy behind him, Humphreys retained a lifelong admiration for Blavatsky and her teachers, and even edited the third edition of the *Mahatma Letters* in 1962.

Humphreys, like his master Suzuki, did not reject the West and its religions, but sought the evidence in them of the experiences that lay closer to the surface in the East. They found these especially in the Romantic poets, and in a few of the less churchly mystics. Jesus' teaching of unconditional love naturally appealed to them, being so close to that of the Mahayana, but the doctrinal structures erected after his death appeared to them a disaster for the Western psyche.

The quotation from Suzuki's early essay, given above, illustrates a further link between East and West, and specifically between Buddhism and the Gnostic theology that informs the Western magical tradition. Suzuki speaks first of the negation of God and of the *atman,* then of the supreme "suchness" experienced in Nirvana as an "Eternal Motherhood" radiating infinite love. Bennett, in his interview with the editor of *Light,* spoke of the gods and of the paranoid delusions they suffer of being eternal and having created the universe. This was pure Gnosticism. There are many Gnostic schools, but their common thesis is that God, as generally worshipped, is an impostor, neither supreme nor eternal: he is the Demiurge who has this world temporarily in thrall. Usually they point to Jahweh, the god of the Hebrews, as an illustration of this entity. Then, if they are Christian Gnostics, they say that Christ was an emissary from a higher plane, come to recall humanity to the *deus absconditus,* the true god whose nature is love. If we substitute for the malign Demiurge the grandiose but deluded inhabitants of the Buddhist heavens, and for the true god Suzuki's "Eternal Motherhood," the similarity is apparent. Then, in parallel with the Buddhist teaching that only the human state offers the chance of enlightenment, there is the Gnostic doctrine of the divine spark from the *deus absconditus* latent in humanity and awakened through *gnosis.*

H. P. Blavatsky was, of course, a Gnostic of this type. Her *Secret Doctrine* was perhaps the most substantial statement of a modern Neognosticism. Her pupil Mead was quick to see the connection. In the second article cited above, he says that Buddhism was from the start a religion of *gnana* or gnosis, using contemplation and yoga rather than prayer. Mead recognized in the boasting Demiurge of Gnosticism the image of the Hindu god Brahma, to whom the enlightened Buddha was superior. That man is essentially higher than the gods seemed to Mead "a doctrine of magnificent hope, only equalled by certain gnosis forms of the early centuries."[41]

The same Gnosticism appears in the Cosmic Philosophy of Max Theon, the man who gave the impulse for starting the H.B. of L. His pupil Mirra Alfassa recalled that:

> to Theon, the God of the Jews and Christians was an Asura. This Asura wanted to be unique; and so he became the most terrible despot imaginable [. . .] Theon always said that the "Serpent" had nothing to do with Satan, it was a symbol of evolution [. . .] and that the earthly paradise was under the dominion of Jehovah, the great Asura who claimed to be unique, who wanted to be the only God. For Theon, there is no such thing as a one and only God: there is the Unthinkable. It's not a "God."[42]

Theon knew, as Mead and Suzuki did, that there is an esoteric Christianity and an esoteric Judaism that both culminate in an "Unthinkable" rather than in a personal god. It is the "Godhead" of Dionysius the Areopagite and of Meister Eckhart, and the "Ain Soph" of the Kabbalah. And for Theon, too, the one definite thing to be said about this Unthinkable was that its influence is experienced as Love.

What distinguishes the occultist from the Zen Buddhist, and from the Hinayanist, is that he is still interested in those ultimately unreal beings who fill the heavens or the "aethyrs." Hence comes the whole apparatus of planetary magic, the summoning of god-forms, etc., that occupied the Golden Dawn and other magicians. It was this that Alan Bennett put behind him when he went to the East. Had he gone to Tibet instead of to Ceylon, he might have encountered a form of Mahayana Buddhism much closer to the magic he had renounced: the esoteric schools of Tantra. The essence of Tibetan Tantric practice is the playing, as it were, with these god-forms who are illusory and known to be so, in order to use them as a springboard to the Unthinkable. Tantrists may be Buddhists, Hindus, or Bön-Pos by religion, but they are all practical occultists.

It seems, in conclusion, that in the early years of the twentieth century there was an emerging common ground between occultism, Buddhism, and the Western Gnostic tradition. East and West had parted, but only on a certain level. The London spiritualists could not stomach Hindu philosophy, nor could the Christian esotericism of a C. G. Harrison be reconciled with the Hinayana Buddhism of an Allan Bennett. But it had always been the intention of the Theosophical Society to overcome the barriers between religions and peoples, indeed "to form a nucleus of the Universal Brotherhood of Humanity, without distinction of race, creed, sex, caste or color."[43] Blavatsky went to the East in 1879, but within seven years she was back in Europe, making every effort to create, in her *Secret Doctrine,* a unitive view of human origins and destiny. Certainly she believed that the West had better look to the East if it wanted to learn what real philosophy was (or to relearn what it once knew). With equal certainty she despised every form of institutional Christianity. As a result, her Society, its members, and its offshoots became the main vehicle for Buddhist and Hindu philosophies to enter the Western consciousness, not merely as an academic study but as something worth embracing. In so doing, they paved the way for both the best and the worst of the oriental gurus who have taken up residence in the West. They introduced into the vernacular such concepts as karma and reincarnation, meditation, and the spiritual path. Together with the Western occult tradition, the Theosophists have provided almost all the underpinnings of the "New Age" movement, their exoteric reflection, in which there is definitely no parting of the hemispheres.

But these efforts themselves are something characteristically Western. Like the efforts of the mythographers treated in the opening chapters, they could never have happened elsewhere. No previous civilization has ever had the interest, the resources, or the inner need to hold the entire world in its intellectual embrace; to take the terrifying step of renouncing, even blaspheming, its own religious tradition, in the quest for a more open and rational view; to publish freely those secrets that were formerly only given under the seal of initiation; and, in short, to plunge humanity into the spiritual alembic in which we find ourselves today.

Appendix A

Transcription of Raja Rammohun Roy's letter to Robert Dale Owen

48 Bedford Square
April 19th 1833

Dear Sir,

Not having been sufficiently fortunate yesterday to find you, or any of your friends, at home, I feel induced to make one or two remarks in writing to which, from what I heard from you on Tuesday night, I think you will agree. They are as follows:—It is not necessary, either in England or in America, to oppose Religion in promoting the social, domestic and political welfare of their Inhabitants, particularly a system of Religion which inculcates the doctrine of universal love and Charity. Did such Philanthropists as Locke & Newton oppose Religion? No! They rather tried to remove the perversions gradually introduced in Religion. Admitting for a moment that the Truths of the Divinity of Religion cannot be established to the satisfaction of a Freethinker, but from an impartial inquiry I presume we may feel persuaded to believe that a system of Religion (Christianity) which consists in Love and Charity is capable of furthering our happiness, facilitating our reciprocal transactions and curbing our obnoxious passions and feelings, I grieve to observe that by opposing Religion your most benevolent Father has hitherto impeded his success. He, I firmly believe, is a follower of Christianity in the above sense though he is not aware of being so. Allow me to send Hamiltons East Indies (1st Vol) in which you will find, page 35 line 3d, that more than two thousand years ago the wise and pious Brahmans of India entertained almost the same opinions which your Father now offers though they by no means were destitute of religion.

My desire to see you and your Father crowned with success in your benevolent undertakings has emboldened me to make these observations;

a freedom which I hope you will, in consideration of my motives, excuse. With my best Compliments to your Father and kind regards for Mrs Owen and Miss Owen I remain with my best wishes for your success Dear Sir,

Yours very faithfully
Rammohun Roy.

P.S. I am now troubled with a strong attack of Influenza, which prevents me from sitting for a few minutes or writing a few lines.

RR

Appendix B

Transcription of Hargrave Jennings's letter to Bulwer-Lytton

London:
36, Gloucester Street,
Warwick Square,
S.W.
July 1st, 1870.

My Lord:—

I am in the present only putting into execution a design which I had formed to myself and a pleasure which I had promised myself now of many years standing—I also add a deep honour.

I cannot hope to recal to your remembrance, for you have doubtless years ago forgotten the circumstance, which was very small as regards yourself although very great as regards me—but I will now with your permission briefly narrate it.

Eight-and-twenty years ago, a very long time ago—a very long time as measured as a period—a very protracted space, (and sometimes very melancholy), as noted and recalled as experience—a very young man who had just given to the world, with the usual thoughts of it, an anonymous first poem—you yourself, my Lord, know well what these feelings are—received from one of the grandest leaders in literature, of whom, by the bye, the young author had the most intense secret admiration evidenced by the first of all flatteries, imitation, the following letter which he copies now, it having been carefully preserved as his highest literary testimonial, (though he has had abundance of these since), and lying before him at this moment.

The subjoined is the letter referred-to.

"Sir Edward Lytton-Bulwer begs to thank the author of 'Astolfo' for the honour and pleasure conferred on him by the present of a poem full of power and beauty, and evincing talents which might probably find yet greater field in subjects of more human interest. Fulham: Friday, May 1842."

I am aware, my Lord, of all your continuous, undaunted, and noble efforts in the cause of literature and in advocacy of the interests of the struggling literary men who endeavour to sustain it; and who in this country—and I suppose it is the same in every other—just as it seems in proportion to their valours, needs and sensibilities suffer, sometimes bitterly, and are made to suffer. In great part this arises from the difficulties of obtaining that adequate money recognition on the part of booksellers and the public and trade—valued that shall ensure them even a livelihood. True literary men, who never were yet found to covet money or to adopt those commercial methods the likeliest to obtain it, form a class which the world does not understand. And the world, naturally inattentive, certainly permits that all the substantial, that is, the permanent rewards of the toil of literary men shall be diverted anywhere than in their own individual, "never-ending, still-beginning" direction. From some such reasons as this forgetfulness and this active selfishness and disregard among the publishers, and from the difficulty which I experience, though I have had a lifetime of literature, journalistic and otherwise, I have failed in securing any other at any time than very fitful and precarious emolument, although I have been very industrious and have had much literary negative success, and have from principle and practice for a lifetime been excessively economical and careful as befitted a man of letters whose wants are, (or ought to be,) very easily and cheaply supplied—leading in truth, the life, (unmarried), of a poor gentleman and scholar, as both which in every respect I hope I may claim to be considered; by birth, by profession and associations for the former; by education and hard study, past and present, for the latter.

My Lord, with every possible respect, and truly with great diffidence and with every expression of admiration for you literary and personal, I have the honour to ask your patronage and to solicit your interest, (if I am found worthy), to assist to procure for me some moderate, modest position or place, where as secretary or librarian, or as some such lettered officer, (for duties resembling which I am very fit), I might serve, if possible, some individual or some society or association, with the same zeal which I have always evinced in business, and with the devotion to their interests which, (though I say it), it is my nature to feel towards those with whom I am brought in contact and for whom I entertain due, dutiful, deserved regard.

The work, "*The Rosicrucians*", which accompanies this letter, and which in addressing the famous author of "*Zanoni*" I need not expatiate upon as entailing great labour and penetration, and unflagging pains, consumed no less than twenty years silent, unsympathised—with attention—gradually piled as it was from book to book, from suspicion to suspicion of truth concerning the subject, from discovery to discovery, from fact to fact, from light to light. And as the end and test I assure you, my Lord, that I could not be prouder of the sympathy and the approval of any man in Europe than of your own, (when I shall boast of such), should patronage be the result of your favourable judgment and recognition of my "*Rosicrucians*".

My work, which was a year carrying through the press, has just been published by Mr. John Camden Hotten of Piccadilly. It is now an accomplished memoir and a justification of those renowned men the Rosicrucians; and this long-appearing book I have now the very great honour, accompanied by a private feeling of delight, to lay before your Lordship, with a hope that it may reach your hands safely and be read by you at your kind leisure and with indulgent interpretations.

My Lord, I beg to remain, with the expression of gratitude for infinite literary enjoyments which the reiterated perusal through a lifetime of your books has afforded me—

Your Lordship's
Most Obedient and Obliged Servant,
Hargrave Jennings$_{x}$

The Right-Honourable
the Lord Lytton,
&c., &c.

Notes

NOTES TO CHAPTER ONE
(THE WORSHIP OF THE GENERATIVE POWERS)

1. A long extract from the diary appeared in Goethe's *Life of Hackert* (*Gedenkausgabe* [Zurich: Artemis Verlag, 1950], XI, 489–525), but the full text was unknown until Claudia Stumpf discovered it in Weimar in 1980; see Knight 1986, 7–8.
2. Beckford's relations with occultism will be treated in Chapter Five.
3. Date given in *Dictionary of National Biography*, s.v. Knight.
4. Knight 1986, 66.
5. Knight 1986, 61.
6. *Collection*, IV, 39n. On D'Hancarville's (and Knight's) influence on British literature, archeology, and orientalism, see Hungerford, 220–221; Mitter, 84–85.
7. Boulanger, II, 20–21.
8. Boulanger, II, 56.
9. On Townley's erotica, see D'Hancarville, I, 82–84.
10. On the Dilettanti, see Towers, 43–51.
11. *Monumens de la vie privée des douze Cesars* (1780), *Monumens du culte secret des dames romaines* (1784), and *Veneres uti observantur in gemmis antiquis* [also titled *Veneres et Priapi*] (1785). All were published with fictitious imprints.
12. *Biographie Universelle*, s.v. Leblond.
13. *Monumens du culte secret*, iv–v.
14. *Monumens du culte secret*, xv.
15. *Monumens du culte secret*, xx.
16. D'Hancarville, I, xxiv.
17. D'Hancarville, I, xiv.
18. D'Hancarville, I, xvi–xvii.
19. D'Hancarville, II, 447–448.
20. Much of the incomplete third volume of d'Hancarville's *Recherches* is a commentary on this.
21. D'Hancarville, I, 60.
22. D'Hancarville, I, 65–66n., gives the source as *An Embassy to the Emperor of Japan*, 274–275.
23. D'Hancarville, I, 67.
24. D'Hancarville, I, 71, 87, 103.

25. D'Hancarville, II, 59.
26. Knight 1974, 27.
27. Knight 1974, 44.
28. Knight 1974, 48.
29. Knight 1974, 15.
30. Knight 1974, 75.
31. Knight 1974, 48.
32. Knight 1974, 43.
33. Knight 1974, 104, citing Herodotus Book II.
34. Knight 1974, 33.
35. Knight 1974, 68.
36. Knight 1974, 68.
37. Knight 1974, 71.
38. Knight 1974, 68–69.
39. Knight 1974, 27.
40. Knight 1974, 109.
41. Knight 1974, 111.
42. Mathias 1808, 67–69n.
43. *Quarterly Review* XV (1815–1816), 534.
44. Knight 1796, 55.
45. Letter of 3 September 1810; British Library, Add. Ms. 43229, f.72.
46. Letter of 15 August 1812; Add. Ms. 43229, f.133.
47. Letter of 3 Sept. 1810; Add. Ms. 43229, f.72–72'.
48. Undated letter (Autumn 1809?); Add. Ms. 43229, f.41.
49. Letter of 28 Sept. 1809; Add. Ms. 43229, f.58'–59.
50. This was intended to be an introduction to the Society of Dilettanti's *Specimens of Antient Sculpture,* but owing to delays in printing, Knight published it first privately, in 1818, and then in separate numbers of *The Classical Journal* from 1821 to 1823. I cite the first public edition in book form, specifying paragraphs to facilitate reference to Alexander Wilder's edition of 1876.
51. Knight 1836, paragraph 6.
52. Knight 1836, paragraph 173.
53. Knight 1836, paragraph 177.
54. Knight 1836, paragraph 77.
55. Knight 1836, paragraph 82.
56. Knight 1836, paragraphs 135, 132.
57. Knight 1836, paragraph 90.
58. Knight 1836, paragraph 65.
59. Knight 1974, 63n.
60. Knight 1836, paragraph 60.
61. Knight 1836, paragraph 62.
62. Knight 1836, paragraph 34.
63. Knight 1836, note to paragraph 85 (deleted in Wilder's edition).
64. Knight 1836, paragraph 231.
65. Knight 1836, paragraph 232.
66. Knight 1836, paragraph 234.

67. Jones, 253.
68. Burrow, 477.
69. Wilford 1792, 365.
70. Moor, 385–390nn.
71. Wilford 1798b, 300.
72. Wilford 1798a, 241.
73. Maurice, II, 156.
74. Maurice, V, 879.
75. Maurice cites as source of this story *Sketches of the Mythology and Customs of the Hindoos*, printed in 1785 but never published. See Maurice, II, 165–166.
76. Wilford 1808, 39–50.
77. O'Brien, xii–xiii.
78. O'Brien, 50–51, 103–105.
79. O'Brien, 109.
80. O'Brien, 110.
81. Charles Vallancey, author of *Collectanea de Rebus Hibernicis* (6 vols., Dublin, 1770–1804), cited in O'Brien, 253.
82. O'Brien, 258.
83. O'Brien, 290–293.
84. O'Brien, 311.
85. O'Brien, 503.
86. O'Brien, 500.
87. Carlile 1845, 96.
88. "Bro. O'Brien" is mentioned in Martin 1860, 301.
89. On the publishing history of Knight's work, see Fraxi, 7–8.
90. On Sellon, see Fraxi, 379–396.
91. Jennings 1884, xxv.
92. Sellon, *Annotations*, 71.
93. Sellon, 27–28n, 66.
94. *BCW*, XIV, 177.
95. Inman's often-reprinted *Ancient Pagan and Modern Christian Symbolism* (London, 1869) contains the essential points of Inman's theory and their illustrations.
96. Inman, I, 89.
97. On Davenport, see Fraxi, 82–88.
98. Jennings 1895, 57.
99. See Andrew Ramsay, "Discourse upon the Theology and Mythology of the Pagans," annexed to *The Travels of Cyrus* (first ed. 1727; reissued Albany: Pratt & Doubleday, 1814).
100. See Blackwell's *Letters concerning Mythology* (London: s.n., 1748).
101. See Bryant's *A New System, or, An Analysis of Ancient Mythology . . .*, 3 vols. (London: T. Payne et al., 1775).
102. See Faber's *The Origins of Pagan Idolatry Ascertained from Historical Testimony and Circumstantial Evidence*, 3 vols. (London: Rivington, 1816).
103. See Leland's *The Advantage and Necessity of the Christian Revelation shewn from the State of Religion in the Ancient Heathen World . . .*, 2 vols. (3rd ed., Glasgow: University Press, 1818).

104. See Landseer's *Sabaean Researches in a Series of Essays, addressed to Distinguished Antiquaries* . . . (London: Hurst Robinson, 1823). The dedicatees include Payne Knight and Sir Joseph Banks.

NOTES TO CHAPTER TWO (THE CULT OF THE SUN)

1. Dupuis 1781, 1–2.
2. Court de Gébelin 1773, 205–226.
3. Dupuis 1781, 72.
4. Dupuis 1781, 79.
5. Dupuis 1781, 89.
6. Boulanger 1770, 206.
7. For the history of the work, see Dupuis 1795, III, 355n; *Nouvelle Biographie Générale*, XV (1856), s.v. Dupuis. References here are to the quarto edition of the *Origine de tous les cultes*.
8. Dupuis 1781, 79–80.
9. Dupuis 1795, I, vii.
10. Dupuis 1795, I, viii.
11. Dupuis 1795, I, ix–x.
12. Dupuis 1795, I, 245.
13. Dupuis 1795, I, 4.
14. Dupuis 1795, I, 43.
15. Dupuis 1795, IIa, 141.
16. Dupuis 1795, IIa, 140.
17. Dupuis 1795, I, 48.
18. Dupuis 1795, IIb, 116.
19. Dupuis 1795, IIb, 123–124.
20. Dupuis 1795, IIb, 5.
21. Dupuis 1795, IIb, 177.
22. Dupuis 1795, IIb, 195–196.
23. Dupuis 1795, III, iii.
24. Dupuis 1795 III, iv.
25. Dupuis 1795, IIb, 166.
26. *Biographie Universelle*, s.v. Dupuis, 322.
27. *Biographie Universelle*, s.v. Dupuis, 319.
28. English extracts include *Was Christ a person or the sun? An argument from Dupuis* . . . (London, 1857); *Christianity a form of the great solar myth* (London, 1873); *On the connection of Christianity with Solar Worship* (trans. T. E. Partridge, London, 1877).
29. *The Ruins, or a Survey of the Revolutions of Empires* (London, 1795).
30. Volney 1890, 153.
31. Volney 1796, 16–23; also in Volney 1890, 179–182.
32. Estlin 1797, 6.
33. Estlin 1797, 37.
34. Estlin 1797, 42.
35. Estlin 1797, 40.

36. Estlin 1797, 48–49.
37. Priestley 1797, Letter II.
38. Priestley 1797, Letter IV.
39. Priestley 1799, 310.
40. Priestley 1799, 291–292.
41. The society included the future Lord Liverpool, George Canning, Lord Henry Spencer, and Robert Montgomery, who records this in Montgomery, 120.
42. *Notes & Queries* VII/xii (5 September 1891), 185–186.
43. For his political views, see Drummond 1795.
44. Drummond 1805, xv.
45. Drummond 1806, 126.
46. Letter of 13 August 1805; British Library, Add. Ms. 43229, f.73'–74.
47. Anonymous 1820.
48. Author of *Oedipus Aegyptiacus* (Rome, 1652–54), to whose title *Oedipus Judaicus* evidently alludes.
49. Madden, I, 96.
50. D'Oyly 1812, 12, 22, 25.
51. D'Oyly 1812, 5.
52. D'Oyly 1812, 16–17.
53. D'Oyly 1812, 26.
54. D'Oyly 1812, 34.
55. Q.R., 24.
56. Vindex, 5.
57. Vindex, 5.
58. Q.R., 21n.
59. Vindex, 3.
60. Vindex, 10.
61. Vindex, 29.
62. Vindex, 8–9.
63. Vindex, 84.
64. Vindex, 93.
65. D'Oyly 1813, 196.
66. Q.R., 28–29.
67. Townsend, 15.
68. Townsend, 20–21.
69. Townsend, 33.
70. Townsend, 39–40.
71. Drummond 1821, 11.
72. Drummond 1821, 34–36.
73. Drummond 1821, 38.
74. Drummond 1824–29, II, 162.
75. Drummond 1824–29, II, 171.
76. Drummond 1824–29, IV, 424-425.
77. Madden, 96–97.
78. Holland, 204–205.
79. Holland, 244.
80. Madden, 97–98.

NOTES TO CHAPTER THREE
(THE BLASPHEMERS)

1. Q.R., 22–23.
2. Paine 1819, 5–6. Ironically enough, Paine's gravestone ended up at Knebworth, Bulwer-Lytton's home. See Escott, 192n.
3. Tomalin, 70.
4. Letter dated 1819; British Library, Add. Ms. 43230, f.332'–333'.
5. Hone, 41.
6. Hone, 43.
7. *Notes & Queries* I, iii (21 June 1851), 508.
8. See the statement of his conversion (written 1834) in Hackwood, 311–317.
9. Carlile, *To the Reformers of Great Britain*, 12.
10. Carlile 1821, 6.
11. Carlile 1821, 9.
12. Carlile, *Every Woman's Book*, 2.
13. Carlile, *Every Woman's Book*, 3.
14. Carlile, *Every Woman's Book*, 5.
15. Carlile, *Every Woman's Book*, 6.
16. Carlile 1831, 9.
17. Fenton, 94.
18. Paine 1819, IV, 47.
19. Carlile 1845, xii.
20. Aldred 1913, 162.
21. Carlile 1845, 92.
22. Owen 1830, 3.
23. Owen 1830, 9.
24. Aldred 1942, 9–10.
25. Aldred 1942, 20.
26. Taylor 1841, 61.
27. Taylor 1857, 224.
28. Taylor 1857, 226–227.
29. For the rumor, see *Notes & Queries* V/vii (17 March 1877), 213; VI/x (13 December 1884), 472; Charles Bradlaugh's reply in VI/xi (24 January 1885), 78.
30. Fox, v.
31. Fox, xii.
32. Fox, xiii.
33. Fox, 47.
34. See Walter, passim.
35. Sangharakshita, 7.
36. Sangharakshita, 8–9.
37. Sangharakshita, 18.
38. Sangharakshita, 19.
39. Sangharakshita, 24.

NOTES TO CHAPTER FOUR
(THE SHOEMAKER AND THE SQUIRE)

1. Mackey 1824a, 25.
2. Mackey 1824a, vi.
3. For a diagram of precession and more on Mackey, see Godwin 1993, 196–202.
4. Mackey 1824b, 28.
5. Mackey 1824b, 8.
6. Mackey 1824a, 45.
7. Mackey 1824a, iii.
8. Mackey 1825, 72.
9. Mackey 1834b, 26.
10. Mackey 1825, 8.
11. Mackey 1826, 3.
12. Mackey 1826, 4.
13. Mackey 1826, 7.
14. Mackey 1826, 4.
15. Mackey 1826, 14.
16. Mackey 1839, 65.
17. Mackey 1834, 22.
18. Biographical information on Da Costa from Waite 1970, I, 167–168.
19. Da Costa 1975, v.
20. Mackey 1826, 43–45.
21. Mackey 1826, 46.
22. Mackey 1826, 48.
23. Mackey 1832, 22–24.
24. Mackey 1832b.
25. *BCW* XIV, 548. This source contains long extracts from the *Notes & Queries* items mentioned below.
26. Mackey 1836, 18.
27. Mackey 1839, 61.
28. *Notes & Queries* I/viii (10 December 1853), 565–567.
29. *Notes & Queries* I/viii (10 December 1853), 566.
30. *Notes & Queries* I/ix (25 February 1854), 179.
31. Mackey 1839, 72.
32. Higgins 1836, I, 636n.
33. Higgins 1829a, 142n.
34. Higgins 1836, I, 816.
35. Higgins 1836, I, 442, 596, 665.
36. Higgins 1836, I, 435–436.
37. Letter of 9 August 1830; British Museum, Add. Ms. 24869, f.116. See also the remark in Higgins 1836, II, 270.
38. Carlile 1845, iii.
39. Katz, 57–69.
40. Higgins 1836, I, 723.
41. Higgins 1836, I, 768. There are many pages on the Culdees in *The Celtic Druids*.
42. Higgins 1836, I, 652–653.

43. Higgins 1836, II, 145.
44. This idea is credited to Sir William Jones in Higgins 1829a, 18.
45. *Southern Review* 7 (August 1829), 1–46.
46. Higgins 1826, 77, 81.
47. Higgins 1826, 43.
48. Higgins 1826, 64.
49. Higgins 1826, 59.
50. Standish, 23.
51. Hughes, 5n.
52. Hughes, 42.
53. Higgins 1833, vii.
54. Higgins 1833, 95n.
55. Higgins 1833, viii.
56. Higgins 1829b, vii.
57. Higgins 1829b, 2.
58. Higgins 1829b, 12.
59. Higgins 1829b, 16–17.
60. Higgins 1829b, 29.
61. Higgins 1829b, 31.
62. Higgins 1829b, 47.
63. Higgins 1829b, 51.
64. Higgins 1829b, 83.
65. Higgins 1829b, 101–103.
66. Higgins 1829b, 107–108.
67. Inchbald, iv.
68. Inchbald, 2n.
69. Inchbald, 58.
70. Wyatt, 9.
71. Beverley, 2.
72. Higgins 1829c, 1.
73. Beverley, 53.
74. Higgins 1836, I, 681n.
75. Higgins 1836, II, 449.

NOTES TO CHAPTER FIVE (MAGICIANS AND REVOLUTIONARIES)

1. Cited from Heisler, 38–39.
2. See the *Jewish Encyclopedia* for an outline of Falk's career, with his portrait by Copley; a lengthier treatment in Roth, 139–164.
3. See Scholem 1974, 310–311.
4. Scholem 1974, 282.
5. For an anecdote concerning Falk and Aaron Goldsmid, see Mackenzie 1987, 213–214; also 626–627.
6. Schuchard 1975.
7. Schuchard 1975, 234.
8. Schuchard 1975, 236–237.

9. Schuchard 1987, 17.
10. Schuchard 1992, 45.
11. Schuchard 1975, 353; 1987, 18.
12. Viatte, I, 204.
13. Schuchard 1987, 18; Viatte, I, 205.
14. See Waite 1970, I, 93–99.
15. Faivre 1969, 212n., quoting a letter of Kirchberger, 1795.
16. Viatte, I, 207.
17. Schuchard 1975, 351–355.
18. Schuchard 1975, 361.
19. See Brodhurst; Paley, 51–70; Oliver, 88n.
20. See de Loutherbourg's *Catalogue*.
21. Viatte, I, 184, quoting from the Comte d'Allonville's *Mémoires secrets de 1770 à 1830* (Paris, 1838), I, 145; also, on Falk's pupils, see Viatte, I, 110–111.
22. Schuchard 1975, 328, citing the *Jewish Encyclopedia*, s.v. Falk.
23. *Arcana coelestia*, n.5110, cited from Swedenborg 1896, 40.
24. Hindmarsh 1790, 269, 272, 306.
25. Hindmarsh 1816–17, 189.
26. Hindmarsh 1818–19, 312.
27. Hindmarsh 1818–19, 314.
28. Schuchard 1975, 318.
29. Schuchard 1975, 256.
30. Quoted from Schuchard 1992, 42.
31. Schuchard 1992, 42–43.
32. On Rainsford, see McLean 1990.
33. See his statement of belief in McLean 1990, 134.
34. "Obituary of Manoah Sibly," in *New Jerusalem Magazine* (Boston) XIV (1841), 310–314; "Memoir of Manoah Sibly," in *New Jerusalem Magazine and Theological Inspector* (London) I (1826), 1–3.
35. Debus, 278. See also Curry, 134–137, for another appreciation of E. Sibly.
36. Howe 1967, 25.
37. *The Astrologer's Magazine* ran from August 1793 to January 1794, as a continuation of *The Conjurer's Magazine* (1791–1792), which I have not seen, the British Library's copies having been destroyed in the war or lost.
38. *The Astrologers' Magazine* I (1793), 20.
39. Sibly 1807, 1082.
40. Sibly 1807, 1088–1089.
41. Sibly 1807, 1101–1102.
42. Sibly 1807, 1121–1125.
43. Sibly 1807, 1117.
44. Sibly 1814, 12.
45. Sibly 1814, 27.
46. Sibly 1814, 76–77.
47. Sibly 1814, 152.
48. Sibly 1814, 304–305.
49. Sibly 1824, part 1.
50. One such landscape is illustrated in Lister, pl.2.

51. Oliver, 88–92.
52. Chapman, 189.
53. The quotations that follow are from Beckford's undated letter to Louisa, printed in Oliver, 173–181.
54. Oliver, 181. Oliver follows this with the French text of the Orleans story, as told by Jean-Louis Soulavie in 1801.

NOTES TO CHAPTER SIX (NEOPHYTES AND INITIATES)

1. Wordsworth, *The Prelude*, Book XI.
2. I rely on Howe 1967, 23, for the description of the issues of 1791–1792.
3. See Howe 1967, 24.
4. See Raine 1968, I, 388n., for reference to a theory that Barrett was the editor of the *Conjurer's Magazine*.
5. Barrett, II, 140.
6. Wellcome Institute, Ms. 1073.
7. Wellcome Institute, Ms. 1073, f.3–3'.
8. See Hamill, 20–21.
9. Schuchard 1975, 436–437, 493–494.
10. For Bacstrom's charter, see Waite 1960, 284–287. For Tilloch's charter, see McLean 1979, 25–29. The charter is analyzed in Waite 1924, 549–560.
11. Hogart, 234.
12. Waite 1924, 555.
13. Waite 1924, 563.
14. Higgins 1836, II, 301.
15. McIntosh 1992, 97.
16. Katz, 36–37.
17. Galtier, 174.
18. Galtier, 177.
19. Katz, 61–62.
20. McIntosh 1992, 176–177.
21. McIntosh 1992, 175.
22. Westcott 1966, 4–5.
23. Bulwer-Lytton changed his name and style several times. Born plain Edward Bulwer, he was made a baronet (Sir Edward Bulwer, Bart.) in 1838, then in 1843, when he inherited his mother's estate at Knebworth, added her name (Sir E. Bulwer-Lytton, Bart.). In 1866 he was created Baron Lytton of Knebworth. His son Robert was the first Earl of Lytton.
24. Galtier, 175, 177.
25. See McIntosh 1980, 124–125.
26. On *Zanoni*, see Wolff, 159–232.
27. Escott, 253.
28. Lytton, *Zanoni*, 93.
29. Lytton, *Zanoni*, 176.
30. Lytton, *Zanoni*, 87–88.

31. Lytton, *Zanoni*, 228.
32. Cited in *Light* IV (5 January 1884), 4–5.
33. Lytton, *Zanoni*, 301.
34. Lytton, *Zanoni*, 79n.
35. Lytton, *Zanoni*, 392.
36. Lytton, *Zanoni*, 250–251.
37. Lytton, *Zanoni*, 329: "It is only the dead who never return."
38. Quoted in Campbell, 2.
39. Lytton's annotations to Townshend's letters, in the Hertfordshire County Record Office, D/EK.C.1.
40. From "Irregular Lines," in Bulwer 1820.
41. Cited in Schuchard 1975, 526.
42. Information from Miss Sybilla Jane Flower, Lytton's biographer.
43. Anonymous 1841.

NOTES TO CHAPTER SEVEN (ARTISTS AND ASTROLOGERS)

1. See Schuchard 1975 for some painters not mentioned here: Francesco Bartholozzi (310), Thomas Stothard (323–324), George Cumberland (325–326), William Sharp (412–413), John Martin (535–536), John Ruskin (549–550).
2. Blake, 551.
3. Irwin, 22, 51.
4. See Paley, 65–67, with illustrations.
5. The illustration of the Eidophysikon, by Edward Francis Burney, is shown in Lister, pl.28, together with an account of the sound effects. The title of the image is from Cannon-Brookes, 19. Another item in the Eidophysikon was "The Cataract of Niagara."
6. On Cosway, see Daniell.
7. Schuchard 1975, 326–327.
8. On Graham, see Schuchard 1975, 333–336.
9. *The Spiritualist* XIII (1878), 280.
10. Raphael 1825b, 210n., 215, 232, 240; Schuchard 1975, 387.
11. Binns, 477.
12. Information from Dr. Stephen Lloyd, who is preparing a catalogue of Cosway's sale.
13. See Scholem 1971, 131–133; 1974, 287–309.
14. Scholem 1974, 293–294.
15. On Palmer and the Irvingites, see Lister, 87, 91; Cecil, 53.
16. Schuchard 1975, 501–504.
17. Sketchbook in British Museum. Quoted from Peacock, 129; illustration, 31.
18. Bury, 33.
19. See *Prospects* . . .
20. Schuchard 1975, 490.
21. See Varley for full title.
22. Prospectus, quoted from Bury, 60.
23. Varley, 45–47n.

24. *Mentor Stellarum* seems to have appeared during 1813; I have seen only a collection, paginated 1–140, bound with its evident continuation: *The Monthly Correspondent*, dated January through August 1814.
25. *Monthly Correspondent* I/5 (1814), 187.
26. *Monthly Correspondent* I/7 (1814), 283.
27. Ms. note in Corfield's hand in British Library copy of *Antijacobin Review*, 90.
28. *Antijacobin Review*, 92.
29. Ms. note in British Library copy of *Antijacobin Review*, 52; see Howe 1967, 25–26.
30. Ms. note in British Library copy of *Urania*, iv.
31. J. Corfield, *Eccentricities, Maxims, Reflections, Anecdotes, etc.* (1825), Ms. in British Library, 10163 ee 37.
32. See Wilson 1819; Ptolemy.
33. Ptolemy, xi–xii.
34. Wilson 1819, xx.
35. Oxley 1830, 178.
36. Oxley 1848, note at end.
37. Oxley 1830, 183.
38. See Raphael 1825b, 461.
39. See under Kirchenhoffer.
40. *The Straggling Astrologer* 9 (31 July 1824), 144.
41. *The Straggling Astrologer* 2 (12 June 1824), 30.
42. Raphael 1825a, 71.
43. Howe 1964, 30.
44. *The Straggling Astrologer* 14 (4 Sept. 1824), 218.
45. Cecil, 54.
46. Raphael 1825b, 190.
47. *The Straggling Astrologer* 17 (25 Sept. 1824), 263.
48. Raphael 1825b, 243.
49. See Howe 1964, 13, and many references to Graham in Schuchard 1975. Howe 1964, 16, says that Zadkiel–Morrison was a Mercurius, but I think it was more likely Zadkiel–Palmer (see below).
50. Raphael 1825b, 228n.
51. Raphael 1830, 8.
52. Raphael 1830, 9.
53. Wellcome Institute Library, Ms. 4639.
54. Raphael 1831, 490–498, 632–638.
55. Raphael 1834, vii.
56. See Howe 1967, 32.
57. Bulwer-Lytton seems to refer to this substance in Chapters 82 and 83 of *A Strange Story*.

NOTES TO CHAPTER EIGHT (ANIMAL MAGNETISM)

1. Mesmer, 14. The definitive work on the subject of this chapter appeared too late for me to make full use of it: Alan Gauld, *A History of Hypnotism* (Cambridge University Press, 1992).

2. Bell, title page.
3. Martin 1790, 5; 1791, 5.
4. Schuchard 1975, 334.
5. Martin 1791, 7. Other sources give the date as 1788.
6. Martin, *Wonders*, 8.
7. Winter, 17.
8. Winter, 15.
9. Schuchard 1975, 333.
10. Bell, 57.
11. Podmore 1963a, 85.
12. Franz von Baader, *Ueber die Extase oder das Versücktseyn der magnetischen Schlafredner* (Leipzig: Reclam, 1817), quoted in *Archiv für den thierischen Magnetismus* (Altenburg and Leipzig) I/3 (1817), 114–118.
13. *Archiv für den thierischen Magnetismus* I/3 (1817), 119–120.
14. *Archiv für den thierischen Magnetismus* VI/3 (1820), 170ff.
15. Dupotet, 321n.
16. Goldsmith, 193–194.
17. Colquhoun 1833.
18. On Chenevix, see Lang, 6.
19. Dupotet, 322–323.
20. Goldsmith, 194–195.
21. Sandby, 89.
22. Podmore 1963a, 124–125.
23. Colquhoun 1833, 88–89, quoting Kluge's *Versuch einer Darstellung des Animalischen Magnetismus* (1815).
24. Colquhoun 1833, 104.
25. Colquhoun, I, 101.
26. Ms. note on Townshend's letters to Bulwer-Lytton, Hertfordshire County Record Office, D/EK C.1.
27. Townshend, viii, 4.
28. Letter of 29 February 1840, in Hertfordshire County Record Office, D/EK C.6.
29. Dupotet, iii.
30. Dupotet, 17–18.
31. Elliotson 1832, title page.
32. Dupotet, *Introduction*, p.327.
33. Podmore 1963a, 127–128.
34. Podmore 1963a, 128.
35. *Zoist* I (1843), 24–25.
36. Elliotson 4–5.
37. *Zoist* III (1845), 75–76.
38. *Zoist* III (1845), 152–154.
39. *Zoist* I (1843), 51–52.
40. Podmore 1963a, 139–140.
41. *Zoist* VI (1848), 113.
42. *Zoist* V (1847), 44.
43. Podmore 1963a, 172.
44. Letter from Townshend to Elliotson, 25 November 1851, in *Zoist* IX (1852), 402–414.

45. Podmore 1963a, 173.
46. Gauld, 240.
47. Jung-Stilling, 45.
48. Jung-Stilling, 63.
48. Jung-Stilling, 44.
50. Podmore 1963a, 99–109.
51. On Lord Stanhope, see Newman, 223–249, and Mayer.
52. *Zoist* XIII (1855), 107.
53. *Zoist* X (1852), 194.
54. Earl of Stanhope's Appendix to Edward Binns, *The Anatomy of Sleep* (London: John Churchill, 1845), 477.
55. Earl Stanhope, *Letter on the proposed alteration of the Corn Laws* (1827), quoted in Barnes, 211.
56. Letter of 4 December 1843, in *Zoist* II (1843), 80.
57. Summarized from Stanhope 1836.
58. Sandby, 92.
59. Summarized from Daumer.
60. Steiner's statements, scattered in his lectures, have been collected and summarized by Paul M. Allen in his (unpaginated) Foreword to Wassermann.
61. Kaspar's likeness to the Grand Duke Karl (portraits in Mayer 482–483) is very persuasive.
62. See genealogies in Mayer, 635, 636, 638.
63. Quoted in Allen, Foreword to Wassermann.
64. Allen, Foreword to Wassermann.
65. Steiner, *Things in the Past and Present in Human History*, cited from Christopher Bamford's notes in Harrison 1993, 201.

NOTES TO CHAPTER NINE
(VISIONS IN THE CRYSTAL)

1. The best all-round guide is still Besterman 1924.
2. Ms. Harley 6482. See McLean 1990b, 20–21.
3. Raphael 1831, 33–44.
4. "Crystal-seeing in Lancashire," in *Spiritual Magazine* N.S., I (1866), 516–522.
5. "Of the making of the Crystal and the Form of Preparation for a Vision," in Barrett 135–139; illustration, 128.
6. On Hockley, see Hamill 1986.
7. Anonymous 1896, 106.
8. These details are from Hamill 1986, 11–13.
9. See R.A.Gilbert's list in Hamill 1986, 30–32.
10. See Hogart, 226–234.
11. Information in this paragraph is from Hockley 1849.
12. Hockley 1850, 60; see Hamill 1986, 200–216.
13. Anonymous 1896, 102.
14. Hockley's Crystal Ms., vol. 6, 124–126, transcribed from the copy in Irwin's *Rosicrucian Miscellanea,* Grand Lodge Library, Freemasons' Hall, London.
15. See especially *ML* 1924, 22 (letter VI).

16. See Hockley's obituary in *Light* V (1885), 585.
17. Hamill 1986, 36.
18. Letter to Bulwer-Lytton, 21 July 1853; Hertfordshire County Record Office, D/EK C.19.100.
19. Dialectical Society Report, 184–185.
20. Schuchard 1975, 541–542.
21. Schuchard 1975, 543.
22. Anonymous 1896, 107.
23. See Hamill 1986, 145–183.
24. From *Rosicrucian Miscellanea,* ff. 273–274.
25. See Longford, 418–427.
26. Godwin 1992a.
27. Anonymous 1896, 101.
28. On Morrison, see Howe 1967, 33–47.
29. Howe 1967, 34–35.
30. Morrison 1871.
31. See Morrison 1868.
32. Zadkiel 1842, 16–22. From this book, it appears that Morrison had read, but does not mention, Samson Mackey.
33. "Mesmerism," in *Zadkiel's Almanac, or Herald of Astrology* for 1845, 42–48.
34. "An Account of Visions seen in Lady Blessington's Crystal," in *Zadkiel's Almanac* for 1851, 47–64.
35. *Zadkiel's Almanac* for 1851, 55–56.
36. Bury, 58.
37. Sadleir, 268.
38. See the Gore House Sale catalogue by Phillips, 7 May 1849. There are no occult or philosophical works among the many books, and no crystals are mentioned. Perhaps they were sold privately.
39. Ms. note on Lady Blessington's letters to Bulwer-Lytton, in Hertfordshire County Record Office, D/EK C.26.
40. Sadleir, 261.
41. Madden, II, 197.
42. *Zadkiel's Almanac* for 1851, 46.
43. Bulwer-Lytton's Ms. note, on D'Orsay's letters in the Hertfordshire County Record Office, D/EK C.9.
44. Sadleir, 272; Madden, II, 194–195.
45. Letter appended to John Elliotson, "Triumph and Reward of Dr. Esdaile," in *Zoist* VI (1848), 113ff.
46. Lane, I, 414n.
47. Lane, I, 417.
48. Thomas, 105–106.
49. Besterman 1924, 160.
50. Gregory, 355.
51. Besterman 1924, 20.
52. Gregory, 370–371.
53. Copyist's transcript sent to Bulwer-Lytton, in Hertfordshire County Record Office, D/EK C.19.98. Published by permission.

54. Letter from Lord Stanhope to Bulwer-Lytton, 29 June 1853; in Hertfordshire County Record Office, D/EK C.19.97.
55. Letter from Lord Stanhope to Bulwer-Lytton, 19 July 1853, in Hertfordshire County Record Office, D/EK C.19.99.
56. Mackenzie 1878.
57. Mackenzie alludes here to *Dr. Rudd's Nine Hierarchies of Angels. How to bring a visible appearance of them into a Beryll Glass, &c.* Hockley's 1834 transcription of a copy lent him by George Graham, which had been bought at the Cosway sale, is in Cambridge University Library, Psychical Research Society collection, Z 1834.11. The text is contained in McLean 1990b, 173–225.
58. Mackenzie 1878, 312.
59. Mackenzie 1878, 312.

NOTES TO CHAPTER TEN (HYDESVILLE AND AFTER)

1. Often drawing on the classic account in Hardinge Britten, 27–42. See also Ernest Isaacs, "The Fox Sisters and American Spiritualism," in Kerr and Crow, 79–110.
2. See Sprigg and Larkin, 249–150.
3. Podmore 1963b, I, 81–91.
4. Hardinge Britten 1970, 39.
5. For a thorough treatment of spiritualism from a sociological approach, see Braude; Owen 1990. As an objective history, Oppenheim's book is unequalled.
6. On Mrs. Hayden, see Podmore 1963b, II, 4–7.
7. See Hamill 1986, 145–183.
8. On Owen's spiritualism, see Podmore 1923, 604–614.
9. *The Rational Review* 4 (1853), 199, 246.
10. *The Spiritual Telegraph* N.S. III (1853), 34–39.
11. *The Spiritual Telegraph* N.S. VI (1854), 139; confirmed in Ashburner, 317.
12. Elliotson, "The Departed Spirits," in *Zoist* XI (1853), 191–201.
13. J. W. Jackson, "Table-moving, Rappings, and Spiritual Manifestations," in *Zoist* XI (1854), 422.
14. Obituary of Elliotson in *Spiritual Magazine* N.S. III (1868), 475–476; see also Hardinge Britten 1884, 135.
15. On Home, see Podmore 1963b, II, 223–243.
16. See Hardinge Britten 1884, 139–142; Podmore 1963b, II, 142–144.
17. Lytton is mentioned as one of those who has investigated Mrs. Hayden in "W.R.H.," "The Manifestations in England," in Brittan 1853, 19. W.R.H's. letter is dated 4 February 1853.
18. Letter of 21 July 1853, in Hertfordshire County Record Office, D/EK C.19.100.
19. Letter to Bulwer-Lytton, 25 July 1853; in Hertfordshire County Record Office, D/EK C.19.101.
20. Letter of 8 December 1853, in Hertfordshire County Record Office, D/EK C.7.160.
21. Wolff, 263. This remains the best study of Bulwer-Lytton as occultist.
22. Lytton 1925, 67–9.
23. *The Spiritual Telegraph* III (1853), 446.

24. Elliotson, "On Medical Anti-Mesmerists," in *Zoist* VII (January 1850), 382–383nn. The whole letter is given in Wolff, 237.
25. Howe 1967, 42.
26. Cooke, 60.
27. Howe 1967, 45–46; Schuchard 1975, 545.
28. B. Coleman, "The Rt. Hon. Lord Lytton upon Spiritualism," in *The Spiritual Magazine* N.S. II (1867), 541–543.
29. Dialectical Society Report, 240–241.
30. *The Spiritual Magazine* VIII (1873), 130.
31. Olcott 1972, 453–454.
32. See Christopher Bamford's exhaustive Introduction to Harrison 1993, 7–59.
33. Harrison 1993, 85.
34. The only reviews I have seen were an incredulous one by A. E. Waite in *The Unknown World* I (November 1894), 174. and a very negative one in *Light* 16 (10 October 1896).
35. Sinnett 1895. Godwin 1990–91, 40–41, gives additional material from later Theosophists.
36. Sinnett 1895, 15–16.
37. Sinnett 1896, 437.
38. *ML*, 209–210 (Letter XXVIII).
39. Blavatsky 1877, II, 403.
40. Blavatsky 1877, II, 306–308.
41. Léclaireur, 319. Another French adherent of the provocation theory was Papus; see a summary of his views, without references, in Vulliaud, 110–11.
42. Mani, 26 October 1911, 461.
43. Harrison 1993, 85.
44. Guénon 1982, 23.
45. Guénon 1952, 20.
46. Guénon 1952, 27.
47. Introduction to Hardinge Britten 1970, xvii.
48. Guénon 1982, 95; 1952, 20.
49. The posthumous *Autobiography* (Hardinge Britten 1900) is mainly about Emma's travels as a medium, and tells virtually nothing of her private life or background.
50. Hardinge Britten 1900, 5.
51. I learned this in London, 1989, in conversation with the late Mr. Mostyn Gilbert, Dingwall's fellow psychical researcher.
52. See Podmore 1965b, II, 5, 20–21.
53. Hardinge Britten 1900, 9.
54. Hardinge Britten 1970, 254.
55. Hardinge Britten 1900, 101–102.
56. Hardinge Britten 1860, 21.
57. Hardinge Britten 1860, 24.
58. Hardinge Britten 1860, 26.
59. Hardinge Britten 1860, 61.
60. Hardinge Britten 1860 116.

NOTES TO CHAPTER ELEVEN (FROM THE ORPHIC CIRCLE TO THE GOLDEN DAWN)

1. Dialectical Society Report, 111.
2. Hardinge Britten 1870, 564. I think he may have been the Hon. Roden Noel, who also supplied Robert Dale Owen with information on the Cambridge "Ghost Club." See Owen 1860, 33–34n.
3. Welton, 5.
4. See Caithness 1876, 131.
5. These comprise most of the first six chapters of *Ghost Land.*
6. *The Western Star* I (1 July 1872), 53–54.
7. Letter to *Light* IX (10 August 1889), 383.
8. *ODL* I, 193; photograph opposite 198.
9. Introduction to Hardinge Britten 1970, xvi.
10. See *ODL* I, 147–184.
11. Calculated from the two dated events mentioned in Louis' autobiography: the Hydesville phenomena of 1848, and the Sepoy Mutiny of 1857.
12. *Ghost Land* 19. In the *Western Star* version, Austria's father works in Bombay for the East India Company. *Western Star* I (1872), 62.
13. *Ghost Land*, 33.
14. *Ghost Land*, 34.
15. *Ghost Land*, 22–23.
16. *Ghost Land*, 39–40.
17. *Ghost Land*, 88.
18. *Ghost Land*, 100.
19. *Ghost Land*, 258.
20. *Ghost Land*, 101.
21. Hardinge Britten 1900, 4.
22. Sirius, "Occultism Defined," in *The Two Worlds* I/1 (18 November 1887), 3–4. I am grateful to Christian Chanel for bringing this article to my attention.
23. "Occultism in England" [= extract from *Ghost Land*], in *Two Worlds* I (1888), 422.
24. On Mackenzie, see Howe 1972 and the introduction by R.A. Gilbert and John Hamill to Mackenzie 1987.
25. Cooke 1863, 274.
26. F.H., "Spirit, Who art thou, and Where?" in *Biological Review* 1 (October 1858), 15–18.
27. *Biological Review* 2 (November 1858), 36.
28. Morrison, "The Hindu Gods," in *Biological Review* 3 (December 1858), 84–94. Quotation from 91.
29. Mackenzie 1987, 253, s.v. Globes.
30. S.J., "What is the light within us?" in *Biological Review* 2 (December 1858), 39–41. Quotation from 40–41.
31. See Mackenzie's farewell to S.J. in *Biological Review* 4 (January 1859), 144.
32. See Levi 1991, 121–123.
33. Text in *The Rosicrucian* II/20 (May 1873), 27–34; also in McIntosh 1972, 117–123.
34. Mackenzie, "Spiritualism in Paris," in *The Spiritual Magazine* III (February 1862), 94–95.

35. Personal communication, 27 August 1993. I am grateful for permission to give these details from Mr. Parisious's unpublished researches.
36. See Howe 1972a, 251n, 255n.
37. Westcott 1900, 6.
38. See McIntosh 1980, 110.
39. Westcott 1900, 7.
40. Westcott 1900, 33.
41. I am grateful to Mr. Nicolas Tereshchenko for drawing my attention to the "Secretary-General's Report" in which this is stated.
42. *The Rosicrucian* 14 (October 1871), 181.
43. Information from Mr. Tereshchenko.
44. Yarker's letters to Lytton and the "Obligatory Meeting" summons are in the Hertfordshire County Record Office, file D/EK, under "Rosicrucian Society."
45. The reference is probably to Yarker, 84n. Yarker added that he was sending Bulwer-Lytton a copy of his book.
46. Westcott 1900, 15ff.
47. See Levi 1991, 186.
48. Howe 1972a, 264n.
49. Westcott 1900, 8–9.
50. See *Zadkiel's Almanac* from 1844 onwards.
51. E.g., *Two Narratives illustrative of magical and Cabbalistic Science*, Ms. in the hand of Mackenzie, dated 1863, in Warburg Institute Library.
52. Francis Irwin had a special swastika bookplate made in commemoration of his son Herbert, who died in 1879. An example is in Irwin's *Crystal MSS* in the Warburg Institute Library.
53. E.g., Irwin's bound volumes of *Light* in the University of London, Senate House (Harry Price Library). See Hamill 1986, 62–63.
54. Mackenzie 1987, s.v. "Suastica, Most Ancient Order of, or Brotherhood of the Mystic Cross."
55. See Hamill 1986, 22f; Howe 1972, 257–260.
56. Howe 1972a, 260.
57. Irwin's *Crystal MSS*, part 3, f.5.
58. Howe 1972a, 259, from Ms. in Grand Lodge Library.
59. Howe 1972a, 258–259.
60. Hamill 1986, 23.
61. Mackenzie 1987, 453.
62. Krezulesco-Quaranta, 47–48.
63. *Ghost Land*, 88.
64. Hamill 1986, 16.
65. Howe 1972a, 259.
66. Howe 1972a, 272, says that the "prospective members" in August 1883 were Irwin, Yarker, Ayton, and Holland. See also Howe 1972b, 31. Ms. Geraldine Beskin, curator of the Yarker Library, named the members (in order) as Holland, Mackenzie, Yarker, Irwin, Hockley, Cox, Westcott, and Mathers, in her lecture at the Theosophical History Conference, London, 1989.
67. Howe 1972b, 39n.

68. Gilbert 1983b, 8.
69. Information from the Yarker Library, thanks to Roger Parisious.
70. Gilbert 1983a, 25.
71. Mackenzie 1987, 627.
72. Information given out at the Theosophical History Conference, London, 1989.
73. Howe 1972, 8–9.
74. Information kindly provided by Mr. Tereschchenko, who is preparing a manuscript on the subject.
75. See Gilbert 1983a, 35–37. On the nature of such initiation, see Tereshchenko, 79–86.
76. See Colquhoun, 32–39, for a sympathetic account of the process.

NOTES TO CHAPTER TWELVE (THE WAY TO CHRIST)

1. See bibliography under Neander.
2. For a fuller version of this chapter, see Godwin 1992b.
3. Greaves 1845, II, 11.
4. Pestalozzi, 165.
5. Pestalozzi, 176.
6. Greaves 1845, II, 9.
7. Greaves 1845, I, xiii.
8. Greaves 1845, II, 231.
9. Greaves 1847, 56.
10. Greaves 1845, II, 216.
11. Greaves 1845, II, 144.
12. Greaves 1845, I, iv–v.
13. Greaves 1845, I, 32f.
14. *Contrasting Magazine* XVII (22 September 1827), 133.
15. Greaves 1847, 88–89.
16. Steiger, 234.
17. Steiger, 120, 190.
18. Published under the Greek name "Thuos Mathos": an anagram.
19. W. H. Wilmshurst attributes the whole book to her in his Introduction to South, 1960, (4).
20. South 1846, 42.
21. South 1846, 27, 3.
22. South 1846, 49.
23. In G. R. S. Mead's magazine *The Quest* 10/2 (1919), 213–225.
24. South 1960.
25. South 1960, (6).
26. All letters quoted in this chapter are in Dr. Williams's Library, London.
27. Letter of 27 November [1848?].
28. Letter of 4 January [1853?].
29. Letter of 19 September [1853?].
30. Letter of 3 November 1874.
31. Walton, vi.
32. Walton, xx.
33. Walton, i.

34. Biographical note by C. C. Massey in Penny 1912.
35. Steiger, 234.
36. Letter to Walton, 27 October 1865.
37. See Saint-Martin in the Bibliography. Penny also translated Saint-Martin's *Man: his true nature and ministry* (London, 1864).
38. Letter of 19 May 1863.
39. Letter of 24 May 1863.
40. Letter of 21 September 1865.
41. Letter of 2 September 1866.
42. Steiger, *Memorabilia*, 188.
43. On Levi's openness to visitors, see McIntosh 1972, 134.
44. For Mackenzie's account, see McIntosh 1972, 117–122.
45. Letter of 9 June 1867.
46. "Böhme and Swedenborg." *Light* I (18 June 1881), 186–187.
47. Letter on "Emanations of the World Soul." *Light* I (10 December 1881), 399.
48. "Communicating Spirits. Their claims to recognition." *Light* II (21 January 1882), 27–29.
49. "Communicating Spirits." *Light* II (18 February 1882), 75.
50. "Vicarious Suffering." *Light* II (17 June 1882), 286.
51. "Esoteric Views of Church Doctrine." *Light* II (29 July 1882), 355.
52. "Communicating Spirits." *Light* II (21 January 1882), 27–29.
53. Letter on Reincarnation. *Light* VII (15 January 1887), 32.
54. "Have animals souls?" *Light* VII (19 March 1887), 128–129.
55. Letter on Baader's Theory of Sacrifice. *Light* VII (11 June 1887), 261.
56. "Dissolving views." *Light* VII (29 October 1887), 518–520.
57. "Blood Sacrifices." *Light* IX (23 March 1889), 140; 6 April, 168–169; 15 June, 290; 6 July, 324.
58. Massey's obituary of her appeared in *Light* XIII (30 December 1893), 618, and was reprinted in Penny 1912, xxi–xxvi.
59. Vaughan, I, xix.
60. Steiger, 191–193.
61. Steiger, 195.
62. Steiger, 252–254, confirmed in Sinnett 1986, 38.
63. Not to be confused with his contemporary Gerald Massey, the mythographer, to whom he was unrelated.
64. Massey 1909, 114.
65. Massey 1909, 17.
66. Steiger, 253.
67. Massey 1909, 66.

NOTES TO CHAPTER THIRTEEN (ROSICRUCIAN PRETENDERS)

1. The *National Union Catalogue* gives the year of Randolph's death as 1874, probably misled by Clymer. The correct date is 29 July 1875; the place, Toledo, Ohio; the coroner's verdict, suicide. See his obituary in *The Spiritual Magazine*, 3rd Series, I (1875), 474–475.
2. Randolph 1872, 18.

3. Randolph 1872, 19, says from age 12 to 20; the same work, 4, says from 15 to 20.
4. Randolph 1872, 19.
5. Randolph 1932, 165–166.
6. Barber: Randolph 1871a, 121; physician: 1860, 63; orations: 1932, 88; Reformatory Party: 1872, 8.
7. Letter of 1 January 1853, in *The Spiritual Telegraph* I (1853), 421–422.
8. "From one of the Ancients," letter dated 24 June 1853, in *The Spiritual Telegraph* I, (1853), 333–335.
9. Letter of 21 July 1853, in *The Spiritual Telegraph* II (1853), 20–22. Quotation from 20.
10. Randolph 1860, 50.
11. "Harmonial Convention," in *The Spiritual Telegraph* IV (1854), 49–58.
12. "Clairvoyance and Psychometry," in *The Spiritual Telegraph* VI (1854), 54.
13. *The Spiritual Telegraph* VI (1855), 95–96.
14. Clymer gives the name as Fontaine. Clymer 1949, III, 192.
15. *The Spiritual Telegraph* VI (1855), 54.
16. Many are collected in Randolph 1872.
17. Randolph 1892, 8.
18. Compare the extracts from Randolph 1872 in Clymer 1949, III, 174–192, with the original.
19. Clymer 1949, III, 190–191.
20. Randolph 1939, 21.
21. See Podmore 1963b, II, 22–23.
22. Randolph 1939, 113. On Bielfeld, see Welton, 62.
23. Randolph mentions that at the time of his Paris séances, Home was still staying in Cox's Hotel in London, which dates them to the spring or summer of 1855. See Randolph 1939, 114.
24. Randolph 1939, 259–263.
25. "Mr Randolph's Visit to England," in *Yorkshire Spiritual Telegraph* 17 (August 1856), 211–212.
26. "Mr Randolph's Visit," p.212, says he is expected to be in London by October 15, or perhaps a month earlier, and gives a *poste restante* address in Great Portland Street.
27. Podmore 1963b, II, 26.
28. Obituary of Randolph in *The Spiritual Magazine* 3rd Series, I (1875), 474–475.
29. Randolph 1867, 36–37.
30. Randolph 1867, 48.
31. After the present book was completed, Mr. Deveney kindly showed me a draft of his forthcoming biography of Randolph, enabling me to correct several statements in this chapter.
32. Randolph 1860, 57–58.
33. Clymer (Randolph 1939, 170n.) places Randolph's second journey to London, Paris and the Orient in the spring of 1858. Randolph 1872, 74, claims three years' absence from America, beginning in 1857. This cannot be true; see next paragraph.
34. Randolph 1860, 32, 56; 1871b, 102–103.
35. Hardinge Britten 1970, 242–243.
36. The book published as Randolph's *Magia Sexualis* or *Sexual Magic* is a misleading compilation by Maria de Naglowska.

37. Randolph 1871b, 36, gives Cora's age in 1861 as six; in 1872, 3, his daughter is about 15.
38. Randolph 1871b, 43.
39. Randolph 1888, 113.
40. Randolph 1888, 162.
41. Randolph 1888, 67.
42. Sandburg, III, 263.
43. Letter of 14 October in Boston Public Library, Ms. A.1.2. vo.34, 88.
44. Randolph 1872, 19, 51.
45. Randolph 1867, 2.
46. Mary Jane returns to the *Utica City Directory* in 1867–68, after two years (1864–65, 1865–66) in which neither Randolph is listed. Perhaps she was in Louisiana with him. She is styled "widow" in 1868–69 and 1869–70, then disappears.
47. Randolph 1872, 67.
48. Randolph, *Mediumism*, 18.
49. Randolph, *Mediumism*, 4.
50. See biographical note in Randolph 1939, 267n.
51. This is Mr. Deveney's conclusion, to which his forthcoming biography of Randolph will supply supporting evidence and arguments.
52. "Pioneer Rosicrucian Workers in America, Number One. Pascal Beverly Randolph," in *Mercury* 2/4 (19 February 1917), [2].
53. Randolph 1872, 73.
54. The preceding sentence is omitted from Clymer's edition of *Eulis*; see Randolph 1978, 56.
55. Randolph 1874, 47.
56. Randolph 1874, 48.
57. Randolph 1874, 169n, 221n.
58. Randolph 1874, 218.
59. Randolph 1874, 48.
60. Randolph, *Mediumism*, 5, 18, 36.
61. Randolph 1874, 219–220; 1861–62, 77.
62. Randolph, *Mediumism*, 5; 1892, 69–70.
63. Unpublished, but circulated in manuscript by Randolph and later by the H.B. of L. See Chanel.
64. These biographical details are from Jennings 1873a, 341–342.
65. Jennings 1895, 14.
66. The story is told in Jennings 1883, viii–ix.
67. See his entry in the *Dictionary of National Biography*.
68. Letter from Jennings to Bulwer-Lytton, 1 July 1870.
69. In his letters to Fryar.
70. They include: *My Marine Memorandum Book*, 3 vols., 1845; *The Ship of Glass, a Romance, with Atcherley, a Novel*, 3 vols., 1846; *The Opera; or Views before and peeps behind the curtain*, 1847 (never located); *Pebblestones by Peregrine* (supposedly edited by Jennings; never located), 1853; *War in London or Peace in London*, 1859.
71. Jennings 1858, vii–xi.
72. Jennings 1858, 34–35.

73. Jennings 1890, 21. The previous citations from *The Indian Religions* are of portions not taken on into the second edition, which is cited henceforth.
74. On the question of priority, see Almond, 29–32.
75. See Almond, 35.
76. Jennings 1890, 32.
77. Jennings 1890, 68.
78. Jennings 1890, 49.
79. Jennings 1890, 32
80. Jennings 1890, 35.
81. Jennings 1890, 51.
82. Jennings 1890, 51.
83. Jennings 1858, 138–167; absent from the 1890 edition.
84. Wright, 90.
85. Crowe, *The Night-Side of Nature* (1848); Christmas, *The Cradle of the Twin Giants* (1849); Ennemoser, *History of Magic* (English trans. 1854); R. D. Owen, *Footfalls on the Boundary of Another World* (1860).
86. These are three of the eight Conclusions in Jennings 1863, I, 276–278.
87. Jennings 1861, I, 296–297.
88. Jennings 1861, I, 11–12.
89. Jennings 1861, II, 126–132.
90. See Chapters 10–12 of Jennings 1870, and Chs. 18–23 of Jennings 1890, which reproduce Jennings 1861, II, 152–345.
91. Higgins 1829, "New Preface," unpaginated.
92. Jennings 1861, II, 361–362.
93. Randolph 1892, 61–71. Most of the extracts were also incorporated into Jennings 1890.
94. Jennings 1861, II, 346.
95. See Westcott 1900, 29.
96. Jennings 1861, II, 352–353.
97. Jennings 1861, II, 360.
98. *The Rosicrucian* II/22 (November 1873), 65ff.
99. Jennings 1895, 44.
100. Note in Jennings 1877, verso of title page, where the dates 1850 to 1870 are given. In Jennings 1895, 42, Jennings says that *The Rosicrucians* was written in 1868–69.
101. See Jennings 1861, II, 347, where Jennings says that he would like to quote for his epigraph Higgins' *Anacalypsis* "on the ubiquity of Tauric, Phallic Doctrines."
102. Jennings 1861, II, Ch.viii; 1870, 81f.
103. O'Brien, 112.
104. Jennings 1873b, unpaginated Introduction.
105. Jennings 1873a, 123.
106. Jennings 1883, 80.
107. Jennings 1883, 326.
108. For a full bibliographic analysis of the series, see Godwin 1991, 65–66.
109. Jennings 1884, xxvi.
110. Jennings 1884, xvii.
111. Jennings 1884, 230–231.
112. Jennings 1884, 213.

113. Much of *Phallicism* was incorporated in the third (1887) and later editions of *The Rosicrucians*.
114. Letter of 12 December 1883; Jennings 1895, 17.
115. Letter of 17 April 1886; Jennings 1895, 37.
116. See Fryar's affectionate dedication to Morrison in Welton.
117. I have not seen the pamphlet. See letter of 29 July 1878, sent from Bath by "One of the Six Hundred," on "Visions in Mirrors and Crystals," in *The Spiritualist* XIII (9 August 1878), 71.
118. Welton, 5.
119. Information from Mr. Deveney.
120. Jennings 1895, 11.
121. Jennings 1895, 12–13.
122. Advertisement in *The Medium and Daybreak*, 3 July 1885, 431.
123. Randolph 1892, 59.
124. Welton, 153.
125. Welton, 53n.
126. Letter Fryar, 7 December 1883, in *Letters of Hargrave Jennings*, 16.
127. Letter of 18 August 1885; Jennings 1895, 33.
128. "New dispute against women, by which it is proved that they are not human beings." See also *The Rosicrucians*, 4th ed., 416.
129. Letter of 18 August 1885; Jennings 1895, 34–35.

NOTES TO CHAPTER FOURTEEN (ENTER MADAME BLAVATSKY)

1. Johnson 1990, 1–2.
2. The only modern study of Rawson's life and work is Johnson 1988.
3. Rawson 1988, 210–211.
4. Sinnett 1913, 124–125.
5. Sinnett 1913, 125–126.
6. Peebles 1874, 78.
7. See *The Theosophical Movement 1875–1925. A History and a Survey* (New York: Dutton, 1925), 69.
8. See Johnson 1994, ch. 8.
9. Rawson 1988, 211.
10. Galtier 1989, 144.
11. This was not exactly the same as the "Ancient and Arabic Order of the Nobles of the Mystic Shrine," known in the US as the Shriners.
12. Johnson 1988, 232; Blavatsky 1877, II, 313–315.
13. Blavatsky 1877, II, 2. On Lady Hester Stanhope, see Johnson 1990, 109–113.
14. See Godwin 1989, 5–6.
15. Michal, 14.
16. Note in HPB's *Scrapbook*, published in *BCW* I, 73.
17. Letter to Prof. Hiram Corson, 16 February 1875, quoted in *BCW* I, lv.
18. *ODL*, I, 75.
19. *ODL*, I, 75–76.
20. Mackenzie 1987, 461.

21. Blavatsky 1877, II, 308n.
22. Blavatsky 1877, II, 307; cf. Mackenzie 1987, 309.
23. Mackenzie 1874, 107, 109.
24. Howe 1972a, 264.
25. In "Lodges of Magic" (1888); see *BCW*, X, 125n.
26. Biographical note by Sotheran's widow, quoted in Johnson 1990, 44.
27. Johnson 1988, 232; Board 1988, 153.
28. Johnson 1988, 233.
29. This was stated by Laura Holloway in 1915; see *BCW* I, 527.
30. Johnson 1990, 57.
31. Johnson 1990, 53.
32. Johnson 1990, 19.
33. Freethinkers' Convention, 57–58.
34. Freethinkers' Convention, 150–174.
35. Santucci, 134–135.
36. See Felt's account in *The Spiritualist*, 8 February 1878, reprinted in *ODL* I, 126–131nn.
37. See Rawson 1988, 211.
38. Blavatsky 1877, I, 127–128.
39. *ODL,* I, 130–131nn.
40. Extract from *New York Dispatch* in *The Rosicrucian* 18 (October 1872), 233–237.
41. *The Rosicrucian* II/14 (April 1879), 92.
42. Copied into the Irwins' *Rosicrucian Miscellanea*, Grand Lodge Library, London.
43. Blavatsky's letter is published in *Theosophical History* IV/6–7 (1993), 172–177.
44. Lytton, *Zanoni*, 214.
45. Lytton, *Zanoni*, 226.
46. Solovyoff, 256–257.
47. *ODL*, I, 76.
48. *ODL*, I, 71–72.
49. *ODL*, I, 25.
50. *LMW*, II, 19–21 (Letter 3, with facsimile, omitted from later ed.).
51. *LMW*, II, 60.
52. *LMW*, II, 31 (Letter 9).
53. *LMW*, II, 34 (Letter 9).
54. *LMW*, II, 38 (Letter 11).
55. *LMW*, II, 40 (Letter 11).
56. *LMW*, II, 52 (Letter 20).
57. See *BCW*, I, 103, 115.
58. *BCW*, I, 269.
59. See, for example, *BCW*, X, 124–125.
60. Communication from Mr. Deveney, 1993.
61. See especially *BCW*, I, 126–127.
62. *BCW,* VIII, 76, citing an article published in France in 1887.
63. Biographical information from Charlton Templeman Speer, in Moses 1933, v–xxii.
64. Moses 1933, 182.
65. Page references are to Moses 1933.
66. *ML,* 43 (Letter IX).

67. Published in *The Spiritual Scientist*, 15 and 22 July 1875; see *BCW,* I, 101–119.
68. Page numbers in *BCW*, I.
69. Some extracts from Olcott's letters were published in *Light* during July 1892, but ceased on Moses' death later that year. Blavatsky's first letter to Massey has been published in *Light* 113/1 (1993), 19–26.
70. See the letter from Olcott to Massey published in *Theosophical History* V/1 (1994), 5–9.
71. See *BCW*, VI, 271, 280, 291–292.
72. Letter from Papus to Alfred Erny, dated April or May 1898, kindly shown me by Daniel Caracostea of the Paris Société Théosophique.
73. *ODL,* I, 111.
74. See his letter in *Theosophical History* V/1 (1994) 5–9.
75. *Light* XII (23 July 1892), 356.
76. Meade, 343.
77. Letter reprinted in *The Spiritualist* IX (25 August 1876), 39.
78. Letter of 22 December 1875, in Irwin's *Rosicrucian Miscellanea*, 80.
79. *Rosicrucian Miscellanea*, 84.
80. Quoted in *ODL,* I, 325.
81. *ODL,* I, 327.
82. *ODL*, I, 325.
83. *ODL*, I, 320.
84. *LMW*, II, 42 (Letter 12), 44 (Letter 13).
85. Godwin 1993, 82–83.
86. *Ghost Land*, 349–350.
87. *BCW*, I, 142.
88. Sinnett 1913, 50.
89. Johnson 1990, 152–153.
90. On *Art Magic*, see *ODL,* I, 185–201.
91. Page references to *Art Magic.*
92. *Two Worlds* IV (27 November 1891), 646.
93. Page references to Caithness.
94. Letter to Colonel Bundy, 8 January 1884; Ms. of extracts in College of Psychic Studies, London.
95. In whose library, Blavatsky told Massey, she started to write *Isis Unveiled.* See her letter to Massey, cited in note 71 above.

NOTES TO CHAPTER FIFTEEN (WISDOM FROM THE EAST)

1. On their visit, see Massey's account in *The Spiritualist* XIV (24 January 1879), 41–42.
2. *ODL*, II, 4–9.
3. *Bhagavad Gita*, 8.
4. *Bhagavad Gita*, 9.
5. *Bhagavad Gita*, 10.
6. *Bhagavad Gita*, 24.
7. Mukherjee, 141.

8. Mukherjee, 105.
9. Most of what follows is taken from Singh and Collet.
10. Mukherjee, 118, 141.
11. See Jackson, 33–34, 49–50.
12. Roy 1887, I, x–xi.
13. Sisir Kumar Das, "Rammohun: His Religious Thought," in Roy 1974, 71–91.
14. See Guénon 1945, 322–325, on "Vedanta Westernized."
15. *BCW*, III, 56; from "The Brahmo Samaj," in *The Theosophist* II/6 (1881).
16. See "Triumph and reward of Dr. Esdaile," in *Zoist* VI (1848), 113ff.
17. *Encyclopaedia of Religion and Ethics*, II, 820.
18. On Ramakrishna, Keshub, and the Brahmo Samaj, see Isherwood, 157–166.
19. *BCW*, IV, 110.
20. *BCW*, III, 58.
21. See the entry on his son, Sir Vitthaldas Damodar Thackersey (1873–1921) in *DNB of India*, III, 334–345. This says that both father and son were members of the Indian National Congress, but the son not so anti-British as Moolji.
22. Ransom, 98.
23. But see the doubts expressed in Gomes, 228.
24. *ODL*, I, 395.
25. Dayananda 1976, 64.
26. Dayananda 1984, 469.
27. Dayananda 1984, 42.
28. See *BCW*, VI, 48–53.
29. See their tributes in Dayananda 1984. Others in the volume include Max Müller, Leo Tolstoy, Romain Rolland, Rabindranath Tagore, Dr. S. Radhakrishnan, Annie Besant, and numerous modern scholars.
30. For essential details on Dayananda and the Theosophists in India, see Johnson 1990, 161–169.
31. Letter to *The World*, in *BCW*, I, 238.
32. Letter to William Henry Burr, 19 November 1877; in Gomes 1987, 78.
33. Letter to *La Revue Spirite*, October 1878; in *BCW*, I, 402.
34. For the definitive study of the subject, see Almond.
35. Buchanan, 179–180.
36. Buchanan, 258.
37. "On Singhala, or Ceylon, and the Doctrines of Bhooddha, from the Books of the Singhalais," *Asiatic Researches* VII (1801), 32–56.
38. Joinville, 402.
39. Moor, 221.
40. Moor, 244.
41. See Almond on this and on many other points.
42. Hodgson, 440.
43. See Almond, 72–74.
44. Alabaster, 4.
45. Alabaster, xliv.
46. Alabaster, xlv.
47. Alabaster, xxxvii–xxxviii.

48. *The Spiritualist* X (25 May 1877), 245, citing *New York World*, 30 April 1877; on the California temple, see *Spiritualist* XI (14 September 1877), 125; *BCW*, I, 247–248.
49. Blavatsky 1877, II, 320.
50. See Johnson 1994.
51. Peebles 1870, 16.
52. *Buddhism and Christianity Face to Face* (Colombo, 1873), summarized in *Light* XXIX (23 October 1909), 508; see also *BCW*, II, 138–140, 523–524.
53. So stated in the summary in *Light* (see note 52).
54. *The Spiritualist* XIII (5 July 1878), 8.
55. Blavatsky 1877, I, 242–243n.
56. Ransom, 21, 169.
57. *The Spiritualist* XI (31 July 1877), 103–104.
58. See Blavatsky's scathing remarks in *BCW*, I, 282.
59. *The Spiritualist* XII (8 February 1878), 67.
60. *The Spiritualist* XII (24 May 1878), 249.
61. Quoted in Ransom, 143.
62. *BCW*, II, 98–104.
63. *BCW*, XI, 189.
64. *BCW*, II, 102.
65. *BCW*, XI, 414.
66. *ML*, 52 (Letter X).
67. Row, 465.
68. *BCW*, XIV, 418.

NOTES TO CHAPTER SIXTEEN (THE HERMETIC REACTION)

1. *ODL*, III, 93.
2. Maitland 1913, I, 40.
3. Maitland 1913, I, 26.
4. Maitland 1913, I, 57.
5. The Rev. Kingsford later came to Paris to join his wife, as did their daughter and a governess.
6. Maitland 1913, I, 222.
7. Maitland 1913, I, 69, 107–110.
8. Maitland 1913, I, 217.
9. Maitland 1913, I, 242–243.
10. Maitland 1913, I, 253.
11. Maitland 1913, I, 276.
12. Maitland 1913, I, 317–318.
13. Maitland 1913, I, 324–325, 334–338.
14. Maitland 1913, I, 286.
15. Maitland 1913, I, 438.
16. Letter of 11 March 1884, in Maitland 1913, II, 167.
17. Maitland 1913, I, 345.
18. Maitland 1913, I, 355–356.

19. Maitland 1913, II, 16.
20. *Light* II (11 March 1882), 112.
21. *Light* II (4 March 1882), 103–104.
22. *Light* I (9 April 1881), 107.
23. *Light* II (18 March 1882), 128–130.
24. *Light* II (3 March 1882), 104.
25. *Light* II (18 March 1882), 130.
26. Blavatsky 1925, 26 (Letter XIV).
27. See *BCW*, IV, 119–122.
28. See *BCW*, IV, 182–186.
29. *BCW*, IV, 122.
30. Parallels, as explained to Lady Caithness by Anna Kingsford, 3 July 1882; see Maitland 1913, II, 73; Kingsford 1923, 342–343n.
31. *Light* II (9 September 1882), 407.
32. Sinnett 1907, 197.
33. Maitland 1913, II, 119.
34. Letter of 8 June 1883, in Maitland 1913, II, 119.
35. Sinnett 1986, 25.
36. Letter of 5 November 1883, in Maitland 1913, II, 148.
37. Blavatsky 1925, 51 (Letter XXV).
38. Letter of 23 August 1883, in Blavatsky 1925, 52 (Letter XXVI).
39. *ML*, 346 (Letter LIX), received by Sinnett in July 1883.
40. Perhaps he did not know that she developed occult powers in order to kill the scientists who practiced vivisection, believing that she had succeeded in killing Claude Bernard, but failed with Pasteur. See Maitland 1913, I, 250; II, 269.
41. *ML,* 402 (Letter LXXXV).
42. *ML,* 405 (Letter LXXXVI).
43. Blavatsky 1925, 66 (Letter XXIX).
44. See Godwin 1989, 10.
45. The Wildes: *ODL*, III, 94; R.A.S. meetings, *Light* IV (11 July 1885), 330.
46. Mead 1949, I, 15.
47. Maitland 1913, II, 31.
48. Maitland 1913, II, 168.
49. See Christopher Bamford's note in Harrison 1993, 210. Maitland published a pamphlet in 1882 entitled *How the World Came to an End in 1881*.
50. Maitland 1913, II, 301–302.
51. Bamford, notes to Harrison, 1993, 210.
52. The reference is to I Corinthians 1.23.
53. Gilbert 1987a, 106.
54. See Bibliography under Chanel.
55. In Part Four of "The Hidden Hand" (Godwin 1990) I followed these sources, but Mr. Chanel, who has written a dissertation on Theon ("Max Théon et la Philosophie Cosmique," Ecole Pratique des Hautes Etudes, section V, Sorbonne, 1994), has since persuaded me that they are untrustworthy.
56. H.B. of L. 1988, 4. Another version in Guénon 1925, 217–218.
57. Davidson 1881, 19, 190.
58. Davidson 1881, 37.

59. Davidson 1881, 193.
60. "The Bhattah Mirrors," in *The Theosophist* V/3 (December 1883), 72–74; Blavatsky's commendation in *BCW*, VI, 6–8.
61. *The Occult Magazine* II/15 (April 1886), 31.
62. *BCW*, I, 421: Olcott records the arrival in 1878 of Ayton's translation of Trithemius' prophecies. Hockley also studied Trithemius; see Hamill 1986, 80.
63. Compare Barrett, II, 135–140.
64. Guénon 1970, 21.
65. A much more complete account will be found in Chanel.
66. A second volume followed posthumously. See Burgoyne 1980.
67. *Two Worlds* IV (8 May 1891), 301.
68. See Godwin 1989, 26.
69. See Howe and Möller, 87.
70. Howe and Möller, 136, citing Reuss in *Oriflamme*, Jubilee No. (1912), 15.
71. Howe and Möller, 214.
72. Lewis received an OTO diploma from Reuss in 1921, but does not seem to have had a closer relationship. See Howe and Möller, 247.
73. See the report in *Light* VI (19 June 1886), 283.
74. See announcement in *Light* VI (10 July 1886), 303.
75. Colquhoun 1975, 76.
76. Gilbert 1987b, 3.
77. Gilbert 1987b, 7.

NOTES TO CHAPTER SEVENTEEN (THE PARTING OF EAST AND WEST)

1. Harrison 1929, 24n says that it was not Vienna, but another important city on the Danube.
2. Harrison 1993, 86–87.
3. Harrison 1993, 89.
4. Henderson, 1956, 240.
5. Massey 1909, 3.
6. Massey 1909, 59; see also 208–209 on Massey's debt to Oliphant.
7. Massey 1909, 66.
8. Mr. Johnson points out to me that Blavatsky's birth coincided with strange omens in the sky, which convinced Nat Turner that God had given him a sign to begin what was to be the largest slave uprising in American history.
9. Johnson 1994.
10. See Leadbeater's *Man: Whence, How, and Whither* (Adyar: TPH, 1913), and, co-authored with Besant, *The Lives of Alcyone* (Adyar: TPH, 1924) and *The Masters and the Path* (Adyar: TPH, 1925). For a description of Leadbeater's methods, see Gregory Tillett, *The Elder Brother. A Biography of Charles Webster Leadbeater* (London: Routledge & Kegan Paul, 1982).
11. Lutyens, 272.
12. The contradictions within Krishnamurti's own life are amply displayed in Radha Rajagopal Sloss, *Lives in the Shadow with J. Krishnamurti* (London: Bloomsbury, 1991).

13. Harrison 1929, 32.
14. Harrison 1993, 167.
15. Brunton, 77.
16. Bennett 1902, 1 and title page gives his name as Allan Bennett McGregor. See Colquhoun 1975, 79–80, 118 for further explanations.
17. Until 1885 Mathers lived with his mother in a rooming house near Bournemouth. From then until his marriage in 1890 he lived in London on a small allowance from Wynn Westcott. See Colquhoun, 72–73.
18. Grant 1972, 102; See also Symonds, 191; Howe 1972, 106–109.
19. Symonds, 39.
20. Brunton 76.
21. Bennett 1902, 1.
22. Symonds, 40.
23. Symonds 59.
24. Brunton, 77.
25. Bennett 1904a, 503.
26. Bennett 1903a, 28–29.
27. Bennett refused to use the Sanskrit "Nirvana," saying that it applied only to a lesser state of "absorption into Brahma." Bennett 1903b, 115.
28. Bennett 1911, 33–34.
29. Bennett 1904b, 557.
30. The interviewer identifies Ananda Metteya as Allan Bennett *MacGregor*.
31. Interview with Dudley Wright, *Light* XXVIII (9 May 1908), 225.
32. Bennett 1903b, 126.
33. Brunton, 78–79; Bax, 313.
34. Grant 1972, 85.
35. Bennett 1903b, 133–134.
36. Mead 1909, 585.
37. Mead 1910, 697–698.
38. Mead 1910, 706.
39. Suzuki, 113.
40. This account is from Humphreys, 32, 42, 50–51, 63.
41. Mead 1910, 700.
42. *Mother's Agenda*, III, 56, 455; quoted in Levin, 20–21.
43. First Object of the Society, revision of 1896, from Ransom, 551.

Bibliography of Works Cited

Alabaster, Henry. *The Wheel of the Law. Buddhism illustrated from Siamese sources by the Modern Buddhist, A Life of Buddha, and An Account of the Phrabat.* London: Trübner, 1871.

Aldred, Guy. *The Devil's Chaplain. The Story of the Rev. Robert Taylor, M.A., M.R.C.S.* Glasgow: Strickland Press, 1942.

———. *Richard Carlile, agitator. His Life and Times.* London: Pioneer Books, 1913.

Almond, Philip C. *The British Discovery of Buddhism.* Cambridge: Cambridge University Press, 1988.

Anonymous 1820. Review of Townsend's *Oedipus Romanus* in *Edinburgh Monthly Review* 3 (1820), 60–61.

Anonymous 1841. *De Divinatione per Crystallum. Concerning the Treatise upon Divination by the Chrystal or Berill Glass . . .* Cambridge University Library, Ms. SPR Z.1841.6.

Anonymous 1896. *The Great Secret and its unfoldment in Occultism. A Record of forty years' experience in the modern mystery,* by a Church of England Clergyman. 2nd ed. London: Redway, 1896.

Art Magic, or Mundane, Sub-Mundane and Super-Mundane Spiritism. Chicago: Progressive Thinker, 1898. (First ed., 1876)

Ashburner, John. *Notes and Studies in the Philosophy of Animal Magic and Spiritualism.* London: Baillière, 1867.

BCW. H. P. Blavatsky. *Collected Writings.* Ed. Boris de Zirkoff. 14 vols. Wheaton: TPH, 1966-85, except for Vol. 5, published Los Angeles: Philosophical Research Society, 1950.

Barnes, Douglas Grove. *History of the English Corn Laws.* New York: F. S. Crofts, 1930.

Barrett, Francis. *The Magus, or Celestial Intelligencer; being a complete system of Occult Philosophy.* London: Lackington, Allen & Co., 1801.

Bax, Clifford. *Inland Far. A Book of Thoughts and Impressions.* London: Lovat Dickson, 1933. (First ed., 1925)

Bell, Dr. John. *The General and Particular Principles of Animal Electricity and Magnetism.* N.p.: Author, 1792.

Bennett, Allan. "The Faith of the Future." *Buddhism* I/1 (September 1903), 6–38. [1903a]

———. "Nibbana." *Buddhism* I/1 (September 1903), 113–134. [1903b]

———. "News and Notes." *Buddhism* I/3 (March 1904), 497–503. [1904a]

———. "The New Civilisation." *Buddhism* I/4 (November 1904), 529–560. [1904b]

———. "The Training of the Mind." *The Equinox* I/5 (March 1911), 28–59.

———. *The Wisdom of the Aryas.* London: Kegan Paul, 1923.

———. *The Religion of Burma and Other Papers.* Adyar: TPH, 1929.

———. *A Note on Genesis.* York Beach: Samuel Weiser, 1976. (First ed. in *The Equinox* 1/2, 1909)

Besterman, Theodore. *Crystal Gazing.* London: Rider, 1924.

Beverley, R. Mackenzie. *A Letter to Godfrey Higgins Esq. in answer to his "Apology for the life and character of Mohamed."* Beverley: M. Turner, 1829.

Bhagavad Gita. The Bhagvat-Geeta, or dialogues of Kreedshna and Arjoon; in eighteen lectures. Tr. Charles Wilkins. London: C Nourse, 1785.

Binns, Edward. *The Anatomy of Sleep.* 2nd ed., with annotations and additions by Earl Stanhope. London: John Churchill, 1845.

Blake, William. *Complete Writings.* Oxford: Oxford University Press, 1966.

Blavatsky, see *BCW.*

Blavatsky, H.P. *Isis Unveiled.* 2 vols. New York: Bouton, 1877.

———. *The Letters of H. P. Blavatsky to A. P. Sinnett, and other miscellaneous letters.* Ed. Trevor Barker. New York: Stokes, 1925.

Board, David. "The Brotherhood of Light and the Brotherhood of Luxor." *Theosophical History.* 2/5 (1988), 149–157.

Boulanger, Nicholas. *Examen critiqué de la vie et des ouvrages de Saint Paul. Avec une dissertation sur Saint Pierre.* London, 1770.

———. *L'Antiquité dévoilée par ses usages* Amsterdam: M. M. Rey, 1772.

Braude, Ann. *Radical Spirits. Spiritualism and Women's Rights in Nineteenth-Century America.* Boston: Beacon Press, 1989.

Brittan, S.B., ed., *The Telegraph Papers* [extracts from vol. I of *The Spiritual Telegraph*]. New York: Partridge & Brittan, 1853.

Brodhurst, J. Penderel. "A Faith healing academician." *Magazine of Art* IX (1886), 101–103.

Brunton, Paul. "A White Yogi." *The Occult Review,* April 1940, 75–80.

Buchanan, Francis. "On the Religion and Literature of the Burmas." *Asiatic Researches* VI (1799), 163–368.

Burgoyne, Thomas H. *The Light of Egypt, or The Science of the Soul and the Stars.* 2 vols. Albuquerque: Sun Books, 1980. (First ed., attributed to "Zanoni," 1889, 1900)

Burrow, Reuben. "Memorandums [sic] concerning an old building, in the Hadjipore District." *Asiatic Researches* II (1790), 477.

Bury, A. *John Varley of the "Old Society".* Leigh-on-Sea: F. Lewis, 1946.

Caithness, Countess of. *Old Truths in a New Light.* London: Chapman & Hall, 1876.

Campbell, James L., Sr., *Edward Bulwer-Lytton.* Boston: Twayne Publishers, 1986.

Cannon-Brookes, Peter, ed. *The Painted Word. British History Painting: 1750–1830.* Woodbridge: Boydell Press, 1991.

Carlile, Richard. *Every Woman's Book.* Undated pamphlet.

———. *To the Reformers of Great Britain.* Undated pamphlet.

———. *An Address to Men of Science.* London: R. Carlile, 1821.

———. *A New View of Insanity*. London: R. Carlile, 1831.

———. *Manual of Freemasonry*. London: William Reeves, n.d. [1845]. (First ed., 1825)

Cecil, Lord David. *Visionary and Dreamer. Two Poetic Painters: Samuel Palmer and Edward Burne-Jones*. Princeton: Princeton University Press, 1969.

Chanel, Christian, John Patrick Deveney, Joscelyn Godwin. *The Hermetic Brotherhood of Luxor. Initiatic and Historical Documents of an Order of Practical Occultism*. York Beach: Weiser, 1995.

Chapman, Guy. *Beckford*. New York: Scribners, 1937.

The Church of Light: Its History and Principles. Los Angeles: Church of Light, n.d.

Clarke, Michael, and Penny, Nicholas. *The Arrogant Connoisseur*. Manchester: Manchester University Press, 1982.

Clymer, R. Swinburne. *The Book of Rosicruciae. A Condensed History of the Fraternitas Rosae Crucis* . . . 3 vols. Quakertown: Philosophical Pub. Co., 1946–49.

Collection of Etruscan, Greek, and Roman Antiquities, from the cabinet of the Honble William Hamilton, His Britannick Majesty's envoy extraordinary at the court of Naples. 4 vols. Naples: 1766. [By Pierre-François Hugues d'Hancarville]

Collet, Sophia Dobson. *The Life and Letters of Raja Rammohun Roy*. Ed. and rev. D. K. Biswas and P. C. Ganguli. Calcutta: Sadharan Brahmo Samaj, 1962. (First ed., 1900)

Colquhoun, Ithell. *Sword of Wisdom. MacGregor Mathers and 'The Golden Dawn.'* London: Neville Spearman, 1975.

Colquhoun, J.C. *Report of the Experiments on animal magnetism made by a committee of the medical section of the French Royal Academy of Sciences*. Edinburgh: Robert Cadell, 1833.

———. *Isis Revelata: An Inquiry into the origin, progress, and present state of animal magnetism*. 2 vols. Edinburgh: Maclachlan & Stewart, 1836.

Cooke, Christopher. *Curiosities of Occult Literature*. London: Hall, Smart & Allen, n.d. [1863]

Cosway, Richard. *A Catalogue of the very curious and valuable Assemblage of Miscellaneous Articles* . . . London, 22–24 May 1821.

Court de Gébelin, Antoine. *Allégories orientales ou le fragment de Sanchoniaton qui contient l'histoire de Saturne, suivie de celles de Mercure et d'Hercule, et de ses douze travaux, avec leur explication, pour servir à l'intelligence du génie symbolique de l'antiquité*. Paris: l'Auteur, 1773.

Crowley, Aleister. *777 and other Qabalistic Writings, including Gematria and Sepher Sephiroth*. York Beach: Samuel Weiser, 1977.

Curry, Patrick. *Prophecy and Power: Astrology in Early Modern England*. Princeton: Princeton University Press, 1989.

Da Costa, Hippolyto Joseph. *Sketch of the The History of the Dionysian Artificers. A Fragment*. London: Sherwood, Neely, & Jones, 1820. Reprinted Los Angeles: Philosophical Research Society, 1975.

Daniell, Frederick B. *A Catalogue Raisonné of the Engraved Works of Richard Cosway, R.A. with a Memoir by Sir Philip Currie*. London: Daniell, 1890.

Daumer, G.F. *Enthüllungen über Kaspar Hauser*. Frankfurt a. M.: Meidinger, 1859.

Davidson, Peter. *The Violin*. Glasgow: Porteous Bros., 1871.

———. *The Violin*, 3rd ed. London: Pitman, 1881.

Dayananda Saraswati. *Autobiography*. Ed. K. C. Yadav. New Delhi: Manohar, 1976.

———. *World Perspectives on Swami Dayananda Saraswati*. Ed. G. R. Garg. New Delhi: Concept Publishing Co., 1984.

Debus, Allen G. "Scientific Truth and Occult Tradition: the Medical World of Ebenezer Sibly (1751–1799)." *Medical History* 26 (1982), 259–278.

D'Hancarville, P.-F. Hugues. *Recherches sur l'Origine, l'Esprit, et les Progrès des Arts de la Grèce sur leur connexion avec les arts et la religion des plus anciens peuples connues; sur les monumens antiques de l'Inde, de la Perse, du reste de l'Asie, de l'Europe et de l'Egypte*. 3 vols. London: B. Appleyard, 1785.

Dialectical Society. *Report on Spiritualism of the Committee of the London Dialectical Society, with the evidence, oral and written, and a selection from the correspondence*. London: Longman, 1871.

D'Oyly, George. *Remarks on Sir William Drummond's Oedipus Judaicus; being a sequel to Letters to Sir William Drummond*. London: W. Bulmer, 1813.

———. *Letters to the Rt. Hon. Sir William Drummond relating to his observations on parts of the Old Testament, in his recent work, entitled Oedipus Judaicus*. London: W. Bulmer, 1812.

Drummond, Sir William. *Philosophical Sketches of the Principles of Society and Government*. London: W. Bulmer, 1795. Published anonymously.

———. *Academical Questions*. London: W. Bulmer, 1805.

———. "An Examination of Mr. Dugald Stewart's Pamphlet relative to the late Election of a Mathematical Professor in the University of Edinburgh." *The British Critic* XXVII (1806), 124ff. Published anonymously.

———. *Memoir on the Antiquity of the Zodiacs of Esneh and Dendera*. London: A. J. Valpy, 1821.

———. *Origines; or, Remarks on the origin of several empires, states, and cities*. 4 vols. London: A. J. Valpy, 1824–1829.

Dupotet de Sennevoy, Baron. *An Introduction to the study of Animal Magnetism*. London: Saunders & Otley, 1838.

Dupuis, Charles. *Mémoire sur l'origine des constellations, et sur l'explication de la fable*. Paris: Veuve Desaint, 1781.

———. *L'Origine de tous les cultes, ou Religion universelle*. Paris, An III [1795].

Elliotson, John. *Address, delivered at the opening of the medical session of the University of London, October 1st, 1832*. London: Longman, n.d. [1832]

Encyclopaedia of Religion and Ethics. Ed. James Hastings. 13 vols. Edinburgh: T. & T. Clarke, 1908–1926.

Escott, Thomas. *Edward Bulwer, First Baron Lytton of Knebworth*. London: Routledge, 1910.

Estlin, John Prior. *The Nature and Causes of Atheism [. . .] To which are added, Remarks on a Work, entitled Origine de tous les cultes, ou Religion universelle*. Bristol: N. Biggs, 1797.

Faivre, Antoine. *Eckartshausen et la théosophie chrétienne*. Paris: Klincksieck, 1969.

Fenton, S. J. "Richard Carlile; his Life and Masonic Writings." *Ars Quatuor Coronati* 49 (1936), 83–121.

Fox, W. J. *The Duties of Christians towards Deists: A Sermon, preached at the Unitarian Chapel, Parliament Court [. . .] on Occasion of the Recent Prosecution of Mr. Carlile, for the re-publication of Paine's Age of Reason.* London: R. Hunter and D. Eaton, 1819.

Fraxi, Pisanus [=Anthony Ashbee]. *Index Librorum Prohibitorum.* London: Privately Printed, 1877.

Freethinkers' Convention. *The Proceedings and Addresses at the Freethinkers' Convention held at Watkins, New York., August 22d, 23d, 24th, and 25th, '78.* New York: D. M. Benjamin, 1878.

Galtier, Gérard. *Maçonnerie Egyptienne, Rose-croix et néo-chevalerie. Les fils de Cagliostro.* Paris: Editions du Rocher, 1989.

Gauld, Alan. *A History of Hypnotism.* Cambridge: Cambridge University Press, 1992.

Ghost Land; or Researches into the Mysteries of Occultism. Illustrated in a Series of Autobiographical Sketches. In Two Parts. Tr. and ed. Emma Hardinge Britten. Boston: for the Editor, 1876.

Gilbert, R. A. *The Golden Dawn: Twilight of the Magicians.* Wellingborough: Aquarian, 1983. [1983a]

———, ed. *The Sorcerer and His Apprentice. Unknown Hermetic Writings of S. K. MacGregor Mathers and J. W. Brodie-Innes.* Wellingborough: Aquarian, 1983. [1983b]

———. *A. E. Waite, Magician of Many Parts.* Wellingborough: Crucible, 1987. [1987a]

———. *The Golden Dawn and the Esoteric Section.* London: Theosophical History Centre, 1987. [1987b]

Godwin, Joscelyn. *The Beginnings of Theosophy in France.* London: Theosophical History Centre, 1989.

———. "The Hidden Hand." *Theosophical History* N.S. III/2–5 (1990–91), 35–43, 66–76, 107–117, 137–148.

———. "Hargrave Jennings." *Hermetic Journal,* 1991, 49–77.

———. "Queen Victoria and the Crystal." *Occult Observer* II/2 (1992), 27–28. [1992a]

———. "A Behmenist Circle in Victorian England." *Hermetic Journal,* 1992, 48–71. [1992b]

———. *Arktos: the Polar Myth in Science, Symbolism and Nazi Survival.* Grand Rapids: Phanes Press; London: Thames & Hudson, 1993.

Goldsmith, Margaret. *Franz Anton Mesmer. A History of Mesmerism.* Garden City: Doubleday, Doran, 1934.

Gomes, Michael. *The Dawning of the Theosophical Movement.* Wheaton: TPH, 1987.

Grant, Kenneth. *The Magical Revival.* New York: Samuel Weiser, 1972.

Greaves, James Pierrepont. *Letters and Extracts from the Manuscript Writings of James Pierrepont Greaves.* 2 vols. Ham Common: the Concordium, 1843; London: John Chapman, 1845.

———. *The New Nature in the Soul. From the Journal of James Pierrepont Greaves.* London: John Chapman, 1847.

Gregory, William. *Letters to a Candid Inquirer on Animal Magnetism.* London: Taylor, Walton & Maberly, 1851.

Guénon, René. "F.-Ch. Barlet et les sociétés initiatiques." *Le Voile d'Isis* 30/64 (April 1925), 217–221. [1925a] Translation in Chanel.

———. "Quelques précisions à propos de la H. B. of L." *Le Voile d'Isis* 30/70 (October 1925), 592–595. [1925b] Translation in Chanel.

———. *Introduction to the Study of Hindu Doctrines.* Tr. M. Pallis. London: Luzac, 1945. (First ed., 1921)

———. *L'Erreur Spirite.* 2nd ed. Paris: Editions Traditionnelles, 1952. (First ed., 1923)

———. *Formes traditionnelles et Cycles cosmiques.* Paris: Gallimard, 1970.

———. *Le Théosophisme, histoire d'une pseudo-religion* Enlarged ed. Paris: Editions Traditionnelles, 1982. (First ed., 1921)

H.B. of L. *Textes et Documents secrets de la Hermetic Brotherhood of Luxor.* Milan: Archè, 1988.

Hackwood, F. W. *William Hone, His Life and Times.* London: T.Fisher Unwin, 1912.

Hamill, John, ed. *The Rosicrucian Seer. Magical Writings of Frederick Hockley.* Wellingborough: Aquarian, 1986.

Hardinge, E. [Britten]. *Six Lectures on Theology and Nature.* Chicago: for the Author, 1860.

Hardinge Britten, Emma. *Nineteenth Century Miracles; or, Spirits and their work in every country of the earth.* New York: William Britten, 1884.

———. *Autobiography of Emma Hardinge Britten.* Ed. Margaret Wilkinson. Manchester: John Heywood, 1900.

———. *Modern American Spiritualism.* New Hyde Park: University Books, 1970. (First ed. 1870)

Harrison, C. G. *"The Fourth Mystery" Birth and Death.* London: Rider, n.d. [1929]

———. *The Transcendental Universe. Six Lectures on Occult Science, Theosophy, and the Catholic Faith. Delivered before the Berean Society.* Introduction and notes by Christopher Bamford. Hudson: Lindisfarne Press, 1993. (First ed., 1894)

Heisler, Ron. "Introduction to the Hermetic Adepti." *Hermetic Journal,* 35 (1987), 34–41.

Henderson, Philip. *The Life of Laurence Oliphant, Traveller, Diplomat and Mystic.* London: Robert Hale, 1956.

Higgins, Godfrey. *Horae Sabbaticae.* London: A. J. Valpy, 1826.

———. *The Celtic Druids.* London: Rowland Hunter, 1829. (The first, engraved title page is dated 1827.) [1829a]

———. *An Apology for the life and character of the celebrated prophet of Arabia, called Mohamed, or The Illustrious.* London: Rowland Hunter, 1829. [1829b]

———. *To R. M. Beverley, Esq.* Doncaster: Charles & James White, 1829. [1829c]

———. *Horae Sabbaticae.* 2nd ed. London: R. Hunter, 1833.

———. *Anacalypsis, an Attempt to Draw Aside the Veil of the Saitic Isis; or an Inquiry into the Origin of Languages, Nations and Religions.* 2 vols. London, 1833–36.

Hindmarsh, Robert. "Inquiry into the Nature of Astrology." *The New Magazine of Knowledge* I (1790), 231–306.

———. "A comparison between Jacob Bohmen and Emanuel Swedenborg, particularly on the subject of divine influx." *The Intellectual Repository for the New Church* III (1816–17), 188–190.

———. "Observations on astrology, the science of palmistry, and the transmigration of souls." *The Intellectual Repository for the New Church* IV (1818–19), 305–314.

Hockley, Frederick. "On the Ancient Magic Crystal, and its Connexion with Mesmerism." *The Zoist* VIII (1849), 251–266.

———. "Remarks upon the Rev. George Sandby's Review" [of Cahagnet's *Celestial Telegraph*]. *The Zoist* VIII (1850), 54–67.

Hodgson, B. H. "Notice of the languages, literature, and religion of the Bauddhas of Nepal and Bhot." *Asiatic Researches* XVI (1828), 409–478.

Hogart, Ron. Charles. *Alchemy. A Comprehensive Bibliography of the Manly P. Hall Collection of Books and Manuscripts* . . . Los Angeles: Philosophical Research Society, 1986.

Holland, Lord. *The Journal of Henry Edward Fox (afterwards fourth and last Lord Holland) 1818–1830.* London: Thornton Butterworth, 1923.

Hone, William. *The Third Trial of William Hone.* London: W. Hone, 1818.

Howe, Ellic. *Astrology, a Recent History.* New York: Walker & Co., 1967.

———. "Fringe Masonry in England, 1870–1885." *Ars Quatuor Coronatorum* 85 (1972), 242–295. [1972a]

———. *The Magicians of the Golden Dawn. A Documentary History of a Magical Order 1887–1923.* London: Routledge & Kegan Paul, 1972. [1972b]

———. *Raphael or, The Royal Merlin.* London: Arborfield, 1964.

———, ed. *The Alchemist of the Golden Dawn. The Letters of the Revd. W. A. Ayton to F. L. Gardner and Others, 1886–1905.* Wellingborough: Aquarian, 1985.

Howe, Ellic, and Möller, Helmut. *Merlin Peregrinus. Vom Untergrund des Abendlandes.* Würzburg: Königshoven & Neumann, 1986.

Hughes, T. S., *A Letter to Godfrey Higgins Esq. of Skellow Grange, on the subject of his "Horae Sabbaticae . . ."* Cambridge: Richard Newby, 1826.

Humphreys, Christmas. *Both Sides of the Circle.* London: Allen & Unwin, 1978.

Hungerford, Edward Buell. *Shores of Darkness.* New York: Columbia University Press, 1941.

Inchbald, Rev. P. *Animadversions on a work, entitled "An Apology for the life and character of Mohamed . . ."* Doncaster: Charles & James White, 1830.

Inman, Thomas. *Ancient Faiths Embodied in Ancient Names.* 2nd ed. 2 vols. London: Trübner & Co., 1872. (First ed., 1868)

Irwin, David. *John Flaxman 1755–1826.* New York: Rizzoli, 1979.

Isherwood, Christopher. *Ramakrishna and his Disciples.* New York: Simon & Schuster, 1965.

Jackson, Carl T. *The Oriental Religions and American Thought. Nineteenth-Century Explorations.* Westport, CT: Greenwood Press, 1981.

Jennings, Hargrave. *The Indian Religions, or, Results of the Mysterious Buddhism,* "by an Indian Missionary." London: T. C. Newby, 1858.

———. *Curious Things of the Outside World. Last Fire.* 2 vols. London: T. & W. Boone, 1861.

———. *The Rosicrucians, Their Rites and Mysteries.* London: J. C. Hotten, 1870.

———, "ed." *One of the Thirty: A Strange History, Now for the First Time Told.* London: J. C. Hotten, n.d. [1873a]

———. *Live Lights or Dead Lights. (Altar or Table?).* 2nd ed. [1st not known]. London: John Hodges, 1873. [1873b]

———. *The Childishness and Brutality of the Time. Some plain truths in plain language.* London: Vizetelly & Co., 1883.

———. *Phallicism, Celestial and Terrestrial, Heathen and Christian; its connexion with the Rosicrucians and the Gnostics and its foundation in Buddhism. With an Essay on Mystic Anatomy.* London: Redway, 1884.

———. *The Indian Religions or Results of the Mysterious Buddhism. Concerning that also which is to be understood in the divinity of fire.* London: Redway, 1890. (Much enlarged from 1858 ed.)

———. *The Letters of Hargrave Jennings [. . .] Forming the unabridged Correspondence with the Editor of the* Bath Occult Reprints, *between 1879 and 1887.* Bath: Robert H. Fryar, 1895.

Johnson, K. Paul. "Albert Leighton Rawson." *Theosophical History* 2/7 (1988), 229–251.

———. *In Search of the Masters. Behind the Occult Myth.* South Boston, VA: Author, 1990.

———. *The Masters Revealed. Madame Blavatsky and the Myth of the Great White Lodge.* Albany: State University of New York Press, 1994.

Joinville, Mr. "On the Religion and Manners of the People of Ceylon." *Asiatic Researches* VII (1801), 398–445.

Jones, Sir William. "On the Gods of Greece, Italy, and India." *Asiatic Researches* I (1788), 221–275.

Jung-Stilling, H. *Theory of Pneumatology.* Tr. Samuel Jackson. London: Longman, 1834.

Katz, Jacob. *Jews and Freemasons in Europe 1723–1939.* Cambridge, Mass: Harvard University Press, 1970.

Kerr, Howard, and Crow, Charles. L. *The Occult in America.* Urbana: University of Illinois Press, 1983.

Kingsford, Anna, and Maitland, Edward. *The Perfect Way; or, The Finding of Christ.* 5th ed. London: Watkins, 1923. (First ed., 1882, published anonymously)

Kirchenhoffer, Hermann. *The Book of Fate: formerly in the possession of Napoleon.* London: G. Berger, 1822.

Knight, Richard Payne. *The Progress of Civil Society. A didactic poem in six books.* London: W. Bulmer, 1796.

———. *On the Symbolical Language of Ancient Art and Mythology.* With a Preface by E. H. Barker. London: Black & Armstrong, 1836.

———. *A Discourse on the Worship of Priapus and its Connection with the Mystic Theology of the Ancients.* Secaucus, NJ: University Books, 1974. (First ed., 1786)

———. *Expedition into Sicily.* Ed. Claudia Stumpf. London: British Museum Publications, 1986.

Kretzulesco-Quaranta, Emanuela. *Les jardins du songe: Poliphile et la mystique de la Renaissance.* Paris: Les Belles Lettres, 1986. (First ed., 1976)

Lane, Edward William. *An Account of the Manners and Customs of the Modern Egyptians . . .* 2 vols. 3rd ed. London: Charles Knight, 1842.

LMW. Letters from the Masters of the Wisdom. Ed. C. Jinarajadasa. First Series: Adyar: TPH, 1977. Second Series: Chicago: Theosophical Press, 1926.

Lang, W. *Mesmerism, its history, phenomena, and practice with reports of cases developed in Scotland.* Edinburgh: Fraser & Co., 1843. Published anonymously.

Léclaireur, Jean. "Le Secret du Comte de Saint-Germain." *Le Lotus Bleu,* September 1895, 314ff.

Levi, Eliphas. *The Doctrine of Transcendental Magic.* Tr. A. E. Waite. York Beach, Maine: Weiser, 1991. (First English ed., 1896)

Levin, Martin. "The Gnostic Cosmology of Max Theon." *Eco-Gnosis* 2 (February 1988), 8–23.

Lister, Raymond. *British Romantic Painting.* Cambridge: Cambridge University Press, 1989.

———. *Samuel Palmer and 'The Ancients'.* Cambridge: Cambridge University Press, 1984.

Longford, Elizabeth. *Victoria R.I.* London: Pan Books, 1966.

Loutherbourg, J.P. de. *A Catalogue of all the valuable Drawings [. . .] Together with [. . .] extensive library of scarce books.* London, 18–20 June 1812.

Lutyens, Mary. *Krishnamurti. The Years of Awakening.* London: John Murray, 1975.

Lytton, E. Bulwer-. *The Haunted and the Haunters.* With an Introduction and an account of the Haunted House at Willington by Harold Armitage. London: Simpkin, 1925.

———. *Zanoni.* Philadelphia: John Wanamaker, n.d.

———. *Ismael, an Oriental Tale. With Other Poems.* London, 1820.

ML. The Mahatma Letters to A. P. Sinnett. Ed. A. T. Barker. New York: Frederick Stokes Co., 1924.

Mackenzie, Kenneth R. H. "The Aims of Rosicrucian Science." *The Rosicrucian* 24 (March 1874), 105–112.

———. "Visions in Mirrors and Crystals." *The Spiritualist* XII (29 March 1878), 151–154; supplementary note: "Crystallomancy," 28 June 1878, 312.

———. *The Royal Masonic Cyclopaedia.* Wellingborough: Aquarian Press, 1987. (First ed., 1877)

Mackey, Samson Arnold. *The Mythological Astronomy of the Ancients Demonstrated . . .* Norwich: R. Walker, 1822. Reprinted Minneapolis: Wizard's Bookshelf, 1973

———. *The Mythological Astronomy of the Ancients; Part the Second: or the Key to Urania . . .* Norwich: R. Walker, 1823. Reprinted Minneapolis: Wizard's Bookshelf, 1973.

———. *A Companion to the Mythological Astronomy . . .* Norwich: R. Walker, 1824. [1824a]

———. *A Reply, intended to be made to the Various Disputants, on an essay on chronology, which was read at the Philosophical Society of Norwich . . .* Norwich: R. Walker, n.d. [1824b]

———. *A New Theory of the Earth.* N.d. Issued with *A Companion . . .* but paginated separately. [1825]

———. *Man's Best Friend, or the Evils of Pious Frauds.* Norwich: R. Walker, for the Author, 1826.

———. *The Two Zodiacs of Tentyra, and the Zodiac of Thebes; explained.* Norwich: Author, 1832. [1832a]

———. *A Lecture on Astronomy . . .* London, 1832. [1832b]

———. *The Original Design of the ancient zodiacal and extra-zodiacal constellations [. . .] Also, further remarks On the long Zodiac of Tantyra . . .* Norwich: R. Walker, 1834. [1834a]

———. *The Age of Mental Emancipation* [No. 2]. Issued with *The Origin and Design.* [1834b]

———. *The Age of Mental Emancipation.* [No. 1] *In which is shown the exact agreement of Geological discovery with the ancient astronomical observations of the Hindoos.* Norwich: R. Walker, for the Author, 1836.

———. *The Age of Mental Emancipation, No. 3, in which is shown the natural cause of the spiral motion of the axis of the earth among the stars* . . . N.p.: J. Lemmon, for the Author, 1839.

Madden, R. R. *The Literary life and correspondence of the Countess of Blessington.* 3 vols. London: T. C. Newby, 1855.

Mahatma Letters. See *ML.*

Maitland, Edward. *Anna Kingsford. Her Life, Letters, Diary and Work. By her Collaborator.* 2 vols. 3rd ed. Ed. S. H. Hart. London: Watkins, 1913. (First ed., 1896)

Mani, Swami Narad, "Chef de l'Observatoire secret européen de la 'True Truth Somaj' d'Adyar." "Baptême de Lumière; Notes pour servir à l'Histoire de la Société dite Théosophique." *La France Antimaçonnique,* various numbers from 25th year, no.43 (26 October 1911), to 26th year, no.9 (29 February 1912).

Martin, John. *Animal Magnetism examined.* London: Author, 1790.

———. *Wonders and Mysteries of Animal Magnetism displayed.* London: J. Sudbury, 1791.

Martin, Robert. "Ancient Symbolism Illustrated (with Engravings)." *Freemason's Magazine and Masonic Monitor,* N.S., I (1859), 289, 330, 350, 369; II (1860), 162, 249, 268, 301, 429.

Massey, Charles Carleton. *Thoughts of a Modern Mystic.* London: Kegan Paul, 1909.

Mathias, Thomas. *Pursuits of Literature; a Satirical Poem.* 14th ed. London: T. Becket, 1808. (First ed., 1794)

Maurice, Thomas. *Indian Antiquities.* 5 vols. London, 1793–94.

Mayer, Johannes. *Lord Stanhope, der Gegenspieler Kaspar Hausers.* Stuttgart: Urachhaus Johannes Mayer, 1988.

McIntosh, Christopher. *Eliphas Levi and the French Occult Revival.* London: Rider, 1972.

———. *The Rosy Cross Unveiled. The History, Mythology and Rituals of an Occult Order.* Wellingborough: Aquarian, 1980.

———. *The Rose Cross and the Age of Reason. Eighteenth-Century Rosicrucianism in Central Europe and its Relationship to the Enlightenment.* Leiden: E. J. Brill, 1992.

McLean, Adam. "Bacstrom's Rosicrucian Society." *Hermetic Journal* 6 (1979), 25–29.

———. "General Rainsford. An Alchemical and Rosicrucian Enthusiast." *Hermetic Journal* 1990, 129–134. [1990a]

———, ed. *A Treatise on Angel Magic, Being a Complete Transcription of Ms. Harley 6482 in the British Library.* Grand Rapids: Phanes Press, 1990. [1990b]

Mead, G. R. S. Review of Shanti-Deva, *A Manual of Mahayana Buddhism. The Quest* I (1909–1910), 584–585.

———. "Spiritual Reality in Progressive Buddhism." *The Quest* II (1910–1911), 692–706.

———. *Thrice-Greatest Hermes. Studies in Hellenistic Theosophy and Gnosis.* 3 vols. London: Watkins, 1949. (First ed., 1906)

Meade, Marion. *Madame Blavatsky, the Woman behind the Myth.* N.Y.: Putnam, 1980.

Mesmer, Franz Anton. *Mesmerism. A Translation of the Original Medical and Scientific Writings of F. A. Mesmer, M.D.* Comp. and tr. George J. Bloch. Los Altos: William Kaufmann, 1980.

Michal, Victor. *Le corps aromal.* Paris: "tous les libraires," 1854.

Mitter, Partha. *Much Maligned Monsters: History of European Reactions to Indian Art.* Oxford: Clarendon Press, 1977.

Montgomery, Robert. *Oxford, a Poem.* Oxford: Henry Slater, 1835.

Monumens du culte secret des dames romaines, pour servir de suite aux monumens de la vie privée des XII Césars. Caprée: Sabellus [actually Paris], 1784.

Moor, Edward. *The Hindu Pantheon.* Los Angeles: Philosophical Research Society, 1976. (First ed., 1810)

Morrison, R. J. *The New Principia; or, True System of Astronomy.* London: J. G.Berger, n.d. [1868]

———. *King David Triumphant! A letter to the astronomers of Benares.* London: J. G.Berger, 1871.

Moses, W. Stainton. *Spirit Teachings through the Mediumship of William Stainton Moses ("M.A., (Oxon.)").* 7th ed. London: London Spiritualist Alliance, 1933.

Mukherjee, S. N. *Sir William Jones, a Study in Eighteenth-Century British Attitudes to India.* Cambridge: Cambridge University Press, 1968.

Nahar, Sujata. *Mother's Chronicles.* Book 3: *Mirra the Occultist.* Paris: Institut des Recherches Evolutives, 1989.

Neander, Hermann [=Samuel Borton Brown]. *True Resignation. How Man must die daily, in his own will, in Self . . .* By Old Jacob Boehme. London: Whiting & Co., n.d. [1860?]

Newman, Aubrey. *The Stanhopes of Chevening. A Family Biography.* London: Macmillan, 1969.

ODL I-V. Henry S. Olcott. *Old Diary Leaves.* 5 vols. Adyar: TPH, 1928–41.

O'Brien, Henry. *The Round Towers of Ireland, or the History of the Tuath-de-Danaans.* New ed., with Introduction by W. H. C. London: W. Thacker, 1898. (First ed., 1834)

Oken, Lorenz. *Elements of Physiophilosophy.* Tr. Alfred Tulk. London: Ray Society, 1847. (First ed., 1810)

Olcott, see *ODL.*

Olcott, Henry S. *People from the Other World.* Mokelumne Hill, Ca: Health Research, 1972. (First ed. in *New York Daily Graphic,* 1874; in book form, 1875)

Oliver, J. W. *The Life of William Beckford.* London: Oxford University Press, 1932.

Oppenheim, Janet. *The Other World: Spiritualism and Psychical Research in England 1850–1914.* Cambridge: Cambridge University Press, 1985.

Owen, Alex. *The Darkened Room. Women, Power and Spiritualism in Late Victorian England.* Philadelphia: University of Pennsylvania Press, 1990.

Owen Robert. *The New Religion; or Religion founded on the immutable Laws of the Universe, contrasted with all Religions founded on Human Testimony.* London: J. Brooks, n.d. [1830].

Owen, Robert Dale. *Footfalls on the Boundary of Another World.* Philadelphia: Lippincott, 1860.

Oxley, Thomas. *The Celestial Planisphers, or Astronomical Charts.* Liverpool: Davis & Dickson, 1830.

———. *The Gem of the Astral Sciences.* London: Simpkin & Marshall, 1848.

Paine, Thomas. *The Age of Reason.* London: R. Carlile, 1819.

Paley, Morton D. *The Apocalyptic Sublime.* New Haven: Yale University Press, 1986.

Peacock, Carlos. *Samuel Palmer. Shoreham and After.* London: John Baker, 1968.

Peebles, James M. *Seers of the Ages, embracing Spiritualism, past and present.* 4th ed. London: J. Burns, 1870.

Peebles, James A. "A Séance on the Great Pyramid." *The Spiritualist* IV (13 February 1874), 77–78. (Reprinted from *The Banner of Light,* 10 January 1874)

Penny, Anne Judith. *Studies in Jacob Boehme.* London: Watkins, 1912.

Pestalozzi, J. H. *Letters on Early Education, addressed to J. P. Greaves, Esq.* London: Longmans, 1851. (First ed., 1827)

Podmore, Frank. *Robert Owen. A Biography.* London: Allen & Unwin, 1923. (First ed. 1906)

———. *From Mesmer to Christian Science. A Short History of Mental Healing.* New Hyde Park, NY: University Books, 1963. (First ed., 1909) [1963a]

———. *Mediums of the Nineteenth Century.* 2 vols. New Hyde Park, NY: University Books, 1963. (First ed., as *Modern Spiritualism,* 1902) [1963b]

Priestley, Joseph. *Letter to Mr. Volney, occasioned by a work of his entitled Ruins, and by his letter to the author.* Philadelphia: Thos. Dobson, 1797.

———. *A Comparison of the Institutes of Moses with those of the Hindoos and other ancient nations . . .* Northumberland: A. Kennedy, for the Author, 1799.

Prospects, Charter, Ordinances and Bye-laws of the Royal Institution of Great Britain. Together with lists of the proprietors and subscribers. London: Royal Inst., 1800.

Ptolemy. *The Tetrabiblos; or, Quadripartite of Ptolemy, translated from the copy of Leo Allatus.* With critical and explanatory notes by James Wilson. London: Wm. Hughes, n.d.

Q.R. *Remarks on Additional Letters to the Rev. G. D'Oyly [. . .] by Vindex., Biblicus, and Candidus.* London: Law & Gilbert, 1814.

Raine, Kathleen. *Blake and Tradition.* 2 vols. Princeton: Princeton University Press, 1968.

Randolph, Paschal Beverly. *The Unveiling: or, What I think of Spiritualism. To which is appended his world-famous Medicinal Formulas.* Newburyport: William H. Huse, 1860.

———. *The Grand Secret; or, Physical Love in Health and Disease.* San Francisco: Pilkington & Randolph, 1861–62.

———. *The Guide to Clairvoyance, and Clairvoyant's Guide [. . .] Also, a special paper concerning hashish . . .* Boston: Rockwell & Rollins, 1867.

———. *The Wonderful Story of Ravalette. Also, Tom Clark and his Wife, and the curious things that befell them; being The Rosicrucian's Story.* Boston: Randolph Pub. Co., 1871. [1871a and 1871b]

———. *P. B. Randolph, His Curious Life, Works, and Career. The Great Free-Love Trial . . .* Boston: Randolph Publishing House, 1872.

———. *Pre-Adamite Man: demonstrating the existence of the human race upon this earth 100,000 thousand years ago!* Toledo, OH: Randolph Pub. Co., 1888. (First ed., by "Griffin Lee," 1863)

———. *Seership! The Magnetic Mirror. A practical guide to those who aspire to Clairvoyance-Absolute.* Toledo, OH: K. C. Randolph, 1892. (First ed., 1874)

———. *Soul! The Soul-World: The Homes of the Dead.* Ed. R. S. Clymer. Quakertown: Confederation of Initiates, 1932. (First ed., as *Dealings with the Dead,* 1861–62)

———. *Ravalette. The Rosicrucian's Story.* Ed. R. S. Clymer. Quakertown: Philosophical Publishing Co., 1939.

———. *The Immortality of Love. Unveiling the Secret Arcanum of Affectional Alchemy.* Ed. R. S. Clymer. Quakertown: Beverly Hall Corp., 1978. (First ed., as *Eulis,* 1874)

———. *Mediumism; Clairvoyance; Second Youth and how to gain it?* N.p., n.d. (copy in College of Psychic Studies, London, SM 258, 6)

Ransom, Josephine. *A Short History of the Theosophical Society.* Adyar: TPH, 1938.

Raphael. *Urania; or, the Astrologer's Chronicle, and Mystical Magazine.* London: A. Sweeting, 1825. [1825a]

———. *The Astrologer of the Nineteenth Century.* 7th ed. N.p., n.d. [1825b]

———. *The Royal Book of Dreams.* London: E. Wilson, n.d. [1830]

———. *The Familiar Astrologer.* London: John Bennett, 1831.

———. *Raphael's Sanctuary of the Astral Art.* London: Wm. Charlton Wright, n.d. [1834]

Rawson, A. L. "Mme. Blavatsky: a Theosophical Occult Apology." *Theosophical History* 2/6 (1988), 209–220. (First ed., 1892)

Roth, Cecil. *Essays and Portraits in Ango-Jewish History.* Philadelphia: Jewish Publication Society, 1962.

Row, T. Subba. *Esoteric Writings.* Adyar: TPH, 1980. (First ed., 1895)

Roy, Rammohun. *The English Works of Ram Mohun Roy.* Ed. Jogendra Chunder Ghose. 2 vols. Calcutta: Oriental Press, 1885, 1887.

———. *Rammohun Roy. A Bi-centenary Tribute.* Ed. Niharranjan Ray. New Delhi: National Book Trust, 1974.

Sadleir, Michael. *Blessington-D'Orsay: A Masquerade.* London: Constable, 1933.

Saint-Martin, Louis-Claude de, and Kirchberger, Baron de Liebistorf. *Mystical Philosophy and Spiritual Manifestations. Selections from their correspondence.* Tr. E. B. Penny. Exeter: William Roberts, 1863.

Sandburg, Carl. *Abraham Lincoln. Vol. III: The War Years.* N.Y.: Harcourt, Brace, & Co., 1939.

Sandby, Rev. George. *Mesmerism and its opponents, with a narrative of cases.* London: Longmans, 1844.

Santucci, James A. "Forgotten Magi: George Henry Felt and Ezekiel Perkins." *Le Défi magique.* Vol. I, pp. 131–142. Lyon: Presses Universitaires de Lyon, 1994.

Sangharakshita (D. P. E. Lingwood). *Buddhism and Blasphemy. Buddhist Reflections on the 1977 Blasphemy Trial.* Glasgow: Windhorse Publications, 1989. (First ed., 1978)

Scholem, Gershom. *The Messianic Idea in Judaism and Other Essays on Jewish Spirituality.* New York: Schocken, 1971.

———. *Kabbalah.* New York: Dorset Press, 1974.

Schuchard, Marsha Keith. "Freemasonry, Secret Societies, and the Continuity of the Occult Tradition in English Literature." Ph.D. diss., University of Texas, Austin, 1975.

———. "Yeats and the Unknown Superiors: Swedenborg, Falk, and Cagliostro." *Hermetic Journal* 37 (1987), 14–20.

———. "The Secret Masonic History of Blake's Swedenborg Society." *Blake, an Illustrated Quarterly* 26/2 (1992), 40–51.

———. "Yeats and the 'Unknown Superiors': Swedenborg, Falk, and Cagliostro." In *Secret Texts,* ed H. Ormsby-Lennon and M. Roberts. N.Y. AMS Press, 1994.

Sellon, Edward. *Annotations on the Sacred Writings of the Hindus.* London: Privately Printed, 1865.

Sibly, Ebenezer. *A new and complete illustration of the occult sciences.* London: J. Adland, 1807. (First ed., 1787)

———. *A Key to Physic and the Occult Sciences.* 5th ed. London: W. Lewis for G. Jones, 1814.

———. *The Wheel of Wisdom.* Transcribed by Frederick Hockley, 1824. Wellcome Institute, Ms. 3203.

Singh, Iqbal. *Rammohun Roy. A biographical journey into the making of modern India.* 2nd rev. ed. 3 vols. in 2. Bombay: Asia Publishing House, 1983.

Sinnett, A.P. "The Phenomena of Spiritualism considered in the Light of Theosophic Teaching." *Transactions of the London Lodge of the Theosophical Society* 23 (March 1895).

———. *Some Fruits of Occult Teaching.* London: TPS, 1896.

———. *Esoteric Buddhism.* 8th ed. London: TPS, 1907. (First ed., 1883)

———. *Incidents in the Life of Madame Blavatsky. Compiled from information supplied by her relatives and friends.* London: TPS, 1913. (First ed., 1886)

———. *Autobiography of Alfred Percy Sinnett.* London: Theosophical History Centre, 1986.

Solovyoff, Vsevolod Sergyeevich. *A Modern Priestess of Isis.* Abridged and tr. Walter Leaf. London: Longmans, 1895.

South, Thomas. *Early Magnetism in its higher relation to humanity as veiled in the poets and the prophets.* London: Baillière, 1846. Published anonymously.

South, Mary Ann. *A Suggestive Inquiry into the Hermetic Mystery, with a dissertation on the more celebrated of the alchemical philosophers.* Rev. ed. New York: Julian Press, 1960. Published anonymously. (First ed., 1850; first issue of this ed., 1918)

Sprigg, June, and Larkin, David. *Shaker Life, Work, and Art.* London: Cassell, 1988.

Standish, Henry. *Remarks on the Horae Sabbaticae of Godfrey Higgins Esq.* Doncaster: Sheardown & Son, 1826.

Stanhope, [Fourth] Earl. *Truths relating to Caspar Hauser.* London: James S. Hodson, 1836.

Steiger, Isabel de. *Memorabilia. Reminiscences of a Woman Artist and Writer.* London: Rider, n.d. [1927?]

Suzuki, D. T. "The Development of Mahâyâna Buddhism." *The Buddhist Review* I (1909), 103–118.

Swedenborg, Emanuel. *Compendium of Swedenborg's Theological Writings.* London: Swedenborg Society, 1896.

Taylor Robert. *The Diegesis; being a Discovery of the Origin, Evidences, and Early History of Christianity.* 2nd ed. London: J. Cunningham, 1841.

———. *The Devil's Pulpit: or Astro-theological Sermons.* New York: Calvin Blanchard, 1857.

Tereshchenko, Nicolas. "Israel Regardie (1907-1985) and the 'Golden Dawn'." *ARIES* 4 (1985), 71–87. Expanded version in *Bases de l'ésotérisme: Fragments de gnose.* Paris: Trédaniel, 1993, 59–102.

Thomas, Northcote W. *Crystal Gazing, Its History and Practice, with a discussion of the evidence for telepathic scrying.* London: Alexander Moring, 1905.

Tomalin, Claire. *Shelley and His World.* London: Thames & Hudson, 1980.

Towers, Eric. *Dashwood. The Man and the Myth.* N.p.: Crucible, 1986.

Townsend, George. *The Oedipus Romanus; or, an attempt to prove, from the principles of reasoning adopted by the Rt. Hon. Sir William Drummond, in his Oedipus Judaicus, that the Twelve Caesars are the twelve signs of the Zodiac. Addressed to the higher and literary classes of society.* London: A. J. Valpy, 1819.

Townshend, Rev. Chauncey Hare. *Facts in Mesmerism, with reasons for a dispassionate inquiry into it.* London: Longmans, 1840.

Varley, John. *A Treatise on zodiacal physiognomy; illustrated by engravings of heads and features; and accompanied by tables of the time of rising of the twelve signs of the Zodiac; and containing also new and astrological explanations of some remarkable portions of ancient mythological history.* London: Author, 1828.

Vaughan, R. A. *Hours with the Mystics.* 3rd ed. 2 vols. London: John Stark, 1888.

Viatte, Auguste *Les sources occultes du romantisme. Illuminisme - Théosophie, 1770–1820.* 2 vols. Paris: Honoré Champion, 1979. (First ed., 1927)

Vindex, *Letters to the Rev. George D'Oyley [sic], [. . .] in answer to his attack on the Oedipus Judaicus.* London: D. N. Shury, 1812.

Volney, Constantin François. *The Law of Nature, or Principles of Morality, deduced from the physical constitution of mankind and the universe.* Philadelphia: T. Stephens, 1796. (First ed., 1793)

———. *The Ruins, or a Survey of the Revolutions of Empires.* New York: Peter Eckler, 1890. (First English ed., 1795)

Vulliaud, Paul. *Histoire et Portraits des Rose-Croix.* Milan: Archè, 1987.

Waite, Arthur Edward. *The Brotherhood of the Rosy Cross.* London: Rider, 1924.

———. *The Real History of the Rosicrucians.* Mokelumne Hill, CA: Health Research, 1960. First ed., 1887.

———. *A New Encyclopedia of Freemasonry.* New York: Weathervane Books, 1970. (First ed., 1921)

Walter, Nicholas. *Blasphemy in Britain: the practice and punishment of blasphemy, and the trial of 'Gay News.'* London: Rationalist Press Association, 1977.

Walton, Christopher. *Notes and Materials for an adequate biography of the celebrated divine and theosopher William Law . . .* London, 1854. Published anonymously.

Wassermann, Jacob. *Caspar Hauser, the Enigma of a Century.* Trans. Caroline Newton. Blauvelt, NY: Rudolf Steiner Publications, 1963. (First ed., 1928)

Welton, Thomas. *Mental Magic.* Ed. Robert Fryar. London: Redway, 1884.

Westcott, W. Wynn. *History of the Societas Rosicruciana in Anglia.* London: Privately Printed, 1900.

———. *The Rosicrucians, Past and Present, at Home and Abroad.* Mokelumne Hill, CA: Health Research 1966. (First ed., 1900)

Wilford, Francis. "On Egypt and other countries [. . .] from the ancient books of the Hindus." *Asiatic Researches* III (1792), 295–463.

———. "On the Chronology of the Hindus." *Asiatic Researches* V (1798), 241–296. [1798a]

———. "Remarks on the names of the Cabirian Deities, and on some words used in the mysteries of Eleusis." *Asiatic Researches* V (1798), 297–301. [1798b]

———. "An Essay on the Sacred Isles of the West, with Other Essays connected with that Work." *Asiatic Researches* VIII (1805), 245–368; IX (1807), 32–243; X (1808), 27–157 (called "Origin and Decline of the Christian Religion in India"); XI (1810), 11–152.

Wilson, James. *A Complete Dictionary of Astrology.* London: Wm. Hughes, 1819.

Winter, George. *Animal Magnetism. History of its origin, progress, and present state; its principles and secrets displayed, as delivered by the late Dr. Demainauduc.* Bristol: George Routh, n.d. [1801]

Wolff, Robert Lee. *Strange Stories and other Explorations in Victorian Fiction.* Boston: Gambit, 1971.

Wright, Brooks. *Interpreter of Buddhism to the West: Sir Edwin Arnold.* New York: Bookman Associates, 1957.

Wyatt, Rev. George. *A Letter to Godfrey Higgins Esq., chiefly in reference to certain arguments unfavourable to the Christian priesthood and the Christian religion . . .* Doncaster: Charles & James White, 1829.

Yarker, John. *Notes on the Scientific and Religious Mysteries of Antiquity; the Gnosis and Secret Schools of the Middle Ages; Modern Rosicruciansim; and the Various Rites and Decrees of Free and Accepted Masonry.* London: John Hogg et al., 1872.

Zadkiel. *Zadkiel's Legacy, with Essays on Hindu Astronomy.* London: Sherwood & Co., 1842.

Index